ADVENTURES OF NIMON
Volume Two

Raymond Hoche-Mong

MONTARA, CALIFORNIA

ii

Raymond Hoche-Mong
835 George Street, POB 370937
Montara, CA 94037-0937

Publisher's Note: I have tried to recreate events, locales and conversations from my memories of them. In order to maintain their anonymity in some instances I have changed the names of individuals and places, I may have changed some identifying characteristics and details such as physical properties, occupations and places of residence.

Book Layout © 2014 BookDesignTemplates.com

Editing by Christine Myers, ladymyerswordsmithing.com

Cover Design by Debbie Brady

Cover Formatting by Eileen Swift

Adventures of Nimon/ Raymond Hoche-Mong. -- 1st ed.
ISBN-13: 978-1530746293

CONTENTS

iv

vi

Photographs

To Emily Darden, and to Dominique and Michel

who have been patient with me.

Acknowledgments

Several people have given me encouragement and also have shared information to help me write this autobiography. I will mention a few but will have to leave out a number of names because listing them would convert this book into an enormous volume.

I began writing it in 1995 as a letter to my children but then my daughter, the English and Medievalist scholar, suggested that a book would be more appropriate. Since that comment, my daughter has been invaluable in helping me manage my thoughts. I am grateful for her support.

Someone sent me a quote stating that if I wanted to be a writer I needed to marry an English major. I did. I married Emily, she has become over the years my best critic and editor of all my writings both professional and personal.

Because I have not kept a journal or notes but relied only on recollections, I am grateful to all who have contributed details; especially the many who have helped me remember facts, incidents, the names of people, project details, and sundry other necessary historical bits and pieces. I will mention a few and hope that those not included will forgive me because they are not forgotten.

I am happy to note Dr. Rebecca Jernigan, a friend of many years and an avid fan. Dr. Stuart White a colleague during our graduate academic years and still a person I turn to when I need to discuss important issues. Drs. Denis Slavich and Ronald Brooks, and also Robert Jackson, who have given me support and crucial details on issues that were related to my work on projects. In addition, I cannot omit Barry and Margaret Pugh from the list; both have been stalwart supporters for many years.

In addition, I am indebted for the information and direction shared with me by Glenn Plymate, Charles Sands, Umberto Bozzo, the Reverend John Schively, the Right Reverend William E. Sanders, the late Reverend Therrel Holt, the late Right Reverend and Lord Peter Walker, the late Reverend and Attorney Donald Mackenzie Williamson, the late Colonel Lawson Wynn xii

(USAF Retired), and the late Ralph Finch (retired mayor of McCaysville, GA), Newell (Do) Anderson — my last living college classmate. What is notable in this acknowledgement is the number of dear friends who have terminated their travels around the Sun!

A note of gratitude for Nancy Key for her generous hospitality to share her house and to allow me to work without interruption.

Eileen Swift has applied her graphic design talents to the formatting of the cover and I also appreciate the attention to details and creative enthusiasm she has imparted beyond being an invaluable friend.

Readers of sections of the books such as Emily Oppegard, Dr. Kate Hodgson, James and Ellen Ellingsworth, and James Harrington have been most helpful in sharing suggestions, photographs, anecdotes, and various tid bits for enriching the book.

My editor Christine Myers has been helpful in many ways, especially in searching for a publisher, tending to details that turn a story into a book, and for being the reliable administrator, something that I cannot possibly want to do. Christine has the patience of an angel and the good judgment of a genius.

This autobiography could not have been written without the wisdom, the astuteness, the editorial management, and the love and support of Emily my "tractor", associate, world traveling partner, and wife.

Finally, any errors are my responsibility and any interpretation of facts is simply the result of my perspective; we each have our own way of accepting reality.

I have shared many tasty meals and expansive conversations with Raymond. He engages both with élan. Nourishing body and mind; taking time to break—or make—bread, RHM draws out tales that reveal a companion's underlying passion and often the chance to share the works created to express it. RHM seeks the ebb and flow of creative process, with its potential for deep, connecting recognition. For Raymond, this is an everyday act, an art of living, connecting people to one another, to themselves, back to the places within from which so much originates.

Emily Oppegard, Artist

PART FOUR

The Principality of Liechtenstein

Of all the places in the world why would I select Liechtenstein as a destination? Liechtenstein is nonpareil. It is an independent country and it is fascinating, beautiful, small, hospitable, interesting, and enigmatic. This small principality has a revenue producing high technology business, and an industrial base of other value-added goods that are commercially amazing. Yet Liechtenstein appears to be simply a pastoral community with dairy cows grazing in green meadows surrounded by mountains with ski slopes, hiking trails, bird sanctuaries, and a picturesque segment of the Rhine River. It is quiet. It is peaceful. It is enchanting.

Just outside the capital city of Vaduz, Prince Hans-Adam owns a vineyard and a fine restaurant named the Torkel. Located in the midst of grapevines and overlooking the mountains that Liechtenstein shares with Austria and Germany, the restaurant not only offers superb cuisine, but also provides an atmosphere of serenity, good service, and warmth. I have never felt like a stranger at the Torkel because of the way guests are treated. No one hovers over you, but service is responsive and unobtrusive. Of course there are other excellent restaurants in the principality, and most of them are careful to provide both good food and a fine atmosphere.

Were it possible and were I fluent in German, I would make Liechtenstein my home. Many years ago, Prince Hans-Adam invited me to live in the

Principality and I have not totally discounted his invitation. There are several restrictions applied to a foreigner who wishes to establish residence in the principality. First of all, one needs to be invited by a resident. One needs to have an income earned from outside the principality or to have the where-withal to start a business in the country. Seeking employment in the principality is rarely possible unless one has a specialty that is exceptional. One may rent or purchase a condominium apartment; no house and no land ownership are allowed. These restrictions are not terrible and are acceptable to the few who have funds available and seek either to retire or to start a business there.

Liechtenstein is a jewel reflecting many brilliant rays from its polished facets. Hence I keep returning to the Principality of Liechtenstein and main-tain, at least at Christmas, some communication with its ruler, Prince Hans-Adam of Liechtenstein. Years later, I had the opportunity to meet and dis-cuss the state of Liechtenstein with the Prince and others in government when I was working on the technopolis project. I was also fortunate to be invited to meet with his family.

Chocolates, Feathers, and a Principality

After landing in Frankfurt, Germany I went immediately to one of the six restaurants we had selected to meet Emily, who had arrived several hours earlier from San Francisco and had been exploring the "airport city." We had scheduled approximately 30 days of holiday in Europe. Our plan was to rent a car, observe a show of trained birds of prey, stop in Ulm, then Munich to visit Dachau, proceed through the Black Forest, on our way to Liechtenstein and then rest for a few days in the Principality. After that we were to cross Switzerland, stopping in Neuchâtel to eat palée, a local fish from Lake Neuchâtel, and to sample some chocolate at Milia Walders' (Mrs. Hans Wal-ders) sweetshop; these two delicious bits of exquisite foods were suggested by Michel Thomet, a colleague from Bechtel, who was born in that canton. We would cross a portion of the Alps passing through Geneva, and then de-scend to Lyon for lunch before ending this portion of the trip in Montignac,

Lascaux, and a visit with Jacques Marsal. The core purpose of this trip was to visit the small chocolatiers on our itinerary and taste the exquisite chocolates that they fashioned.

Indeed, in Neuchâtel we ate palées, tasted the wonderful chocolate truffles prepared by Milia Walders, then onward north we enjoyed Liechtenstein and the Torkel restaurant. To this day Emily remembers the delicious pork chops prepared by the Torkel's chef. It was a memorable meal made still more memorable by the addition of the wine from the Prince's vineyard. But that's a comment that will be restated later on at the proper time since I'm getting ahead of my story.

Arriving at Frankfurt airport on time from Riyadh, Lanarca, Cyprus, and then Athens, I made my way to meet Emily. She was waiting for me and had forewarned the waiter that I would order a tall beer having arrived from Saudi Arabia. I had not seen Emily in almost three months, so it was good to see her again and I was looking forward to our holiday. After picking up a rental Fiat we headed for the small town of Neu Isenburg, about an hour away from the airport. I had found a small hotel that would accommodate us comfortably and which would put us on the proper route for the birds of prey performance the next afternoon.

Both Emily and I were tired from our flights; hers was a long ten-hour across several time zones, and mine was a seven-hour flight across three time zones. Exhausted, we fell asleep after a few short moments of conversation. In the middle of the night we were awakened when our door was flung open and there stood a tall man in his jockey shorts, but in the light we could see his face. Apologizing profusely, the man quickly withdrew and closed the door (the next door to ours was the shared toilet). After he was gone we looked at each other and burst into laughter. Who was that man? After making certain that our door was fully locked we tried to resume our sleep, but it was impossible because of the time change or jet lag.

At breakfast, we entered the dining room and as we located our assigned table we looked straight into the face of our night intruder. He was quite embarrassed and immediately got up from his chair and left the room. We sympathized with him but no damage had been done to either party.

After breakfast we loaded our red Fiat, and purchased for the trip a bag of Johannesberren berries, small red and black berries, similar to currants, that are delicious but a little tart. Leaving the small town, we headed south to Burg von Guttenbergwhere the trained birds of prey would perform. Arriving in plenty of time, we found good seats overlooking the valley. Because I had forgotten the details of this phenomenal visit with the birds I asked Emily, since she had made the arrangements, if she had details of the event with the birds of prey. Here is what Emily gave me:

"On the 22nd of July we drove along the Black Forest Hohenstrasse to Burg Guttenberg where we lunched at the Falcon Aerie and saw an hour's flight of Sea Eagles (seeadlern) vultures, and a fine falcon. Then we toured the adlergarten. (The) castle had been in the same family since 1449."

As is the German custom, the show began on time and the performances were excellent. Eagles, hawks, falcons, vultures, and several other types did their acts of flying, chasing, retrieving, and returning to the arms of their trainers. It was a lovely afternoon on a clear cool day and the performance of the birds was unforgettable.

After the show, we continued south towards Ulm to visit one of the tallest cathedrals in Europe that was constructed without a foundation. Typical of German architecture, the cathedral was adorned with extremely baroque decorations and with too many statues depicting bloody religious saints. It was too much for the eyes to absorb. Looking for a konditorei (patisserie) we ran into a down-feathers store and met the owner, whose name was Tony. Tony was such a delight that I bought my first down comforter from him and in the process received a thorough education in feather quality, use, and variations.

We went to the konditorei and enjoyed good pastries accompanied by dark black cups of German roast coffee. It was in this condition that I experienced for the first time the electronic urinal and faucet operations. Move away from the urinal and the flusher does its thing. Put your hand under the faucet and water is released at the correct temperature for washing. At first I was puzzled because I could not understand how the water started pouring and then ceased miraculously. My stupidity was overcome after a few tries and several hand washing attempts. When I returned to our table and related my experience to Emily, she immediately went to the ladies room to experience firsthand this new electronic technology. She was as amazed as I. Of course today the electronic dispensing faucets are common, especially now that we are concerned about not wasting water.

That evening we found a lovely hotel on the outskirts of Munich where the waitress, the daughter of the owner, had spent a few months in California as an au pair. Our room, the meals, the beer (I still have a gift glass from that hotel), and the view were phenomenal. We made that hotel our headquarters as we explored the surroundings of Munich. The next day it was to Dachau that we headed. Dachau, the concentration camp where the presumed enemies of the German National Socialist Party (NAZI) were incarcerated and either executed then incinerated in gas ovens on site, or shipped to other concentration camps for the final solution. Dachau is a hideous reminder that Robert Burns was correct when he talked about "Man's inhumanity to man," as the millstone forever hanging around civilization's neck. That visit is engraved in my memory and nothing will erase it. Nothing.

Much as I'd like to think of Dachau as an exception, a unique incident in the history of civilization, I am aware that it is not. The graves in China, Uganda, Cambodia, Zimbabwe, Congo, Serbia, Rwanda, and in other places are again a reminder that Burns' words were absolutely justified when he wrote them in his poem, "Man was Made to Mourn," in 1786. Humanity is a long way from attaining humaneness, if ever.

When we left Dachau we went directly to the National Beer Hall where Adolph Hitler almost stopped a bullet at a rally for the members of the embryonic Nazi party. The hole made by the bullet in the upper beam is still visible. The course of history would surely have been changed had Hitler's heart or head stopped that bullet.

Munich is a lovely city and the English Garden is quite beautiful and still well maintained. The capital of Bavaria, the most conservative of the German states, Munich commands an important place in politics, industry, and tourism. The city is clean, well ordered in its traffic, and openly friendly to foreigners. The many beer halls indicate that Munich is the home of several beer producers of the famous German brews.

We left the Munich area a few days later to drive to Liechtenstein by way of the Bodensee, the large lake that separates Germany from Austria. It is on the southeast border of Switzerland that one finds the Principality of Liechtenstein with its capital of Vaduz. The princely castle of Prince Franz Joseph and his son, Hans-Adam, hangs on a cliff overlooking Vaduz. The castle has been the set for several movies, especially the terribly funny and politically incorrect, *The Mouse that Roared.*

The drive to the Bodensee was in a drenching downpour that forced us to take cover in a park building to wait for the end of the deluge. Soon, the clouds moved away, the sky cleared, and we continued our drive to Liechtenstein and to our hotel on the eastern bank of the Rhine River. Our hotel was located in Schaan, a small village north of Vaduz. With dinner reservations made for 1930 hours, we had an hour and a half to rest, get a shower, and even look around the grounds that were on the edge of a farm on the Rhine River. A more deliciously romantic setting would have been hard to find. When the time came we drove to the Torkel restaurant in the Prince's vineyard just a couple of kilometers south of our location.

At the restaurant, Emily was surprised that the Maître d'hôtel knew my name. I explained that I had made the reservation by telephone and had discussed the menu and the wine in detail with him. The dining room was exquisitely decorated and possessed enough Rubens to make one drool (later we discovered that the Liechtenstein family had been ardent collectors of Peter Paul Rubens works). A bit of pink coloring on the drapes and the tablecloths added to the cheerful ambiance. We were seated at a table that overlooked the vineyard and, at my request, a bottle of the Prince's "Claret" (British name for a Bordeaux) was brought to our table. The wine was a Bordeaux-Claret but with a touch of hardy Pinot, or something akin to that. It was particularly delicious. A taste of heaven could not have been better. Dinner consisted of pork chops for Emily and for me sweet breads — the test for every chef! Dinner was superbly prepared, delivered, and seasoned. It was a princely repast indeed.

Vaduz, the capital, is the least attractive part of the Principality because it is a point of meeting for tour buses filled with tourists who want to set foot in this tiny and enchanting place. Yet in Vaduz, as I mentioned above, one can find the world's largest collection of Peter Paul Rubens. Entering the gallery in central Vaduz, one is immediately surrounded by enough Rubens to satisfy even the most avid collector. The exhibit is free to viewers and in the event that a tourist wishes to have a visa stamped in his/her passport, the cost is less than a Swiss franc: a token price for the traveler.

Leaving Vaduz, one immediately climbs on wonderful roads towards the lush higher elevations. The view is extraordinary and the countryside below is pristine. If ever there was a jewel country on this planet, the Principality of Liechtenstein takes first place. But what makes this small postage stamp size country tick? Several years later I made it the focus of my research when studying the raison d'être of the several city-states.

Farms are spread over most of the countryside. The population totals approximately 30,000 to 35,000 souls. Census numbers indicate that approximately 5,000 workers from Austria and Switzerland commute daily to work in the Principality, but they cannot reside in it permanently. What makes Liechtenstein economically viable? There are several items that are manufactured and several knowledge-based resources that emerge from the Principality. Liechtenstein manufactures high quality tools, produces premier foodstuff, makes high temperature ceramics, and develops leading-edge technology in informatics, programmatic, and plasma films, and other high tech commodities. In addition, tourism is an important revenue generator for the Principality.

Its history informs us that in the 1930s Liechtenstein was on the verge of bankruptcy. Until 1933, Liechtenstein was attached to Austria but as Germany's National Socialist Party began courting that country Liechtenstein considered separation. Unhappy with the values of the Nazi party and its influence, Prince Franz Joseph pulled his two small cantons nation from the Austrian grip and attached them to neutral Switzerland. The change was salutary because it prevented Germany from annexing the Principality to itself when Austria became part of the Third Reich. In addition and soon after separation from Austria, the Prince called a general meeting of his elders to decide what paths should be taken to gain solvency. After all, they could not go on forever selling off a Rubens here and there to cover their debts; and agriculture and dairy farming were not sufficient to keep Liechtenstein financially afloat. These were difficult times for the Principality, especially since converting the Austrian currency to the strong Swiss francs impoverished its coffers further.

What do we make that is of excellent and unsurpassed quality? Hans Joseph asked. This was a multi-dimensional question posed by the Prince to the Elders of the Principality. In the mid-30s, when the Principality broke away from its concordat with Austria because of the Nazi political atmosphere, answers had to be found, and found immediately. The question required examination and assessment of capabilities, skills, and resources. The Principality was nearly bankrupt. Unemployment had reached 70% of the labor force, the state coffers were nearly empty, and further financial penury would have given Hitler's Nazi Party ample reason for taking over the Principality of Liechtenstein.

After obtaining a new concordat with the Swiss, that was valid only if the Principality did not have to be on the dole, the Prince and the Elders looked at what could be done in short order to resuscitate the small state. The elders identified several products that included ceramics, tools, foodstuffs, and knowledge-based products; all of these had value-added qualities and required available skills to support them, skills that were readily available in the two cantons. The Prince lent the elders enough seed money to establish the development mechanism to revitalize the economy. Agreements with the Swiss allowed the Principality to remain neutral, to adopt the Swiss franc as its currency thus stabilizing its monetary system and strengthening its small banking operation, and allowed access to Swiss universities, academies, and trade schools. In return the Swiss saw in Liechtenstein a potential banking and intellectual kinship. In less than three years the economy was revitalized and was sustaining a 3% growth, unemployment was reduced to less than 2%, and investment from foreign sources began to be secured. Two private banks were opened for business on a similar footing as the Swiss banks but with a few exceptions: interest paid was higher than the Swiss, money-laundering accounts were forbidden, and depositor's anonymity and protection ceased when criminal issues were involved. The Swiss warned the bankers of the Principality that these variances would affect them negatively. They have not.

Today (2010) the Principality of Liechtenstein has a robust economy and Prince Hans-Adam II, the current Head-of-state, an economist and a graduate of the London School of Economics, is continuing to move his people towards newer leading-edge technologies. In a certain sense, Liechtenstein is akin to California's Silicon Valley, except that it has neither a university nor an airport. Education is a high priority for the residents of the Principality, and college graduates who attend European universities, indicate that over 70% of the adult population possesses a diploma. Adam's son, the Prince Regent, Erbprinz Alois, directs day-to-day affairs.

A drive through the Principality reveals more cows than industrial activity, yet a great deal of production is going on behind the façade of green farms, pristine valleys, charming family houses, and an atmosphere of shocking quiet. By no means is the Principality attempting to hide its industries, it is just that the planning is superb, the ecological considerations are foremost for the people, and the citizens like a beautiful yet efficient setting. Crossing from the Austrian to the Swiss borders by automobile takes 35 minutes on Sunday morning. Crossing from the Swiss border across the northern edge of Liechtenstein to the southern edge and back to the Swiss border will require several hours of driving over the mountain, and in winter the crossing may have to be done with a four-wheel drive, chains or on skis!

Several years later I had the good fortune to meet Prince Franz Joseph and his family, and later had an extensive meeting of several hours with the current ruler, Prince Hans-Adam; that story will be told in due time. It is sufficient to say that I visited Liechtenstein several times and have learned a great deal about this extraordinary small acreage of Europe sandwiched between the Rhine River and the Alps.

The Quest for Good Chocolate

We left Liechtenstein after breakfast for the drive to Neuchâtel and Auvernier, on the French side of Switzerland. The transition from the German Swiss region to the French Swiss region is immediately noticeable: the lavatories are much less tidy on the French side. We arrived in Neuchâtel soon after lunch and went directly to Michel Thomet's house to visit his mother but unfortunately she was away on holiday. We left the house, which is located atop a hill and may be reached by car or by long staircase; we took the stairs. The view from the top was splendid overlooking the whole city of Neuchâtel and the lake of the same name. After this short visit to Thomet's house, we located Mrs. Milia Walders, the woman who commands a reputation for producing the best chocolate in Switzerland. She does indeed.

Milia Walders had known Michel Thomet since he was a small boy in short pants scooting down the Grand Rue on his bicycle. Often he was rewarded with a chocolate truffle or some other piece of dark chocolate. Her shop has the scent of heaven for chocoholics like Emily and me and I explored many shapes of dark chocolate, especially the hard chocolate-coated truffles. We bought a kilogram or two of chocolate for our enjoyment as we traveled west.

After our gourmand visit with Milia, we headed towards Auvernier, and what should have been our pension. On the way to Auvernier, we passed by, without stopping, the plant of the Suchard Chocolate Company. Arriving in Auvernier we soon discovered that our pension was closed for the season even though I had made reservations months earlier for several nights' lodging. The owner simply ignored my reservations and on the closed door we didn't even find a note of apology. Walking over to the Restaurant du Poisson we inquired if there was a hotel they could recommend and to reconfirm our dinner reservation for that evening. We were in Auvernier to sample the local specialty of the palée fish from the Lac de Neuchâtel. One of the attendants at the restaurant recommended a small hotel up the hill and overlooking the vineyard a short distance from where we were. Up we went in our little red Fiat to the hotel. It was a charming hotel and we were given a room with a small balcony facing the vineyard and within hearing distance of the church bells. It was a lovely location and our room was comfortable and spacious and the bathroom was well equipped and sparklingly clean.

After a refreshing shower we went for a walk to begin our exploration of this pleasant lakeside village. We discovered several book binding firms specializing in elite small run books. We looked at numerous exquisitely bound books on flowers, animals, and one in particular was intriguing to me because it was a portrait book by the renowned photographer Joseph Karsh. Bound in hand-sewn leather and inscribed in gold leaf hand calligraphy lettering, this large black and white portrait book was scheduled for only 25 copies. Each copy was pre-assigned to a premier library of the world. Emily was examining a tiny book with dimensions that were no more than 4 x 6 centimeters. The book was bound in a type of satin material and contained the hand-drawings of an illustrator's commentaries on symphonies he had heard. A delightful miniature of a book to have but which would pose problems for a reader with poor eyesight. We examined several other books and would repeat the expedition the next day at other binderies. It was, however, time now to have dinner.

At the Restaurant du Poisson, we were seated at a table located by a large window with a fine view of the lake. The waiter served us immediately several fillets of palées on a silver tray, and that was impressive. When we had eaten a few delicious bites of palées, the waiter returned to explain that these were fish found only in the Lac de Neuchâtel and nowhere else. To maintain the stock of fish in the lake, the canton had authorized a group to farm-raise palée for restaurant consumption; no one could tell the difference in taste between the farm-raised and the wild variety.

We enjoyed our fillet and found that we were to be served other portions of palée and, yes, with every new service we received new dishes, knives and forks, wine glasses, and serviettes. I believe that we were served three helpings or about nine fish for each of us. Each palée is approximately the size of a small hand, flat, and not thicker than 1/3 inch. When that main course was completed, a small salad was served made of freshly steamed vegetables and seasoned delightfully with herbs, olive oil, and grape-seed vinegar. After that mouth-clearing dish, a chocolate raspberry ganache dessert was served that was laced with cognac and whipped cream. Our white wine was delicate, crisp, and quite dry. It was a local French-Swiss wine of good but not memorable quality. The palée was, however, memorable and I'd like to return to experience another meal of this delicate fish from the Lac de Neuchâtel.

Years later I can still remember the dinner, the service, and the ambiance. It was a memorable event that will always entice me to return to the Restaurant du Poisson because of the excellent food and what came with it. There are few restaurants that leave me with a lasting impression, an impression that I want to re-experience a second or third time. I suppose that I can count the number of restaurants that are extraordinary on one hand. These restaurants do not have to be plush, expensive or recognized by testers and tasters; they just need to be able to affect me, and affect me in several ways. I can remember a fine little hole-in-the-wall restaurant in Brussels and another old historic place in Ely. I can recall a "greasy spoon" place in Daly City that offered a fine breakfast but unfortunately was closed because of city redevelopment. I miss that breakfast nook and wonder what happened to the short order cook who was entertaining as she flipped eggs, bacon, and potatoes on the grill. I remember Wing Fat, the little quasi-Mandarin Chinese restaurant in San Mateo that offers the best won-ton soup this side of food heaven. Then there is the Café Barbet in Chaumont and the chef is Mme Petrie, near Lyon. Time marches on and the new replaces the old but sentiments are very hard, if not impossible, to replace.

The next day we returned to Neuchâtel to chat with Madame Milia Walders and to explore the town known for producing the best spoken French in Europe. Several academies teach proper French to students from France, Canada, America, England, the Soviet Union, and, of course, Switzerland. Boarding schools serving the children of the rich and famous are the mainstay of the economy of the town. With the abundance of students and scholars in town, patisseries, ice cream parlors, and cafes are found on almost every street. The adult population is quite active and working either in small businesses, with the schools, the academies, or at the Suchard chocolate plant located between Auvernier and Neuchâtel.

To me the Swiss, be they from the German, French, or Italian sector, have a similar trait, a cachet, and a quality that sets them apart from other people. I can only describe this characteristic as one of acute self-importance. The Swiss make personal welfare and personal interests their primary or only concern, sometimes at the expense of the needs of non-Swiss. In addition, it is their understanding that the correct basis for an ethical code is every person's concern for his or her own best interests. Their neutrality on the world's scene is not because they are pacifists or are concerned about the welfare of other nations, but it is a tool that gives them economic benefits. In product developments, the Swiss are master marketers. They are such good marketers that they have convinced the world that their products are supreme and above all others in quality. With a mix of "justification by works" from John Calvin's theology, and strict authoritarianism from Roman Catholicism, the Swiss have developed a self-image, which they project quite well in their marketing, that makes them appear to be extraordinary and excellent craft people.

Near the city of Neuchâtel there is a small military contingent and because the Swiss are reservists until their 60th birthdays, several men in uniform were seen carrying their weapons. Military service is not a part-time task for the Swiss. I was informed that a Swiss military man keeps his weapon at home or in his office at all times. The Swiss is ready to respond to a call at a moment's notice. While eating lunch in a restaurant, we saw several military men at table. We assumed that lunchtime was time to take a break from the rigors of military defense duties. We saw several soldiers carrying the complex Swiss Army knives on their belt. My own gigantic Swiss Army knife, which matched theirs, was in my attaché case.

As for chocolate, Milia Walders' product was unquestionably the best that was produced in the region, if not in the whole country. Saying au revoir to Mme. Walders, we left this lovely region and headed west. It was time to move beyond the Alps to cross Geneva and enter Haute Savoie in France. The drive in the Fiat would be interesting because we were to climb onto higher ground then descend to lower land towards Lyon, the heart of fine French cuisine.

We arrived in Geneva a little past nine in the morning. I had seen much of this international city so a long stop was not a priority on my schedule. I was anxious to get into Lyon to enjoy a good hearty lunch. That evening we were to be in Montignac, hence we had a long drive ahead of us. But lunch in Lyon was my goal before pushing further west to Dordogne.

Out of Geneva we stopped near Chamonix and Les Houches, then drove on to the small village of Les Houches that was the seat of my ancestors, a most peaceful place surrounded by the Alps and in sight of the dazzling Mont Blanc. It felt good to be on that small part of the Planet; somehow I could feel the warmth and the memories in my veins. I don't know if DNAs ever call one to remember one's heritage, but I felt summoned. I could have stayed in place forever. Haute Savoie is the place where the roots of the Hoche clan were to be found at one time. WWII changed all that, as I indicated in an earlier segment.

Leaving Chamonix we began our descent from Haute Savoie to the Upper Rhone valley and into Lyon. On the road, traffic was heavy and slow on the descent. We could not even maintain the normal speed limit; in fact we never reached the 60-kilometers/hour speed. At noon we were still a long way from Lyon. At two o'clock I decided that it was time to find a restaurant and stop for lunch just on the outskirts of Lyon. A small, attractive place came into view and we stopped. At the door I was welcomed with words from a waiter that told that lunch was over. There were still several tables full of eaters. I was further informed that we were too late for Madame Petrie to serve us. I asked if I could speak with Madame, and without waiting for permission, I proceeded towards the kitchen and bypassed the waiter who had greeted us at the door. I spoke to Madame Petrie in my best and most polite French. I must have had a pathetic look on my face. What some of my friends call a "petit Raymond a faim" look! She considered my request for a moment, inquired if I was American or French. My reply was that I was both. She thought for a few seconds more, and then asked me to sit at a table next to the door leading into the garden. This was to be a set menu and wine with no other choices offered. "Merveilleux!" I said. After escorting Emily to our table, I was happy to sit and be served, especially when I saw what fare was brought to the other guests.

Lunch was an experience in heavenly eating. I cannot begin to describe it because justice for it would not be possible. All I can say is that several years later, Madame Petrie's restaurant and her cooking were reviewed in a major and well-known food magazine and rated at the top of the list for small country-style restaurants in the Lyon region. Madame served us and she described every dish with such flair that compliments were inevitable and certainly honestly earned.

What we were served started with a wonderful Potage Crème de Cresson (cream of watercress soup). Crisp bread and a bottle of true Bourgogne Pinot were keeping us company as we relished the superb soup. The next dish was Côtes de Veau aux Herbes (veal chops with basil, thyme, and tarragon) accompanied by Timbale d'Asperges (asparagus mold) and Harricots Mange-Tout à l'Ètuvée (beans with onions, lettuce, and a touch of cream). For dessert we were served a Clafouti aux Mûres (mulberry flan) and a small glass of Cassis liqueur. The lunch was finalized with coffee.

It was a find that will not be forgotten and because I normally do not forget names of people I like, I can remember Madame Petrie's name — I can even recall her splendid face. The restaurant was so memorable that the name still swirls around my head: it is L. Barbet, Café Restaurant. Café Barbet is located in Chaumont, just north of Lyon. I am certain, however, that I can find the auberge again, even after decades have passed. Something that excellent cannot be forgotten. Of course, Lyons is the culinary heart of France.

After Lyon was traversed, we headed directly to Montignac and Lascaux. We were expected by Jacques Marsal to arrive in the early afternoon if the crossing through Clermont-Ferrand would not be infernal. Emily was driving this leg of the trip and all attempts to cross the Grand Massif in the past had incurred delays. This crossing, however, proceeded without delay and we arrived in Montignac when the sun was still on the horizon. After checking in at the small Hotel de la Grotte — a less than comfortable place, but adequate for our use — I telephoned Marsal to announce our arrival. He asked us to come to the gate of the grotto of Lascaux at eleven o'clock the next day. We were to see the magnificent Lascaux a second time, and that was another high point for this trip.

With a lot of daylight still remaining for the day, we drove to Rocamadour to look at the gorge, have a drink, and revisit the ancient monastery. The gorge at Rocamadour is fascinating because it is a deep cut into the calcareous rock formation that is predominantly found in the Dordogne area. Because we had been driving since our fabulous lunch, we decided to have a drink on the veranda of the café, which overlooked the gorge. As we walked to our table I saw that a small chocolate shop was located in the café; unable to pass it I ordered a hundred grams of truffles. At our table Emily and I each took one in anticipation of the good chocolate taste that would envelope our taste buds. Simultaneously, Emily and I reached for paper napkins so we could spit out the vile tasting chocolate. It was awful and not fit for consumption. Never have we tasted such terrible chocolate. The chocolate was obviously neither tempered correctly nor were its ingredients mixed well. To clean our mouths, we each ordered double espressos before our Campari arrived. The remaining chocolate truffles were deposited into a trash bin.

Returning to Montignac we stopped at "une épicerie" to purchase something for our dinner. We were beyond having a full meal and I was not interested in looking at a menu. So to the grocery we went. After purchasing some local cheese, several specialties from the Périgord Noir such as ham, black truffle mushrooms in olive oil, celery root rémoulade, a loaf of bread, pâtés de foie gras d'oie (for me because Emily does not eat it), and a bottle of St. Emillion from Bordeaux we headed for our room and its ancient velvet drapes. Spreading the food on a small table and using facial tissues instead of napkins and our Swiss Army knives we went to work feeding ourselves. The French épiceries, especially in the Périgord Noir, offer some fine selections for the lazy cook. Regional cuisine features truffles, which are unearthed among oak trees by trained pigs and dogs between November and March, and fine pâtés de foie gras. Geese are penned in November and force-fed corn (maize) cooked with fat and salt; geese and ducks are slaughtered by Christmas for foie gras. The wings and thighs are seasoned and canned as confit. Wild boars are occasionally raised for pâté.

The next day after our café au lait and two or three croissants each and some creamy chèvre accompanied with a few slices of Dordogne ham, we headed for the grotto of Lascaux, Jacques Marsal and his Alsatian dog, Loof.

Second Visit in the Dordogne

As we had arranged by telephone, Jacques met us at the gate of Lascaux and took us directly into the grotto where we saw paintings and drawings that had not been shown to us during our earlier visit. We saw the raw etching on a wall of the head of a lion, which was estimated to date from twenty-nine thousand years ago. The duration of our stay in the grotto, because there were only three of us, lasted a whole hour and ten minutes. Again the experience was tantamount to being in a cathedral and experiencing the serenity of holiness. The semidarkness, the aroma of the soft moist earth, the paintings that bespoke of earlier beings who struggled to carve or paint memorable remnants of their lives, touched us deeply. Once again my heart was pounding in my chest. I was witnessing the creative process of human beings who had stood or crouched in this grotto some 20 to 29 thousand years before my time. These were vivid reminders left by folk who walked, talked, ate, laughed, and hoped just as I did. They had the urge to create art as best they could, with finger drawings, etchings, paint brushes made of animal or even human hair, pigments found in the grotto, airbrush touches emanating from bent straws and blown by human breath, and employing techniques that were the product of their ingenuity. Indeed what I witnessed was the result of humanoid creativity that separated humans from lesser creatures, who perhaps also may have been creative but not to the same extent, where the event of harmony, perspective, and composition was implicit in the final result.

Out in the open air we discussed various aspects of what research was being done on Lascaux and what particularly Jacques was promoting. A video crew was scheduled to tape a documentary on Lascaux and he, Jacques, was going to be one of the leading commentators. I have not seen the whole tape of the documentary; although clips of it have been shown on several occasions on French television, unfortunately none have been shown in the United States.

Because Jacques had a delegation coming to discuss future aspects of Lascaux as part of a larger program for the grottos of the Dordogne, we said goodbye and continued our travel in search of the best chocolate. Montignac had a small chocolatier owned by Mr. André Perrault, a student of La Marquise de Sevigne who made wonderful truffles with cocoa imported from Gabon. We had ordered two kilograms upon arriving in Montignac. Our chocolate truffles would be available the next day.

It was time to do some exploring in the Dordogne and to visit several other grottos such as Cougnac, Péche Merle, and others, which we did. We left Montignac and stopped in Les Eyzies to see the small but significant grotto of La Mouthe that had one of the few drawings of the human figure. The keeper himself, Mr. Blanchard, looked like a genuine early edition of a Neanderthal man. Mr. Blanchard, who owned the grotto, was a character in his own right. I remember clearly that he kept potatoes and onions inside the entrance of the grotto. With the tiny flame of a small oil lamp he helped us see the drawings. They were exquisitely detailed and each small painting stood as a monument to the work of a fine artist. La Mouthe is not a very well known grotto because it is not on the obvious tourist path.

There are other things near Les Eyzies for visitors to see, for example the large Cro-Magnon sculpture carved on the chalk ledge of the gorge's wall. It is an impressive piece of sculpture dating back to 15 thousand years, and it does attract many visitors because it is so much in the open. Though La Mouthe is hidden, and is located on private land and furthermore the keeper is not too interested in making it accessible to tourists, he cooperates readily with scholars who can produce credentials as we did, especially those who speak French and hand him a few dollars (preferable to francs at that time).

After visiting La Mouthe we wandered about town where a weekly farmers market was held. Lots of luscious fruit and vegetables were on display, grills were set up for meats and sausages, and in a large tent we found a woman deep-frying beignets, those light little flour and egg puffs doused with powder sugar and syrup of honey and cognac. Eaten hot and with a good cup of coffee they are wonderful. We consumed several while standing and discussing where we might head next. Our next stop was the tables with all the colored silk cloths. All the silk cloths came from Italy but the colorful designs were French. We wanted to acquire several meters but our little car was already quite full, including the large box that contained my feather bed cover from Ulm.

In the late afternoon, we stopped to visit friends of Lawrence Beasley, Jean and John Laurie who had rented a house not too far from Les Eyzies. Our visit was short but enjoyable, and we talked about how pleasant it would be to have a place in the Périgord. Their rental house was possibly built in the 15th century and had a small garden. The house itself had been renovated in recent years and provided all the comforts that would make living in the Dordogne quite pleasant. I could easily live in such a house. Jean was writing a novel, her third I believe, and John, who was on an extended sabbatical from university, was enjoying reading and learning French. They had set aside a year for this period in France. After saying our goodbyes, we headed for a country restaurant in Thon where we knew that authentic French country meals were served at a nominal price. We were right. The meal was excellent and included fresh river trout, lightly cooked vegetables, crème au chocolat, and a local vin de table.

Now quite satisfied, we went for a walk then headed to our pension to prepare for the early morning departure for Notre-Dame du Haut, Ronchamps, in the eastern portion of France. On this particular visit to the Dordogne, we stayed on the outskirts of the small town of Sarlat in 1980 at La Chapelle, a pension near honking geese raised for pâté de foie gras.

This was a different experience than the one we had in 1979 when we were staying in Sarlat at the hotel Albert. On Tuesday when we had arrived at the hotel Albert, we were shown our room, then the kitchen and instructed on how we would find our breakfast — the baker would bring the croissants before we awaked — this was done because the staff was scheduled to have a day of rest on Wednesday. We were also given a key to the main door of the hotel and a telephone number to call in the event of an emergency. We felt quite at home in this 40-room hotel all by ourselves. Only in France does something like this occur. We prepared ourselves for breakfast with no difficulty the next morning, the croissants were delivered as promised, the baker prepared the coffee when he made his delivery, and set out several cheeses for us. We were on our own for only one day; after that day the service resumed and was quite good and hospitable.

We would now be leaving Sarlat for the eastern part of France, to visit the marvelous church of Notre-Dame du Haut designed by the Franco-Swiss architect, Le Corbusier (Charles Edouard Jeanneret-Gris). Indeed, we were crisscrossing France, going from east to west and then back to the east but that was the only way we could arrange some time with Jacques and be rewarded with another visit to the grotto.

We had estimated that the drive to Ronchamps would take about three to four hours. Because it was now Thursday, we would do the driving on Friday and be at Ronchamps a day ahead and in plenty of time to attend the morning Eucharist on Sunday at Notre-Dame du Haut; it was important that we set off early the next morning to allow for possible delays. We had to cross the Monts Faucilles and then proceed towards Belfort, the nearest city to Ronchamps in the Haute Saône.

Notre Dame du Haut

In the morning we collected our truffles from Mr. André Perrault and braved the French roads across France to Ronchamps and Notre-Dame du Haut. The drive was longer than we had expected but still we managed to arrive early in the afternoon and find that the hotel we had considered was simply unacceptable to us — the toilets lacked seats and the rooms were situated directly over a very noisy bar that reeked of cigarette smoke. We abandoned it after one look at the room. Off we went to look for another hotel, perhaps one nearer Ronchamps and the church. I was not about to spend the night in a horrible place just because it called itself a hotel.

We drove further up the hill and through a wooded area that looked strikingly like the Black Forest. Fortune offered us a small attractive hotel nestled among tall trees in the hamlet of Champagney, a mere two kilometers down

ADVENTURES OF NIMON · 21

the hill from Ronchamps and the church. We stopped and asked if a room was available. One was. The room overlooked a small flowing creek that ran through the woods. It was perfect. It was large. It was most pleasant. Moreover, the owners were friendly, hospitable, and a delight. After unpacking we asked if an aperitif was obtainable. Again we ordered Campari and soda, some cheese, olives, and a piece of baguette bread. The owner, Mr. Kembs, came to chat with us and soon we had a delightful time discussing various subjects that spanned art, architecture, education, political conditions, and aviation. He was a main supporter of the local elementary school and at one time had taught political history at the university in Mulhouse. We talked about the changing aspects of the Saar Valley area, the German influence and legacy, and the blood of dead soldiers that had soaked the ground of this great industrial region through the years. Mr. Kembs' family came from Kembs, a town located Southeast of Mulhouse and known for its dairy farms and cheeses.

Because dinner would not be served until 2000 hours and the summer light was still quite bright under a cloudless sky, we decided to walk about and investigate the surrounding woods. Emily's newly acquired fondness for birds was satisfied and my interest for simply enjoying the quiet and the scent of the woods fulfilled my needs. By the time the dinner hour arrived I was starved. The menu du jour was exactly what I wanted and I washed it down with a half bottle of pinot noir. Our placemats, covered in acetate, were made and drawn by the local school children. They were works of art and to our pleasure, at every meal we were given different placemat masterpieces. The ones that had been displayed were neatly kept for another day and another diner. The subjects on the mats ranged from animals, to sketches from stories the children had read, to nature morte, and cartoons. We stayed at the hotel three days and invariably looked forward to new and different placemats. In addition to the placemats, the service, the setting, and the food personally prepared by our hosts was exceptional.

After dinner we repaired to bed because we were exhausted but contented. The day had been enjoyable but it was time for sleep. On Saturday we walked into the woods, investigated the creek, and checked out Notre-Dame

Du Haut with its magnificent view of the valley below. It started to rain in the afternoon so Emily and I returned to the hotel and obtained a hot teapot and a few cookies, and enjoyed another session of good conversation with Mr. Kembs. We discussed the idea of the European Common Market and what it would do for France and Europe. He found it stupid of Charles De Gaulle, who attempted to exclude Britain from the Market. After all is said and done, the British helped De Gaulle in many ways during WWII, and helped liberate France from Nazi occupation. I agreed with Mr. Kembs who also envisioned a united Europe, a European Union, after the Common Market matured for a few years. Much of what was developing politically in terms of economic changes for Europe would prove to be the salvation of the continent and possibly the end of Western European conflicts.

The next day would be Sunday and the Eucharist at Notre-Dame du Haut was scheduled for 10:00 a.m. I did not want to be late for it. After a shower Saturday night, we went to bed but soon discovered that the sheets were slightly damp. Cool and damp for an evening that was not terribly warm caused us to feel a little bit uncomfortable. We soon fell asleep anyway.

Before heading up the hill to Notre-Dame, for breakfast we were served hot coffee, croissants, strawberry jam, cheese, fresh raspberries, and hard-boiled eggs. We mentioned to our hosts that the sheets had been a little damp. After a long apology, our host explained that because it had been damp for several days, he had been unable to get the laundry completely air-dried. He hoped that today's sun would help dry his laundry and he would see to it that we received crisp dry sheets for a comfortable sleep. In fact, although the sheets were less damp on the second night, they were not completely dry, but the hotel was so pleasant that the problem was negligible. We have since learned that clothes dryers are not standard in Europe — but they should be.

We drove the few kilometers to Notre-Dame du Haut. Photographs do not do it justice. Le Corbusier was an architect's architect, an artist in the real sense without the pretensions, the claims of artistic superiority, which usually plague people in the design profession. Le Corbusier's architectural style is generally known as the International Style. White cubic shapes and the avoidance of ornaments identify the International Style; Le Corbusier's style draws heavily on the purism of early Modernists, the proponents of simplicity, and is generally seen in the architecture of Ludwig Mies van der Rohe and Richard Alan Meier. It includes simple geometric masses, many of them pure white or nearly white.

The high walls of the Church of Notre-Dame du Haut curved almost like the nuns' headpieces of the sisters of Notre Dame and were painted a stark white and reflected crisply the bright sunlight. Curves, sharp edges, and peaks worked impeccably in unison to lift one's eyes towards the heavens above. Built on a hill and incorporating the remains of the old church, which had been destroyed by bombs during WWII, Notre-Dame du Haut overlooked the valley below and reminded visitors that the concept of "resurrection" was more real than imagined. Like a phoenix rising from the rubble and ashes of its destruction, the church structure stood as a sign that defeat in this case was succeeded by victory. Both the inside and the outside indicated a simplicity that said, "less is more," following Mies van der Rohe's motto.

In the nave the pews were placed on the right side of the structure, with nothing on the left but the entrance door and narthex. The sanctuary was large, open, uncluttered, and quite unlike anything seen in Roman Catholic churches; it had no statues or devotional aids. The altar, which allowed celebration facing the people, was made of a finely sculptured wooden table of hand-polished oak, from a tree that had been felled by the explosive force of a detonating bomb during an air raid. No railings had been constructed to separate the people during communion from the altar and sanctuary. Two candlesticks bracketed the altar thus leaving it uncluttered. The lighting was brilliant and accented by the square or rectangular windows gracing the side, front, and back. No window had been built behind the altar on the east wall, and this architectural design precluded the bright light that overcomes a sanctuary and often blinds communicants sitting or standing in the nave.

Above the sanctuary, however, there was a deep skylight directing a beam of outside light directly onto the altar. Neither pulpit nor lectern cluttered the space that allowed readers to hold their reading material in their hands and face people directly. Preachers are forced by the design to move about as they deliver their pearls of wisdom. They cannot hide behind a pulpit and pontificate; they must speak intimately to their listeners. This approach to preaching was emphatic enough that to this day I can recall the sermon; it was about Jesus being the *moteur*, the motor, of the world. Even Emily, whose knowledge of French is limited, could understand the message because the preacher's body language, visibly seen without a pulpit, was intimate enough to convey the theme of his address. Communion was administered in both kinds, bread and wine; again, I suspect this was the norm because the building forces intimacy for communion and injects corporateness. Emily remembers that an infant named Solange was baptized that day and wonders about her subsequent life.

After the Eucharist, I was able to speak with the priest who was kind enough to tell me much about the building and its history. For example, Le Corbusier filled the walls with the rubble left from the bombed old church's structure and that was the reason that the walls were thick. Outside, the remaining rubble was collected into a mound, covered with topsoil, and planted with flowers. Not one piece of rubble was hauled away to a dump. The candlesticks were fashioned from pieces of marble from the altar of the old structure. The current door was re-fashioned from oak that was part of the portal of the old church. The floor was constructed from crushed stone and concrete rubble bonded together with epoxy.

After the service we walked around the property again, then drove down the hill to the village of Ronchamps to have lunch and explore other places. The area around and near Ronchamps is mainly an industrial center of manufacturing and steel smelting. This is the robust part of France. Heavy industrial manufacturing is the order of the day in Lorraine around Metz. To the south the area down to Mulhouse and northeast to Strasbourg (now the seat of the European Union Parliament) is also industrial. One can see and feel the atmosphere of blue-collar workers with restaurants serving hearty meals centered on meat, large pieces of vegetables, bread, and beer. No sauces or dainty dishes can be found, except in the fancy hotels serving visiting delegations from Paris, Lyon, Luxembourg, Brussels, and other cosmopolitan cities. I like that part of France because it is less affected by tourism than other more genteel parts such the western coast from Arcachon to Biarritz.

Chocolates in Luxembourg

Early Monday morning we headed for the Duchy of Luxembourg, and the city by the same name. It would be a drive through some winding hill roads, the woods of the Ardennes, and many cemeteries holding the dead from battles in WWI and WWII. This is territory that has been the battleground for many bloody encounters, and which is marked by memorials from people long dead, and individually forgotten. Soon we reached the entry into Luxembourg. After finding our hotel in the suburb of Hespérange, which was situated eight kilometers from the center of the capital city of Luxembourg, we unpacked and prepared to head for the Centre de Ville and lunch. The sky looked dark and grey indicating that rain was soon expected. After locating a parking place in a lot that was surrounded by sheer cliffs, we climbed the steps to the center of the city. It started to rain. We took refuge under a store's canvas canopy and the downpour of rain followed soon after. By some good fortune we were in front of a chocolatier, one that we had not known even existed. We entered to sample the products but mostly to wait for the rain to cease. Mme. Alice Oberweiss owned the shop, and we soon discovered that she was a fine chocolatière!

Mme. Oberweiss had been making chocolate truffles for many years using brut Belgian bulk chocolate, which she preferred to any other. The cocoa was mainly from Uganda and Côte d'Ivoire from Mexican beans, which she preferred. She informed me that ever since the miserable Idi Amin ruled Uganda, she had switched to a brut that employed a southern Mexican variety, which she found to be much superior to anything she used before. All her chocolates were made by hand except when she used rollers to temper it. She employed Egyptian sugar because she found the taste to be excellent. Other sugars were not as fine to the taste, and she never used pineapple or beet sugar because they were too acidic. Mme. Oberweiss told me that she had visited the United States several times. She had a sister living in Virginia and one of her sons had attended the University of Virginia to study international law. Another son had earned a degree in nutritional chemistry from the University of Montreal and was expected to take over the chocolate business in time; he was already a fine chocolatièr.

After our serendipitous meeting we concluded that she produced one of the finest chocolate products found in Europe. Her chocolate was smooth, evenly textured, fully exuding the flavor of the dark and pure cocoa, without the added tastes of extraneous substances. It had sugar but it was not overwhelmingly sweet or bitter like most Swiss or French varieties. Until we found good chocolate available in the United States, such as early Scharffenberger (before Hershey acquired it) from Berkeley, California, we ordered all our truffles from her and from Mme Walders. Every so often I corresponded with Mme. Oberweiss, but she has retired and left her store to her son and daughter-in-law, who is, I am informed, also an excellent chocolatière.

The Duchy of Luxembourg is larger than the Principality of Liechtenstein. The capital city of Luxembourg was manageable on foot and we took advantage of that option to explore the main streets where the banks and the offices of the European Economic Union (the name predates the European Union) were. We walked to the gates of the Palace enjoying the gardens, the architecture — which resembled very much that of Paris, and the palace guards in their colorful uniforms. The Duchy is much more formal and its palace is grander than the Principality of Liechtenstein. Returning to our car, we drove a bit into the countryside where we saw a few dairy farms and some industries. But the Duchy is not blighted, as both industrial and political affairs make it quite active and prosperous.

Back at our hotel we were surprised to see that one of the owners was African. In conversation with her we discovered that her husband was an aircraft pilot who flew for CargoLux and who not only owned the hotel, but also was starting the new Air Afrique, an airline that would serve Africa from the Duchy, which has an international airport (Liechtenstein neither has nor needs one). A while later I met the pilot, Claude, who was European. Claude had flown for Sabena, the Belgian Airline, and had married Sophia, a Congolese, while serving as a line pilot on the Brussels-Kinshasa route. Sophia was born and educated in Belgium but had worked for Sabena in Zaire, now the Congo. Both Claude and Sophia spoke French fluently, but among themselves they spoke a language that sounded harsh to my ears, and which later I learned was a Flemish dialect.

We were so well hosted by both Claude and Sophia that we added a day to our stay, and would have added more days had our schedule permitted it. Claude and I had extensive conversations about flying, air traffic control, airport service and safety, and seat and freight revenue in Africa. At the time he preferred flying the Boeing 747-200 series but expected that soon he would change to the newer -300. Claude was not convinced that the Airbus was quite what suited his needs and he was not interested in re-training his pilots to fly a different aircraft. Over wine and cheese we had several good chats. Claude had been flying for over 30 years and had accumulated more than 20,000 hours, mostly over Africa, the Middle East, and South America. A few years later, I learned that Air Afrique had grown to become a profitable freight and passenger airline but had been purchased by a consortium and that Claude had retired to manage his hotel in Hespérange.

After Luxembourg we drove across the border to Cochem, Germany. This was a short two-hour drive through lovely country adjacent to the Mosel River, a tributary to the Rhine River that joined it at Koblenz.

The Mosel City of Cochem

The region of the Mosel River is famous for its white wines, its lovely countryside, and its quiet, relaxing atmosphere. A reservation for a week's stay awaited us at an historic hotel, Alte Thorschenke, in the small city of Cochem on the Mosel River. Cochem is approximately a two-hour drive west of Frankfurt am Main's airport, the Frankfurt International Airport. We only had seven days remaining in our vacation and wished to make the most of our remaining time by going to the airport only the morning of our last day.

After crossing the border between the Duchy of Luxembourg and West Germany (in 1981 Germany was still not unified) we were stopped by German custom officials who insisted on examining our car and the contents of all of our boxes and packages. This was a confrontation I did not expect, did not relish, and never have. Crossing borders almost always makes me uncomfortable and uneasy, because in many countries border guards and custom officers are unpleasant, domineering, and imperious with little cause because most travelers are quite honest and the few who are smugglers, terrorists, or illegal people know so many tricks of the trade that they are able to make fools of the border staff.

At any rate, after repacking the cumbersome down comforter, we were allowed to enter Germany and to continue on our journey to the Mosel region. We arrived at our hotel, an old and impressive structure that dated from the 15th century. Our room was on the top floor. It was large and overlooked the ancient city but was close enough to the electric train that we could hear it as it swished by at nearly full speed. Our bathroom was large and possessed all the amenities that we could possibly need. The bathtub was huge: twice the width and length of any ordinary tub we had ever used. The floor creaked when I walked, but the wood was original dark oak and glisteningly clean. Emily and I liked our room, the hotel, and the area. One problem we encountered was that the hotel did not have any off-street parking, which meant that we had to find on-street parking and hence empty our car of all of our possessions. That caused us a small confrontation with the night clerk on the morning of our departure.

After unpacking, we headed downstairs to the restaurant and ordered lunch. Fortunately the menu was in German, English and French, which made it easy for us to order what we wanted. Because I ordered a beer to drink with the meal, the waiter (who I later discovered was also the owner) gave me a strange look and asked me again if a beer was what I wanted. He brought us lunch and the beer but his look indicated that I had committed a faux pas. I was puzzled but a few days later I would learn all about my sin. Until judgment day I took a sip of my beer. The beer was bottled and did not particularly make me happy or satisfied. I find that German beers are less pleasing to me than Belgian or British Ales. Casket beers in German beer halls are much better than those in bottles; I suspect that is so because they are still live beers producing fresh aromas from their hops and live taste to the palate.

After lunch it was exploration time. When we drove into town, several galleries had attracted my attention, so off we went to make new discoveries. The galleries were well stocked with works from local artists, some of whom were painting nearby. One small painting particularly interested me. I examined it and discussed the work with its creator who was painting just a step away. After chatting with the artist for a while, I asked if I could reserve the painting for a later decision on purchasing it. He saw no reason not to agree. Before leaving Cochem I bought the lovely painting and have it often hanging on the wall of our dressing room.

We continued our exploration and stopped at a culinary shop and bought a much-needed paring knife that I've used for more than twenty years. The town borders the Mosel River and the riverbank and hill on the opposite side have many vineyards and some of the winery's names are world famous. We walked along the riverbank, stopped at a Konditorei to rest our tired feet and enjoy a cup of coffee and a pastry. The weather was lovely and the setting was out of a travel brochure. We continued our walk and explored several interesting sites, including shops selling wine, furniture, clothes, books, and musical instruments. None of the shops were selling junk or tourist mementoes. It was obvious that the community was targeting upper-end tourism.

On the return walk, which we made through the town, we wondered if there was a train for us into Koblenz where I wanted to check with Mercedes Benz for parts for my old '59-190D car. After crossing the railroad track, not on a crosswalk, we were stopped by a guard who shouted at us, waiving his hand and touching the rifle slung over his shoulder. His shouting of "verboten" became louder and his body language more pronounced and threatening. It then occurred to us that he was terribly upset because we had crossed the rail tracks at an unauthorized place. We turned around, and soon enough he became quiet. We never did find out about the train schedule; it just became less important.

The next day we drove to Koblenz for the information on the Mercedes. In Koblenz we found that the post office clerks (certainly more friendly than the guard) were more than willing to share information, direction, and search the address of a supplier when asked. We found the Mercedes distributor of dated cars and I was able to obtain a catalogue with prices.

Across the street we saw a MB dealer with a new Jeep-style four-wheel-drive vehicle. I was surprised to see MB making such a vehicle and had thought that one would not need an expensive off-road car such as this one to explore rough places. The car was beautifully designed, the seats were covered with leather, and the inside was well appointed. I was impressed and even thought that someday I might succumb to my deepest emotions and purchase such a car. As Emily and I were inspecting the car and imagining how we might use it, the salesman came over to speak with us. He spoke English and joined our conversation by kindly answering many of my questions. "Could the car withstand the harsh mountain roads of Western America, and the long freeways driven at high speed?" I asked.

He replied immediately, "Sir, the car was designed for the Eastern Front in WWII and made the campaign against Russia. It withstood the bitter cold weather of the Russian winter and conquered the bad roads of the Soviet Union." He paused to catch his breath, and tenderly touched the shiny hood of the car.

"It is a lovely car," I said. Then I added, "But the Wehrmacht lost the war!"

The salesman looked at me with his piercing blue eyes. He stood erect and towered inches over me. "Yes the Wehrmacht lost the war," he took a deep breath, "but the car did not." I thanked him and we shook hands as I said goodbye. He gave me a brochure that I've kept to this day. In the year 2000, twenty years after I saw the Jeep-like car in Koblenz, the MB 500 became available in California.

The week in Cochem was spent mostly exploring, eating, and reading. On one occasion we went to an interesting restaurant for authentic German fare where no English or French was spoken. The waitress tried to take our order and neither Emily nor I could figure out what we wanted. I saw one item and asked what it was. The waitress tried several times to explain what it was then in exasperation she put her hand on her hip to indicate that the meat came from that part of the animal; it was beef because she used her fingers to show us what horns looked like. Sign language does come in handy when words are nonexistent. It was a very good meal; I ordered it several more times during my stay in Cochem.

On our last evening in Cochem, we decided to have a full dinner at the hotel. I had already made arrangements for an early departure and had paid my bill ahead. The dinner was going to be paid separately with a credit card. We ordered dinner and when time came for me to order beer, the manager inquired why I did not order wine, the local specialty. Before I could answer he left our table and returned with a whole bottle of chilled white wine. "It is on the house with my compliments," the manager said. The manager was determined that I sample the local treasure, the golden wine of the Mosel region. I explained that I did not dislike wine, but knew so little about Mosel wine that I could not even select a good name. "I would have come to your assistance, kind sir, if you only had asked me," he replied. Judgment day did not call for condemnation: the manager was most kind to this beer-drinking American. It was a fine Johannesburg Riesling, dry and crisp. After dinner he brought me a glass of a white dessert wine that I found to be light and not sweet, and clarifying to the palate. I thanked the manager-owner of the hotel and left him a large tip for his staff. Had I made up for my faux pas?

We left Cochem very early the next morning, but in the process of moving our luggage and boxes, the night clerk-guard stopped us by waving his arms, tightly gripping my arm, and raising his voice but never shouting. I suppose that he was thinking that we were escaping without settling our bill. It took a bit of discussion but after showing him my receipt, he became calm and helped us carry our stuff to the car. Security was a serious business in Cochem.

The drive to the Frankfurt airport was easy, quick, and without incident. At the appropriate time, we boarded a Lufthansa flight to San Francisco, via Dallas-Fort Worth (DFW). Because of a strong tail wind, our flight arrived an hour earlier at DFW but we had to wait on the apron before we could park at an empty gate; what hour we gained, we lost on the hot tarmac.

Return to America and Thinking of Judas

An autobiography or memoir must include, I suppose, even the inner discussions that are rattling around in one's mind during the long hours of flight in the aluminum tubes called airline cabins. Books and magazines are good company on airplane flights but the best company is the thoughts that are generated inside one's head. Ideas, concepts, historical cameos remembered, meetings with friends, bits of conversations, are all part of the mental tableaux that entertain one in the silence of the night, especially on long intercontinental flights. It is the silence in one's brain that offers the best entertainment, at least for me.

A flight of approximately ten hours from Frankfurt to DFW keeps one's mind active, especially since sleep is not what I do when flying. As usual whenever I depart Germany I always think of WWII and the human conflicts that were either connected to it or exacerbated by it. Human cruelty has always been something difficult for me to comprehend. I have trouble understanding cruelty emanating from Christian, Jewish or Islamic behavior — and from other persuasions. These three religions in particular have more or less foundations of good human values; they consider the individual important, and have respect for human dignity. I cannot understand how human cruelty grew out of the very fabric of these religious convictions. When the treacheries and the killings that result are classified as being noble aspects of these cults, I have the most trouble. They trouble me because I see these religions claiming to offer the means to a better life, a better civilization, and a better human nature. How so?

Did the killing mentioned in the old religious texts of Judaism, Christianity, and Islam help fashion humanity into a better fabric? On the contrary; they became examples that could be tolerated as long as we understood them as a means to an end, an end that may be virtual and no more. In ethics, evil means employed to achieve a desired end are not acceptable. The deaths of martyrs in the Roman coliseums are historical events that cannot be accepted without regret. The modern deaths of Islamic fundamentalists in the Middle East for reasons that are uncertain cannot be ignored and dismissed. Outside the religions of the Book, we cannot avoid thinking about the Buddhist monks immolating themselves during the Vietnam War, during the occupation of Cambodia, and under the dictatorship in Myanmar; these acts were performed at best as a questionable moral testament and at worst a stupid act. There are other examples of martyrdom and none are excusable, especially when we accept that religion is supposed to be life enhancing and not life-denying. They are in a sense suicide. Does this immolation further the cause of enhancing life or does it just snuff out a life that might have become creatively healing?

From my perspective I doubt that death of any kind is a means to a good end. Even in accounts of heroic events, I find that death is an unnecessary issue, a wasted act, even an idiotic consequence that makes the point poorly. Let's see the waste of the sacrificial event when death is its consequence. The word sacrifice comes from "making sacred," bringing about a connection with the Holy, and the Holy is that which is understood as nourishing life and not death. A sacred place is a life-giving place where one encounters the Holy. Only in speech that connotes a poor understanding of both language and the meaning of the concept itself is sacrifice equated with death or the act of killing. This is obvious in the pronouncements found in the New Testament when Jesus mocks the whole process of animal sacrifice in the Temple to satisfy and pacify God, the source of the Holy. Yet Jesus himself in the Gospels is placed in a position by his redactors wherein he is killed to fulfill, we are informed, a sacrificial requirement that is believed to be dictated by ancient scripture.

It appears to me that something is terribly amiss in the justification of this killing when the argument for it is based on the human interpretation of "the word of God in scripture." Jesus is executed, we are told in the canonical texts and by many writers and that it was a "sacrifice" to God — even a ransom payment to God so that humanity might be saved — whatever that means. The cause for the killing of Jesus has many facets, none of which satisfy me. Moreover, quoting scripture to justify the killing of Jesus is a poor attempt for mitigating his death; in fact it is a way to rationalize support from dubious passages of scripture (for example an obvious reference is found in

Isaiah 53: 7-10) for a reprehensible act. Let me make clear: As I understand God, I am certain that God neither wanted Jesus killed nor did God require Jesus' death for a ransom. Jesus was killed by human beings for their own reasons, which included, among many reasons, expediency. Jesus was a dangerous person who interfered with the status quo. I stand firm by my statements in spite of what is written in the canonical texts, and even if I am classified as heretical. So be it!

I see three options available to me for understanding the meaning of the Biblical texts. First, I can be a naïve reader of the Bible and accept all that is written literally, and that the text is written by the very hand of God. Second, I can be a disclaimer of the Bible and be convinced that the text emanated from the mind of human beings and that nothing occurred outside the human mind — solipsism at its best. Third, I can be a critical reader of the Bible and hold that perhaps there is that which is called God, but that It is encountered by human beings in forms and ways that are relative to their position in the universe; that is to say, that the encounter with God is an experience of that which is "real" but it may not be mediated in forms that are necessarily "of reality." Admittedly, my position lies between that of the disclaimer and the critical reader, in essence options two and three, and a mixture of options two and three.

I am fascinated by the mystery of the universe but I do not want to use the worn out and simplistic cosmological argument to prove the existence of God. There are too many pitfalls in this approach because it is "I" who interprets what "I see" in the universe. When my interpretation is correct, physics, cosmology, and astronomy are my tool, but when it is incorrect am I in astrology? Much too dangerous an approach for today's thinking. The disciplines of physics, cosmology, astronomy, and philosophy are still struggling to comprehend what the universe is all about. Physicists are currently struggling to understand the content of the universe, especially gravity, weak/strong forces, and electromagnetism; the make-up of the universe in terms of string, patchwork universe, multiverse and the function of each as they attempt to tell us more about what envelops us. Even theology is attempting to resolve the issue of the creation and the universe. All I can say to give me some consolation is that in this vast, cold, and dark cosmos, we who exist on one of the smallest planets (there are inevitably more such small habitable planets in the cosmos) — perhaps in one of the smallest solar systems — have a consciousness of the universe. Indeed, I am gratified that in me the universe has entered my "conscious" state, and that through me it has begun to be consciously thought, appreciated, and explored. Would that all other human beings would share in that consciousness, not just a miniscule minority. The rest, the large majority of humans, are more intrigued by making war, by killing other living creatures, and in general by indulging in loathsome behaviors. The magnificence of the universe and the conscious thoughts of it that emerge in the few humans who think about it suggests that we are in awe of the whole process of creation. Then come the human acts of killing a life for causes that are unjustifiable, especially when such causes are given to "pacify or appease" a god, a god who we claim is the god of love.

Dinner was served on Lufthansa's transatlantic flight to DFW. Nevertheless the thinking exercise continued. At 39,000 feet there isn't much to entertain you except what's floating in your head, and what floats may need to be captured and examined. In this case it was one of several biblical episodes. My revulsion of the necessity for slaughter goes to many accounts mentioned in the Bible and to those same accounts forming the very structure of the theological framework of Christianity. I am mindful of what a Chinese friend of mine said after a Eucharistic service. "Raymond, why is Christianity so taken by the cruel death of Jesus? The Cross seems to be the central theme of what Christians believe," she observed in puzzlement. Susan He was interested in Christianity and she recognized that I was too. She was, however, curious as to why the cross, the symbol of Jesus' death, is the focal point of all that is said and done.

"On the night he was handed over to suffering and death...." Susan wondered where was the joy of the good news when it was prefaced by such a sentence? As perhaps one voice crying in the wilderness, I keep reminding people that Christianity is truly a message of joy, but that often this joy is sublimated by singularly focusing on the death of Jesus.

Of course I do know that human beings wrote the scriptures and the writers were overly concerned with death, the pending end of the world, and their historic affinity with sacrifice. But it seems to me that with the appearance of Jesus on the scene and the proclamation of his several benevolent messages, deadly sacrifices would be cast aside. Both the Roman and the local Jewish citizenry, however, could not leave death alone or cast it out of their religious framework.

I'm particularly puzzled by the rationale given by classical interpreters of the Gospels for justifying the purpose of Jesus' crucifixion as a necessary requirement for effectively obtaining redemption for humanity. What was it that humanity was being redeemed from? If it was from "original sin" then they were beating a dead horse because humanity remains in essence unmoved from its self-interest. People are still, and will continue to be, focused on self-rewards, self-aggrandizements, and self-satisfactions at the expense of others so much as to espouse despicable means, which are reprehensible, errant, and corrupt in essence.

Humanity has yet to adopt the position that Jesus offered of "loving one's neighbor as one's self." That call from Jesus has yet to be understood by human beings and no amount of redemption seems to be working. If we are redeemed from being alienated from God, then why are we still corrupting the Holy in our politics, our ethics, our behaviors, and our treatment of this planet? No, I see Jesus' crucifixion as the work of a humanity that refused to accept his pure personality and was unwilling to make the necessary corrections to preclude selfishness and to delete its own self-generated evil.

Placing ourselves in the context of Jesus' time, we must recognize that his homeland was under the sword of the Roman Empire, the convictions of the Sadducees, and the religious fanaticism of the Pharisees. The Sadducees gained influence in Judea after Judea became part of the Roman Empire in 63 B.C. They opposed a group of Jews called the Pharisees in religious beliefs and practices. Unlike the Pharisees, they accepted only the written law of the Hebrew Bible, and refused to recognize the Oral Law as binding upon them. In addition, the Sadducees did not believe in immortality, as the Pharisees did. They said that the soul died with the body. They also believed that all people had free will and were responsible for whatever good or evil befell them. In this mix of Roman, Sadducee, and Pharisee beliefs, the people of Jesus' homeland were struggling to understand not only their culture but also their historical and dogmatic foundation for their allegiance to God.

Perhaps someday humanity will realize and understand what Jesus was about. There are some glimpses that at the end of this dark tunnel a light shines brilliantly. Perhaps this is less optimism than hope, or even trust that Jesus' mission was not for naught. When would that hope emerge into reality? I don't know. But I do know that religion of any content offers more problems than are necessary or useful.

In this same context, I cannot understand the function of Judas Iscariot, who has the role of the betrayer. Was he necessary to fulfill the scene for the death of Jesus? He appears to be a key player in setting the drama in the right form. Someone had to act as the connection to the authorities and Judas was elected, or destined, to do that. Jesus, however, could have stopped him, couldn't he? Jesus himself could have gone to the authorities, thus circumventing Judas's betrayal, and precluding his suicide and his defamation in history. The whole issue of Judas has a bad smell. Constructing a theological apologia based on the behavior of Judas Iscariot seems to be disingenuous, not quite honest. I am unable to believe that Jesus used Judas as a means to an end. This is not the quality of person that Jesus projected. The redactors and the subsequent apologizers of the Passion narrative have done Jesus a disservice when they portrayed Judas as a treacherous pawn in the scheme of salvation. My research convinces me that Judas was an earnest follower of Jesus, but a follower who had a mind of his own and who could arrive at decisions that were different from group mentality and it is this quality in him that Jesus found attractive. I suspect that it is high time that the Church corrects its shameful interpretation and restores Judas' place gracefully in history. If Judas did alert the authorities, I'm more inclined to accept that it was done in partnership with Jesus, and, perhaps, at Jesus' command. If that is heresy on my part, then let it be so. I am more concerned about the phenomenal goodness of Jesus and his graceful acts, than in the misinterpretations produced by a few of the Church's so-called theologians.

Theology suffers from a lack of rational discipline. Unlike philosophy or physics that follow strict rules of peer analysis, theology is its own judge and jury floating in a sea of "belief." Who can argue with a theologian? Theologians have been the brunt of contested arguments for eons, but they remain firmly implanted on their pedestals and few have been toppled off. Their pronouncements are enviable because they have the scepter of belief and the allegiance of their devotees supporting them. Who can move the Pope, the Patriarch of Russia, or any other theologian, minister, teacher, denominational leader, or mullah one iota towards changing their positions?

Why was Jesus' death necessary? Some theological explanations state that God needed to be appeased because of the sinfulness of human beings. Jesus paid a "ransom" to God for humanity's appalling behavior. Are theologians saying that God required a ransom of sorts? Would a father ask for his son's life as a ransom? Let's assume that Abraham was a real human being for the sake of discussion. The account of Abraham's willingness to execute his own son, Isaac, at God's request to appease God may be understood more readily if we recall that he had a good, solid relationship with God. God made Sarah, Abraham's aged wife, fertile so she could bear Isaac when she was supposedly past her birthing possibilities. Abraham had been promised that he would live to see his offspring abundantly multiply. Wasn't Isaac to be a key player in this expansion of the generations of Abraham? So one suspects that Abraham was cognizant that this execution would be a moot trial of his trust and would certainly not culminate in the literal death of Isaac. In the scheme of the narrative, Isaac is the product of God's idea and not of Abraham's. It was the God of the Old Testament who promised that Sarah would overcome her barrenness and bear an offspring. The reason for Isaac was that Abraham's descendants would have a chance to populate the world:

> *...your wife Sarah shall bear you a son, and you*
>
> *shall name him Isaac. I will establish my covenant*
>
> *with him as an everlasting covenant for his offspring*
>
> *after him. (Genesis 17:19;cf., 15:14-16)*

The descendants of Abraham and Isaac lived in a covenantal relationship with God, became en-thusiastic (theos means god in Greek, hence en-theos means in-godded or in contemporary language enthusiastic — to be filled with God's being) followers of God, and practiced monotheism. Recalling that sacrifice is the making of something sacred, we can deduce then that Abraham was asked to make Isaac sacred and not to execute him. The culmination of the test and of the ceremony, yes the ceremony, occurred when Abraham was directed to a ram caught in a nearby bush. I interpret this ceremony as if God said to Abraham, "Listen carefully and understand that sacrifice has nothing to do with killing, but if you must kill, then go after the ram and prepare it as an enthusiastic offering for Isaac and his mission, and have a banquet in thanksgiving." The myth tells us that Isaac lived many more years and became the father of many progenies.

In contrast to Isaac's sacrifice, the issue is quite different with Jesus and God the Father. Would the benevolent, loving, omnipotent, and omniscient God the Father demand his Son's life as ransom? Why? To redeem miserable, selfish, and ingrate humanity? It all sounds improbable and foolish. Justifying Jesus' death by the redactors of the Gospels to be a mere execution by a local authority that was totally corrupt, even more corrupt than Rome's, was apparently not sufficient. The drama had to be expanded, the backdrop enhanced to include the opening of graves, the rending of the Temple curtain, and the quaking of the earth. The innocent Jesus died on a cross like a common criminal. Jesus died, as he surely expected and anticipated, to fulfill his goal, his mission, and his purpose and to establish the process that might bring about a change to the human heart. Even though he appeared innocent by not having committed any crime, he was inherently guilty of being a revolutionary of the worse kind dedicated to changing the status quo by changing the mindset of the people. He was dangerous to the Romans because he challenged their allegiance to the Emperor in the light of his monotheistic description of God, his father. He was dangerous to the Sadducees because he promised life after death, which they did not accept, and he questioned their religious beliefs as being void of any content. Moreover, he discounted the fanaticism of the Pharisees as being merely form without function. Indeed, he was dangerous, very dangerous because he thought little of the ancient Hebraic law; he injected human behavior with love and deleted fear; and he repersonalized the awesome God of Abraham, Isaac, and Jacob into his Father, Abba. This personalization of the Hebrew God to the people was tantamount to blasphemy, especially when Jews were prohibited from pronouncing even the word for God and traditionally substituted another word for it.

Thus Jesus established the process that might bring about a change to the human heart, and I cannot overemphasize that this is a process, a work in progress, and not an instantaneous event and certainly not a fait accompli as is often expounded from pulpits. But I shall go further with the issue. Redemption, if that's the word used, means that a process was started to change the human heart, and the culmination of which is still a long way off. Redemption is not limited to an individual, although the redemption of humanity demands redeeming many individuals, if not all individuals. Liturgically, every mention of redemption is a universal aspiration, for all mankind; it is not redemption from something but a change into a new attitude, a new mode of behavior, a new life filled with love, service, concern, reconciliation, bonhomie, and dignity.

Indeed if the death of Jesus is crucial for discerning the proposition that death is to be terminated and that resurrection (however it is defined) is to have a genesis, the process could have been accomplished without Judas (the unwilling pawn) or the ransom (payola, bribery, blood money) issues. Moreover, why did the ransom issue have to be brought to bear on the saving action? Is God the Father a kidnapper, who must be paid his due? Is God in need of payment before he can act? What kind of God have we before us? Surely the God who created the Universe is not petty, does not need the energy of a single life to motivate him/her/it?

It is preposterous to think that Jesus was the ransom payment to God the Father (his father) to obtain, nay, to purchase our salvation, our redemption. A loving God needs no payment to shower his love on his creatures. Not that much different from gravity requiring your weight to recognize that it is a force. Acting upon you is sufficient for gravity to be a force to contend with — to attract you is its own reward (I wish neither to carry this analogy further nor to equate God with gravity). After all, the reason his creatures are the way they are is because they are not automatons or zombies. It is understood that human beings, all creatures, are defined by the laws that circumscribe them, hence they are free to a certain extent, and can exercise their freedom within that context. Within that circumscribed limit, humanity has the freedom to obey and to disobey, to agree and to disagree, to follow and to digress. Humanity has the latitude to object and to acquiesce. Humanity has the free will to accept or to reject whatever it was that validated the personal expression of independent thinking. Independence offers both the possibility for doing good as well as for doing nefarious deeds. A loving creature (if it be Creator, God, or whatever) that has granted that right understands the consequences and should be prepared to love in spite of heinous actions.

What of Adolf Hitler, Saddam Hussein, Joseph Stalin, Pol Pot, and thousands of other tyrants? Many tyrants are in sheep's clothing and appear to be paragons of virtue. Humanity is not perfect. Humanity has been given freedom to act, but actions may be good or bad, benevolent or criminal. Retracting that freedom would make humanity behave, I suppose, but that is not how the human mold was cast. So tyrants do surface at times, and we humans should be prepared to limit their actions. Now, how God deals with tyrants is fortunately not my problem. But drawing another human being into the fray to make a divine point is pointless. Combining the lives of Hitler, Hussein, Stalin, Pot and the others still does not reduce the value of the life of Jesus. In sum, I consider the possibility of ransom to be absolutely unethical and irrelevant.

The biggest part of the problem about Jesus' death is that we do not understand the purpose of the victimization. If Jesus died simply because he was a convicted man accused of breaking the law and living under a rigorous and unfair legal system it would be acceptable. Indeed he was living under a double legal system that often operated at cross-purposes. For example, Pontius Pilate, the Roman administrator, was willing to release Jesus but the Jewish religious authorities felt threatened by this person who rejected their law, who rejected their current legal system. Jesus, after all, reminded them that "the law was for man and not man for the law;" in other words, the old law, the law of the Torah, was no longer absolute but had been replaced by the law of love. This was unacceptable to a bureaucratically directed community that shunned grace, and that operated and survived by enforcing the old law of the Torah.

In later years the death of Jesus took a more dramatic position for the new followers, the so-called Christians. Perhaps a simple death for being caught at cross-purposes with the Sanhedrin, the Sadducees, and the Pharisees would have appeared to give historical theologians little fodder for developing an elaborate scheme to obtain redemption. Many theologians have not been able to accept that Jesus died merely at the hands of a violent old-style religious system that would not accept that God was simply a loving God. The Sanhedrin authorities, the 23 members of the political and civil council that came mostly from among the Sadducees, could not tolerate a person of Jesus' ilk who challenged the old Law of the Torah. No, the synoptic writers or others had to conjure the betrayal scenes, underscore Judas's role (if he had a role), and dramatize the event on the hill of Golgotha. That Jesus, the man, died on the cross as any man wrongly accused would, was neither sufficient for the synoptic writers and others, nor was it for the hearsay-historians of the times. As I intimated earlier, an inconsequential criminal execution was not sufficiently dramatic and provided little fodder for the drama of salvation.

Jesus died on a cross as any convicted man would. He was, however, unjustly convicted by a legal system that was petrified by his forward thinking and by his extraordinary knowledge of God, and by his unquestioned allegiance to God. The drama of Jesus' betrayal adds not one iota of clarity to the mystery of his life. Jesus' life was a sacrifice, an overt act of holiness, a radical coming face-to-face with the sacred, a sacrifice because it forced human beings to encounter and to be confronted directly and unequivocally with the presence of the Holy. Jesus was both man and eternal Son of God whose death at the hands of humans does not delimit his intimate connection with God. He died as the Paschal Presence on earth who...

broke the bonds of death and hell and rose victorious from the grave. How wonderful and beyond our knowing, O God, is your mercy and Loving-kindness to us, that to redeem a slave, you gave a Son. (The Exsultet)

Perhaps in years to come, theologians (and the Church) will mature to the point of restoring Judas Iscariot to a position less heinous than the one he occupies. Even he deserves to be the recipient of the love, the grace, and the forgiveness of God. To paraphrase the parable of the adulterous woman: all those without sin, please raise your hand!

My Interest in Ocean Conservation

Because of good tail winds we arrived at San Francisco International Airport a few minutes ahead of time. Our ride home was waiting for us and off we proceeded to Montara. Now it was time to unpack, review the pile of mail that had accumulated while we were away, and attempt to sleep. I was able to catch just a few hours and was awakened at early dawn. After a cup of coffee the brain continued its exploration.

Was it an article in a magazine or the chance meeting in Jeddah, Saudi Arabia with Jean Michel Cousteau and his Vice President of International Affairs, Charles Vinick? I am not certain but anyway I became acquainted with Jean Michel and began to follow with great interest the oceanic research of the Cousteau Society. A few months after my acquaintance with the Cousteau Society, I was called to give assistance on a project in the Bahamas. It was on Andros Island that I ran into a member of the Monterey Bay Aquarium (MBA), John Racanelli, who was there to assist the local marine protection group. John was not a scientist but a training manager and close assistant to Julie Packard, the founder of MBA. John invited me to visit the yet unfinished facility of the future Monterey Bay Aquarium and to meet Ms. Packard.

On a short trip back to San Francisco, John Racanelli asked me to come for drinks at the home of the Packards in Palo Alto that evening. There I met Mr. and Mrs. Packard, Steve Webster, Julie, and several other people. As an employee of Bechtel I was sufficiently interesting for the clan to share information about the "new" aquarium to be constructed. The story was that Julie and Steve, graduate students at Stanford, were interested in developing a teaching and research aquarium dedicated to the protection of the Monterey Bay. Mr. Packard offered 50 million dollars for the project but ultimately added another 80 million to open the facility. It was a most extraordinary evening and I have always been grateful to John for making it possible. Let me continue!

As a graduate student and a member of the Episcopal Diocese of California's Future Planning Council, I had been fortunate to meet George Lockwood. George was a marine scientist who had come to the rescue of the California abalone by farming them. With the support of the Department of Fish and Wildlife, U.C. Santa Cruz, and U.C. Davis, George had created an ecologically sound model abalone farm off the coast of Pacific Grove, California. Later he was invited to Hawaii to develop an ecologically sound scampi shrimp farm. His techniques for scampi and abalone farming were lauded as being harmless to the environment and to similar animals in the wild — a great concern to marine scientists. My interest in marine ecology was increasing daily as I read more and more and also received papers from George on the subject. George was an enormous help when I was working in the Commonwealth of The Bahamas years later to help the authorities restore the conchs that had been depleted by over harvesting. Five years later, in 1990, I was informed that the conch population was increasing in the waters off The Bahamas and that the farming had been declared environmentally acceptable, all thanks to the advice shared by George Lockwood and his people.

Upon my return to San Francisco in April 1982, I telephoned John Racanelli at MBA. John invited me for lunch, to see for myself the developing aquarium, and to meet key personnel. When I arrived, I was immediately reintroduced to Julie Packard and Dr. Steve Webster, the chief scientist for the aquarium. Not much of the aquarium was constructed when I visited in 1982. The million gallon tall tank was in place but not filled. The old power plant was cleaned, enclosed, and preserved as a part of Cannery Row's history made famous by the novels of John Steinbeck and the writings of Doc Ricketts. Several pumps and pipes were in place, and much concrete was visible. At lunch I was given a quick sketch of the history of Mr. Packard's gift to his daughter Julie for building the aquarium. I was reminded how it all began as what appeared to be an informal conversation around the family coffee table in the Packards' home in Palo Alto. Being present at the Packards' was a revelation of how an idea can be realized when enthusiastic people with available funds support it!

Julie Packard's interest in marine science started long before she entered Stanford University. As an avid diver in Monterey Bay, when she was a young girl she thought that the Bay was a treasure that had to be preserved, and that one way to preserve it was to confront people with its splendor. The seed for an aquarium grew and matured as she matured into a scientist. In fact, at Stanford, she studied marine biology and graduated with a master's degree in the subject.

It was at university while she was completing her master's degree that she met Steve Webster, who was finishing his research for his doctorate in marine science. Both Steve and Julie became partners in the aquarium project; she became the Executive Director and Steve, the Chief Scientist. The team has worked well over the years. The Monterey Bay Aquarium opened to the public in 1984, and since then has been host to approximately 50 million visitors. I am proud to have been associated with the Monterey Bay Aquarium all these years as a donor and as an avid promoter of its mission. It is a mission that focuses on protecting the Monterey Bay, teaching all age groups, and showing that ecology is not a strange and remote concept. It was with the help of the Monterey Bay Aquarium that the Monterey Bay Marine Sanctuary (MBMS) was identified by Congress and given legal status.

Through the years I have tried to get Bechtel Corporation involved in giving funds to the Monterey Aquarium but my attempts were ineffective, yet I do know that one or two members of the family are donors. Aquarium staff have been most helpful in helping me identify needs and programs for non-Monterey projects, such as the coast off The Bahamas Islands, the bay off Bari, Italy, the Black Sea and Azov Sea nexus off Kerch, Crimea, and a potential project that never developed off Cape Mohamed, in Egypt. Their graciousness has been offered to me any time I called upon them, especially from Julie Packard, Steve Webster, and the now-retired aquarist David Powell. Today I consider myself a donor of record and feel good that I am able to support such an exemplary institution that performs such conscientious environmental services to the world by way of its focus on the California Monterey Bay.

My interest in the health of the oceans did not stop with the Monterey Bay Aquarium. When I met Jean Michel Cousteau and Charles Vinick, I also received an introduction to the work of the Cousteau Society and its research. I had the privilege of boarding the twin-wing-mast boat that was designed especially for sailing the high seas without the cumbersome canvas sails impeding the delicate work of the researchers. The boat is a sleek white vessel that seemed to slice through the water like a sharp knife. I took Emily and a colleague from Bechtel, Gordon Linden, and we toured the vessel from one end to the other and even watched the French chef prepare a superb lunch for the crew. Anchored at a pier in San Francisco, the vessel attracted visitors from many places on its public relations visit. We were part of the few honored guests invited to step on board. It was a marvelous experience and one that further convinced me that we earth dwellers had better tend carefully to the oceans of this planet.

Perhaps, had I known about marine science I would have opted to study that discipline at university? Having had no mentor to guide me, I selected disciplines, such as physics, philosophy, and theology, that were as important and were as critical as marine science, and those disciplines gave me an appreciation for Creation, for this planet Earth, and for the responsibilities that we human beings have to protect it all.

Of course the older I am the more I wish that I had the energy, the wisdom, and the years ahead to learn more about the many disciplines that tell us human beings a bit more about this planet, the Milky Way, dark matter, and the universe. Because time and energy are limited commodities, we do our best to learn as much as possible about this splendid creation, this universe.

Through the years I have continued to be interested in the protection of the oceans. I am a member of the National Marine Sanctuary Program directed by the National Oceanic and Atmospheric Administration, and also a local member of the Monterey Bay and Gulf of the Farallones National Marine Sanctuaries. These two sanctuaries are part of a group of 14 national marine sanctuaries; two more have been added to the list and funded by Congress. My specific interest is the protection of pelagic fish such as the tuna family of albacore, bigeye, skipjack, yellowfin, and bluefin, the latter being the largest and the fastest of all the tunas. Other pelagic fish, fish that swim near the surface and roam over great distances of the oceans, are anchovies, capelin, herring, mackerel, menhaden, and sardines. Pelagic fish are threatened because they are overfished and are the first to suffer from pollution since they swim near the surface of the ocean where upwelling of bottom food is found.

Many of the fish caught in waters over the continental shelf are taken from regions of upwelling. Upwelling occurs during certain seasons when winds blow surface waters near the coast offshore. The colder bottom waters are rich in nutrients because all food of one sort or another ends up settling on the bottom, then when the winds are right they churn the water, which then make the food rise to the surface near the coast. More nutrients are found in proximity to coasts because the land acts as a barrier that prevents further movement except to promote settling. This upwelling provides nutrients for the growth of tiny organisms that fish feed on, thus promoting growth of the fish population. Upwelling also brings to the surface toxic waste that enters the oceans from industrial and agricultural sources.

Upwelling takes place chiefly along the coasts of Peru, western North America, Northwest and Southwest Africa, Somalia, the Arabian Peninsula, Antarctica, the Northwest Atlantic, and a few other coastal locations. During the years when El Niño affects the weather pattern, especially over the Pacific Ocean, the Eastern coast of Asia contributes to upwelling and with it toxic industrial waste in enormous quantities comes to the surface from farm-

ing fertilizers, factories, and the general mismanagement of the coastal waters. In the 1980s large amounts of mercury were discharged from a Japanese
industrial plant near Tokyo; this heavy metal ended in much of the upwelling
along the shelf of its coast and later spread throughout the world's oceans.
Tuna and especially the bluefin variety roaming the Pacific Ocean absorbed a
sufficient amount of the mercury to make them inedible for human consumption, although dolphin and other marine animals did eat tuna. Tuna with
residual mercury was found in the North Atlantic, thousand of miles away
from Japan. Because mercury is a carcinogen, bluefin tuna was banned from
sale in North America and in Europe for two decades, although the Japanese,
disregarding the ban, continued to consume them and pay a high price
($50,000 to $80,000) for some fish.

Fortunately, the level of mercury in tuna has decreased greatly and fishing them has improved sufficiently to allow them to regain their numbers.
The organizations I support monitor the oceans quite seriously and push for
world legislation and control to protect the oceans and the marine life residing in it.

A New Chapter and a New Companion

In December 1982, Trudy telephoned me to ask me if I would file for the
dissolution of our broken marriage. She wanted to marry her high school
sweetheart, Tom Sayne. Thomas Sayne had a doctorate degree from Yale
University and was currently head of the German department at the University of California, Riverside. She had dated Tom when we courted in
Knoxville but the relationship did not progress after she met me. I remember
that he had come to Knoxville to visit with her during the winter break of
1961. She would meet him in the early evening but by 11:00 p.m. she would
meet me for a midnight date.

That said about our early relationship, I was ready to accommodate
Trudy and filed for dissolution immediately. Trudy wanted to be married to
Sayne in June 1983, and because in California it takes six months for the dis-
solution to be finalized, I found a lawyer who would file the papers

immediately. We had been estranged for five years and all our finances were completely separated, hence the legal issues were resolved and the process was smooth. On December 15, 1982, after going to court with my attorney and answering several questions asked by the judge, my attorney filed the necessary papers. One pointed question asked by the judge was why I insisted on joint custody of the children. My answer was simple and to the point: "Your honor, I have roots in Europe and if you do not award me joint custody, I will board the 6:20 p.m. British Airways flight to Heathrow this afternoon with my children, and never return to America."

He looked at me for the longest moment. Trudy had made no appearance in court and for that negligence I had to pay a $50 fine, which I paid gladly, but her no-show gave me an advantage before the court. "Dr. Hoche-Mong I believe you. Your request is granted." The dissolution was finalized on 15 June 1983. Trudy married Sayne soon after the final decree was issued, but her marriage lasted a mere six months.

Freed of the burden of a poor marriage I was now considering what I would do with my life. My position at Bechtel had improved greatly and my service at St. Edward's Episcopal Church was enjoyable, especially since John Schively, the rector, was a fine person to work under. I was assisting at St. Edward's Church in San Jose and working closely with John who gave remarkable freedom to my own approach and did not feel threatened by my style or my popularity with a large group of parishioners. I would drive to San Jose on Sunday mornings and take Michel and Emily with me. On the way down in the faithful blue Mercedes, I would place Michel on my lap and let him steer the heavy car on the highway. He always did a perfect job as driver, especially since he was only 13 or 14 years old.

Yet, all was not well and events were not velvety. John was having marital difficulties and his son's declaration that he was gay added to John's problems. At St. Edward's, John was considering resigning to get his personal and marital life in order. I had dinner with him one night in San Mateo and tried to dissuade him from resigning but was unsuccessful. A few days after our dinner I received two telephone calls, one from C. Shannon Mallory, the bishop, and another from Don Koenig, our mutual friend. They both informed me that John had resigned his cure as rector of St. Edward's. My colleague, the other assisting priest on the staff, Billy Joe Hoover, was appointed interim rector. Billy was a non-stipendiary priest employed by Lockheed Space Industries, and lived close to the parish in San Jose. It was a good appointment and Billy was an excellent interim rector for the parish. John's departure was a sad occasion for me.

My own situation was not difficult but needed some attention. At Bechtel I had begun to carve a good position for myself, and the future looked much better than it had been. I was beginning to be recognized as a talented person who could get things done and who was creative in several disciplines, which included aviation and the development of the knowledge city or region. I was, nevertheless, struggling with what I wanted to do with my life. I had the idea to own and operate a bed and breakfast, which would give me some financial independence in case my employment at Bechtel went sour; it would also give me a platform of revenue when I chose to become an independent consultant upon retiring. That I needed a larger house and an employee or a willing mate to help me in the endeavor was obvious. Loneliness for me was not much of a problem because I was working on many projects, both with Bechtel and for myself. Yet it would be in order and would be comfortable for me to have a partner, a mate, and an understanding lover.

Emily and I were friends with a strong bond between us. I was still very reserved about expressing my love for her, because the experience with Trudy had not been very encouraging. I admit that I was a bit closed to love and very much in a mode of self-preservation. Yet, I was hoping that this would change and it has. Emily had done some extensive traveling with me; we have enjoyed many places and many serendipitous occasions. Emily is a wonderful fit as a mate. Aware that I was not perfect and was also mostly an impossible person to live with because of my attitude, my values, my creativity, and my demands on life, I gave my relationship with Emily a great deal of thought. Emily seemed to accept my disposition, my peculiar attitude, my orneriness, and the fact that I was a curmudgeon on occasion. Yet we managed to get along quite well both at work, privately, and when we traveled.

Emily understood that I was keen on my children and that they were my primary concern.

We both had handicaps of one sort or another. Mine was that I distrusted any intimate long-term relationship. Hers was alcohol but it appeared to be under control. She went through a long-term detoxification program to overcome her dependency. Her support therapist had informed me that Emily would never be cured, but that her dependency could be controlled. I was hoping that it would work out for her and that she could get rid of her alcohol problem, once and for all. That dependency has been difficult for her to overcome, if she can overcome it ever. It was a problem with me because my margin of tolerance for drunks is quite thin, if not nonexistent. In the intervening years, Emily has been as good about not imbibing as she could be, with, however, a few occasions when she fell "off the wagon," as it is said. When drunk she is another person. To see a loving person turn into a confused, incoherent, and idiotic individual is devastating to me. Emily has, however, been able to put her dependency aside by mostly avoiding alcohol through force of will, prayer, and recognition that it was ruining her life and our relationship. Emily has finally started to attend Alcoholic Anonymous meetings on a regular basis and that seems, I hope, to improve her disposition greatly. At this moment, I await to see what the future will offer us.

After long conversations with Emily, which began in 1980, to explore the possibility of owning and operating a bed and breakfast, and after planning for it informally, we began to search for a suitable building. Training was not an issue for me, for us. It was quite clear to me that our B&B was going to be developed our way, would reflect our ideas, and would host guests as we understood hospitality. I was determined to have a house that was large enough for my books, my art, and ample room for living comfortably. I also wanted a house with history, sufficient rooms for guests, space for a large kitchen, an ample common room, and a large garden. My current house in Montara was large but not large enough to convert into a bed and breakfast. After calling on several realtors and being shown houses that were unsuitable or not in places of the Bay Area that I liked, I was almost on the verge of abandoning the whole issue and because I was traveling a great deal for

Bechtel, my time was limited for house searching. On a bright Saturday morning, a morning that makes one thankful to be living on the edge of the Pacific Ocean and after I had explored two quite unsuitable houses, my realtor, Jan Grey, asked me if I was willing to look at a "white elephant."

"Where is it?" I asked with a tone of impatience.

"It's on George — the extension between 3rd and Sunshine Valley Roads," she replied hesitantly.

"The house with two turrets?" I asked.

"Yes, it is the house with two turrets."

My reply shocked both Jan and Emily. "If it is in sound structural condition, I'll buy it." Both Emily and Jan looked at me and were puzzled by my direct reply. I knew the house from the outside, I had seen the garden around it, and knew people who were familiar with the house and some of its history. After all it was one of a kind. The house was designed in the style of an Italian villa, but had been subjected to many additions that gave it an interesting and beautiful architectural presence. Emily and I did buy the house. The year, 1983, was a year full of surprises and new beginnings.

After admitting that we cared for each other, Emily and I were married on November 6 at St. Edward's at the main Sunday Eucharist with the Reverend Dr. Earl Count, priest and anthropologist, officiating. A few weeks earlier we acquired the building with the two turrets that ultimately became our home and the Goose and Turrets Bed and Breakfast. In addition to what was already occurring, we purchased our beloved aircraft N4004R, the Piper PA-32-300. So many things happened that year that I almost lost the thread of events. Emily had obtained her Private Pilot license on "square root day" (9/9/81) and was ready to act as copilot on flights of exploration.

The Goose and Turrets Bed and Breakfast was still a long way off before it took shape as a workable, if not revenue producing, business. Much inside had to be torn out of the nearly century old building and much had to be constructed and reconstructed to bring it up to approved building code, to make it structurally sound, to make it livable, and to create a five-room bed and breakfast out of it. The building had to be restructured, new foundations added, the upstairs — our eventual quarters — had to be reconfigured with an attic, dressing room, shower and bath, and toilet. Downstairs a new kitchen had to be constructed, and several other bits and pieces had to be tended to before we could begin to invite guests or to live in the house comfortably. We had an immense task ahead but with the encouraging assistance and direction of our dear friend Donald Koenig the project had possibility. In addition our friend and real estate broker Roberta Fickles assured that we had made a good investment, especially for the low price we paid.

Don, a pilot also, had just retired as chief inspector of the San Jose Planning Department. His wife Geraldine, who was not quite ready to have him home all day, encouraged Don to take on our project, which he found challenging, exciting, and creative. I doubt if Emily and I would have been up to the challenge without Don's invaluable assistance. Don gave us the hope, the strength, the knowledge, and his priceless insight. In the process of reconstructing the house, Don became a close friend and often we would take a day of rest to fly my Red Bird for the traditional $100 hamburger.

As a form of a delayed honeymoon, Emily and I decided to head for England and France for a four-week holiday. Because Dominique and Michel were also having school breaks during the month of December, I proposed that they both meet us at Heathrow the beginning of the third week of our stay. In essence that gave Emily and me two weeks to visit Cornwall, and then two weeks with the children. For Dominique and Michel, my intent was to show them Ely Cathedral, Paris, and then Lascaux. Jacques Marsal was to host us in Montignac and explicate to Dominique and Michel the nuances of the great grotto of Lascaux, which they had never visited. This would be the first time that Dominique and Michel would travel without an adult to Europe. We met them at Heathrow after they had a most pleasant flight on Pan American Airways.

For the first two weeks Emily and I explored Cornwall from top to bottom. It was a marvelous time spent in sunny and stormy days, calm and violent weather. In St. Ives, we found a lovely room in a family run B&B. Our room was perched on the third floor overlooking the Irish Sea. During storms the waves would lap at our third floor windows with such force that we were certain that water would do in the house. Our hosts assured us, however, that the house had withstood storms for more than four centuries. They were not a bit concerned and soon neither were we.

Staying in one location for several days proved to be a clever decision. After a few days, it was time for laundry. We found a proper coin operated laundromat in Bude but when we arrived I decided that if I took all my clothes off, Emily could wash them too. Covering my self with a blanket, I undressed in the car and waited patiently for my clean clothes to be delivered by Emily. The whole process worked well, until another car pulled up next to me; fortunately the occupants soon left their car to use the washing facilities and the tension dissipated.

After doing our laundry it was time to do something about lunch. What does one eat for a quick lunch in Cornwall? Pasties. Pasties are dough pockets (similar to Italian calzones) with meat, potatoes, and vegetables all baked together to form a nice, neat lunch snack. We were on our way to Mousehole (pronounced "mouzall") located at the very tip of England on the Channel, a couple of miles from Land's End. This was a small fishing town with much history and beauty. Stopping on the road at a bakery we purchased two pasties that we couldn't eat right away because there was no proper place to park the car for a picnic, so we decided to place the pasties over the car's heater vent. We drove on to Mousehole, and soon forgot about the pasties. Arriving at Mousehole, we found a spot near the small beach and remembered our pasties: they were hot, delicious, but way too big for both of us to eat at one sitting. With my ready Swiss army knife, we divided one pasty, and kept the whole one for another snack. Off we went exploring Mousehole, its harbor, fishing dock, several book and antique stores, and its enormous Father Christmas. We did not expand the British economy because we did not want to carry anything in our bag or small car.

The visit had been a good way to goof off after months spent purchasing the future Goose and Turrets and currently thinking about all the repairs, deconstruction, and construction that would be necessary to make the old building ready, not only for our own occupancy, but for the anticipated guests at the B&B. Much of the pleasure of this holiday was diminished by my concentrating on who would be hired to make the building not just livable but also in compliance with the legal codes. On top of that I was feeling the discomfort of not being able to manage my bladder well. I was having a problem with the inability to empty it when I needed to.

Our next tourist stop was Penzance, where that night I wanted to taste some renowned home-brewed ale made by two brothers. In the Old Pub, built in the 12th century or earlier, we ordered our ale and spoke to the mother of the brothers. With two pints of dark chocolate-colored ale we sat in the smoky pub until eight o'clock waiting for dinner to be served. The time was a little before six. Two hours before dinner, and I cannot drink without eating. To the car I went to rescue the other pasty, which was also warm and delicious — in fact it became our dinner for the evening!

Penzance did not display any pirates, as Gilbert and Sullivan would have us believe, but it did show us that the community was unafraid of fires. In many of the shops, this being the week prior to Christmas, displays with lighted candles were the norm. Because it was past eight o'clock at night, the shops were closed for the day, yet the candles were left to burn prettily and no one seemed to attend the window displays. The displays were delightfully festive but we kept wondering about the possibility of fire. None occurred and none were expected to occur. A local couple walking by stopped to look at the window display and informed us that these were beeswax candles and that they were secured to put themselves out when all the wax was consumed. I suspect that a pirate ghost, invisible to us tourists, was looking after the candles in the many shops we saw. Anyway, I hoped so.

Soon it was time to drive to London's Heathrow International Airport to meet Dominique and Michel. Our plan, after we met them, was to drive to Cambridge where Nan Youngman had located an apartment for us not too far from the village of Trumpington, where my old school, Victoria College, used to be. Currently the property was an open field that was being readied for the construction in the future of an artery connecting a local road to the motorway leading to London. The Pan Am flight was on time and both Dominique and Michel where happy but tired. We drove to Cambridge and unpacked in our apartment. After dinner, a bath, and chocolate dessert, the kids went to bed and we went to the local pub for me to sip a house-brewed pint of ale and for Emily to have a non-alcoholic drink.

The next day it was a visit to Nan and then lunch at the Old Fire Engine restaurant across from the main entrance to Ely Cathedral. Both the lunch and the cathedral were awesome to Dominique and Michel (who had seen it on a previous visit). That afternoon after returning Nan to the Hawks (her house and property) we drove on to Cambridge and King's College, where Dr. Norman Pittenger met us. Emily and I went to tea at Aunt Annie's Tearoom, and the kids went with Pittenger for an extensive tour of King's College, its study area and the renowned Chapel with its Rubens behind the altar. Michel, on a previous occasion, had met Norm who had given him an extended tour of the University, the Camb River, the suite where I studied, and King's Chapel. The tour was repeated and both Dominique and Michel loved the campus. After their tour we went for a long walk around Cambridge where I showed the kids where I lived when I did my research on A. N. Whitehead at King's for my doctorate in 1973. We walked to 77 Maid's Causeway, where my apartment was located and where I spent months studying and simultaneously avoiding Trudy's constant harping. "I am bored. You have something to do. I thought we were going to have a vacation!" was the repeated refrain. Sadly I remembered that wail but now its echo was buried in the past never to be heard again.

We stayed in Cambridge just for one more day before making our way to Oxford. Oxford is approximately a three-hour drive from Cambridge passing through several small towns and villages, mostly to avoid the traffic on the main roads. It is a beautiful drive but not a particularly leisurely one.

The next morning it was time to head for Oxford and to Mrs. Rebecca Trace's B&B on the outskirts of the city, in Banbury. Mrs. Trace's Rectory Farm was in a sense the model for my bed and breakfast, and she was also the spark that helped me see the possibility of an actual B&B in Montara. Mrs. Trace and her husband, Jeremy or Jerry, had taken an old Oxford faculty house and converted it into a comfortable but unpretentious home with three bedrooms for guests. The two common bathrooms had huge tubs, towel warmers, ample lighting, toilets, and lots of fluffy, thick towels. The dining room was their dining room and was furnished with solid oak furniture inherited from their parents. The sitting area was located in the old library, richly endowed with 19th and 20th century authors. Both Rebecca and her husband were the product of Oxford University and each had books covering their particular interest; hers was in literature, and his in history.

Jerry was also a connoisseur of ale, live ale, which means ale that has not been capped in a can or sealed bottle. On several occasions Jerry shared with me a pint of Old Hookey, the live ale from the nearby brewery made especially at Christmas. He also directed me to the Star Pub to have a pint or two of ale under the able Jack, the wonderful and enjoyable publican who often watched the "google eye," the name given to the television by his wife.

That night, Dominique became a little ill so she quickly went to bed after sipping a hot cup of tea and a few dry biscuits prepared by Mrs. Trace. The rest of us went to the Thatched Roof restaurant in Warmington, a village a few miles north of Banbury. The Thatched Roof is located directly across from the estate of George Washington's family. The restaurant offers a traditional English fare with no Continental imitations or pseudo French dishes. Straight English food washed down with English ale or, if one prefers, English wine. Michel outdid himself by eating a gigantic chocolate pudding dessert topped with double cream.

The next day Dominique had regained her exuberance and we all went to explore what Oxford offered. Balliol College, St. Mary's Church where Thomas Cranmer preached his famous last sermon "my dear children..." before being taken to the stake to be burned alive by order of Queen Mary, Bloody Mary, the eldest daughter of King Henry VIII and Catherine of Aragon. We walked the very steps that Cranmer took to the heap of faggots gathered for his forced immolation. I had walked to the same spot in 1973 and wanted both of my offspring to experience the solemnity of what had happened to Thomas Cranmer. Both children were silent and in awe and had read the play that I had written, *The Crowning Winter.* The play, written in 1974 as part of my doctoral comprehensive examination, explored the last days of Archbishop Cranmer before his burning at the stake on a wet morning in 1556 not too far from St. Mary's Church, Oxford, along with Bishops Nicholas Ridley, and Hugh Latimer, both colleagues and supporters.

After Oxford we drove to Dover with a short stop to visit Canterbury Cathedral in Kent. We attended Evensong and enjoyed seeing the grand cathedral, especially the grave and the altar where Archbishop Thomas à Becket was murdered in the 12th century. In 1989, a commemorative plaque was dedicated in the Cathedral's crypt for Archbishop Thomas Cranmer. I had wondered for several years why there was nothing commemorating the life and work of the great archbishop, the man who so defined the character of Anglicanism and its liturgy, if not also its understanding of theology. I was pleased to see that at least a plaque had been placed in the mother church of the Church of England. The visit to the old Cathedral was memorable all the more so because Michel left his brand new English-style cap on a pew; it was never retrieved. Michel has not forgotten the loss of his cap.

After Canterbury, it was to Dover that we continued on Christmas Day. Christmas and its twelve days are considered to be holidays, and hence most of the shops, restaurants, and businesses are closed. When we arrived at the Hotel Dover, conveniently situated near the docking platform of the Channel ferry for France, we found that we could return the rental car and walk easily back to the Dover Hotel. Our ferry to France was scheduled to depart the next day at noon. In the meantime we had to look for a restaurant that would supply us dinner. There were no local restaurants open to serve us. There was neither any Indian nor Chinese restaurant, which are usually open during the Christian holidays. We discovered quite soon and fortunately that the hotel restaurant, although closed to the public, had two tables with quantities of food on them. The whole set up looked quite festive but we could not understand why the restaurant was closed to us, the only guests that night on Christmas night. I went in search of the manager, who was also the owner. When I met him, I was informed that all the restaurants in town were closed for Christmas but that we were invited to share the hotel staff's party and eat to our heart's content. What a fantastic invitation this turned out to be! We had a wonderful time and the food was superb. We all enjoyed the meal, the festivities, and the conversations that emerged. The kids went to bed and we continued with the party. In the morning at breakfast we discovered that the wonderful dinner we had enjoyed the previous night was complimentary.

Because the weather made the water of the English Channel too rough for the operation of the hovercraft, we boarded a small ship that bobbed with every wave and every gust of wind as it carried us across to France. I am not too fond of ships or of sailing, and the sea or ocean intimidates me just a little. I suppose that because I fly, the water is as unfamiliar to me as altitude is to a sailor. I remember chatting with a Navy pilot who was qualified for instrument night landings on carriers, who assured me that he works very hard at making each landing perfect because he too was petrified of the water or the idea of ditching in the ocean. To me the sea is cold and wet and a foreign medium. After a couple of hours on the ship, we were in sight of the coast of France. Calais was just around the bend of the land. "Voilà la France," a little boy shouted. Indeed, France was just a few minutes away.

When we docked on French soil, Michel reminded me that I should be careful with my French because he did not want to be embarrassed! There is nothing more difficult than having a smart kid. Inside the terminal we searched for the Avis rental car representative but found the counter closed. Fortunately, a National car representative was willing to rent us a car, a much smaller car than we had booked with Avis. We took the car and soldiered on towards Paris. Our plan was to spend three days in Paris, then proceed to Montignac, our destination, with one intermediate stop along the way after our stay in Paris.

In Paris we decided to stay at the Hotel Helder, which is located just a few blocks from the Place de l'Opéra off the Boulevard des Italiens, a very central location. Paris would offer the kids a chance to do some investigation on their own. Dominique was 18 and Michel was 15, old enough to do things on their own without Daddy tugging at their chains. Dominique wanted to investigate the shopping and movie areas and Michel wanted to revisit the Pompidou Center and the Quartier Latin. With city maps in hand Dominique and Michel escaped the paternal eye. We were to reassemble at the Centre Pompidou at 1800 hours. In the meantime Emily and I decided to visit the new Picasso gallery, several other art centers, the Cluny to see the embroideries, and several bookstores on the Left Bank of the Seine. Lunch was enjoyed in a small restaurant near the Place Saint Séverin, in the depths of the Latin Quarter.

After completing our exploration we proceeded to the Pompidou Center first to enjoy the activities outside the building that often included lectures, comics, sidewalk performances, and music, then inside, where there was an exhibit of Magritte's works. The Pompidou Center is an extraordinary building and one of the first architectural works to openly display and color-code its utility infrastructure. The Italian architects Renzo Piano and Gianfranco Franchini, the British architect couple Richard Rogers and Sue Rogers, designed the Pompidou Center. I have always been amazed at how all these architects were able to work together to produce such an extraordinary building. In normal circumstances, architects are known to be prima donnas; hence managing this club of creative people would be tantamount to directing a team with several Maria Callas-level divas. The Centre Beaubourg, as it is locally known, is a magnificent site for young and old — there is no room for boredom in the area. One can see everything from plays and singing to acrobatic stunts in the plaza, and then let the eyes follow the structure itself. Hence heating and water pipes, electrical conduits, cables and operating systems are all out in the open for all to see, which also makes repairing them easy. The building looks inviting, open, and conveys a sense of intimacy because all its parts are visible.

At about 5:30 p.m. I started looking for Michel and Dominique inside the Pompidou Center. Soon enough I found Michel, hunched over, and sitting on an inside step outside the lavatories. He was very sick with an acute case of diarrhea. Fortunately, when I travel, I always carry Lomatil pills with me just for diarrhea. After taking a pill and returning once more to the toilet, Michel seemed to regain his composure. Before we left the Pompidou Center, Michel was well but declined to have dinner. Soon Dominique joined us and quickly informed me that she wanted to skip dinner and instead see a movie. Off she went with instructions to knock at my hotel room door when she returned from the show. Michel just wanted to go back to the hotel. After depositing

Michel at the Helder hotel, Emily and I went to the Opera Pizza for a light meal of fruits de mer and their famous profiterole dessert.

The next day, with both children in good health, it was to the Louvre, Bois de Boulogne, the Eiffel Tower, and several other places of interest for all of us. Breakfast was always of fresh Parisian croissants, lunch was saucissses and frites, dinner that evening was a Plat de Fruits de Mer. Tummies satisfied, we took a walk along the Seine and Dominique romanticized about living in Paris and other dreams that surface from a young girl's imagination. The next day we were to be off quite early to Montignac and I felt that possibly a cold was attempting to access my body.

Using the autoroute south we headed towards the Dordogne and Montignac, but once out of the capital we had to take a secondary two-lane road to continue our journey. By early afternoon I was tired so we decided to spend the night in Aubigné, the hometown of La Marquise Françoise de Maintenon, mistress to King Louis XIV, and the name given to one of the schools where mother taught in Cairo, the Cours Maintenon. In Aubigné we found a small hotel with two rooms overlooking the chateau of La Marquise. A short walk to town took us to a pharmacy where I obtained some medicine to squelch the cold. By morning the cold was history and I was feeling my proper self again.

Again after croissants (Michel consumed six and Dominique five) and café-au-lait we continued south to Montignac, where Jacques Marsal expected us. We arrived at the gate of the Grotto de Lascaux at eleven o'clock. Hugs and more hugs and pats on Louf's head preceded our entry to the grotto, which, as I mentioned, neither offspring had seen. Of course the idea of visiting a grotto with "ancient" art was beneath Dominique's artistic taste. Michel was quite ready to see the art, and in fact was excited to forge ahead in the darkness. As I said, Dominique was reflecting the temperament of the all-knowing teenager: "Ancient art from our ancestors?"

Once inside the grotto both Dominique and Michel were in awe. Their eyes were wide open after becoming accustomed to the low light intensity and we could hear the oohs and ahs, exclamations of amazement. They had heard me speak of the splendor of the grotto, had seen some pictures of the art on the walls, and had heard Marsal elaborate on the history, technique, and restoration program. Now, they were absorbing the actual work of art produced by early human beings of the Cro-Magnon era. Dominique immediately altered her negativity and was quickly taken by what she recognized as superb. Needless to say, as recently as my birthday in 2002, both Dominique and Michel admitted that seeing the grotto of Lascaux was one of the most memorable experiences of their lives. We remained in the grotto for just over an hour, a bit longer than is at times permitted with five breathing human beings, but Jacques felt that no damage was possible because he would circulate additional dry air in the afternoon since he expected no other visitors.

When we surfaced from our visit inside the grotto, Jacques informed us, as planned, that we would be eating dinner at his house that evening at 1900 hours. We left the grotto to return later that evening but in the time left before dinner we toured the area around Montignac to show Dominique and Michel a few sites. After our tour, we went to the hotel to rest before arriving for the grand dinner. Dominique and Michel took off on their own to look about and to discover things to do, one of which was to locate the fine chocolatier, Mr. Aubert, and to purchase chocolate truffles: they consumed 100 grams of truffles each but were kind enough to bring back one for each of us.

We arrived at the home of Jacques and Nounou (his lovely wife) Marsal exactly at 1900 hours. The aroma flowing from the kitchen was heavenly. The table was set and reflected the tastes of a family that considered eating a primary reason for living. Jacques had cooked the majority of the meal, but both Nounou and Jean Claude had contributed substantially to the repast. The fare would be totally of food of the local region and would include Dordogne ham, black truffle and other mushrooms from the Périgord Noire, that Jacques had gathered early that morning, wine from Sarlat — a town located a few kilometers south of Montignac — and several cheeses of the region, plus one dessert cheese made by Madame Marsal. The Porto (port) was a specialty made by Jean-Claude Pinheiro, Jacques's nephew and co-resident in their house. The dinner was exquisite, a royal degustation. The dessert cheese was light, nearly floating over our plates, and had sweetness that made our palate rejoice for another morsel. As for the Porto, Jean Claude was a master port craftsman. It was a glorious meal and the company was just as glorious. I am so fortunate to have met Jacques and to have been able to invite him to California for a few lectures that helped him fulfill a dream to visit America.

The next day we left Montignac to make our way towards Vezelay in the Yonne department in Burgundy. It was now December 31st and we were headed to the Hotel des Fleurs located near the superb Basilica of Sainte Marie de Madeleine. We arrived at the Hotel des Fleurs in the early afternoon of New Year's Eve 1983 and just in time to enjoy a short visit to the Parish Church de Notre Père. Returning to the hotel we reconfirmed our dinner reservations for 2200 hours and asked both Dominique and Michel to grab a few hours of sleep so they could stay awake for the wonderful dinner we anticipated. Chef Robert, the owner of the hotel, was a recognized culinary artist and I hoped to be regaled with delicate dishes of local specialties. One of the charms of France is that meals are always anticipated with great yearning because one can expect delicious food, well prepared and memorable in taste.

At 2200 hours, all four of us entered the dining room and soon we were eating local escargots drenched in butter and estragon (tarragon). We had local slices of Burgandy ham cured in the warm wind of the valley and drenched in a clear sauce of garlic, capers, and grape oil. The wine was a robust Rhone variety of pinot noir, chewy and solid tasting. The main course comprised lamb and an assortment of splendid vegetables *al dente* with a light white wine sauce. Chocolate handmade petits éclairs closed the meal. After sending the kids to bed, we awaited the midnight call to open a bottle of Veuve Cliquot champagne. There were several couples in the dining room and each of us offered a toast to a glorious 1984, the year that was anticipated by all who read the futuristic novel by the same name. Cheese assortments followed the toasts, and then we all gathered around the fire for more celebration. It was nearly two o'clock in the morning when we returned to our room for a few hours' sleep.

For me 1984 was to be a difficult year that included my first bout with prostate impaction, construction and renovation of the newly acquired Goose and Turrets (which hadn't been named yet), a drastic change in department at

Bechtel, and the creation of a bed and breakfast — something for which neither Emily nor I had any experience but only hopes and ideas. I had put all these concerns aside while in Europe, but now the moment was drawing close to a time when returning home was inevitable.

The purchased house was a disaster in need of much improvement. The upstairs floor, our future quarters, the kitchen, and the main floor, were concepts to be realized. As I mentioned earlier, the foundation of the house had to be reconstructed and stabilized and the roof had to be raised a few fractions of an inch to put the new foundation structure under tension. The sidewalls had to be converted into shear tension supporting walls to terminate the existing ongoing racking movement of the building east and west walls. That was not all there was to do. Rooms on the main floor had to be recreated for our future guests, in fact they had to be cleaned, floors repaired, and made livable. The kitchen was a dirty, slimy, unsanitary mess that needed to be torn apart, gutted and reconstructed from scratch. Moreover, we needed to hire a contractor to do the work upstairs. Public bids had to be put out, and a contractor needed to be selected. I had no experience for such tasks. I would have to consult and rely on my dear friend Donald Koenig and would then have to accept his judgments.

There was much to think about. When I attended the New Year's Day Mass at the Basilica of Vezeley I prayed for help with my concept of a bed and breakfast and the building that was to house it. The task before me was enormous and daunting. On top of that concern, I was having great difficulty with my bladder and often I could not urinate.

On January 3rd we drove to Paris' Orly International Airport for the return trip to San Francisco on Pan Am at 1400 hours. It had been a glorious month and I was very happy to have been able to give Dominique and Michel another visit to Europe, a holiday punctuated with several small and memorable experiences. As for Emily, already a good traveler, she was able to see, experience, and enjoy many additional encounters with both the English and the French, cultures that have contributed much to the world.

We arrived at Orly in plenty of time to return the car, obtain our boarding passes, purchase a few odds and ends from the duty free store, and buy a copy of *Le Monde Diplomatique*. The flight back to San Francisco was long and in daylight, hence little rest was possible. From past experience I shared the discomfort that plagued the pilots who had to endure the sun shining in their eyes for ten hours. Quite often flying over the Pacific Ocean I had endured the hot and bright sun glistening mercilessly in my eyes — no sunglasses are sufficient to relieve the discomfort. Often we would place above the instrument panel sunshields made of aluminum foil taped to the screens, and these would block the sun from our eyes and, of course the view; that trick, however, is not dangerous over the clear Pacific Ocean. I presumed that the pilots of Pan Am would not use that trick over the crowded North Atlantic Ocean, as we did over the Pacific.

Thoughts at 39,000 feet over the North Atlantic

Once we were all settled in the big Boeing 747-200, I took out from my attaché case a copy of J.A.T. Robinson's book on the Gospel of John that I had purchased at Blackwell's Bookstore in Oxford. I had read three-quarters of the book and was intrigued by Robinson's thesis that, perhaps, the Gospel of John may have been written earlier than was assumed. John Robinson intimated that the gospel might have been written in the mid-first century for an already established Christian congregation as a dramatic narrative, structured around simplistic questions, some of them with multiple meanings, and complicated responses that pointed to a complex corpus of theology. To me, then in 1984, I felt that the writer of John was responding to a series of questions posed by someone not mentioned at all in the text. It was not until 2002 that I learned that perhaps John was responding to the text of new documents found in Egypt purported to be written by an author who could be Thomas. Research is still being done but all indications suggest that John is a linear reply to questions or issues raised by the author of Thomas' Gospel. Thomas asks a series of questions that are an attempt to define Jesus and his purpose. John takes it upon himself to answer these questions directly but never revealing the questioner. Thus we encounter complex answers to what appear to be rather simple questions.

The Gospel of John is an important key for understanding the history of the Eucharist. It is also of importance for understanding the mood of the people in the mid-first century, especially when the author of the gospel refers to the "Jews." During the writing of the gospels, all the gospels, the people living in Palestine (Israel and Judea) were known as a nation of Jews. Many of the Jews were religiously Jews, and many were simply national and cultural residents living within the border under Roman authority, and some, like Paul of Tarsus, were Jews with Roman citizenship. Hence, when the authors of the gospels, especially the author of what is called John's Gospel, refer to Jews, care must be taken not to assume that religious Jews were invoked in that nomenclature. Even today in the 21st Century there is a clear distinction made between Jews of the religion and cultural Jews who are not practicing Judaism, the religion, but proclaim to be historically connected Jews. The same distinction should be applied when Jews are mentioned in the gospels. In that vein, the Christian Church ought to be clear as to whom they are denigrating in their canonical gospels and epistles. I am certain that mention of Jews in the gospels does not necessarily imply that religious Jews should be singled out as enemies of Christianity; some were but also many were not. That many of the Jewish citizens were upset with Jesus because he invoked drastic changes in the social and ethical structure and the ancient laws is no doubt true. Yet many followers of Jesus were Jews and were known to be Jews who were members of the group that followed the man from Nazareth. Christianity cannot accuse the Jews, the religious sector of the nation, to be explicitly the enemy. The "people" were the enemy, whom the authors of the gospels call "Jews." This name, Jews, caused many complications that clouded the meaning of John's message in his Book of Revelation or Apocalypse.

I mulled this problem for several hours until I was interrupted by dinner, the in-flight movie, and conversation. I was also interrupted by pain in the lower part of my body in the area of my bladder. "Too much tea," I thought. "The tea that I have consumed, probably because it was acidic may be causing me problems in the bladder." Little did I know what was to be expected and how I would feel in the coming days.

Excellent Friendship with Koenig

Upon my return to Montara, I immediately telephoned my friend Don Koenig to seek his advice. The reconstruction of the building was weighing heavily on my mind, especially since I knew little about the process. The idea of hiring the right construction crew haunted me during my entire holiday. How would I know which construction crew was the right one, the best one, and, of course, the most honest one?

When I returned a local realtor had suggested a contractor that I soon interviewed and from whom I obtained a bid. I had gotten the bid for the reconstruction of the upper floor but I suspected that because it was extremely low it was consequently inadequate and perhaps fraudulent. My only alternative was to seek advice from Don Koenig and I was hoping that he would be willing to help me. I called Don and asked him to come to Montara to look at the bid offer and to examine exactly what had to be done to the house, especially to the upper floor, and how to arrest the racking of the east and west walls.

Don took one look at the bid and threw it into the trash. Before I could ask him, he took it upon himself to become my construction manager. All of a sudden I felt that a heavy load had been lifted off my shoulders. Don hired his ex-son-in-law to do the construction and promised that he would supervise him through every step of the way. He did just that and much more. The Goose and Turrets would never have reached the condition it is in now without Don's watchful eye, his support, and ultimately his direction. That in the long term it cost him, or better contributed, to his demise by way of a stroke and heart problem. I am sincerely sorry. He did smoke a great deal and that did add to his ill health, but hard work, worry, and reduced stamina did the rest. Don died soon after the task was completed and the Goose and Turrets B&B was born from its incubation period of two years.

That I learned a great deal from Don is the least I can say. I am grateful for his friendship, his help, and his sense of humor, his inquisitive mind, his graciousness, his trust, his aircraft piloting skills, and his affection. The little chapel in the East turret, which Don helped build, was officially consecrated as the Chapel of the Transfiguration and was dedicated to Donald Koenig, while he was still alive. Don helped create that chapel, and behind one wall is his hammer that was inaccessibly lodged between the studs and remains there for posterity as a reminder of his wonderful sense of friendship.

Don Koenig was a saint, a dear friend, a funny person, a great pilot and just about the best pal a person could have. I miss him when I think of him but I go into the Chapel of the Transfiguration and there he is in full presence with hammer in hand, a smile on his face, and a good suggestion.

The European Community (EC)

I will elaborate a bit on the reconstruction of the Goose and Turrets at a later time but for the moment let me switch to Bechtel's less than desirable attitude and behavior. In a sense it was Bechtel's peculiar attitude that gave me the impetus to proceed decisively and rapidly with the evolution of the Goose and Turrets. During the Reagan administration and the slump in the economy, Bechtel's reaction to the construction and engineering market was difficult to forecast. I also realized that Bechtel did not know how to market itself; in fact it considered marketing a futile endeavor. For Bechtel, its name and connections, especially with governments, were deemed sufficient by its management for booking work. Times were changing however.

Competition from South Korean, Japanese, and Filipino firms offering to do construction at a cheaper rate was displacing Bechtel in many areas, especially in the Pacific Rim. With the advent of the European Union, American firms were at a disadvantage if they were not associated with a European firm or were established as practically European. Bechtel had offices in London and Paris but neither was known to be European. The London office was the principal office in Europe but it was mainly concerned with projects that were already Bechtel's and sought no new projects in Europe. When the construction management of the tunnel under the Channel was awarded to Bechtel, another office was established in Kent and was apparently totally independent from the London office. Moreover, Bechtel had been awarded the Channel project because of its association with the World Bank, the prime lender, and not because the Europeans allowed it to bid on the project. When Bechtel proposed Bob Polvi, an American, as the project manager, both the French and the British refused to accept him because they wanted a British or French citizen, or at least a European to manage the project. Fortunately, Bechtel had a fine and competent project manager on its staff who had dual citizenship. Joseph Anderson, a Scotsman who possessed American and British citizenship and who spoke French was found to be acceptable to the Franco-British consortium.

Events at Bechtel gave the opportunity to position myself as interested in working in Europe. Soon with Joseph Anderson, Robert Jackson, and others I was assigned the responsibility to look into the EU and how it would affect Bechtel and also was made manager of all technopolis programs.

I had several meetings with Joe Anderson and knew him very well from our work in Jubail. A few years after this debacle, when I was working on European Union management affairs, Joe and I had several discussions on how we could get Bechtel to establish itself as a European firm. The task was impossible to accomplish because, although Bechtel claimed to be a global firm, it was essentially myopic and parochial in vision. I was surprised, at the time that I was shuttling between San Francisco, Brussels, Paris, and London, that the Paris office had never made any attempt to meet with some of France's top government or company officials. The Paris office remained an isolated island in the most British sector of that city and was totally unconnected to anything that dealt with French businesses. When work developed in the old French colonies of Africa, such as Gabon, Algeria, Tunisia, Morocco, and others, the management supervision was always transferred to a small office near Marseilles or to the San Francisco office, even bypassing the London office. In sum, Bechtel did not nurture a European image or presence, even when it had appendage offices there.

It was not until Howard W. Wahl, senior vice president and director, arrived to take the helm of the Paris office, and with the help of the resident French attorney Maurice Cori, that my pleading that Bechtel needed to have a bona fide European resident office, that its directors back in San Francisco agreed to establish a Bechtel Europe Company, but it lasted merely three years and was reduced to a skeleton office when Riley Bechtel became chairman and president upon the retirement of his father, Steve Bechtel Jr. That was a great disappointment to me and in a sense contributed to the planting of the kernel for my eventual retirement. Another factor leading to my unhappiness with how Bechtel under Riley's direction limited the firm's work in Europe and elsewhere was the demise of Robert (Bob) Jackson as my immediate manager. Bob was a long-term employee, an economist, and a fine project manager who understood marketing, and the necessity of establishing broad contacts with leaders of countries around the world.

Bechtel Corporation was not in the mode of marketing itself. In past years, Bechtel was sought after to do projects around the world, especially after WWII when both Europe and South East Asia were still undeveloped as industrial tigers. By the mid-80s, the world situation had been altered and Bechtel was competing with others in the field of engineering and construction. Projects were usually awarded to local firms, firms that were resident or associated with firms that were resident in the area where the project was to be built. As I said earlier, Bechtel had an office in Paris but was not a resident firm in France. In addition, Bechtel's resident office in the UK — in reality it was merely an extension of the San Francisco office but the British did not mind — was not seen as representing a European resident firm. Both the French and German governments were sensitive that Bechtel (a German name) was not willing to show that it was a prima facie European firm.

Soon after Steve Bechtel Jr. retired, Howard Wahl retired too because he was diagnosed with muscular dystrophy; this was a year or two before my own retirement in 1993. When the European Economic Community was finally amalgamated as the European Union (EU) it was too late for Bechtel to claim that it was a European firm, and projects in Europe began to elude the firm's grasp, especially after it completed the Tunnel, not only with a cost overrun but a two-year schedule extension. It was a sad and complex situation that cost Bechtel in its ability to project its professionalism in the developing regions of the world.

Plymate and the Victims of Management Changes

Now another story unfolds, and this one concerns Bechtel (1985 and before my involvement in Europe as shown in the previous paragraphs) and its attitude towards its employees, the lifeblood of its future as a profitably productive company. The work I was doing in support of the new Dammam International Airport in the Eastern Province was exciting but the management approach by Bechtel left a great deal to be desired. The work at Riyadh's airport was moving forward towards completion and all attention was shifting to Dammam, in the Eastern province. The airport was eventually to be named King Fahd International Airport to honor the reign of the current king of Saudi Arabia. The airport group at Bechtel was poorly managed, and the San Francisco support group was in a state of chaos. Supervisors, managers, and leading personnel were put into places of authority not because they were competent but because they had connections, mentors, and godfathers in the right place. The consequences of this condition provided fertile ground for absurd management policies and the demise of several good people who were experts in airport creation, management, and operations.

One of the first victims of this management fiasco was my friend and department manager in the aviation group, Glenn Plymate. Glenn had been the airport director of the Metropolitan Airport of Oakland for several years before being invited to come to Bechtel to establish a department that would be responsible for developing a program to incorporate Management, Operations, and Maintenance (MOM) as a logical flow onto airport construction and to extend its profitable involvement for years after the construction was completed. The idea was not quite part of the general approach that Bechtel used but Ivan Nealon, a senior vice president and an avid aviation supporter, had been able to convince Steve Bechtel, Sr. that it was a good idea because it would provide the firm with work beyond the "turn-key" stage of completion.

Once hired by Bechtel, Glenn recruited several of his colleagues in the airport arena. He also complemented his new department with an aviator with commercial and military experience and that person was I. To that eclectic group he added security people, parts people, maintenance and procurement specialists, and a fully staffed publication group under Emily's supervision. All in all it was a fine group rich in knowledge and experience. The MOM group performed admirably and the Saudi client was more than satisfied. In fact, in Riyadh, when the new airport was nearing completion, the Saudi Airport Authority moved to develop its own MOM by creating a local firm called Al Akiel, which would use "seconded" Bechtel employees to establish the momentum, then set the mode of operation, and duplicate the approach used by Glenn's MOM group. To guide the task, which in a sense was rather simple because it would be tied to the jurisdiction of MOM in San Francisco, the future director of Riyadh, Saad Tassan, asked Glenn for the loan of a temporary manager. The main task of the person assigned to lead the way would be diplomatic in nature. Glenn sent his second-in-command, Barry Craig, to do the job. Barry had been an airport manager in Ohio, was quite presentable, and had traveled to Riyadh, but was neither bright nor could he follow simple orders. In addition, Barry had an ego that was much larger than his intellect. He was also unwilling to show any courtesy towards Saad Tassan. What made Barry a worse problem was that Glenn recruited a permanent manager from San Jose, California. Frank Coffey, retired director of San Jose airport, was a prima donna who was also unable to treat the Saudis with respect. To add fuel to the fire of mismanagement, when Frank Coffey was given his walking papers, he was replaced with another of Glenn's friends, Jim Mettler. Jim had been on the staff of Los Angeles' Airport Department. A retired and prominent manager of this gigantic airport authority, Mettler's credentials were excellent but the damage caused by both Barry Craig and Frank Coffey was irreparable. Mired in this mess was Glenn. Mismanagement of a portion of an important project is nearly unforgivable. Barry Craig, sensing that his days were numbered, proposed to Bob Polvi, the current project manager, that a tour of major airports of the world might be of value to the Saudis. Polvi took to that idea and appointed Barry as the guide for the tour and eventually found him a spot in business development.

To retrace the steps a bit, Barry went to Riyadh to help the development of Al Akiel and to work with Bob Polvi, a jovial construction type who was an excellent taskmaster with building crews but a poor diplomat (he was the one who released the construction firms before they fulfilled their spare part requirements, the problem I was recruited to correct). The combination of Barry Craig and Bob Polvi's departure to become president of Bechtel Civil Company (BCiv) soon torpedoed any creative plan that Glenn had managed to put in place.

First, Barry treated the soon-to-be Riyadh's airport director like dirt; Saad Tassan, the appointed director-to-be for the new airport was ignored, intimidated, and reduced in meetings often to the level of a child who was to be seen but not heard. Bob supported the attitude established by Barry.

Second, Barry ignored all recommendations that Glenn proposed to help the Saudis and, especially, to Tassan for managing the airport. Barry injected his own shallow ideas that often backfired with disastrous consequences. He suggested that Al Akiel "hire" the seconded Bechtel employees and put them directly under its control. Barry's idea was to win favor from the Saudi Airport Authority in the hope that he could become CEO of Al Akiel. Once Barry's proposal for hiring the expatriates was accepted by the Saudis, all the Bechtel employees submitted their resignation rather than leave Bechtel and the protective umbrella that was theirs under the original benefit plan.

Third, Barry belittled Glenn in the eyes of the Saudis and in the eyes of Polvi.

Fourth, Barry influenced Frank Coffey and Jim Mettler and in the process destroyed their credibility and Glenn's to boot. The consequence of Barry's perfidiousness was that he was elevated by Polvi (recently appointed the new president of Bechtel Civil Company) to become manager of Airport Business Development and thus Glenn's position was further undermined and his status destroyed.

Fortunately, the existing manager of Airport Business Development, Stuart Hill, a prince of a person and well connected in aviation circles, had been promoted to head Bechtel's London office as Manager of Transportation Development. Stu was responsible for including Bechtel both in the Channel Tunnel and in the new Hong Kong International Airport. With Barry in the management seat, Bechtel obtained no more airport projects around the world. This lack of airport development projects was sufficient to dislodge Barry out of his position. He was assigned to work as business development manager in the new nuclear cleanup department but that department lasted less than a year and Barry was shown the door out of Bechtel in 1984.

In the meantime, to save face in front of the Saudis, Glenn was reduced to managing a much smaller MOM group that was quite insignificant in its contribution to not only the completion of Riyadh's King Khaled International Airport, but also to the emerging work for King Fahd International Airport, in Dammam, Eastern Province. As was explained earlier, the MOM group had been removed from BCiv and injected in Bechtel Operating and Service Company (BOSC) under the leadership of Dr. Leon Ring and his assistant Michael L. R. Bishop. Circumstance could not have cooperated more impeccably to create a team with less good sense and limited foresight. The metaphor for this staging is the format of the Greek Tragedy. Glenn became the fall guy so that Bechtel and all its minions could save face in front of the Saudis. Saad Tassan was the only person who was able to see through this charade but he had no authority yet.

Just about this time I was working on two fronts: one was the remnant of MOM and the other as assistant to the new airport manager of Riyadh, Dr. Ronald Brooks. Ron was the replacement to Bob Polvi when he was elevated to become president of Bechtel Civil Company (BCiv). I was traveling back and forth between Riyadh and San Francisco. During one of my short stops in San Francisco, a three week break to prepare for Jacques Marsal's presentations on the splendor of Lascaux, I arrived at my office which was located in what was called the China Basin complex, a building some distance away from Bechtel's home office building. Glenn came to see me. He informed me that he had been demoted to assistant manager and that the new manager would be Jim Camier, a section supervisor from Riyadh whose claim to fame was that he had been manager of a passenger terminal at Sky Harbor International Airport, Phoenix, Arizona. At noon, Glenn's wooden desk was moved out of his office and placed in a cubicle off the bullpen. Camier's desk was brought in — a metal desk because he did not have the grade to warrant a wooden one!

Camier was a pleasant sort but totally unsuited for the task of managing MOM, even in its remnant form. Jim just did not know what was to be done to keep the group busy; moreover, he did not know what was needed to make an airport function properly. There were gate checking counters to be located, security checking points to be identified, personnel to be identified, interviewed, and hired, and a complete keying system to be designed, coordinated, ordered, installed, and tested. None of these tasks was on his agenda nor did he understand their importance. We waited. Ron Chandler, who knew Camier from Riyadh, was as puzzled as I about the replacement. Ron, an experienced airport manager, knew a great deal more about airports than Camier would ever grasp. Neither Ron nor I could see how Camier was ever going to become the knowledgeable and dynamic leader necessary for the revitalization of MOM. Camier was the wrong man for the task. It was quite obvious to both Ron and to me that MOM was soon to be discarded in as short a time as possible.

A week after the change of management occurred, Glenn came to me and informed me that he had been called for a meeting with Leon Ring and Michael Bishop; the topic was to discuss personnel changes. His meeting was scheduled for ten o'clock the next morning, Tuesday. The next morning I stopped at Glenn's desk and offered him a cup of coffee. "I think that I'm going to be sacked," he announced. I agreed that these were ominous times for MOM and for his career. To pass the time we discussed the Roman tradition of thumbs up for death or down for life in the arena. He said that thumb up was for life and down was the sign of condemnation for the victim. At any rate, when the time came he went to the meeting, not sporting a sad look, but with a smile on his face.

Just before noon, Glenn returned from his meeting and as soon as he spotted me his right thumb went up — way over his head. Recalling our discussion earlier, I went over to his place and asked point blank: "Are you in or out?"

"Thumbs up means that I'm to die. I'm sacked," he paused then added, "I will instead retire." And so another good asset at Bechtel was stupidly discarded. Glenn had made mistakes; sending Barry Craig to Saudi was a poor decision. Many of his immediate subordinates were poor choices. Neverthe-less, the work produced by MOM was excellent because Glenn had also had the vision of collecting a fine team of bright people as second tier personnel, and this group overshadowed the miserable performances of his upper eche-lon people. The "Yellow Books," a somewhat biblical looking set of books defining every aspects of MOM tasks, was such an excellent work that sev-eral airports borrowed it and the FAA and ICAO recommended it as being imperative for sound airport management. Yet the architect of this work was now being dismissed without so much as a note of thanks. In less than two weeks Glenn Plymate was gone and Bechtel lost MOM, one of its more lu-crative tools in the airport business.

The writing on the wall was clear. I could not continue working with MOM under Jim Camier. Jim was doing a lot of traveling to Dammam and in his absence I was put in charge of the expiring department. In that position I was able to obtain information that indicated that MOM was to be terminated and that Camier's days were numbered. It was time for me to find a new home within Bechtel. It had already dawned on me that my future at Bechtel depended on my becoming indispensable in many areas! I had started the process while in Riyadh and Ron Brooks knew my plan because he was also looking at his own future.

New Casualties and New Vision

I returned to Saudi Arabia and completed my several tasks for Ron Brooks including the last phase of the certification of the Riyadh airport. Be-ing authorized by both the FAA and ICAO to certify airports was the first step in my becoming indispensable at Bechtel. Thus while in Saudi Arabia, I received a phone call from Michael Wakelin and a telex plus a phone call from Mortimer Dorris, the department manager, asking me if I had any inter-est in transferring to their planning department. My friend Steve Gomes had suggested to both Wakelin and Dorris that I would be open for an offer be-cause I was dissatisfied where I was. Soon I returned to San Francisco and not too long after I changed departments. I started working on something that I felt would be acceptable to Bechtel, would make me invaluable to the firm, would give me great satisfaction, and would contribute much good to strategic regions of the world that were economically problematic.

My new interest was "infrastructure" with all its ramifications. Because infrastructure is the fundamental core of any project I was certain that it would also be the key to making me as invaluable as possible to Bechtel Corporation. The planning department was perfectly suited for incorporating elements of infrastructure services within its charter. The conversation with Wakelin was cordial, but I soon discovered that he was not the key person in the planning group (Mort Dorris was the actual manager of the group), although he did have vision and could stitch new ideas in the Bechtel fabric. I mentioned to Michael that by adding infrastructure to the department's tasks much would be gained because of the core requirements through the research, planning, implementation, operation, and potential next-steps phases. I also suggested to Mort Dorris, when he phoned me in Riyadh, that my interest in his department would be more accented if the department could accept "infrastructure" as its operating-functional title, and I could be a floating resource person rather than a "planner." I said pretty much the same thing when he phoned me the second time a day later, obviously after he had consulted with Dorris. Wakelin bought the idea and soon made it his own. In the telex responding to Mort Dorris I pretty much said the same thing to him. Mort's reply was direct and suggested that I immediately make preparation to transfer to his department.

Now that I was back in San Francisco, I called Mort to inform him that I was back at China Basin and to explain that I was under BOSC's control and any move for me had to be sent through Leon Ring's administration. Indeed, I did alert Mort that I was willing to transfer to BCiv when that would be possible; otherwise I would only be on loan. He thought that he could work that out after I was physically moved into his planning department. I was satisfied that a good move was about to come my way. The next day Mort Dorris invited me to have lunch with him at One Market Place restaurant. We had a good meeting and I accepted his offer to move me to his department and to work on the Gabon project, which allowed me to use my French. At the lunch I mentioned *again* that the Planning Department should change its name to the Infrastructure Department because then it could assume any project it deemed capable of tackling; it would have no limits because infrastructure was the *core* of any project. Dorris listened, took notes, but said little to my suggestion.

As I thought about Glenn's demise in recent time, I began to see a pattern that was being established by Bechtel. Other good men were cast aside besides Glenn. I will point to three other casualties: Robert Jackson, Denis Slavich, and Stephen Gomes. These three men were assets but with a different vision than the old staid construction-engineering approach that was endemic in Bechtel. A fourth man, Ron Brooks, who rose to the level of senior vice president and director (the only Afro-American to reach that position), found it best to resign after 18 months. His vision to expand aviation in a new form, such as direct point-to-point travel with smaller aircraft, thus bypassing for most short distances the hub system, was never allowed to be discussed. What a waste!

Returning to recounting what was occurring at Bechtel to some fine people, I will begin with Robert Jackson. Bob Jackson was a superb and creative economist who was also a wonderful project and department manager. For a few years, after Mortimer Dorris's retirement, he was also my immediate manager and the one who spoke kind words at my tenth anniversary as a Bechtel employee. As far as Bechtel was concerned, Bob was too much interested in marketing, going after new products that would increase the firm's work scope and define the needs that the future would and could propose. One example will suffice to make the point. In 1987 Pan American had contracted with several firms for the development of an ester-type sensor or such equipment to identify explosive material in cargo and baggage. Two firms were researching that issue, one in Europe and the other in Maryland. The equipment was demonstrated at the Paris Air Show but the manufacturers needed some support from airport builders. Bechtel was an airport builder. Bechtel was not interested. The German firm Consult AG, also an airport builder, was interested and signed a protocol with Pan Am. The equipment was installed at Heathrow, Frankfurt, and Paris but it was never installed at Jeddah or Riyadh and in the long run, Bechtel lost the right to participate in the ongoing research and the return on the investment. Had the sensor been installed when it was developed at Frankfurt airport, the disaster over Lockerbie, Scotland, might have been averted. Today, such equipment is being used in the United States and all major airports, especially after September 11, 2001, but at an enormous price. Bob Jackson was royally mistreated and reprimanded for proposing that Bechtel get involved in this research, and any support from Joseph Violet, a Bechtel expert on such matters, was ignored and rebuffed. Joe Violet was an expert in explosives and pushed hard to have Bechtel support the research but was not successful. I brought back reports from the Paris Air Show to see if I could convince Bechtel to invest just one million dollars in either the European or American sensor; I was aiming for Bechtel to acquire a small partnership in the R&D. Success eluded me also. The reason given by Bechtel was that the firm did not want any involvement in equipment that was not absolutely proven for the task it was designed to do. Research, development, and marketing were anathema to Bechtel's narrow perspective. The firm that began with a team of mules in the latter part of the 19th century had not quite progressed to current technological developments. My relationship with Bob was excellent, close, and mutually appreciated. I worked with Bob for many years, and continue to keep in regular communication with him and his wife, Mitzi.

I suspect that Denis Slavich's fateful dismissal was not too different from that of Bob Jackson. Denis was chief financial officer and a director of Bechtel. When young Riley Bechtel was given the reins at Bechtel, Denis, who had initiated a Future's Group under the leadership of Bob Jackson, was dismissed in the most ignoble manner. I suspect that Denis was considered to be competition by Riley and a challenge to his leadership.

The purposes of the Future's Group were to research, obtain or create forecasts, and explore possibilities for future projects, which might add to Bechtel's booked work. In a sense, it was an effort to look at what was coming down the pike for engineering, construction, and management. Bechtel did not approve of this approach for doing business. Forecasts, marketing, and exploration were not part of Bechtel's approach. The company was convinced that it was too well known, too big, and too exclusive to be reduced to doing marketing in any shape or form. Today it is suffering from that arrogance.

As for Slavich's dismissal, it is too embarrassing to bear repetition but I am no longer a Bechtel employee. At a formal dinner given for some occasion, the subject of which is irrelevant, Denis Slavich and his wife, Debbie, were invited as part of a group of Bechtel management personnel. Riley sat next to Debbie Slavich and in the course of making conversation Mrs. Slavich was informed that her husband's days at Bechtel were numbered. Denis had not been informed, had received no formal notice, and had never been approached by Riley on this matter. The fact that Denis was not just any employee, but a director and the CFO should have afforded him a bit more courteous approach by Riley. The root cause of the dismissal, I assumed, was because Denis was in competition with Riley for the position of president. When Riley was assured of his presidency he did Denis in. About a month later, Slavich was cast out of Bechtel.

Because he was an excellent and competent front person to open doors, to meet people, to obtain introductions to the upper management of firms, and that he was a good speaker who often overshadowed many of his superiors, Stephen Gomes was given the boot by Bechtel. Steve and I had worked closely to obtain the first runway approval from the FAA, a runway that was designed to be built in Southern California in Moreno Valley.

No one before us at Bechtel had ever been able to get approval from the FAA for a new airport. As a reward, Steve Gomes was dismissed because he suggested that the news of a new airport should be part of a marketing drive in many national professional magazines to promote the name of Bechtel. In addition, Steve tried to move Bechtel to enter the business of converting Air Force military bases that were scheduled to be closed by Congress to civilian use. This was a touchy affair because many Representatives in Congress were against the closure of military bases in their districts and several were friends of Bechtel. Steve tried to convince Bechtel to make the case for the conversion but resistance from several sources was enormous. Steve's argument for

convincing Bechtel was reason for his demise. He was given 30 days to vacate his office with the excuse that "Bechtel had no more work for him." I
had work for him in the Intellectual Property and Technopolis arena, but I
was directed that he could not be transferred to my projects and the comptrol-
lers would not accept any job number that I gave him. In as much as that was
the case, when he left Bechtel I proceeded to send work his way for almost
three years, and he was able to complete a major part of a project I managed
in France and in Italy for me.

After 18 years at Bechtel one's store of less-than-pleasant occurrences
could fill a large book. That is not, however, my purpose in this recollection.
Bechtel has produced some fine professionals, developed some extraordinary
ideas, and managed several magnificent projects. Yet it is puzzling to see
competent people shown the door of the firm while less than adequate employees continue to accumulate seniority. It is a puzzle and one that I neither
can nor wish to resolve, but which in many ways has shaped my thinking.
Poor management, the lack of vision, restricting research and consequently
development of new products and ideas, and encouraging marketing, principally self-promotion in the market place, will invariably bring about a type of
corporate atherosclerosis in a firm.

As for me, I found Bechtel to be a good environment where I could expand, apply, and put my creativity to good use. I learned to manipulate my
position with the company and found great satisfaction in the process. Indeed, some wise director reminded me and others during the occasion of my
departing luncheon that: "Raymond did not work for Bechtel...no, Bechtel
worked for him!"

What Bechtel offered to those who were willing to work was an environment for creativity that spanned the entire world. Yet one had to work hard to
prove oneself at every level. The challenges were enormous because with
every new idea one was required to prove that it was valuable and that the
results were worth the effort. Yes, upper management in the image of the
directors had to be convinced, and convinced again and again, of the value
inherent in the idea. It wasn't easy. It wasn't a giveaway. It demanded thorough preparation every step of the way. There were failures, some of which

were caused by the attitude of those who manned the helm. There were successes because of the impeccable preparations that went into the tasks, the program, and the implementation. Of course, I was at times frustrated — as I was by the limited thinking displayed by Frank Cain. I was also gratified by the good thinking I witnessed from Slavich, Jackson, Plymate, Wakelin, Wahl, Anderson, Hill, and many others. Bechtel was a job shop and hence allowed a creative person to establish many platforms for interesting possibilities.

City States and Principalities

As I mentioned earlier, after taking stock of the situation at Bechtel I soon decided that I would change my approach and develop a strategy where Bechtel would work for me rather than I work for it. To implement that strategy I needed to amplify my value to Bechtel. My bag of tricks included such tools as editing, publication, aviation, airport management, city and regional understanding, and the ability to evaluate an entire project or program. I was at heart an aesthetician — I could evaluate a project as a whole and envision its future — as such I decided to follow through as I had discussed with Steve Bechtel Jr. years earlier. Obviously these tools were not without value, and it was quite known that Bechtel particularly needed help in the evaluation of projects and programs.

In my estimation I concluded that my value would be accented in the area of infrastructure, because of my ability to work with multi-disciplinary tools, hence I accepted the offer to work with the now-new Infrastructure Group of Bechtel Civil Company (BCiv). But I also needed to be an expert in a discipline that other people did not possess. Building airports, maritime ports, highways, power-generating complexes, or new cities required knowledge of two disciplines: regional economic development and infrastructure.

Regional economic development entails knowing how a region can be made to attain its highest potential. Any region resembles an organism, and an organism depends on its infrastructure and the supporting infrastructure of its environment. I thought about these ideas a great deal. Then it occurred to me that the best way to learn more about regional economic development and infrastructure was to look into the very structure of the city-states.

Following this line of thinking, my first decision was to move out of airport projects and into regional planning. The Planning Department, which changed into the Infrastructure Department under Mort Dorris, at Bechtel looked interesting to me, and its manager and assistant manager were keen on my idea of infrastructure and regional economic development. I had worked with the planning folks prior to my going to the Peoples Republic of China (PRC), and had helped the group when it was engaged in work in Gabon, Africa. After establishing myself in the Planning Department and asking that it be officially recast as the Infrastructure Department, I started working with the group full time. To do justice to the story, a story that is not linear, I will have to cover several stages, some of which have already been narrated.

After reading several books and articles on regional economics, the emergence of city-states, and the making of a first-class city I decided that I would spend my next holiday looking firsthand at the European city-states. Because I had been to Singapore, Hong Kong, and Macau in South East Asia I decided to concentrate on the European city-states and principalities. I chose Andorra, Monaco, San Marino, and Luxemburg. Liechtenstein was also added to the list, which we had visited earlier. Liechtenstein was not technically a city-state, but it would serve as such in my research. I asked Emily if she was interested in doing such an itinerary and her reply was positive and enthusiastic. We both set about planning the trip but in detailing the route and comparing it with the time available, we decided not to visit Luxemburg because we had had a good glimpse of it on our chocolate excursion; we also removed San Marino because I had explored it several years earlier. We discounted Andorra because we had also explored it during our Niaux grotto visit a few years earlier. The list had been reduced to Monaco and Liechtenstein and a lot of fun in between. We did obtain a great amount of data from the city-states I had discounted and that data was sufficient to serve my purpose. Compiling data from Singapore, Hong Kong, Macau, San Marino, Luxembourg, and Andorra, plus the material we gathered from our visits to Liechtenstein and Monaco, we developed a major file of extraordinary information, a file that would put Bechtel in my debt.

The Small City State: Liechtenstein

After landing in Frankfurt we proceeded by car in a green Peugeot 404 towards the Swiss border by way of the Black Forest and the Bodensee (known as Lake Constance) to arrive in Vaduz, Liechtenstein. We had to stop for a while on the shore of the Bodensee to let a thunderstorm and its load of rain pass us by. The drive through Austria to the crossing point at Feldkirch was lovely, especially after the rain. Once past the gate into Liechtenstein we proceeded towards Nendeln, Schaan, and Vaduz, the capital made famous to some extent by the fine film *The Mouse that Roared*. Liechtenstein's landscape is beyond belief. When one speaks of a pastoral environment one need only mention Liechtenstein. It is pastoral at first sight but behind this pastoral façade one soon discovers a churning engine of research, high technology production, precision tool manufacturing, laboratories immersed in micro and macro physics, earth science development, food preparation for preservation, canning, and freezing, and extensive exploration work in viniculture.

Liechtenstein is a country that possesses no university, no airport, no belching factories, no oil or prized minerals, and no police. With a population of less than 25,000 plus a daily transient work force of approximately 5,000 people, Liechtenstein has one of the highest per capita income levels in the world. Liechtenstein is the Silicon Valley of Europe. Fuel injection computers for automobiles were designed and first produced in Nendeln. Precision tools and plasma research are part of the work performed in Triesen. High temperature ceramics are being researched and produced (many for Space vehicles) in Schaan. The high level physics researched in several facilities located in pastoral settings in Malbun count among the top in the world and contribute much to the work performed at the Conseil Europeen pour la Recherche Nucleaire (CERN), Argonne, Los Alamos, Livermore, and other renowned centers.

I soon discovered that Liechtenstein, as I have recounted earlier, was not a dormant little ski resort where the rich and famous spent time wasting away their lives. I was fortunate to have had meetings on two occasions with the governing body of Liechtenstein. I met with the late Prince Franz Joseph and his family and I also had several meetings with the current ruler Prince Hans-Adam in 1988. Beyond these occasions I was able to meet with finance and planning ministers, directors of economic development, and other key people in Liechtenstein involved with the future of the Principality.

After Liechtenstein we drove through Switzerland and south to the French Côte D'Azur to enter the Principality of Monaco. Indeed Monaco is quite different from Liechtenstein in many ways. Monaco exists because of the good graces of France. Its very existence depends on the continuing line of its princely family. If and when the line stops, so does Monaco's independence, and the principality's existence is likewise terminated.

Revenue is produced in Monaco by the few contract laboratories working on marine research, by the tourist and gambling industry, by the Grand Prix automobile races held on its local roads during the racing season, and by its tax-free shopping centers. Monaco is home to the Jacques Cousteau Marine Research facilities and to several other less famous marine enterprises. Monaco is not a driving engine economically. It is mostly a supporting entity devoted primarily to tourism and the "good life." Once beneficent France closes the tax loopholes, if the ruling Grimaldi family of Prince Rainier ceases to exist, then so will Monaco. At such time the coastal community will be absorbed by Nice and will join the Côte D'Azur as another tourist haven — not particularly a bad thing but certainly not an indication that Monaco is self-sufficient and master of its own economic destiny.

For my future purpose I leaned more towards the example of Liechtenstein and would employ much of its mode in the later development for our Dynapolis research, which will be explained later.

On and Away to China

After our return to the Bay Area from the visits to the city-states and tending to the demands of the Goose and Turrets and other tasks, many of which
called for destruction followed by construction and several trips to hardware,
building material stores, and architectural salvage depots in our newly acquired little red Mazda 2000 truck, work at Bechtel in the aviation group
continued for a while. I knew that I was about to abandon the airport group
but before doing that I gave Ron Chandler an offer that I had received from
American Airlines. American Airlines wanted to construct a people-carrier
train at Dallas-Fort Worth (DFW) International Airport. I telephoned American Airlines Chairman and CEO, Robert Crandall, and received exactly what
was required from Bechtel. American Airlines needed an experienced airport
director who could work with their construction and engineering people to
guide them during the design and installation of the shuttle so that general
operation of the gates would not be interrupted and the passengers would not
be inconvenienced. Ron Chandler had the perfect résumé for that job. Chandler had been director of Santa Ana Airport, now known as John Wayne
Airport. The airport was a multi-runway facility that managed heavy airline
traffic. When I asked Ron, he immediately accepted the task and made preparation with his wife Dawn to relocate to Dallas. The work called for Ron,
through a Bechtel contract, to assist American Airlines, as project director, to
continue its operation while it built the new passenger shuttle light rail serving its three terminals. I expected the project to last three years, if not longer.
Hence to fight the good fight for MOM was a futile endeavor. With Ron's
departure and my transfer to the planning group, the final nail in MOM's cof-
fin was hammered.

As I mentioned earlier I had been approached by Mort Dorris and then by
Michael Wakelin, of the then-Planning Department for BCiv to join the department. The group was soon to change its name to Infrastructure and I was
excited by the possibility of working in such an eclectic group that could influence changes all over the world.

I had helped the group in the past on small projects and had worked with Gordon Linden, a planner, and Stephen Gomes, a developer, and both had done some work for me in MOM. Was I really still interested? Indeed, I was, but I was under BOSC and not with BCiv. Dorris informed me that he would take care of making the transfer, but after I moved to his department.

This would be a lateral transfer for me, hence no salary or grade increase. The opportunity to depart from the declining airport group was sufficient reward and incentive for me. The proper two weeks were scheduled for the transfer. I would begin the first Monday of July 1985. I notified Jim Camier and Ron Brooks. Ron informed me that he still wanted access to my brain whenever he needed it. That was indeed a morale booster for me and Mort agreed that Ron could borrow me from time to time. Camier was in the clouds and didn't quite understand the impact of my departure and that he was losing a proficient aviation person who had proved himself and who had good relations with the Saudis, FAA, ICAO, and other critical institutions.

I moved to the Bechtel building at 45 Fremont and perched myself in a corner office on the 27th floor. I was asked to review the planning work that was to be submitted to President Bongo of Gabon. It was interesting work, especially the proposal to build a "presidential" city near Lara. A note in the plan advised that no development would be made near or on the highlands as a precaution not to disturb the mountain gorillas. I liked that and hoped that it was not just paper decoration to satisfy the World Bank governors, the World Wildlife Fund (WWF), the African-Wildlife (AW) groups, and several American and British environmentalists. I was certain that the French residents in Gabon or the representatives from the French government did not have much interest in the welfare of gorillas. I did underscore the issue of mountain gorilla protection and added a memorandum to Mort and to Maurice Cori of the Paris Office, which would be conveyed to President Bongo. The memo was sent to Bongo by way of the Bechtel project manager Mike Zaharias, a Greek-American engineer, who was fluent in French and sympathetic to the issue. I then sent a memo to the president of the World Bank, and copied WWF and AW.

A few days later Wakelin came to see me. He asked if I had cleared my memoranda with anyone. I replied that Mort Dorris was aware and had given me the green light to go ahead. Wakelin informed me that I was causing a lot of commotion in Gabon and that Bechtel's John Neerhout, senior director, would not be too happy with my actions. I replied that the gorillas would love me!

The next day, Mr. Neerhout's administrative assistant, Brent Sherfy, called me to his office. I went to see Brent and he immediately informed me that I should pursue the topic of protecting the gorillas because Mr. Neerhout did not want Bechtel to fall prey to the WWF, WA, or any environmental group. As I was leaving, Neerhout came out and Brent introduced me to him. "Young man I trust that you will work hard at protecting the wildlife, especially the mountain gorillas, of Gabon," he instructed me. Turning to Brent he said, "Write a memo and give it to this man so there'll be no arguments about Bechtel's keen responsibility for protecting wildlife," and he left the office. I showed the memo from Neerhout to both Mort and Mike Wakelin. To date, Gabon has remained one of the foremost protectors of the mountain gorillas and is a standing example to Congo, Rwanda, and Uganda, which border the mountains where the gorillas dwell.

The mountain region of central Africa is a tinderbox of conflict, especially in Rwanda, where mass killing occurs regularly between the various tribes. In all fairness, the mountain gorilla is still in danger of extermination, eradication, and oblivion because civil strife in Congo (then Zaire) and Rwanda (although there is peace in Rwanda between Hutu and Tutsi) is still quite tenuous. Yet the intent to save the mountain gorilla is strong, supported by external forces, and funded somewhat better than it was.

My work reviewing the plans proceeded at a good pace and included working with several competent people, including the architect Charles Sands with whom I had no small acquaintance since we had worked in Riyadh on the airport and spoke French. The transfer to the planning group had not included a departure from BOSC, a company that was also having a diminished standing in the eyes of Bechtel's upper management. In late September as I arrived to my new location with the now-Infrastructure Group, a telephone call from Mort (his office was across the aisle from me and within hearing distance) asking me to come to his office startled me.

Forced Holiday

Dorris immediately asked me when I entered his office if I had any vacation time left. That question surprised me because I had just been transferred to his department. Nevertheless, I replied that I did and could use some because Emily's parents were visiting us and my presence at home would help the remodeling project of the house. "Raymond, take a week off," Mort informed me.

"Why?"

"Raymond, don't quibble with me. Take the week off but before you do, tell Ron Brooks where you can be reached." I was puzzled. Mort noticed my questioning look and continued, "Go now and you'll understand in a week or ten days."

I breathed heavily.

"Leave right now and I'll have Suzanne Knutssen (the department's administrative employee) prepare the necessary papers for you. Leave now."

Mort picked up the phone and started a conversation with an unknown person. I left for Montara after leaving a message for Ron Brooks. I also advised my friend Steve Gomes that I was leaving on vacation immediately. He was puzzled too. I telephoned Emily to tell her that I was starting my vacation. She too was puzzled.

The week at home allowed me to enjoy Emily's parents, Sarah and Paxton Morrow, who were visiting. In addition, I took the time to tear down the old kitchen; in fact I removed all the cabinets. Don Koenig came over from San Jose to help me, and added new supports for the roof crossbeams that were not sufficiently anchored. Soon the task of installing the new cabinets began. The new cabinets had been delivered and were stored in the living room. The work continued without interruption until a call from Mort informed me that I should be reporting to Ron Brooks for work on the following Tuesday. I phoned Ron Brooks and confirmed that he wanted to see me for a new project but he gave me no specifics. Soon after that phone call, Steve Gomes called. He wanted to know if I had been informed about my new project.

"Steve, there seems to be an enigmatic process at hand. I neither know about my new project nor do I understand what it is that forced me into a week of unscheduled vacation — not that I'm complaining about that bit of rest."

"Raymond," Steve said, "You are slated to go to China to help in the planning of a new airport."

"Oh! So what is the secret?" I asked.

"It's not a secret, but BOSC has been causing some trouble and you are in the midst of it. Has Mort Dorris informed you?"

"No," I replied.

"He will when you return on Tuesday. Also come see me after you speak to Ron." I was left hanging in midair.

On Tuesday I went directly to Ron's office. Ron was waiting for me. "Chief," he said, "Will you go to China?"

"To do what?"

"First answer my question: Will you go to China?"

"Yes!"

"But you're on record stating that you'd only go to places that serve desserts?"

"Yes. Maxim's has opened a new restaurant a couple of weeks ago in Beijing and the Lido Hotel has engaged Henri Moliere as a pastry chef."

He laughed a deep and long laugh. "OK," he added after catching his breath. "I want you to do the design of all the navigation, weather, control, and runway systems for this new airport in Wenzhou, just across the Taiwan Straits."

"Looks interesting," I said.

"What will you need?"

"May I hire a translator-interpreter of my choice? Please ask the Bechtel office to prepare six persons that I can interview when I arrive."

"Done, Chief!" (Ron always called me by that title) and he puffed on his stogy and let out a plume of smoke.

Then he explained in detail that an airport was being planned for Wenzhou, across the straits from Taiwan, and that Bechtel had been given the task of developing the preliminary plans. He wanted me to be in charge of planning the requirements for all telecommunication, navigation, weather, and approaches-departures for this new airport. In addition, I was to assist the project architect, Charles Sands, as deputy project manager. I would be based in Beijing and would work directly with the Chinese authorities, China Aeronautic and Airport Commission (CAAC), China Aviation Engineering Institute Authority (CAEIA), and their assigned engineers, architects, and aviation specialists. I would be working also with Jim Webb (resident Bechtel aviation manager in China and my good friend from Riyadh days) and several others of whom I had some knowledge.

"Ron, I'll go but I'm not sure that I understand why I had to take a vacation last week."

"Chief, Mort will explain after you leave here. Now give my secretary your passport, go get your immunization shots and cash advance, and tell me when you can leave for China — but make your own airline reservations. I know that's what you want to do." He handed me a stack of documents to review. As I was leaving his office Ron called, "Keep me informed and go visit the archeological sites that you are so interested in!"

I went to see Mort Dorris. "Mort, what is the issue at hand?" I exploded impatiently.

"Raymond," he took a letter from his center drawer and handed it to me. The letter was to me from Leon Ring, president of BOSC. The gist of it was that by reading it I would be informed that BOSC could no longer afford me and was thus laying me off as of the end of the week; that was the day that Mort ordered me to start my vacation.

"Raymond," he continued, "if you had seen that letter I would have had no choice but to lay you off since Ring out-ranks me. But by not showing it to you I could phone Ring and tell him that you were gone on vacation and had not seen the letter. This way you were safe. Now you are heading for

China. You are on loan to Ron Brooks. Your line manager is Michael Wakelin, manager of the infrastructure group, I am your department head, and Ron Brooks is your operational manager — but you are still attached to BOSC — sorry about that."

I would soon be out of BOSC upon my return from China. Suzanne Knutssen would arrange that change.

Settling in and reviewing the material that Ron had given me took the rest of the week. Emily and I discussed when I would leave for China. My time depended on when I finished the kitchen — that task would take two weeks — and when Emily's foot would be out of the cast (she had broken her ankle when attempting to clean Michel's room and fell off a stool, not wanting to bring in a small ladder). Finally I decided that I would leave the last week of October and be exposed to the brunt of the Chinese winter.

I booked my flight from San Francisco International on Japan Airlines by way of Tokyo, with an overnight stay in that city, and an outbound flight to Beijing. An overnight in Tokyo would permit me a fine dinner of sashimi and all the accompanying goodies. It seemed to me that I was not too anxious to arrive in Beijing or even to the People's Republic of China; China was such a strange and different land and was a little frightening, yet terribly exciting to me.

The kitchen was completed in time. I saw Ron and informed him that I was ready to leave. Was there anything in particular that he wanted me to do for him? No. We discussed the project, the contract, the schedule, CAAC and CAEIA. I reminded him that we had agreed that I could hire a translator-interpreter just to serve my needs since I would be doing a great deal of committee and aviation interfacing. Indeed I could, and he added, "Had you not brought this up, I would have. Jim is already informed that you may hire anyone you might need. He'll have six candidates for you to interview."

"Ron," I sat down, "I'm still attached with BOSC and I want out. BOSC is a sinking ship."

"Chief," he stood up and there was six-feet-plus of the man towering over me, "if your separation comes to naught, I'll make you my operations manager. You'll be out of BOSC, I promise." Then he added, "The executive board knows that BOSC needs to be disbanded and it'll be done as soon as Leon Ring resigns."

The People's Republic of China (PRC)

The flight across the Pacific was long. Arrival in Beijing after the overnight stop in Tokyo was exciting and a bit strange. I was met at the airport by Bechtel's Max Muller, business development manager for China, and taken directly to the Lido Hotel Complex (franchised Holiday Inn).

Max was a friendly and most competent employee and I had known him for several years. He, with Jim Webb, manager of airport projects in the PRC, had worked hard to obtain the first airport project for Bechtel in China. Jim was a colleague who had also been with me in Saudi. His wife had died of cancer, and Ron had sent him to China to keep him busy and to change his venue from Mobile, Alabama to Beijing. Jim, unlike most construction engineers, was a gentleman and courteous to a fault. I liked Jim very much. It was Jim Webb who had seen to it that I had a good group to interview when I requested an administrative assistant who could act as my interpreter and translator. It was Jim who predicted that after I interviewed the lot of six candidates ultimately I would hire Yujun (Susan). He died in 1990 in bed in Alabama and Max Muller died in Hawaii in 2004.

The next day I was taken to the CAEIA office for an introduction. The weather was cold, snow was falling, and the outside temperature was 10° Fahrenheit. After the initial formalities and an overview given by Charlie Sands (architecture) and Jerry Light (power utilities) of what had been accomplished, I was taken to meet the Chinese directors of CAAC. They discussed what we were under contract to produce and I explained to them what support I required from them. It was agreed that I would have a vehicle with a driver and that I could begin to interview candidates for translation-interpreting the next morning at the Lido Hotel.

The third morning at 8:00 a.m. a staff person from Bechtel's central office called me from the Lido lobby to inform me that I had six candidates to interview. After interviewing the first three, who were women, I was discouraged. None of them wanted to work on Saturday because they had to attend indoctrination classes that day or pay a fine. Moreover, none of them was interested in working on Sunday as a guide so that I could see a few historical sites in and around Beijing. The fourth candidate was a young boy who did not speak English well enough to be of help to me.

All the candidates I had interviewed wore the customary blue garb that Mao Tse-Tung had instilled in the population. This garb consisted of a pair of baggy blue slacks and a blue jacket with a high collar. A blue cap adorned the head and in front above the bill was imprinted or sewn a red star. The outfit was silly, ill fitting, and as stylishly designed as prison work clothes.

The fifth candidate arrived, sans the blue uniform. With her hands on her hips, a broad smile on her face, and a look that suggested that she could easily take command of any situation, including this one, she did not hesitate to tell me that she would be able to work on Saturday and Sunday if I needed her and paid her for overtime.

"How can you say that you can work on Saturday when you are supposed to be indoctrinated?"

"I don't attend the stupid indoctrination sessions. I just pay the fine of three yuans [40 cents] and I'm left alone," she informed me.

"What about Sunday?" I asked.

"I can work on Sunday if overtime is paid." There was a pause, then she added, "but what is it that you want to do on Sunday since the office is closed?"

I laughed and she joined me in recognizing the possible implication of my request. I quickly explained. "I want to see several sites in and around Beijing, especially the digs and museum at Zhoukoudian where the remnants of Peking man were discovered."

"I can do that," her hands still on her hips and a twinkle in her dark, pretty and large Asiatic eyes. "You may call me Susan, but my real name is Yujun He," she added.

"I have one more interview before I can make a final decision." I told her, and then stood up.

"I will wait outside," and she left.

The next and last interview was of a man who spoke good English but could not work on weekends because he had a wife and child. He had been one of Susan's classmates and had great regard for her.

"You may call me Ken if you wish to hire me." I liked him but I needed someone like Susan who not only could work weekends but who had presence, audacity, and a sense of humor. Susan was hired and a week later I hired Ken also. Ken Kie would be working only on textual translations.

One of the first assignments I gave Susan was to find me a good hotel where only Chinese was spoken and only Chinese guests were registered. The Lido Holiday Inn was not where I wanted to stay in China. I wanted to experience Chinese culture as much as possible. Susan found me the Foreign Chinese Hotel. This was a hotel that catered to Chinese citizens from Taiwan, Hong Kong, Singapore, America, and other nations harboring the Diaspora.

"If I'm not with you how will you manage to deal with the hotel or the restaurant, and the taxis?" Susan asked. "They all speak Chinese and know no English!"

I explained after smiling to her, "We will use 3x5 cards," I said. "On one side we will write in English and on the other side we will write in Chinese." I looked at her and her eyes were large, as she understood the process. "I'm informed that most all Chinese can read, is that correct?"

"Yes." After a short pause, "When do we start?"

"Now, as I take you for tea downstairs."

"That's a good trick." She touched the stack of cards on the table. "Very intelligent idea!"

I liked the accommodations at the Foreign Chinese Hotel and my room was comfortable; the service and the food, with the exception of breakfast, were excellent. I just could not abide Chinese breakfasts; especially since the menus for breakfast, lunch, and dinner were indistinguishable. Chinese Mandarin food is very tasty but I do not want all three meals of the day to have absolutely no distinction. I want breakfast to be lighter but substantial. Cold fish soup, tepid chicken, won ton with rice or whatever accompanies them is just not to my liking. I was able to have my driver take me to the Great Wall Hotel operated by the Sheraton company or to the Toronto, a Hyatt Hotel, for a good western breakfast. We also made arrangements to have a western-style breakfast at a small hotel where Jim Webb was lodging. I managed to have good breakfasts with my colleagues and for lunch we went to the cafeteria at the Beijing Culinary School not far from our office. We were introduced to the Mongolian Pot stew and to Pijoo, the Chinese beer, which is quite good and served in liter bottles.

Susan was an extraordinary asset for my work and for the project. She was quick, smart, pleasant, and a joy to have as a colleague. Her translations were dictionary correct, as was her spoken English. She needed to gain some knowledge of common and technical, especially airport, usage of English-American, which was still impossible to experience in the People's Republic of China. One day, during a break over midmorning tea, I asked if she had considered graduate language school to further her education. She informed me that she could not attend graduate school in China because she was past the age (35) when students were accepted. This was a surprise to me. It never occurred to me that she was older than 35 because she looked to be in her mid-20s, more or less. Then I learned that she had been sent to Manchuria for 10 years to work on a sheep farm during the terrible period of the Cultural Revolution.

Not being one to waste time or to give in to overwhelming odds, she had used English-as-a-second language tapes and a small tape recorder sewn in her long coat to learn the language. Both the tapes and the recorder with batteries were obtained from the Foreign Store through the help of a friendly foreigner (usually Singapore Chinese expatriates) who would go to the store and buy the items for Susan. I also purchased several items for my Chinese friends that they could not obtain through their own stores. When the Cultural Revolution ended and she was able to return to Beijing, she entered the Language Institute to obtain her bachelor's degree in English. Upon graduation the government assigned her to teach school, a profession that she disliked and for which she was emotionally ill suited. Moreover, she could not abide or even tolerate the regular indoctrination sessions that teachers were to receive and then had to convey to their young students. She quit. Leaving a government-assigned position in China puts one immediately among the ranks of the unemployed and unemployable — a class of misfits. Susan was not one to remain unemployed or inactive for long. She soon found among the hordes of foreign companies invading China that she could obtain translating and interpreting jobs. In her search she applied at Bechtel for an opening and when I asked to interview translators she was included on my list. As fortune would have it, over the years Yujun (Susan) He and I became very close friends and she was able to come to the United States for further education and ultimately to settle here, earn a master's degree and then obtain her American citizenship.

The airport project moved along well. All of us put in long hours but we were careful not to work on weekends. I was especially unwilling to work on the days that I could use to see the sites that for too long had been impossible for westerners to visit. There was the Great Wall, the Ming palace and burial grounds, the Forbidden City, Tiananmen Square, the Zoological Garden, Zhoukoudian, Tianjin, Zhuoxian, Tong Xian, the Sound Wall, and a score of other marvels that most westerners had read about but had not experienced because of the closure of China in 1949. I gave a list to Susan, asked her to hire a taxi (I didn't want to use the company car and driver) and to locate the way to all those exciting places. Susan produced splendid itineraries and I (we) reserved Sundays for out-of-city excursions, and Saturday for in-city adventures.

One bright and cold Sunday we planned to visit Zhoukoudian by way of the Marco Polo Bridge. The taxi arrived early with Susan and off we went for our adventure. I had asked Charlie Sands to join us with the condition that he not smoke in the car. He agreed. We drove out of Beijing and onto the two-lane road that led to Zhoukoudian. At the Marco Polo Bridge we stopped for water and a short sightseeing visit. It was at the Marco Polo Bridge that the Japanese were finally stopped in 1938 by the Chinese forces. "Enough was enough" was the Chinese stance. This was when General Chennault intervened with his famous Flying Tigers Group. We continued to Zhoukoudian, the excavation site, and the museum. The site was where the Peking Man had been discovered and where Teilhard de Chardin had worked as a paleontologist on the archeological site. The Chinese had kept the site in good order and well protected from vandals and robbers. It was an amazing display of bones and remnants of material, some with pre-historical significance, and some of negligible value to researchers but of interest to lay people.

The museum was impeccably kept. All glass display cases were clean and well organized. The only problem I found was that the Chinese inscriptions were transliterated on the signs directly into the western alphabet, but were not translated. This little service offered no assistance because although one could read the sign, one could not understand what it indicated in English. Susan was of enormous help to me in making sense of the signage. She had done some research on the Peking Man prior to our visit and had acquired quite a bit of knowledge on the subject.

It was almost past lunchtime and the nearest village was several kilometers away. Charlie had gone off for a smoke. Susan and I were sitting in the garden even though the temperature was in the high teens. We talked about her time in Manchuria, her family, and her aspirations. I mentioned that one of my hopes while in China was to be invited to someone's home for a visit and to meet Chinese in their informal setting. Spending time in a hotel and working with Chinese was good and satisfying but I wanted to experience the intimacy reflected in a Chinese home, with family and social conversations. I shared my feeling about wanting to meet the Chinese in a less touristic atmosphere. We also discussed her future education.

Her time in Manchuria became a milestone in her refusal to accept anything that Communism proposed or that the current government defined as beneficial for the Chinese people. Her ideas were certainly contrary to official and party thinking, but Susan was not a revolutionary. Her rebelliousness took a quieter mode of action: she just did not do what was required of her when she considered the source to be silly. She simply ignored the party system and its indoctrination. The same characteristic emerged a few years later when she was employed by Scientologists to translate passages from the book written by the founder of the movement, L. Ron Hubbard.

When we discussed her aspirations, her hopes, and her future a somber look was visible on her otherwise joyful face. "I suppose that I'll go from job to job and avoid government assignments of any type. I doubt if I'll ever marry because it will be hard for me to adjust to the contrary opinions of a husband who will simply accept this corrupting political system." This was a note of self-condemnation that the future held absolutely nothing of value for her, either socially or personally. We explored further that aspect of her negative perspective. "My official education in China is terminated by my age," she said with great sadness. "As a Chinese citizen with no money or possibility of learning more in a university, I have no choice but to live from job to job and hope that the present governmental conditions change in my lifetime."

After a spell of silence, I said, "Susan, what about learning in a foreign country and obtaining an advanced degree to help you sharpen your American English?" I could see that my comment saddened her even more.

"How will I go? Where will I go? Then what do I do?"

I asked her point blank if translation was a passion that could turn her into a professional. Her honest response was that it was not, but that it allowed her to learn more, much more than was possible if she spoke only Chinese.

"Would you leave your family to study in a foreign country?" Tears welled in her pretty Asiatic eyes and a deeper sadness covered her round face.

"Yes," she replied. Then she added with great emphasis, "that is a dream that will never come true."

I replied with a tone of conviction so she would believe that these were not just words, "I'd like to help you make that dream come true." She looked at me. Her tears channeled down her cheeks.

"It's impossible," she said.

I interrupted her, "There will be many obstacles but will you be tenacious enough to stick with me as we overcome each one?"

She looked at me with a fixed stare, "What is 'tenacious'?" she asked.

I explained that it meant to stick firmly to a decision or plan without changing or doubting it.

"Susan, it will be difficult but I must know that you really want to study in a foreign country, perhaps America." Her reply was clear and to the point.

"I will." Then she added, "Why are you doing this? Are you honest and serious?"

"Susan," I said, "I think there is much more to you than shows. You seem to have the spark that will offer great contributions to mankind and I believe in you and that you are a good person."

Charlie Sands who found us sitting in the garden interrupted our conversation for the moment. He was hungry. We were all hungry. Even the taxi driver was hungry. The intimate conversation would hold until a later time.

After a few kilometers of driving we entered a village where a small farmers' market was in full swing. All types of vegetables, poultry, small birds, pigs, and crafts were being sold. It was interesting to discover that in Beijing the primary vegetable available in the winter was bok choy (a member of the cabbage family), but in this village several kinds of fresh produce were being sold. Susan explained that this produce was grown on family plots and not on government collective farms, hence the great variety. What was more surprising was that spring and summer vegetables were available in the cold of November. Susan again reminded me that the Chinese farmers were using a crude but efficient greenhouse system to grow these vegetables, vegetables that brought more income when sold out of season. During the Cultural Revolution and even before, at the height of the communist authoritarian government, farmers abandoned greenhouses on the collective farms. Once family farming was again permitted to compete with government farms and collectives were abandoned, families reconstructed their greenhouses to obtain extra revenue. "Private industry requires more imagination, and imagination rewards one with better profits," Susan advised.

There were several vendors selling roasted meats and noodle soups but Susan was adamant and would not let us touch the food sold on the street. She had spotted a small restaurant and headed towards it to check on its quality. When she returned, I had already purchased a dozen winter pears that had the fine scent of jasmine mixed with a slight touch of cloves. I had eaten one or two a few days earlier and was anxious to have some more. I had paid the vendor with "foreign" yuans or Rimibis as they were called, and literally RMBs. Susan reminded me that I should not have done that because it supported the government's attempt to isolate the Chinese people from foreigners with this two-currency system, which was illegal in the hands of the population. But the general population liked these RMBs because they had more value and could be used by foreigners in government stores to buy objects that could not be found in domestic shops by the locals.

At any rate, we followed Susan after she accomplished her detailed inspection and entered the restaurant. It was a clean village restaurant with long tables and each table could accommodate eight eaters. A menu was posted on the glass wall separating the kitchen from the dining area. Many of the names of dishes posted, Susan could not translate, so I suggested that we go into the kitchen to see for ourselves what it was that we wanted to eat. She went to speak with the head cook or chef and she was told that we could do that. The chef was a large man with a big belly, a jolly smile, and a wonderful disposition. He showed me several dishes that he was preparing and even offered me samples to taste. He was making a pork dish with wild garlic (I found some growing in my garden in Montara) and some sauce that had a tantalizing aroma. I selected several dishes and the chef assured Susan that he would prepare fresh food for us and would not give us the dishes already prepared.

Charlie Sands agreed that he would accept any dish I selected. I ordered several dishes, including soup, rice, and Pijoo. Just as I was about to return to the dining area, the chef approached to shake my hand and informed Susan that I was the first American to "grace his humble kitchen." Then he added that the meal would be complimentary. I hugged him and insisted that I wanted to pay for his food but could I give him dollars. Then I gave him a couple of my business cards, and he promptly glued one to a piece of cardboard and posted it on the inside window of the restaurant for all passersby to see. Below the card he wrote in Chinese, Susan told me, that his restaurant serves Americans. It was a lovely lunch and none of us got sick. I left $20.00 as a gift that Susan informed me was worth a lot and the chef would be proud to show the bill to his friends. I asked Susan if she could glue a $1.00 for display under my business card. She checked and was told that it would be a wonderful addition.

After lunch we returned to Beijing to look at the pandas at the Zoological Garden. I must admit that the zoo was not as impressive as I had been told in old literature. The animals were poorly kept, especially the pandas. The cages were too small, dirty, and devoid of anything for the animals to entertain themselves with. The new approach of open spaces for the animals had not reached China. I complained to a keeper when I saw that the Asian elephants were chained. I got some excuse that this was only a temporary occurrence. After a stern warning in Chinese by Susan, the keeper agreed to unchain the elephants, but I doubted if that would last too long. It occurred to me that China still had a long way to go before it would grant animals their simple rights to live healthily in captivity — even human beings were generally denied their dignity and inherent value. Life was cheap for both animals and humans. Times will change that, especially when education permeates deeper into the culture. But for the near future the PRC was pragmatically a Fascist nation and neither human beings nor animals had any rights. At the moment, although literacy is quite prevalent among the people, education is still aimed at the very top layer of society. I suspect that the real Cultural Revolution, which might bring democracy to China, is still to come and enormous obstacles currently restrict the course for liberty, dignity, and enlightenment. A special type of democratic rule will come to China, but perhaps not in our lifetime. Both economics and environmental issues will push the Chinese to reassess their government. Deng's statement: "To be rich is glorious!" has a great deal of value and much attention, but crass wealth is not sufficient as an empowering, driving force to bring major improvements to a people.

The Curved Wall of Sound

Leaving the zoo we went to the "sound wall" or "whispering wall" to listen to our voices travel more than 200 meters along a curved, polished stonewall. Susan was at one end of the wall, and I was at the other, and our whispers could be heard clearly. It was amazing. Charlie Sands praised the architect. I praised the acoustic engineer. Susan praised the generations that lived long before Communism corrupted China. I reminded Susan that generations before Communism were not any more civilized than the current ones. China, the early source of science, ethics, philosophy, cuisine, and education, had fallen into misery and had contradicted Confucius and his teaching of benevolence, education, and good will for all. Instead China had adopted the pronouncements of Xunzi, who influenced Chinese philosophy best with his belief that human nature is basically evil. His ideas are presented in the book Xunzi (or Hsun-tzu), most of which he wrote himself. In the book Xunzi minimizes the dignity of human beings, limits education to a few males, and promotes an isolated China so that it would not be corrupted by foreign influences.

It was time for tea. After the long and exciting day, I invited Susan to join us for tea in the French Patisserie at the Lido hotel where every Sunday afternoon they served tea and excellent pastries. It was wonderful but Susan could not finish her second small Éclair — too rich for her Chinese taste (after living in America her tastes have changed tremendously because now she is accustomed to whipped cream and chocolate). But that reminds me that few Chinese used dairy products or ate tomatoes, cheese, or even delicate pastries when I first visited China. Currently the story is a bit changed, ice cream, whipped cream, cheeses, and other western fares are quite available in China, especially in Beijing, Shanghai, and a few other cities. I'm certain that these enriched and calorific Western foods have affected the health of the Chinese. But I am one who believes that good-tasting food and a shorter life are better than bland nourishment and a long life. Honestly I live to eat rather than eat to live! Flavors and spices are the accents that enrich life.

Chinese cooking is, nevertheless, varied, refined, and excellent but imbued with salt and soya sauce. There are clearly two cooking traditions in China: Northern Chinese (Mandarin) cuisine, which is complex yet delicately prepared and served; and Southern cuisine, which is popular in American Chinese Restaurants. Mandarin cuisine is quite different from most Chinese foods served in American Chinese restaurants, which serve mostly southern cuisine of the type eaten in Canton and Hong Kong. One of the great and visible differences I soon discovered was that Mandarin-style food is served in small individual plates and not mixed together as is often the case for southern-style cuisine, especially as served in America. I admit that I much prefer Mandarin cuisine and how it is served than its southern Cantonese form. Eating in restaurants in Beijing gave me the experience and a little knowledge about how to order Chinese food in America.

I also experienced authentic Peking duck, which is nothing like what is served anywhere else outside Beijing. Peking duck is truly a delicate dish. It is an exquisite dish requiring meticulous preparation and calls for using a young duck that has been raised on a controlled diet of selected greens, some grain, and fruit. The duck is cooked whole and lavishly seasoned; aficionados tell me that it is rubbed with honey, tented, and suspended from the head over a wood fire to allow the fat to drip onto the hot charcoal to add to the flavor. When it is ready to be served, the duck is brought over to the dinner table and displayed whole to the diners.

At this stage the duck is golden, its juices make it glisten, and the hot steam sends buds of aroma out to tantalize the awaiting eater. When both sight and smell have been satisfied, the duck is taken back into the kitchen to be cut in thin slices and lightly reheated. When it is brought back to the table the aroma is even more tantalizing than earlier. It is then served with its juices on a heated plate over some leaf vegetables. The diner is well rewarded when Peking duck is served.

In Beijing I was introduced to Peking duck in the famous restaurant known as the Sick Duck Restaurant! The restaurant was given the name because it is located across from the general hospital and in earlier days physicians associated with the hospital ate there. The name remains operative although the hospital ceased to exist in 1919.

My second experience of eating Peking duck came after an invitation extended by the Civil Aviation Administration of China (CAAC) when they gathered our team to show its appreciation for our cooperation and work on the Wenzhou Airport. The feast was splendid but noisy and the drinking truly followed the confused Chinese format of mixing beer (pijou), fruit wine, and Ma Tay (similar to vodka but almost pure ethanol alcohol).

The third experience I had was more my style. I went alone deliberately to eat, at my pace, the fine bird and to wash it down with a bottle of wine.

Indeed, I'll walk ten kilometers for a good Peking duck. Since those days I've had Peking duck in Manchuria in 2003 and I admit that it was just as good.

A Luscious Silk Carpet

Ever since my arrival in Beijing I had been looking for a pure silk carpet. I wanted one that showed bright colors and had no traditional boilerplate design; I wanted an original. Jim Webb took me to several carpet dealers and even to a carpet show. None of them caught my eye. Price was the least of my concern. Delicate, handcrafted beauty was my target. I was looking for a carpet that had an extraordinarily tight weave; nothing less than 300 threads to a centimeter. One evening while visiting the Toronto Hotel, I was introduced serendipitously to Mr. Al Young, a Chinese-American carpet buyer who told me that Tianjin was the place for silk carpets and I could hitch a ride with him the following Monday. I accepted his offer and went with him to Tianjin.

He took me to a silk carpet manufacturer who informed me that his people could have a carpet (6x9 feet) finished in three weeks and that I could contribute to the design. The manager, Mr. Mengzi, showed me sample patterns he had designed. These designs were in watercolor on silk fabric. I looked at several patterns, many of which featured a light blue that I found pleasing. Soon, I selected several drawings that formed an overall design for the carpet. I gave him an advance of $20 and he promised to bring the carpet to the Toronto Hotel in Beijing in exactly three weeks. I was incredulous that such a carpet could be completed in that short a time. I allowed him a month but he assured me that it would be finished and delivered in three weeks.

After the selection was made he introduced me to several weavers and to a team of women weaving a carpet that was nearly completed. The tight weave and the craftsmanship were superb. The silk was smooth, the design brilliant, and the weave impeccable. The women worked on the carpet as the frame hung on a wall; in other words, the work was performed, not as the Persians do it on the floor, but perpendicularly on a wall. I was introduced to the two ladies who would create my carpet. The women were in the their mid-40s, well-groomed, and appeared happy to create new designs. Their working room (and also the whole facility) was clean, tidily kept, and filled with light from large windows. The room was warm, and a pot of hot water for tea was available in one corner. I felt that the women who would create my carpet were decently employed and kindly cared for. My escort, who was from Chicago and a Chinese American, Mr. Al Young, acted as my interpreter, which of course, I found to be very kind and accommodating.

After we left the factory, Mr. Young had to visit a few other factories, which allowed me to learn a bit more about carpets, quality, and design. It was obvious that I had contracted for my carpet with one of the best in the city. By all measurements, I had been visited by good fortune not only in the person of Al Young but also in the kind folks of the Tianjin Enterprise Carpet factory.

After a good dinner of Mongolian roasted meat and vegetables, we returned to Beijing, arriving at my hotel at 11:30 p.m. It had been a long day and a long ride on medium quality roads and little traffic. I said goodnight to Al Young, thanked him and his driver and slipped the driver $10. The next time I spoke with him was on a brief stop in Chicago six months later, when I invited him to lunch and gave him a photograph of the carpet.

At any rate the carpet was delivered to me on the day Mr. Mengzi promised. He had one of the women with him and I offered to take them to dinner. The carpet was superb. The price was surprising. I was charged all of $600 for a 6x9-foot carpet handcrafted in pure silk. I asked Mr. Mengzi where he wanted to eat but he chose the Toronto Hotel's dining room for a "genuine American hamburger, fries, chocolate sundae, and tea." I joined him in celebration but I had beer instead of tea. Even though the carpet was 6x9 it folded nicely into my business sample bag for the return trip to America. I was ecstatic over the ownership of such a lovely carpet.

Back at my office many of the Chinese workers asked me where I would hang the carpet and I replied that it would be on the floor at the foot of my bed. "On the floor?" they all questioned.

"Yes, on the floor so I can walk barefooted on it and enjoy the feel of silk under my feet." Because I had two single beds in my hotel room, I laid the carpet on top of the bed I did not use. There wasn't much room on the floor to spread the carpet completely, at least not without putting some furniture on it. So I just admired it on the next bed and often ran my hand over it to feel the softness of the silk and to appreciate the beauty of the delicate design.

Friendly Chinese Encounters

One of the fascinating experiences that I enjoyed in China was the friendliness of the people — listening to their stories, and learning about their relationship with the Communist Party and its inhibiting approach to their lives. In any team organization there was always to be a "cadre" person watching over them. The cadre person represented the power and the control of the Party over any process.

For example, I remember designing one of the navigation transmitting sheds that would house the glide slope transmitter, auxiliary battery, small generator, and link box to public utilities. The glide slope transmitter is a relatively small unit that emits a signal to guide approaching aircraft down to the runway touchdown area. Enclosed in a container, the glide slope unit is controlled, in terms of off/on and for minor adjustments, by the operator in the control tower.

In the design of the shed, I was required to include room for two beds, a toilet, a dining table, kitchen, and common area for a crew of cadres that would monitor the unit round the clock in three shifts. "What would they be doing?" I asked. The cadre leader of our group, Mme. Zhuzh, responded by informing me that they would monitor the unit. "There is nothing to monitor," I insisted.

"We must monitor the equipment in case of a power problem," she replied.

"But the controlling switches are in the control tower, and the operator there can monitor the equipment," I responded. After much discussion for an argument that I could not possibly win, I agreed that the design would be done in accordance to strict Party specification. After all, I thought to myself, with 1.2 billion souls in China, this would be one way to employ unskilled labor.

Mme. Zhuzh was a pleasant person who looked after us in the office and provided anything we needed including assigning Chinese technical workers when we needed them, people such as draft designers, electrical specialists, water technicians, and many other skilled supports. In addition, she was responsible for furnishing the tea we drank, the cookies we ate, and the chocolates we consumed. We called her our Mother Hen!

Working with Chinese was an experience that I cherish and never will forget. Every member of the team was hardworking and always willing to share or give assistance when it was necessary. Working ten hours was not an apparent hardship. They were willing to see the project completed even if it meant working long and late hours. We Americans did put in much overtime but we were under contract and we received an enormous salary compared to what the Chinese received. Yet the Chinese worked side by side with us and never complained as far as we were concerned.

Approaching one weekend when it was imperative to have some civil engineering design completed and the American civil engineer, Tomas Csoboth, was overwhelmed with what he had to do, the lead Chinese engineer, Dr. Rueben (Ben) Wang, volunteered and worked over the weekend to make certain that by Monday the design was completed and precisely done. Indeed this support embarrassed Tomas but Dr. Wang worked because it was necessary — and he considered himself part of the team.

Incidentally, Dr. Ben Wang ultimately married Susan. In 1999, Ben became an American citizen and I helped him obtain his first US passport. This was a very proud moment for my dear friend Ben — and for me. Susan was given her citizenship in 2004 and the event was held in San Francisco.

A Homecooked Meal in Beijing

Accommodations for the Chinese were not the best in the world. Apartments were badly designed and mostly uncomfortably small and lacking in western-accepted conveniences or even basic comforts.

Susan invited me for dinner to her family's home one Sunday evening. The plan was that her brother would meet me at my hotel early in the afternoon and show me the Forbidden City, then we would take a taxi and go to his family's apartment for dinner to meet Susan, her other brother and his wife, the young niece, Yihe, and the parents — the entire family living in the small apartment of three rooms. I was excited that I would see the inside of a Chinese apartment, meet a Chinese family, and eat genuine, family-cooked Chinese food.

Susan's brother, Yulin He, was a wonderful guide and a wonderful person whom I hope to meet again. A graduate engineer in mechanical and production engineering, Yulin was moving rapidly to become an entrepreneur managing his own business. He spoke excellent English and knew the Forbidden City quite well. Acting as a guide, he took me in tow and showed me the City from point to point explaining much of the history and the arcane aspects — many not given to visitors. It was informative and fun for me. When we completed the tour, the lecture, and the engineering and historical commentaries, we took a taxi to his parents' apartment.

When we reached the apartment I was introduced to the family. Susan's mother, a petite, attractive woman, greeted me with a warm handshake and a sunlit smile. The family was gathered in one room and was waiting for me. Indeed, I was the guest of honor. I felt like royalty, a very special and privileged person. With Susan acting as the interpreter, the conversation covered much territory. They were as curious about me as I was about them. Dinner was superb: delicate in flavors, complex in forms, textures, and aromas, and utterly divine in tastes. There were several dishes and each delivered impeccable culinary zest, flavors, and aromas. It was a banquet of impressive magnitude. All the food had been prepared before my arrival and laid out on the table on top of warming stones. This way we could talk and learn about each other without interruptions. Susan's father, whom I met later when he visited us in Montara, was absent because he was mildly indisposed.

After dinner I had the opportunity to look at the apartment as I took photographs of the family. The apartment was about 30 feet long in the shape of a corridor, with small rooms on both sides. Each room had a window overlooking the street on one side or a playground on the other side. The rooms were well ventilated and had windows that allowed a lot of light, especially sunlight in the afternoon — I suspected that the morning sun was visible on the other side. At one end of the corridor, there was a shelf with a gas stove on it. Next to it was a sink on the right side and on the left there was a smaller shelf made of tiles for food preparation. This was the kitchen.

At the other end of the corridor was the toilet-shower combination. The toilet was a floor type unit typically found in Asian countries. Above the toilet was a shower delivering both hot and cold water with a mixing faucet. Thus the toilet acted both as the drain and as the platform for taking a shower. When taking a shower it took care not to step into the toilet or slip on its uneven edge. This was the bathroom.

The apartment was primitive by western standards but it did provide sufficient amenities to allow people to live comfortably under the operative Chinese system. The He family had lived in that apartment for most of their married life and had raised all their children in that location. Two offspring had finished university, and one was buying a taxi as part of his new business. Against adverse political conditions, the He family, as did other families, had managed to continue their lives, raise families, and stay out of trouble. It was not so much that they were politically correct in their approaches but that they let the system work for them whenever possible. Chinese who were not members of the elite ruling group did suffer greatly and were still suffering under the Communist system, but each was able to try to make the most of what was, and still is, a bad situation.

Years later I learned that Mr. He had owned a successful trucking company with a large fleet of General Motors heavy trucks before the Communist Party took over the government of China. When the Communists came to power they confiscated Mr. He's trucking company and took away his license to work. He could work for the government, of course, but because he had been a capitalist and self-employed, he was belittled and often mistreated. During the Cultural Revolution he was incarcerated and often forced to do hard work. In the early 80s he was given early retirement on the condition that he never open his own business or participate in politics. I was fortunate to meet him and his wife in 2000 and was privileged to take him flying over the San Francisco Bay Area in my aircraft. More will be narrated about our meeting with Mr. He and his wife in Montara when they came to visit us with Susan and Ben.

The dinner and meeting with Susan's family was an event that I will never forget. Being in the home of a Chinese family and sharing a common meal, perhaps less common than most, was an enriching experience for me. I was deeply touched by the warmth, the friendship, and the indelible bond that emerged from that encounter. Susan and I continued our conversation about her education, and I began to develop a deep fondness for her. Having met her dear family gave me an insight into her thinking and her aspirations. She wanted to improve her English but she also wanted to receive more education. In China, all the doors to advanced education for her were closed. Remaining in China would give her no possible opportunity to extend her knowledge. Susan was too creative a person to be condemned by a system that offered little room for future development. Susan's mind was too good to waste.

A Short Flight Training Course

The Wenzhou Airport project design was finished the 10th of December and immediately submitted for review and approval to CAAC's directors of airport construction. On 15 December 1985 I received a letter from CAAC advising that the design was approved without changes but they wanted an explanation as to why the Instrument Landing System (ILS) was only applicable to Runway 30 and why Runway 12, the other end of the runway, did not have one. "What would happen if winds favored Runway 12 on rare occasions?" CAAC asked. A phone call soon followed the delivery of the letter asking for a meeting the next morning at CAAC Headquarters. Charlie Sands and Jim Webb placed the request into my hands. I was elected to respond to CAAC because airspace design, hence approaches, were in my domain. I called on Susan to be prepared to help me explain the issue to CAAC.

The next morning at seven we were on our way to CAAC Headquarters for a 7:45 meeting. I brought with me a flip chart board and a few felt pens to draw the approaches when explaining the process. The directors arrived on time and after tea (always a requirement) and informal conversation, they sat down for the explanation at exactly eight o'clock. I explained the ILS process, the placement of the localizer at the end of Runway 30, hence at the approach end of Runway 12, and the positioning of the Glide Slope system for Runway 30's ILS.

"That is all well and good," one of the CAAC directors exclaimed, "but what about an approach in inclement weather to Runway 12 when the winds do not favor Runway 30?"

My response was short and direct: "Either use the ILS for Runway 30 then circle to Runway 12 and land," I said then paused for a moment. "Or do a Back Course localizer approach to Runway 12 using the localizer signal for Runway 30 — of course minima for height clearances and visual runway visibility will be increased."

"What is a Back Course approach?" the same director questioned. "Do we need to add new instruments in our aircraft to use the Wenzhou Airport?"

I couldn't believe that CAAC did not know about a "Back Course" approach. I proceeded to explain what a Back Course approach entailed and how it was done, and that no additional instruments were necessary either in the aircraft or on the airport, but pilot training was required. Moreover, I stressed that a Back Course approach was quite simple but that pilots needed training to learn to read instruments backwards. I stressed the word and repeated it several times to allow it to sink in.

"That's impossible," the doubting CAAC director said. "How can you read instruments backward?" he said raising his voice and pointing at me.

"It is not impossible," I responded, "I have done it many times in my airplane."

The CAAC director stood up and asked, "Are you in the military?"

After a pause, I assured him that, "Were I in the military I would have been forbidden to be in the PRC." I continued, "No, I am not, but I have done that approach in my own aircraft." I paused for a moment and emphasized, "And also in other aircraft!"

"How could you have an airplane if you are not in the military?" I explained that I owned my own single-engine aircraft, that I was not in the military, and that I had performed the Back Course approach in mine and other aircraft several times. It took some convincing to have them accept that in the United States one can own an aircraft. "Bechtel gave you an aircraft," the doubting director stated, still standing and red in the face.

"No, it is my airplane." Then I pulled a photograph of my red aircraft from my file — I had anticipated the question. I had brought the picture with me just to remember what it was that I had left at Hayward Airport. I explained that I was sole owner of my aircraft and that no one had given it to me. I drew a schematic of how a Back Course would be made and explained the details as best I could. As much as it was difficult to understand, the directors finally ended the issue of ownership. The problem of performing the Back Course, however, still lingered as an issue of doubt.

Finally in exasperation I said, "If you have an airplane available at Beijing International Airport, I shall demonstrate how it's done." This was said simply to end the discussion. One of the directors reminded all present that it was time for lunch. Lunch was served in the conference room and fortunately no alcohol was accompanying the food — an unusual fact in China. After lunch ended, at around two, the doubting director informed us that an airplane and crew were awaiting us at Beijing International Airport. I was asked to accompany the CAAC team, but Susan was told that she could not come along. I was now without an interpreter.

A senior line pilot with CAAC Airline was to help with the demonstration and with the interpreting. The pilot spoke good American English and was happy to participate in the demonstration. When I arrived at the airport I was confronted with a twin-engine aircraft that looked like a Soviet Ilyushin 14 but with some noticeable changes. I had neither seen that type before that day, except in an album, nor was I familiar with the Chinese version of the USSR's model.

We entered the aircraft and the pilot led me to the copilot's seat while he occupied the left seat. The copilot took one jump seat and the doubting CAAC director occupied the other. The CAAC director had strapped on a belt with a gun — I guess in the event I commandeered the aircraft. The right seat was my choice because I knew nothing about this particular aircraft. After start up and the normal conversation with the tower and what I was certain was air traffic control, the captain released the brakes and we started rolling towards the active runway — Runway 30. As we taxied, the captain asked me what I wanted him to do even though I had given him a briefing before we boarded the aircraft.

I gave him my instructions, which was that he fly straight out for 20 to 25 kilometers, make a 180-degree turn to a heading of 120 degrees, which is the opposite track for Runway 30. Once established on that heading, I asked him to dial in the localizer frequency and to give me the yoke. He would continue to handle the power levers, but we disconnected the autopilot. We took off on a heading of approximately 300 degrees. When 20 kilometers out, I asked the captain to tune in on the localizer frequency and then execute a 180. The pilot was to tell me when he was on the localizer — I could monitor the needle as well on the copilot's side, but I wanted him to see it too. When we were stabilized on the incoming course, I asked if I could take over. He agreed. I pointed to the VOR dial, which becomes the ILS dial when tuned to the latter, and showed him that the needle was to the right of the center (doughnut), then I adjusted the course to bring the needle into the doughnut by stepping on the left rudder pedal — exactly the reverse of what usually is required. In normal cases one steps on the rudder pedal that is on the side of the needle but in a reverse course (Back Course) one steps on the opposite side of the needle (the pedal).

I descended to Runway 12 but did not land. The pilot reduced power as we descended and we lowered the landing gear in the event that I overcontrolled — which I did not. I called for takeoff power and flew about 50 meters over the runway, and then I handed the aircraft back to the captain. We turned to 300 degrees and flew back to return to the 120 degrees direction for another attempt. This time the captain would fly the Back Course approach. The captain stabilized the aircraft and as sweet as pie repeated the approach flawlessly. He smiled and exclaimed: "I fly the Back Course!" I was smiling also.

The captain repeated the Back Course approach several times and then asked me to swap seats with the copilot so he could perform the Back Course. The copilot executed several Back Course approaches. Each pilot, when stabilized on the localizer, repeated a mantra in Chinese of "back course" that when translated into English reminded them to guide the aircraft in the opposite direction than the needle indicated. Fortunately, the exercise was performed in clear and visibility unlimited (CAVU) weather and with practically no wind.

Upon landing we repaired to a bar where we celebrated with several rounds of drinks that were paid for by the doubting director of CAAC who was now happy and without his gun belt. The chief pilot introduced me to several other pilots and he informed them a new procedure was to be added to their training, a procedure that I had invented! "No, no, no," I repeated, "it is a standard procedure that predates me by many years."

A few days later I received a letter thanking me for teaching the Chinese pilots "the complicated procedure required to execute a Back Course approach." As a result of that training exercise, the CAAC had saved approximately 150,000 USD by not installing another ILS at Wenzhou Airport.

The design for the Wenzhou Airport was approved. I was asked when I returned to San Francisco to draw several drafts of ILS and Back Course approaches to be submitted to the proper authorities at CAAC for final approval and then after approval, to have them incorporated into the PRC's airspace system.

The Farewell

Monday morning several tasks awaited me at the office. Mme. Zhuzh, the leader of the Chinese team, was planning a party which included a dinner sponsored by CAAC, China's equivalent to the United State's FAA. The party was scheduled for the following Friday and would be held in the conference room of the building we were occupying. Mme. Zhuzh always meticulously organized parties, receptions, dinners, and friendly gatherings. The planning of such events was a major part of her duties as lead cadre for the Party.

No work was to be done the afternoon before the party because we were to attend a musical performance in the theatre of the Petroleum University performed by its students. The fact that none of us from Bechtel understood a word of Chinese did not matter much. We would enjoy the music, the dancing, and grasp perhaps tidbits of the story. Our interpreters would come to our rescue. Susan assured me that I would be bored not only by the poor performance but also by the content of the musical. I wasn't that bored because my interest zeroed in on the choreography and the direction, which were elementary but good and quite entertaining.

At any rate after the performance at the Petroleum University we were taken to a restaurant to celebrate the successful termination of our assignment on the Wenzhou Airport. The main dish would be, of course, the traditional Peking duck and several other delicacies, such as snails, sea cucumbers, a variety of small fish, and a splendid selection of vegetables, many of which I had never tasted. It was a delicious fare and one that is not easily forgotten. We could not escape the several rounds of alcohol gulps. Fortunately I was sitting next to a large potted plant and could quietly drain my glass into the pot. Several of my colleagues were not as fortunate or as careful hence they lost a certain level of coherency. When time came for speeches it fell on me to make the required departing soliloquy because I was sober and still quite coherent. The Authorities had provided the party with a translator who was able to make my American address understandable to the Chinese executives present. After much applause and hugging we were driven to our hotels. It had been an interesting three months in Beijing and my experience served me well in understanding the PRC and its zeal to become a powerful nation in the new century that was just fifteen years around the corner.

I sat in my room with the window open so I could hear the noise of the city of Beijing. It was obvious that I was to depart the PRC in a few days but there was a lingering feeling that I wanted to return and would do so at the first opportunity. I thought about Susan and also Ben and their attention to my needs and to the requirements of the task. Could I be of functional help to Susan? I would try with all my might to see her come to America. But then what would happen to her? Would she be accepted in a college and could she handle the demands of the language in an American environment?

Here I was just a few days from my return to California. I was hoping to be at home by Christmas and to serve at St. Edward's at the Christmas Eve service. It was only a couple of weeks away. What would await me at Bechtel when I returned, especially with BOSC? Little news had come my way while I was in China about the state of affairs in San Francisco. Would I have to scramble for work, interesting work, especially in the arena of knowledge-based economic regional development? Would my idea for creating a bed and breakfast emerge as a successful reality? All this and more floated in my head.

Well, my stay in Beijing had been good and productive. A new chapter would be unfolding soon. The future was ahead but its offerings were still a bit out of focus. It was time to turn the lights off and obtain some sleep. Tomorrow would bring new hope, new challenges, new encounters, and new risks.

The Departure from the PRC

On December 20th the central Bechtel office in Beijing informed me that my return flight reservations to San Francisco by way of Hong Kong and Honolulu had been lost because of a computer glitch. Because of the Christmas holidays, space on US-bound aircraft was scarce. I wanted to return home, but I was prepared and willing to spend several more days in China. Susan was also willing to work with me as a guide and companion while I explored more of the region.

I had made a plan of what I wanted to see and places I wanted to visit with Susan. Manchuria was top of my list, especially the cities of Haerbin and Qiqihar (which I was able to visit in 2003 on a proposed project). I also wanted to accept the invitation extended to me by the bishop of the small

Anglican community in Nanjing, and of course an architectural and historical visit to Shanghai was a must. Susan had agreed that for Manchuria we would use a commercial flight, but for Nanjing and Shanghai we would obtain good seats in business class (no first class existed, but business class offered the same privileges as first without intimating any social discrimination) on the train.

Two days later, and to my surprise, I was handed a return ticket to San Francisco by way of Shanghai. I would be arriving at San Francisco International Airport on 24 December 1985. I phoned Emily from Tokyo to inform her of my new arrival date but mistakenly told her that my aircraft would be landing at 10:00 p.m. I was wrong in my time conversion but fortunately Emily was able to count a lot better than I and soon recognized that I would be arriving in the morning at that hour.

Indeed, I was sad to leave China, Susan, and the friends I had made there. I enjoyed my stay in China and especially my association with Susan and her family. We had developed a bond that will be sustained for the duration of our lives. I hope to return to China in the not too distant future. China for me was an exceptional opportunity to meet people who had suffered immensely but who had not lost hope, who still had a vision for a better life ahead, and who could manage an oppressive situation with a smile and a shrug.

Remembering without Notes

Many years ago I remember that there was a man who discarded his American passport and requested one from the United Nations. I don't believe that he was ever issued one. This incident is striking for me because I don't belong to one country. I was born in Africa, was educated in Europe (Britain is still part of Europe), and established roots in the United States of America. The USA is my adopted country and I'm glad for that, but I am still somewhat of a foreigner. I look at the world with different eyes than Americans. My view of reality is tinted by my history and by how I interpret events. Reality is not what others see but is quite different for me because I translate what I see, the facts I encounter and their meanings into what suits me, into what I can understand, and into what I can make my own. My general perspective is less American and more European and colored by the experiences I have acquired through my extensive travels.

I've been accused often that I dramatize events, and that I dramatize them differently than they were. Perhaps. But it is true that for me all events are scenes from a play and the play is life as I view it. It is not that I can imagine what never happened; rather it is that what happened is many layered. Life is a complex event that possesses many shades, many aspects, many parts, and many approaches to truth. Alfred North Whitehead reminds me in his *Dialogues* (page 16), "There are no whole truths; all truths are half truths. It is trying to treat them as whole truths that plays the devil." Thus I see life as a series of half truths, perhaps because I've never encountered a whole truth. But for me that embellishes life rather than diminishes it. Like a diamond glistening in light, it has many facets, and each reflects a different set of photons. I see some and you see others, and yet the diamond is.

I can spend hours alone in a place without a book, a magazine, or whatever and always know that I have what's in my brain to entertain me. I keep thoughts alive in the giant theatre that spans the distance between my ears. Never do I run out of material. In a real sense I am my own source of entertainment, my own interpreter of reality, and my own collector of memories and of their explication. The few who have read parts of this work have suggested that it is more a memoir than an autobiography. I accept that editorial judgment.

Readers please remember that it is my life. More is to come filled with recalled "half truths!

PART FIVE

Another Airport Planning Project

A major change occurred in my work and in my attitude when I returned from the People's Republic of China in December 1985.

Back in San Francisco I continued to support the Wenzhou Airport project for a few more weeks. Mort Dorris had retired while I was in China and the new department manager was Robert (Bob) Jackson, whom I hardly knew. I was still attached to BOSC and trying hard to get out of that miserable web of incompetent parasites.

One morning as I completed a phone call with Jim Webb who had called me from Beijing, Suzanne Knutssen, the department project administrator, informed me that I was invited to lunch a few days hence at the World Trade Center to celebrate my ten years with Bechtel. I knew about these affairs. It was customary for one's company president or department manager to say a few kind words on one's behalf. "Suzanne," I said, "I will not attend that lunch if anyone from BOSC accompanies me."

"Raymond," she said in her wonderful Swedish accent, "this is a command performance. You must attend unless you are ill and if you are ill it will be rescheduled."

"Suzanne, I will not attend if someone from BOSC accompanies me. That's that!" Suzanne left without saying a word. It never occurred to me that this encounter with Suzanne would be the augury of a long and warm friendship. I did not know Suzanne well except by name and position and only because she tracked the hours for the several projects, and while I was in China, I would telex the hours of the team to her.

The next morning Suzanne came to me again. "Raymond, let's go for coffee," she said. Now I had never gone for coffee with Suzanne Knutssen before that day. At coffee she informed me that Bob Jackson would introduce me for my tenth year anniversary.

"How can he? He does not know me and I'm still in BOSC under the thumb of Leon Ring." She smiled that broad, full, and sunny smile that only Suzanne could offer. She reached into her pocket and handed me my transfer paper from BOSC to BCiv and hence into the Planning Infrastructure Department.

"Bob Jackson wants to see you after we have coffee. Your line manager is Michael Wakelin, and Bob is your department manager." I hugged Suzanne and kissed her cheek.

After my coffee with Suzanne I immediately went to see Bob Jackson. Bob reminded me of my uncle, Mathieu. Bob was quiet-spoken, direct, and most understanding. Because he would be introducing me he wanted to know a few details about me, what I would be doing, and what I had done. I was still working on the Wenzhou Airport but was close to completing the project. I did not know what was next on my agenda. Would I let him know what was next on my plate, and soon? I would.

Before noon, both Steve Gomes and Michael Wakelin came to me to ask if I would help with a presentation to a client who wanted to build a cargo airport in Southern California to serve the growing airfreight industry. That afternoon I went to the presentation and met Iddo Benzeevi, a new client and ultimately a friend, in spite of the fact that he was anti-Arab.

The location of the airport was to be in Moreno Valley, not far from the city of Riverside, and approximately 60 miles east of Los Angeles and 40 miles west of Palm Springs. Moreno is a valley surrounded by high mountains and not far from March Air Force Base. I told the client that the idea was good, the purpose would probably produce revenue after the capital costs were recuperated, and that the freight industry would welcome an airport away from Los Angeles International and Ontario International Airports. The terrain was a valley surrounded by hills and mountains. To the east there were hills to 3,000 feet and to the north there was St. Jacinto Mountain, which tops 10,000 feet. The valley floor, although sloping from north to south, was fairly flat and devoid of trees, boulders, canyons, or creeks. From north to south, the terrain where the runway would be built sloped approximately 150 feet. It was not a naturally level piece of land and would require leveling for a runway but approaches and departures had clearways.

After the terrain was examined on the topographical chart Iddo asked, "Can a 10,000-foot runway be constructed?"

I looked at Iddo and asked how much money he had but did not wait for an answer. "An airport can be built in the middle of the Pacific Ocean if you are willing to bear the cost." I was thinking of Kansai in Japan, which was being built on a man-made island in Enshü Bay. After some initial calculations I added that a runway and taxiway could be constructed on the property and that there was sufficient space left for a cargo terminal and other airport-related buildings. "Yes," I said, "a good cargo airport can be built on your Moreno Valley property."

I called Bob Jackson after the presentation and informed him that we had a contract to be signed to start the phase study of a 1.8 million dollar project. The contract also included some initial marketing; how did he feel about marketing? He supported the work proposed all the way. The initial planning design contract was signed that afternoon and I was asked to lead the design both for the land and the airspace requirements. Dr. Steve Gomes would be project manager and I would be program manager. It was a good team.

Unfortunately, Steve Gomes from the very beginning did not get along well with Jackson. The chemistry was not there. Steve was very good with clients and could open doors to new ventures easily; he was not, however, good at following up with written details and keeping his superiors informed of developments. Yet Steve and I get along quite well and still remain good friends.

In my capacity as program manager I dealt mostly with Bob Jackson and the client but Steve was responsible for dealing only with the client. The clients, Benzeevi and Cohen, had difficulty working with each other. Benzeevi was a bright Israeli-American entrepreneur who could grasp issues immediately. Cohen did not understand the first thing about regional development and even less about airports. The critical mix in the client did not exist; fortunately Iddo was able to overcome the deficiencies.

We proceeded with Moreno Valley and even obtained the approval of the Federal Aviation Administration (FAA) for a 10,000-foot runway with Category 1 Instrument Landing system (Cat 1 ILS) on both approach ends that could be upgraded when and if necessary in the future to higher categories. Moreno Valley was the first airport approval ever received by Bechtel from the FAA. The runway was designed to support the footprint of an aircraft with 55,000-pounds/square inch of weight — ample for a DC-8 or a B-727 or heavier. Marketing progressed well and retired military personnel who were residents of the valley were supportive of the project until the Defense Department suggested that March AFB, not more that 20 miles from Moreno, be closed as a military facility. The shift against Moreno Valley materialized when retirees assumed that March AFB could be converted into a civilian cargo airport and they would have priority in both employment and housing on or near the Base.

After a year's worth of work by Bechtel and supporting firms, the new Moreno City Council, stacked with retirees from March AFB, voted to disallow the construction of the Moreno Valley airport. This decision came about after the previous Council had fully endorsed the airport and its effect on the region. One of two newly elected council members called for another vote on the airport and was able to persuade the whole Council to change its vote; thus rejecting the airport construction. Hence after 1.1 million dollars were spent, the Moreno Valley project was stopped. In 2003, Moreno Valley was suffering from 18-20% unemployment; March AFB was partially decommissioned and used mostly by Air National Guard Air Refueling Tankers, but with a few civilian aircraft. The civilian team in charge of March AFB was working to attract business, but no businesses would come to March until the toxic sites were cleaned. The Defense Department claims it could not clean them until more Congressional funding was committed to that purpose. With the economy in the doldrums and the intrusions into Afghanistan and Iraq, it was unlikely that funds would be allocated for March AFB in the near future.

Thus in less than a year a good project was dynamited by a city council that hoped for a Defense Department gift that never materialized.

My next project was helping in the conversion of Pease AFB, Portsmouth, New Hampshire. This project was a marketing effort for me mostly to see if freight carriers and aircraft maintenance firms were interested in establishing themselves at Pease. The surrounding community did not want Pease to become an alternate airport for Boston's Logan International Airport. I was able to interest Pan American Maintenance Division and Airbus Maintenance Group. The Delta Connection was willing to provide a commuter link to Logan if the community authorized it and if the passenger seat-mile-revenue (SMR) factor made it profitable. The community accepted four flights by commuter aircraft without restrictions. Airbus established a maintenance satellite to service their manufactured aircraft. Pan Am went bankrupt but was able to sell its maintenance equipment located at John F. Kennedy International Airport to ASIO, an Asian firm willing to relocate at Pease to service Boeing and other aircraft. The New Hampshire Air National Guard had established an active squadron of air tankers at Pease. To date, Pease is operating quite well and appears to be profitably managed.

Pease AFB was my last airport project for Bechtel. It was time for me to move into new uncharted terrain, new adventures, and new creative endeavors. I did — soon enough.

The Dynamic City

After Pease AFB I returned to San Francisco to find that the Planning Department (at my often-given suggestion to Mort Dorris and Bob Jackson) had become the Infrastructure Department. The reader having heard this piece of information many times should recognize that changing a department's name and task is tantamount to changing its sex! Infrastructure was a more appropriate title for a department that operated in many disciplines and served many purposes. Readers should remember that when I first arrived in the Planning Department with Mort Dorris as its head, I had suggested to him and Mike Wakelin that a more appropriate name would be something that incorporated "infrastructure." My thoughts were that then we would be able to expand our work to include more than just planning, which was done anyway on each project. This change was to my advantage, especially as I moved more into straddling many disciplines and hence to become almost indispensible to the firm. In my introduction to, and my meeting with, each member of the department, I counted out of the 18 members only four planners. The rest were architects, economists, mathematicians, public policy specialists, agronomists, physicists, and one financial expert. I certainly was not a planner but more of a multi-disciplinary professional. Thus I suggested that the department assume the title of infrastructure. I was pleased with the new name: it made more sense and it opened doors that were often closed because of the limiting scope that planning offered potential clients.

My interest at the time had moved from airports and aviation to what an airport really was: a self-contained city. My focus was to expand my understanding of what made a city, how a city emerged, what made a city viable, and what the economic underpinnings of a city were.

You will recall that Emily and I had taken a few weeks to look at city-states in Europe. I had, of course, been to Singapore, Hong Kong, and Macau (though to the latter only for a day). Macau was a small piece of Portuguese real estate on the coastal mainland of China that thrived primarily on gambling and illicit trade. Neither China nor Portugal offered a semblance of governmental control over the activities that surfaced in Macau. Macau was a tourist haven and the home of numerous shady organizations that traded anything and everything that was illicit. Soon to be returned to the PRC, it was not a place where foreign industries were willing to establish themselves for the long term. Businesses and industries need a modicum of controlling laws and statutes to maintain a stable, safe, free, and encouraging environment.

Singapore is a tightly governed city-state that has been converted into an economic generator of major importance under personal restrictive laws that dictate the behavior of its citizens to the nth degree. Several interesting things are forbidden on Singapore's streets and public places such as smoking, gum chewing, and ice cream cones. Furthermore, no criticism of the government either in public or in the press is permitted; no littering on the streets; and of course no illicit drugs are to be used or sold in Singapore. Any violation of these laws would produce punishment that includes whipping in public, jail, forced labor, or expulsion. An interesting environment for business ventures, yet businesses love to establish themselves in Singapore because skilled and professional workers are available, are responsible, and are tightly controlled by the laws of the state. Singapore is safe and security is excellent. Air access to the island of Singapore is abundant and Singapore International Airlines (SIA) is the provider of excellent passenger and cargo service. By guaranteeing a safe and orderly environment, a tightly practiced legal and statutory system, and a stable, if restrictive, government, Singapore manages to nurture a vibrant economy based on good technology, banking, transshipping, and a skilled and professional work force.

Hong Kong, unlike Singapore, is a chaotic beehive of small businesses doing well. It was to be returned to the PRC but Hong Kong furnished laws, statutes, and a safe environment for businesses to grow. Hong Kong functions on a lax and quite simple municipal system. In addition, an agreement between the United Kingdom and the PRC was being fashioned that allowed the coastal location to continue as it had since its colonial days for the next 50 years. That 50-year extension allowing capitalism to continue provided some encouragement to industries willing to make Hong Kong their base. Of course the projection is that Communism in the PRC will not last too long — at least it will experience a radical change towards economic liberalism. The financial world is hoping that the tail, typically Hong Kong and the growing Sino-economy, will wag the dog of Chinese Communism out of existence.

As was indicated in earlier portions of this writing, the European city states all had characteristics that made them unique. Andorra, high in the Pyrenees Mountains, is a ski resort in the winter and a general tax-free shopping haven year round. Andorra produces nothing of consequence except leisure, cheap goods made elsewhere, and a tax haven locality. Governed loosely by both Spain and France, Andorra is a territorial tax loophole befitting both adjacent nations. As a tourist haven in the winter and a shopping magnet year-round it does produce respectable revenues. Andorra's tax advantage is being altered and even reduced with the establishment of the European Union, but because Europe is not quite a federation with taxes monitored by the Union, the small mountain community can still offer some advantages, at least for a while longer.

Monaco, the cliff-side Principality on the edge of La Côte D'Azur of France, and overlooking the Mediterranean Sea, is a gambling center offering many casinos for the rich and famous. Beyond the gambling it is also a tax refuge, home of the world class Grand Prix auto racing event, several marine research institutions such as the Cousteau Institute, financial investment corporations, a few luxury yacht builders, and the fine International University of Monaco.

San Marino on the east side of Italy is a pleasant, small tax-safe place that exists because it offers Italian investors a site where they can legally protect their wealth without having to go to banking institutions in Switzerland. A serene location in the beautiful mountains of Montefeltro and not too far from Rimini and the Adriatic Sea, San Marino offers a good place to locate a retirement villa and provide a quiet life but not much more.

The generator of high technology activities, high temperature ceramics, research, and the production of innovative methods for preserved food is the Principality of Liechtenstein. Nestled in the Alpine mountains near the Swiss, Austrian, and German borders, Liechtenstein stands as a dynamo of creativity and sound economic foresight. Liechtenstein is the example, par excellence, of how to maintain a dynamic, healthy, safe, free, liberal, and beautiful environment while at the same time generating revenue through productive endeavors.

Emily and I had assimilated all this information and had discussed the pros and cons that are attached to a small state, when one afternoon Dr. Ronald B. Brooks came to me and said that he had been informed by colleagues and his soon-to-be wife Nassmah that I knew much about "city-states." I admitted that I had visited most of them at my expense because I was interested in the characteristics of a small state managing its future in the current developing global economic environment. "Prepare a tight outline of the requirements for a successful city-state," Ron asked me. He wanted the information ready by the next morning.

OK, I could do that but in the confusion of moving from one office to another, I soon forgot about it. The next morning while driving our little red truck to work I remembered Ron's request when I saw an advertisement that mentioned the words "city in transition": it was a promotion for the Bay Area Rapid Transit (BART). Quickly I asked if Emily had a notebook available and could we jot down some bulleted sentences for an outline on city-states. By the time we parked the red truck we had a two-page outline that described the requirements for a successful city-state. Arriving at my office I found Ron Brooks waiting for me. "Come with me, Chief," he said.

"Where are we going?" I asked.

"To the executive board meeting in Polvi's office," he said as he took my arm to make me follow him. Bob Polvi was president of BCiv.

"Here is the outline you asked for yesterday, but in draft form," I informed him as we were walking towards Polvi's office.

"Keep it ready," he said.

"But won't you need to look at it before you make the presentation?" I said. He stopped and looked at me. He was taller and larger and I felt small, very small.

"YOU are making the presentation. Keep it simple and short. Answer the questions clearly and succinctly," he instructed me.

In the conference room, which was attached to Polvi's luxurious office, I made the presentation to the Board of BCiv on the possibility of creating a city-state, a group of nine senior vice presidents plus two Saudi representatives, the Moroccan Consul General to Los Angeles, and the Business Attaché to the Moroccan Ambassador. After the presentation was completed and the questions had been asked and answered, Ron asked me to step into the outer office and help myself to a cup of coffee and doughnuts. I did as I was told. Thirty minutes or so later Ron stepped out of the conference room and asked me to meet him in his office at eleven o'clock.

I returned to my office and Emily was curious about the presentation and its purpose. I replied that the presentation appeared to have gone well but I did not know what its purpose was. While I was speaking with Emily, Wakelin walked in to ask what Brooks wanted. I told him about the presentation and who the people present were. "Why did you not call me?" he asked.

"Michael," I said, "Ron kidnapped me as I arrived and I did not know what he expected of me."

"Well, what was the topic?" he was a bit angry.

"City-states," I replied.

"What city-state?"

"All of them," I replied. "And now I'm going for a mocha and then to Ron's office."

Promptly at eleven I was in Ron Brooks' office. He motioned me to enter. Polvi was with him. Ron explained that the Saudi government was concerned that Iran might close the Strait of Hormuz, the gate to the Persian Gulf. They had negotiated an agreement with Morocco to fill deep, empty sulfur caves with surplus oil to protect the world economy in the event of an Iranian move to starve the West of oil. This storage of oil was to begin immediately. In conjunction with the storage agreement with Morocco and as a pay off, Tangier was to be converted into a free "city-state" with a permeable border to help the economy of Morocco and all costs for this conversion would be paid by the Saudi Government. As a free city-state, Tangier would be able to circumvent several of the hidebound Shari'ah laws that prevented the Royal Islamic Kingdom of Morocco (and Saudi Arabia, although that was intimated but never mentioned) to have revenue-producing financial banking institutions.

Would I do the research and produce a justification for Tangier? That was the gist of it all. "Ron," I said, "a justification to create a city-state from the coastal, and historically mercantile, port city of Tangier will require that it be compared with other regional potential locations." This was no easy project. Creating a city out of what had become a port in modern times was a major endeavor, but not an impossible one. I looked at Ron and I guess he could see that I was thinking. He nodded. I continued, "It seems to me that I need to look at Malta, Cyprus, Gibraltar, Crete, and several other locations. Then I must compare them to each other and to Tangier. When that is accomplished I need to look at statutes, laws, environmental conditions, educational prospects, financial lures, and transportation advantages, among other items that I've not yet considered but that will surface once the research is underway." I paused. "What currency will the new city-state use? Who will be its entrepreneurs and what guiding structure will make possible free and productive enterprises? There are so many issues to research and I need to make a general plan that will help me gain some direction, even if it must be altered and revised often." My head was spinning with the thought of creating a country — it was exciting, orgasmic. "I will need to have a team to help with the research," I added.

Ron looked at Polvi and both looked at me. Polvi said quietly (and he was never one to speak in a whisper), "We've got the right person. Go ahead."

Ron looked at me and asked, "How large a team do you need? This is to be a secret project. No one except Bob Jackson is to know about it — and I will inform him. No one is to hear or read what you produce about the project."

I thought for a moment, and then said, "I'd like to have Emily on the team because she has already helped with the first phase of the research on existing city-states and she is a first-class researcher." After a pause for further thinking I continued, "I need an economist that I can trust and hence I want Richard (Dick) Stauffer. I also want my administrative assistant and typist Ligia Zelaya who I trust implicitly. That's the team. I want billable hours for three or four months."

"You've got it Chief, but remember that it is a secret project. One word of it gets out and the Saudi Government will retract its support," Ron warned me. "No one is to know. Not even Wakelin or your department colleagues." Then he added, "When can you begin?"

I looked at both Ron and Polvi then said, "I have already!"

As I walked out Ron said, "Frank Nettleton will monitor the hours for you and give you the administrative support that you'll need, but he does not and will not know the real focus of your work. He'll assume that it has to do with Riyadh's airport."

I needed to get out of the office. Both Ron and Polvi were cigar smokers and cigar smoke permeated the room even if no one smoked in front of me.

My first task was to recruit and brief Emily, Dick, and Ligia, then to stop whatever they were assigned to do. Dick was in my department so that was easy. Emily was in the publication department and that was in another division that would not release her to work under me, her husband, as part of my team. Michael Wakelin, who was titled my line manager had to be convinced that I was taking his Chief Economist for three or four months — Dick Stauffer outranked me but he was willing to work under my direction. Wakelin was curious and inquisitive, and being very much a political creature who always played the corporate game but often produced nothing tangible, he wanted to know all the details. When I explained that it was a secret project that even he, my line manager, was not permitted to know, he went immediately to speak with Bob Jackson, the department manager. Ron Brooks already had informed Bob about the sensitive project. Wakelin was instructed to leave the team alone to do its work. When he returned to my office he was not happy and his eyes showed it.

Getting Emily released from her department was a bit testy. I made an appointment to meet with her manager, Louise Forbush. Louise would not allow the transfer. We chatted a bit about other items long past because we knew each other and at one point we had dated and had dinners a few times. No intimacy card was going to be played for this transfer. I thanked her and went to see Ron Brooks. He immediately dictated a memorandum to Louise Forbush placing Emily under his jurisdiction, and making me her line manager. "Take this letter to Ms. Forbush and let me know if she still offers any resistance." Louise immediately caved in and accompanied me to Emily's location to inform her that she was released and hence on loan to Dr. Ronald Brooks for the duration of the project but that she was to report to her immediately at its completion. She was to move to a new location on the 30th floor of 45 Fremont, adjacent to my office, the next day. And thus the project began with a superb team of excited participants.

The product that emerged took a little over three months to complete and was written, on purpose, in non-Bechteleeze language and was received well by all the parties involved. Entitled "Towards the Dynapolis," it was a genuinely creative work that examined the social (type of citizenship), financial (how to create a new money), economic (monetary strategies and type of currency to be used), transportation (full gamut of access and connection in and out of Tangier), infrastructure (supporting logistics for all aspects of a dynamic state), legal and statuary (safety, control, operation, judiciary, etc.), environmental precautions (protection of the surroundings), and government (democracy, oligarchy, dictatorship, etc. — what form and the manner that it would be put into place).

There are a few anecdotes that might be of interest to the reader. The research for the Dynapolis was performed before the advent of the Internet; hence it was either done by way of libraries or by direct interviews of key people. To develop the governmental material we researched how some of the existing city or small states managed. We interviewed government personnel from Singapore, Hong Kong, Liechtenstein, San Moreno, Malta, and Andorra. We asked how corporations and new firms could be created, registered, and how they would be taxed, regulated, and permitted to trade.

We interviewed many representatives from institutions to learn more about the various issues that we were researching. For example, for the financial questions we contacted banks, investment firms in San Francisco, in New York City, in Boston, in London, in Tokyo, in Singapore, and in Berlin. At one point my telephone bill was just below $7,000. To obtain in formation on how a new nation could create its new currency we needed to interview a number of economists and financial resource people.

Dick Stauffer, the economist working on my team, decided to contact several professors at Stanford University, at the University of California in Berkeley, and at Yale University. We drove to both Stanford and Berkeley to discuss the question of the creation of a new currency. After many hours of conversation I was not happy with the approach of using the "basket currency" method, which called for selecting several known currencies and pegging the new currency's value to the mean or average value of what was included in the basket.

Not being an economist I allowed myself much leeway to show my ignorance. I telephoned Harvard University and was directed to the Massachusetts Institute of Technology department of economics. I spoke with Professors Lester Thurow and Robert Heilbroner who joined the phone conversation from the New School of Social Research. Professor Heilbroner suggested I contact a friend of his at the Treasury Department, Robert Green. Mr. Green was not available but his assistant suggested I telephone Princeton University and talk with an associate professor who had done some work and written a few pamphlets on currencies. His name was Dr. Paul Krugman, and I was immediately connected with his office when I telephoned the main operator at Princeton University. Dr. Krugman was most helpful and was able to speak to me in plain English. He suggested that I consider the value of what the new nation was going to produce, what the products would cost and what they would be sold for and what profit I expected to collect from the sale. It was my responsibility to establish the values and compare them with what other countries were charging. If we were to sell a ton of sardines what value would we place on that and how would it compare with what Spain, France, Morocco, or Malta would demand. Once that value would be established for this item, we would price another product and another and another and so on. After that exercise was completed we would begin to have a certain value for our currency, which we had decided to name the "Dole." Of course, the dole never materialized because the new nation was not given birth. The Saudi government decided not to fund its creation. At any rate I learned how a new currency could be created and I enjoyed my discussion with the young associate who was quite pleasant, clear, responsive, knowledgeable, and funny. Incidentally, Dr. Paul Krugman received the Nobel Memorial Prize in 2008 in economic sciences in part for his explanation of the patterns of international trade and geographic concentration of wealth. He did this by examining the effects of economies of scale and of consumer choices for diverse goods and services. The question on the creation of currencies was coincidentally just up his alley.

The final product was distributed to just a select group of readers for comments. One copy was sent to John Neerhout, executive vice president, director and corporate sponsor of BCiv. Neerhout was known as a terror, a tough person to please, a stickler for details, and a searcher for weak points. Yet, one morning a few days later, I received a phone call before my usual coffee escape from none other than John Neerhout. He asked a few questions about the team, the mode of research, and how we managed to maintain the confidentially of the assignment, then he congratulated the team and me and added, "That's the most readable product I've ever received from Bechtel." I shared that compliment with my team. A few hours later a memo arrived stating exactly what he had said to me.

The unfortunate result that followed the completion of the research was that because politics in the Persian Gulf had been altered by the end of the Cold War and local events, the Saudi Government decided not to proceed with the oil storage, and the King of Morocco chose to abandon the idea and direct his attention to working more closely with the European Union as a vassal state supplying labor as needed to European countries, especially to France and Spain. Iran became less of a belligerent nation as its engagement in a war with Iraq occupied its attention for eight years. Then Iraq's Saddam Hussein invaded Kuwait and the direction of the geopolitical world took a different course. The price of oil declined for a period but not for long, transportation of crude oil was less threatened, the US Navy made its presence known in the Gulf, and Iran decided that the time was not right for a show of power (time will show that the political and economic conditions were not settled).

The Dynapolis was not a wasted effort, not at all. Much of what had been learned in the research and in the strategy to create a dynamic state went into my understanding of what emerged as the Technopolis, the emerging Centers for Advanced Technologies (CAT), and the further understanding of what makes a city viable, fiscally strong, and attractive to investors, residents, and immigrants. Much of this will be explained below.

Economic and High-tech Programs

With the completion of the Dynapolis I turned my attention to a new development in the arena of high technology. I was interested in knowledge and
all that emerged from that inexhaustible resource. Japan had started to build a
community around advanced high technology, research, education, and innovation. But Japan was unable to foster much development in that arena
because it was in the midst of a financial crisis, a crisis that lasted a decade.
In the meantime, after looking at the Japanese model and California's Silicon
Valley, both France and Italy began to develop communities where high
technology was being encouraged and where technology firms, mostly from
the United States, were establishing themselves in anticipation of the creation
of the European Union (EU), the follow-up to the European Economic Union. These technology communities were patterned loosely after Silicon
Valley, the California high technology Mecca first initiated by Stanford University when it created the Stanford Technology Park, wherein Hewlett
Packard (HP) was given latitude after its birth in a garage.

The French named their parks "Technopoles." The Italians named their
parks "Technopolis," using their own spelling. Technopolis was the generic
name used by the associations dealing with these parks. In certain locations
the word "science park" was interchangeable with technopolis because it was
easier for the public to understand. No matter, the idea was that in these locations knowledge was the economic driving force and the communities that
emerged would be revenue producing.

There existed a confusing factor, however, in that often these European
parks were in reality real estate parcels of managed land that were sold or
leased to firms producing high-tech products such as hardware and software.
Much as these parks were driven by knowledge to produce revenue, they
were managed by firms as real estate ventures rather than collegial communities. To encourage greater high-tech participation, space was allocated for
start-up enterprises, called "incubators." Incubators were given a certain
number of months to produce a new or supporting product that would bring
about revenue and convert the incubator (sometimes) into a commercially

viable firm that would subsequently either lease or purchase property in the park. It must be indicated that in reality these Technopolis parks were quite unlike Silicon Valley because they were managed by corporate firms or quasi-government entities. Silicon Valley in California, however, was neither managed nor controlled by any entity; each firm located in the peninsula that connected San Francisco to San Jose cared for itself. Rather than being planned, Silicon Valley (which has no exact address) was a serendipitously spontaneous coming together of creative minds, many originally from Stanford University, some from the Bell Laboratory in New Jersey, a few from the University of California at Berkeley, and yet some from Europe who came to the San Francisco Bay Area because the business climate and the weather were better for innovative thinking.

Silicon Valley, except for the unique Stanford Technical Park, which was for a short time but is no longer managed, survives and expands because firms settling or emerging in the San Francisco Bay area are free to purchase or lease property wherever it is available. There is no management dictating where firms may settle (except for municipal building codes) and how much they must pay for purchasing or leasing property. The forces of the market are the ultimate controlling factors. Hence in real terms, Silicon Valley spans the area that pretty much consists of the whole San Francisco Bay Area and includes such major cities as San Mateo, Belmont, Menlo Park, Palo Alto, Los Altos, Mountain View, and Cupertino. In addition there are smaller cities that are located between the ones mentioned and even some that are located in the East Bay towards Hayward. None of these cities are managed to facilitate the creation of knowledge and revenue thereof. The magnet that attracts people in the knowledge industry to the Bay Area is the amenities, weather, collegiality, and working circumstances that exist in the region.

I was curious about the European process and wanted to obtain firsthand information on how the Technopolis programs functioned. After making arrangements to visit several in France, in particular the newest part called Sophia Antipolis in Valbonne, I prepared an outline of my itinerary for Bob Jackson's approval and gave it to Michael Wakelin for his review. A day later Wakelin informed me that Jackson was neither in favor of the itinerary nor interested in pursuing such a study. I was puzzled because I could see Bechtel becoming a partner in the development and construction of these parks and I could also anticipate Bechtel marketing the knowledge emerging from these parks creatively as the company became more active in the EU, when that union became a reality, which was imminent. I anticipated these parks becoming part of the economic infrastructure of France, Britain, and Italy, and, of course, of other European countries. Moreover, in conversation with Jackson I had the distinct impression that he was interested in knowledge-driven programs.

Entrance into France and the USSR

I waited a few days before challenging this rejection, but in the meantime I directed my attention to the opening of the USSR, now that Mr. Gorbachev was Secretary General of the Communist Party. The year 1985 was a momentous year for the USSR and for the rest of the world. President Ronald Reagan had foolishly declared the USSR to be the "Evil Empire." From my personal research and reading, I saw the Evil Empire becoming economically exhausted and slowly slipping into bankruptcy. I was certain that the threat of Soviet power was slowly diminishing because it was financially bleeding and had nowhere to turn for an economic transfusion. The USSR produced nothing of value to export to the global market except oil, and its intellectual resources were tightly monitored, controlled, and restricted from being exported. Moreover, its currency was not convertible and with that impediment it was economically isolated from the wealth that resided in the foreign market. So like a terrier, I pursued my goal for getting access through the gates of the Soviet Union but that would be accomplished through a serendipitous encounter later.

In addition, at a reception given by the French Consulate, I had met the Russian technology attaché and we had become sufficiently friendly that he was amiable enough to keep me abreast of what was developing in the USSR now that Mr. Gorbachev was in power.

One morning, not too many days after my conversation with Wakelin and his negating my suggestion, while riding up in the elevator with Bob Jackson I asked him what was it that he did not like about doing a study of French Technopoles. I explained immediately and before he could answer that I thought that such a study would be advantageous to Bechtel. Bob gave me a puzzled look then said, "What study?" I further explained that I was interested in visiting the several Technopoles in France and was willing to write a book on what I learned.

"What are Technopoles?" Bob asked as we stepped off the elevator and he beckoned me to follow him. In his office, we discussed the subject in great detail but he indicated that he had neither seen my itinerary nor the supporting information for it. I was puzzled. Then I asked him why he had rejected the material on my proposed trip, the one that Wakelin had showed him. "Raymond," he said, "there must be a misunderstanding here. I did not reject anything." Then directly he asked, "When do you want to go and for how long?"

My reply was short, "As soon as I can finalize the appointments. I expect to be gone for a month."

He looked at me through his clear metal-rimmed eyeglasses. "I think it is advantageous to Bechtel to be on top of such developments, especially in Europe. Here, use this overhead charge number for the trip." And he wrote the charge number on his snowflake and added: "Raymond has my OK for travel to Europe to study the French Technopoles." Then he asked me if the word was correctly spelled!

I walked straight into Wakelin's office and showed him the snowflake. He said, as he walked about his office, that Bob must have changed his mind, now that he had had time to think about the possibilities that such a trip offered Bechtel. "Yes, Michael," I replied skeptically and walked out of his office. After informing Emily that I would leave soon after Labor Day, I proceeded to finalize the appointments with the French Chargé d'Affaires, at the Consulate in San Francisco and DATAR, the representing French government entity.

Soon after Labor Day, I was on an American Airlines flight to Paris after a short stop in Chicago. In Paris I met Senator Pierre Nöe and his assistant, Daniel Moy (we still correspond regularly). Pierre, even as a senator, was director of Cité Scientifique Parcs et Technopoles, Ile de France Paris-Sud. Pierre Nöe gave me detailed information about how the Technopoles program functioned under the format approved by the current president, François Mitterrand.

After Paris, I flew to Bordeaux to meet with a delegation from the newly established Technopole near the University. After the meeting and a tour of the embryonic Technopole I rented a full-size Citroen and drove the hour and a half to Montignac for the weekend. There I met my friend from Lascaux, Jacques Marsal, his wife, and nephew Jean-Claude Pinheiro. This would turn out to be the last time I saw Jacques. He died a few months later of leukemia in July 1989. Losing Jacques was like losing a part of me. He had become a dear and wonderful friend and we had planned to return him to America for another lecture tour, this time with his wife. At any rate, while in Montignac with Jacques I was able to revisit the Grotto, enjoy several meals with him and his wife, one meal with Jacques and Jean-Claude, and several hours of good solid conversation. Thinking about Jacques even now several years later brings tears to my eyes and a choking surge in my throat. But I wish to recall my visit because it was a time of great enjoyment for me.

Before dinner on Saturday, Jacques had asked me to come to the Grotto at Lascaux for a visit. When I arrived Louf greeted me at the gate with the door key in his mouth and Jacques followed. He led me to the Grotto, down the steps, and gave me his small flashlight. Once my eyes grew accustomed, he left me alone. I was in the Grotto for nearly two and a half hours — the longest stay ever for me. The Grotto was like a temple to me, a holy sanctuary, and offered a sacred connection with human history, the history that touched all human beings, and especially me. I revisited every painting, absorbed every color, nuance, and scratch. I inhaled the special scent of the temple grotto and in particular the aroma of its clay. I looked at the floor and imagined my artistic predecessors inside painting, the darkness disturbed only by the flame of a simple oil lamp.

My imagination ran wild. I could visualize a human being concentrating on painting a bull, a deer, a small black horse — looking back every so often to allow distance to refocus the eyes and examine the creative work. "It is good," was the painter's comment. The assistant, for there was a need for an assistant to help in holding the oil lamp and make it cast its delicate light on the area being painted, to hand pigments to the painter, and to help in other ways that would allow the artist to better execute the work of art, nodded.

I was so engrossed in the magnetic and intimate surroundings that I did not hear Jacques's return. He told me later that he had stood some few meters away for quite a while watching me absorbed in what I was focusing on. He had sensed that my response to the quiet beauty of the Grotto had been and was very much similar to his. Perhaps that was a polite exaggeration on his part, for to him the Grotto of Lascaux was his life. Chevalier Jacques Marsal had dedicated his entire life to the protection of this unique memorial of the artistic history of human beings. Before he died, his gift to me was the moments he granted me to spend time in Jacques's personal Grotto. To me the Grotto of Lascaux was Jacques Marsal's Grotto.

On Sunday he insisted on taking me to a "restaurant de campagne" located a few kilometers from Montignac on the bank of the Vézere River. Jacques ordered the local fare that was accompanied by a rich local wine that I wish I had noted. Jacques was knowledgeable about local food, especially mushrooms, wines, hams, and how these were to be prepared. Eating with the Marsals was an adventure in culinary excellence. It was a fine and memorable "casse croute" with a dear friend and his lovely wife Nounou. Jacques died in 1989 and after all these years I still miss him. Mme Marsal died in 2001. Both were far too young to die.

The next day after telephoning Jacques and saying "au revoir," which was never to be, I left to drive to Toulouse and another encounter with representatives from the local Technopoles. In Toulouse I was also taken to the Airbus complex to review several new aircraft. The visit included Matra, Motorola, Aerospecial, and other industries that were established in the five communities that make up the larger region of Toulouse on the banks of the Garonne, Louge, and Ariège Rivers. In Toulouse I met with Joël Olivier, Secrétaire

Général de Labege-Innopole and Jean Barcellini, Président Directeur Général of the Technopole Toulousaine, SEML-SA, and on loan from Motorola France, assigned to create the techno-park that would bring together the surrounding six municipalities of Toulouse. In addition, and as my guide for my stay in Toulouse, I met Françoise de Veyrinas, Chargé de Mission of the Bureau Regional d'Industrialisation for Midi-Pyrenées.

That evening I had dinner with Françoise de Veyrinas and was further informed about the program that was in place for the Technopole Toulousaine. Françoise was a product of the University of Lyons and Oxford University. With graduate work in political science at Princeton University for a few years, she was quite knowledgeable about American attitudes and politics. Originally from the Toulouse region, she returned to the area to assist in its movement into the knowledge industry. Françoise was a charming, lovely woman, a great conversationalist, and a most pleasant dinner partner.

The next morning I left Toulouse and drove to Valbonne, a community west of Nice, to see the extraordinary development of the new Sophia Antipolis Technopole, created to a large extent by French Senator Pierre Laffite and Dominique Fache. Sophia Antipolis is named after Sophie Glikman-Toumarkine, the wife of Pierre Laffite, founder of the Technopole.

The drive to Nice took me through Montpellier, Nîmes, Arles, Aix-en-Provence, Cannes, and then into Nice. Bechtel made my reservations for a hotel in Nice's neighboring municipality of St. Laurent, when they should have been made for the one located directly in Sophia Antipolis. This glitch caused a bit of a problem for me, which was fortunately not serious, although it might have been, had I missed my appointment.

I was to have a lunch appointment with Dominique Fache at the hotel in Valbonne. Dominique was a student of Dr. Glikman-Toumarkine, professor of Russian literature at the Sorbonne and mentor to Fache and wife of Laffite. Dominique's responsibility was the development of Sophia Antipolis as a knowledge community, a technopole. I was to have lunch at the hotel in Valbonne but not the one in which I was registered as a guest. Let me preface this by saying that Dominique, a cherished friend now, can be a bit prickly if things do not fall in place as he planned them. Taking some time to reach

Sophia Antipolis early to obtain a preliminary look at the complex, I passed by a hotel that was part of the same chain as the one in St. Laurent. At noon, the time of my appointment, it occurred to me that perhaps I was staying at the wrong hotel. Entering the hotel I asked if a Mr. Fache had made reservations for lunch. Indeed the reservations had been made for 12:30 for two for lunch. By a stroke of luck I was at the exact location, and even a bit early.

Soon after noon, Dominique Fache walked in and asked the reservation clerk if I was in. The clerk directed him towards my table in the bar. This was a happy encounter because Dominique and I started our friendship with punctuality yet it would have been different had I not been at the right hotel. Had I stayed at my hotel to await Dominique I suspect that our friendship would have begun on a less amiable footing. We have become long-term friends and worked in association on several projects in France, Italy, England, Russia and most recently, in 2006, in Clovis, California. Dominique is fluent in Russian and English, is married to Olga, a beautiful Russian, and they have two lovely children.

The tour of French Technopoles after Sophia Antipolis included visits to Grenoble, Lyon, Lille, Amiens, and Chartres. All in all I spent five weeks in France gathering an enormous amount of information. But the most important portion of this venture was being invited by Senator Pierre Nöe to meet President François Mitterrand in his private villa at Massy, not too far from Versailles. Nöe had asked me if Bechtel was implanted in France in anticipation of the EU's inception and whether the firm had presented its credentials to the government of France. My reply surprised him when I said no. He then offered to find an occasion when I could meet President François Mitterrand at his villa in Massy. I was thrilled. When I returned to Paris, being driven by Daniel Moy, the Secrétaire Administratif of the Ile de France Sud and an aide of Nöe, I asked Mr. Cori, the manager of Bechtel's Office in Paris, the important question "Has Bechtel ever presented its credentials to the government of France?" Maurice Cori admitted that Bechtel had never considered that to be important.

I telephoned Bob Jackson and asked him the same question and why Bechtel had not presented its credentials to the French Government. He informed me that he would check and report to me as soon as possible. At midnight my time in Paris, Bob phoned me to tell me that Bechtel was still an American firm and had never officially registered in France. Why was I asking the question? I told Bob that maybe, just maybe, I would have an opportunity to meet the President of France. He told me to go ahead because this would be an opportunity that should not be discounted. I thanked him and tried to go back to sleep, which is an impossible task for me once I'm awakened.

The next morning Pierre Nöe telephoned me while I was having breakfast and announced that Daniel Moy would come for me at 10 a.m. Daniel came on time and took me directly to Pierre's office in Massy. Coffee was served and I was introduced to Catherine Sauvageon, program director for GA, the firm assigned to putting together the technical program for the science park. I was also introduced to a lovely woman by the name of Renée Claret, manager of Promopole for SEM Saint Quentin en Yvelines; a group involved with technical incubators for the technopole. The discussion was very enlightening and I gathered a great deal of information and many nuances about how France was addressing the issues around high technology and its implantation.

A little after noon Pierre suggested that we prepare ourselves for lunch. He announced that he and I had a lunch appointment and that he was uncertain as to when we would return to his office. We climbed in the car and Daniel drove us to a remote place where a lovely villa was situated at the end of a long row of tall Italian Cyprus trees. As the car stopped, Pierre told me that the President of France, François Mitterrand, had invited us for lunch. I was a bit stunned and short of breath. I had this warm tingle all over my body. I was to be in the presence of the President of the Fifth Republic, the first member of the Socialist Party to be elected head of state.

When we entered the villa and were escorted by a butler to the library, Mitterrand was reading one of Churchill's history books in English. Nöe and I were greeted and Mitterrand especially reached out to take my hand. The President wore a white shirt and grey sport slacks, on his nose were gold half-reading glasses, and on his head the hair was white and sparse. His eyes were clear but reflected the age of a person who had done a great amount of reading, looking, and visually taking in life and its multiplicity of events and occasions. He was not tall but his stature was impressive and his handshake was that of a powerful person who was in command and who expected respect. Because I had never met or been around a president of France, I looked at him for a moment longer than etiquette might have suggested. Mitterrand noticed. Mitterrand responded by sizing me up too. "Un Americain qui parle Français." This was not said as a question but as a fact that he appreciated, especially after I learned that he had little regard for Ronald Reagan, the current president. Mitterrand took my arm and led me to a deep and comfortable armchair. Pierre took another chair next to mine with a small table separating us.

As soon as we were seated, a lovely lady entered the library and served us aperitifs; much later I learned she was his mistress of many years. She was most attractive and about Mitterrand's height and had a figure that was slim, well proportioned, and eye-catching. Her face was sculptured with angular bones and her nose was small and pointed but not beaked. Her hair, grey as it was, was bundled on the back and held together with a silver clip. After serving us each our drinks, a fine Blanc Fumé, she took the other deep and comfortable armchair and offered a toast to "notre Americain." Her voice was soft but clear and also commanding. I never heard her name and Mitterrand always addressed her as "ma chère," but never as "ma chéri." (The first term is polite and the second amorous).

Our conversation covered, for the first few minutes, the expansion of Technopoles, and the subsequent increase in high tech research in France. We discussed knowledge as a renewable revenue resource. This was a good omen for France, Mitterrand pointed out. The conversation lingered a few more moments on technology, knowledge, privatization of enterprises, and the future of research and the products that could emerge in the next decades for France and the world.

Soon enough, as Pierre had alerted me, the conversation moved to art in all its dimensions. M. Mitterrand was exquisitely informed, as was expected, about the art in the grottos, especially Lascaux, and he knew Jacques Marsal.

Pierre had briefed the President that I had been involved in research in the grottos, especially in Lascaux.

Lunch was served on the veranda by a butler, but the lady who had served the aperitifs was not seen again that afternoon. She disappeared once we moved to the veranda. In fact the next time I saw her was on television after Mitterrand died and she was walking in his cortege, as it was moving through Paris. I saw Mme. Mitterrand and his daughter following the cortege, and next to his wife were the lady and her daughter. It was amazing to see wife and mistress, with their respective daughters walking in quiet harmony behind their beloved president, husband, lover, and father. Both women wore black dresses and large hats, and the daughters wore light grey dresses and small berets. It was apparent that the French accepted the fact that Mitterrand had a double family and the arrangement posed no problem, friction, detraction or distraction. Mitterrand was a person of size and nothing obscured that for the French. Mitterrand was as big as life when he was President. As an elected member of the Socialist Party, Mitterrand was one of the most liberal and market savvy presidents that France has had since the emergence of the Fifth Republic. Mitterrand at first nationalized banks and firms until they were placed on a firm financial footing and then turned them over to the free market as independent entities. Government's role was to prevent the collapse of the finances during tight economic times, and the market always required some control, some guidance, and a regulatory system to keep it honest and to dispense with greed.

I met Mitterrand twice more for lunch during my several visits to France and Paris. I spoke with him by telephone on four other occasions at his request. He was a most kind, interesting, and charming person with a sharp intellect and a quick sense of humor. I felt honored to have known him and I was grateful that Pierre Nöe had been kind enough to introduce me to the great man, a man who moved France from its small-mindedness, the heritage from the Gaullists, to a visionary posture that looked at the EU, the UK, America, and high technology not as enemies but as cooperating forces, allies challenging the global market. Mitterrand, the supposed socialist, at the beginning of his administration threatened to nationalize industries and banks unless they removed the hangers-on, the deadwood, and demanded that labor work and not play as if it worked. Mitterrand raised the level of France to that of an active participant in world technology, finances, and the unification of Europe. Unfortunately Mitterrand died before he could complete his work and reach his goal. France has returned to the position it is in now in the first years of the 21st century: labor is ineffectively producing, technology is mired in re-engineering projects, market success is dependent on cut-prices, long-term loans to buyers are strangling its economy, and the current president Jacques Chirac has an imperious attitude that is mimicking the Gaullism of the 1950s.

When I reported to the Paris Bechtel office to inform them of my research into how France was strategically developing high-tech centers and the products that were anticipated from them, I was told that I had a phone message from M. Mitterrand's secretary asking me to return the call. The President wanted to know if he could obtain a copy of the report of my research. I assured him that indeed he could and would as soon as I had completed it, but it would be written in English. That was quite all right with him (I knew that) because he was fluent in English and in American. After the conversation ended, the manager of the Bechtel Office, Maurice Cori, informed me that Bechtel had never met any of the Presidents of France. Bechtel had established an office in Paris and then one in Fos-sur-mer in the early 1950s. I was surprised. But I was always most grateful to Pierre Nöe for making the encounter with M. Mitterrand possible.

After my introductory meeting with François Mitterrand I telephoned Bob Jackson and related the main elements of the encounter. Bob asked me to brief Howard Wahl, senior director, who was scheduled to manage the Paris office soon. I knew Howard well and also was aware that he was on some project in Ann Arbor, at the University of Michigan. I telephoned and briefed him then he showered me with many accolades.

Upon my return to San Francisco, I immediately blocked time to write and complete the report that also contained several photographs of the Technopoles I had visited. When the report was completed and after clearing the "proprietary" issue with Bechtel's legal department, the President of France received a copy of my report that was entitled Centers for Advanced Technologies (CAT). An image of a large black cat on the cover emphasized the acronym CAT.

The survey of French Technopoles opened new avenues for Bechtel and for the infrastructure department because it let in a vision that suggested that the firm could be involved in Information Technology (IT), and that IT offered longer-term projects for the construction and engineering company. I was appointed, by Bob Jackson, manager of the Technopolis and High Technology Infrastructure and given sufficient hours to continue my contacts with European high tech complexes, the European Economic Union (EEC), and to begin exploring what products and ideas were surfacing from the arenas of high technology in the world. Moreover I was given the green light to work with the EEC and support its endeavor to form the European Union (EU). Now that Bechtel was legitimately in France as a European firm the numerous avenues for projects were unlimited. This was a huge task. At my suggestion, Bob also directed me to become intimately acquainted with the governing body of the future European Union, the subsequent entity emerging out of the EEC.

When I related the news to Mitterrand that I was directed to become acquainted with EU as it progressed from the EEC he offered to make me a representative of his committee assigned to work with the embryonic EC. I informed the President, with my regrets, that I could not accept because it would have jeopardized my neutrality and responsibility as an American citizen; I was not permitted to work for a foreign government. A few days later it dawned on me that I had not been offered employment, just access. I telephoned the President's office to ask for clarification. After a few moments on the line, an official confirmed that I was to have access only; no employment was to be considered. That was excellent because then I was able to obtain documents and to approach the Organization for Economic Cooperation and Development (OECD), which is an international economic organization, founded to stimulate progress and world trade and that acts as a research arm for the several committees working to develop the framework of the European Union. Access to this entity allowed me to see how the infrastructure of the EC was developing and to share that information with Bechtel.

In addition to my work with the OECD and EU, I was asked to look into how high technology affected the aviation industry. The Air Bus was beginning to indicate that it was becoming a valid builder of transport aircraft and was moving to challenge both Boeing and McDonnell Douglas. What all this meant was that I was traveling to Europe seven or eight times a year and each venture lasted four to six weeks. It was interesting work but it took me away from my own business, the Goose and Turrets B&B, and from Emily. Promotion followed promotion and I found myself working independently as long as I kept Bob Jackson aware of my progress.

It was not enough to visit the centers where high technology was being produced; I wanted Bechtel to be an active participant in the evolutionary process. Joining the International Technopolis Association, the University Science Park Association, and DbF (Silicon Valley's French group of high tech innovators) gave me a more complete picture of what was developing in Information Technology (IT), especially in France, Italy, Finland, the Netherlands, and the UK with SQW, the firm that created the Cambridge Phenomenon. What was becoming clear for me was that IT was a tool, and an important tool, for guiding the regions to attain better economic levels using the instruments of knowledge. In short, I was moving further into the discipline of creating strategies to implement knowledge-based regional economic methodologies.

My interest was sparked by the understanding that IT could become a way for bringing about economic development to any strategic region — regions with potential characteristics for improvement — that had been, for one reason or another, bypassed because of poor management and left in the doldrums because of a badly developed legal and statutory system. The push to move these regions out of their inertia and into the global economic stream could be supplied by IT. But IT was many things and not just the ability to communicate on a higher level through technological innovations. IT was the leading driving tool for all aspects of information innovations — information that fueled knowledge in a gamut of disciplines — that would allow eventually for better quality of life, better education, and inherent personal freedom without destroying the ecology of the environment. Merging my newly acquired knowledge of IT with what I learned about city-states and the dynamic city offered a new approach for improving regions economically.

Working on IT and Technopoles was the highlight of my productive years at Bechtel. Under the leadership of Bob Jackson, an excellent and trusting department head, I moved into several new areas that were often not important to Bechtel, a firm with the mentality of engineers and constructors but not entrepreneurs. I am not saying that the engineering or constructor mentality is poor but often such professionals lack vision and avoid taking risks, even calculated manageable risks. Unless these risks are controlled by a proven formula or an accepted format (then they are obviously no longer risks), they are nevertheless to be avoided. Bechtel was slowly finding itself blindsided by engineering and construction, and financial firms from Asia and Europe, firms that were not only good and willing to accept risks, but offered good results at lower prices.

Korean and Japanese firms could muster a disciplined team of skilled technical people who were hardworking, spoke English and other languages to boot, and worked for lesser wages than could Bechtel's construction workers. Bechtel needed to promote its professional advantages, its intellectual edge, and accept the fact that other firms could do the labor at a reduced cost. What Bechtel could offer was program management, project management, good support for operational supervision, and solutions for problems inherent in mega-projects.

European firms, such as those from the UK, Germany or France could compete in Europe more readily than Bechtel because they were local entities as far as the EU was concerned. For projects in the USSR, the Nordic firms and especially the firms from Finland, such as Pollard and Hake, were more acceptable because they had experience with cold weather construction. Finnish firms knew the Soviet temperament and its centralized system quite well, and could work out financial agreements that Americans were unwilling to accept or were unable to work out through a bartering system. The Finns had been occupied by the Soviets and thus knew not only how they thought and behaved in business, but also their language and their financial structure. American firms and especially Bechtel had to approach business with new tactics, had to employ different marketing tools to acquire new work, and needed to establish a genuine local base in Europe. It was not enough to have an office in London or in Paris, American firms had to become "European" firms.

Moreover, gone were the days when Bechtel could sit back and enjoy being called to do projects by the King of Saudi Arabia, the Chairman of Standard Oil, or the Secretaries of State or Defense. Marketing was a foreign tool for Bechtel. It was often heard that when a marketing department was initiated by a subsidiary company of Bechtel, the next step was the exit door. Marketing was anathema and in a sense demeaning to Bechtel's upper management. The thought was that a first class engineering and construction firm such as Bechtel did not need to market its wares. Wrong. Quite wrong.

Well, Bob Jackson and I attempted to change the mentality that precluded marketing with the help of Denis Slavich, senior vice president, CFO, and director. The attempt ultimately failed but Bechtel learned a great deal in the process, as did we. With marketing expunged from Bechtel's system also went any attempt to look at the future. A projection of potential work for five or ten years ahead was not how it was done. Bob and I began to look at the future in technology, and how technology — the high tech development of the latter part of the 20th century — would affect industry, people, business, and Bechtel in the 21st century.

I began to look first at technological innovations that would affect aviation and what Bechtel could learn from that information. Bechtel National Company, a sub of Bechtel, had started a computer research department to keep pace with what was being developed by firms in Silicon Valley. It was a good idea that had great merit. This was exciting for me and for those of us who looked ahead at new developments. Dr. Harold Forsen was a key player in our strategy to move Bechtel into the high-tech arena, but the forces of upper management were not keen to support us. A board of directors that was not able to see beyond its nose circumvented even Riley Bechtel, the young and new president of Bechtel. Bechtel was an engineering and construction firm and that was that. It might dabble in investments, operation of power and water companies, and tackle certain defense contracts that called for pro-curement support but that was about the limit of its interest and approach to risk. Times were changing because the old approaches were being replaced by the new for doing business such as joint ventures, partnerships, and part-nering — helping out another firm without investing or contracting directly in a project while knowing that in the near future Bechtel could receive simi-lar help, access to a business network, and various degrees of free support.

Because I had focused my sight on high-tech developments, I joined the International Technopoles Association, the University Science Parks Asso-ciation, and the research arm of the EEC known as FAST (Forward Approaches to Science and Technology). The work called also for a fair amount of travel to foreign places. At the same time Bob Jackson and I agreed to look into high technology developments in and for aviation — in-cluding aircraft and security software and hardware — and elsewhere such as in the Soviet Union. There was an East-West conference scheduled in Lap-peenranta, Finland. The purpose was to let the Soviets show the West what elements of high technology they produced for sale. Because of my interest in the USSR, I decided to attend the conference. Again Bob Jackson thought that it was a good idea and that it would be useful for Bechtel in the long run. I booked a flight from London to Helsinki and from there to Lappeenranta, a city that was located approximately 80 kilometers from Leningrad (now St. Petersburg) by train.

Arriving in Lappeenranta, Finland, in mid-January 1987 reminded me of my time in Alaska. When I landed, it was cold, white, and dark as early as three o'clock in the afternoon. Lappeenranta is situated between two lakes and that means that everyone is adept at using ice skates, and because snow is in powder form, everyone can ski. People go to work on either skates or skis; even little kids go to school that way. Lappeenranta is a small town of less than 20,000 inhabitants and most of the work force is involved in some field of high technology from computer components to cell phones to high-end radios, and to ultrasonic computer-aided machining. In addition, several firms specializing in computer controlled high-pressure water cutting techniques for metals, especially titanium, gold, and platinum, have open houses for visitors. It is a most interesting town.

The conference was bizarre in that the Soviets' wares indicated that they were a long way from the finer edge of high technology. What they showed us was rough, badly assembled, and embarrassing to us Westerners and even to themselves after they examined the Western displays of HP, IBM, Apple, Rockwell, Honeywell, and others. One of the good things that emerged from the conference were the discussions, the one-on-one interchanges with the Soviet attendees. I remember a conversation with Dr. V.P. Groshev, Rector of the Plekhanoy Institute of National Economy in Moscow, who insisted that a centralized economy offered more options for innovation in setting the financial pace of a society. Dr. Groshev further argued that a convertible currency for the USSR would undermine its economic strength by allowing currency to flow out of the country and into the coffers of capitalists who would then be able to control the economy and diminish its growth. Indeed a most simplistic understanding of how the economy of the world functions.

Another conversation was with a physicist who was working on a laser-engraving project. He was lauding the developments in laser physics in the USSR as opposed to those of the west, especially in the UK. He had written a paper in which he stated his ideas and one aspect of his theory, but he could not mail his paper to an English colleague to obtain peer review because neither the facsimile machine at the Institute for Advanced Research nor the postal service could guarantee that his paper would reach its destination. The paper was written in pretty good English, and I took the time to read it. After finding nothing untoward in it, I offered to deliver it to his colleague at Cambridge University. Upon reaching Cambridge and meeting his colleague, an American physicist teaching at the university, I found that we had common friends and similar interests. But to the point, the American thought the theory proposed by the Russian was extraordinary and quite advanced but informed me that he would telephone the Russian and advise him to sit on his work for a few years — he expected as did I that the USSR's life was limited. My subsequent visit to Moscow a few months later convinced me that the Soviet enclave's existence was indeed quite limited. The Soviet Union died in

1991, but what surfaced was a confused set of quasi-independent states whose economy depended on fossil fuel and mining. During the transition after the break up of the USSR, the laser researcher was able to go to Cambridge and further develop his ideas. He never returned to Russia and I introduced him to the Beckman Institute laser researchers located on the campus of the University of California, Irvine.

At any rate, the conference in Lappeenranta was an eye opener for me because it allowed me to see firsthand how technology in the USSR measured up vis-à-vis the west. I also recognized that after all the superficial pride displayed by the members from the USSR, there was a sensitive element of humility that was obvious once in-depth conversations took place. The Soviet members did not appear to be happy people. Joy was an element that was markedly invisible in their eyes. They were noisy and raucous after a few drinks and they craved companionship with western attendees. There was a sense emanating from our Soviet friends that the conditions in the Soviet Union were not at all well. Many questions were asked about the standard of living in the western countries; the freedom experienced in scientific circles; and, of course, the political climate in our respective countries. President Ronald Reagan and Prime Minister Margaret Thatcher were looked upon as anomalies that neither understood the course of changes that were occurring in the Soviet Union nor the depth of the economic crises that were emerging. The situation in Afghanistan, dreadful as it was for the Soviet Union, was merely a blip in the downward spiral of the static and ossified economy.

Dr. John H.W. Cramp, director of ICI's Chemicals & Polymers Division agreed with me that several of the Soviet attendees indicated in one manner or another that they would willingly join us in the west. Two Finns, Ali Saravita and Topio Poranen of Kareltek Technology Centre, hosts of the conference, made the point that the bankruptcy clock of the Soviet Union was ticking and not much time was left on it. Indeed, not much time was left because in less than five years the dissolution of the USSR would become a reality.

After the conference I took time at the invitation of a Finnish engineer, entrepreneur, and principal of Oy Symbion AB, Fredrik Eklöf, to travel north to Oulu on the Gulf of Bothnia, and to Peãloaivi; these towns are located north of the Arctic Circle in the heart of Lapland. It was in Peãloaivi that I tasted my first reindeer filet. Before leaving for the North Country I had rented a parka in Lappeenranta to allow me to go outdoors; my fleece-lined coat was sufficient for Lappeenranta but would not be adequate in the Arctic area. In Peãloaivi the temperature in late January was a chilling minus 35 degrees Fahrenheit (minus 37.2 degrees Centigrade). It was cold but refreshing. Laplanders were working on many jobs and reindeer were kept in fenced areas, although outside Peãloaivi, I saw several reindeer free and roaming without any obvious human control. I was informed, however, that according to the law the reindeer are not really free but are under ownership, at least by common agreement in the Nordic counties.

My real introduction to Finland and its interest in high technology and revenue from the knowledge industry came about at a conference in Montpellier in 1988. What I saw in Finland in 1987 in IT subsequent to my visit to Lappeenranta was a drop in the bucket, but yet there was an interest as my visit to Oulu indicated.

In Oulu, I visited an up-to-date Technopole with several incubators working on program developments for the communication industry. One or two incubators were specifically addressing requests from Nokia, the upcoming cell phone firm. The Gulf of Bothnia was frozen when I approached it from the small hotel where I was staying in Oulu. Oulu, which was a small city of less that 15,000 but now has a population more than 30,000, is still an active fishing port and the home of Technopole Linamar and a university satellite. Again, Finns in Oulu, if not involved in reindeer farming or in fishing, work mainly in high tech and computer program research and development.

This experience is further reinforcement for me that IT can be a fine tool for ecologically sound economic regional development, even in secluded locales, and that IT may be a decisive driving force for providing education to remote regions. Incidentally, when I revisited Oulu in 2006, I saw not one PC; all the computers used were Apple Macintosh instruments of the latest generation. In sum, I found the Finns to be creative, hardworking, and conscientious, and willing to tackle the vicissitudes and gains, if any, of the global economy. I witnessed a dynamic society lifting itself out of the doldrums from years under the boot of the Third Reich and the oppressive rule of the Soviet Union. If my count is correct I paid more than half a dozen visits to Finland and at every visit I was charmed and impressed further with the attitude of the Finns, their intellect, the art and craft quality of their work, especially in silvers, porcelain, and architecture, and the beauty of their land.

Added to the task of exploring European technology, was my inroad into Russia and the building of an initial connection with the Kurchatov Nuclear Energy Laboratory Institute in Troitsk. The latter had offered me an open door into the Soviet Union's Atomic Energy arena. My schedule for travel was extensive. I managed to be in Europe or elsewhere approximately five to six months of the year — a difficult time because the building for the Goose and Turrets Bed and Breakfast had been purchased but required much work for renovations, code requirements, and structural reinforcement. Dear Emily was left with much of the work, the supervision, and the planning for the B&B. For instance, the roof of the building had to be raised to allow for new foundations to be constructed and the existing kitchen had to be gutted and replaced with a new and semi-commercial cooking arrangement. Much work was ahead and much travel was on my schedule, but much of what was happening was fun, informative, and interesting. I had to be ready for events or contacts that were serendipitous in character. I cannot forget that I also had an exciting position with Bechtel and Bob Jackson, my superior, was a superb person.

Russian Connections

Senior Vice President Tom Flynn, the manager of Bechtel's Public Relations, phoned me one morning in 1987 to ask me if I could meet with two Russian scientists who were visiting the San Francisco office. I was briefed that they were interested in IT and the economic reshaping of their knowledge city.

I was busy with preparations for a trip to France and Morocco. "Why me?" I asked.

"You have spoken with Riley Bechtel about looking at the USSR for future work and he thought that you might be the one to meet with these Russians," he replied to my question. "Michael Wakelin and Chris Hartzell will accompany you to the meeting and they will make the general presentation listing Bechtel's wares and accomplishments."

"What's the need of having me present at the meeting if both Mike and Chris are there?" I asked. I disliked dog and pony shows, especially when the presentations were going to be featherweight. This would be another most boring meeting where Bechtel had no special interest in it.

"Riley thinks that you should be present and in fact he wants you to host the meeting," Flynn informed me. "Moreover," he added, "they are interested in science cities, which is your area."

My answer was a simple, "Okay."

At the meeting I was introduced to two Russians. One of the two, Dr. Dimitri Sobolenko (Dima), ultimately became my dear friend for the past several decades. He is deputy director of the Kurchatov Institute in Troitsk; working directly under the leadership of Dr. Viacheslav Pismenny, better known to me now as Slava. The second Russian was Dr. Andre Y. Sebrant who acted as the interpreter for Sobolenko. After the preliminary formalities were completed by Mike Wakelin, I listened to Chris expound on the superlative qualities of Bechtel and the work he had performed as a planner. Then I introduced myself and called for tea to be served. When tea was served and the Russians relaxed, I asked what was it really, and I stressed the "really," that the two Russians wanted from Bechtel?

Andre informed us that they had visited the San Francisco Exploratorium and wanted to develop something similar for the young high school age students in Troitsk. Sobolenko still maintained his silence and I wasn't certain that he understood the import of my question. Except for shaking my hand he had not spoken one word to us. Any comment he needed to make he muttered *sotto voce* to Andre who possessed good English.

The meeting was going nowhere. Mike immediately announced that Bechtel could build anything that they needed and the company could help them with planning issues and project management. Chris joined in and announced that theme parks were one of Bechtel's specialties and that he was working on one of Disney's parks in Florida. "The Disney project, a 250 million dollar initial phase, will be completed by the end of the year," Chris told them. Chris went on and described how the theme park was configured and how it would attract visitors. It was invariably a marketing approach to the Russians.

It was obvious to me that both Michael and Chris were on the wrong track with these two gentlemen from the USSR. I could see that their eyes offered blank looks. Sobolenko whispered something to Andre. Sensing that the meeting was becoming obviously uninteresting to the Russians, Mike stood up and said goodbye and added that if they needed any help with defining a project, "my staff will gladly be available to assist you, gentlemen." With that last, he left the room. Chris said more about the Disney project, which in my estimation was too rich a project for the Russians and certainly not germane to them.

Just before we were on the verge of rising from the conference table to terminate the meeting, I asked Dr. Sobolenko directly, "Tell me about Troitsk and the Kurchatov Institute."

Finally Dr. Sobolenko broke his silence. In halting but understandable English, Dr. Sobolenko informed me that the Kurchatov Institute was the principal defense laboratory of the USSR and was chartered to work on plasma, laser, and nuclear and particle physics research, and also that the "tokomak" reactor was one of their principal efforts. Approximately 4,000 scientists were involved in the laboratories and they all resided in Troitsk, a community of some 6,000 residents, most of which had doctorates in scientific disciplines. Sobolenko's explanation was clear and to the point but he peppered his comments as if he were writing a theorem. He often used the phrase "and as following" to link ideas together. He was quite explicit in his explanation.

"Is all your work under tight security?" I asked.

"No. About fifty percent is not part of any security control," Sobolenko replied.

"What type of work is not under security control?" I asked.

"The chemical laboratories, the basic physics first tier research, some part of the optics research, the equipment research, design, and manufacturing, and repair shops are open areas."

"Will I be able to enter these laboratories were I to visit Troitsk?"

His English was getting better although it was punctuated with many "aahhs." He looked more at ease. He even smiled a few times. "Yes. I tell you following: if I go with you or another person come with you, you can see many sections." There was a pause in our conversation. Tea was replenished and we all enjoyed a moment of informality.

"Tell me about the chemical laboratories and the equipment shops, Dr. Sobolenko?"

"You can call me Dima," he said with a broad smile, "my friends call me such, instead of Dimitri."

I responded by saying, "please call me Raymond." Our conversation proceeded with a thumbnail description of what was being done in Troitsk. It turned out that the chemical labs worked mostly on pharmaceutical research and the physics labs did fundamental research in nuclear energy applications, while the equipment shops developed the necessary equipment needed for all the laboratories of the Institute.

Dima continued his explanation by stating in English and without Andre's help that he was impressed with the Exploratorium and was hoping that something like that would be created in Troitsk. He added that many of the students in the schools were very interested in science but laboratories for teaching were not available in Troitsk.

"Why not let scientists and technicians take a few students, as interns, to use on 'real' projects?" There was a pause. I continued, "Working closely with scientists and technicians, the students will experience real success and real failures and all the corrective measures that go with that process. They will learn on actual projects about innovation, frustration, completion, rewards, supervision, and team work."

Dr. Sobolenko gave me a penetrating look that has become his trademark. He smiled, and then laughed and his shoulders moved up and down as if to indicate coyness and joy. "Very is good," he said in English without using the interpreter. "We try do that. It is good idea and I very like it." He looked at me and spoke to his interpreter Andre, then he said: "You say following program: we take student as helpers in laboratories with scientist to work on real problems. Yes?"

"Yes," I affirmed. "Dr. Sobolenko, this way they learn about real research, not fake or play research."

"Raimon what, aahh, fake research?" he asked.

"You know, research that is not research but wastes the student's time because he knows and you know that it makes no difference what the results are." He repeated to himself and to Andre several times the words "real research."

"Very good idea," Dr. Sobolenko said as he pointed his index finger at me. "Most excellent idea." Then he asked me to tell him how interns work in America and how they are supervised. He asked if I had ever been an intern and I replied that I had been one when I attended university and worked at Oak Ridge. "You worked Oak Ridge?" he asked. "Oak Ridge very famous nuclear place with many scientist like Troitsk."

We discussed a few more details then exchanged business cards, telex numbers, and personal telephone numbers.

"You could help us makes such a program?"

I replied that Bechtel could.

After escorting the two Russians out of the conference room, I returned to my office. I wasn't in my office more than ten minutes when the telephone rang. It was Dr. Sobolenko calling me from the Bechtel lobby and thanking me for the several suggestions I had shared with him and asking me if I would accept an invitation to visit Russia and meet the director, Dr. Viacheslav D. Pismenny. If I would telex him the necessary information from my passport he would send an invitation for a visa to the Consulate of the USSR in San Francisco. His English was quite understandable. I accepted and followed through with the information he requested.

Once in my office I thought that I had better brief Jackson before either Michael or Chris would give their reports.

About a month after my meeting with Dr. Sobolenko, the invitation arrived via a telex. I went immediately to Bob Jackson to show him the invitation. Since he had been apprised of the discussion and the possible invitation he was pleased that I had been invited but because Bob had other commitments and could not accompany me, he suggested that perhaps Michael Wakelin could join me for the trip to Russia. I agreed and then Bob offered to finance the travel expenses rather than make the Russians pay for them. "The Russians are not in the money. We'll give them a break since they'll bear the internal expenses for you," he assured me.

I went straight to Michael and told him that he was to accompany me to Russia and that we would leave San Francisco in April (1988) and fly to Moscow by way of London. "Why are we going to Moscow?" he asked.

"Because we are invited and there may be a project that might follow," I replied and left him.

The trip to Moscow was approximately three weeks away and much preparation was needed before we made the trip. I briefed Riley Bechtel and Denis Slavich, the two senior people interested in establishing a footing in the USSR. I was still involved with Ron Brooks and the planning for the establishment of Tangier as a city-state, even though the Saudis had cooled off a bit on the idea. Ron wanted me to stop in Tangier on my next jaunt to Europe to see if there were any possibilities local investors might be found who were interested in the idea. I suggested that I could stop in Tangier after my visit to Moscow. I made arrangements with the director of the chamber of commerce of Tangier for my visit. Preparations were made to my satisfaction: I would spend ten days in Tangier and Morocco, and within that week I would also visit Larache, Rabat, and Casablanca. I would also spend a few hours in the Spanish possession of Ceuta, located east of Tangier and which is a thorn in the flesh of Morocco.

Before leaving for Moscow I was given an assignment that took me to Chile for a week. This was not a trip that I had expected. The transition time between my return from Chile and the departure for London was a mere 36 hours. I will say more about the Chilean excursion in the next portion of the text.

On a Sunday afternoon in April 1988, I boarded British Airways for the flight to Heathrow (LHR). Michael was flying on Pan Am a few hours later and would meet me at the Windsor Hotel in Windsor. The flight was uneventful but restful in first class — a suggested upgrade from business class by Bob after my long flight from Chile. From Heathrow I reserved a Mercedes limousine to take me to Windsor and to fetch me the next day from the hotel. Michael arrived an hour or so later and met me at the hotel.

After a cup of tea and a few moments to decompress, Michael asked me again why we were going to Moscow. I explained all over that there was a possibility of a project, even a long-term project in Troitsk.

"But they did not seem interested when I left them at the meeting," he replied.

"You left too soon and you did not listen to them."

"But they were saying nothing of importance."

"Michael, had you just listened instead of talking you would have perceived what they were asking."

He mumbled something incomprehensible then asked me to come with him to meet his cousins who lived in Windsor. As it turned out, Michael's cousin Catherine was an actress on the legitimate stage of London, and her husband was a screenwriter for several television shows performed both in the UK and the United States. Our conversations were lively and focused mostly on theater. A few hours later and post Wakelin's family gathering, we returned to the hotel for dinner and an early turn-in.

The next day the limousine fetched us on time and we boarded the flight to Moscow after buying some Scotch, chocolates, cheeses, coffee, and other items to distribute as gifts to our Russian hosts. We arrived in cold, grey Moscow in the early evening of April 1988 and were met by Dima Sobolenko who gave me my first Russian bear hug. I had not stepped on Russian soil since 1956, just three years after Joseph Stalin's death and during the leadership of Nikita Sergeyevich Khrushchev, the revisionist leader of the Communist party, the great clown with the shoe at the meeting of the United Nations, and the architect of the Cuban Missile Crisis. On the way to Troitsk we were shown the gigantic sculpture of Yuri Gagarin, the first cosmonaut, fashioned completely in titanium. Impressive but a bit vulgar, especially if one knows the market value of titanium and the contemporary Russian economic condition.

In Troitsk we were shown our apartment and given a schedule that was as tight as it could be because of the long meetings planned. After the usual wine, vodka, beer and food, and introduction to several people, Dr. Viacheslav Pismenny, the director, arrived to greet us. There was no question that Dr. Pismenny was the top person in charge of all operations in this scientific community, this brain branch of the larger Kurchatov Atomic Institute complex. It had many facilities throughout the USSR, and especially one in Gorki (Nizhniy Novgorod) where Andrei Sakharov, the physicist who promoted peace, was restricted by order of the Kremlin (more about that further on).

Our meetings took place mostly in the evening, starting with dinner, and continued into the early hours of the morning. Dr. Pismenny, better known as "Slava" and who became my dear friend, was keen to transform Troitsk from a defense community under the thumb of the Ministry of Nuclear Energy, into a productive, revenue generating, high technology, commercial engine free of government control. Slava took us to see property controlled by his Institute adjacent to a nearby river and across from the Kurchatov Institute. The property across the road from Troitsk was approximately 300 hectares of open land and was supposed to have a housing development. We were also taken to the newly constructed hospital, which needed — Slava said and we agreed — to be torn down and rebuilt because it was badly designed.

During the day he organized for me, after reading my resume and learning that I was a priest, a visit was arranged to Zagorsk (Sergey Prasad) the principal Lavra (ecclesiastical and educational center) of the Russian Orthodox Church. I was able to attend part of a service and meet a few monks, priests, and seminarians (all had completed their military obligations and were university graduates). Zagorsk is a holy center for Russia's Orthodox community and is the ecclesiastical see of the Patriarch of Moscow. It was amazing to me to witness a vibrant, dynamic, and energized complex in the heart of the USSR and in proximity to the capital city of Moscow.

Christianity was outlawed in the USSR but when Gorbachev took the helm of the government he relaxed the law and permitted the Orthodox Church to function as long as it did not cause trouble. In a very short time the Orthodox Church established itself in abandoned churches, built new churches, and began to gather the faithful openly for worship services. It was amazing to see the number of seminarians studying for holy orders, especially when all of them had completed their military service and were university graduates. I was informed that at Zagorsk there were approximately 1000 seminarians studying and that the program was for three years. This was quite a change for a nation that since its inception had forbidden Christianity. It was also amazing that Slava picked up from my vita that I would be interested in what Christianity was about in the USSR. Slava himself was not a practicing churchman, but his mother and his wife Valentina were church folks.

Many things on this, my second visit to Moscow, would surprise me. It was still very much the USSR with its central government, exclusive dollar shops for foreigners, paltry groceries, dilapidated vehicles, rutted roads, miserably maintained fuel service stations; the shabbily dressed people everywhere; the trash mounds in elevators, on sidewalks, and in gardens; and the constant checks by the security police.

Moscow was weighted down by enormous apartment houses, some half a kilometer long and 15 to 17 stories high. Inside the apartments, residents were careful to keep their quarters clean and well managed, but in the public areas one encountered filth, graffiti, and a general lack of maintenance. The dilapidation and lack of care were impressive, sobering, and embarrassing when foreigners were visiting. Public places in the USSR were badly maintained as a general rule. Slava's zeal to modernize Troitsk was one that interested me because his idea was to improve the quality of life for the citizens of the USSR and this would be a tough task to perform but certainly a worthy one.

In those late night discussions and after our tours to several industrial locations, it was beginning to be clear to me that the Soviet Union was sliding rapidly into financial bankruptcy. I remember reading that the quickest way to analyze the economic situation of a city or a region was to see what trucks carried, what was sold in shops, and what people bought or sold, if anything. Old and badly maintained trucks were mostly not fully loaded with goods, shops displayed empty shelves, not a few men and women sold wilted vegetables and others sold used clothing and dirty kitchen wares on the sidewalks, and the few cars on the roads were clunkers ready for the junk yard. It was obvious that the USSR was sliding into economic stupor, and very quickly.

It didn't take a genius to observe that no part of the infrastructure worked well. Food was not grown efficiently and what was harvested was not delivered on time, as it was needed, or was parked to be soaked rotten by the rain or the snow. Productivity was practically negative. Workers labored little and were drunk most of the time. Craftsmanship was non-existent; objects were badly assembled, misassembled, and/or left without the needed parts.

Nothing worked well. Telephone service did not function well, and when it did, it was on an irregular schedule. The Kurchatov Institute had built its own teleport to avoid the national telephone system, and this teleport was shared with Moscow State University and the Academy of Science. In my few days in Russia I observed a nation in decline. Science and the military were still in good order but little besides these two had any effect on the general quality of Soviet affairs. Afghanistan was becoming the "straw that would break the camel's back;" it was draining the USSR of what little remained of its cash wealth.

Mind you the USSR, principally Russia, enjoys a geography that spans eleven time zones, hence it is not poor in natural resources, although it has effectively corrupted much of it by practicing bad stewardship of the land it occupies and of the people who make it a nation. The USSR was simply miserably managed by apparatchiks who had no understanding of the value of their nation's wealth, assets, and resources. It was sad to witness such wanton waste and overt mismanagement. Time was running out on the great Union of Soviet Socialist Republics.

In detailed conversations with members of the Academy of Science it was obvious too that the satellite republics were in no better economic shape than Russia, the Motherland. I was witnessing an empire that was slowly caving in. Much can be learned from such an example. A country exhausts its greatest natural treasures, its human population, by making their lives miserable; it exhausts its natural ground-extracted wealth by mismanaging it; it exhausts its citizens' intellectual savings by restricting their creative urges; and it exhausts the financial wealth by spending much too much of the percentage of its gross domestic product (GDP) on the military. A great power is only powerful when its economy and its intellectual wealth are in full bloom and productive. (Listen America and digest it).

At the heart of Moscow stands the Kremlin. This old red stone fortress was the center of the Soviet Union's government until that nation dissolved itself in December 1991. Inside its walls, the perimeter of which stretches almost 2.4 kilometers, are beautiful cathedrals and palaces, as well as government buildings. Many of the cathedrals date from the 1400s. Many czars are buried in the Cathedral of the Archangel Michael. The Grand Kremlin Palace was built in the early 1800s as an imperial residence and later was the meeting place of the Supreme Soviet, the parliament of the Soviet Union.

Red Square lies just outside the Kremlin walls. The Square is a large plaza, about 0.4 kilometers long, and its name in Russian means "beautiful" and "red." Huge military and civilian parades were held in Red Square in order to celebrate various special occasions. On the day I was there, a meeting of VIPs was being held and many speeding cars, most of them Zils, were entering through the main gate. Near the main gate, and just outside the Kremlin's wall, is located Lenin's famous tomb guarded with the fascinating sentries who perform a superb march to and fro — a military-choreographed ballet. A similar ballet is performed by guards at the flame of the Unknown Soldier located near another wall of the Kremlin.

Opposite the Kremlin on Red Square is GUM, the country's largest department store. It was completed in the early 1890s and remodeled in 1953. The initials GUM come from three Russian words that mean State Department Store. Unfortunately GUM, the pride of the Soviet establishment, was empty of merchandise the day I visited. St. Basil's Cathedral — a Russian church famous for its many colorful, onion-shaped domes — is also on Red Square and Stalin had threatened to destroy it several times, but he died before he could authorize its destruction. Around Red Square are several sites commemorating the character and accomplishments of Communism.

My interest in Communism and its accomplishments was paper thin so I walked around and chose to stand on the spot where the young German pilot landed a Cessna 172 in front of the Kremlin and thus embarrassed the entire Soviet military. He was able to penetrate the Soviet radar line of defense without being detected, a protective electronic barrier that was believed to be impregnable. He entered the USSR from the Baltic Sea and thus was totally undetected by the air defense facilities. The USSR is poorly protected from the north because it assumes, as it always did, that it is too cold for an enemy to breach its border from the frigid northern region. The pilot was arrested and the aircraft confiscated and I understand that even Mr. Gorbachev enjoyed the humor of the penetration, yet he had to detain the young pilot for several months to save face. The news that leaked after the arrest of the young German pilot was that several high-ranking officers in charge of the defense system were removed, jailed, or demoted. The young pilot was returned to Germany with the promise that he was not to be treated as a hero by the Bundesrepublik Deutschland. Of course the German people could not adhere to that impossible condition and after he set foot on the homeland he received a hero's welcome. The flight club that owned the confiscated aircraft wrote off its value and the pilot was not charged for either its cost or its value.

Author at the Kremlin

As we were shown around Moscow, I was also taken to a shoe factory where the previous month the manager had received a commendation for out-performing his assigned quota of 10,000 or so shoes that year. The commendation was short lived, however, because an audit of the factory showed that it had indeed produced the quota and more, but only in left foot formats. He was sacked and sent to a mine somewhere in the North.

Two more incidents accentuated the condition of the demise of the USSR when I was in Moscow. As part of our tour of the city we were taken to lunch at the premier hotel of Moscow, the Moscovi Palace (to be torn down, I understand in 2003, and rebuilt as a modern hotel), a Grand hotel operated by Intourist, the USSR's tourist organization and watchdog of foreigners. Just as we entered the lobby I spotted a Diners Club ATM machine and because I had arrived from Chile and had not had time to obtain some dollars, I went to the dispensing machine, slipped in my card, and punched in my pin number to obtain some cash in dollars. Please remember that this was in the Spring of 1988. Several of my hosts followed me and looked on as I managed the dispensing machine.

"What you do?" I was asked.

"I'm getting some dollars to spend."

"How you do that?" was the query. I only needed $200, but for the sake of demonstrating both taking and returning cash, I punched the numbers for $400. After a few seconds the machine dispensed crisp dollar bills and a receipt. My host was puzzled but said nothing. The machine asked if I wanted another transaction, for which I placed half the dollar bills I had received in an envelope supplied by the ATM and re-entered them into the machine. At this point my hosts were absolutely puzzled.

"What you do with money you printed?"

"No, no, I did not print any money. This is genuine US cash from my account in America. I am taking it because I need cash." I continued to show him what I was about to do, "But because I don't need too much and to show you how it works, I asked for two times what I needed. Now I am depositing the extra cash back into my account."

"How machine know from which account is from America?" I further explained that Diners Club in Moscow would service the ATM on a schedule and that the machine was connected by telephone or by Internet to the home office of Diners. I continued to explain as Michael Wakelin followed me and displayed a big smile.

"No money has been printed and Diners will credit my account correctly."

My Russian friend then said taking a business card from his pocket, "Like magic. I put card in the slot and get money also?"

"No, no, you need to have a special card given to you by the company, and you need a PIN — a personal identification number — before the system will give you or take any money."

We discussed the credit process, the ATM system, and the fact that I could obtain dollars (or in some cases local currency) practically anywhere in the world when an ATM was available, which could recognize my plastic cards, such as the one from Diners Club or Master Card, Visa, etc. I wasn't certain that my explanation was convincing or even clear. The whole credit card system was foreign to most Soviet citizens but soon they would get the hang of it and all of Russia would operate with plastic cards.

We had made our return airline departure from Moscow, but once in Tro-itsk it was obvious that we would have to depart from St. Petersburg instead because we were invited to tour that beautiful city with its Neva River, the St. Peter and St. Paul complex, and the Hermitage. I telephoned BA for my flight out and Pan Am for Wakelin's. I was informed that Aeroflot was acting on their behalf but they could not change our flights. We would have to go to the airport on the day we were to depart and attempt to make the necessary change. Moreover, Aeroflot could not access the computers of BA or Pan Am. I immediately asked my host if I could telephone my office in San Francisco. With permission granted, I called Ligia Zelaya and asked her to access both BA's and Pan Am's reservation computer and change our departure airport from Moscow to St. Petersburg. In less than three minutes the changes were accomplished to the amazement of all present. How could someone in San Francisco not affiliated with the airlines access their computers and change the departure flights in just a few minutes?

On my recent trip to Moscow, I've discovered that electronic tickets are still not available from Russia and that credit cards are not accepted by regional commuter airlines in either Russia or Ukraine. I say this because in 2002, 14 years later, reform had not yet happened throughout.

Our translator for the duration was a young physics PhD, Mikhail Per-siantsev, also known as Misha. Misha was a delight as a person and he was a young man of extraordinary intelligence and foresight. Because he was interesting and spoke fluent English we had several extensive conversations on politics, physics, life, and Americans and America.

One evening before we were to take the night train to Leningrad (now St. Petersburg) we discussed democracy and its weaknesses. Slava was away at a meeting but was expected to return for dinner and before we were to be taken to the railway station. Soon enough, Slava made his appearance and he exclaimed with great jubilance something in Russian. Everybody listened and many cheered and clapped their hands. After the commotion was reduced, Misha translated the news to me immediately and told me that nuclear physicist and peace promoter Dr. Andrei Dmitriyevich Sakharov, who had been incarcerated in the city of Gorki for several years until Gorbachev released him, had been unanimously elected back into full membership in the USSR's Academy of Science. For his efforts to promote human rights and world peace he received the 1975 Nobel Peace Prize.

Dr. Pismenny was thrilled that this had happened as he had voted for Sakharov's reinstatement. Of course we celebrated with several shots of vodka and some singing. It seems to me that Russian men have wonderful voices and are born with the capacity to carry folk tunes. A month later, in 1989, Sakharov was elected to the newly formed Soviet legislature, called the Congress of People's Deputies, which was the precursor of the new Russian Dumas, the parliament. Unfortunately, Sakharov died in 1990. Yelena Bonner, his wife, published Sakharov's memoirs immediately.

Misha escorted us to the railway station and we arrived just a few minutes before midnight to board the train to Leningrad, which was scheduled to leave for the eight-hour trip north. Michael Wakelin went to our reserved couchette and Misha and I chatted until the train started to move. Misha informed me that he was going to California during the summer to teach in a high school. Was he taking his family? I asked. Yes he was. I listened to his evaluation of the general conditions in the USSR and his ultimate intentions to spend more time in Information Technology (IT). When the train started to move slowly, "Misha," I said, "You will not return to Russia." We were moving slowly. He made no attempt to reply but simply hugged me tightly. The train started to move faster. We looked at each other and much was understood.

Misha did come to California, and yes, he has yet to return to Russia. He and his family, including Daniel, his American born son, now have American citizenship and hope to visit his native Russia soon. His parents Igor and Natasha, both respected scientists and his sister, a physician, visit him in Massachusetts often. Misha is the senior scientist for an IT firm anchored on Boston's famous Route 128, the Silicon Valley-like portion of this city.

When we arrived in the morning we were shown our apartment in Leningrad and then we were taken to the Hermitage. Our guide, who spoke excellent English, was Professor of Art at the University of Leningrad and one of the curators of the museum. The official name of the museum is the

State Hermitage Museum. The Hermitage, also known as the Winter Palace, is a collection of several buildings and extends about 0.8 kilometers along the banks of the Neva River. The museum has almost 400 rooms, with about 3 million pieces of art from different civilizations, historical periods, countries, and peoples. The Hermitage is globally known for its exquisite collection of European paintings by renowned masters. It also has outstanding collections of classical antiquities from Greece, Crimea, and Ukraine, as well as wide-ranging collections of Russian art and the art of the Far East. When I visited the Crimean section of the Hermitage I did not know that a decade later I would be intensely involved in the restoration of the antiquities and the protection of the archeological finds in Kerch, Crimea. Fortunately, I had several opportunities in later years to revisit the grand museum.

Italian architect Bartolommeo Rastrelli designed the exterior of the Winter Palace in the late Baroque style of the 1700s. The palace was built between 1754 and 1762 on a site where several earlier palaces had stood. The interior was designed during the late 1700s and early 1800s, primarily in the Classical style.

Czar Peter III became the first resident of the Winter Palace. After overthrowing the czar in 1762, Empress Catherine the Great lived there until her death in 1796. Catherine founded the art collection when she imported about 225 paintings by Dutch and Flemish artists in 1764 to decorate rooms in the palace. Catherine had a long, narrow building, called the Little Hermitage, built along the west side of the Winter Palace from 1764 to 1767. The building soon housed much of the imperial art collection. From the mid-1700s to the mid-1800s, several more buildings were added to the palace complex, which makes the Hermitage a long and narrow set of buildings standing on the bank of the Neva River. Behind the Hermitage is a vast plaza often used for government assemblies and parades.

During the October Revolution of 1917, the Hermitage was the headquarters of the provisional Russian government. Between 1917 and 1922, the Winter Palace and the other Hermitage buildings were converted into a state museum at the command of Lenin, who fortunately for Russia and the world, appreciated art and history.

We also visited the Neva River, which was still frozen, and the beautiful sculpture commissioned by Empress Catherine of Peter the Great on horseback. It is a wonderful and very well executed sculpture of the great Tsar, who tried to reform his country, who built St. Petersburg, and who brought some element of western culture to Russia. Nevertheless, Peter died a frustrated man because the task of reforming Russia was not completed to his satisfaction. I suspect that Russia may be impossible to rule and to reform. Russia, as a vast land of eleven time zones and numerous ethnic groups, who are totally unrelated in custom or ideology, appears to be beyond reform, especially under a central government — later in a free society that may or may not happen. Ruling Russia is a daunting task. Even in 2009, the elected Russian government had great difficulties ruling the country and bringing about a democratic society. The President and his Prime Minister were acting in a rather authoritarian manner and ignoring much of the democratic avenues that had been established after the dissolution of the USSR.

With half a day left for me before my flight to London, I was taken to see the historical palace-museum in the town of Pushkin named after Alexander Sergeyevich Pushkin, the beloved Russian author and poet. The town is famous because its population withstood the long siege by the Nazi military during WWII. Pushkin is a lovely, quiet town of small houses and well laid out streets with gardens, trees, and brooks. Not a bad location for a villa, I thought.

Soon it was time for me to fly to London, where Margaret Pugh was scheduled to meet me at Gatwick International Airport. Barry Pugh was working in Saudi and I had invited myself to their home for a few days of rest before continuing my trip to Morocco.

I was pleased with my visit to the USSR and called Bob Jackson to inform him. Bechtel, if it played its cards well and partnered with a Finnish firm, could develop much lucrative work in the USSR. A month after my visit to Troitsk I made a point to visit Helsinki to talk with two firms that were well positioned in the USSR. The firms were Polar and Hakka; with the latter I had previously established an interest in partnering with Bechtel.

There was much work to do, but I was jubilant that a small door had been opened in the USSR.

On the way to London I composed a memo that I hoped would ultimately end up on Riley Bechtel's desk informing him that the USSR was economically on the edge of collapse. I gave the USSR until 1994 before it would disintegrate completely in fragment states or suffer a violent revolution that would alter the shape of Europe and Asia. I was more willing to foresee the former rather than the latter, because leadership was lacking to incite revolution. Neither Gorbachev nor anyone had the political size to generate a revolution. Mr. Gorbachev was sufficiently astute to recognize that the USSR was in economic chaos and that it needed to jettison its European satellites at once. He also needed to refashion radically the Soviet Union's economic fabric by establishing free market and private property laws. The memo concluded by noting again that Bechtel should be poised to enter the USSR or whatever states emerged from it. Moreover, I suggested that sooner rather than later, Bechtel should open an office in Moscow — and certainly before 1994 when it would be after the USSR's swan song.

Arriving at Gatwick International Airport I was met by Margaret Pugh who drove me to her home in Chichester. Long before the age of cell phones, the telephone rang with a call from Emily as soon as I arrived at the Pugh's home. She related the message that Dr. Pismenny had telephoned my office in San Francisco to inform me that he was coming to Bechtel the following Monday and wanted to see me. That was exciting news, but it also meant that I had to postpone or cancel my visit to Helsinki and to Tangier, Morocco. That was not such a bad trade, because I could reschedule both destinations quite easily, and Hakka would understand the value of the postponement.

Chilean Exploratory Assignment

One must regress every so often because developments do not surface in exact chronological order. The visit to Santiago, Chile was made ten days before going to Moscow.

During the hectic days before my visit to Moscow, I received a call from the Aviation Department asking me to fly to Chile to review the proposed expansion of Santiago's International Airport. Charles Sands, my good friend and a fine airport architect, would accompany me (we had worked together in Saudi and in China). This was to be a tight schedule. I would be in Chile for a week, return on a Friday, be home on Saturday with just enough time to have my laundry done and pick up a file from my office, and catch a flight out of San Francisco Sunday afternoon for Heathrow.

Charles and I left for Chile on a night flight on LAN Chile from Los Angeles in first class with a stop in Panama, and arriving in Santiago mid-morning. We were met at the airport and taken to the Crowne Plaza Hotel to rooms that overlooked the beautiful city that is located at the foot of the towering Andes Mountains. Our task was to review the plans of the proposed expansion, the possible merger of Ladeco Airlines with LAN Chile, and air-space configuration over the airport and how the expansion would affect it. We would be meeting with several groups, including members of the International Civil Aviation Organization (ICAO), especially Carlos Boctor (a Bechtel colleague on loan to ICAO), and with Guillermo Gomien, Chile's Minister of Aviation, and the airlines affected by the expansion, especially American Airlines, which was a 40% owner of LAN Chile. From LAN Chile I met Rene Dussert, general director of the airline and from Ladeco, I met Ernesto Silva, president and chief executive officer. My hosts in Santiago were Herman Uribe, Aviation Consultant, and Harold Rogers, his partner in Uribe and Rogers Co. I also met Armando Navarro, director of Aviation Planning for the City of Santiago.

During my week I was able to have Harold Rogers, a pilot, take me for a flight in a rented Cessna 172 around Santiago. I was able to take control of the aircraft and overfly the International Airport after obtaining clearance from Air Traffic Control (ATC). After returning to the GA airport, a Chilean designated aviation examiner, Miguel Horn, came on board to give me a flight check for the 172. We took off heading south and then I was asked to make a left crosswind turn. I did as instructed but then I looked straight ahead at the sheer side of the Andes Mountains reaching 24,000 feet into the sky. I quickly turned downwind, headed north, and then parallel to the mountain range. It was a sobering experience especially when I noticed that I had gained 1,000 feet by the lifting force of the western offshore winds attempting to climb the massive mountain range. We flew for about 45 minutes and during this time I made several stalls and steep turns, and then returned for a soft landing at the GA airport. The examiner endorsed my log and declared that I was authorized to fly the skies of Chile; this is tantamount to a reciprocal license. In fact, a few weeks later I received a letter indicating an official endorsement by Guillermo Gomien.

I met with several Bechtel employees and some friends who were part of ICAO, and working with Charles Sands was a pleasure. I met an attorney who was a friend of my friend Randolph Linehan. Señor Jose Luis Santa Maria Zañartu, an attorney specializing in international law of mergers and acquisitions, invited me to the Polo Club for lunch to sample several local wines and to watch a game between a team from Chile and one from Dubai; Chile's team took the trophy.

Santa Maria invited me to see Santiago in the evening, enjoy dinner at one of his favorite Italian restaurants, and experience several Chilean wines with the meal. It was a wonderful evening and I became deeply fond of Santiago and the Chilean people. Santa Maria and I discussed the Augusto Ugarte Pinochet dictatorship known as the "black years." It was obvious that Chile had suffered a great deal under Pinochet's rule, but it was also recognizable that the Chilean economy and work ethic had been given a boost under the general's control. Chile was quite business-oriented and was less prone to having a lackadaisical approach to employment, productivity, and loose work ethics. Work started at 8:00 a.m., banks and businesses were open at that time and remained open until 5:00 p.m. with no siesta break after lunch. Unlike every other South American nation, Chile's workers were productive. Laziness was not something that I encountered. Chileans appeared to be a hard-working, civic-minded, and organized people. It was clear from our conversation that Señor Jose Luis Santa Maria had not been a supporter of Pinochet and had had some grave personal difficulties during the dictatorship.

I have not been too fond of visiting South American countries; having been to Argentina, Brazil, and Venezuela, my view of the Latin people was not terribly positive. Authoritarianism and dependence on hierarchical control was the signature of governments in South America. It wasn't dictatorships that controlled the lives of the people, it was the military that held the reins of authority, and the corrupt Roman Catholic Church judiciously supported both. In fact, even the non-Roman Catholic segment of Christianity played along willingly with the military. In Chile, I encountered a different mentality. With Pinochet no longer heading the government (the shadow of his firm hand was quite recognizable although he was no longer in command), the new democratic administration was honestly attempting to restore freedom and a market economy to the wounded nation. Even the church hierarchies had been a headache to Pinochet because he could not obtain their support as the Argentinean military could. Chile was a nation wounded by revolts, the assassination of its duly elected socialist president, Salvador Allende Gossens with the heinous help of the Nixon administration, and the implantation of Pinochet as dictator followed by nineteen years of military rule.

Thousands of people were known as the disappeared (desaparecidos), the unaccounted men and women who were abducted by the military secret police because they disapproved of the Pinochet junta for one reason or another. A few days after my arrival and after much discussion with Chilean colleagues, my point of view began to change to empathy with understanding. Pinochet was dreadful and his administration was cruel, harsh, and unforgiving, yet he did purge Chile of the Marxists, the Maoists, and the corruption that was a principal part of the business culture. He forbade bribing, insider trading, and the enriching of those in the shadow of power. It is revealing to know that Pinochet himself did in fact loot the country and several foreign bank accounts were found to bear his name.

Chile, unlike many other South American countries, was relatively clean and crime was at a minimum. Business could be done without greasing the palm of every individual involved, even of those peripherally connected. My short stay in Santiago was a delightful experience that changed my long-held perspective of Chile for the better. Yes, the Pinochet rule was a horrible era for Chile, but out of his dung germinated a lovely rose: a robust economy and a magnificent country.

Could this improvement have been accomplished without the rule of Pinochet? Do foreign powers have the right to interfere in the affairs of nations and remove legally elected leaders and even self-appointed leaders such as dictators? If the United Nations is to be an effective body for overseeing the affairs of member nations in the global arena, does it have the ethical right to interfere and do its members, collectively and independently, have a similar right to interfere in the governments of other nations? These questions will become more germane as globalization becomes more prevalent.

My non-Bechtel connected host, Santa Maria, who was a bit more conservative than the current administration but not, as I indicated, a supporter of General Pinochet or of his junta, pointed out that Chile's economy was growing at a healthy 6.25% per annum. Indeed a healthy sign that compared well with other strong economies. With wine, agriculture, high technology development, and innovative new businesses, Chile was almost a copy of California, and considered the Golden State to be its example and mentor. I promised myself to return to Chile again, which I did in 1993.

We departed Santiago at midnight and arrived in San Francisco in the early afternoon the next day. Flights to and from the Southern Cone of South America are long and run from 14 to 16 hours and include a stop in Panama. Emily picked me up at San Francisco International Airport (KSFO) and we made a quick trip to Bechtel to drop off some files for Ligia and to pick up my Russian folder.

My account of the visit to Russia has been given in the previous section but what hasn't been discussed is the comparison. Chile was a bustling nation trying to recuperate its self-respect and to move ahead into the globalization process. The USSR was stagnant and declining rapidly into becoming a third world country from being the second most powerful nuclear power. The infrastructure of Chile was being improved on a daily basis, streets were being repaired, telephone service modernized, airports improved and expanded, buildings — especially apartment structures — were being upgraded, markets and shops were overflowing with goods of both imported and domestic origin, and the people were working, singing, and enjoying their new status as free citizens. In comparison to Moscow's GUM and the shopping area around it that was devoid of goods and impoverished, the shopping area of Santiago was bustling with activity and with shoppers buying goods of every sort, every price, and from every source, even at midnight. Russians were dour in appearance, market stalls were empty and grubby looking, streets were filled with potholes and were badly in need of resurfacing, the transportation and communication infrastructure needed to be overhauled, and on the whole it indicated that Soviet citizens were leading a very hard, sad, and miserable life. To be a Soviet citizen was tantamount to being cheated by destiny.

The USSR was on the verge of imploding. Chile was being reborn. I could feel the zest of the people as they worked, went about their business, ate in restaurants, and walked the streets or shopped. Yes, I saw a few beggars and a handful of homeless folks, but they were mostly in the poor district of Santiago, and a program of urban restructuring was redeveloping even those districts. Santiago was not quite out of the Pinochet grip but it was attempting to move ahead, and rapidly. The city offered some hope, and I could see that the country's government was bent on improving the lot of the citizens.

Some Thoughts and Comments

Long flights on airlines and mediocre movies shown allow me to read and to think. To think is one of my favorite pastimes. I've often stated that what is between my ears is the greatest resource of my entertainment. On my return flight from Santiago, a night flight in a slow Boeing 707, my mind scanned many subjects and stopped at how I visualized God. I remembered a luncheon conversation with my colleague Bernard Catalinoto at Bechtel.

Bernard was a bright mathematician who specialized in global mapping systems and he was also the father of a young son who kept asking questions about God. Bernard was a lapsed Roman Catholic who had been totally uninterested in theological questions prior to becoming a father. He would join

me for lunch to discuss the large, and often prickly, issues that made life exciting. He was searching. He was questioning. He respected my position as a
priest and as a philosopher with a background in physics. Roman Catholicism
had not helped him with answers to his questions. Bernard had studied in
Italy and there he had found himself running further and further away from
the Roman Church. As a result Bernard had abandoned the Church and all it
stood for.

Bernard had, however, not abandoned his personal relationship with God
or what he considered to be God, which he never defined. Who among us can
define God? Like the rest of us he could not. Roman Catholicism, especially
the strict, doctrinaire type, had turned him off completely from religion. He
was, as I am, unhappy that the Church — yes even the Episcopal branch —
has been unwilling to march boldly into the realm of new thinking and new
understanding. It is not a matter of abiding with morality, but much more
than that. It is that the morality — whatever that is — of the current religious
community is ineffective and unreasonable. A few examples given here may
help clarify the point.

At a time when human beings are multiplying too rapidly on this planet,
it is unconscionable for Roman Catholicism, Islam, and other like-minded
religious bodies to oppose birth control. As I have insisted earlier, ethics
(some might wish to include morality too) are a social lubricant to help society operate more effectively, for people to live better lives, and to fashion the
human condition to be more in tune with reasonableness. Thus one hopes that
curbing unchecked births, controlling overpopulation, protecting the environment, granting women their rightful place in society, and letting folks
with different sexual orientations — orientations that are not of their creation
— merit some support from religions and should be accepted by religious
institutions. Of course there are other issues that the established religious
community refuses to tolerate, consider, acknowledge, and accept. The list is
too long to include here.

Bernard was always keen to discuss many issues of belief with me. When
his son asked a question about God, Bernard hadn't a clue how to answer
him, either positively or even negatively. Doctrinal answers did not satisfy

him. He was too inquisitive to accept doctrine simply because it was the stated position of the church or part of the corpus of organized religions. Indeed, we often discussed stated doctrinal issues. One day he asked me about how I related to God and if there was such a being.

My reply was that I understood God as a process intrinsic in the universe — that God is the essential element of creation. I was willing to accept Tillich's "ground of all being" as long as it included all creation with no exceptions, even in the context of a multiple-universe. I shared my liking for Rudolf Otto who saw the Universe as holy and where every part is inescapably reflecting God's presence and participation. This position was akin to William Temple's assertion that we live in a sacramental Universe and that all in this Universe is sacred, holy, and hallowed. But what does holy mean? For me it implies that creation is "special," that it is not unimportant and irrelevant in the great scheme of all there is. For something to be identified as holy means that it is, in the particular sense, not like anything less but singular, distinct, exceptional, extraordinary, unique, and beyond the ordinary. I lean to the more dynamic approach of the same thoughts that identify God as "process," ongoing creation, forever evolving beyond the Big Whimper of termination. For me the so-called Big Bang, the Singularity, the genesis of the current universe, loses its historical meaning of initial time when we see it processively to become a more modest, though still important, turning point in the history of the universe. I agree with the scientist Gabriele Veneziano of CERN that the Big Bang is but one of many interesting phases in the life of the universe; it is a turning point, a rite of passage, like turning twenty-one.

The universe for me then is of a piece. The birth of the universe is a natural event and God is inextricably part of that event. The universe (or multiverse) is a process, not a thing. It just keeps right on happening, right on emerging; it may never have started even when considering the origin of the singularity, and it will almost certainly never cease. Like "ole Man River it just keeps rolling along!" To me God is not a figure with anthropological form, but an event that gathered all of Creation including God in it. God is Being, but not anthropological being. God is greater than "a being." God is the fullness of being and forever becoming. Hence, God is process, developing, revising, evolving, creating, generating, harmonizing, and attending to all aspects, large and small, of creation. Moreover, God is love in all its dimensions, all its ramifications, all its consequences, and all its particulars. God has no bargain with evil or its devilish or satanic personification. Evil is the product of human selfishness. Evil is the product of human beings missing the mark set by ethical conventions. A convention, an agreement, perhaps an ethical understanding that delimits human beings from trespassing into or harming the self of other human beings.

Bernard accepted what I said and we discussed further the issue of God as process. He liked that approach because his mathematical sense of reasoning accepted that as ongoing for him. He had read some of the works of Alfred North Whitehead, Alan Guth, Edward Witten, John Wheeler, and Stephen Hawking, especially their mathematical treatises. He understood process and recognized that it is an ever-evolving movement, which may bring about progress and may not. Yet the human contribution to process was effectively needed because it could make a difference in how the occasions were aligned to produce an event that might turn out to be ethical, loving, and good.

Bernard thought about what I said, then asked, "What defines an ethical issue?"

My reply was, "When two human beings are, for instance, stranded on a desert island, the presumption is that for self-preservation they will agree — develop a convention — that neither one will exterminate the other. If that is not agreed at the outset, then life for them is not worth living because neither will ever rest for fear that the other will attempt to kill him. Self-preservation is not the condition from which evil surfaces, but it is the tool that may fashion it. Once self-preservation overrides all other issues, relationships, associations, and elements of life fall prey to malevolence — the action to deliberately cause great harm, pain, or upset because others become object. When that surfaces then only the self (supreme subject) or the self's purpose assumes ultimate importance. Bang! Its will surfaces and the mark is missed."

Bernard Catalinoto's subject matter was put to rest for a while. I asked myself: but where does the person of Jesus fit in this understanding of God?

My thoughts were interrupted by breakfast. The flight attendant brought me a cup of coffee, something I had not had much of in Chile because tea is the national beverage. The coffee was exactly what I wanted: black, decaffeinated, and hot. I had another five or six hours before we landed in Los Angeles because we would have a fuel stop in Colón, Panama. The food on LAN Chile was excellent, at least in first class, and the service was superb.

After a short stop in Colón to refuel the Boeing 707, we re-boarded and my thoughts wandered back to Jesus and the little that was known about him from the Gospel accounts, from both the canonical and the non-canonical texts, and from the Pauline Epistles. The dating of Paul's writing placed them close to the time of Jesus, but the synoptic gospels (Mark, Matthew, and Luke) were written much later. John's text has caused much consternation. Traditionally the dating of John placed it towards the end of the first century. New research, however, placed it much earlier because it is now thought to have been written for a liturgical community that was quite informed about Jesus. Then there was the question of both the so-called Q-document and the non-canonical gospel of Thomas and others. It was known that the Q-document had influenced Mark, and perhaps Matthew as well. What influence the recently discovered Thomas text had on the writers of the canonical gospels is still debated. The Thomas text consists of a series of sayings indicating perhaps that there was a discussion with the writer of John's gospel. In all likelihood, John's gospel is a reply to Thomas and is aimed at dismissing the opinions of its author. At any rate, one thing was certain: Jesus loomed high in all the documents. He is an enigma that warrants a great deal of thought. What was the purpose and mission of Jesus? Why was it crucial for Jesus to make his presence known in that particular period in history? What was his relationship to God, whom he identified as the Father or Abba? Is Jesus unique as the single emissary of God, not just as a prophet but also as the singular Son of God? Aren't there many who acted in that role — and who have different names?

The idea held by religious conservatives that the death of Jesus was to be a ransom payment for the sins of human kind is unacceptable to me and to many. It is ludicrous to think that God needed to receive a ransom, and that he chose Jesus as the perfect payment to satisfy the indebtedness that human-kind owed God. What kind of benevolent God would need a life, Jesus' life, as a form of ransom? That God needed payment challenges sound reason. Even the allegory of Isaac and Abraham is acceptable because Abraham was convinced, we are told, that the God that had helped Sarah become pregnant was not going to take the life of his offspring, in the final analysis, just to prove a point. So the act was possible and Abraham played the part to the hilt. He was willing to slash Isaac's throat, or at least to act as if he would. For what purpose would God destroy Isaac's life? To make a point? Is a hu-man life only a voucher for making a point in a dialogue? Was he such a little God that he would resort to such a savage act? No, the drama was that Abra-ham understood quite well that the test proposed by God for using Isaac was merely to obtain his complete allegiance. Understanding this relationship with God, Abraham accepted his part.

Jesus addresses another issue, an issue that is more important than the ransom theory long supported by many wrong-headed theologians in the es-tablished Church. Jesus was too dangerous at the time to keep alive. The power of Rome recognized that it was unable to cope with what Jesus pro-claimed peacefully, principally that Caesar and all who stood with him were of little importance in the presence of God.

The Sadducees and the Pharisees were afraid that in Jesus their claim over the people would be dissipated into nothing. The future for them was more important than Jesus, and besides, Jesus may have been an impostor, a charlatan, and a revolutionary. Not only were the Sadducees and the Phari-sees frightened that Jesus would develop a new sect that would challenge their authority, but they were petrified that Rome would move to abolish their religious independence, their tradition, and their authority. A near dissolution of their religion had occurred during the Exile period, centuries earlier. Now they wanted to prevent that from recurring and Jesus' life was a good way to appease the Roman authority and to help the Sadducees and the Pharisees maintain their tight hold on the Jews. Jesus was expendable. Who could prove that Jesus was divinely recognized? He was one of many who had come as preachers and that included John the Baptist, that troublemaker who had identified Jesus as the singular emissary from God. There were scores of others who claimed to be emissaries of one god or another. No, Jesus was executed not because he was connected to the divine being known as God, but because he was a potential political cause of great trouble — for everybody.

Jesus was an agent of change, and change is terrifying to people of all persuasions, particularly those of a conservative bent. Jesus was offering a new paradigm for living, for society, and for self-fulfillment but that offer was rejected out of fear, out of distrust, and out of a communal refusal to change the status quo.

The enemy was change and the communal target was Jesus. Moreover, the community in Jerusalem did not consider that Jesus' approach was valid; his approach suggested that major changes were necessary, and both the rulers and ruled could not accept that drastic change. It is interesting that when Pilate allowed the populace to liberate one of the accused, they chose Barabbas, the known criminal, rather than Jesus. The community knew what power Barabbas had at his disposal. Indeed, he was a criminal, a thief, and an unsavory character but Barabbas was a known entity. Jesus? Jesus was strange, different, dangerous, and offered more, much more, than the community could reasonably and emotionally accept. Transpose Jesus, or someone like him, in today's community and see what conclusions you would reach. Would you accept him or would you cast him out of your sight as a dangerous agitator or charlatan?

But what is the connection between Jesus and God? Let me return to an earlier comment about the issue of ransom. If Jesus is the ransom that God needed before the people could be restored to God's good grace, then Judas Iscariot is a vital pawn in that scheme. Judas is paramount for the strategy to make Jesus a martyr for the ransom. Without Judas, or someone like him, how could Jesus be found and arrested? If that is the case, then Judas acted as a means to an end required by God to initiate his requirement for ransom (and atonement?). Again it diminishes God's love if we accept that the love and the grace that ensues from that love required a ransom through the death of

Jesus, the victim of a divine scheme for restoring human kind to full status. What is that status to which human kind is to be restored?

From this perspective Judas was merely a pawn and as such his part requires a bit of forgiveness from Christians and from the Church. Judas is a pathetic person — maybe he was a devoted zealot determined to act for whatever was his cause — and the Church has been unwilling to offer him any aspect of forgiveness. In the eyes of the Church, Judas is a betrayer, a low life creature who turned against the Son of God. But is he? In the scenario chosen for the culmination of the deed of redemption, is it a scenario chosen by God or perhaps by Jesus to bring about his own martyrdom? Judas plays a significant part, a part that is emphasized at the Last Supper and recognized in the Garden of Gethsemane. Judas is given a role to perform, wittingly or not; he performs it to the hilt and becomes a historic villain. Iscariot's role is devoid of blame even if he acted as the tool or the fool for the purposeful and intentional demise of Jesus — for whatever reason. Could not a mere arresting officer in the service of the existing authorities do what Judas was asked to do, thus avoiding the whole issue of condemnation of Judas? Again, is a human life merely a token to be used to satisfy a scheme? What happened to Christian gracefulness, forgiveness, and redemption? Are the betrayal, arrest, and killing of Jesus the stuff that is part and parcel for a course in manipulation? Finally, I hope for the redemption of Judas and for the Church to erase all the negative commentaries about him.

Now why was Jesus killed? Looking at his crucifixion I must always remind myself that Jesus the man was condemned to die a violent death, painful and humiliating. His accusers claimed that he assumed that he was exclusively the Son of God, and hence by inference the King of the Jews. Neither title were his to assume, and he knew it. He was put to death and did not defend himself because he recognized that it would be a useless effort to refute them, and not because he was following a script written by God. I see the use of the passages from the Hebrew Bible, the Old Testament, to justify the death generally as prophesy historicized rather than as prediction fulfilled.

I am also troubled when I imagine that Jesus saw his own death as salvific. I think that Jesus recognized that he had challenged the domination system in the name of God. Another approach: If Jesus had merely been a mystic, teacher, healer, or offerer of compassionate service, I doubt that he would have been executed. Jesus was these, but he was also a God-intoxicated voice of religious and social protest who had been a magnet to his following. In Roman times this was sufficient cause to get arrested and executed by authorities that did not wish to have their position questioned, especially by a social revolutionary with credentials that could not be authenticated.

Let's discuss Jesus and who he was or even who he thought he was and his connection with God, whom he called Abba, Father. When I bring Jesus' temple action and the Habourah meals (this is the unique meal that requires the presence of a stranger, whereas the Berakah, the Seder, and other like meals are in-group or family repast) eaten on many occasions by his followers and especially at what we call the Last Supper, I recognize that at the heart of Jesus' prophetic persona lay not merely the announcement of God's kingdom, but the implicit claim that he was thought to be the king who had arrived. There were many other royal movements or assumed royal movements in the first century; Jesus' movement, however, is not quite like any of them, but neither is it too dissimilar. Jesus came with a divine claim not of earthly power but of having a divine and direct connection to God. To assume that just because the early Christians considered Jesus the messiah, the chosen Son of God, any indication that Jesus himself viewed himself as such is an assumption made from later Christian understanding.

Historically, we see Jesus as head of a movement through which he was convinced that the expected kingdom was forthcoming. Indications are aplenty that Jesus regarded his own work not simply as pointing forward to his kingdom but actually inaugurating it. More centrally and perhaps metaphorically, I see Jesus as the Christian messiah, the Anointed One. "Jewish mystic" and "messiah" describe how I understand Jesus before and after the Easter event. This affirmation suggests an inherent negation, principally that I am not persuaded that the pre-Easter Jesus considered himself to be the messiah. As for the post-Easter Jesus, I find that I rely greatly on the documents produced by writers of the first and second centuries and my own understanding of Christianity — ergo my personal conviction about Jesus.

I see Easter as utterly central to Christianity and with it comes a two-fold understanding of the event: Jesus is alive, and Jesus is Lord. Now whether Jesus is the divine spark enkindling all humanity or with the making of a different magnitude, is an issue that will only be comprehended in later ages — in the age when all questions are plainly answered! Both claims are essential: Easter means that Jesus was experienced after his death, and that he is the Christic Presence — several notches above human beings. This last sentence leads me to the empty tomb and I say emphatically that the tomb has no relevance for me. But resurrection is relevant, especially in terms of Jesus'.

Briefly, resurrection in a first century Jewish and Christian context is quite a different notion. Succinctly put, "resurrection does *not* mean resumption of previous protoplasmic or corpuscular existence, that is to say the reconstruction of the particles that make up the human body, but the entry into a new kind of existence," as Dr. Marcus Borg states in several of his writings.

Any details of what this new kind of existence implies is beyond my capacity, but neither can I say much about what occurred before the Big Bang or the puzzling Singularity (the beginning of the beginning) amidst it. Nor can I say much to answer questions about what existed before the singularity, and not any theoretical astrophysicist can add any meaning to any answer in response to such questions (this subject is explored further in later pages). Moreover, I don't know any theologians who can give me a clear and reasonable, yes reasonable, theory that would satisfy the questions: What existed, if anything, before the Singularity? What about God?

Returning to Easter, it is necessary to understand that it is not about factual resuscitation but about resurrection. Thus for me the historical basis of Easter is quite simply this: the followers of Jesus, both then and now, continue to experience Jesus as a living reality after his death. Consequently I see the post-Easter Jesus as an experiential and phenomenological reality. One must be cautious, however, because unethical proponents and manipulators of both people's experience and quests for Jesus have corrupted much of this "experiential and phenomenological reality." Each one of us must be the filtering agent to prevent us from falling into the classical corruption, and the test is when we try using a bit of reason. The "experiential and phenomenological reality" package of Jesus is a difficult one to open and understand, yes, understand, because impostors wrap it attractively. There are no gimmicks necessary to open the package. There are no short cuts. Even prayer is not an easy tool to use — and who and what is the focus of the prayer? Prayer offers the opportunity to distill our thoughts, to observe some time for concentrated thinking, and to listen to what may be called the inner voice. It takes discipline but not the discipline of rote or mechanical exercises, rather the discipline of including the divine in all our affairs. That does not mean calling outwardly on the divine every instant but simply grounding us, as Paul Tillich says, in the "ground of all being."

What about God's image in this scenario? When we are told that God (the God who is love) demands a ransom and the only payment he will accept is the life of a human being, innocent or not, do we question it? Not much different from the Aztecs, the Incas, and the Pharaohs, and their "sacrificial" executions to appease the gods, gods that they created. Killing human beings to appease gods is neither new nor unique. The Scythians were accustomed to sacrificing hundreds of men and horses to appease their god or to accompany their fallen leaders. Indeed, there is nothing new or extraordinary with the approach of killing human beings for some divine reason. The Christian Church followed suit without missing a beat. Yet the focus of the Church has always been life, love, and grace, but with the scenario of the killing of Jesus to satisfy God's demand, the effect of divine goodness is surely dissipated.

The thinking process continued even after a small interruption for refreshment. The flight attendant was wondering why I was not asleep. I explained to her that my brain was actively engaged in sorting out ideas. Fortunately she never inquired about the subject matter because that would have demanded an exposition that would have lasted until landing in Los Angeles. She went on with her duties and left me to reenter my head.

Is there another option that we might consider to explain the death of Jesus? I think so. Let me explore the relationship that existed between God and Jesus before this alternate option is examined concerning the death of Jesus. I understand God as being the process of creation. By that I mean that he (she/it) participates in the ongoing élan vital to creation, forever evolving even before the Big Bang, the Singularity, of the universe and continuing after the culmination of the (known?) universe. Tillich's "ground of all being" is a good way to describe God, but I want to add the quality of "process" because it keeps God in the dynamic realm.

There is purity and surgical dexterity in Jesus that is quite noticeable in the accounts of the Gospels. Jesus has an approach to reality that cuts through the legal, ossified, and hierarchical doctrines that were, and are still, in common use by religious organizations. For example, consider the response Jesus gave to the gathered crowd when the adulterous woman was accused; his response when he dealt with a sick person on the Sabbath; and his response when asked who was greater, Caesar or God. There are many more examples indicating that Jesus was moving towards a new approach to God, an approach that considered God's love as being primary in any relationship.

I am convinced that Jesus had a particular relationship with God because he understood that God the creator was a God that/who penetrated the entire universe. Teilhard de Chardin, the Jesuit priest, paleontologist and philosopher understood that quite well when he upset the Roman Curia, and was censored for stating that God was universal, could not be delimited by Rome, and that he "penetrated the entire universe." For Archbishop William Temple, there are no isolated sacred places in the universe because the whole universe is sacramental, and no part of it can escape God's influence. Rudolf Otto saw the whole of creation as being holy with no exception. Jesus saw that he had a special relationship with God because he accepted his responsibility as a human being and was devoid of any need for self-aggrandizement. Jesus recognized life as being inseparably and processively connected to the "ground of all being," to the God of Creation, to the process of emergence, and to the coming (becoming?) kingdom. Thus Jesus uniquely walked, lived, and behaved entirely in the knowledge that God was the primary source of his existence. He was unequivocally the Son of God (the connected life to God, "the ground of all being") and consequently the Son of Man (the connected life to all living creatures) personified. Drawing from the superstring theory, all life is connected and interconnected by the bits of energy that are present, vibrating, and pulsating dynamically in all things, perhaps even in God if he (she/it) is the source of all energy, and energy itself predates the known universe and its Singularity.

But death on the cross for such a devoted human being is an enigma unless we understand that no society, no hierarchy, no organization wants to be told that what it is promoting is in error or off the mark. Moreover, few institutions want to be shown their mistakes or want to be corrected. Very few individuals are happy to be corrected, are pleased to be alerted when they make mistakes, or happy when they are given instructions that will help them change their course of action. Perhaps it is a matter of pride, and a fear of being humiliated, and/or a quality of hard-headedness that prevents corrections, however kindly and gracefully presented, to be accepted. In that regard, Jesus was a serious problem to existing supremacy, both to Jewish and to Roman authority (and to the revolutionary Jewish zealots of the period). After all, the Jewish hierarchy knew what was best for its people. The hierarchical Church knows what is best for its members, does it not? The doctrine of Papal infallibility (First Vatican Council of 1870 by Pope Pius IX) was a sure sign that the Roman Church was terribly concerned about those in its realm who thought independently and who might challenge the authority and knowledge of the papacy. The minimal exegetical work being permitted in Ko'ran is an indication that Islam's authority wishes not to be questioned and that its sacred text cannot be picked apart or examined. Judaism also shies away from exegetical scrutiny of its scriptural corpus. Many religious leaders do not want their opinions challenged lest they might have to alter their doctrinal positions, most of which are firmly ingrained so as to enhance their power. Many religious leaders anchor their arguments in scriptural verses to protect their wrong-headed ideas from questioning. Yet most readers of scriptural books know that justification or support for any opinion can be found in these books. The attitude challenging ingrained doctrines is anathema to sound religion or coherent thinking, and totally different from what the scientific community calls "examination by peers." In science a theory, a solution, a speculative argument is normally published in order that other scientists might challenge it, and it is in the challenging exercise that propositions are asserted as valid and sound or invalid and unsound. Religion stands firmly outside that approach.

Galileo learned that lesson the hard way when he was told that his theory was wrong and counter to the "will of God and the wisdom of the Church," and forbidden to publish any of his scientific and philosophical writings because he questioned Rome's position on the rotation of the sun vis-à-vis the earth and other planets. In 1589, Galileo was appointed professor of mathematics at the University of Pisa. This position required him to teach courses in astronomy on the basis of the Greek astronomer Ptolemy's theory that the sun and all the planets revolve around the earth. Preparing for these courses deepened Galileo's understanding of astronomical theory. In 1592, he took up duties as professor of mathematics at the University of Padua, where he spent the next 18 years. During this time, he became convinced of the truth of the theory, proposed by the Polish astronomer Nicklaus Copernicus, that all planets, including the earth, revolve around the sun. Because of his statements about the earth, planets, and sun, Galileo was censored.

The German priest, Hans Kuhn, was forbidden to teach because he disagreed with Rome's theological conclusion with regard to the beginning of all things, procreation, contraceptives, and celibacy. Kuhn now teaches as a secular professor at the University of Tübingen.

Liberal as it is in most matters and asserting the via media (the middle way), the Church of England was not immune to this tenacity when it refused to give Prince Charles permission to remarry or to marry a woman who was divorced and was an excommunicated Roman Catholic. Because of a literal reading (misreading?) of the Bible, Christians today find ways to exclude women in many parts of the Anglican (and other) Communion and from holy orders; gays from holy orders, especially from the episcopacy; and non-whites from all sorts of positions, entitlements, and benefits. Jesus simply cut through this rubbish — and if we listen carefully, he still cuts through this nonsense — and would have announced that the church was for human beings and not human beings for the church. Jesus understood that calling God by name or as Abba was a reminder that God was intimately connected to all human beings.

Those in authority usually want to wield whatever power is available to control those with less or little authority. Authority cannot be questioned. Authority cannot let itself be questioned. When it is questioned, authority is diminished (even frightened) and reduced to a level that makes it vulnerable, or so it believes. This is true of the Church; it is also true of industry, of institutions, and of government. John Emerich Dalberg Acton was the Cambridge historian who stated that, "All power tends to corrupt, and absolute power corrupts absolutely." Lord Acton was a Roman Catholic who worked and wrote against the doctrine of papal infallibility, which states that the Pope can commit no errors when he speaks from the Chair, Ex-Cathedra, on matters of faith and morals. Is that a classic illustration of the abuse of authority or not? Another example of the abuse of power is found in Ayatollah Khomeini's pronouncements, *fatwah*, threats, rulings, and absolute authority — even above the authority of the duly elected president and parliament of the government — in Iran.

A few years ago as I functioned at St. Edward's parish in San Jose, California, it was my custom to have a few minutes immediately after the homily for the congregation to ask questions. I had followed this pattern quite successfully and without too many difficulties for a few years under the leadership of the rector, John Schively. On one occasion a parishioner accused me of being a "heretic" because I dispensed with the Devil as a genuine force and a fallen angel in creation. I said that the devil was a human creation used often as a crutch to shift the blame for the horrible actions that human beings were engaged in foisting on their fellow earth travelers. I responded to the accusation in such a way that the person understood sufficiently that we disagreed and that the personification of evil was not necessary for Christianity. At any rate, the congregation liked the opportunity to ask questions and I liked the opportunity to clarify points that I had made in my homily.

All went well for several years until John resigned from the parish and a new rector was engaged. Bill Eberly, the new rector, was most uncomfortable with the question period. One Saturday, the day before I was to offer my homily, he called me and ordered me not to have a question session after my address. I stopped asking questions because he was the rector; hence I was a guest and he was the authority and host. I was "forbidden" from asking questions. I subsequently resigned because it was my persuasion that what I was saying combined with what the congregation asked or questioned added clarification to the subject matter. In addition, the discussion that followed was a key element that enriched and contributed to our corporate enlightenment. It removed the aura of pulpit pontification from the liturgy. All of us contributed to the topic of the homily and all of us shared in better understanding the subject matter. Bill Eberly failed to see it that way, and I could neither abide by his restriction nor would I accept the role that made me a pontificating "preacher." I resigned from my position as guest assistant at St.Edward's and a few years later Eberly was encouraged to resign too.

Los Angeles was ten minutes away and it was time to look for my ticket and passport. I had one hour to catch a connecting flight to San Francisco.

Bahamas: Land of Sun, Sea, and Conch

It was February 1997 and I was sitting at my desk reading a report on city developments.

"What's on your schedule for the next couple of weeks?" Marcia Le Winter asked me.

"Why?" was my reply, as I was completing a conversation on the telephone with the Consul General of France in San Francisco. Marcia Le Winter was a colleague with whom at first I had a problem because she assumed that all men were sexists until she discovered that I was not. I respected her and found her to be a fine addition to our group. Marcia was an architect with a degree from Columbia University and she was also a planner. That she smoked cigarettes like a chimney was objectionable to me and to most people in the department but she refrained from smoking in my presence. We respected each other. I liked Marcia and still do. Marcia left Bechtel in 1990 but I still sporadically keep in contact with her. I'll say a bit more about Marcia at a later time.

Marcia continued, "We've been asked to review programs for tourism and a couple of airports in the Bahamas and Bob Jackson suggested that you might wish to participate because you have the experience and are creative in your approaches," was Marcia's reply as she gave me a file and walked out of my office.

I'd never been to the Bahamas and in February 1987 I expected that a short holiday in the West Indies might be good for me. I was planning on setting up a month's visit to France to check other aspects of European programs for IT, but that could be delayed by a few weeks. I reviewed the file that Marcia handed me. Soon enough Michael Wakelin walked over to me and asked me if I had the time to review the project for the Bahamas. "Bob Jackson would like you to evaluate the project and take Marcia with you."

I hesitated now that Marcia was to be involved because she was often difficult as a team player, yet she was competent, bright, hardworking, and I liked her. One of her major drawbacks was that she was superficially a feminist as a result of a bad marriage. I say superficially because she never advocated a dislike for men or assumed the traditional put-upon attitude when she worked with me. We had a shouting match once over a program that I reviewed but we settled our differences and trouble never reared up again. I went over to Jackson's office.

Bob and I discussed the project in the Bahamas and he did ask me to take Marcia along so she could work on the program for tourism. I was to handle the aviation side and anything else that the Bahamian authorities threw my way. Apparently, the Bahamian Minister of the Interior had mentioned something about creating a craft school for young and old in Nassau, the capital of the Bahamas. "Who do you think might be recruited to handle the creation of a craft school program, Raymond?"

Without batting an eye, I suggested Carol Austin. Carol had worked to develop a craft school in Port Moresby, Papua. The craft school had been a success and reports indicated that Carol had been a fine team player. Bob agreed but wanted me to talk personally to the Minister before a decision was to be made. That was reasonable and I agreed. "When can you leave?" he asked me.

"Give me a week and I'll be in the Bahamas for a week or ten days," I replied.

"When are you going to Europe?" He had already signed my travel request for Europe.

"After my return from the Bahamas, I suspect, in March." That was enough time to do what I needed to do in Europe and a week of preparation would allow me to get all my appointments in order. Ligia Zelaya would be of great help in this matter; she was always of great help. I walked over to Marcia's desk and informed her that I had accepted the Bahamian task. She seemed genuinely pleased. "I suggest that we leave in a week and overnight in Miami. Can we meet tomorrow morning to mobilize?" I asked. She was happy to meet the next morning. "I need to get the Bahamas settled before I start on the planning for my trip to Europe. Let's be expeditious tomorrow." She agreed. I went home early that day and informed Emily that another project would take me away for a few more weeks. She wasn't too happy.

We took a flight to Miami a week later. Upon arriving and checking in at the airport Sheraton, I decided to grab a cab with Marcia for Coral Gables and a fresh fish restaurant that I knew from years gone by when I would land at Homestead AFB. After swallowing a dozen Gulf oysters and a fine dish of three soft-shell crabs, I was ready for a walk and then bed. Marcia joined me for the walk. We said goodnight and I went to bed after a shower. The next morning we boarded a flight to Nassau at eight o'clock. By 9:50 I was waiting outside the office of the Minister of the Interior. Promptly at ten o'clock the minister invited us into his office. Coffee and sweet cakes were served and we went to work. By noon our agenda was completed. The minister wanted a plan to increase high-end tourism, a review of the airports on Eleuthera Island, a plan for a craft school, and some ideas for Andros Island, the biggest and most rustic island but the most neglected economically. Marcia was to take on the task for tourism, Carol was to come immediately to plan the craft school, and I was to have responsibility for the rest. I asked Marcia to take on the role of project manager, a task she was happy to assume and for which she was well suited.

After that was settled, I went to see the director of aviation to share with him what I would be doing for the airports and for aviation. He was most supportive and put a twin aircraft (Piper Aztec) and a pilot at my disposal. I had booked a room at the Victoria Hotel for the night, an old-style grand hotel located near Nassau's harbor. Marcia had also booked a room there and planned to fly with me the next morning to Eleuthera Island.

In the early afternoon, tea was served in the garden and because it was February, the weather was wonderfully cool, clear, and fresh. The tea was excellent, as were the goodies and savories that accompanied our several pots of the brew. For dinner we received a recommendation to walk about a kilometer from the Victoria Hotel to a seafood restaurant that specialized in local fish and steamed conch in a salad. The dinner was superb and the conch was sweet and delicious. When I commended the waiter for the fine local fish, he admitted that the conch was imported from the Florida Keys because most of them had been over-fished around the Bahamas. That was a sad piece of news because conch delicacies were the indigenous food of the Bahamians, and tourists came especially to enjoy these creatures in wonderful shells that were often used as house decorations.

After dinner and a walk along the harbor, we settled in the garden. I asked Marcia if she would join me in a brandy. Our conversation did not touch Bechtel or the project but centered mainly on her time in New York at Columbia University, her preppy years at Gulfport School for Girls, Gulfport, Mississippi, and her years living in Venezuela when her father worked for Bechtel in Caracas. Her marriage to a New Yorker had produced two boys but her relationship with her husband had produced antagonism, despair, and unhappiness. She came to hate men and had adopted the façade of feminism until she stopped denigrating the male creature after we had become friends. Marcia was well read, bright, and a good planner with an excellent architectural education. At Bechtel she had been relegated to being a support person and was never given a lead position on any project. She was delighted that I had asked her to be project manager for the Bahamian project and promised that she would do her very best, of which I had no doubt. The Bahamian tasks clinched our friendship and gave me additional respect for her; I also learned that she was not, after all, difficult as a team player.

The next morning we flew to Rock Sound Airport on Eleuthera. Marcia accompanied me to see what Club Med was doing on the Island. I made reservations at the Cotton Club Hotel for us and rented two cars, one for Marcia and the other for me. Off we went and hoped to meet at the hotel later in the afternoon. At Rock Sound I met the airport manager, Jeff Blaine. Mr. Blaine had been a protégé of Juan Tripp, the founder and driving force of Pan American World Airways. Jeff told me that the first Boeing 747 purchased by Pan Am had landed at Rock Sound so that Juan Tripp could see it. At any rate, Mr. Blaine was a good source of information and a fine fellow.

My review included Rock Sound Airport and Governor's Harbor Airport, the main commuter airport for Bahamas Airways. Both airports were adequate for current use, but would need to have their amenities expanded if greater numbers of tourists were to be received on Eleuthera Island. In total, I stayed four days on Eleuthera but Marcia returned to Nassau on the second day by taking a seat on Bahamas Airways. From Eleuthera I telephoned Carol Austin to ask her if she was interested in a long-term assignment in the Bahamas to develop a craft school. She was and would be preparing her affairs to permit her to come to Nassau a few weeks later. After my review of the airports I went to Nassau to pick up Marcia and then to fly to Andros Town, Andros Island.

Andros Island is the largest body of land in the Bahamas and it is sparsely inhabited. There are three towns, really villages, on the island. Andros Town is the largest community and is located midway north but below Nicholls Town, which is established at the very northern tip of the island. Moving towards the south there is Kemps Bay Town and still further south is Snaps Point, which can barely be called a village. Kemps Bay harbors a large fishing community, a few very small hotels, and two or three restaurants and other businesses. I set up my headquarters in Andros Town because that's where I was able to obtain most of the information I needed. Just a few kilometers south of Andros Town is a US Navy ocean testing base where dolphins are being trained to rescue sailors who fall overboard, for mine identification and location, and for sonar research.

I was staying with a couple who owned a bed and breakfast on the outskirts of Andros Town. Jane and Pierce Wesley had obtained their Bahamian citizenship after emigrating from Louisiana to the islands. Pierce was a fisherman who was trying to develop an aqua-farm to raise table fish. Jane was a painter, potter, and a fine cook, especially when it came to conch fritters. There is nothing as excellent as fresh conch fritters laced with lime juice and washed down with a pint of room-temperature draught ale. Pierce was agonizing that his aqua-farm was not doing too well. He had tried to raise conch but the result was not encouraging. He had financial backers, and the Bahamian government was ready to invest a lot of cash in a productive aqua-farm, especially one that could produce conch. Pierce identified the problem as being a lack of knowledge in the technical operation of aqua farming, which requires a great amount of specific experience.

After my conversation with Pierce, I telephoned the Minister of the Interior to obtain his point of view. He immediately assured me that the Bahamian government was quite interested in developing marine farming and would I add this task to my general project; a letter of authorization would follow the next day to my office in San Francisco and a faxed copy would be sent to me also.

It was late afternoon but three hours ahead of California and I was able to call Ligia to have her contact my friend, George Lockwood, in South Carmel, who was a renowned aqua-farm expert. Soon I had George on the other end of the telephone line discussing the fine details of marine farming and his experience producing abalone, shrimp, and oysters under sound ecological conditions. He was willing to accept the project and would be sending me and the minister a copy of his scope of work, his contract, the estimated cost for a feasibility study, and his fees. Once the paperwork had been completed George was willing to fly to the Bahamas to review the sites. I gave George my approval and asked him to fly as soon as possible and I would meet him in Nassau.

George arrived two days later and we met at the Victoria Hotel and discussed his assignment. In 1999 Andros Island Fish Enterprise LLP produced the first conch harvest. Currently, conch farming is established in Snap Point, Eleuthera Point, on Cat Island, on the west side of Andros, and Cape Santa Maria, on Long Island. Obviously, my role was less as promoter of marine farming and more as the one who knew an expert in the field who was a successful marine farmer. George Lockwood was my friend from the days of the Diocese of California Futures Planning Council, and the genesis of the Diocese of El Camino Real. George is a fine person and a great practical scientist who cares for the oceans but he is also a good businessman.

I visited the Bahamas twice more that year, in August and November. I was invited to see, among other ventures, the new hotel in Nassau built to promote the recently constructed aquarium. The Poseidon Undersea Resorts hotel was erected in the Tongue of the Ocean, a strait of sea that separates the islands of New Providence and Andros. Six stories are under water and the guest rooms have large windows overlooking the marine life that parades by. Guests can lie in bed or sit on deep davenports and see marine life peering into their rooms. At night, lights can be directed into the water directly in front of the picture windows for a better view of visiting marine life. I did not spend the night in the Nautilus View Hotel but took time to visit several rooms, which can be reached by glass-walled elevator to show marine life as one descends deep into the ocean.

When I completed my part of the Bahamian project, Marcia and Carol continued their work while I proceeded to do my work in Europe, work that I had postponed. The Bahamian project gave me the opportunity to discover that both Marcia and Carol were competent and creative people but who had not been too well regarded by their supervisors while working at Bechtel. Carol, a professional spinster, was one of the hardest-working women that I encountered during my years at Bechtel. In fact, when the time came for me to manage the First Technopolis Conference in San Francisco's Mark Hopkins Hotel, I asked Carol Austin to supervise the process and manage all the details. Carol did a superb job.

On one of my visits to Nassau, Carol, who was overseeing the craft program, invited me to have a drink in her apartment before we went to dinner. Carol offered me a perfect martini made with Tanqueray gin and three olives; just the way I like it and into which no ice had been inserted because she kept her gin and the glasses in the freezer! I'll never forget her thoughtfulness. As I said, Carol performed magnificently and the conference and craft program were a success. After the conference and when I was in Europe, I learned that she had been put on holding status and after 30 days was laid off; this turned out to be permanent. Carol retired to Kalamazoo, Michigan to tend to family matters and every so often I speak with her on the telephone. The last time I spoke with her she was supervising the construction of her new house and was caring for her elderly mother.

Marcia Le Winter has also been laid off from Bechtel after working with the firm for twelve years. She is currently retired and living in San Francisco. Marcia has invested some funds in a new disposal and recycling process headed by Joseph Anderson, retired Bechtel vice president. I believe that she has been receiving some money from the project; at least enough so that she has not needed to terminate her unemployed status. As with Carol, on occasion Marcia and I speak on the telephone or via email. On rare occasions we meet for coffee or I stop by her condo to share a bottle of wine. I feel enriched to have worked with these two women and to have learned much from them.

Technopolis: The Technically Driven City

My brief introduction to the French Technopoles program moved me to get more involved and certainly to learn more about its effects on the national economy. After attending a key conference in Montpellier, France, and hearing and meeting several international leaders in the arena of high technology community development, I was further impassioned with the idea that high technology, or better still, Information Technology (IT), was the engine that would drive the world's economy for the next generation. The main platform for IT is the knowledge-based revenue producing industry. Knowledge was the veritable driving generator that produced extraordinary economic results. It is knowledge that made Silicon Valley what it is. It is knowledge that sustains the economic momentum of the United States, or Japan, or France, the United Kingdom, and other vibrant communities and regions. Indeed, it is knowledge as a renewable resource that will be the vehicle for an improved human and planetary condition.

As for IT, of course there were deep-seated problems with the way IT was used. For example, IT needed a system of laws and appropriate policies that could protect and guide its integrity; too many charlatans were making hay of IT to the point that a big financial balloon was developing that one day might burst (as it did in California and Massachusetts in 2001) and depress many economies. Moreover, IT was not understood well by the general public, and many investors in it were doomed from the start because stock buying spurred by avarice overwhelmed reasonable financial planning; fortunes could be made quickly and could be dissipated just as quickly.

Important issues needed attention. IT was driven by small groups of creative young entrepreneurs who had no business savvy. Few countries had the basic statutory infrastructure to support these entrepreneurs. IT innovations did not emerge from major established companies, but from incubators created by young people who had no business track record, no financial knowledge, and no marketing skills to place their ideas and their products on the market. From Hewlett-Packard (HP) to Apple, Dell Computer, Sun Microsystems, Intel, and Oracle, these firms began as small, insignificant, and tentative entries into the market. Because the United States supports small businesses with possible loans and statutory incentives, and because when their products have merit they can register as public entities to obtain more funds through the sale of shares (stock offerings), such entrepreneur-driven incubators are able to blossom and become giants in IT. Added to that is the availability of major investors known as venture capitalists (VC) or angel capitalists (AC) who are willing to sink money into these incubators and bear the risks involved to bring an idea to market. VCs are not found in every country and many countries have laws that preclude them. In the United

States incubators and VCs are encouraged by the simple fact that creativity and risk are how new businesses develop and grow.

In France, for example VCs are not encouraged, and only the government has the legal means to support and encourage incubators. Hence, the French were interested in how Americans treated incubators, especially in Silicon Valley and along Route 128 near Boston, and I was interested in the defined, structured science parks that the French and many European nations promoted just to encourage IT incubators. Europeans approached IT with the tools of real estate, setting aside special zones for promoting the creation of incubators, whereas Americans simply relied on good location, the entrepreneurs' enlightened self-interest, the financial resources that were available when in proximity to VCs, and the supporting universities — preferably private institutions that were not encumbered by public charters that restrained their willingness to invest in potential risky ventures.

Stanford University gambled on its students, William Hewlett and David Packard, when they developed an oscilloscope in Packard's parent garage. Eventually, Stanford set aside some land as the first science park to permit Hewlett-Packard (HP) to expand into what surfaced as a major force in the IT industry. But the Stanford Science Park is a small part of what emerged as Silicon Valley and its revolutionary work pattern, creative force, and free enterprise approaches — with no government, state, or city intervention except for building codes, business licenses, and traditional operating and financial requirements.

Apart from the small firm of HP, several other firms large and small chose to locate their research units in the Stanford Research Park (SRP). Of course, as the years moved ahead, SRP became the leaven for further implantation of IT firms, both new and old, in the region north and south of Palo Alto known as Silicon Valley. Silicon Valley (it is not found on any cartographic map) became the Mecca for IT development — unmanaged development. Property in the region of Silicon Valley (silicon such as that used in early computer chip manufacture) was bought, sold, and leased by commercial real estate firms under the existing laws of California. No managing entity, government or otherwise, controlled either the work performed in Silicon Valley or the type of residents who moved into the region. In essence, market forces controlled both who worked and who resided in Silicon Valley. Communities such as San Jose, Mountain View, Los Altos, Redwood City, Menlo Park, Woodside, San Mateo, and Burlingame became the hot zones of Silicon Valley's development.

Soon other communities joined the expansion when real estate around the Peninsula became limited and prices soared. IT developers, scientists, technicians, and manufacturers were interested in choice location with good infrastructure, good weather, good schools and universities, and amenities that offered good quality-of-life, hence the San Francisco Bay Area was attractive to them. As the marketer Regis McKenna, who helped Apple become a byword in IT, informed me: "No one in knowledge will locate in the Sahara or the Gobi desert!"

Because Technopolis programs established by governments in Europe encouraged technical incubators to search for technological developments that were substantially new, the tendency was to have entrepreneurs of all types flock to the science parks. Mixed in with genuine researchers were also many charlatans. Competition to produce innovation was fierce and for every success there were scores of casualties. Many incubators succumbed soon enough because of unworkable ideas, and many entrepreneurs lost the financial support from their governments. The problem was worldwide and not limited to Europe. Japan's Ministry of Industry, Technology, and Innovation (MITI), the source of funds for innovators, not only required that incubators work under the umbrella of large companies (a similar statutory approach exists in France) but also controlled the funding and the entrepreneurs' business plans. Consequently many entrepreneurs found it necessary to escape to the United States, United Kingdom, and Canada where they found better business climates for incubators to develop, where risk management was considered an implicit part of the creative process, and the free market was open to receive their products.

My research on science parks and their conditions took me to France, which touted itself to be on the leading edge of innovation (after Mitterrand's presidency it began to slide into decline). France protected itself robustly but in the process invoked such delimiting laws and statutes that creativity in IT was practically destroyed because many of the innovators chose to escape to more friendly regions. Consequently after President Mitterrand, entrepreneurship slowly lost its innovative zeal in France, in spite of the fact that the word is rooted in the French language. The United Kingdom, Canada, and the United States were the happy recipients, in the long run, of this French brain drain. The brain drain did not just emanate from France, but many excellent scientists, entrepreneurs, and innovators from Japan, other Pacific Rim countries, Germany, Italy, Russia, the People's Republic of China, and India found that moving to the United States, the United Kingdom, and Canada offered better environments for creativity. Again the IT generated financial heat (too much money chasing too inconsequential products — hardware and software), and that heat expanded the bubble, which soon would burst because of its over-size in 2001-2002.

It is a curious turn of events that while many entrepreneurs were seeking to come to the United States to share their creativity and engage themselves in "start-up" enterprises, the administration of George W. Bush began, after the destruction of the World Trade buildings, to reduce the immigration option, close the entry means for these bright people, and make funding greatly more difficult. It was tantamount to using a sledgehammer to kill a fly. The pretext was because of national defense, security in all its phases, and reduced competition by starving the technical arena of qualified, bright, innovative, and essential people. Firms in the United States and especially in Silicon Valley began to be starved of technically astute people. That problem has not been resolved yet in the first decade of the 21st century. This politically complex issue made my work in the IT arena of the world much more difficult and put me often in situations where I was constantly asked why, when, and how the United States would open its doors, especially since it was a country that not only could use the foreign brain supply but that had the stature to promote further knowledge development, to make funding possible, and to proffer a market.

After offering several presentations at Bechtel to get the company to include Technopolis on its list of interests, I was assigned as manager of the program within the parameters of the Infrastructure Department. Because Technopoles in Europe were framed in technical parks that were managed, controlled, and funded by the government, I saw an opportunity for Bechtel to enter as designer, constructor, operator, investor, and, best of all, recipient of some of the research.

I was not, however, convinced that Bechtel really understood or was interested in Technopolis. Bechtel's construction mentality apparently placed a veil over anything that was not concrete and reinforcement bars. Yet I proceeded to move further into the community of people who promoted Technopolis and its agenda. The International Association of Technopoles, also known as the International Association of Science Parks (IASP), was one association that I insisted on joining, or rather joining on behalf of Bechtel. Another association was the Association of University Research Parks (AURP) based in the United States but incorporating several members from the IASP.

The tug-of-war with Bechtel was a debilitating waste of energy and added much to my consideration of early retirement from the firm. At any rate, I pursued the program and developed many lasting friendships with people involved in IT, its peripheral programs, its economic effects, and its regional developmental possibilities (on which I thought Bechtel would capitalize immensely). Umberto Bozzo, Dominique Fache, Robert Hodgson, Pierre Nöe, Henri Thibiant, Daniel Moy, and a score of others have become cherished friends. Dr. Riccardo Petrella, of whom I have spoken earlier, was one of the most exciting and challenging persons in the IT arena. He was also a phenomenal person able to write and communicate in several languages. In Brussels I would spend hours talking with Riccardo discussing many subjects and exchanging anecdotes, bits of history, and political issues.

Not willing to assume the risks that could surface if they allowed a free hand similar to that of Silicon Valley, and to a lesser degree Route 128 in Boston, foreign governments monitored, controlled, and managed what became known as Technopoles or Technopolis. France, Italy, Finland, the Netherlands, Germany, Australia, Canada, Japan, and other countries developed parks for IT development. The Japanese became the first to establish government sponsored and controlled science parks under the umbrella of MITI. France soon followed the format, as did Italy and others. All such IT parks were managed and funded by government entities, and governments employed the majority of the people who were members of IASP. On several occasions at conferences I pointed out that the activities in Silicon Valley were purely controlled by market forces and not by government sponsorship, with the exception that at times firms did obtain public grants and did bid on government projects. The message was received but the prospect of allowing enlightened self-interest, and to some extent the free market, to act was shunned and the necessary policies and statutes were unavailable. Entrepreneurship laws in many countries were suffocating creativity with results that, as I mentioned earlier, many French and other nationals immigrated to the United States (overcoming the obstacles placed by the George Bush administration), to the United Kingdom, and to Canada. It was puzzling to me to know that as much as "entrepreneur" is a French word, the climate for the promotion of what an entrepreneur does is almost non-existent in France.

As a European country, the United Kingdom was different in that it promoted and offered unencumbered conditions for free enterprises, especially in IT. Much credit must go to Prime Minister Margaret Thatcher, a strong opponent of socialist policies, who worked to reduce government control over the British economy. Thatcher's government supported a free market and removed government from that arena.

A good example of the forces of free market at work is in Cambridge. What became known as the Cambridge Phenomenon emerged as the result of Trinity College of Cambridge University opening itself to supporting entrepreneurship, and released some of its land to incubators (just as Stanford University had done in California), for the development of a science complex and a technical park. Firms flocked to Cambridge, purchased land, built facilities, and placed their research centers in that domain to be close to the driving power of research evolving from Trinity College and other Cambridge University colleges. By the 1990s, Cambridge had become a premier center for IT, and the region's economy was strengthened enormously. In fact, Cambridge became a model for Oxford, Birmingham, Newcastle, and

Edinburgh. Only estate agencies monitored the land for development in the United Kingdom just as real estate agencies in the United States monitored land acquisition, all for market-based fees or commissions but with no control on what the new owners did and produced. Real estate agencies in America, the United Kingdom, and Canada simply found and sold land for IT buyers; they exercised no management control over them.

If land management is the operating entity for a science park, as is the case in Europe, then it all boils down to having a real estate managing group act as the authority over the tenants! In all my presentations and conversations I indicated that the Technopolis program will never take off as long as it is managed by estate agents, because they are only focused on sales and leases, not on IT products. At any rate, I became disillusioned with both IASP and AURP because both directed their attention primarily to estate management and not to ideas, concepts, creative options, and incubating generators of IT. I was convinced that Europe would not any time soon achieve the independence that prevailed in America, the United Kingdom, and Canada.

As a member of both IASP and AURP, I became acquainted with IC^2. IC^2 was created by Dr. George Kozmetski, one of the cofounders of Teledyne, a major technology firm later acquired by United Technologies, and a professor at the Business School of the University of Texas, Austin. When Kozmetski retired from industry, he created IC^2 as a catalyst for developing entrepreneurs in IT. One of his prized pupils was Michael Dell, founder, president, and chairman of DELL, the computer manufacturer. Dr. Kozmetski became an influential force in the development of centers for IT, and for giving IT entrepreneurs the necessary training for promoting their ideas. Working for George Kozmetski was Dr. Raymond Smilor, who was the first one of his doctoral candidates, then installed as the director of IC^2. Ray Smilor managed the programs and was editor and publisher of all publications produced by IC^2.

While with Bechtel and under the management of Bob Jackson, I worked often with IC^2 staff and especially with George and Ray on several conferences and presentations. IC^2 was an active member of both IASP and AURP and as such was present at all conferences sponsored by them. In 1988, Bechtel and IC^2 joined forces to inaugurate the First Technopolis Conference in San Francisco (and the last I might add). The Conference attracted 40 speakers and catered to an audience of six hundred and was held at the Mark Hopkins Hotel on Nob Hill. It was a most successful conference. Two years later, when IC^2 and I suggested that Bechtel host another conference, the replacement for Jackson, Frank Cain, turned it down. Of course Frank Cain, a senior vice president and a favorite of Riley Bechtel had a myopic vision and could not appreciate the value of delving into IT development.

At the first and only Conference on Technopolis sponsored by Bechtel and IC^2 and which I managed with the invaluable help of Carol Austin, several IT luminaries were present, among whom were: Michael Dell, Steve Jobs, Larry Ellison, Viacheslav Pismenny, Gordon Moore, Harry Nichols, Dominique Fache, Bob Hodgson, Umberto Bozzo and others of the same caliber. It is regrettable that none of the presentations were published either in audio form or in a book. IC^2 had offered to publish the material but our miserable leader Frank Cain dismissed it as unnecessary and fruitless, and so it went into oblivion!

But some momentous events do not go readily into oblivion. When the Conference took place and since I was its host, I had the opportunity to have both lunch and dinner with Steve Jobs at the Mark Hopkins. Our time together was memorable. Steve was courteous, interesting, communicative, and most charming. We discussed his goals and his interest in offering the best, the very best, product to his clients. We talked about his strangeness and his focus on great design and coherent engineering development. He was insistent on creating a product that was of a piece, practical, beautiful, and well made. I still can hear Steve insist on producing a computer that was menu-driven and that did not require a computer engineer to operate it. "Even young children should be able to operate our computers and these computers should have lots of graphic capabilities," he insisted. I agreed.

In terms of the practical effects of the Technopolis program, I was able to acquire a project in Montpellier and rescue one in Bari, Italy. The first one was to resolve a conflict between France Telecom and the Antennes Tech-

210 · RAYMOND HOCHE-MONG

nopole (teleport facility) in Montpellier that served the Centre National de la Recherche Scientifique (CNRS) at the hospital. Montpellier prides itself on having the oldest continuously operating medical school in the world, established in the 14th century and still functioning, though renovated several times. Montpellier's medical school focuses primarily on African tropical diseases and supports many of the ventures of Doctors Without Borders and the work performed by indigenous physicians in regions where laboratories are nonexistent. The teleport is used for examinations of patients via video and computer data transfer. France Telecom would not permit the use of the teleport, yet it could not provide the broadband services needed by the hospital and its researchers. In negotiations I asked if France Telecom would allow the use of its utilities to connect to satellites. Once they accepted that avenue, we had the teleport connection go through France Telecom, and then all communication was shifted to the satellite network. In this way France Telecom services local access and the teleport of Antennes Technopole provided the rest of the service. Voilà! The problem was solved and Bechtel was able to complete the construction of the teleport with the support of AT&T.

After the teleport issue was resolved, George Frêche, the mayor of Montpellier and the principal mover behind the IT development in his jurisdiction, wanted to attract an American private university to his area. Working with Frêche and Harvard University, I was successful in establishing a postdoctorate branch of the University. Moreover, Massachusetts General Hospital agreed to an interchange of medical scholars with Montpellier. Eventually, Mass-General established a research center for African diseases in Boston, working closely with Montpellier's research teams. At present, both Mass-General and Montpellier are collaborating to find a vaccine to counter the Ebola virus, which causes hemorrhagic fever and ultimately death of the infected person.

Venice

To narrate this phase of my history, I will need to approach it from the reason I traveled to Venice, and then I will share the details of the lovely trip.

Michael Ryan, President of IASP and Director General of Plassey Technological Park in Limerick, Ireland, had invited me to attend the major
International Association of Science Parks (IASP) Conference held in Montpellier, France. IASP wanted me to meet several of its members and
especially wanted Bechtel to be involved in its global effort of uniting all the
IT-promoting parks. Michael was an amiable person who was well respected
by the French members who preferred an Irishman to anyone else. The European Union was emerging, and Ireland was viewed as a poor but friendly
nation standing in juxtaposition to Great Britain. I had accepted the invitation
to attend the Montpellier conference.

Consequently, because I was going to Montpellier, my department head
figured that it would be cheaper if I presented Enrique Diaz's paper in Venice
at the Scuola Grande di S. Rocco — an historic building dating back to the
16th century — for the Technopolis project. Enrique was not a colleague that
I considered simpatico; we were often at odds and I particularly did not like
his approach to planning or how he treated clients. Nevertheless I accepted,
although I had not read the paper, which had yet to be written! In fact I received the paper by fax 14 hours before I was scheduled to present it. Had I
read the paper earlier, I would not have presented it, although I would have
gone to Venice merely for a holiday visit. Later when I was working for Dr.
Bozzo, I learned that the person who was scheduled to be my colleague at the
presentation of this paper was Mario Marinazzo; he too had received the paper a day earlier and had decided that it was awful but it was too late to alert
me or rewrite it. To avoid his embarrassment — he did not know me —
Mario called in sick and left me holding the bag. I soldiered on but did not
give the content of the paper much support. I did announce that I was only a
spokesperson for Sr. Enrique Diaz from Bechtel Corporation.

Every so often one is placed in an embarrassing position and, like entering a box canyon, escaping out of it is impossible. The presentation in Venice
became my box canyon. As I approached the podium of the Scuola Grande di
S. Rocco with the text of a poorly written paper in my hand, I realized that
we are spectators to our own awareness. I was going to be my own spectator
as I read this paper written by Ivan Ivanek under the direction of Enrique

212 · RAYMOND HOCHE-MONG

Diaz. Enrique was the project manager of the then-Italian *Tecnopolis* (Italian spelling) project. It was just as if I was watching someone else performing. It was eerie. Here I was at the podium and yet I was looking sympathetically at myself reading the words of the paper. I disagreed with every word because the premise was wrong.

Enrique was proposing that Tecnopolis needed two new buildings if it wanted to expand its influence in the Bari area. Of course Bechtel would be called upon to build the new facilities! My position was that Tecnopolis had all the facilities it ever needed; what it needed was a program to make IT part of every business in the region, and this did not call for new buildings. Yet here I was proclaiming Enrique's premise. Why? Because I had been asked to make this presentation to save money for Bechtel, and because it was assumed that because I was part of the IASP community, my words would carry more weight.

As an aside, I accepted the assignment because I thought a holiday in Venice with Emily was worth the difficulty I would be encountering. I soon found out at the Q&A session that I was not able to be convincing and to show that I believed the words I had spoken. Sitting in the audience was the general manager of Gianfranco Dioguardi Engineering and Construction Company who spoke French fluently but whom I did not yet know. He asked me if I thought it would be necessary to expand Tecnopolis for future development with IT. My reply was that expansion was necessary but not in terms of building, rather in terms of information capabilities, networking, entrepreneurship, active marketing, and subsequently, these to be supported by the tools of high technology. My emphasis was clear and succinct: Bari did not need new buildings, and even though I recognized that Dioguardi E and C was in the building business, in this case for IT's expansion no new buildings were necessary; and I was saying this even when I had yet to visit Bari. I left the podium and did not have a chance to meet my questioner, until much later when I was involved in the project.

On the day of my departure from Venice, Umberto Bozzo, the director general of Tecnopolis Novus Ortus of Bari, telephoned me at the hotel to ask if I could schedule a visit to Bari. My response was that if I were made project/program manager of the Tecnopolis project I would schedule a visit to Bari, but not before. When I returned to San Francisco all hell broke loose because Dr. Bozzo had telephoned my superiors asking that I assume the project/program management of the Tecnopolis project, thus replacing Enrique.

Enrique, Wakelin's golden boy, was very unhappy with me, especially because I was against his suggestion of adding more buildings to Tecnopolis. In fact Enrique, as the project manager, was loath to pay my expenses from Montpellier to Venice because I had Emily with me and because I had rented a car instead of purchasing an airplane ticket. As I figured it, a car would carry both of us but an airline ticket would be for one person or I would have had to pay for Emily's seat — in fact a car was much less expensive for the client, Tecnopolis.

Soon after the storm and the removal of Enrique from the project, I was given the job of becoming project/program manager of the Tecnopolis project. After a telephone call to Umberto, I scheduled my visit to Bari. Umberto had been informed by Gianfranco Dioguardi, who was president of Tecnopolis, which I indicated by the tone of my address that I was not in favor of what Enrique Diaz was proposing. Soon after being made manager of the Italian Tecnopolis, Umberto asked me to write a brief summary of my ideas for him. I sat down and wrote a one page summary explaining that the facility was to be focused on knowledge, creative developments, revenue production, and innovation; not on buildings, land expansion, or further construction. To the paper I attached a memorandum that it was my intention to make a thorough examination of the Bari and Apulia region, to list all the businesses, the industries, the tourist establishments, the academic institutions, the harbor, the fishing businesses, and speak with as many civic leaders as was possible. Then I asked if Dr. Bozzo would arrange that effort before I arrived. My first visit to Bari took place in late February 1988.

Camargue, Cote d'Azur, and Lago d'Iseo

It is necessary to backtrack to Montpellier now that the stage has been set for Bari, Italy. Another reason to backtrack is because I want to share with the reader a few items of the wonderful trip that was mine to travel by automobile from Montpellier to Venice.

We traveled to Montpellier in 1987 from Paris on the Très Grande Vitesse (TGV) train. Emily had never ridden this wonderful train so I booked our trip in first class and with lunch served as France sped by the car's window. Seating was face-to-face with a well-appointed table between us. Lunch was a multi-course repast served with wine or another beverage of choice. Coffee and dessert followed as the meal ended with pousse-café liqueur, again of choice. The track was nearly noiseless and there was little side swaying of the cars, thus conversation or reading was possible.

The TGV should be the envy of the western world, especially America. It puts the American Amtrak system to shame and adds to the embarrassment of how the United States looks upon passenger rail travel. I agree that America is a bigger country than France, but traveling at approximately 300 kilometers per hour or more on smooth, quiet, well maintained, and precisely engineered track would make travel over this large country pleasant, attractive, and profitable. In addition, the TGV offers superb service in all classes and maintains comfortable sleeping compartments for overnight trips, all at a reasonable price.

It is obvious that France understands that public transportation produces revenue not directly through the sale of tickets, but through the fact that it pulls people away from their cars and allows firms to reduce their parking facilities if the employees do not need to park their cars. On another level, the traveler who leaves his car behind and uses the TGV is less stressed upon arriving at his destination and reaches the town or city center of his choice, rather than far away, as it is for airports.

Anyway, the TGV is an experience that is its own reward. I have used the TGV to travel to Brussels, Bordeaux, Lyons, Nice, Nîmes, and to Montpellier. We arrived in Montpellier and found that the train station was merely two blocks from our hotel and a half block from the car rental agency we would use three days hence for our travel to Venice. In 1999 I had the opportunity to travel from London to Paris on the Channel TGV and found it delightfully restful, and the travel time was only three hours from city center to city center, with no airports to suffer through.

Montpellier lies west of the city of Nîmes and northwest of the Rhone Delta. The Rhone River, a major artery of France, pours itself into the Golfe du Lion. The delta of the Rhone is important in many ways. West of the delta is the ancient town of Aigues-Mortes, an historic walled city that is as generously beautiful as it is quaint. East of the delta are the salt ponds, the small town of Salin-de-Giraud and across the Grand Rhone River lies Port St. Louis, a major commercial and fishing harbor. Between Salin-de-Giraud and Aigues-Mortes is found the great expanse of the Plaine de la Camargue, an extraordinary natural reserve that is home to black bulls, white charolais cattle, white horses, other mammals, and birds of many varieties.

La Camargue is the historic home of the "cowboy," the riders who care for the black bulls of the corrida de toros, the charolais cattle, and the horses, both wild and tamed. Because cowboys control their mounts with the left hand (in French "la gauche"), and because the bulls of La Camargue are often bred for the arenas and the ranches of France, Spain, Portugal, Brazil, and Argentina, the word has been converted in Argentina into slang Spanish, as gaucho, the legendary and romantic cattle cowboy of the Pampas of Argentina.

We walked to our hotel and got settled. After some freshening up we walked to the conference center. On the way we obtained a good look at what Montpellier offered but it was not the time to be tourists.

The IASP conference was excellent and although the presentations were in many ways dealing with strategies to rent property, because I was new to the group, I found it quite educational. I met several people who eventually became my friends and with whom I still keep a running correspondence. My dear and enigmatic friend Dominique Fache was present wearing his red socks to amuse the socialist-leaning mayor, George Frêche. Umberto Bozzo, Michael Ryan, and many others, all members of IASP, were in attendance. It was enjoyable to meet and get acquainted with so many people from various parts of the planet. In the Q&A session I stressed that real estate matters were to be left out of the IT arena and thus relegated to the enterprises that required property; but that it should not drive the knowledge agenda. It was in Montpellier that I met my Finnish friends for the first time. The Finnish representative had heard my comments about removing real estate issues from the whole technopolis endeavor but stressing knowledge as the instrument for revenue development. That approach rang a bell that would be of interest to Finland's quest for more involvement in IT. The conference proceeded on time and on track and the schedule was terrific, the subject matter loaded with information, and the folks in attendance enlightening.

On the second day there we had a moonlit evening past midnight; taking the opportunity, Mayor George Frêche led a group of us through the historic part of the city, pointing out the famous edifices and their contribution to the history of the city of Montpellier. People in the apartment buildings peered out of windows or balconies to listen to Frêche lecture and then wave to or otherwise greet us. We ended the tour almost at sunrise and topped it with excellent café-au-lait and many croissants. Sleep was unimportant because we were all very excited and impressed with the history of Montpellier, the oldest medical teaching institution in Europe. If the University of Bologna is the oldest academic institution in Europe, as I said earlier, Montpellier is the oldest medical center of learning on the Continent.

That afternoon I had the opportunity to meet several delegations and one in particular was most interesting. It is normal for the delegation to offer to the conferees brochures, national food products, sweet things and chocolate, and trinkets. The Finnish delegation offered airline-size bottles of Finlandia vodka. Many of the conferees stuffed their pockets with several bottles. I was singled out and asked to meet with the chief of the Finnish delegation the next morning to listen to a proposal.

The next day, when the conference ended, I met with the Finnish delegation in one of the seminar rooms to listen to a proposal. As I indicated previously, the key person who headed the delegation had been impressed with my short comments at the Q&A session and had heard me discuss technopolis in conversation with others. My discounting of property management had been important for him and for his vision of IT in Finland. I was promptly invited to visit Finland to further discuss the potential of developing a knowledge-based program for the country. The proposal was fascinating and I accepted the invitation. In brief the Finnish chief inquired if I would come to Finland to assist in developing a long-term plan for the promotion of their nascent knowledge industry. Would that be just for Helsinki or for the whole country? The chief assured me that it would be for the whole country. Finland had completed its obligation to the USSR with its final debt payment; now it was free and could direct its attention to its own economic future. A copy of the proposal with a contract was to be faxed to me in San Francisco in a few days. I telephoned Jackson and asked him to keep an eye out for it.

It was time to head east to Venice and places in between; this was the fall of 1988. The reason we headed to Venice was to give a lecture for Bari's Tecnopolis, which was mentioned above. For the trip, we rented an automobile and booked a room for three nights in Arles, another historic city on the edge of the departments of Gard and Provence.

Arles has been built around the ancient Roman arena where until a few decades ago, bullfights instead of wild animals and gladiators, were part of the entertainment for the citizenry. Our hotel room overlooked a noisy alley within walking distance of the arena, the city market, and the business sector. My plan was to spend one day investigating Arles, and one day discovering the wonders of La Camargue. My plan was executed precisely and fully.

We had an introductory visit to La Camargue, Aigues-Mortes, Salin-de-Giraud, and Stes. Maries-de-la-Mer. Aigues-Mortes is a splendid historic walled city with fine restaurants serving the specialty of La Camargue, filets de taureaux (bull), a cut of grilled tenderloin that has absolutely no fat and is served with fresh vegetables and the inevitable and terrific pommes frites, which turned out to be our dinner. Lunch was eaten in Salin-de-Giraud where we had barbillon and the foundation of genuine bouillabaisse, rascasse from the Golfe du Lion.

La Camargue greeted us with a rich variety of birds, flowers, horses, black bulls and charolais. One day does not do justice to the delta of the

Rhône River but that was all the time we had on this first visit. As it turned out I was still involved with a proposed project to establish an IT center in or around the city of Nîmes and hence made many visits to this part of the country while still working with Bari's Tecnopolis project. But I will tell more about the proposed Nîmes project in a later piece when I describe my work from 1989 to 1991.

After our fine visit to La Camargue we proceeded towards Nice but stopped at Valbonne to show Emily the technological park of Sophia Antipolis and where Dominique Fache had a principal hand in its creation. We took time to spend a couple of days in the coastal community of St. Laurent where I had stayed on an earlier visit.

St. Laurent has a fine long beach and is located across the runway that serves the International Airport of Nice. On one of my earlier visits to the Côte d'Azur, I had been asked to review the airport and its over-water approach to the runway. I thought that from the beach vantage point of St. Laurent, photographing the approach would be a cinch. Wrong! During the day the beach is crowded with sunbathers and most of the women are topless. It is impossible to focus on the approach to the runway without capturing in the photograph one or two women as they sunbathed nues aux naturelles. I was not able to obtain any acceptable pictures but I enjoyed the exhibition.

From St. Laurent we took a side trip to St. Paul to absorb the art of Magritte, Alberto Giacometti, Joan Miró, Henri Matisse, and others at the Aimé Maeght gallery. The gallery was designed by the architect from Massachusetts, Josep Luis Sert and dedicated to André Malraux in 1964. My eyes were satisfied and my senses quivering with contentment. After the Maeght and a quick lunch we drove the few kilometers up the hill to Vence to see the Chapel of the Rosary of the Dominican Nuns of Montéils, planned and designed by Henri Matisse. On the afternoon we chose to visit the chapel, the street was being repaired and the dust and noise were overwhelming, but once inside the building it was another world, an aesthetic world that enveloped me with color, silence, and exquisiteness. I did not want to leave and in my inner being I never have left the chapel of Henri Matisse — it has joined other awe-inspiring places in the treasure chest of my heart and memory.

The next morning we had breakfast in Nice to see the many magnificent sculptures by Sasha Sosno, a friend of Dominique Fache who had introduced him to me. Sosno's signature is an aesthetically placed cavity inside his sculpture such that one is able to see through the solid mass of his creation; hence, the sculpture incorporates the surrounding view through its aperture.

Nearing noon we proceeded across the border to the Italian Riviera and on to Milan and beyond. We stopped for lunch (there are no small lunches in Italy) in Arenzano on the outskirts of Génova. After lunch we turned in a northern direction to skirt around Milan and then east towards the Alpi Orobie, passing through the wine and herb country of Bergamo and stopping for several days at Lago d'Iseo. At the hotel Ca' Blanca di Lago, we were able to view the great classic movie *Gone with the Wind* with Scarlett, Butler, and Ashley speaking in Italian; it was humorous and fortunately the southern accent was imperceptible.

The region of Lago d'Iseo is a fine producer of both wine and marble. The quarry of marble has been mined for several centuries and promises to supply the wonderful carbonate stone for several more centuries. At the foot of the Orobie, the valley produces some of the finest wine grapes. Food in the region is exquisite. We found that even the basil pizza at the Tennis Club restaurant was exceptional. We visited several wineries to taste the drink of the gods, and one of the wineries suggested that we indulge ourselves for lunch at La Fiorita. It was a sumptuous lunch with prosciutto, veal, fresh tomatoes with basil, vegetables, salad, cheeses, and dessert. More than either Emily or I could eat but the custom of the restaurant was to serve until the customer stopped the food from arriving at the table with a firm "per favore basta (please stop)!" I soon discovered that in Italy, at most good restaurants (tratorios), the food keeps coming unless the customer makes a move to stop its delivery.

It was time to point the car towards Venice. I had allowed five days of play in Venice before the Conference at the Scuola Grande di S. Rocco. Emily had to return to San Francisco at the end of the four days but I was to remain for the duration of the Conference and then head to London for a meeting with Stu Hill on some aviation work that Bob Jackson wanted me to look into. As I drove the kilometers to Venice, past the beautiful villas of Verona, Vicenza, and Padua, I kept thinking that my calendar and my plate were quite full for the next year and onward.

Exciting projects and much traveling for me marked the years from 1988 through 1992. I remember being surprised when I received my American Airlines mileage statement to learn that I had accumulated more than 500,000 frequent advantage credit miles and that did not consider the miles on British Airways. That indicated a lot of flying, a lot of airline meals, many airports, and that I had slept in many beds. Moreover, I was concerned that my cholesterol level may be higher than it should because one never knows how fatty the food is and how it is prepared.

We arrived at our small hotel in a water taxi (I had booked an inexpensive room to save Enrique's project money). After unpacking and getting our bearings we walked to Piazza S. Marco, the hub of Venice's tourist sector. Venice is either a walking island or a boat riding island, it is not an automobile haven and never will be. On the second day of our stay we learned about the waterbus system and purchased passes and obtained a schedule. The waterbus proved to be excellent transportation to get around Venice and its schedule was quite dependable. Much of Venice we explored by waterbus with a great deal of walking filling the gaps of the system.

One of the most enjoyable places we visited was the Collezioine Guggenheim at S. Gregorio. The Guggenheim art collection was one of the fullest and richest I had seen in many years and it was well displayed with natural light bathing the pieces. The Guggenheim villa was built on the Canal Grande across from the Palazzo Pisani, and east of it, the Piazza S. Marco. Quite close to the Guggenheim we found the Anglican Church of St. George's and chose to participate in the Sunday Eucharist, which was to be celebrated two days hence.

Venice was a marvelous place for a short period but I'm not sure that I could accept a long stay there; everything in Venice is damp and the buildings all reek with a sort of mildew smell. On the fifth day I accompanied Emily to the Marco Polo airport for her flight to London and on to San Francisco. When I returned to my hotel the Tecnopolis paper had arrived by DHL and I began to read it at the café located near my hotel on the Rio di S.Trovaso in preparation for the next day's presentation at the Scuola Grande di S. Rocco. As I indicated earlier, the paper was poorly conceived and badly written. I had to do a great deal of editing without changing the ill-conceived content.

Aviation and European Union Consult

After I made my presentation at the Scuola Grande di S. Rocco, the next day I took an Alitalia flight to London to meet with Stu Hill, Manager of Aviation Business Development at the Hammersmith office of Bechtel. Stu was a walking encyclopedia of aviation contacts. He had received a call from Bob Jackson to recruit me for a special investigative project. When I arrived in Stu's office the next day, he informed me that I was to research four issues:

1. What were the latest developments in aviation surfacing from the Europeans?

2. Could Bechtel help the emerging European Joint Aviation Authorities (JAA)?

3. Would I help place Bechtel on the list of "European" firms before the European Union (EU) agreement was finalized?

4. If the EU accepted Bechtel's help in its emergence, would I see to it that Bechtel continued to support the future work of the EU, especially in infrastructure?

I was particularly weary of the last issue because I couldn't believe that Bechtel would commit itself to any long-term association with the EU.

Stu assured me that for these tasks I had the blessing of Riley Bechtel and an open balance of funds for performing the job. I didn't believe that Bechtel could be so visionary; hence I insisted that Riley Bechtel, the heir apparent to both the chairmanship and presidency of the company, write me a memorandum specifying my tasks and subsequent funding for them. Stu smiled and indicated that I was pushing a bit too hard.

"I don't trust Bechtel," I replied, "at the first opportunity and after all my contacts begin to trust me, the rug will be pulled from under my feet." Stu agreed that historically Bechtel was prone to act that way. "Stu," I said, "I have work to do. I like these new tasks, but I want to make certain that I, you, and Bob Jackson receive the appropriate support from Riley."

Soon after our meeting I wrote a fax to Riley asking for greater details, his intention, and what funding was allocated to me. I copied Stu and Bob.

"You will not get a reply," were Stu's last words as he left me in his office. I went back to my hotel room at the Gloucester, Harrington Gardens, off Cromwell Road. I was expecting to return to the Continent in three days on the following Monday.

At 8:30 a.m. the next morning, Stu Hill telephoned me. A faxed memorandum had arrived from Riley Bechtel stating that I had his support, what funds had been allocated for the tasks, a job number to charge my time and expenses, informing me that Bob Jackson was to be my line manager, and that the English legal firm associated with Bechtel in London would support the effort.

"I have never witnessed that before in my 25 years at Bechtel," added Stu over the phone. He asked when was I coming in and said he would have an office assigned to me when I arrived. It was Thursday and I arrived at Hammersmith at eleven o'clock. In my new office, Stu's secretary, Jane, had piled a stack of contacts and files for me to review; she had also left me a note informing me that I was to share her with Stu. A few minutes after seeing Stu and getting my bearing for the project I returned to my new office to begin the process of untangling the tasks ahead, planning the appointments, and making sense of what I was plowing through.

Stu took me to Ken Turnbull's office to introduce me to the general manager of Bechtel London. I had known Ken Turnbull in Beijing, PRC because he was the on-site manager of Bechtel PRC. Ken was English, a senior vice president of Bechtel, and an able and visionary man who was mostly frustrated by Bechtel's attitude in Europe, especially from a firm that engaged in global projects and prided itself as being international. Ken greeted me and assured me that if I needed anything I was to let him know.

By mid-afternoon I had decided to stay in London for a week then head to Brussels to meet with the new director of the EU's Department of Aviation, Mr. Ellwood Martin. I wrote a telex and asked Jane to dispatch it to Mr. Martin's office.

Finland and the National Plan

As I was preparing to follow through with Mr. Ellwood Martin, Jane, Stu Hill's secretary, gave me a telex. I read it. It was from Bob Jackson informing me that he had signed the contract for the Finnish project and that I was to put every task in abeyance and fly to Helsinki as soon as possible. Just as I had finished reading the telex, the phone rang. It was Bob. "Raymond the Finnish economic planning project is most important for our department and for Bechtel." We discussed the contract and I agreed with Bob that it was not only important but also interesting. After writing a note to Stu I booked a flight to Helsinki for the next day and sent a telex to Mr. Jaaskelainen Kyosti, chair of the National Planning Commission informing him that I would be arriving the next day and that I had booked a room at the Ramada Hotel; I also gave him my flight and airline information.

Upon arriving at Helsinki International Airport, a driver with a sign bearing my name signaled me. After checking in at the Ramada, I was whisked to Espoo where the Commission was meeting in a small building that was part of the University of Helsinki. After the introduction I was briefed and handed a schedule. Was I happy with the schedule? I was asked. The work would be intense and the group was ready to participate fully to what was planned. I was given a stack of papers, an outline of what had been accomplished, and an invitation to dinner for that evening. By 1500 hours I was returned to the Ramada and informed that a driver would come for me at 1900 hours.

Once in my room and after room service brought me tea and a sandwich, I read what I'd been given. In brief the Commission wanted a plan for the economic development of Finland; the goal was to make the country a knowledge producer. They expected that the plan would help them develop the means for a knowledge-based revenue producing economy and that was exactly where my interest resided.

After I'd digested all data that had been given to me and after we'd had a few meetings and my ignorance had been dissipated a little, it was time to open the discussions for a long-term plan for Finland. In essence the recent history of Finland was that the nation had been finally rid of the oppressive presence of the USSR but that an expensive extortion toll had been paid for that liberation. Financially, Finland was at the point of bankruptcy and its Gross Domestic Product index was nearly zero. Apart from timber production, fishing, and some basic manufacturing the country was struggling to make ends meet. There were three firms that were attempting to be more productive. Nokia was moving from shoes and tires to something in IT, especially communication hardware. Marimekko textiles, iittala and Arabia glassware, two excellent ceramic and tableware manufacturers with a long history of aesthetic designs were ramping up production to improve their revenue from export. In the arena of construction, especially cold weather construction, both Hakka and Polar were known for their excellent work and were often sought after in the northern and southern hemispheres, below the Arctic and Antarctic circles, for their expert talents.

In advanced education, the University of Helsinki was being staffed with world-class members of the faculty with the aim of attracting more students and in strengthening its humanities and architectural design departments. The University of Tampere was focusing on science, especially physics and astrophysics and was beginning to make a good name for itself by being equated with Cambridge, Berlin, Princeton, and California Technical University (Caltech). Because Finland has very cold winters, I suggested other universities needed to be located to permit people to learn in locations that were not too distant from their residences. I further advanced the idea that attention should be also focused on the good Samis, the Laplanders, who lived above the Arctic, especially north of the city of Rovanimi.

In my review of what was at hand I saw great potential for major improvements. With some of the staff I went to visit the several entities mentioned and learned from their leadership what the current outlook was, especially for developing the knowledge industry.

In the committee sessions I suggested that one of the main tasks was to develop a plan to improve education, especially in the primary and secondary levels. It was implicit in my encouragement that foreign language needed to be taught in the early years of school. I suggested that both English/American and French languages needed to be taught at the earliest levels. My reasoning was that Finnish was a most difficult language and of not much value in the commercial and scientific world (the members agreed with no objections). In addition, I suggested that computer literacy would be a required asset in the not too distant future.

I stated in strong terms that education was the only viable investment that would always bring back good returns to the country. Education was to be the goal for the future, and that future started now and not later. As quickly as the Finns could reach the upper level of the 90th percentile in reading, writing, and all aspects of mathematics, the sooner the country would climb out of its economic depression. Finland had to move from having a large percentage of unskilled workers to one that was skilled and professional. I further suggested that elderly workers who could not be retrained for IT needed to be given funds and some necessary civic tasks to keep them at a comfortable level until they died. I cautioned the committee that this approach was neither communism nor socialism but simply accepting the fact that some people were too old to be retrained, especially since they had been bypassed by developments in the current knowledge industry.

The next stage was to encourage large and small firms to assume IT as possible options. For that to become the tool for national improvement, funding had to be available for entrepreneurs to do their thing. For funding from various sources was necessary to stabilize the political arena because it was needed to attract venture capital and make it available, to support angel capital with tax incentives, and to allow creativity to emerge from all sectors of the population. Finally Finland had to develop a good transportation system, a reliable infrastructure, and governmental policies to encourage and support the momentum of economic development for all sectors of the population. Again, I emphasized that education was the starting point for Finland.

Finally, I suggested that the tourism industry needed to be encouraged and given the support necessary for it to attract visitors and inevitably revenue. Tourists were the best ambassadors and eventual marketers for a nation.

The committee took what I had shared with it and established a ten-year plan with check stages wherein Finland would be moving ahead. The committee also considered joining the European Community and the common currency. Further more, the committee invited firms to send representatives to work with their members. A few weeks later, after my departure, Jaaskelainen Kyosti informed me that a bill had been drafted and sent to the *Eduskunta* (Legislature) then it would go the President for immediate action as Law. My understanding was that the bill was voted and became law and was promptly implemented.

When I left, a detailed plan had been prepared and I must say that in later years I was amazed at how specifically they followed the plan.

My time on this round in Finland spanned three weeks. I returned several times over the years and have become quite familiar with the country to the point where I would not mind residing somewhere in this lovely and functional piece of Nordic real estate. In later years, I was invited several times again to review what had been accomplished.

Brussels, Paris, and the Eurotech Complex

When I returned to London and sorted out my in-box, Jane told me that I was to head to Paris soon. I agreed, but decided first to return to San Francisco to see Emily and tend to some personal chores. Two weeks later I returned to London and had not been at the Hammersmith Bechtel office more than a few moments before my traveling orders materialized. Jane offered me a cup of tea and a small sandwich. I started to eat and was chatting with her when, a few minutes later, Howard Wahl, director, senior vice president, and manager of Bechtel Paris, telephoned me. He wanted me to come directly to Paris the following Monday for a meeting with a gentleman who was interested in creating a private science park. "Howard, I can be in Paris towards the end of the week but I need to be in Brussels first," I informed him.

"Raymond, Mr. Charles Osborne, an American living in Paris, wants a meeting on Tuesday morning," he replied. I thought about it for a moment then replied that I could be at the Paris office for an early meeting but after lunch I wanted to grab the train to Brussels. It was fine. Howard would arrange the meeting for nine o'clock on Tuesday. Before the end of the day, the EU director of aviation, Mr. Martin, had returned my telex and affirmed that he would meet with me on Wednesday morning in his office.

The next morning I returned to the office to finish looking through the stack of contacts that Jane had piled on my desk. Stu came in and asked me if I would have a late lunch with him and his wife. Jane came over and asked me if I had any correspondence for her. "Give me 30 minutes, Jane," I said. I wrote a telex to Bob Jackson informing him of the plans ahead and about Wahl's request. I wrote a telex to Pan American Airlines in New York asking for access to their research facilities in Berlin. Then I made a few phone calls to my IASP contacts in France, especially Pierre Nöe and Dominique Fache. At 1:00 p.m. Stu asked me if I was ready to join him. After grabbing some papers and informing Jane that I would phone her every day, and after giving her the name and phone of Ligia Zelaya, my Girl Friday in San Francisco, I followed Stu. We hailed a taxi, drove by his apartment and were joined by his wife, then headed for Covent Garden to eat at Rule's, an historic, charming, outstanding, and authentic English restaurant.

With pheasant and swedes (rutabagas) as the main course and accompanied with an English wine from Sussex county we enjoyed our fine lunch. I had known that the English made a good quality wine but I did not know how good it was. The pinot noir was superb with a chewy feel and a taste that lingered on the palate and drifted up the nose. Our conversation dealt with what was developing in Europe. The European Economic Community (EEC) was being metamorphosed into the European Union (EU), a tightly agreed union of a dozen nations under a directorate located in Brussels and a Parliament located in Strasbourg. Europe was attempting to actively change its nationalistic mentality to a loose federation-type union. Stu suggested that I get acquainted with the directorates of the emerging EU.

In aviation, a major force was surfacing in Aerospatiale, the incubator of Airbus Industries, which was expected to be a major challenger to Boeing, Lockheed, and other American and Canadian firms. Funded directly by the various EU governments, Airbus had little financial worries and could jump developmental hurdles with ease and few monetary worries. In the UK, British Aerospace Company (BAC), later to become British Aerospace Enterprise (BAE), although a partner with Airbus, was also an independent designer and manufacturer of aircraft for both civil and military clients.

Airports and airlines were going through some momentous changes in Europe. British commercial airports were being turned over to a quasi-private company called British Airports Authority (BAA). This meant that the government no longer controlled either the day-to-day operations or the future planning and budgets of the commercial airports. British Airways (BA), the flag carrier of the UK, was privatized. Several commuter lines were either consolidated into Midland Airways or spun off as private trunk airlines. Into this field entered a new private airline, Virgin Atlantic, which was started by the young entrepreneur Richard Branson, who owned a record company. Virgin Atlantic was to attempt to become a direct competitor to BA initially on the Atlantic routes.

To top these changes in industry and government, it was also apparent that the USSR was crumbling and its European satellites would be spun off to become independent nations no longer under the umbrella of the Soviet Union. The first crack in the breakup of the USSR occurred with the opening of the Berlin Wall in November 1989 (I had arrived in Berlin two days after the wall was opened and was informed that the first person to escape was an East German Border guard); the length of the barriers totaled about 110 miles (160 kilometers). It was hailed as a historic event that symbolized the collapse of Communism in Eastern Europe. In October 1990, East and West Germany were united into the single non-Communist country of Germany. Berlin was reunited into a single city. By 1992, nearly all of the Berlin Wall had been removed; and of course on 31 December 1990, the USSR ceased to exist. On

1 January 1992 Russia and 14 republics created the Commonwealth of Independent States (CIS).

It was in this dynamic environment that I was asked to operate. My mission was to learn what was emerging, to develop a network of associations with the new EU department heads, introduce Bechtel to the EU and to the private companies that were surfacing every day, and to offer Bechtel's services to governments and private industries. I had already seen to it that the USSR was in my sight; what I needed to do was to establish Bechtel as a bona fide European company.

Both Stu Hill and Bob Jackson gave me carte blanche to move into the European scene as I saw fit. Moreover, Howard Wahl had already begun to present Bechtel to several department heads and ministers of the EC. With my hotel reservations confirmed at the Metropole Hotel in Brussels, I made additional reservations for Paris at the Pavilion de La Reine located at the Place des Vosges (les Colonnades) after booking an early flight on BA from London to Paris Orly for Monday. My intention was to arrive early in Paris, check in at the hotel, then go the Bechtel office to have a preliminary meeting in the afternoon with Howard Wahl to learn what Mr. Charles Osborne had in mind and find out where Howard had arrived in his attempt to place Bechtel on the EC agenda.

Once all these arrangements had been made, I took the train from Liverpool Street station to Cambridge to visit with Nan Youngman. Sunday morning I would attend the Eucharist at Ely Cathedral, and then have lunch at the Old Fire House Restaurant. Mid-afternoon I would catch the returning train to London to make myself ready for the hop to the Continent the next day. Laundry needed to be tended to, plus I wanted to have dinner with Patrick Gavigan, a dear friend that I had met at Nell McVeigh's ranch in St. Helena. Fortune did shine its face on me and my plan turned out exactly as I had expected with one additional gift: I was joined at lunch by Bishop Peter Walker and his wife. Bishop Walker and his wife, Jean, were delightful people. He was diocesan bishop of Ely (Cambridgeshire) and a most interesting and intellectually rich person who was quite knowledgeable about philosophy and art, and friends with Bishop George Bell of WWII fame and a sponsor of

T.S. Eliot, Dietrich Bonheoffer, and a keen student of Archbishop William Temple. I maintained my friendship with Peter and was often on the phone with him discussing issues that were important to both of us. I look to him as the last of my mentors. Bishop Walker died in 2009.

The flight to Paris was quick and painless. After checking in at the Pavilion de la Reine, I hopped the Metro for the Bechtel Office. Howard Wahl greeted me and we sat in his office for the briefing. Mr. Charles Osborne, an American who lived in Paris, wanted to create a science park near Nîmes in the Department du Gard. Osborne wanted Bechtel's assistance in this project. According to his introductory letter Osborne had the necessary funds to begin the preliminary search for land and for the feasibility study. It all seemed quite on the level at this stage and Osborne would be at the meeting in the morning at nine o'clock. Howard and I decided to continue the discussion on both Osborne's project and Bechtel's sudden interest in the EC over lunch, so we crossed the street to the Entrecôte Restaurant, which specializes in filets. Howard was concerned that Bechtel's executive board of directors was being difficult because it felt that the EC was not important enough for the company to warrant all the effort required to establish itself as a bona fide European firm, although it had become registered in France as Bechtel France! But to some members of the executive board France was not the EC. After all Bechtel was a well-known firm and possessed a reputation that should have opened doors without having to appear to be a European enterprise. Howard understood that the EC was simply attempting to give itself an identity. In addition, the EC was looking at giving the domestic firms a chance to compete without being overwhelmed by foreign corporations: the EC was looking for a level playing field for continental companies to operate on. I encouraged Howard not to abandon his vision of establishing Bechtel as a local company and I added that I would see him the next morning at the meeting. We decided to revisit this subject when I had more time and less on my plate.

I took the Metro to Le Forum des Halles to say hello to Charles Vinick, vice president of operations who was working for the Cousteau Group and was building a mock deep-water-and-space theme park to show visitors how it was to dive deep in the ocean and rise high up into space. Much as the model and the lectures were excellent, it did not attract enough visitors to make the project financially worthwhile. A couple of years later the Cousteau exhibition was closed, and Paris was that much the poorer for not having supported it. Perhaps if the experience had been placed in another city and did not have to compete with all that Paris offers, and especially the new and gaudy Disney Park, it might have had a chance to survive.

Arriving at 8:30 the next morning, I was directed to the conference room to await Mr. Charles Osborne. Osborne arrived promptly and was accompanied by a friend who was in finance and who had worked in London for many years. Osborne was a tall man with an overbearing demeanor, a loud voice, and horribly bad French, which he insisted on using. The project was a science park to be built on a pie-shaped piece of land in Nîmes. We were assured that the mayor of Nîmes and his administration were firmly behind the project that Osborne was hoping to create there.

When he completed the presentation, I asked him if he was willing to let Bechtel review the site he had picked and prepare the feasibility study. No feasibility study would be necessary because his consortium had already decided that the land was acceptable, the mayor had approved the use of the land, and anyway, he was certain that Bechtel would find the land perfect for the project.

I sighed audibly because I had heard those words of assurance before when I dealt with clients. "Mr. Osborne, I want to look at the property and I insist that a feasibility study be prepared before Bechtel or I will commit to converting your hopes and aspirations into a science or technical park."

Osborne looked at Wahl as if to ask for his support to shut up this pipsqueak. Wahl's response was that Bechtel had to do what it had to do, and that Dr. Hoche-Mong's request was not out of the ordinary. "We can go to Nîmes tomorrow, doctor," Osborne blurted out.

"I can't. I have an appointment in Brussels that cannot be postponed."

"But this is important Raymond," Osborne said with an imploring tone and addressing me by my first name.

"I can be in Nîmes next Monday and not any earlier," I replied to him.

"OK. I'll come pick you up at your hotel for the earliest flight to Nîmes. We can return back to Paris the same day. I have a friend who can pick us up at the airport and show us around the property." We settled that bit of travel planning and moved to finances, always a touchy issue, and a minefield that requires careful maneuvering. Osborne gave Wahl a check for $10,000 as a retainer that would be placed in his account for the project. It was nearly lunchtime and Charles Osborne invited us to join him for lunch at the Paris Ritz Hotel.

After lunch and a few minutes of conversation with Howard Wahl, I took the Metro back to my hotel and packed my bag; I had the hotel call a taxi, which whizzed me to the Gare de l'Est to catch the train to Brussels. In Brussels I was to be met by Mme. Eliane Camus, Kalaa Mpinga's mother-in-law. Kalaa was Zairian, now Congolese, and an intern at Bechtel who was assigned to work with me on some projects. Married to Caroline, an Afro-Belgian beauty, Kalaa and his wife were in America to improve their education and professional skills. Kalaa was an agronomist and Caroline was attending classes at Heald College in graphic design. Kalaa was a tall, handsome African who spoke with an impeccable French accent, had a fine sharp sense of humor, and was an embryonic entrepreneur very much interested in benefiting his country. Kalaa was one of the protégés of President Mobutu Sese Seko who ruled the nation as a dictator until 1997. Kalaa had asked his mother-in-law Eliane Camus to be my guide in Brussels and that she did admirably (I'm sorry to say that I have lost contact with her).

When I arrived in Brussels I was looking for an elderly black woman of African origin holding up a poster with my name written on it. Surprise! Eliane was a most attractive fair-skinned blond woman in her late forties or early fifties who spoke fine French. Carry-on luggage in hand, Eliane escorted me to her Citroen sedan parked just outside the exit gate of the station. Off we went to the Metropole Hotel where I had booked a room. After I registered at the hotel and deposited my belongings, Eliane met me in the bar for a glass of fine Belgian beer.

Belgium is a country whose national drink is beer, which comes in many flavors and many tastes. I chose a dry hoppy beer and Eliane selected a raspberry flavored beer, which I found repulsive — but to each his taste. After the beer and much conversation I suggested that Eliane join me for dinner. She accepted and we walked across the street then turned left onto a small square that was framed by four- or five-storey 18-century empire style houses that reminded me of postcards. At the square, Eliane directed me to an excellent restaurant. Dinner was outstanding as was the Flemish beer that accompanied it. We returned to the Metropole and stopped in the bar for a Cognac and further conversation before she left to return home. I went to bed for a good night's sleep to be ready for the next day's meetings with the several directors of EC.

The story I obtained from Eliane was that she had fallen in love with a Congolese diplomat stationed in Brussels. After a tempestuous courtship that led to the birth of her daughter Caroline, the diplomat was returned to Kinshasa for an important government meeting. Late in the night after the meeting in Kinshasa, Eliane's lover was found dead, probably murdered by enemies of President Mobutu. Mobutu sent Eliane sufficient funds for a lifetime of comfortable support for her and for her daughter, even though she had never married the diplomat. Eliane was Roman Catholic but a great admirer of the Greek Orthodox liturgy and of astrology; in fact she made a small living as an astrologist. I did not have her tell my fortune; although she told me several times that she would do it as a favor to me. "Thank you, but no thanks," I would cordially reply. Eliane was a delightful person who often met and escorted me when I had to visit Brussels.

When I finished a breakfast of Belgian waffles soaked in raspberry syrup accompanied with a side dish of sausages, I informed the concierge that I did not need a taxi to take me to the EC complex. I poured myself another cup of coffee and as in most of Western Europe it was delicious. Breakfast finished, I headed for the EU complex of buildings, which were not too far from my hotel. Walking to the aviation unit was enjoyable and refreshing in the cool morning air. I arrived at the Department of Aviation and found Mr. Ellwood Martin's office. I had a few moments to spare. At the appointed time, Mr. Martin's secretary escorted me to his office.

Martin was a tall Scot who had a lovely brogue. He had been in aviation most of his life, starting as a pilot with Caledonia Airways and when that company was absorbed by BA he continued flying the line. After, as a second career, he earned a degree from the London School of Economics and was given a position with BA in system management and control, a department that was responsible for training pilots, dispatchers, and route planners, and in tracking and managing aircraft traffic over Europe and the Atlantic. When the EC was organized, he was hired in the new office of air traffic management. Martin's task was to coordinate the air traffic of 15 nations, many of which were not members of the EC. When the EU was indicating that it would emerge in 1990, Martin was appointed by the embryonic European Parliament as Director of the Aviation Department with responsibility for managing aviation traffic on the Continent, even traffic that originated from non-member nations. When Martin took over the task of managing air traffic, the skies of Europe were fragmented and control was practically impossible because each nation insisted on controlling its own airspace. Martin's approach was to consolidate the management of air traffic under one authority and only one authority. Britain was the first nation to accept such control because it had had enough trouble with the Spanish Air Traffic Control Center managing the space over the North Atlantic. Spain and France followed the British decision soon after when they discovered the wisdom of having one authority to oversee the North Atlantic routes. It was common knowledge that removing the management of the North Atlantic from the Spaniards was a move in the right direction because it removed the system from the control of a temperamental group. Soon the other members signed on and then non-members accepted a single authority after a few aircraft collisions occurred over Romania and Norway.

Martin had obtained approval for a single authority for the airspace over Europe, but the task was still unmanageable because the technology was not in place. ICAO had suggested that Martin contact the American FAA, but that organization was in dire trouble under the leadership of President Ronald Reagan who had slashed its funding appropriation and had terminated the employment of (really he had fired) 14,000 air traffic controllers. The Reagan mismanagement of aviation caused grave consequences for both airline and general aviation traffic because the congestion in the skies was impeding the safe flow of traffic from point to point. Airline revenues dwindled by 15 to 20 percent at a time when commercial airlines had committed themselves to new aircraft because of forecast increased passenger and freight demands. For general aviation, the Reagan action had started to destroy the entire small aircraft industry. Often flight plans for a particular flight had to be filed 36 to 48 hours ahead with Flight Service. Over that length of time and circumstances, weather and needs can change so much that the original flight plan must be cancelled and a new one filed. On several occasions several flight plans were filed before Flight Service accepted one, and even then it was often revised several times in flight. The problem was chaotic, irritating, and very costly for all aviation.

My own experience on one occasion when I was trying to depart Santa Barbara IFR produced a 36-hour delay that eventually forced me to take off into a cloud hole VFR because I could not receive the necessary clearance. So Martin was looking for help from a major firm to design and engage subcontractors to make the management possible. Bechtel was one management firm that could fill his demand. Bechtel, however, was not a registered European firm and that was important to Martin and the EC. "Can Bechtel do the management job?" he asked.

My reply was positive and direct: "I will see to it that Bechtel registers also as a European firm before the EU is finalized at the end of the year." He accepted and assured me that Bechtel would be in the running for a bid once it became a European firm.

I walked back to my hotel to telephone Howard Wahl in Paris and then Ken Turnbull in London and lay before them the problem of parochialism that Bechtel was facing in Europe. Howard confirmed that he had already encountered this problem and was working with a German firm, Mannesmann, to develop an association that would lead to a merger-acquisition arrangement. He wanted to see me in his office when I returned to Paris. I was taking the train back to Paris on Friday morning and would remain in the City of Light until Osborne picked me up at the hotel.

The call to Turnbull produced little information. Turnbull could not see what difference it made if Bechtel was an American or a European firm; it produced excellent work and that was that. Well, as much as America would not let a European firm own more than 25% of an airline, the Europeans preferred to work with a domestic firm — this was a sign that the Continent was restyling its identity. It was obvious to me that soon after the EU was established, America would be faced with an enormous competitor, not only in the firm Airbus, but with many other firms and political entities. Europe was coming into its own and would soon establish its own uniform currency as a contender for global accreditation against the dollar. I could see that it was no longer the old docile Europe that waited for America to instruct it and guide it. Europeans had discovered that as a united body they could move about more easily to attain certain common goals, they could make decisions suitable for their needs, and they could look America in the eye as their power increased on the world's scene.

Back in Paris, I met with Howard Wahl who briefed me on the Mannesmann-Bechtel negotiations. Bechtel's CFO, Denis Slavich, who had a larger and more comprehensive world view, supported the European merger with Mannesmann, but not many other members of the board did so. The board could not see the value of a European presence, especially in association with a German firm.

That evening when I spoke with Bob Jackson (he was on the roof of his house repairing a gutter) he asked me to continue what I was doing and said that he would inform Riley Bechtel about the potential projects and about the firm becoming a European entity. He also informed me that the Maltese Consul General in San Francisco had called to have me visit Malta when my schedule permitted it. Apparently, the Honorable Charles J. Vassallo, Consul General of Malta, had heard me speak at a meeting and thought that the Government of Malta could use Bechtel to develop its economy in the arena of IT.

Eventually, I met Mr. Vassallo, who was later more intimately known to me as "Uncle Charlie," and who was a charming person and a permanent resident of San Bruno, California. Uncle Charlie owned a small manufacturing plant producing small fasteners and was also part-time consul of Malta. Malta was not that active diplomatically in California so Uncle Charlie, a Maltese citizen with dual nationality, was able to cover the position of Consul for Malta and also manage a business.

Bob would telex me the details and I could follow through whenever time permitted me to visit Malta. I then called Emily to give her an overview of what I had been doing (I called her every day) and mentioned that I might be going to Malta. She was happy that I would be going, and yet she was unhappy that she could not go because she'd always wanted to go to Malta.

Shoes, Olives, Art, Bari, and IT

The reader will recall that a few weeks after the IASP Conference in 1989 and the subsequent work in Montpellier, I assumed the Bari project in Italy. In Bari, Bechtel had supervised the construction of two buildings for the Tecnopolis Novus Ortus of Bari. Once the buildings were built the client wanted to expand Bechtel's service to create and also implant IT firms and then develop further scientific work. In essence this was a creative marketing effort to help Tecnopolis expand its programs. Bechtel's proposal to Bari through Enrique Diaz was to add several new buildings that the client did not feel were necessary, nor did I. I met, for the first time, the Director of Tecnopolis, Dr. Umberto Bozzo, in Montpellier, although I had heard his name and had been informed of his excellent work in Bari by Dominique Fache. We discussed his problem, and I proposed that we develop a test marketing approach to see what IT firms might be interested in establishing themselves in Bari or in the region of Puglia but not specifically on Tecnopolis ground.

Two months after presenting the paper (in Venice) that suggested that Tecnopolis continue its building expansion (a position with which I disagreed emphatically), I was given the program management of the Tecnopolis and was invited by Umberto to come to Bari, Italy, in September of 1990. I arrived on a Saturday afternoon and was met at the airport by Umberto who took me to the Nicoli Sheraton Hotel. He felt that I needed to rest that evening but said that he would come for me the next day after church and we would go to his office to plan the program for Tecnopolis.

Bari is the capital of the Puglia (Apulia) region, one of Italy's political regions or departments. Bari, the largest city of the department, is a trade and manufacturing center surrounded by 19 communities or villages of which Vallenzano is the most active and the home of Tecnopolis. As early as the 400s B.C., Bari was an important town and a major seaport on the Adriatic Sea. Bari has been destroyed and rebuilt three times by invaders. During WWII Bari and Brandisi were bombed repeatedly to scuttle both the Italian and German war ships berthed there. Brandisi was a launching port for the Allied forces when they invaded Albania and moved on to Greece and further into Eastern Europe. Brandisi and the territory north of the city was also the center for making what were commonly called "Spaghetti Westerns" starring Clint Eastwood and other eventually famous actors.

Each year, thousands of pilgrims visit the Church of St. Nicholas, which was founded in 1087. The Bari throne in Bari, Italy, may have been created for a meeting of Pope Urban II and church leaders in 1098. The throne extends the tradition of working in precious metals to stone carving, with figures sometimes cut virtually in the round. Other marble furnishings with relief images include pulpits, choir railings, shrines, and table altars. The original Saint Nicholas of Christmas fame is buried there.

On Sunday afternoon when we met in his office, Dr. Bozzo gave me an outline of what he had in mind and I offered suggestions for achieving his goal. In essence Umberto wanted to attract IT firms and incubators to Bari and to the Puglia region. I added that because Tecnopolis was approaching its first decade of existence, it was time to consider what the next ten years would be like. We agreed on the strategy I suggested and shook hands. It was now late Sunday afternoon, so after our long meeting Umberto invited me to have dinner at his home and to meet his family. Umberto announced that he would come for me at 2000 hours; that was 90 minutes hence. He drove me back to the Nicoli Sheraton Hotel so that I could refresh myself.

Before I get lost in the repast I was given at his house, I want to describe parts of what developed in the Bari Region because of our influence upon it.

Tecnopolis acted not only as a creative force but also as a catalyst for the emergence of new programs.

Umberto, a graduate in engineering from the University of Bologna (UB), one of Italy's finest, became interested in IT when he was working for the developing European Economic Community (EEC) market in Brussels under his mentor Dr. Riccardo Petrella, EEC Director General, Science, Research, and Development. I met Petrella in his office in Brussels, an office that was wall-to-wall books. Riccardo was fluent in six languages, a regular contributor to *Le Monde Diplomatique*, head of the Future and Advance Systems for Technologies (FAST) program, and professor of economics at UB and the Sorbonne, Paris. Riccardo was an extraordinary man and I always remember his keen sense of humor and agile brain. I went to meet Riccardo because Umberto suggested that it was important for me to know him.

My appointment with Riccardo was scheduled for 1600 in his office and after dinner and several cognacs at his house I returned to my hotel at 1:30 a.m. the next morning with a head filled with exciting knowledge and hope that the world would eventually find peace. Now, at least once a year I receive a note from Riccardo and a copy of his latest book or article written in French, English, Italian, or Spanish. At present, Riccardo is retired but still teaching at the Sorbonne and continues as a consultant to the current EU.

A few years after he started with the EU, Umberto Bozzo was recruited by the Italian government to establish the first science park in the country. After much research, Umberto decided to implant a science park in Bari and "partner" it to the small University of Bari. Naming the science park with the Italian corresponding term and spelling of Tecnopolis, it became a generator of IT in the Mezzogiorno part of Italy. Tecnopolis was the catalyst that changed Bari and Puglia in a major way. When I was introduced to Tecnopolis, Umberto was at the height of his success having been its director general for nearly a decade. Umberto now wanted to move further ahead in IT and especially to reform and make improvements in the region and also in the towns surrounding Bari. What was there to do in Bari or Puglia and how were we to do it? We decided that we needed to import and implant other IT firms in the region and in the town of Vallenzano, the home of Tecnopolis and to see what could be done with the small local industries and businesses. Soon we were able to attract International Business Machines (IBM) and Apple. Digital followed within six months of Apple's implantation. Not long after these three IT firms arrived, the Italian Space Agency (ISA) with Fiat and Augusto purchased land west of Bari in Puglia and Basilicata to develop a space control and design complex working hand in hand with Tecnopolis, the European Space Agency (ESA), and the American National Air and Space Administration (NASA).

But before that land could be useful to ISA, approximately 330 olive trees had to be transplanted or they would be destroyed. Many of these trees were 300 years old or more, give or take a decade here and there. Planted when the region was less populated and land ownership was not too strictly defined, they were scattered over a large area. The government of Puglia, at Tecnopolis' insistence, had identified several thousand hectares of appropriate land for these trees if they could be transplanted and relocated. A daunting task for us to accomplish if we did not want the trees destroyed. Umberto obtained some funds from the EU and from several olive and olive oil cooperatives. But could the trees be relocated? Experts from the EU assured us that the Puglia trees were of excellent quality and needed to be saved if at all possible.

After placing several telephone calls to universities in the United States I was directed to the faculty at the University of California, Davis. Because California is one of the major producers of olives and olive oil from trees transplanted from Italy, Greece, and Spain the faculty had the knowledge to help us with our problem. With the help of the faculty and the mechanical support of the construction company of Gianfranco Dioguardi we were able to transplant 230 trees and suffered a total tree casualty of only five — the remaining trees left in their original place were to be tended by several farmers. The new Apuglia Cooperative has grown to the point where it now exports olive oil to firms in California, New York, New Orleans, and other centers of good cooking under the name of "Apuglia's Tecnologically Cold Pressed Olive Oil" produced in Bari, Italy. The pits are ground for fuel in a cogeneration plant producing electricity for small cottage industries.

Part of my task for Tecnopolis was to see what the science center could do to improve the lot of small businesses in the region around Bari. The Bari region is known for its small cottage industry of shoe manufacturing. There were several shoe manufactures within the city limit of Bari and a couple of them were not too far from Tecnopolis in the suburb of Vallenzano. I asked Umberto if he could take me to one or two of the shoe cottage factories located nearby. Assigning Mario Marinazzo, his second in command who drove an old Morris car (no one in Italy would steal such a dilapidated car he assured me), we went to a small seven-person factory near the coastal village of Trani. Mario selected that one because he knew the family and assured me that it was one of the better shops and one of the less financially endowed in the region.

The factory was making shoes for one of the major Italian name brands. The shoes were exquisitely handmade. The grandfather, who was a cobbler by trade, still ran the family team. All his workers were related to him with the exception of the sewing machine mechanic who was on loan from the manufacturer and had the task of making certain that the machines worked properly during their high usage of the day.

I watched the operations being performed from the initial cutting of the leather to the final polishing and boxing of the shoes; they made both men's and women's shoes but mostly women's. Grandfather Roberto and father Mateo were kind to explain to me every step of the production. Marketing was not a problem because they produced all they could on demand and had a backlog of three to four weeks supplying the name brand firms. The team spoke no English, but kindly listened to my halting Italian. Mario spoke good English and was a great interpreter.

"May I ask a few questions?" The team was pleased with my interest in their small family business. "What is your most delicate and tedious operation and which one is prone to failure because of a simple misstep?" I asked.

Without batting an eye, grandfather Roberto informed me that cutting the leather was the most tedious and delicate.

"Why?"

He replied, "Because we have to cut the entire pair from the same leather. If we do not, the shoes will not have matching leather patterns. No; they will look awful!" He grimaced to make his point. I looked at him but then he turned serious and nudged his son Mateo to explain the cutting operation.

"Each pair of shoes must be cut from the same piece of leather, and each skin can produce only a certain number of pairs of shoes. What leather is not used for making the shoes is obviously wasted but we still have to pay for it because we buy skins by weight," he shook his head and pressed his hands as if he were going to pray. "Waste is not good, and the cutting operation produces the most waste even when we do not make mistakes."

He further explained the cutting operation, the scissors and how sharp they had to be, and that it took training to be able to eyeball how many pairs of shoes could be cut from one skin. "How many pairs of shoes can be cut from one skin?" I asked as I touched the skins that lay on the cutting table. Mateo showed me the waste bin with several pieces of skins, and many had a lot of leather still left for other uses. "What do you do with these pieces of leather?"

"Some parts may be used for decorations and in wing-tip styled shoes, other parts can be used for small purses, money pouches, and key holders but not much profit comes from these items," Mateo informed me. I looked at the skins again and spread my hand on one piece to feel the suppleness and see the color tone in the light of the nearby window. These were wonderful pieces of fine leather.

"How many pairs can you cut out of this skin?" I asked. It was a piece approximately 60 by 50 centimeters (24x19 inches).

"At most four pairs of shoes," he replied after examining it carefully.

"Do you have a computer in the factory?"

Both Roberto and Mateo rolled their eyes skyward and jabbered in rapid Italian. Mario stepped into the conversation and informed me that they had no computer because this was a family factory and not one of the American factories that can produce millions of shoes per day.

"I understand Mario but please ask them if they have any objections to computers."

"No, no!" Mateo spoke slowly to me, then in English, "We no have computer. Too much money and we no have money."

Taking a look at the entire operation and seeing each employee attentive to his or her task, I asked him if I could borrow the piece of skin that I was playing with and which could only produce four pairs of shoes from a typical shoe pattern.

Of course I could borrow it but what was I going to do with it?

"I want to see if a computer assisted design (CAD) program could do better than four pairs of shoes," I spoke in my best Italian and made certain that Mario explained my intention by repeating what I said.

"Per favore. Accettare cuoio (please accept the leather)!" and he pressed the leather in my hand and gave me a broad smile.

After obtaining the pattern for a pair of men's shoes, I thanked them and went directly with Mario to Tecnopolis. Being excited I rushed to ask the CAD technicians what they could do with the area of the leather. The supervisor of the CAD group, Augusto, took one look, took a few measurements, re-measured, and placed the leather on the work plate. "Come back in an hour," he said to me.

Less than an hour later he called me on the phone as I was chatting with Umberto. Umberto and I walked to Augusto's office and we were greeted with a piece of paper that matched the surface area of the skin and on it where outlines of six pairs of shoes that were obtained from the typical pattern given to me. Leaving Umberto in his office, Mario and I took his car and sped to the shoe factory to share with Roberto and his son Mateo what a CAD system could do to reduce his waste and increase his profit. After the jubilant reception and a few small glasses of Grappa, Roberto asked if Tecnopolis could help him acquire a CAD system and would they be able to instruct his son. That was exactly the goal and charter of Tecnopolis. Mario took the lead and in rapid Italian settled the approach and offered to lend Roberto the funds to purchase a Macintosh computer with a CAD attachment. Until the computer arrived, Tecnopolis would help Roberto and Mateo prepare several leather skins and also furnish the training.

Back at Tecnopolis I faxed Apple in Paris and gave the marketing manager, a friend I knew, the option to help the cottage people in Bari. By morning he had a computer with CAD in a DHL package for Bari. It arrived the next day and soon Tecnopolis staff was training Roberto and Mateo. Apple charged less than $2,000 for the equipment and offered reasonable installment payments.

Soon after Tecnopolis helped Roberto's shoe factory, other small family shoe manufactures approached Mario to inquire if the same innovation could be made available to them. Tecnopolis proved able to help others become adept at using technology in their manufacturing processes. A side effect of this venture was that Apple Computer established a presence in Vallenzano not only to promote their hardware and software but also to work closely with Tecnopolis in research, development, and especially in training.

Umberto was keen to develop incubators in the Bari/Vallenzano region of Puglia. He assigned an associate to work with me to achieve that goal. Dr. Annamaria Annicchiarico was director of research and development and given the specific task of nurturing incubators in IT. Annamaria worked diligently and creatively to encourage entrepreneurs in establishing small promising firms in various niches of the larger metropolitan region. I helped her refine her strategy, draft her marketing plan, and begin contacting potential people who were interested in creating incubators. Annamaria was quite successful in establishing and nurturing a half dozen incubating enterprises located in and around Bari.

Another program suggested by Umberto was the development of technologies that would be of interest to the Italian (and European) space agencies (ISA and ESA). For this task Umberto assigned Dr. Luciano Schiavoni, Director of Technological Development. The ISA was establishing a complex in a region of Basilicata, not too far from Bari. Luciano traveled to California and together we went to Pasadena to meet with members of NASA at Jet Propulsion Laboratory. After intense and detailed discussions, plans were drawn to develop a support complex connected with Tecnopolis; less than a year later, in 1991, Tecnopolis became a key player in the ISA's program. With some assistance from me, we brought into play Boeing Space Division and confirmed a protocol agreement with Tecnopolis.

Because of the work and enthusiasm that Tecnopolis was generating in the Bari region, the University of Bari was forced by the Ministry of Education to spin off its technological college and with the help from Tecnopolis create a Polytechnic University in Vallenzano. The reaction from the University was not positive, especially towards Tecnopolis, which it considered to be its opponent and antagonist. Approximately 2,000 students were siphoned from the University of Bari to create the Polytechnic University. The Minister of Education in Rome made Dr. Gianfranco Dioguardi, who was president of the board of Tecnopolis and mentor to Umberto, dean of the civil engineering department of the emerging Polytechnic University. This appointment did not further endear Dr. Bozzo to the University. But the problem was not so much that the University of Bari was losing a number of its students but that its prestige appeared to be waning — which was not really the case. In two years the student body of the University of Bari increased by 3,000 students, and the Polytechnic University added another 2,000 students. Bari was proving to be a dynamic location where both education and technological advancement were charting a good future for Puglia and the Mezzogiorno part of Italy. Caught in the crunch of this educational pressure cauldron between the University of Bari, the Polytechnic University, and the Ministry of Education, was the dynamic Umberto Bozzo. Over a glass of wine one evening I warned Umberto that his days were limited because of what was developing in education. He smiled and agreed but admitted that he needed to move on to other challenges, issues, and projects. Umberto was hoping to start his own firm and begin the process of slowing down a bit.

In 1994 Dr. Umberto Bozzo came to the Goose and Turrets to discuss his situation vis-à-vis his role at Tecnopolis. Dear Umberto was ready to abandon the Tecnopolis, especially because Professor Gianfranco Dioguardi had resigned as president of the board of Tecnopolis and also as dean at the Poly Tech, and the Ministry of Education assigned a new rector for Bari University. The new rector was totally uninterested in what Tecnopolis was offering to the University and to the community, and in fact viewed Tecnopolis as an albatross around his neck because it appeared to lure students away from classical education and into modernism and science. For a while the rector of the Technical University was supportive of Tecnopolis. At the start of the new semester in the autumn of 1993, the Ministry of Education promoted the rector of the University of Bari by making him also the rector of the Poly-technic University and transferred the previous rector to Naples. This appointment placed the two institutions in conflict with each other but under the same leadership. In December 1994, Umberto submitted his resignation from Tecnopolis Novus Ortus.

My workdays in Bari, while Bozo was still director, were from Sunday to Sunday and the work began after Umberto and his family returned from Mass, but every so often I had a Sunday all to myself because the family went off to visit friends.

On one particular Sunday I was completely free. No appointments. No meetings. No unfinished work to do in my hotel room. Sunday dinner was often with the Bozzo family but I was not scheduled this time. I was free. The rental car company Avis had assigned me a red Lamborghini as a midsize automobile for my pleasure, and pleasure it was. It was my thought to drive towards Naples to visit some old haunts, and return via the coast towards the heel of Italy. Breakfast was a hearty meal at the Palace Hotel (I no longer stayed at the Nicoli Sheraton because it was too far from the city center) and my car was fueled for the fun drive to Naples. I was in a bit of a hurry be-cause I wanted to visit the city where, in my youth, I had met an angel by the name of Ivetta Arletta. I wanted to see the house on the hill of Santa Lucia, drink a Campari and relish again the few days I had spent in her house and enjoyed her warm hospitality. I knew that Ivetta had died many years ago, but still I wanted to visit her house, smell her flowers, and look at Naples and the enchanted Isle of Capri. Italians drive fast cars fast on excellent winding roads and I did the same. There was no good reason for me to nurse the Lam-borghini. I pushed it to over 150 kilometers per hour, pushed on some stretches way beyond that speed and relished every kilometer, every curve, and every squeal of the fat Pirelli tires.

Naples was in sight with a haze of yellow over it. Naples never did offer clean air for breathing. If the air was not heavy with a yellow tint it was not Naples. Over a hill I got a peek of the blue sea and a bit less yellow tint. There was a brisk breeze that pushed the smog inland and away from the coast. That was good, at least for me. Capri would be visible and the Santa Lucia would be clear and sparkling as I remembered it. After getting lost a few times in my attempt to reach my goal, finally I located the Corniche road that led me to the Santa Lucia district and to my destination. A right turn here, a left one there, a climb up a steep hill then a left turn parallel to the coast and there was Arletta's villa almost as it was several decades ago. I parked the car. It was mid-morning. I looked at the veranda, the flowers, and the house, especially the small balcony of my room. Someone entered the veranda, a woman my age dressed in white and with waist-length salt and pepper hair. She saw me and approached the balaustrata (balustrade) of the veranda. We looked at each other and I was a bit embarrassed thinking that I appeared to be peering into her house, which I was. In my best Italian I said "Excuse me but once I visited this house many years ago and my hostess was a wonderful lady whose name was Ivetta Arletta."

The woman on the veranda looked at me carefully then said with a genuine American Georgia accent, "You're an American?"

"Yes, ma'am," I replied. "Sorry to bother you but I was just admiring once again this wonderful villa and remembering the good time I had in it." I was about to leave but thought that it would be polite to introduce myself.

"We are the Cortlands from Atlanta, and I am Mrs. Eunice Cortland. We live here part of the year and currently own the villa." I said something polite and explained what I was doing in Italy. "Honey," Mrs. Cortland called to her husband, "Come meet this charming American from California."

Mr. Cortland joined his wife. He was a tall, heavy-set fellow with a thick crop of white hair. We greeted each other and exchanged thoughts about Italy. "Have you had brunch?" Mr. Cortland asked me. And so here I was once again invited into that lovely villa to share a meal.

The interior of the villa was nothing like it had been when Arletta was living in it. The furniture was Italian-modern and a bit informal. The art was different and the carpets were of the type purchased at Macy's or Lafayette. Yet I was warmly welcomed and the meal was good. The Cortlands had never met Arletta but had heard that she had lived in the house, was an author, and was quite wealthy.

After the brunch, the Cortlands gave me a tour of the house and I was pleased to step once again into what had been my room. After my tour and a cup of good Italian coffee I said goodbye and left the villa. Climbing into my Lamborghini I headed straight for the harbor. No *Pace* ship was in sight; the ship was probably refashioned into fenders for Toyota or Fiat cars! I had not expected to see the old passenger ship but looking at the dock where she once had been tied was sufficient for me.

A short drive south took me to the Yacht Club where Arletta used to have her yacht moored. I could not locate it and no one knew anything about it. With my visit completed I decided to drive the coast to the heel of Italy then turn north towards Bari. The return drive was done at a much slower speed, but not at a crawl. I was back in Bari by 1730 and had plenty of time to park my car, take a shower, and enjoy a cup of tea. There was a note for me at the concierge desk asking if I would have dinner with Umberto; it said also that I would be fetched. It had been a fine day and I was tired but the invitation sounded good. My brain was busy sorting out the historical from the contemporary impressions. I was much older than when I first saw Naples. My life had taken an unexpected turn and here I was working on a project, a project that I never imagined I would do. At the time I was in Naples, education was a distant option; a professional discipline was still further away from my thoughts. I knew little of what I would or wanted to do apart from flying.

The quest to fly seemed so infantile an idea now as I looked back. I am a little embarrassed that I could not offer anything more substantial than a passion for flying. Was there no depth in my thoughts? Was my vision so limited? After all, piloting an aircraft is not much of a contribution to society. In fact I never considered pilots to be the intellectual cream of hominoids. When conversation with pilots about airplanes or flying occurs, I would often run away. I wanted to fly, not talk about flying. Yet flying and knowing aviation has served me better than I would have expected, and it has even served society. My contribution has been minimal, but it is a contribution nevertheless, I think.

I waited for Umberto in the lobby with a Campari in hand and thought of the days long ago when I was in Naples and on my way to the New World. At the time I had no idea what the future would offer and then bring to my life. It has been a good life, an interesting life, a productive life, and a happy life. Looking back I could see little of what would emerge to give me a life that made me proud. Education had come my way to give me a deep understanding of what learning is. Fathering two great and admirable children gave me enormous satisfaction and honor. I thought of Emily, my wife, friend, business partner, avid co-explorer, and loving mate; I was immediately moved and phoned her even though it was early morning and she was in the midst of finishing breakfast at the B&B. She was happy to hear from me. Life, my job, my adventure, my financial state, and my hopes for the future were on a solid foundation. Onward I continued and hoped to continue for several more years. I did, however, consider retirement as a real possibility.

Umberto and Anna came for me as scheduled. We headed to a small restaurant by the Adriatic Sea a few miles south of Bari.

The Bozzo Family and Bari

Now it is time for me to return to my first encounter with the Bozzo family and dinner at their home. Umberto arrived a few minutes before 2000 hours. His house was located in a gated section of Bari where security was strict. His house was designed as a cross between a villa and a townhouse. The interior was beautifully appointed and displayed much original art. Paintings, sculptures, books, and tapestries rewarded the eyes in every room. The furniture was relatively modern and quite comfortable reflecting the Italian touch for design. Anna, Mrs. Bozzo, had greeted me in Italian because she spoke no English, but had a little French. She gladly accepted my Italian. Alessandro, the young son, spoke a great deal of English and was helpful when I needed him and when Umberto was not available. Anna and Umberto were quite familiar with the art in the Dordogne grotto and had visited many of the other grottos, but not Lascaux.

Dinner was typical Apulia fare and was accompanied by a local wine. Being present in my client's home was an unforgettable experience, especially because I was treated like one of the family. Anna was very much interested in the art of early human beings and she had collected quite a library on the subject. Dinner was excellent as expected, and I was surprised and touched to see the General Director of Tecnopolis helping Anna with the cooking. One of the memorable items was a plate of fresh mozzarella cheese served as part of the dessert course. The dessert was Anna-made cannelloni filled with hand-whipped rose-scented crema dulci. Espresso coffee, decaffeinated especially for me, was soon served accompanied with a small glass of clear grappa — the Italian brandy of the gods.

Until 1993 when I retired to start my own firm, G.T. Ideas, I worked on Technopolis as a Bechtel employee. When G.T. Ideas was created my very first client was none other than Tecnopolis, and I worked with it until 1995. There was something very exciting in the work with Tecnopolis and with Umberto. What made my work exciting was that we bounced ideas off each other and thus developed a vision for Tecnopolis and the economic improvement of Puglia.

Puglia is geographically a lovely region bordering the Adriatic Sea. The principal cities are Bari and Brandisi to the south. As I mentioned earlier, for those readers who like Clint Eastwood, they will recognize that many of his early Westerns were filmed in the rugged area north of Brandisi, a location that resembles Arizona or Western Texas. Puglia is an historically poor area that has always been regarded as economically deprived. Yet Puglia produces some of the best grapes for wine, extraordinary olives for oil, big, juicy, and tasty red tomatoes for fresh eating (but not for sauces), and an abundant harvest from the sea — if the Adriatic is cleaned and detoxified. By improving the economy, education, airport, and the coastal water, Puglia began to carry its own burden without funds from Rome and the strings that usually accompany such "charity." Progress, however, is difficult to achieve because it entails changes, and those who are married to the conservative political position often reject change. What Umberto was trying to do was bring about progress, economic improvement, and rekindle the innate spirit of Italian entrepreneurship.

Umberto, a native of Puglia, knew what would be possible and what his people would accept. I learned a great deal working with Umberto Bozzo. In particular what I learned was that patience is imperative in project development and that if one avenue is closed then a turn to another avenue may offer a clearer shot at the goal. After the complex debacle caused by the rector of Bari and the Technical University, Umberto resigned his position as Director General of Tecnopolis to create his own company. For a few years he offered his services as a consultant to emerging technical parks in Sicily, Sardinia, and Southern Italy. In the year 2000 he refocused his attention on Puglia to create an entrepreneur group interested in bringing about changes in the economy of the region by helping willing and creative people create new businesses. In my last conversation with Umberto he informed me that he had been hired to chair a group of successful entrepreneurs in Puglia and that soon he planned to have a major conference to discuss what economic advancements have been generated in the region, what new markets have been opened, and how they would promote the region in the international arena. Dr. Bozzo was obviously back in the saddle in Bari, his home, and was moving the community ahead to new goals, new achievements, and new ventures.

In March 2004, before my scheduled trip to China, Umberto emailed me asking if I would participate in a conference he was scheduling to explore new goals for Apulia's business people. I accepted and hoped that his plan would emerge soon. It did not. The new government of Prime Minister Silvio Berlusconi was too right wing to allow the plan proposed by Umberto to be developed.

The Maltese Misjudgment

When I returned to London after Bari, I was reminded that I still had to respond to the inquiry made by the Maltese Consul General in San Francisco, the Honorable Charles J. Vassallo. Mr. Vassallo had obtained an invitation for me from Prime Minister Eddie Fenech Adami to visit Malta for the purpose of helping the Maltese government nurture economic development through the implantation of IT on this small but strategically located Mediterranean island.

My schedule indicated that I had seven days before I was to meet Prince Hans-Adam Liechtenstein in Vaduz. A whole week was sufficient for me to set up appointments in Malta to investigate what it was that the government wanted Bechtel to do. I called the Minister for Economic Development and Infrastructure, the Honorable Michael Falzon, in Valletta. I was immediately connected to Mr. Falzon who was gracious to invite me to come when I was able. We agreed that I would arrive the following Monday and that I would stay five days. His office was prepared to make all the arrangements for me but asked that I make the flight reservations to suit me.

Mr. Sandro Raniolo, his calendar secretary and aide, would meet me at the Luqa International Airport, located a short distance from Valletta. I telephone Ligia Zelaya in San Francisco and asked her to make the flight reservations and to fax the details to Mr. Sandro Raniolo. I would go to Malta and spend five days in discussion with the authorities, but I also wanted to familiarize myself with Malta. Early in WWII, the aircraft flying me to England had landed in Malta in the dark of night for a refueling stop but I had seen very little of the two major islands of Malta and Gozo and nothing of tiny Comino and Cominotto Islands.

Once all arrangements had been made I was becoming excited about the trip. Several decades earlier I had set my two feet on this British possession but not for a moment had I imagined that I would return years later to check into the possibility for potential projects in this now-independent country.

My flight from London took me to Rome where I boarded Air Malta for the short flight to Malta. Malta is an island country in the Mediterranean Sea, about 60 miles (97 kilometers) south of Sicily. It is one of the most densely populated countries in the world. Malta was once a British crown colony but in 1964 Malta became an independent country. Valletta, on the island of Malta, is the capital with the main seaport and airport.

My arrival at Luqa International Airport was before noon in May 1990. Mr. Sandro Raniolo promptly met me at the gate, whisked me through customs and passport control, and escorted me into a large Mercedes. I was taken to the Crowne Plaza Hotel overlooking the Mediterranean Sea on the north side of Malta in a section called Sliema. I had a corner room that was sumptuous and offered an unimpeded view of the sea on one side and the city on the other. Located on the sixth floor, it was quiet and comfortable and it also had a small balcony where I could sit and enjoy the pleasant air. A bottle of local red wine and a tray of various cheeses greeted me. Attached to the bottle was a welcoming note from Minister Falzon who reminded me that I was to be his guest for dinner that night at his villa.

After unpacking and showering I reviewed a folder that Sandro had given me. In the folder were several statistical reports, a draft summary of the work that Bechtel was requested to do, and a letter asking Bechtel to participate in half the cost of the feasibility study. From the documents before me, I estimated that the whole project would amount to approximately 10 million US dollars spread over three to five years. Much of the project dealt with converting the existing port into a transshipment facility for container ships, and Bechtel was asked to manage the conversion, the infrastructure elements, and possibly to create in the process a technical park on land adjacent to the port but not connected to the marine facility. Not a bad project! From the tone of the description, it was obvious that Bechtel would possibly be asked to do other projects as well.

Picked up again in the Mercedes, I was taken to the minister's villa in Saint Paul's Bay, several kilometers north of Valletta and Sliema. The Honorable Michael Falzon and his wife Christina met me at the entrance of the villa and escorted me to the library's balcony, which overlooked the blue Mediterranean Sea. There were several members of Parliament present, including Prime Minister Eddie Fenech Adami (PM). Scotch or gin and tonics were to be served as if they were the national drink. I asked if Scotch was available and immediately a bottle of Glenlivet 21-year old single malt was brought to me. That was much better for my palate and I greatly appreciated it.

After the introductory chitchat was exhausted, Michael Falzon directed the conversation to what Malta needed to improve its economy. I was informed that because Malta had good relations with the Arab countries and the Europeans, it could become a competitive transshipment port, if only its facilities were updated to accommodate container ships. Malta, which prided itself on having an excellent university modeled after the prestigious English institutions, needed to create a technical or science park for innovations in IT to germinate. I thought to myself when I heard this: "Did the virus of Silicon Valley contaminate this island also?"

More conversation ensued on the economic subject that I found interesting and cogent. Dinner was served and the conversation was redirected to personal affairs, travels, children, and approved bills still pending the PM's signature. The PM remained aloof but most affable, never playing his hand openly. After dinner, port was served and we all moved again to the balcony under a dark, overcast sky. We also broached the subject of knowledge-based developments and their potential for generating revenue. With an excellent university, the ability of most residents to speak several languages (including English), and proximity to the mainland of Europe, it was quite possible that Malta had the right mix for creating a knowledge-based industry. It was also possible that Malta could become part of the EU, when it emerged. The PM broke his silence and agreed, then offered a toast to me.

It was time for me to be taken back to my hotel; it had been a long day.

In the morning, Sandro came for me at 9:00 to take me to the meeting in the office of Michael Falzon. After being introduced to his staff, Michael introduced me to the Minister of Finances (old Exchequers) Mario J. Azzopardi (MF), to Director General of the Port (DGP) Marin Hili, to the General Director for Government Land Management (GDLM) Vincent Grech, to Director of Aviation (and nephew of the PM) Saviour V. Fenech, to Director of Education Dr. Frederick Fearne, to Personal Assistant to the PM Dr. Richard Cachia-Caruana, and to the keenest and toughest person of the group, I soon discovered: the Advisor to the PM, Dr. Patrick G. Staines.

The DGP announced at the outset that the budget permitted that Malta expend no more than 8.5 million dollars over a three year period for the planning of the port, the infrastructure, and the concept for the technical park. After the work gained momentum, the minister informed me, it would not be inconceivable for Parliament to allocate additional funds, but only if all indications showed that employment in IT would increase. Falzon added that he would personally lobby for additional funds downstream. He also reminded me that he hoped that Bechtel would share the cost of the feasibility study, which shouldn't be more than $100,000 in total. Dr. Staines informed me that Malta would pay $50,000 up front to urge Bechtel to take the job and share in Malta's economic improvement. Falzon reinforced what Staines said by personally assuring me that Malta would pay up to $50,000 if Bechtel would pay the rest. Now that payments were said clearly and repeated I was sure that a project was at hand and that Bechtel's cost would be $50,000; a reasonable investment for a 10-million or more project. I felt comfortable that the project would be a reality.

I absorbed all this information and replied that I would advise Bechtel by fax immediately and wait for a reply. From my position, I felt that Malta was offering a fair proposal, but I didn't voice my thoughts to the members. I did, however, ask to see the site as soon as possible. Falzon assured me that after lunch I would be given a complete review of the site and the city of Valletta. We adjourned for lunch and further discussion on the subject resumed. At lunch we were joined by the PM who greeted me warmly and sat next to me.

First course was a shellfish salad and a lovely local white wine. The PM spoke of the time when he lived in Cairo, Egypt as a boy. He had been a schoolboy at the English School in Heliopolis, whereas I had been a student at Victoria College in England and not at the Shubra District extension of the school in Cairo, which I had visited but never attended. Mr. Adami had read for his degree at King's, London then had obtained his economics degree from the London School of Economics. We exchanged tidbits of information on various subjects including my own background, but none dealing with the request given to me. At the end of lunch the PM invited me to attend the evening session of Parliament the following night but this evening I was to join him for dinner at the Club. Lunch finished, I was ushered into the Mercedes to follow the DGP and the GDLM.

Heading to the port area we passed an old fortress and a very busy ship-yard. Ship repairing is one of the important revenue producers for Malta; other revenue producers are agriculture and fishing. Terrace farming over much of Malta makes the countryside look like giant steps. The balmy climate attracts many visitors who also come to view some of the world's finest examples of Baroque and Renaissance art and architecture. Tourism is becoming an important revenue producer for Malta. Tourists come to Malta by air and by private yachts; few cruise ships are welcomed to the islands. After viewing the harbor and the surrounding available land nearby I was given a tour of the Capital. I asked to see the airport and to meet its director; that, I was told, would come another day.

Back at the hotel I prepared a fax and sent it to Michael Wakelin and Bob Jackson. I urged Bechtel to accept the offer and agree to pay for half of the feasibility study; a small investment would make possible a large return and earn good will. When that was completed I donned my swimsuit and took a quick dip in the Mediterranean Sea. After a shower and fresh clothes I called for tea to be served on my balcony. It was a lovely afternoon. At six o'clock Sandro telephoned that I should be ready at 1930 to go to the Sporting Club as the guest of the PM. I was ready.

The British leave their mark in the most extraordinary manner, especially when they create a culture attached to such things as afternoon tea, Windsor tie knots, and Sporting Clubs. The Sporting Club of Valletta, although not built along a river such as the Nile, was nevertheless quite similar to the one I frequented in Cairo as a boy. The PM Eddie Fenech Adami greeted me with his wife and we headed to the private lounge where Scotch was served to me. No proposal discussion marked the evening; instead I learned a great deal about the political system of Malta.

Unlike when I saw him during the day, now the PM was open and willing to participate in and encourage small talk. We reminisced about our years in Egypt, WWII, England, France, and the fascist government in Italy that ended in 1945 with the demise of Mussolini and the subsequent birth of the republic. We both were sad that we had not maintained our Arabic, but we were young and more interested in English as a useful language. He had worked hard to keep his Maltese crisp as I had with French. When port was brought over, we admitted that we had much in common rooted in our youth.

Mrs. Fenech Adami was a lovely lady and quite able to hold her own in conversation. Her primary subject was philosophy. She had attended the Sorbonne in Paris and was fluent in French. She was writing a book on Malta's contribution to ideas, philosophy, politics, and especially on their influence on the current emerging cultural dimensions of the islands. My comment to her was that she had taken on a complex subject and that it would demand much of her energy. Unfortunately, cancer struck and she died less than two years after we met and the book was neither finished nor left in a condition to be finished by a redactor.

Malta is a parliamentary republic and fiercely protective of its independence, especially after many centuries of foreign occupation. I had learned from earlier reading that Malta was not interested in ever being subjugated again. The president is head of state and is appointed by parliament to a five-year term. The prime minister is usually the leader of the majority party in parliament; he is the country's most powerful official. A Cabinet assists the prime minister in carrying out government operations. The voters elect the 65 members of the House of Representatives to five-year terms.

Most of Malta's people speak a language called Maltese, a West Arabic dialect with some Italian words. Both English and Maltese, however, are official languages. Nevertheless, Maltese is used in the courts. The country has both Maltese and English newspapers. Roman Catholicism is the official state religion of Malta. Malta has compulsory elementary education for all children from six to sixteen years old. The country has both public schools and Roman Catholic schools. By law, the teachings of the Roman Catholic Church that are taught in Catholic schools must also be included in public school courses. Instruction is given in both English and Maltese. The University of Malta is in Msida, near Valletta.

The PM and I discussed the history of Malta and I was told that remains of late Stone Age and Bronze Age people had been found in limestone caverns on the islands. Rough stone buildings from early ages have also been discovered in Malta. The Phoenicians colonized Malta in about 1000 B.C.E.

Temples, tombs, and other relics of the Phoenicians still stand. Greek, Carthaginian, Roman, and Arab conquerors followed the Phoenicians into Malta. Then the PM asked, after he learned that I was very much interested in the art of early human beings, if I wanted to visit some of the archeological sites on the main island and Gozo.

"Of course," was my reply.

"I will arrange a visit for you," he assured me.

The dinner and the conversation were in good taste and not of much strain on me. Sometimes such "official" events are a strain because they are boring and unproductive in terms of intellectual bons mots.

The next day, I was shown the Luqa International Airport and was impressed with it. Although it was small in overall size, it was adequate operationally for flights into the country. The director of Civil Aviation, Mr. Saviour Fenech, showed me the weather farm and the equipment facilities for the navigational aids. The navigational aids could have used some upgrading but I was assured that a plan to do that was in the works. The runway, taxiway, and apron were well maintained.

The terminal was clean and functioned properly, except for one problem that occurred after one passes through passport control to leave the country. Before arriving at the departing gate, there is a requirement to pay an airport exit fee of five local pounds. Departing passengers often keep very little local currency when departing a country. With no local pounds in my pocket I was forced to call Sandro and borrow some money when I was ready to depart. I did not, however, notice this problem when I toured the airport.

That evening I attended a long session in Parliament and although the official languages are English and Maltese, many of the arguments were in Maltese. Sandro was kind enough to help with a general translation of what was being expressed. Apart from the regular domestic issues, especially the complaint that Malta imports more goods than it exports, there were discussions about the possibility of a partnership with the European Union. As a small country Malta was unable to offer the EU the advantages of a large financial institution but it could cooperate as a trading bridge with North Africa. The problem that Malta currently faced was that all the North African countries were in deep economic and political distress, and as such did not offer many advantages. Good relations with Libya did not add much to Malta's credit since Italy had good relations with Muammar Muhammad al-Kaddafi too, but he had been a scourge to the Europeans. Nevertheless, Libya did produce oil and supplied both Malta and Italy.

The discussion went on for several hours and I grew tired and a bit bored. Malta, I thought, needed to examine its economic plan carefully to develop a national strategy to move it forward in areas that were financially possible for it. Information Technology was a good area for it to apply itself, as was transshipping. Education was another hidden jewel, especially since it was polyglot and could offer good education and training to many nearby countries. Because it had a fairly good telecommunication infrastructure, which could and should be upgraded soon, it could develop itself as a center for space and financial transactions. Anyway, it was time for me to head to the hotel and call it a day. I asked Sandro if he would drive me back.

A fax waited for me at the hotel's reservation desk. The fax was from Michael Wakelin informing me that Bechtel was not willing to share the fee for the feasibility study. I went to my room and called Wakelin to ask why not, and who had made the decision. His response was that he had discussed the issue with Enrique Diaz who had voiced his opposition. "What about Jackson?" I asked, a bit hot under the collar. "He is my line manager, what does he say?"

"Bob Jackson has been moved to a new position and although you are still under him, the Maltese project, if there is any, will be under Frank Cain, the new department manager."

I paused to allow time for me to absorb this news. "When did this change occur?" I asked. Michael then told me that the change had been effected at the beginning of the week but that I would continue to work under Bob Jackson and my tasks had not changed. "Of course my task has changed. I'm chasing a project and now I'm told that Bechtel will not participate one iota to make this multi-million dollar project a reality."

In his typical, quiet, pseudo-English voice, Michael informed me that Cain was not willing to spend a dollar towards the project in Malta. Either the

Maltese government paid for the feasibility study or there would be no project. Cain was not willing to subsidize Malta.

"That's the stupidest thing I've ever heard. For a mere $50,000 Cain will
forego a multi-million dollar opportunity!" Michael's reply was unenlighten-
ing. Now I had to inform the Minister for Economic Development, the
Honorable Michael Falzon, that Bechtel was not willing to share the price of
the feasibility study with Malta. For Bechtel it was to be all or nothing!

I sat in the balcony looking at Valletta and the sea for a long time, and
then I took a blank fax form and wrote Wakelin that I would not inform the
Maltese Government quite yet, but would hope that Bechtel would reconsider
its position. I just couldn't quite accept Cain's position. My disappointment
was causing me to hurt inside. After other encounters with him I discovered
that Frank Cain was an egocentric, megalomaniac, mental midget.

The next morning after I had a quick swim in the sea, a shower, and a bit
of breakfast, Sandro picked me up for another meeting with Mr. Falzon and
then a tour of the university, which was located not far from the capital in
Msida. Mr. Falzon asked me if Bechtel was willing to participate in the cost
of the feasibility study. I lied and said that, although I had sent my department a fax, a reply had not yet arrived.

Did I want to use his telephone to ask my superiors? Fortunately, the
time difference made it impossible for me to reach Wakelin or Cain. I said
that I would call my office that night. Mr. Falzon continued the conversation
by giving me an outline of what specifically the government of the Republic
of Malta was interested in creating and developing:

1. Upgrading the port to make it suitable for container ships.

2. Developing a place for a science park and helping Malta create an IT
incubator nest to nurture a critical mass.

3. Preparing the university to adopt a research protocol in order to help it
enlist faculty and students interested in fostering science, technical creativity,
entrepreneurship, economic research, and marketing.

Because Malta was currently mainly dependent on agriculture and tourism it had to move quickly to acquire new tools and skills for the emerging
global economy. I agreed with him. Mr. Falzon was certain that such work

could readily begin with a $10 million budget. Furthermore, he assured me those lenders in the EU such as the World Bank, the European Bank for Development, and the IMF would not be difficult to convince for additional grants, especially if a firm like Bechtel were working with Malta.

"Perhaps, but Bechtel is not in the financing business," I reminded Mr. Falzon.

"Of course not," he replied, "Bechtel will be paid directly and on time. We are just hoping that Bechtel would help us maneuver through the financial search."

I assured him that Bechtel could do that but there would be a cost for that service. He nodded his head and said, "Of course."

We discussed each of the three points in his plan. When we had exhausted the subject and he reminded me to telephone Bechtel on the issue of the feasibility study, we adjourned. I followed Sandro and Mr. Falzon to the car.

The Catholic National University of Malta had an impressive looking campus reminiscent of an English university. I was led to the Rector's Office and introduced to the Rev. Professor Peter Serraeins Inglott. Professor Inglott was a tall, handsome man in his mid-fifties whose academic specialty was molecular biology. He had obtained his undergraduate degree in Malta and his doctorate at UC Berkeley.

After spending several years in research and teaching in California, he decided to return to Malta where he was given a position as professor of microbiology and the use of a modern laboratory. He increased the number of students in his field at the University and soon found that he was up against a controlling academic board that was not interested in modern scientific research but preferred to remain solely in the staid field of classical academics, away from science. After a couple of years of conflict, the PM and Mr. Falzon intervened and expanded the board to include several members who were forward thinking. Soon the board began to look at Dr. Inglott as a potential rector who would lead the university into the new areas. It was at Inglott's urging that the issue of a new protocol was raised when the board met in the summer. Not only had the board agreed to consider the possibility that a new protocol would be adopted but they asked the rector for his resignation and elected Dr. Inglott in his place. This brief history was shared with me over lunch.

"I want Malta to reach out to new research not only in the disciplines of biology but in other disciplines that are emerging every day in science. I also want the graduating students, the future scholars of Malta, to be familiar with classical learning, literature, philosophy, and all the necessary tools that enlighten a creative mind," Inglott affirmed as he looked at me. He continued after glancing at Mr. Falzon, "We will hit a wall soon."

In my innocence, I blurted, "Why?"

Falzon looked at me and said, "There are forces that wish that the university remain a monastic center of untarnished learning."

Inglott added, "What this entails is that the Roman Catholic Church, of which I am a part, is the real government of Malta, and prefers that the university remain outside the realm of biology, cytology, quantum, and evolutionary science."

There was a deadly silence for a long period. I broke the silence by making a bold statement: "This is an academic cancer that must be dealt with or it will devastate not only the university but all of Malta. We have some of this problem in the United States. It is not so much the Roman Catholic Church, although it is a force to contend with, but more difficult to fight is the Fundamentalist Conservative Right Wing Puritan (FCRWP) movement."

Inglott smiled and acknowledged that when he was working at the Laurence Livermore Laboratory, "The acronym FCRWP was often changed to For-Crap."

No business appointments were scheduled for me for the evening. Sandro was instructed to show me the nightlife in Valletta and to take me to an upscale restaurant. Tomorrow, before my flight for Zurich, which departed at 4:00 p.m., I was to be driven to Marfa to board the ferry for Gozo Island. I had dinner with Sandro but declined the visit to the nightspots of Valletta. Going to bed was preferable.

In the morning, after packing, Sandro came to fetch me. Sandro asked me if I had contacted my department and I replied that I was unable to discuss the subject because everyone was in some sort of meeting.

The crossing to Gozo Island took less than 30 minutes on the ferryboat. Once on Gozo I was seeing a place that resembled a village from the Phoenician, Greek, Carthaginian, Roman, and Arab periods of human history. The Phoenicians colonized Malta in about 1000 B.C.E., and temple walls, tombs, and other relics of the Phoenicians still stand and are incorporated into newer dwellings inhabited by contemporary Maltese citizens. The Arabs have left many frescoes on buildings and these are preserved and still in good condition. From the Greek and Roman occupations, sculptures remain in courtyards, parks, and entrances to institutional buildings; most of these are in a fair state of preservation.

Gozo is principally a fishing and agricultural island. The streets are not really made for cars, although there are a few automobiles on the island; small trucks and motor scooters are, however, more prevalent. Donkey or mule-drawn carts are common carriers for goods and people. There is a sense that history has ceased to be made in a rush and that time is unhurried. When I spoke to shopkeepers, people in a café, and vegetable merchants, I was gratified to hear them admit that they were content to be separated from the rush and bustle of the "big island." It didn't matter to them what the people of Malta thought or did as long as they were left to tend to their lives in their own way.

I noticed a modicum of enlightened self-interest that was refreshing, which was not selfish or egocentric. One café client informed me that many writers, artists, and scholars come to Gozo to express their creativity on this island of contentment. He, himself a writer from Ireland, lived most of the year on Gozo because he could write poetry without being overwhelmed by the rush for financial gains. Did he not want remuneration for his poetry I inquired? Yes he did, but not as much as his Irish patriots who were focused on financial gain now that the EU was willing to use Ireland as a deep well from which to draw labor, unskilled and skilled, for manufacturing goods to be sold on the global market. He and several of his cohorts, writers, and painters, who were with him on Gozo, preferred the simple life that was available on this tiny island. We spoke for several moments and he was kind enough to show me around and to introduce me to other artists and to fishermen.

I could not wander too far because my time on Gozo was limited, but I did obtain a taste of what made the island such an attractive, peaceful place, a non-disturbing location where the brain can work overtime without being cluttered by the noises made by a striving society. I did envy my poet not so much because he was a poet but because he was able to live for his art, his passion, on an island that required little in terms of monetary support. I could enjoy living on Gozo and I suppose that the weather, especially the heat of summer, could become acceptable. Thick Roman walls do keep an abode quite well insulated from the heat of summer. Of course I know little about the winter weather in the mid-Mediterranean. Anyway, it is unlikely that I would transplant myself to Gozo because Liechtenstein is too appealing and it was my next stop.

It was time for me to leave Gozo to reenter the world of finances, rushing people, airplanes, and chronometric life. My Swissair flight to Zurich was three hours away and I had an appointment with royalty to keep the next day.

I need, however, to close the venture into Malta by saying that Bechtel was adamantly unwilling, mostly because of Cain's negative attitude, to participate in the project. After telephoning Bechtel and pleading that Malta was a viable opportunity and exhausting my list of reasons as to why the island was worth the time and money, I closed the issue. I telephoned Mr. Falzon and expressed my apologies for not being able to bring Bechtel on line as an initial partner. I was disappointed and several years later when I left Bechtel I tried again to see if I could get the Maltese project on board but even with the assistance of Uncle Charlie Vassallo, I was not invited to become a consultant for Malta. I was greatly saddened because I liked Malta and the people I had met during my short but extensive visit. To me Malta will stand as a lovely island and a place I might revisit.

Frank Cain, however, will remain as the least reasonable person I've ever encountered and he can join the club of lesser human beings with Clarence

Rupert Haden, my nemesis in the Diocese of Northern California. To this day I cannot understand why Riley had appointed Cain to replace Jackson. Cain, in my appraisal, is a mental midget. In the final analysis now I find that I'm no longer bitter about Haden or Cain; in fact, they have passed into history.

Liechtenstein: Brilliant Jewel

It was October 1987 and I was on a flight to Zurich and had in my attaché bag an invitation to meet with the prince of Liechtenstein. Whether this was my third or fourth visit to Liechtenstein does not matter much, what is important is that on this visit I was to meet the ruling prince and his family. I had an eleven o'clock appointment with Prince Hans-Adam II to learn more about the history and the economic development of the Principality.

The flight on Swissair took me directly to Zurich, Switzerland where I rented a car and drove to Vaduz, Liechtenstein. The drive was about an hour long and simply a small road sign and no more marks the border. After registering at the small Hotel Schaan that overlooked a vineyard and receiving the information that my dinner reservation at the Torkel Restaurant was for eight o'clock and that the prince's secretary had reconfirmed my appointment with His Serene Highness, I went to my room to wash and change clothes.

As I entered the main lobby downstairs on my way out — I had about an hour before my reservation at the Torkel — I stopped to peruse the books in the adjoining library. In the library was a handsome gentleman in his seventies who said hello to me in crisp English. We chatted a bit. He was driving back to England in his 1930 Rolls Royce coupé-boat motorcar. He had exhibited the car in Vienna and was returning to the UK by way of Zurich, Lyons, Paris, London, and Luton. Luton is a well-established center of automobile manufacturing. The amazing issue about the car was that his father had purchased it new in 1930 and apart from maintenance, tires, new valves and cylinders, and incidentals, the engine block was the same original block that the factory had installed in the vehicle. He was keen to show me the car but because I had a Torkel reservation we made an appointment for me to look at it after breakfast the next morning.

The Torkel restaurant was just as splendid as I remembered it. My table was prepared on the veranda and the prince had been charming to send me two bottles of his wine for my dinner. After escargots nurtured on grape leaves from the prince's vineyard, I was served lamb shank done in wine, tarragon, and basil with baby carrots and haricots mange tous (green beans). The shank was perfect, just perfect. After the lamb a small salad was served followed by dessert, coffee, and Cognac.

After a good night's sleep and a late awakening for me, I descended to the dining room for a light breakfast — that was all I needed after my fine dinner. The English gentleman and his wife invited me over to their table. We introduced ourselves properly this time. He was Lord Henri of Luton and she was Lady Mary. I had never met a lord whose estate still carried his family name and whose town was still named after him. Professionally, he had been an engineer for the Rolls Royce firm until it fell on bad times. Now a retired gentleman dairy farmer, he traveled, exhibited his historic motorcar, and was writing his memoirs. Lady Mary was devoted to working on several charitable endeavors. As promised, Lord Henri gave me a very personal show of his wonderful automobile and gave me a ride in it to boot.

Lord Henri shared an anecdote that a few miles east of Zurich the car developed a problem with the fuel pump: it worked intermittently. Stopping at a petrol station he called RR in Zurich. The RR mechanics arrived within the hour, tented the car as it was parked in the parking lot of the petrol station, and proceeded to make the necessary repairs. Soon the car was in good working order. The tent was removed. The mechanics departed and no bill was given. RR does not want their cars to be seen stranded for mechanical reasons, thus they immediately tent their vehicles!

We said our goodbyes; he was heading towards Zurich and I to the Castle, which appeared to be hanging above Vaduz.

Arriving at 10:40, I checked in at the Castle's gate, showed my credentials, and entered into a conversation with the guard who was a most interesting fellow. When not guarding the Castle, Mr. Dieter Kessler taught sailing on the Bodensee (Lake Constance) and the Rhine River. Mr. Kessler was the proud owner of Segelschule Liechtenstein, a sailing firm. Mr. Kessler and I chatted a bit and he was kind enough to invite me sailing but I declined because my schedule was tight. A few minutes before eleven o'clock the prince's secretary arrived to escort me to the prince's grand office that over-looked Vaduz. Prince Hans-Adam greeted me with an extended right hand and showed me to a seat on the couch. He sat in an armchair to my left. There was no desk between us and the formalities were immediately dispensed with. Coffee was served and delicious small pastries combined well with the hot, strong coffee.

I wanted to know about the history, the economic situation, the education of the people of the Principality, and the answers to several questions that I had written so as not to forget them in my excitement at meeting royalty. Prince Hans-Adam told me that his father, Prince Franz Joseph II, had died in 1989. He, Hans-Adam, succeeded his father and has ruled since 1984. The Princess Mother was still alive and doing quite well.

On the political side, the prince informed me that Liechtenstein is a con-stitutional monarchy. It is ruled by a prince, himself, who is the head of the House of Liechtenstein. The throne always passes to the prince's eldest son. What happens if no sons are produced and only daughters were available? That was not an issue since it would be resolved by a constitutional amend-ment which he was already sponsoring as he sponsored and signed into law the amendment to allow women to vote in general elections in 1984.

The people elect the 25 members of the Landtag (parliament) to four-year terms. The Landtag passes laws, prepares the national budget, and sets tax rates. The prince must approve all the laws with his signature. If, how-ever, the prince chooses to veto a bill, the Landtag can overturn the veto by a 20-vote majority. A five-member Collegial Board headed by a prime minister handles government operations. Its members are nominated by the Landtag and approved by the prince. Liechtenstein has two political parties, the Patri-otic Union and the Progressive Citizen's Party. Unlike Austria, from which Liechtenstein separated in the mid-1930s, it has no right-wing leaning party or factions.

The people in Liechtenstein, like the Austrians and the Swiss, are de-scended from a Germanic tribe that settled in the Alps. Until the 1930s, most people farmed for a living. Now more than half of them are factory workers, technicians, scientists, or craft workers. Less than 10 percent of the people still farm for a living.

Liechtenstein offers free education to all its citizens and has the highest literacy level of any nation on the planet, yet it has no universities or colleges. There are two academies in the Principality, one for music and the other for handicapped children.

Since about 1950, Liechtenstein, at the urging of Prince Franz Joseph, has changed from a farming country to a highly industrialized and technological one. As a consequence of this change, it has one of the highest standards of living in the world. We broached the subjects of finance, long term economics, world and local politics, and the future of the Principality vis-à-vis the EU. The prince was negotiating to join the European Free Trade Association (EFTA), an economic organization of European nations. Liechtenstein became a member of EFTA in 1991.

I turned to the prince and asked about his education and his family. He had obtained his undergraduate education in Zurich reading history and political science, and his doctorate at the London School of Economics. His wife, the princess, is a graduate from Heidelberg in philosophy. He has two young boys and a girl, so the line of heirs will continue without amendments.

It was approaching noon and I felt that my time with the prince was about to come to a close. "But we haven't talked about you and your interests," the prince reminded me.

I said a few things about myself and indicated that I was not wishing to take up more time than he had allotted for me. He had several questions, especially about knowledge as a renewable revenue producing resource, and was particularly interested in my comments about his art collection which included works by Pieter Brueghel the Elder, Sandro Botticelli, Rembrandt, and Peter Paul Rubens. The collection was visible to the public in Vaduz at no charge. As I arose from my seat the prince placed his hand on my shoulder and said, "I do have an appointment waiting for me and I should not make my visitor wait since he is my prime minister. Are you free later this afternoon?"

"Yes I am and I shall be happy to return if that is your wish," I added.

"Well then it is settled. Do come for tea at fifteen hundred hours and we can talk some more."

I accepted with great joy and left. As I walked through the guard area, the guard smiled and said, "We will see you this afternoon." I smiled back and saluted him. In the time it took to walk from the prince's office to the gatehouse, the guard had already been notified that I would be returning!

It was time for a bite to eat for lunch. I continued on the road that led from the Castle on up the mountain to the village of Steg. Steg is a small village of charming houses with decorated windows just a few kilometers from Vorder-Grauspitz (approximately 3,000 meters), the highest peak of the Alps in Liechtenstein. A guest at the hotel had told me that there was an inn with a good restaurant in Steg. Steg is located at the 2,000 meter level and overlooks the western part of Liechtenstein and the Rhine River.

I found the inn; in fact it was on the road. My lunch included a potato-cabbage soup with a piece of sausage and dark bread. My table was on the veranda and I could see beyond Vaduz, beyond the Rhine River, and well into Switzerland. After coffee and a piece of fruit tarte, I continued to drive to Vorder-Grauspitz and into Austria. I stopped the car and absorbed the view, breathed the cold fresh air, and ate a little snow. It was a magnificent sight. No photographs could have captured what my eyes were seeing. It was exhilarating. After a while standing and admiring the view I took a little walk and could feel the crunching ice under my soles. I must have walked a fair distance because I could no longer see the road or hear the cars. It was quiet and serene.

Finding a rock I sat and thought about life and the wonders of being alive. Here I was immersed in nature almost atop the world and mindful of the extraordinary beauty that enveloped me. It must have been a long time that I sat on the rock thinking of what was in front of me and also of my warm encounter with Prince Hans-Adam. I was fortunate to have met him, and especially to be invited again, and for tea with his family. Life is full of wonders and most of them come serendipitously. A bird perching on a rock directly across from me broke my solitude. It was a blue bird with some dark brownish feathers on its head and tail. I looked at it and then glimpsed the time on my watch. Time to head back to the Castle, I said to myself. I wanted so much to postpone the departure, but I knew that I would be back here.

When I arrived at the Castle gate, the guard had been changed. A new man asked me to wait until someone came for me. A young man arrived and escorted me not in the direction of the prince's office but to the residence portion and royal quarters. A large wooden door opened as we approached and Prince Hans-Adam came forward to greet me by taking my hand in both of his. As we walked toward the library, I explained that I was honored to be invited into his home and that I wasn't quite sure why this privilege had been extended to me.

The prince looked at me and said, "We haven't finished our conversation and I wanted to know more about your interest for visiting Liechtenstein and how you came to be interested in our little country."

"Liechtenstein is a jewel of a country, and I want to know as much as possible about it. This small nation is a phenomenon that fascinates me, amazes me, and surprises me." As best I could I explained that I had studied several city-states and small nations but found the Principality to be an ex-traordinary example of sound management, good and controlled economic environment, political freedom, and a most attractive location. I did not want to gush with too much admiration or sound too utopian in my adulation.

When we entered the library I was immediately received by the prince's mother, the Grand Princess of Liechtenstein; the prince's wife, Princess Maria; and a young prince age ten or twelve, Eric-Josef. The beauty emanat-ing from the prince's mother seized me; she was a most extraordinary woman and her age had not diminished the splendor that I had seen in photographs taken decades ago. Hers was a classic and regal exquisiteness that painters have sought to capture forever. I had never been in the presence of such se-rene, sculptured, and overwhelming magnificence. I knew that I was being rude but I could not help but stare at the Princess Mother. I had to pull myself together and quickly. The prince helped by introducing me to all present. He then added that I was on a quest to learn as much as possible about this little country.

"Dr. Hoche-Mong, do tell us a little about yourself?" The prince asked me. "You are not a native of America. Your accent is not quite American." I sat down and was handed tea in a lovely Sevre porcelain cup. "I have been to America several times..." the prince mentioned that he had met with President Jimmy Carter in the White House.

It was my turn to offer a sketch about myself. After the self-portrait, Princess Maria asked me if I had visited the gallery. The conversation moved to art, aesthetics, and on to process philosophy. Princess Maria had read many of the works by Alfred N. Whitehead and after some comparative comments we moved to Liechtenstein. I asked the Grand Princess to share with me some highlights of the history of Liechtenstein.

An attendant served tea again. It was an excellent black tea. The savories and pastries were outstanding.

The people in Liechtenstein, the Grand Princess informed us, are like the Austrians and Eastern Swiss. They are descended from Germanic tribes that settled in the Alps in the A.D. 400s, but the region was possibly inhabited for 3,000 years before that settlement. Charlemagne, king of the Franks, controlled the area in the late A.D. 700s. After his death in 814, the region was divided into two independent regions, Vaduz and Schellenberg. Both regions later became part of the Holy Roman Empire. Johann-Adam Liechtenstein, a prince from Vienna, acquired Schellenberg in 1699 and Vaduz in 1712. "We are his descendants and we still rule Liechtenstein."

The Grand Princess continued her history lesson. Until the 1930s, most of the people of Liechtenstein farmed for a living. Liechtenstein separated from Austria in 1931 when Prince Franz Joseph recognized that Austria was moving closer to Hitler's National Socialism and the ruling prince wanted nothing to do with this type of political philosophy. He removed his domain from Austria and sealed an agreement with the Swiss government to have a diplomatic, currency, postal, and telephone union with them. Prince Franz Joseph contracted an agreement with the Swiss that they would represent Liechtenstein diplomatically but insisted that his country would remain independent, neutral, and practice self-rule. The prince made certain that in the concordat, Liechtenstein would not be annexed as another canton to Switzerland. The Swiss agreed because the concordat would add tax revenue to their coffers; they were not aware that Liechtenstein was practically penniless.

When I asked about the economic history, the Grand Princess explained that when the two regions that make up the Principality of Liechtenstein separated from Austria they were on the verge of bankruptcy. The only funds that remained were those that belonged personally to the Liechtenstein family. Prince Franz Joseph called a general meeting of his elders to discuss the economic future of the Principality. At the meeting the elders listed what it was that Liechtenstein produced, and produced well. Apart from farming, which brought some revenue, products that were made in Liechtenstein included ceramics (especially high temperature ceramics), fabricated metal products, tools, preserved foods, heating appliances, and pharmaceutical products. Today Liechtenstein is a major designer and producer of prototypical electronic equipment and contributor to the information technology arena.

The Grand Princess continued, "In 1932, the prince lent the elders the equivalent of $300,000 in current dollar value (mid-80s) to revitalize the economy by expanding the product line, ensuring that because of the excellence of what was produced competition would be minimized, establishing a marketing plan, and creating a national investment bank."

We discussed the financial directions taken, the goals established, and the working plans for getting Liechtenstein in the black. Sensing in 1936 that war was about to take place, Prince Franz Joseph wanted immediate action into markets before all avenues closed. He mobilized his people to prepare for the worst and so he led them to build whatever was necessary to expand the manufacture of their products. Farms went into high gear, kilns were never given time to cool, kettles were constantly cooking fruit for canning, the small pharmaceutical plants were working around the clock to supply the Swiss with the necessary drugs for their production. All in all Liechtenstein was determined to pull itself out of the red, and wanted to do that before Hitler discovered that it was too poor to resist and had no means to defend itself. The only defense that the prince could consider as viable was economic independence and becoming indispensable.

My cup of tea was never left empty. I was feeling as if I had become part of the family and it was such a lovely family. I still had great difficulty in avoiding staring at the Grand Princess who was a beautiful woman. The younger princess, the wife of Prince Adam, was also strikingly beautiful but not quite as striking as her mother-in-law.

At this pause I asked, "What was Liechtenstein's role during WWII, and how did it survive the Nazi military might?" After a moment I then added with a smile on my face, "The Nazi Panzer force would have overwhelmed the Principality in less than an hour!"

Hans-Adam laughed and replied, "Probably in less than 30 minutes I dare say."

The Grand Princess continued her story and answered my question. "We were neutral and that was an advantage to the German military power because it allowed the Nazi government to place some of its funds in our National Investment bank and invest them on the global market."

I interrupted her by asking, "You mean that you helped Germany invest its wealth, much of it stolen, on the world exchange?"

"Yes," she replied then added, "but you mustn't forget that the Allies, principally France, Britain, and America, also used our banks to expand their investment."

I was not only surprised but also struck by the notion that both sides, the Allies and the Axis, played the same investment game.

"Does that surprise you? What we all need to understand is that the greatest weapon today is not military power but economic might — perhaps America should remember that." This was said during the Reagan years when a significant portion of America's GDP went into building an overwhelming military at the expense of the national economy. I was learning a great deal and the Grand Princess was my teacher. "We are a small and relatively insignificant country with approximately 20,000 souls. We have no army and no police. We remain free because we produce excellent marketable goods. We are also economically almost indispensable because of our banking system, a banking system that is quite unlike that of the Swiss because it is transparent, astute, and global. Moreover, our technology is excellent, refined, advanced, and available to all who need it."

There was a profound lesson here to be learned by all nations. Power did not reside in how many bombers or tanks one possessed but in how a nation managed its knowledge and hence its economy. A nation's value depended on its ability to be indispensable in the marketplace.

The prince asked me about Bechtel and the work that I was doing. We discussed my interest in the city-state phenomenon and the economic characteristics of the small states such as Liechtenstein and Luxemburg. He added, "Don't forget Finland. It is a small state too with a small population, albeit on a large piece of land, yet it stood gallantly and as best it could against the Nazi and Soviet might because of its keen economic strength and educated population." I took that comment into consideration and soon in my work on the economics of small states and their influence on IT, Finland stood as an emblem to be contended.

We talked a bit more about Liechtenstein: its art, its philosophy, its politic, and its wine. I received a personal invitation from the prince to visit his winery and to have one of his technical advisors show me around and see what was being produced.

It was nearly five o'clock and time for me to take my leave. The prince asked me if I had plans for dinner and I replied that I was going to go again to the Torkel. "Go there at eight o'clock. A reservation will be made for you," he said.

I left the Castle and returned to my hotel. I was tired from the wonderful visit with the Liechtenstein family. I needed a few hours of rest to assimilate all that I had learned.

At eight I drove to the Torkel, and, as promised, a table was ready for me. Dinner was once again heavenly as was the wine. When I asked for the bill I was given instead a note card from the prince thanking me for "gracing his home and his humble restaurant." I was impressed by his cordiality and touched by his kindness.

The next morning I received a call from the Director of Economic Development, Toni Jäger, inviting me to join him for a tour of several of the businesses in the lower part of Liechtenstein. I visited plasma laboratories (ionized matter); fine tool and instrument design and manufacturing plants; a ceramic plant known for making, among other items, high temperature tiles used for space vehicles; several computer engineering and manufacturing firms designing units for automobiles, aircraft, and ships; pharmaceutical laboratories; and fruit, vegetable, and whole meals preserving and packaging firms — many of which were also employed by the space industry to feed their human operators.

Over coffee, I was informed that Liechtenstein offers low-interest business loans and income tax offsets to foreign companies established in the Principality. As a result more than 5,000 foreign firms have established their headquarters there. These firms contribute not only to employment but also to revenue and prestige. Two hydroelectric plants furnish more than enough power to the country. Liechtenstein has no airport and the passenger train serving Switzerland and Austria rarely stops in the Principality; most people wanting to travel to the Zurich International Airport use a direct bus or drive a car.

Mr. Jäger told me that the next day I had an appointment with the Prime Minister, Dr. Hubert Büchel. My appointment was for 11:00 in the PM's office in Vaduz. Returning to my hotel I gathered the notes in my head and recorded them into my trip report. That task took almost three hours and brought me up to the time of dinner, which I would have in my hotel in Schaan.

After a dinner of lamb and a brandy enjoyed in front of a roaring fire in the sitting room, I met several other guests from various parts of the world. Most of the guests were technical people working with local IT firms. I listened to the current of conversation and learned much about the special value that this small country had in the global economy. There were representatives from Ford Motor Company, Mercedes, BMW, Lockheed, Cisco, Intel, Apple, Toshiba, and NASA. Each representative was involved in a different phase of technology and how that technology applied to the particular product each produced. NASA was interested in foods, high temperature ceramics, and sensitive controls. Ford was interested in fuel monitoring computers, as were

Mercedes and BMW. Lockheed's and Toshiba's purposes in Liechtenstein were to work on plasma for glass display instruments and screens. Cisco, Intel, and Apple were determining how Liechtenstein's industry and laboratories could offer them support in the manufacturing of high-speed components for computers. The evening conversation did not end until close to midnight; the discussions gave me an invaluable insight into what this tiny Principality was about, what it offered, and who was interested in it.

The next morning I arrived at the office of the Honorable Dr. Hubert Büchel, Prime Minister of Fürstentum Liechtenstein Amt für Volkswirtschaft. Dr. Büchel spoke fluent French and English, but we decided to converse in French. A graduate of the Grande Ecole Administrative de France, Dr. Büchel pursued a doctorate in Economics at Princeton University, New Jersey a few years later. Much of the information he shared with me had already been given to me by the prince. What Dr. Büchel did do was load me with documents supplying me with specific details. He also placed me on his mailing list and for several years I was the recipient of new information on the affairs of the Principality. He further explained to me the close relationship the Principality had with Switzerland, the tax agreement (especially the "salt" tax that the Principality paid, which was nothing more than an agreed name of the surtax for the diplomatic services performed by the Swiss Government on behalf of Liechtenstein), and the differences between the Swiss and Liechtenstein banking systems and in particular the conditions for having an account in one of the banks in the Principality. The banks of Liechtenstein did not maintain the same extent of secrecy that the Swiss banks provided but they did offer, in lieu, greater interest and investment returns. Liechtenstein's banks were not money storage institutions but active revenue generators for its depositors.

Lunch was served in the private dining room next to the PM's office. Our conversation continued but was mostly in response to my interests, Bechtel's interests, and how the embryonic EU would affect the Principality. As far as the EU was concerned, the PM was certain that the EU would be advantageous to his small country because the trading codes, the monetary systems, and the exchange of information would be uniformly shared and easier to contend with. He was more concerned with the voluntary self-exclusion of the Swiss from the UN. Liechtenstein could not join the UN as long as it remained diplomatically attached to Switzerland, and the latter was against membership in the world organization. He felt, however, that when global commerce expanded, the Swiss would inevitably find that they needed to become part of both the UN and the World Trade Organization (WTO). In fact, in 2002, the Swiss began to negotiate their inclusion in both organizations but no agreement was reached.

At the end of my day with the PM, I was again exhausted and my head was brimming full of data. I needed to gather my information in note form and also needed some rest. I decided to have a light dinner at my hotel and record the data I had received. The following day, my last day in this jewel of a country, I wanted to spend as a tourist. Before dinner I telephoned my office in San Francisco to inquire if there was anything I needed to tend to. Ligia informed me that Frank Cain had left a note on my desk advising me to see him upon my return to San Francisco. Ignoring the note because I was not yet under his budget, I also asked Ligia to make appointments for me with Marta Industries, Motorola-France, and Thompson Electroniques. I then telephoned Stu Hill in London and asked for a conference call with Bob Jackson to discuss my next task, which was to visit Toulouse, France, and the Airbus complex.

A few minutes later, Bob Jackson called to inform me that he had been replaced as department manager by Frank Cain but that for the next year, I would remain on Bob's budget and would continue to report to him. We discussed my work in Europe and the direction I planned to take to perform the task. In short, my task was to identify any new technology emerging in Europe; to assist the European Economic Commission in its plan to consolidate 12 diverse nations into one European Community; and to find ways to convince the Europeans that Bechtel was a viable European firm — the latter was impossible unless Bechtel created a European company or merged with a European established firm such as Mannesmann. Stu called a few minutes later reminding me that I was also to look into aviation and airport needs in Europe, especially air traffic management. Again I brought up the issue of

Bechtel establishing a European company and that an office in London and one in Paris did not suggest that it was a veritable European firm.

"Yes, yes, I agree with you," replied Stu.

"Stu, if Howard Wahl is not able to move the board of directors to register as a European firm or merge with or buy into Mannesmann, Bechtel will continue to be an outsider as far as the Europeans are concerned." Stu agreed and promised to discuss the matter with Howard and even with Riley. "Stu, there might be a door in Finland with Hakka Construction and Engineering and that would also offer Bechtel access to the USSR."

"Give Hakka a call and feel them out," Stu told me.

There was a strong feeling in Europe that the EU would be a strong ally with the United States but a competitive one. Europe, as a united unit, would offer a market of nearly half a billion consumers — and that did not include the liberated Eastern Block that would soon be applying for membership in the EU. Consideration also needed to be given to the enlargement of the North Atlantic Treaty Organization (NATO), which offered a united front in defense and the acquisition of the tools for defense. Many American firms such as General Electric, Apple, IBM, Hewlett Packard (HP), and others were moving quickly to become known as European firms, albeit with American roots. I phoned Howard Wahl to inquire how the negotiations with Mannesmann were going.

"It's not Mannesmann that's the problem, it's Bechtel. I'm leaving for San Francisco in the morning to meet with Riley and the directors." This issue wasn't going to be resolved that night so I went to dinner.

I telephoned Frank Cain. He was in Maryland and I caught him as he was starting a meeting. "Raymond, you must return to San Francisco because you are now under my authority and I have no interest in what you are doing." A small pause followed from me. "Did you hear what I said?"

"Yes, Frank, I did hear."

"So when are you returning?"

"Not until I finish what I'm doing for Bob Jackson, Howard Wahl, and Riley."

"That's no longer part of your assignment."

"Tell this to Riley and to Bob. They are still paying for my time, travel, and work." I paused again to make certain that Frank Cain heard me, and then I added, "Have a good day." I ended the telephone conversation.

Frank Cain never did fathom what was being developed, even after he discussed the issues with Riley Bechtel. A few years after this conversation I found myself caught between two forces that pulled me in opposite directions. I found it best to retire.

Well I didn't have to consider retiring quite just yet because the Frank Cain takeover of the department was postponed until 1990. Moreover, I was to remain with Jackson until 1991.

I continued to work in Europe as my tasks dictated. While in England I received a telephone call from IASP asking if I was interested in presenting a paper in Adelaide, South Australia. My reply was in the affirmative. After attending to all my meetings in Toulouse and elsewhere, I interrupted my work in Europe to return to San Francisco and to prepare a paper for presentation at the Australian Conference of the International Association of Science Parks (IASP).

Down Under Land: Australia

The subject of real estate management had become a veritable bone of contention within IASP's membership, especially now that Tecnopolis Novus Ortus had shown that attracting firms and incubators to a location did not require any real estate management of a delineated piece of property. The Italian Tecnopolis had shown that although Vallenzano was the real estate home of the high technology center, the whole Bari region, made up of 19 communities, was part of the complex for advanced technology. In other words, Tecnopolis was the center, the locus of the economic development for the region, and IT firms, laboratories, incubators, manufacturers, educational facilities, financial institutions, etc., could settle themselves anywhere within the whole Bari region as suitable real estate was located for each entity.

Technopolis became merely the attracting entity and not the real estate management firm. The purchase or leasing of real estate was negotiated by interested entities with the owners of the suitable parcels and not with a management firm that had membership in something like IASP.

For Technopolis and for Bari that, at first, was a difficult aspect to implement because the Italian government in Rome, local and provincial governments, and the mentality of the Italians leaned inadvertently towards public control of real estate. It was Umberto's persistence and vision that moved the respective public forces away from controlling real estate or from setting aside certain areas for "technological parks" à la the French model. Of course, in the process, Umberto lost a great deal of support from public officials, which ultimately contributed to his resignation.

Nevertheless, the format for unmanaged real estate not only was useful to incoming firms because they selected their own suitable properties and also formed partnering clusters, but also because it vitalized the entire Bari region and forced the 19 communities and the land owners within them to consider a certain degree of competition, which eventually lowered real estate prices. What proves that the proof is in the pudding is that Umberto Bozzo, more than a decade later, was recognized as having had good ideas and because of that he has been sought after to develop other communities as free-market-driven nuclei for IT.

At their quarterly meeting in Toulouse, the IASP directorship wanted to hear more about the Silicon Valley approach, the Technopolis format, and wanted to compare that model with the Science Park, or Technopole, format of France, the Netherlands, Germany, and other units. In as much as I had been the leaven in refuting the real estate issue, I was invited to present a paper at the IASP conference held in Adelaide, South Australia in November 1989.

After I had received the news of the invitation and because I was traveling in Europe on EU business, I asked Emily, who was in the publication department, to draw together an outline of what I wanted to say using some of A.N. Whitehead's ideas on harmony, events, and occasions for achieving a coherent goal. Emily had heard me speak on the subject so she was ready to put together an outline for me. Using a painting by the artist Paul Klee, we were able to explicate how harmony may develop if all the occasions (elements) are carefully lured into the event (goal). When I returned to San Francisco I finished the paper, the accompanying slides, and made preparations for the trip to Australia.

Because Emily had never been across the Equator or traveled to Australia and because she was on a leave of absence before her retirement, I asked her if she would accompany me to the conference in Adelaide. My frequent mileage account had more than sufficient miles for her to accompany me in business class. I thought that after the conference we would add three weeks to fashion a holiday in Australia. My thought was to fly in to Adelaide, then drive back by car to Sydney to see firsthand some of the country and experience the local color. Emily put together an excellent itinerary that added much zest to our visit and included Flinders Ranges, Kangaroo Island, Mildura (where the Darling and the Murray Rivers join), the Blue Mountains, and all that lies in between, including places where the tenacious and unwelcome pesky Australian flies were abundant.

Before we departed for Australia, Barry Orr, Executive Director of the Technological Development Corporation of Adelaide (TDCA), and the host for the Conference sent his intern to California to meet with me and to be shown parts of Silicon Valley. David Biggs was a young, bright, and energetic American MBA graduate from UCLA who had taken a two-year internship with TDCA. David arrived in my office in San Francisco about three weeks before I was to leave for Australia. David gave me a rough draft of the proposed schedule pointing out that I was to limit my address to 30 minutes with an added 15 minutes for Q/A and discussion. The allotted time suited me well because I had a few slides and each took a few moments for an audience to absorb. We discussed the general agenda and what was in store for the participants during the three-day presentations. Fortunately there would be just in-situ receptions except for one banquet to be held at Innovation House, the main building of TDCA. He advised that Emily, as my wife, was to be a guest at all presentations, dinners, and the banquet.

On that note we proceeded to lunch and then a quick run-through of some of the gems that make Silicon Valley what it is. David Biggs had lived in Southern California but was not familiar with the San Francisco Bay area or with the Peninsula; he must have taken more than a hundred photographs for his file on IT. Ligia had made all the arrangements and the schedule, even to the closing dinner that evening at the Wharf Restaurant, located right on the Embarcadero of San Francisco's Bay.

I was both pleased and proud to have been invited to the Adelaide Conference to discuss a subject that I had thought was of little interest to many of the members of IASP. I knew that a few members and friends, such as Dominique Fache, Umberto Bozzo, and Pierro Formica, supported my position but on the whole many others were content with selling and managing real estate; that approach did not do much for attracting magnet industries, incubators, and developing critical-mass clusters of partnering creators and producers. Would I have a friendly audience or would my presentation be rejected at the outset? I worried that I might lay an egg or worse, have some of the egg on my face. I would soldier on anyway because after the Conference I wanted my three weeks for exploring Australia!

In November 1989 we boarded a Qantas Airline flight from San Francisco via Los Angeles to Sydney, Australia. In Sydney we boarded another Qantas flight to Adelaide, South Australia. Our total flying time was sixteen and a half hours. I suspect that because the time change matched also pretty much the time difference between California and Australia our jetlag was not severe. When we arrived in Sydney to change to a domestic flight we met several of the members of IASP, including Michael Ryan from Ireland's Limerick University Technology Park, Harry Nichols from England's Birmingham University Technology Park, and Dr. Raymond Smilor, professor at the University of Texas, Austin, and Director of IC^2. (As I have indicated earlier, IC^2 was a think-tank established by Dr. George Kozmetski whose goal was the study and promotion of IT entrepreneurship worldwide.) All three gentlemen have become friends and at times we correspond to discuss issues pertaining to entrepreneurship. On several occasions I had lunch with Dr. Smilor in California and we talked about his work in Russia and mine in Ukraine.

George Kozmetski was a brilliant person, a man of vision, and a sensitive creator of ideas and projects. A past starter and partner of Teledyne Corporation, George retired from the firm he started and accepted a professorship at the University of Texas (UT), Austin, in the School of Business. While teaching at UT, he started IC^2, a dynamic think-tank delving into the arena of ideas and entrepreneurship. Soon after the think-tank was opened he hired one of his students, Raymond Smilor, to be its director. George's hand in IT can be most vividly seen in his sponsorship of the computer maker Michael Dell.

Dell was one of his undergraduate students at UT and also was a young man who built computers tailor-made from the back of his 1970 Chevrolet. Recognizing the talents that oozed out of Dell, George staked him in starting his own assembly plant for computers. The story is well known: DELL Computers emerged as a leading PC firm and Michael never finished his degree at UT, but his professor became the first member of DELL's board of directors. Michael Dell's approach, by and large, was to buy computer systems and components from a variety of sources, then assemble them into ready-built computers and sell the finished product. This method of selling computers or other assembled products involves becoming a value-added reseller (VAR). A VAR adds quality through assembly to components that otherwise would have little extrinsic value to customers. In other fields we find that having a whole oak tree is good and cheap to sell, but extracting and manufacturing furniture from that tree adds a whole lot of VAR benefit. A customer wants value from the item purchased, more value than what the raw source can provide, unless the customer is looking at producing something from the raw material to obtain the value-added quality. It is VAR that offers more benefit, more revenue, and more profit than may be obtained from unassembled components or raw material. Michael Dell saw that benefit early and took advantage of it.

At George's invitation, I met Michael Dell and on several occasions when I went to Austin, Texas I had a meal with him, either at his home or George's. On these occasions I learned a good deal about the computer business and the success at placing Dell's product in Costco and other wholesale stores.

Once in Adelaide, and after unpacking our bags at the Hyatt Hotel, I received a telephone call from Michael Ryan asking us to dinner. Michael had been told that Adelaide had a good Greek restaurant and he wanted to try it

before the conference started in the morning. Michael Ryan was president of
IASP at the time and much of his energy would be taken up by the conference, but tonight he wanted to talk to me about the Multifunctional Project
(MFP) for Adelaide that Bechtel was vying for with the now defunct accounting firm Arthur Anderson. The MFP project was to be sponsored by the
Japanese. The intent was to develop an IT complex in Australia but the sub-
intent was to locate retired Japanese folks in Australia and hence out of the
financial current of mainland Japan.

I had been asked by Bechtel to make time while in Adelaide to meet with
the mayor, Michael Llewellyn-Smith, and to attend a private meeting with
would-be Japanese funders and Arthur Anderson planners for MFP. Much as
I was not involved in MFP, I had heard a great deal about the project from
colleagues and from Emily who was also working on it. Moreover, when
Bechtel and my colleague Michael Wakelin targeted the MFP, I was suggested as project manager, a task that I refused because I did not believe the
Japanese were sincere about their intentions; as it turned out my appraisal
was correct.

Dinner with Ryan was delightful in spite of the fact that the Greek cuisine
was far from excellent but the company and the camaraderie made up for it.
Ryan was interested in linking with the MFP. The director of the Adelaide
Technological Park (the host park for the conference), Barry Orr, also was
keen to know exactly how MFP was planned, particularly because it was
funded by the Japanese — and both the Australians and the Irish are wary of
the Japanese. But on another side, the MFP would be draining much of the
energy from possible investments that were now going to the Adelaide Technological Park (ATP).

My concern was that the Japanese had a tendency to open up a region
under the pretext of investing in IT when in reality they wanted a place to
relocate their senior citizens. Investment in such a complex soon dried up
when it became obvious that the project was not to be productive; the relocated Japanese citizens were then left to burden the local economy with their
demands.

A good example of that can be seen in some of the Caribbean islands. The Japanese promised investment, developed complexes using their own labor and construction firms, and relocated several hundred of their own senior citizens. A few years later, the supporting infrastructure needed repairs. At that point, the Japanese washed their hands of the project, leaving and abandoning the domestic economy, which was burdened with the costs and the management of the complexes. I did not wish the Australians to suffer the same fate. Of course I was certain that this might happen in Adelaide but history ignored may be history repeated. I wanted more proof but Bechtel and Anderson wanted a revenue-producing project, especially an opportunity for the engineering and construction firm to build and build.

Our accommodations at the Hyatt Hotel were excellent. Emily, true to form as a travel director, went about to plan for our three-week holiday in Australia. I reviewed the slides, re-read my text and made notes from it because though I was not going to read my presentation, IASP wanted a written text for publication. In looking over the slides, Emily, the editor, noticed that my opening slides were missing. After alerting me that new slides had to be made because I couldn't have San Francisco send me the slides in time for the presentation, she scoured Adelaide for a graphics shop that could make the missing slides in time for the presentation. She was successful: at 8:00 a.m. the next day the slides were delivered to my room.

My presentation was scheduled for 11:00 a.m. and I was ready and primed. The Q/A session would follow the presentation, followed by the lunch break. I was happy with that schedule because it allowed for serious discussion before lunch. My address lasted 20 minutes and the Q/A session went until 12:45. As gauged by other sessions it was a long time but I was ready to defend my position and to explain as forcefully as I could that IT firms did not need real estate management firms to tell them where to implant themselves.

Of course as I expected, the questions began to dwell on who was the "controlling authority" in such places as Silicon Valley or Boston's Route 128 IT complexes. I had covered that issue in the address but obviously there was still some incredulity floating around in the heads of some participants. "Who would manage the complex?"

My answer was crisp and direct: "No one!" Then I added that municipal governments monitored who was where and how they built in those selected locations. The following issues were put into the mix for the selection of a coherent location: the forces of the market were applied, the demands of the firms for good or potentially good infrastructure, educational institutions were carefully examined, the quality of the working force was scrutinized, and the quality-of-life in the region was given much attention.

I'm not certain that I resolved all their concerns as they related to unmanaged IT centers. Cultural changes need to happen in those societies where control is important. The representatives from the UK were keen to shed any control, especially governmental control; Margaret Thatcher was offering new options and better approaches even if they were drastic for the short term. Italy wanted to shed Rome's shackles but that proved to be difficult; however, hopes were high with the emergence of the EU, which promoted a market-economy and movement away from a centralized system.

I think that I concluded the Q/A session with a call for changing paradigms, drastic as that might be for most participants and governments. I cautioned my listeners that I was not against government or the statutes and laws that come with government, but I was not supporting government interceding in all that was developed just for the sake of centralized control. Market forces were as strict as any government and much more efficient, if controls and rules were in place, especially when it came to controlling businesses, research, and the economy.

The conference continued with several great presentations and two in particular given by Ray Smilor and Dominique Fache. Ray in his usual manner of "walk-the-talk" offered marketing points for attracting entrepreneurs. Dominique approached his address by showing how artists make ideational choices when they create a work. I found his address to be rich in creative points for options to guide a firm in identifying a suitable location. On the last evening we were taken by bus to a reception at the Adelaide Technological Park hosted by Barry Orr. The reception turned out to be fun, and Barry was a great host and organizer.

The next day I had a meeting at noon with the mayor of Adelaide, Michael Llewellyn-Smith. Michael was a graduate of Cambridge University and a classmate of Michael Wakelin. Our discussion dwelt mostly on what the Japanese would be bringing to Adelaide.

After our discussion we walked over to a conference where the MFP interested group was scheduled to meet. I listened to the mayor make his cordial presentation to the Japanese representatives. Arthur Anderson's presentation soon followed, as did others — most in a sense drooling for the Japanese candy. I spoke a few words noting that caution was necessary because it all seemed to be too good to be true.

The Japanese Consul General in Adelaide made a short presentation promising the sun, the moon, and the entire firmament of heaven! When questions were called for I got up and inquired how long the Japanese would fund the project and how much control they expected the Australians to relinquish. The answer was hazy and far from satisfactory for me.

"Your honor, you are looking to settle Japanese senior citizens in South Australia but what will Japan offer in return?"

The answer I received was that Japan would pump cash into the Australian economy for several years and would help the Adelaide Technological Park and other IT centers in South Australia and refine them to be technologically smarter for the global economy.

"But Australia has a good technological industry; it is their pride and joy. Moreover, it is not involved in reverse engineering or de-engineering but is occupied with genuine creative technology." I sat down. My bomb had been thrown and the target was hit squarely in the center. The meeting was adjourned and a reporter approached me with a barrage of questions. I avoided saying anything more and left to visit the Anglican Cathedral in Adelaide.

The Anglican Cathedral was located on the edge of Adelaide's inlet. In terms of architecture it was built in simple gothic style without much adornment or clutter. While looking around I met a young priest, Lang Wilberforce, and we chatted for a few minutes about what he did and the complexity of instructing the congregation and the diocese in the use of their new revised BCP, which had been approved at their last convocation. The priest was a Junior Canon and specifically tasked with liturgical instruction, and in that capacity he traveled to the parishes of the diocese.

Escorting me, the priest took me to the sacristy to show me the vestments that had recently been given by the Episcopal Diocese of Chicago. After the sacristy tour he took me to the bell tower for a panoramic view of the city of Adelaide and the harbor. When the tour was completed he invited me for a cup of tea and we chatted for a while. He was most interested and curious as to how I managed secular work and responsibilities in a parish. We ended our conversation too soon because I had to meet Emily and prepare for our drive to board the ferry to Kangaroo Island, where we were to spend three days.

Personal Exploration of Australia's Beauty

After fetching the rental car, loading it, and paying my hotel bill, we drove towards the city limit but soon discovered that our windshield wipers did not function. Not wanting to wander into the rain (which is not a major issue in Australia, but I felt it was sensible of us to have it repaired), we doubled back to the car rental office. A few minutes later with the wipers tightened, we again headed to the city limits and were on our way to the ferry for the crossing to Kangaroo Island. The car rental agent had warned us that the insurance would not cover us on the ferry crossing, "But if you have a mishap and the ferry sinks, you will not be around to worry about insurance!" The crossing was done without any problem.

Before arriving at the ferry loading area, we stopped for a cup of tea because we were a bit early, since it had taken us a short time to drive down to the end of the peninsula. We stopped in Debenham, not too far from Victor's Harbour, at a quaint looking cottage, called the "Pig 'n' Whistle," sporting a sign that promised tea and goodies.

In the cottage, the hostess greeted us warmly and we ordered tea, sandwiches, scones, and the accompanying goodies. Soon a little boy came politely to serve us the sandwiches, scones, and homemade marmalade. The hostess brought the tea and engaged us in conversation. We shared that we were in the process of opening a bed and breakfast and were serving tea to our guests as they arrived at check-in time. We were served an Assam tea, of which she was very proud because it was ordered from a distributor in Massachusetts. Later upon returning to America we discovered that the distributor was Upton, one of our tea suppliers too.

The little boy was a darling of poise, courtesy, and charm. We still often refer to our tea in the little cottage near Victor's Harbour, and the little boy who helped his mother with the hosting. It was a memorable afternoon for Emily and me.

After tea we headed for the ferry and still had a few minutes to wait before embarking. We were ahead of the queue and next to me was a passenger car with a huge and sturdy grill in the front. Too curious to keep silent, I rolled down the window of my car and asked what that grill was for.

"Hey, mate, it's a 'roo-bar. You know, a grill to protect the car if and when we encounter a 'roo."

I paused for a moment to examine the 'roo-bar. "You mean it protects the bonnet against a collision with kangaroo?"

"You got it mate. Don't drive at night unless you have a sturdy 'roo-bar!" he advised. I obeyed his advice and avoided night driving.

It was time to board the ferry to Kangaroo Island. After the loading was complete we went to the tearoom to pass the time in comfort. The crossing was estimated to last approximately one and a half hours. We found a table and soon were joined by another passenger, a kindly gentleman who lived on Kangaroo Island but worked in a vineyard on the mainland during the week as a winemaker charged with controlling the fermentation. As he told us about the Island he warned us against driving at night because kangaroos were mostly nocturnal. He also suggested that we drive slowly because the gravel that had been used to resurface the roads of the island was in the shape of small balls, thus making tire and road adhesion impossible. In other words, it was slippery and foreigners driving on the island often got into trouble because they took turns too rapidly and consequently were prone to slide around out of control. We followed all the advice we were given and had a lovely holiday on Kangaroo Island.

Arriving on Friday evening before dark, we drove straight to Wisteria Lodge in Kingscote, at the center of the island. That night we searched the nearby shore for fairy penguins because the lodge attendant had suggested that we might see a few. We took our travel flashlight and went searching. At it turned out, to our disappointment, we never saw any.

The next morning, Saturday, we drove to the western side of the island and just before the lighthouse we saw a small kangaroo and a young boy. The boy was feeding the kangaroo pieces of an apple; it was obviously a pet kangaroo being cared for by its owner. We stopped and the boy introduced us to Casey, the pet kangaroo. Emily petted the young animal and fed it a few pieces of apple. It had been an orphan and the boy had adopted it as a pet. I took photographs and recorded the event for posterity. The "roo" had soft fur and a friendly attitude. When standing on his hind legs he was approximately 24 inches in height and may have weighed 15 pounds. His eyes were big and round and obviously had evolved for nocturnal existence. This was the first time either one of us had been that close to a kangaroo and that familiar with one. We savored the experience.

The next morning we headed to a national park where several dozen southern sea lions were hauled out on the beach. We chatted with a park naturalist and learned much about their habits on the island. After looking at sea lions and learning a bit more from the naturalist about their special characteristics, we headed for a small beachfront village located not far from the park.

It was a lovely beach, one that would have enticed me to settle there had I not had obligations that did not allow me to retire then and there. The village was built around the arc of a small bay; there were perhaps ten or twelve single dwelling houses, each facing the bay. The beach was immaculate and the ocean offered practically no visible surf. I wondered how it was in the winter when the southern freezing winds spilled over Kangaroo Island with a vengeance. One of the residents stopped to greet us and I asked about the winter weather. Winter winds were not pacific at all, but the surf was never dangerous. Yes, it would get very cold but snow was light and rain normally reached 50 inches. I don't mind the cold so I saved that village in my dream file for future reference!

Sunday morning after packing the car for the trip to the mainland and securing the car's loose battery with rope found in the main trash container, we headed for the ferry to return to the mainland. We stopped for some tea and a sandwich near the ferry building and discovered that our waitress had lived in Santa Cruz, CA and that her brother was a diesel mechanic in Redwood City. After lunch we still had a few minutes before the arrival of the ferry so we entered a pottery shop and I purchased a small mug with an amusing face on it; I often use the mug and remember fondly my short sojourn on Kangaroo Island.

Returning to the mainland we drove to McLaren Vale Lodge, where we spent the night on the shore of McLaren Lake and ate dinner at the restaurant. For dinner I treated myself to half a bottle of South Australia Wolf Blass 1985 Claret and kangaroo steak from a farmed, range-fed animal. I ordered the steak charcoal grilled on the rare side and with no fat; the steak arrived cooked to perfection and doused with an Australian version of Marchand de Vin sauce. Emily had a local cut of pork but appeared to be envious that she did not have the temerity to try something new, especially the tender Australian range-fed kangaroo fare.

On Monday we drove to Burra, an old copper mining town where bauxite is currently also extracted for the aluminum smelters in Saudi Arabia. The name Burra is often given to mining towns but I don't know why. Near Copperhill, there was a mine called Burra-Burra from which was extracted copper sulphate and gold. In Burra we stayed at Emily's father's namesake, the Paxton Square Cottages, which were old quarters for miners when more of them were employed before mechanization replaced many. In Burra we found a small tea place and refreshed ourselves with a cup-o-tea — not quite of the caliber of the "Pig n' Whistle."

After tea it was approaching sunset so we wandered around to explore the small town. Many pieces of old mining machinery were on display as were several plaques noting the miners who had died either in mining accidents or fighting in WWII. I concluded that miners lived a life of "either the fire or the frying pan."

Walking past some jacaranda trees with blue blossoms, we heard hundreds of birds fussing and carrying on. The noise was such that we could hardly hear each other's voices when we spoke. I shall never forget the cacophony that was produced by these birds, many of which had yellow coloring. I can still hear their songs, whistling, and general noises.

For dinner that night we selected the only restaurant-inn in Burra, where we had our first of a series of veal Parmesan dinners of this portion of our trip. A man smiled at us when we arrived and as we were seated. We encountered this same man in Hawker, on our next stop. The man must have been a salesman serving the merchants on the same route we were traveling.

That night in Burra, when the town lights were practically out and the sky was clear with billions of stars in the dark firmament, I called Emily to view the Southern Cross. Emily had never seen the Southern Cross and this was the perfect place to view it because there were no artificial lights interfering. The Southern Cross was to be seen plainly and stood out as a monument in the southern heavenly sky. It was a splendid sight, and enjoy it we did.

The last time I had seen the Southern Cross was some distance north of Perth, in Geraldton, Western Australia. General Parker and I had driven several miles east into the Great Sandy Desert to escape any and all lights of civilization just so we could see the fantastic Southern Cross. I shall never forget the sight, the impression it made on me, and my feelings of diminutiveness as I absorbed the splendor of the firmament. The words of Psalm Eight "...what is man...." humbled me.

That night in Burra I found it difficult to fall asleep. When Emily had gone to sleep, I got up and went back outside to revisit the Southern Cross. I must have stayed out for several hours because soon the lights of dawn began to make the stars of the Southern Cross fade; but once again the impression did not fade away. When I went back to bed I must have fallen asleep because soon I was awakened by Emily reminding me that we had a bit of a drive to do yet that day.

It was to Hawker, home of the old Ghan Railroad, that we headed that late morning. We had made arrangements to spend several days in Hawker at the Outback Motel. The Outback Motel was a pleasant place except for the "modern" telephone system that double-charged us (we cleared that problem a few days after we left but it was a bit annoying because my telephone bill to Bechtel was enormous as it was, and doubling it made it shocking). After unpacking and getting settled we explored the town and found the Old Ghan Restaurant and art gallery.

The town was really a village with little to distinguish it from many in Australia. We could walk all over the town in less than an hour. It had an interesting park, garden, and public swimming pool that we used the next day. There were not too many restaurants, at least none that excited me, except the Old Ghan, which was operated by two quite attractive sisters. The town residents and especially the owner of the motel were quite concerned that the sisters who operated the Old Ghan were not the type that one would introduce to Mom. We found them delightful, cordial, hospitable, and most entertaining. The food was good, the drinks reasonable, the atmosphere pleasant, and the art in the gallery very good.

That night we walked over to the Old Ghan Restaurant (OGR) for a drink and dinner. Entering through the gallery we were taken aback by the lovely aboriginal sculptures and paintings. As I indicated above, I was also taken by the beautiful young hostesses and owners who greeted us warmly and with great charm.

After we were seated, one of the young hostesses brought me my Scotch and informed us that she and her sister, with the financial backing of her father, had purchased the old train station, with the land around it, and the left over rail pieces. They were great supporters of the Aborigines and liked to promote their art and their culture. Many of the town folk were not too crazy about what the OGR owners were doing, especially their way of dressing. "But that's the way it is," one of our hostesses announced. The younger sister was married and was also the cook. The eldest was the manager, bartender, and hostess; both were scantily but not shockingly dressed. The veal Parmesan dinner was superb, the service good, and the atmosphere excellent. Middinner the gentleman salesman from Burra came in and once again recognized us and we him. We smiled. Then he too ordered the veal Parmesan dinner.

When we returned to our motel, the manager inquired where we had dinner. When he was told that we had had a lovely time at the OGR, he indicated that his wife prepared great meals and that we should try her dinners. Moreover, he announced, "nice people do not frequent the Ghan Restaurant!" I suspect that aside from being scantily dressed, the girls' crime in the eyes of the motel owner was that they supported the Aborigines.

The following night we felt compelled to try the motel food (and the owner's wife's) dinner. It was an awful facsimile of the veal Parmesan dish! Next to the last night we returned to the OGR. When we ordered the dinner, the younger sister arrived and in less than 30 minutes she prepared a fantastic meal, but this time we avoided veal Parmesan and had kangaroo piccata, laced with fresh lime juice from OGR's garden. It was good!

The next morning we invaded the local swimming pool and found ourselves the only adults in a gathering of many kids. "Americans," the kids shouted gleefully as they waved at us. We became the VIPs of the swimming pool and had question after question thrown at us about many aspects of the United States. We felt very welcomed and enjoyed the clamor of the kids around us, and even shared throwing and catching the large red pool ball.

One little boy, probably age 11 or 12, wanted to know if America was really like heaven and was it a place that was fun all the time? I thought to myself that since Reagan was president and his administration was slowly sinking us financially, perhaps America could hardly be depicted as being heaven. I said nothing about my inner thoughts but suggested that America had what it took to become like heaven.

On the last night we returned to the OGR and asked to be surprised with the main course. We were served veal Masala, and it too was good. Again the younger sister arrived and activated the kitchen and emerged in less than half-an-hour with the main dish, then left.

Before leaving Hawker I received a phone call from John D. Sullivan, managing director of John Sullivan PTY.LTD, Perth, Western Australia. He wanted to discuss a potential project for some 800 hectares north of Perth. We decided to meet at the Hyatt Hotel, where we were booked in Sydney at the end of our holiday, which would be towards the end of November 1989. Mr. Sullivan had business in Sydney and serendipitously our meeting would dovetail nicely into our schedules.

I wasn't quite certain what Sullivan had in mind or why he called me. Ligia informed me that Sullivan had called my office and she had told him that I was in Australia for the month. He had been in touch with several members of IASP who had suggested that he contact me if he had a mega-project and if he wanted ideas for it. As complimentary as this sounded to me, I was puzzled because Bechtel was often very temperamental when it came to new projects and funding for such projects, especially in Australia where its experience for building was thin, being mainly involved in mining.

Our next stop after Hawker was to be Wentworth near the confluence of the rivers Darling and Murray in Victoria. Thus on Friday, November 24 we left Hawker and passed through Broken Hill, a former Bechtel mining town where work had ceased years earlier, and drove on to the Sportsman Inn Motel. We found the Inn to be comfortable and interestingly surrounded by several large aluminum water tanks. It was here that we learned about what the Aussies call "bore" water.

This water extracted from the subsurface is non-potable because of its very high mineral content. Bore water is used for irrigation, fire protection, and other non-potable uses. However, it depletes the sub-surface water unless it is recharged and in Australia that is a tentative possibility. Potable water is collected from rain in the large tanks that are strategically placed under roof gutters. One must be frugal with stored water from rain because it does not rain often in Australia; the rainy season is extremely short but when it arrives it comes in a deluge.

Our room at the motel was large and comfortable and had a little door over a counter that was large enough to allow a breakfast tray to be slid through it for the guests' breakfast. Breakfast was good and varied to some extent; it usually included eggs, meat, potatoes or fried bread-toast, a fruit, and coffee or tea. Often the meat served was a thick steak. One could not starve and one also skipped lunch; if lunch was to be part of the day, then a lot of the breakfast was ignored.

Not far from Wentworth, the Darling and the Murray Rivers meet at a town called Mildura. It is a charming town shaded with hundreds, if not thousands, of blue jacaranda trees and golden silky oaks. November in Australia being still a month in spring, the trees were in full blossom and lovely to look at. We explored much of Mildura, taking in all the sights, including the large herb garden in the middle of the town where we sampled many fresh herbs.

That evening we decided to try our hand in one of the local watering holes for beer and dinner. Beer is almost the national drink of the Aussies, and in the pub we saw whole families enjoying the brew, the food, and camaraderie — everyone seemed to be well acquainted with everyone else. We were taken in and were included in many of the conversations surrounding us. The noise level was extraordinarily high but no one seemed to mind the cacophony. Yes, we had a good time being introduced to a lively cross-section of Australian local life. It was obvious that the Aussies liked Americans because we were always so warmly received and included in conversations. Even the Ghan ladies always took time to chat with us after serving us.

The next day we had an appointment to have lunch and a river tour onboard a side-wheeler riverboat. It was on this riverboat that we first heard the music and the birdcalls that were recorded by the captain. After lunch, I climbed to the wheelhouse to learn more about the boat and the music. The captain told me that he had recorded the music and birdcalls and he was willing to sell me a copy for a few dollars. Without hesitation I purchased a copy, then I asked if I could make copies of it. If I did not sell the copies I could.

We chatted for a long time and he told me that he was a retired sea captain who had carried ore from Australia to smelters around the world. After his retirement he wanted to do more bird watching and earn a little income. As the master of a paddleboat he could do both and not exert himself or be away from home. He was on the riverboat for only five hours every other day during the spring, summer, and fall, in the winter he properly recorded and mixed in with music the songs of birds that he had gathered in the wild. The sale of those tapes also provided him a small income. To this day we play our tape of birdsongs to start breakfast time at the Goose and Turrets.

From the top deck of the paddlewheel boat I could see both banks of the Murray River and the place where the Darling River merges into it. At this location the Murray was almost half a mile wide and greatly turbid. The captain explained that the river was not very deep and the current was slow because the whole land area was fairly level, but further downstream, as the land sloped towards the ocean, the current picked up some speed. The Murray River, the captain informed me, is Australia's longest permanently flowing river. The Murray River starts in the Australian Alps and winds west 1,609 miles and empties into the ocean southeast of Adelaide. During the southern dry season, the Murray is fed by the country's longest river, the Darling. The Darling River begins in the central part of the Eastern Highlands, the Blue Mountains, and flows southwest 1,702 miles to the Murray. The Darling is dry along most of its course in the Australian winter months, but its flow increases in summer, which is the rainy season. The Darling thus supplies the Murray when most of the other southern rivers dry up.

The captain then added, after a short pause, that we would not go too far downstream because he had to turn the boat around and this area was the widest for that maneuver. Slowly he urged the boat around to return upstream and back to Mildura. We actually watched the old side-wheeler make two U-turns, one to return north and the other to turn south to the dock.

Because we had encountered excellent herbs for our breakfast that morning we inquired where they were grown. They were grown locally and the herb garden was not far from the river. After we docked and said goodbye to the captain, we headed to the herb garden to learn about the local ways of raising the plants and soon discovered that it was not unlike what I've seen in California and, especially, in France. Several common types of herbs were grown, some in greenhouses, and the robust types outside in long raised beds. I sampled several types and even made a small bouquet to take back with me to give the car a more pleasant aroma than what the air conditioner supplied. Jacaranda trees surrounded the several parks of Mildura and because the trees were in full bloom the town was alive with color.

After Mildura, we forged ahead east towards the Blue Mountains where we were scheduled to spend two days. Midway to the Leura, our destination in the Blue Mountains, we stopped in Rankin Springs where we expected to spend the night to rest from the drive. The drive to that point, however, was neither tiring nor long. We stopped nevertheless to inform the innkeeper that we were canceling our reservation. The inn was not at all a place that I wanted to visit, and no one was around to receive my cancellation. I left a note on the office door and proceeded to the local general store where tea was served. Here was a charming owner and a great one for conversation. After learning that we were Americans the owner produced two cookies in the shape of the United States and sprinkled with red, white, and blue sugar. He was proud of these cookies and they were good.

When I asked him if I could use the public telephone to call Leura to alert the hotel that we would arrive a day earlier, we were informed that the only phone was the one outside. He did not have a telephone but always used the public phone. I looked for change for the phone and discovered that one places coins only after the operator specifies how many coins will cover the call. After obtaining the information/operator number, I placed my call and was spoken to by the operator. She gave me the number I wanted and the charge. I neither had enough change nor the correct change to cover the call and she couldn't accept a phone card or credit card for such a small amount as a dollar and twenty cents.

"Mate," the operator told me, "go ahead and make the call. It's on the house 'cause we like Yanks." That was a new one for me. Would an American telephone operator let me call long distance at no charge?

Further Exploration of the Australian Sub-Continent

We continued to Leura and to the Blue Mountains for a three-day visit in the cool and beautiful mountains of eastern Australia. The Blue Mountains Range forms a plateau of the Great Dividing Range and rises about 40 miles (65 kilometers) west of Sydney in New South Wales. Early settlers gave them their name because they usually appear in a bluish haze, the result of fine drops of eucalyptus oil in suspension in the atmosphere. The Blue Mountains cover about 550 square miles. They are bounded by the Emu Plains on the east and the Bathurst Plains on the west. The Blue Mountains rise to about 3,610 feet (1,100 meters) above sea level. The Grose and Cox's Rivers cross the range in deep, steep-sided valleys. Most of the slopes are covered with eucalyptus trees.

A few words about this magnificent tree that is often used as a wind break in the western United States: the eucalyptus that is most frequently planted in North America is the blue gum. The trees grow rapidly and reach a gigantic size, some reach heights that match those of the Giant Redwood trees. Some eucalyptus trees stand more than 300 feet (91 meters) tall. About 600 kinds of eucalyptus trees grow in Australia. Almost all of these trees are evergreen and shed their bark all year. The mature leaves are long, narrow, and leathery. The leaves of the young trees are silver-dollar shape. The flowers are filled with nectar. In Australia, eucalyptuses are the most important timber trees. The jarrah is an Australian eucalyptus with red wood much like mahogany. Australian manufacturers use eucalyptus lumber for ships, railroad ties, paving blocks, telegraph poles, fences, piers, and lovely furniture. In Sydney I have seen furniture, especially tables, made of eucalyptus wood that was absolutely exquisite. The trees furnish a resin, called Botany Bay Kino, which protects wood against shipworms and other borers. The bark of some species of eucalyptus trees furnishes tannin, which is used in medicine. The leaves contain valuable oil that is used as an antiseptic, a deodorant, and a stimulant. In Australian common parlance, the eucalyptus tree is called the gum tree. The cute Australian Koala bear (not actually a bear at all but a marsupial) eats eucalyptus leaves exclusively, but not the type that were imported to America.

When we reached our destination in the Blue Mountains, our reservations were made at a resort complex and our room, although small, overlooked a garden, the woods, and a pool, which I did not use because the temperature was rather cool. The Blue Mountains were mostly a holiday location for Australians.

After settling into our rooms and exploring the small town for a good restaurant, I stopped in one restaurant that offered bar service in a quiet lounge setting. Because I had not had a good martini I chanced it and asked the bartender if he would make me an American martini with Tanqueray gin, please don't ice the drink. What I received was a passable version of a fair drink. When it was time to move to the dining room I asked for the bill and soon discovered that my martini cost 18 Australian dollars, a pretty expensive tab for a drink. But here I was miles away from San Francisco and in possession of a Southern Hemisphere martini, so why would I complain? I enjoyed it and considered myself fortunate to be able to enjoy the gifts of the earth and also to be able to afford it. I gave the bartender a twenty!

Dinner was good but neither memorable nor too expensive. It was still early in the evening so Emily and I decided to take a walk through the town. Passing a liquor store, I stopped to price a bottle of Tanqueray with the idea of making my own martini. A small bottle of Tanqueray gin, a jar of olives, and two glasses came to $22.00 — now I had many drinks at my disposal as there was a refrigerator in our room. In a martini there are one, two or three olives to accentuate the fine taste of the mix of Tanqueray and light vermouth; I like mine with three olives.

As an aside let me say for those who might one day make a martini for me, that the only gin I like, and like very much, is Tanqueray; forget serving me other gins! And don't even try to tempt me with vodka as a substitute.

What we had not purchased, however, were toothpicks to handle the olives; one cannot have free olives in the drink that can only be brought out with one's fingers. So ingenuity was summoned. I broke two twigs from a nearby tree, and with my multi-blade Swiss Army knife I fashioned two toothpicks. This was the genesis of a new tradition of making toothpicks whenever I was in a pleasant, relaxing, and holiday location. At present, I possess many toothpicks from twigs obtained in Russia, Ukraine, France, Spain, interesting parts of the United States, and other places I have visited.

Much of my life revolves around good food and good drink, and not too much of either. Some folks eat to live, but I live to eat. I enjoy the gifts of the Earth and especially of God. What is life without a happy palate, good smells, rich textures for the mouth, and excellent conversations with friends, particularly if they also enjoy food?

The next morning, after breakfast, I thought that it would be more wholesome to leave the car and walk to Leura and explore the small town and its gardens. As in any resort town, we found both vacation houses in some neighborhoods that were crammed together and shoddily built, and some beautiful houses that were well maintained. It was obvious that the latter were houses occupied by full-time residents, most of whom were either local business owners or retired professionals. On the whole, what we saw indicated that Australians were not too different from Americans, except perhaps for the accent, which was less than pleasant to my ears.

I've always had an ear for accents, not that I can duplicate accents that I admire, but to me the common Australian tonic speech is not one that I'd like to possess. Crisp educated Oxford or Cambridge speeches have qualities that I'd like to acquire; even more melodious to me is the Scottish brogue, but with my name, such an acquired dialect would never appear to be genuine or appropriate.

Nevertheless, apart from their speech, Australians are a delightful people; at least those that I've met were wonderfully funny, interesting, welcoming, and hospitably warm.

On our way to look at some of the neighborhoods, we entered a lovely park and because it was springtime, everything was in bloom. There were children playing and adults sitting on benches either talking or reading. Near a seesaw we noticed a metal cage structure of an airplane. It was too good to ignore for a photograph. I asked Emily to sit in the rear seat and I set up my camera for time delay and perched it on a nearby concrete ledge, focused it, cocked it for a 10-second shutter take, and rushed to sit in the front seat. Just as I called "smile" the shutter clicked. Later when the film was developed it proved to have been a successful photo opportunity and the picture hangs in our Clipper Room with the caption, "How we flew to Australia!"

Kids came over to ask us what we were doing. "Flying this extraordinary airplane," I replied as seriously as I could manage my face.

"Flying the aeroplane, mate?" a carrot top girl asked.

"Yep," I said, "and all the way from America!"

"Nah, it got holes and 'tis anchored to good ole earth mate," a dark-eyed boy exclaimed.

"But just think of it this way. I'm a special type of pilot and can whisk about in such an airplane." They looked at me, wanting, I think, to believe me. "Just imagine and see yourself flying like a bird, across the land, the ocean, and in the wind." I looked at the sky and all eyes were also on the sky. Birds were flying above our heads. "Just like the birds but more free because you're able to appreciate what you are doing up there in the air. Floating and sailing in the wind."

The carrot top little girl admitted, "I'd much like to fly too, jus' like a bird."

"You can," I said. "When you are a bit older you can take flying lessons and then you can soar just like the bird. I was about 13 years old when I started. How old are you?"

She looked at me, staring me in the eye for a long moment. "I'm 11 but going on to 12." I could see her brain rushing ahead in excitement at what the future held for her.

"You can surely learn to fly and nothing can stop you if you really want to." We climbed out of the steel cage airplane and the kids scrambled to climb into it. The carrot top girl just looked at the structure and looked at us.

"Can I really learn t' fly mate?" she called out.

"Yep," I replied, "if you really want to." I thought to myself that perhaps that little carrot top child had seen her vision, her goal, and, perhaps, she would end up flying. I'd like to know if she has. Maybe I will someday.

It was just about like that when I looked through the cyclone steel fence enclosing the Waterbeach military training field near Cambridge on the A10. Could I fly an airplane? I thought that pilots were a very special breed of people who possessed extraordinary qualities. They had good eyesight, good health, good responses and other qualities that separated them from the rest of the public. The military selected the very best physical specimens to use as pilots, but what they never revealed was that such pilots were to become "combat" service people. One does not need to be a superman to learn to fly a light aircraft. Anyone with a good brain, and fairly good eyesight and hearing can manage an aircraft, perhaps not in combat, but for pleasure. I hope that little redhead has pursued her dream to become a pilot.

As we walked away to dinner, I thought of another girl, but this time in Texas.

She was the captain of a Boeing 727 flying out of Austin to Dallas Fort Worth (DFW). It was a short flight, but the thunderclouds were right over Austin and our flight was being delayed. Suddenly, the flight deck door opened and the captain came out. She recognized me and I recognized her immediately. She came over and hugged me. "Raymond," she said, "I'm Carol McHenri from Memphis."

Yes, I remembered. She was a pretty young girl that I knew when I was a deacon at St. Mary's Cathedral in Memphis.

"I'm with American Airlines and love my job. Captain of the 727 now based in Oklahoma City but I'm due to switch to the 737 in two weeks and be based in Dallas for the Chicago run."

Yes, I remembered this young person. She had been in my senior youth group and her dream was to be an airline pilot when airlines shied away from hiring women for the flight deck. "You want to fly the big one? Then push the glass ceiling, crack the barricade, and show them that you are a good pilot," I advised.

We had spoken then about persevering, getting her ticket, her rating, accumulating hours by flying in a lot of inclement weather, and applying to the airlines. I had suggested American Airlines because that line appeared to be willing to cross frontiers when others would not. She applied after accumulating flying hours, obtaining her Aircraft Transport Pilot (ATP) rating, and applying over and over again. Finally American Airlines called her in for an interview. She was one of 23 women applying for two openings on the line as Second Officer. She got the position and started as a Flight Engineer on the 727. A few years later she was given the opportunity to be copilot, then a few years later was allowed to be in the left seat. "You gave me the courage to forge ahead, Raymond."

"Perhaps, but you had the talent and the passion and they served you well." We chatted for a few moments until the copilot came out of the flight deck to advise Carol that dispatch was clearing this flight for Dallas. We said goodbye and I've not seen her since. I did, however, receive a note in 2000 that she had been assigned to the Boeing 757/767 and would be receiving copilot training for European flights.

Sydney and Moreton Bay Bugs

After our virtual garden flight we went to a small Italian restaurant for a light dinner, if that is possible with Italian fare. One of my pursuits was to find some national food, apart from kangaroo meat prepared with mushrooms à la Australiene. One day when I asked if Australia had national dishes that represented the culture, the response was: hamburgers and beer!

After our stay in the Blue Mountains we drove down through the town of Penrith and encountered our first four-lane highway into Sydney. I returned the car and took a taxi to the Hyatt Hotel where we would spend four days and also where I was scheduled to have a meeting that afternoon with John D. Sullivan, managing director of John Sullivan PTY.LTD, Perth, Western Australia.

Promptly at 3:00 p.m. I received a call from the lobby announcing that I had a visitor waiting for me in the business lounge. Mr. John Sullivan was a most pleasant person, an entrepreneur who owned his own firm in Perth but who had small projects in other parts of Australia. He wanted to have a "piece of the action" of the MFP. When I informed him that the Multi-Function Project was dead before it was allowed to be born, he quickly shifted to initiating a joint venture project with Bechtel in the field of IT. Perhaps Sullivan PTY could become a partner and help Bechtel develop land in Perth. Well, after much discussion, I informed him that I would consider his proposal, present it to Bechtel, and see what would surface from it. It was obvious that he had neither title to the land nor money to start a feasibility study. What Sullivan presented did not offer much for Bechtel, especially since he had not lined up any potential investors to give the idea momentum.

When our meeting was ended he recommended that Emily and I hop in a taxi and head to an excellent restaurant at South Head Point of Sydney Harbor. John urged us to order Moreton Bay Bugs for dinner. Moreton Bay Bugs are lobsters that are caught in the water of Moreton Bay off Brisbane. Indeed, I had several and found them extraordinary. The restaurant was located on the cliff of the entrance of the Sydney Harbor, at South Head. Sitting down for dinner we could see North Head, ships entering and leaving the harbor, and the lights of the city of Sydney at twilight. Sydney harbor is an active inlet both in terms of ocean ships and in terms of small traffic. Water taxis, bay water buses, private boats, ferries, and small paddle boats used the harbor at all hours of the day and night.

The next morning I spoke to John Sullivan when he called me and discussed several projects that we might find the means to collaborate on if and when Bechtel was willing to invest in the preliminary efforts or when he would locate investors who were interested in long-term projects such as the one in Perth. As a parting note he suggested that we visit the paleontological and anthropological museums in Sydney (both were within walking distance from the Hyatt Hotel), and then the activities around the harbor, such as the craft shops, the zoological and botanical gardens, the Opera house, and more.

I kept communicating with Sullivan for several years but we could never find a project to develop, even after I retired from Bechtel. Sullivan had access to 500 hectares north of Perth but no deep pockets to help us get the project started. Ultimately, I lost contact with John and have never been able to relocate him or his firm. He was a good sort of a fellow and I would have liked to work with him. But as in many "potential projects" the key is gathering a consortium of investors and in this case John was not able to find the right people to support his proposal and I was too far away to help him. The seeds to get the project started in Perth were just not available for John. In my experience, for every dozen potential projects at least eleven are never realized.

True to from, Emily and I set out to explore the city of Sydney. First on our agenda were the paleontological and anthropological museums. The first offered an extraordinary collection of assembled dinosaurs; videos showed their history, the excavation sites, and the work and research that accompanied the extraction of the bones. The anthropological museum dealt fairly and honestly with treatment by the white settlers of the Aboriginal culture. One segment of the museum show encouraged the viewers to exchange roles and act as if the white settlers were the native, original culture in Australia, and the Aboriginals were the invaders. It was not until the late 1970s that the Australian government stopped the ill treatment of the natives and decided by law to give the Aboriginals equal status with the white settlers as citizens. The displays and the documents in the anthropological museum indicated that although the law gave the Aboriginals equal status, much discrimination still prevailed, especially in subtle ways. Racism does not evaporate with the implementation of a non-discrimination law. Just look at the United States: even with an African-American president elected twice we still hear, see, and encounter racism and its effects. In the case of President Barack Obama, he is not a descendant from slaves and yet he is regarded as one. Racism is slow to overcome but I hope that it will be in the very near future.

I daresay that much of the prevailing racism, religious, and national discrimination in the world is caused by insecurity, self-doubt, and a low opinion of oneself. Australia, United States, Japan, the cultures of Africa, and others represent overt discretionary positions among the human races, but what is more critical is the underlying discrimination that runs like a silent underground current throughout human behavior. Often this discriminatory characteristic does not appear obvious at first, but influences many decisions that people make throughout life. The racial distinction is apparent obviously in apartheid, but that racism is also present in nationalism, tribalism, and clanism.

The questions that must be asked are: What have you done to be a member of the white, black, red, or yellow race? What have you done to be born an American, a Mexican, a Japanese or any other national group? The operative answer to these questions and other similar ones is "nothing." Nothing. What have you done to be born in America, Mexico, Australia, or Uganda? Indeed nothing. Yet, you are different and set apart because...?

In the United States there is a second-class classification that is given to all citizens who are naturalized. Native-born American citizens are permitted to access the highest office of the land, the presidency of the United States of America. Naturalized citizens are not eligible, are not allowed, and are excluded from the highest office of the land, even though they can vote for that office. This is indubitably an overt act of discrimination by the Constitution, perhaps not racial discrimination but nonetheless it is discrimination because it assumes that native born citizens are worthy to be president but legally naturalized citizens are not, even when they have added to the wealth of the nation, paid their taxes, served honorably in the armed forces to protect the security of the United States, and otherwise been model, upstanding, honest, and faithful citizens. Moreover, the naturalized citizen has made a deliberate choice to become an American and his or her citizenship is not the product of an accidental birth that occurred within the national borders of the United States.

On this planet Earth, we are all transient citizens and borders do not produce better human beings; it is what is inside the humans that counts and not the race, religion, sex, or country of origin. America is a nation populated by immigrants; even Native Americans (Indians, so called) are immigrants although they arrived several thousand years earlier than most, yet the Constitution dictates that we must discriminate against immigrants when it comes to the highest office, and at times lower positions too although not quite as overtly.

Continuing with our visit of the harbor city, I was very moved by the magnificent display in Sydney's Museum of Anthropology. As I intimated above, the issues that made life for the Aboriginals difficult and the inhumane manner in which both white citizens and the government treated them was not glossed over. I am under the impression that Australian racism has diminished greatly. For instance, Chinese citizens escaping from Hong Kong because of the island's return to the People's Republic of China have been permitted to settle and work in Australia. Australia has also accepted the permanent relocation of people from Laos, East Timor, Vietnam, and Cambodia. No longer are Aboriginals' children taken away from their parents to be educated as "white people." Improvement is a very slow process but it is a process nonetheless.

Sydney, we discovered, was a wonderfully interesting metropolis and the harbor area was one of its jewels. As a major port, Sydney was full of parks, gardens, open spaces, and a well-landscaped waterfront. There was much activity in and near the harbor. Apart from the good transportation in the harbor, there were also very special arts and crafts shops; one of these was a furniture store that specialized in jarrah furniture (red gum wood). The finish and the style of these pieces, especially the tables made of jarrah, were exceptionally beautiful. Had I had the transportation means to ship a table back to Montara I would have purchased one and would have been proud to own and display it.

Soon our visit to Australia and to Sydney would be ending and returning to San Francisco would be welcome after such a long, extensive, and full visit. We were approaching the Christmas season and preparations for the great feast were overwhelming. I wanted to see how a country that celebrates Christmas in the summer acted. No artificial snow or flocked trees were in sight. Summer was a good time for play, to have a holiday, and for enjoying the double celebration of sun, warmth, and Christmas. I was not surprised to find that the northern hemisphere's winter accouterments were missing and of no interest to the Australians — many had never seen snow or been exposed to Christmas in the dark winter December of the north. Emily reminded me recently that once at Ely for Christmas it snowed. Our fellow inn guests were from Australia and became as giddy as children at the sight of snow. Like Dickens!

I also wanted to ride the new monorail, which was part of the public transportation system for downtown Sydney. The ride was pleasant, smooth, fast, and overlooked much of the center of the city.

It is my feeling that a ride in a city's public transportation system offers a special understanding of how a city treats its foreigners. The conductor made change for the tickets either on the loading platform or on the train, and to an American that was surprising. Try obtaining change on a city bus in San Francisco, Los Angeles, or anywhere else in America. What do foreigners do in America when they do not know what the fare is or do not have the exact fare?

The flight back to San Francisco by way of Los Angeles was long but not difficult and I must commend Qantas for its fine service in business class. Back in San Francisco I had but a few days to check mail at the office and then board a flight to Paris for another four- or five-week business trip. Often I remembered that with Bechtel I had just enough time for my laundry to be done before another trip was scheduled. Off I went with my attaché bag and green shoulder bag to catch a British Airways or American Airlines flight to London or Paris. This time I was flying to Paris directly on American in the hope of being able to have my meetings and return in time for Christmas. This was scheduled to be a two-week trip to Paris just in time to see the wonderful Christmas decorations displayed by the shops.

Nîmes: Multipole

In 1989, I arrived in Paris from Brussels. After checking in at my hotel, Le Pavillion de la Reine, I called Howard Wahl, a senior director, at the Bechtel office to see what was at hand. What was at hand was Charles Osborne's project. Mr. Osborne was an American who resided in France and who spoke terrible French and more, he had this idea to create a high-tech (IT) complex in the vicinity of Nîmes. Now the reader must remember that I had had a meeting with Mr. Osborne a few months earlier and a project had been discussed briefly and in general terms and no conclusion surfaced. The real problem was that Osborne did not have the foggiest idea how such a project could be realized. He did have access to Dutch funds but was not able to get his ducks in a row for his project and moreover, he was his own worst enemy. Working with him was tantamount to keeping him as much as possible out of reach; that is to say, off the project. The day we could no longer keep Osborne away from the project, the project suffered a quiet death.

I was to telephone Mr. Osborne immediately. I did just that and we decided that Osborne would pick me up at five o'clock in the morning for the flight to Nîmes to view the proposed site.

Mr. Charles Osborne arrived to take me to Orly Airport for the day trip to Nîmes. I was ready at 5:00 a.m. to catch a 6:30 flight on Air Inter. Arriving at Nîmes Airport, Mr. Henri Thibiant, the retired United States manager of the French glass company St. Gobain, met us. Henri and I have become close friends since the time of Osborne and I am glad that our paths have crossed in spite of the failure of the IT Park project (Henri died in 2012).

Henri took us to the site where the IT Park was supposed to be constructed. The site was pie-shaped and not at all suitable for a quiet research park because it was sandwiched between two major highways, a railroad track, and was under several major high voltage power lines — each obstacle supplied built-in disturbances that would affect delicate measuring instruments. After I explained to Charles that the site was not acceptable because of its problems he replied that the Mayor of Nîmes had given him this site at no cost and had thrown in a 10-year tax offset.

"Good, Charles, build an industrial park if you wish but the site is not suitable for an IT Park," I advised him. "There are high-voltage power lines overhead and several main power transformers close to the perimeter." Osborne got angry. After he calmed down, I suggested that we look at other sites and then speak with the mayor about our intended project requirements.

After lunch Henri, who was quite familiar with both Osborne and the region, took us to two other possible sites. One of the sites was located directly across from the source of Perrier in a magnificent wooded area. I found this site to be acceptable and very suitable for an IT Park, but I wanted Dominique Fache to look into it for us. I called Dominique from Henri's small chateau (yes, a chateau) and described the site and asked if he would accept a retainer for a few weeks as a consultant. Osborne had agreed to send him a check for $3,000 for four weeks work and until he could be placed on a full salary. Dominique accepted and proposed to drive over in a day or two to look at the site and to search through the municipal records for details about the land, the owner, the limitations imposed by the statutes of the Departement, if any, and other potential problems.

That evening before catching the flight back to Paris, we had dinner prepared by Karin, Madame Thibiant. Henri was most helpful in giving me information about Nîmes, the Departement du Gard, Cacharel, the beauty supplies and clothing firm owned by the mayor of Nîmes, Mr. Jean Bousquet, and the political temperament of the municipality. Fortunately the fiasco caused by Osborne's lack of common sense never affected the friendship that surfaced between the Thibiants and me.

Upon our return to Paris I called Bob Jackson (he had yet to be replaced by Cain) to inform him that we would start on the Osborne project after I caught my breath, which meant when I returned to San Francisco and mobilized the supporting team that would include Ray Kingsley, Kalaa Mpinga, Steve Gomes, and Chip Tabor (both Gomes and Tabor soon left Bechtel). I asked Kingsley to become the project manager and, second, to prepare the contract with the technical service agreement and send it directly to Osborne, with a copy to Wahl. The concept plan was completed in October 1989 and the feasibility study was finished a month later. The cost of the feasibility study and the concept development plan would be $250,000 and Osborne deposited that amount in Bechtel's bank.

During the year or so that I was involved with the Nîmes project, I was also acting, at Wahl's recommendation, as a consultant to the European Community (EC), and supporting Howard Wahl's work to develop a European Bechtel presence. My efforts were taxed to their limit. Let me remind the readers again that Bechtel had been located in London and Paris since the end of WWII but had never registered as a European firm; in fact no key Bechtel person had ever had a meeting with either a British or French prime minister or a French president. I found myself flying from San Francisco to Paris and back almost every two weeks for approximately five months. It was not that I suffered from jetlag, but I had trouble getting my laundry done!

I had to juggle many projects during the years of 1985 to 1993, especially in 1989 when I took on the project that was proposed by Mr. Charles Osborne. I called on Ray Kingsley for assistance on the project and delegated to him the task of project manager while he and I managed the program that would realize the concept. Osborne had contacted two French firms, one of which was GTM, an engineering and construction conglomerate; the other was an architectural group, Alliance Architectures. He instructed those firms to create a rendering of what would become the IT Park.

The director general of GTM was Albert Perriguey, a bright but verbose man who was also a chain smoker. He was, however, an interesting and knowledgeable person who knew his profession well. I liked him and found him quite interesting. Albert was also an antidote to Osborne's meandering approach to the project. Perriguey was an engineer with feet firmly planted on the ground; Osborne was flakey, volatile, and filled with braggadocio.

One evening when we were lodged at Le Castellas hotel in Collias, after dinner and when everyone had retired, Perriguey raised some profound philosophical issues that kept us talking past two in the morning — and he had to catch a flight at seven a.m. Still we kept on talking and talking and drinking port. He wanted to know about the "holy" and where to find it. He had experienced the holy on several occasions and wanted to discuss the phenomenon with me. I'll say more about that later. Perriguey, a solid technical person, was nevertheless able to think philosophically and theologically, and appreciated the mysteries that presented themselves to him as he experienced life and its nuances.

The architectural firm and GTM were good, first class organizations but Osborne kept confusing the issues, changing the instructions, clouding the goals of the project, refusing to accept direction from Bechtel, and even going alone and, in the process, causing himself great difficulty. Because of his attitude and his unsettled manner, the investors in Amsterdam lost interest in his project. Moreover, the wealthy Spanish partner who had given Osborne the funds to hire the firms pulled his support.

After we prepared a concept development plan for the IT Park, both Ray and I finally took Osborne aside and pleaded with him to stay out of the project. The firm of GTM, the French construction group, and Alliance Architectures, were pleased that we made it clear that Charles Osborne would step aside although he could maintain the responsibility of raising the funds necessary for the project. Allowing Osborne to continue raising funds was our mistake and the consequential death of the project. Ray Kingsley had calculated that the first phase of the project that included purchasing the land, developing preliminary plan drawings, clearing the land, initiating a marketing effort to find out which firms showed an interest in establishing themselves in the park, developing the feasibility study to satisfy Bechtel and the potential sources of investment, and hiring a local manager who could "bird dog" the tasks agreed upon would cost approximately 3/4 of a million dollars. For the position of the local manager, I suggested to Osborne Dominique Fache who had been instrumental in the creation of the successful park Sophia Antipolis, in Valbonne. To my surprise, Osborne agreed to hire Fache who was to act as both the local representative and the consultant for the group.

Dominique is a prince of a person. He is bright, knowledgeable, visionary, and is very familiar with IT and what is necessary for creating a complex that can nurture its development. Unlike many of his French colleagues who are enamored with the business of real estate, Dominique sees real estate acquisition as the responsibility of the IT firms but that such properties may be collected into a large site, a sort of IT park managed only in so far that a property is acquired, through purchase or long term lease, from a seller or developer. In this case, Osborne's group would be the developer of what Charles called the "Europarc." Parcels of Europarc would be sold or leased to IT firms, be they established or incubators, and they would be responsible for managing their own properties. The necessary infrastructure would be built and would supply all utilities to the perimeter of the properties; within the perimeter, the IT firms would take over. In the case of the leased properties, Europarc would help with the in-property infrastructure connections, for a fee. Europarc would build a teleport facility to make global communication more readily available because France Telecom had archaic equipment, was a nationalized company suffering under impossible management restrictions and offering service at an exorbitant price, and was unable to furnish broadband services. Thus, as I said, Dominique Fache was to be the responsible on-site manager for Europarc, both through its developing phases, and in its ultimate operational phase.

Dominique and Charles both discussed the details of the retainer and their respective roles in negotiations with the mayor, the Departement du Gard, Bechtel, and the city of Nîmes. After we settled the employment by guaranteeing a one-year contract for Fache, he determined to find an apartment locally but would still maintain his townhouse in Nice that he shared with Dr. Michele Verschoore, his titular significant partner. Michele was a physician in charge of the laboratories of L'Oreal, the beauty products firm.

Dominique's first assignment was to make a presentation to the mayor and to the city council of Nîmes. Ray Kingsley and I worked with Dominique on that presentation as we enjoyed Nice and the surrounding region. We found the lovely Hotel Caesar on the Côte d'Azur, I met several of Dominique's friends, saw a performance in the Grand Theatre Regional of Nice accompanied by Michelle, and experienced several restaurants, especially those offering Algerian menus — Michele was born in Algeria and was familiar with North African cuisine. We also toured many of the galleries and absorbed the art every time we had a free moment.

On the day of the presentation, Dominique arrived fully prepared and in his crisp, high French he spoke convincingly to the local representatives of the city and of the Departement of the Gard. We had gathered in a huge conference room in the Hotel de Ville of Nîmes. The scent of the room reminded me quickly that we were in a room where discussions had taken place over many decades, perhaps even a couple of centuries. Would that the walls could speak!

The ceiling was decorated in gold leaf with details of local flowers and reflecting historical events such as the bullfights, the harvests, the Pont du Gard, and many, many other beautiful events. The walls were lined with dark wood shelves and supported books, vases, crystal goblets, and items that reminded visitors of the glorious history of the Gard. Three crystal chandeliers hung from the ceiling and offered bright lights, which gave a gay touch to the large room. Centered in the room was an enormous table which was constructed, I was informed, from the wood of a warship that had been wrecked near the fishing port of Le Grau-du-Roi, on the Gulf of Lions.

We assembled in the historic room and the mayor, Mr. Bousquet, greeted us. I introduced Osborne and Kingsley, and told the body that Dominique Fache was going to make the presentation and that questions would follow. The presentation soon followed. I had asked Osborne to tone down his comments; if he had any, they should be limited to a few words at the end of the presentation. My words fell on deaf ears as far as Osborne was concerned.

Dominique invited an architect friend to show sketches of how the Europarc would evolve as a contributing elegant place in the department of the Gard, home of the famous Roman aqueduct, the Pont du Gard. Nîmes was also the gateway to the Camargue, the great delta of the Rhone River before it emptied itself into the Gulf of Lion and the Mediterranean Sea. Nîmes still has a standing Roman Coliseum in the center of the town that adds much charm and punctuates its grand historical charm. Industrially, Nîmes is also the birthplace of the cloth for denim jeans (De Nîmes).

Dominique reminded those present that the first jeans trousers were made in the United States during the 1850s from material that originated in Nîmes by Levi Strauss, an immigrant from Bavaria. Strauss arrived in California during the Gold Rush and started a business manufacturing sturdy work pants for gold miners. He used brown canvas cloth at first but later made the pants of a tough cotton fabric from Nîmes, France. The word denim comes from the French phrase "de Nîmes," meaning from Nîmes or Nismes, as it was spelled at the time. Strauss dyed the denim a deep blue color called indigo, which became the traditional color for jeans. In 1873, Strauss and a tailor named Jacob W. Davis took out a patent for trousers strengthened with copper rivets at the pockets and other points of strain. Thereafter, the world fell in love with American-made denim pants, jackets, shirts, and other clothing, some of which are currently part of the designer series and quite expensive. Nevertheless, work clothes are still made although many are made not in America but overseas.

Thus it was important for Dominique to emphasize the history of the region, of the city, and to present Europarc as an elegant addition to this famous region of France. Of course, Dominique included as the final sign-off of the presentation the economic advantages that Europarc would bring and the employment by way of new jobs that it would add to the area.

The presentation was a success, but Charles Osborne was a disaster. Charles pushed the mayor by flaunting his connections and dropping names. No one was impressed. Moreover, Charles clouded the issues by implying that he did not need the city's support but would develop the park with or without the support of the locals. I'm not certain if his attitude was because his French was deplorable or because he could not restrain himself from acting as a "big shot." Dominique was able to rescue the meeting and keep the focus on the park and what it would contribute to the region. When Dominique finished, Ray Kingsley, as an economist and in his quiet voice and halting French, was able to redirect the conversation to a more appropriate level of reality. Thus the presentation ended on a good note with the mayor asking us to join him for lunch.

At lunch, Mr. Bousquet sat me on his left and Dominique on the right side, with Kingsley on my side thus precluding Osborne from sitting close by and putting a word in edgewise. I discovered that Mr. Bousquet was keen to have the IT park and that he was willing to facilitate the process both by offsetting the price of the land, any land we chose, and by asking that certain statutes be put in place to help the project further. We agreed that we should meet with the then-mayor of Montpellier, George Frêche, who had been successful in attracting an IT park and helping it to expand quite well. We all agreed that Nîmes was not a competitor to Montpellier.

After lunch I telephoned Frêche, whom I had met the previous year at a conference, and made an appointment to see him that evening at his home. The evening meeting with Frêche was good, and Dominique was an added support, although he wore red socks again to cast his vote against the mayor's socialism, which the mayor took in good humor. Indeed, Frêche would help Nîmes as much as he could because he wanted the region to become economically healthy. We did not stay for dinner because Frêche was expecting visitors from Africa and we did not want to intrude.

As a final note to the Osborne project, which took a year of my time to construct, it ultimately failed and died. Osborne could not assemble his finances, and the few financial backers he contacted were soon turned off by his approach and brouhaha. Even his lovely wife, Katherine, who was quite wealthy in her own right, divorced him soon after Bechtel was off the project. My good friend Henri Thibiant, once Osborne's employer and friend, found it best to abandon him because he was chronically undependable as a promoter and developer.

Bechtel did not come out too shabbily financially from the misadventure with Charles Osborne. I learned a great deal about how business is structured in Europe, how the European Community was expected to function, how the French government operated, and how much it needed the EU's statutes. Moreover, my French, which had been dormant for many years, was given a fresh boost, more modern words, and much practice because of constant usage. I developed many good and lasting friendships and for this alone I'm indebted to Charles Osborne, the American who lived in France but who could not escape his crude Texas manners.

Encountering the Holy

As promised in the previous section, I'd like to relate my conversation with Albert Perriguey at Le Castellas in Collias (more about Collias will be given in the next section). We were exploring the sacred and the holy, and I'm certain that we did not differentiate them. Albert had asked me about how I encountered the holy since I had indicated in my résumé that I was an active churchman in Holy Orders; always an issue that calls for an explanation for those who are searching for their own anchoring point. In the course of our conversation I mentioned that the holy, the *mysterium tremendum,* or, as the Hebrew suggest, the hallow (hiqdïsh), is accompanied by a sense of fear. To recognize a thing as holy is to mark it off by a feeling of dread, not to be mistaken by any ordinary terror, trepidation or fear — that is, to appraise it by the emotion that is associated when encountering the numinous. By the numinous I mean that which is mystical and uncommonly strange to ordinary life. We touch on the mystical or the numinous in our experience of love, deep friendship, and passionate encounters with people, art, food, and special places.

After some reflection, Perriguey inquired about the *mysterium tremendum*. I continued: *mysterium tremendum* is merely the perfectly familiar and common emotion of fear that emerges when confronted by something that is well beyond one's comprehension. For example, when I was left alone in the grotto of Lascaux I was seized by a sense of fear and then of awe as I was riveted by the works of fellow human beings dating from several thousand years before my time. Twenty thousand years before me a person had painted in this underground grotto to express an emotion, to create a picture, and to connect him/herself with something that was greater than the artist. Here I am not at all talking about a "religious" feeling because none of us know much about what early human beings felt "religiously." Rather I'm talking about a resident feeling in human beings that is triggered by awe, the confrontation with *mysterium tremendum* and perhaps even with the numinous.

In the dark grotto, I was a person, a modern person, perceiving the work that the artist had left behind and that had survived intact over the many centuries. Through the art painted on the walls I was meeting the artist, the creator. Much as John Dewey affirmed, art is that which emerges from three sources in conjunction: from the artist, the artifact, and the viewer. It is the combination of these three sources that initiates the mystery of the extraordinary in art. When confronted by the event of human self-revelation, as in art, the viewer is awed — as I was at Lascaux. I encountered the sacred because it seized me, stunned me, disrobed me, and startled me by the effect that this art was ancient but was quite similar to what an artist twenty thousand years later would comprehend. The art had endured the wearing effect of time. It had endured the events that could have been destructive. It had been discovered, unearthed, by a group of boys playing in the woods. What was painted in the grotto had so impressed one of them, the sixteen-year old Jacques Marsal, that he had dedicated his whole life to its nurture. Marsal had encountered the holy, the sacred, long before I had. Marsal had been lured by the holy at a young age and more so than his friends had been, if at all.

Perriguey was asking more questions than I could respond to with brief answers. After more port and cigarettes for him, he wanted to know when I had encountered the holy, the sacred, other than at Lascaux. He volunteered that he had been confronted with what he perceived as the calming and frightening effect of the "holy" when he was in the Basilica of Vézelay years earlier. The Basilica of Vézelay stands atop a hill overlooking vineyards, vegetable farms, and green pastures for raising sheep. Fortunately I had visited Vézelay several times and could appreciate his feelings because the Basilica is a wonderful edifice glistening in natural light, vast open unobstructed space, and a marvelous crypt where relics of various saintly people are kept. Perriguey had visited the Basilica one early morning when it was enveloped in a thick fog and when no one was around to generate any noise or disturbances. Wandering in the large edifice he had felt "un certain quelque chose de superbe" (something that was superb). He continued to explain that he had to sit down because his knees were unable to hold him erect. He found "un siège et j'ai commencé à pleurer" (a seat and started to cry). The emotion was so intense that he felt paralyzed.

He continued that he had returned to Vézelay several times and had only encountered the same intensity of emotion when he visited in the quiet early morning. That encounter with a similar emotion had occurred in a few other places and recently when he took a walk in the Alps and sat on a ledge looking at the summit of the Mont Blanc. When focusing on the mountain, Albert had been smoking a fresh cigarette but had been so mesmerized by the splendor of the mountain cloaked in pure white in front of him that he had forgotten the cigarette and burned his fingers.

We continued to speak about *mysterium tremendum* and how the feeling may at times come over one as a sweeping tide, pervading the mind with a tranquil mood of deepest worship for the source of this event — whatever the source is. Mysterium denotes merely that which is hidden, esoteric, and unknowable, inexplicable. Tremendum surfaces because of a sense of fear, numinous dread, and awe that grasps one by a force that overwhelms, even paralyzes for a time. Perriguey was not overtly a religious man; in fact he was quite cool to his religious roots that were nurtured in Roman Catholicism.

I admitted that I too had encountered similar feelings, particularly inside the grotto of Lascaux, at Ely Cathedral, in my own small chapel, and on occasions when celebrating the Eucharist with a small group. Particularly I remember the evenings at Grace Cathedral, in the dark, when Bishop Kim Myers would gather us for prayer and with a few words release us to wander in the darkness for a few hours. We would complete the evening with the common breaking of bread, drinking of wine, and sharing of the Peace. It was awesome. Often I felt taken up by a force that would lift me out of my own body to observe life from a different vantage — yes, to observe my life from the outside.

The *mysterium tremendum* at times gripped me in places that I either had not visited on earlier occasions, or when circumstances were deeply affecting my inner being. One particular place that often seizes me with deep emotions is in the meadow behind Ely Cathedral. I have found myself avoiding this area because I am gripped with such a surge of feeling that I know that my heart might just stop beating right then and there. The cathedral is a huge structure of many styles of medieval architecture, ranging from Norman to Perpendicular, but mostly unencumbered Norman. It stands on fenland on the west bank of the River Ouse, about 15 miles (25 kilometers) northeast of Cambridge. From the riverbank I can see the greatness of the edifice, the same angle that moved Nan Youngman to paint me an oil canvas of Ely Cathedral. The area just at the end of the meadow near the riverbank offers a gripping view of this Christian symbol reaching for God — not to God, but for God.

Ely Cathedral

On one special occasion I was taken up to the Lantern at Ely and left alone there for several moments while others were taken to the top of the narthex area at the front of the cathedral. I was alone standing high above the sanctuary and surrounded by the wooden structure of the Lantern, which was built in the 14th century. My heart pounded so hard that I felt I might have a heart attack. I sat on a box and decided to be very quiet. It was warm and a bit dusty. Below me I could see the altar. Above me I could see the octagonal shape of the wooden Lantern and the windows that allowed light to enter during the day, and the electrified lights (replacing the oil lamps with reflecting prisms) of the Lantern at night to be visible for miles around the fens. It was late afternoon in June and the sky was clear. Human beings had struggled to construct this wooden Lantern years before power tools and hydraulic lifts were invented. I could feel the thick flow of the holy flowing through my being — like a blanket protecting me from the elements. Not a sound was heard. It was deafeningly quiet. I could neither hear the people below nor those who had left me alone and were walking towards the narthex. Almost like a solipsist I was convinced that I was the only human being left on this planet.

"Raymond, what is happening?" I asked myself.

My reply was, "be quiet and listen." And listen I did. But the beating of my heart drowned all other noises. All of a sudden, I became relaxed, comfortable, strong, and joyful. How long did it last? I don't know, and never will know because much, much later I had to climb down by myself without the group. I did not want to leave this phenomenal place.

On other occasions I have been affected by the *mysterium* when listening to music such as Vaughan Williams's *Fantazia* on Thomas Tallis; Giacomo Puccini's *La Tosca*, especially the aria sung by Floria; Beethoven's Ninth Symphony, especially the one conducted by Leonard Bernstein (other conductors are less affective for me); and even a few popular songs touch me deeply.

Time was moving past us rapidly. I raised the issue that in this mystery the "holy" may have an important part in the events that affect us. I posited that if we understood the universe to be a sacramental entity, in other words, an entity that has a special character, then many aspects of its sacramentality could emerge in various localities. For me, I admitted, the holy in the fullest sense of the meaning combines a complex category of rational and non-rational components — avoiding the trap of sensationalism. I look at the English Archbishop William Temple's extensive and grand work, *Nature, Man and God*, to understand the mysterious qualities of the universe and its makeup. Even when I incorporate the dimensions obtained from physics, both classical and quantum, my conviction is that there is an overt character to the holiness in the universe that does not waver. The French Jesuit and great paleontologist Teilhard de Chardin suggested that the holy penetrates the membrane of the universe on occasions and in certain places like a hand reaching through to touch us. He does not, however, suggest that the holy is outside the universe but rather there are instances when the membrane is overtly opened to the sight of the holy (all this long before the issues of "multiverses" surfaced in popular cosmology). Yes.

Albert Perriguey noted as we talked that the classic understanding of God did not address this issue in terms that he understood. "God was out there, out here, but never where I am, and I am never where God is, or so I thought,"

Albert discerned. I said to Perriguey that if the theistic definition of God were replaced by something such as $E=MC^2$ or the string formulae of vibrating energy bits, the understanding of the preciousness, holiness, and uniqueness of the characteristics of the universe would be little affected; it might be refined and fine-tuned, but not affected greatly. God in non-theistic terms is not localized, delimited to a particular place, but universalized. For example, $E=MC^2$ is a universal law, just as God in those terms is a universal presence and is recognized when we observe its force, its activity, its effect. Yet there is present an intimacy that (as $E=MC^2$, gravity or whatever we call it) relates to us as individuals.

Perriguey was a bit surprised to hear me say that, because he thought that as a man of the cloth I was tied to the image of God as an old man conducting the affairs of the universe, at least of this planet. That I was not tied to the concept, the theistic view, of a super being micromanaging creation opened up a new avenue of discussion for Perriguey. How did I then relate to the Fatherhood of God as depicted in western religion?

How did he relate to Marianne depicted in a light, flowing robe and wearing the Phrygian cap of liberty, the symbol of France? I asked him. Symbolic language has value and purpose, as have myths, so long as they are not converted into actual depictions of reality. Symbols are the actors of language performing the roles that convey the sense of a story. Myths are shorthand tools that are supposed to help explain events, but they should not be confused with historical chronicles. Heaven, hell, Adam and Eve, the Flood, Jacob wrestling with God, Jesus arguing with Satan, the Angel notifying Mary of the birth of Jesus, and others, are all ways to explain certain events and certain concepts but they are not to be taken literally and as facts. None of them reach the level of fact that Yuri A. Gagarin, Alan Shepard, and Neil A. Armstrong bring to history. The events that marked them were not mythical but actual.

Because religion has an enigmatic characteristic, which in itself is wonderful, dramatic, poetic, and liturgical, the tendency is for human beings to remain in that mode even when they are discussing creation in physical terms. Much as creation is mysterious, it is not symbolic or mythological because it is constructed of hard concepts, theories that have to be experimentally or philosophically tested in all manner of ways.

Yes, $E=MC^2$ has been tested experimentally and found to be correct as a physical idea, but the string theory has yet to be tested —but is beginning to pass the philosophical and mathematical tests provided by coherent reasoning. I dare to say that in the brain of every theoretical physicist or scientist there is hidden the kernel of philosophy or perhaps even theology — not every idea can be experimentally tested, although they may be mathematically. In our universe nothing is an entity that puzzles us. In mathematics, zero puzzles us but we know that it is indispensable. Perhaps the holy and the sacred are in that category; they cannot be experimentally tested but they do have some philosophical support, even if only when we examine what emerges from our confrontation with them.

I concluded my conversation with Perriguey by saying that the idea of the holy is not preposterous and that hominoids have encountered special sacred places that have affected them deeply throughout the ages; there is more to the *mysterium tremendum* than can be dissected in the laboratory. In fact, there is more in life and in the human mind than can be placed under the microscope for examination. Once again I must remind readers, as I did Perriguey, that enigmas offer the possibility of solutions but mysteries, by definition, have no solutions, at least not while on this planet Earth or in this Universe. In another Universe, if there is such a place, maybe!

It had been a long day and a long night. We adjourned and Albert Perriguey went to his room to refresh himself for the flight to Paris. I went to my room, and swallowed half a sleeping pill to catch a few hours of sleep before my lunch meeting that was scheduled for noon in the hotel dining room.

Perriguey phoned me at noon to thank me for our conversation and I thanked him for allowing me to share my thoughts with him. We corresponded by mail for several years until I was informed by one of his colleagues that he died the week after he retired from GTM.

Collias: Le Castellas

In 1989, when Bechtel accepted the potential project proposed by Mr. Charles Osborne, I had gone to Nîmes with him to look at the site and begin the scoping process, and in due course had met Mr. Henri Thibiant and a friendship developed with both Henri and his wife Karin. When it was time to have a general meeting with those involved in the Nîmes project and to meet the mayor, Mr. Bousquet, I asked Henri to find me a small and pleasant hotel in a village close to his, which was located in Sainte Eglise. Henri booked me a room at Le Castellas, in Collias. Collias is a small village of less than 1000 residents and is in full view of Le Pont du Gard, a famous Roman aqueduct. Ray Kingsley, my colleague, also had a room booked by Henri at Le Castellas. We both wanted to keep some distance from Osborn and the general meeting in Nîmes but be close enough to be able to participate in the activities that would lead to the development of the project.

The proprietors and operators of Le Castellas were Chantal and Raymond Aparis; their very young daughter Aurelie often entertained the guests with her wonderful antics and joyful disposition. Raymond, a professional hotel manager and restaurateur before relocating in

Collias was busy supervising the kitchen and helping out in a restaurant serving the visitors who came to Le Pont du Gard. Chantal, a delightful and pretty woman, managed the embryonic hotel, enchanted the guests with her warmth, and made me feel special.

Because I had opened the Goose and Turrets B&B in 1986, we often exchanged information about our businesses. Le Castellas was a hotel that also offered an excellent restaurant, whereas the Goose and Turrets provided no in-house restaurant but served a four-course breakfast. Chantal and I had many conversations and many similar likes and dislikes.

As evidence that I felt warmly hosted at the hotel, I gave her a rose bush to plant in her not-yet-landscaped garden. I visited Le Castellas several times when I was with Bechtel, but in 2000 when I returned as a guest with Emily to spend several days on holiday, although the garden had been landscaped beautifully, my rose bush still thrived. In 2000, I gave her another rose bush so that the earlier one would have company.

I seldom saw Raymond Aparis when visiting Le Castellas. He was often busy either earning some additional income at a concession near Le Pont du Gard or managing the wonderful restaurant in the hotel, and soon he was elected mayor of Collias; my association, therefore, as a guest at the hotel was always with the proprietress Chantal. Chantal and I became good friends and in the years following we communicated quite often and more so through the emergence of the Internet. After a couple of visits to the hotel I found that room Number 7 was my favorite room. It was on the second floor and had a large balcony facing a grammar school. The room offered me sun in the morning and cool evenings with a light breeze. The balcony or veranda was large enough to allow me to take my writing table outside and do my work in the open light of the day.

On one of my arrivals, a rather late one, and after a long day of travel and meetings (and too late for dinner), I found waiting in my room a bottle of beer, a wonderful sandwich, and a bowl of fresh mixed berries, plus a welcoming note from Chantal. I've never forgotten that small touch of kindness and warm hospitality. The Aparis family remains dear to me (in 2003, they visited us in Montara).

On a final visit to the Nîmes region of France, after I determined that Charles Osborne was not going to be able to develop a viable technology nucleus because of his undisciplined and egomaniac temperament and his management of the truth, I took a few days off after departing Collias and the charming hospitality of Chantal and Raymond Aparis. My intent was to visit for a day with Dominique Fache and his then-partner Michelle Verschoore, and then head towards Livorno and Florence, in Italy.

Livorno is a major Italian seaport. It is sometimes called Leghorn in jest because it lies at what appears to be the thigh of Italy. Livorno is on the shore of the Ligurian Sea, about 50 miles (80 kilometers) southwest of Florence. It is an important industrial city, with steelworks, glass factories, and automobile plants. The most interesting aspects of Livorno's public buildings included the cathedral, a large temple (Livorno has the largest Jewish community in Italy), the Academy of Sciences, and the Italian Naval Academy complex. The Tower of the Sculptured Lion, a leading landmark, is a relic of the days when the city was a free port.

My interest in visiting Livorno had to do with looking into the roots of my mother's family. The Modiano clan emerged from three locations in Italy: Livorno (the Jewish branch), Florence (the Roman Catholic branch), and Aosta (the Protestant ecumenical, and pro-French branch). There are some documents, especially in public files in Florence, which intimate that the name Modiano and the name Modigliani are the same. Much as it would be a compliment to find a connection to the painter Amadeo Modigliani, who was born in Livorno and settled in Paris, where he died, I have my doubts about the linkage. Both names are common in Liguria and both seem to originate from different sources.

Once in Liguria I looked up the name Modiano in public archives, telephone directories, school registers, and I even spoke to coffee drinkers in cafés. The result was always the same: "Which Modiano do you want?" There were too many and I was never convinced that I would connect with the one sub-branch that would lead me to my grandfather Joseph's family. Because my grandfather was closely connected with the branch of the family that identified with Aosta and the Alps region that bordered France I was not convinced that I would find the correct ties. Moreover, several of the members of the Modiano branch I reached by telephone informed me that North Africa had been a common venue for those who searched for fortune; especially when Italy established Libya as a colony, scores of Modianos went there as pioneers. I knew, at least I had been told, that Joseph Modiano went to Egypt from the Aosta region, but in particular from the northern section closest to the French border. Joseph had been educated in France, had received both his medical and pharmaceutical degrees from the University of Montpellier, and had moved to Egypt only after his wife Angele (a French citizen of many generations whose family was rooted in Lyons) had been deployed by the French government to teach in Cairo, Egypt.

At any rate, I had a good time in that northern portion of Italy. I visited the large Jewish community in Livorno, the large and beautiful synagogue, and the less majestic synagogue of the smaller Orthodox Jewish congregation.

Florence needs no introduction to the reader who has visited that extraordinary gallery of art. To those who have never been to Florence no words can describe what the eyes need to see. It would be complimentary to know that the roots of my grandfather Joseph surfaced in Florence; perhaps they have but it is not important, at least not to me. My concern and appreciation is that somehow from the Modiano branch and the Hoche branch I inherited excellent DNA and subsequently smart, healthy, and stout genes. I suppose that genealogy is not as important to me, because I can do nothing about it — it is too late. What I can do, and have done, is fashion, refashion, and, perhaps, reinvent myself as I live my life.

For instance I am not too terribly concerned that the artist Amadeo Modigliani was born in Livorno, that he settled in Paris in 1906, and that he was a colorful and restless character whose early death was linked to alcohol and drug abuse. I am not even filled with pride that a Modiano was an international correspondent or that a Hoche was a superior general in Napoleon's devastating army — an army that reduced France to bankruptcy and annihilated thousands of human lives. I did feel a tinge of pride when I learned that General Louis-Lazare Hoche was against the carnage wrought by Napoleon's hunger for power in Europe and that he advised against the Russian campaign — he died in Germany before the campaign began to invade Russia. Hoche is looked upon by the Germans and the people of the Benelux as a beneficent leader who was much beloved by those under his authority, both military and civilian. Hoche is seen as someone who protected the people from the dictatorship of the Napoleonic rule.

Thus the words of the poem by James R. Lowell and found in the 1940 Episcopal Hymn comes to mind, "Once to every man and nation comes the moment to decide..." It was time for me to visit old haunts, to see if links could be found to the periods and people long gone. I was satisfied that some connections did exist, but none existed that were of terrible importance to me. Thus after my visit to Liguria, Florence, and Aosta I resumed my work in Bari, Italy. The project in Bari, as I mentioned earlier, was a most gratifying and rewarding task and one that fills me with pride and satisfaction, especially the friendship that emerged with Umberto Bozzo.

Troitsk, USSR

Earlier in the writing I mentioned the visit and the contacts that were developed with the Kurchatov Institute, Dr. Sobolenko, the deputy director, and the director of the Nuclear and Research Institute of the Kurchatov Branch in Troitsk, Dr. Viacheslav Pismenny. Out of my discussions with Dr. Pismenny came a proposal to develop approximately 300 single-family houses, a new research and educational center to teach computer science, and a joint medical facility with the California Beckman Medical Laser Research Center, Irvine.

Bechtel was offered the entire package of design, engineering, construction, and implementation. This was a neat offer by the Soviets and a lucrative project for Bechtel, which was searching to establish a foothold in the USSR. Unfortunately, once again Bechtel muffed the opportunity through Frank Cain's poor management.

In the back of my head I was concerned that perhaps the USSR did not have the funds for such a huge project. But then I suspected that funds could be obtained by the Soviets from the European Development Bank, which was very much interested in establishing a foothold in this large country. In addition, oil was available in the USSR to supply Europe and that would bring some substantial currency for supporting the proposed projects. I also suspected that Dr. Pismenny had access to funds from sources that were separate from the government and that he wanted to develop Troitsk in preparation of the deep financial crisis that was on the horizon for the USSR. Of course all this was tentative thinking on my part and neither Bechtel nor Cain were privy to my thinking, because I had not yet written my memorandum where I stated that I thought that the USSR would implode by 1994. Yet even had I submitted my memo, few on the board of directors would have taken it seriously, except perhaps for Denis Slavich who was keen and understood the political and economic long view.

In nightly conversations with Pismenny when he visited San Francisco a few months later, Slava and I discussed the coming implosion of the USSR and what this would mean to his Soviet home. Dr. Pismenny wanted to be prepared for the new era that he and I expected. Reza Gorbachev was one of Slava's good friends, which gave him an inside track to the General Secretary of the Communist Party and President of the USSR, Mikhail Sergeyevich Gorbachev. Slava was very much aware that the USSR's existence was limited, very limited. But global market demands and loans, especially the reduced price of oil, and the Internet were instrumental elements that caused the demise of the communist empire. Much as Gorbachev tried to prevent the complete breakup of the Soviet Union, on Dec. 8, 1991, the republics of Russia, Ukraine, and Belarus broke away completely from the Soviet Union and formed the Commonwealth of Independent States (CIS). These republics were soon joined by all the remaining republics within the realm of the old USSR, except for Georgia. On December 25, Gorbachev resigned as president, and the Soviet Union formally ceased to exist at midnight 31 December 1991.

Just as this change of authority was taking place in the USSR, there was a major change of management for me at Bechtel. Robert Jackson was asked to resign because he was at cross purposes with the leadership, and in his place Frank Cain was appointed senior vice president of my department. I had a new boss and one with whom I had much difficulty in understanding because of his attitude, demands, and egomaniac behavior. Much like my encounter with Clarence Rupert Hayden in years past, my relationship, or non-relationship, with Cain was a classic déjà vu situation that would give me much anxiety.

After many hours of negotiation still under Jackson's management, and with support from Denis Slavich, the then-chief financial officer of Bechtel, both Bechtel and Dr. Pismenny came to an agreement that the project would begin with a concept development plan (CDP) that would be funded by the USSR, mainly the Ministry of Nuclear Energy. Bechtel would receive USD 160,000 for the concept development plan (CDP), and the CDP was being subsidized in part by the European Development Bank and also several European sources would be tapped to obtain additional funds for the project.

An agreement that I initiated with the help of Harold Forsen had also been made with the US Department of Energy to buy "yellow cake," or raw uranium ore, from the Soviet Union. The sale of such yellow cake to US power firms and to European firms would be sufficient to pay for the work Bechtel was agreeing to do for Pismenny. Pacific Gas and Electric (PG&E), the northern California power firm, was not only interested in the uranium but also needed to have its old hand-drawn drawings revised from their initial design to the as-built configuration. The Kurchatov Institute had a number of engineers who could do the work in Troitsk after some preliminary training.

All these bits and pieces would provide additional cash for the project in Troitsk and Bechtel would receive payment in handsome amounts. After dinner at the Goose and Turrets B&B, a contract between Bechtel and the Kurchatov Institute was signed in January 1990 — 23 months before the dissolution of the Soviet Union.

Soon after the contract was signed and for reasons that are not connected to the USSR, both Slavich and Jackson were forced to resign from Bechtel, but not before Mr. Steve Bechtel, Jr. visited Troitsk and approved the gift of an office building for Bechtel's pied-á-terre branch. Steve Bechtel cut a red, white, and blue ribbon with white stars at the gate of the building and accepted the gift for his firm.

Slavich called me from Moscow and also from Italy as he accompanied Steve Bechtel, Jr. on his European review of several projects. Steve Bechtel was retiring and had turned the entire firm over to his younger son Riley, who became president and soon chairman. Upon Slavich's return to California four weeks later, he was asked to resign by Riley Bechtel, the new president of the firm, and hence to terminate his connection with Bechtel. Jackson, a protégé of Slavich, was also asked to resign not only from his job as head of the Future's Group but also of my department. The news of these resignations hit Pismenny and me like a bolt of lightning. We were left with Frank Cain, a man of little vision and a huge ego.

Events moved along calmly at first. I had a meeting with Cain in his San Francisco office (he shuttled back and forth from Gaithersburg, MD to San Francisco but spent more time in Maryland). Cain had insisted that no work on Russia would begin until the USD 160,000 was deposited in Bechtel's Morgan Guaranty bank account. Cash before work starts was a standard position for Bechtel, and it made sense. Would he accept a partial payment that would allow the team heading for Troitsk to mobilize? Nothing doing, Cain informed me. Payment had to be made in full. I reminded Cain that the USSR was going through some very difficult times because its economy was in shambles and Gorbachev was doing all he could under the circumstances to save the USSR from bankruptcy. Because I had signed the contract and it was my project, Cain permitted no slack and thus I was responsible for making certain that the funds were deposited in Bechtel's account.

I understood Bechtel's standard operating procedure and it usually made sense. At this juncture I had hoped that some slack would be cut for the Russians because they were going through an enormous financial stress bordering on the implosion of the nation (which occurred a few months later) and I was certain that Pismenny was good for the money because he was preparing Troitsk for the time when he'd have to commercialize the city and the Institute. As for Bechtel, it was trying to open the door for future work in the USSR, and if the country went bankrupt there still were a great many projects that would surface and the nation was wealthy with natural resources, especially fossil fuels and minerals, plus it had excellent scientists performing good science. Bechtel's directors and owner knew this quite well and that was reason enough to have allowed me to venture into the USSR. Yet as was the custom of upper management, it did not want quite yet to overrule Cain. They did eventually, after I left the company.

After several calls to Pismenny and receiving assurance that the money would be deposited as soon as he obtained it from the Ministry, I still reminded him that both Bechtel and Russia needed this initial project to solidify our relationship. Time was passing and no notice of a deposit came to my desk. At least every other day I'd call Cain's secretary in Gaithersburg to check if notice from the bank had been received. Everyday, Wakelin would come to me to check the status of the deposit.

"Michael," I would inform him, "no deposit yet."

"Charlie Spink is asking me every time he sees me if the money has been deposited." Charlie Spink was Cain's deputy in the San Francisco office. Charlie was a pleasant sort but he was neither a mental giant nor a man of strong resolve. I kept calling Cain's secretary, Morgan Guaranty, and Pismenny. Pismenny was still in the process of securing the funds but things were very tight in Moscow; the USSR was being disassembled and the satellite nations were unfettering their connections to Mother Russia.

Arriving in my office at 7:45 a.m. on a clear day in March 1989, the first telephone call I received was from the Morgan Guaranty account manager in New York. The $160,000 had been deposited in Bechtel's account. Immediately I called Gaithersburg to inform Cain, but he was in Tokyo; his secretary would give him the message. I alerted both Wakelin and Spink. I walked into the office of Gary Bechtel, President of BCIV, to give him the news. He would inform his brother Riley and his father Steve Jr.

After this I returned to my office before heading for the elevator to get my first cup of coffee of the morning from Pasta Bella, a coffee shop across the street from Bechtel's 45 Fremont building. In the elevator I encountered Tom Flynn, the manager of Bechtel's Public Relations.

"Raymond, any news from the Russians?" he inquired.

"Yes," I replied, being as innocuous as possible to avoid a press release before I could verify the deposit with Bechtel's own in-house comptroller. I said no more and exited from the elevator.

After my coffee I returned to my office to sign a few letters and finish some pending work on a European Union paper I was writing for in-house consumption. At lunch I decided to avoid a meal and headed to the Sharper Image to see if I could find a present for my son Michel, whose birthday was approaching. Returning from lunch I found my office crowded with my colleagues Wakelin, Spink, and Tom Flynn. Spink put his hand on my shoulder, initially I assumed it was a congratulatory gesture, but no it was a warning that Cain had called him and instructed him to fire me. Why?

At this juncture Tom Flynn said that a press release had been made public that Bechtel had landed its first contract with the USSR to convert a defense research enclave into a civilian research and teaching city.

"What press release?" I asked. Flynn affirmed that since I had told him that we had received the funds he could instruct his office to make the news public; the press release had been written weeks earlier and PR was simply waiting for the go-ahead. "You gave me the green light in the elevator," Flynn said.

"I most certainly did not."

"Of course you gave me the news that the funds were received," Flynn replied.

"Tom, when you asked me if we'd heard from the Russians, I avoided a direct answer and said this exact word, innocuous word, to avoid a direct answer: I said, "Yes".

Turning to Spink and the others, "I said nothing about receiving the funds to you. And anyway you don't send out a press release without checking specifically with the people involved." To this Flynn gave a long explanation that only showed he had assumed something from what I had said to him. He was correct in making the assumption, but I had not told him specifically that the funds had been received. At times the 4th Estate is a problem, especially when it jumps the gun and bypasses the correct procedures. "Anyway Tom, what's the problem," and turning to Spink, "why am I being fired?"

Spink thought for a moment then said, "Cain has fired you because he considers it his position to make the announcement that Bechtel had landed its first project in the USSR."

"Charlie Spink," I pointed my finger right into his face, "that's no grounds to fire me. After all it is my project and I made it possible for Bechtel to have a foot in the USSR. If Cain's ego is that enormous then he can make the announcement himself now. Moreover, Charlie, I'll sue Cain for defamation or whatever and clean him to the bone."

"Well, Raymond," Charlie said in an imploring tone, "I suggest you resign to avoid any unpleasant repercussions."

"I will not resign and I will not put up with Cain's stupidity. I'm going to see Slavich, Riley, and Gary." With these words I walked out of my office and was followed by Wakelin, who stopped me by the elevator.

"Raymond, can you find a slot elsewhere at Bechtel?"

"Michael, I will not resign, transfer, or accept this idiotic order to fire me."

Michael continued, "Cain is after you. In meetings he has often indicated that you were uncooperative and usually ignored his authority."

"Michael, Cain is a stupid, spoiled, dim-witted man." Into the elevator I went. Before seeing Denis Slavich, who was still CFO, because Steve Bechtel, Jr. was still CEO and chairman, I picked up the phone and notified Emily that there was a war between Cain and me, and that I had been fired!

In Slavich's office I informed him that I had been fired. He, however, announced that Riley already knew that Cain had gone off the deep end because the four major broadcasting companies CNN, CBS, NBC, and ABC, plus the Japanese Television company had called his office to confirm that Bechtel had received a contract with the USSR and that the person who had "tried to obstruct Bechtel from obtaining that contract had been fired!"

"Raymond you are famous," Denis laughed. Reaching for his phone he called Steve Bechtel, Jr., and spoke to him for several minutes. When the conversation was ended, he turned to me and assured me that I would not be fired because there were no grounds to dismiss me. "Cain will be back tomorrow, so be careful."

"Denis, is anyone in this crappy company going to congratulate me for landing the first project in the USSR?"

"Probably not Raymond. Probably not." Then Denis added, "My days at Bechtel are probably numbered." I looked at him in puzzlement but he put his finger to his lips as a sign that I should say nothing. I left his office. A month later I learned that Slavich was asked to resign the week after Riley became CEO of Bechtel and he was informed by Riley, not directly, but at a dinner when Riley told Debbie Slavich that Denis would no longer be a Bechtel employee by 1 June 1989. At Bechtel the situation was just about as bad as it could be.

After the meeting with Denis I went home. Wakelin telephoned me at home to inform me that I was off the Troitsk project and that Cain wanted to see me the next afternoon at two o'clock. That my stomach was a little upset was the least of my concerns. I was mostly upset that a man like Frank Cain, the apparent fair-haired boy of Riley, could be a director at Bechtel and could represent the firm. I was puzzled and concerned about my own future with the company. The whole issue left a bad taste in my mouth.

The next morning I called the four broadcasting companies to see if I could obtain a copy of Cain's press conference in Tokyo. After the run around and the delays I discovered that these tapes were not released to private individuals but that I could review them if I came to New York at the home office of each broadcasting company. A trip to New York was not quite in my budget at the moment.

When I arrived at the office a little before 2:00 p.m., Wakelin was waiting to accompany me to Cain's office. Cain was sitting behind his desk and when I entered his office he exploded, "I've had a close shave by Riley for not managing my affairs or my loose-cannon employees!" I stood there before him. "I want an apology and I want it in writing today." Wakelin piped in and said that he would see to it that an apology would be forthcoming before the close of business. I looked at Wakelin and then I stared at Cain.

"What apology? An apology for what?"

"Raymond, you hit the media before I could approve the press release and announce the news of the project. I want an apology."

"Mr. Frank Cain, don't hold your breath for that apology. It's never going to be written or voiced. There will be no apology, not now and not ever." I turned around and left the office, slamming the door as I walked out.

Moments later Wakelin came to my office to tell me that Cain was "mad as hell" and that I was not to do anything on the Russian project. Ivan Ivanek was to take my place and I was not to communicate with any of the Russian people. Moreover, I was not going to receive a bonus that year and it was best for me to search for another position at Bechtel. I guess that Riley and Steve Bechtel, Jr. had warned him that I was neither going to be fired nor forced to resign, but that did not preclude making my life miserable. I knew that Dr. Pismenny was due in Oakland at the end of the week and that would give me the opportunity to explain what the undercurrent at Bechtel was.

Fortunately Slava called me upon his arrival and we set a time for a meeting away from Bechtel. I picked him up at the Hyatt in Oakland and drove him to Hayward Air Terminal and to my hangar for a private conversation. I had asked Misha Persiantsev to accompany us and help as a translator. In the hangar I explained what had developed and I apologized for this melodramatic and asinine performance that Bechtel was putting on through Cain and for being removed from the project.

Dr. Pismenny would not hear that I was removed. He was going to speak to Steve Bechtel, Jr. I suggested that we just let the event cool down and that I would find a way to return to the project. As it turned out, Ivanek, who went to Troitsk, was unable to do an acceptable concept development plan and the task was eventually given to me to complete. But ready to play hardball, I refused to take on the Troitsk assignment unless Cain asked me, and asked me personally. Was I pushing my luck?

I need to inform the readers that when the time arrived for me to receive a bonus, the memo was delivered to me with a clear note that it would be $10.00. Knowing that Cain was in his office, I took my memo to his office, bypassing his secretary, I opened the door and found Cain behind his desk. He looked at me. I approached the desk showed him the memo and before his face tore it in pieces and dumped the pieces on his desk. Cain said not a word. I walked out and slammed the door shut.

The Conference in Linz, Austria

In the mean time I had been invited by IC^2 to present a paper on IT in Linz, Austria at the East West Institute. The keynote speaker was to be George Kozmetski, followed by Michael Dell of DELL Computer, and I was to follow the two. This was to be a three-day conference in a charming city known for its famous tortes of the same name, and close to the birthplace of Adolf Hitler. IC^2 was to pay my expenses to Linz and I looked forward to the trip because I planned to enjoy a few days in Vienna, then ride the train that followed the Danube to Linz; this venture would be a small holiday for me after the goings on with Cain.

After I prepared my itinerary and filed my request for travel, carefully filling the cost rectangle on the travel form with a fat red zero, I began to put ideas down for the presentation. After my travel forms had been submitted, a few days later Billo Puri, a colleague, came into my office and asked me if I could attend a conference in Berlin sponsored by the Japanese Ministry of Information, Technology, and Industry (MITI). I looked at my calendar and saw it was 16 November 1990 and decided that since my time in Berlin was to be 3 days after the wall was torn down, the city would be very joyful. I accepted the assignment and obtained the necessary information because I would be offering a variation of the presentation given in Linz. I allowed myself three weeks away from San Francisco for the trip to Europe. The extension cost to Berlin would come out of Puri's project; hence I had to draft my travel authorization to include the change.

When all the arrangements for my travel were completed I took a day off to mobilize my affairs. On the day of my departure I stopped at the office to check my mail and to give Ligia some information about what was still pending on my desk. Spink called me into his office to ask me to take over the Troitsk project.

"Was this your idea?" I asked.

"No it comes from Frank Cain. Will you take the project?"

I laughed. "OK, I'll take the project but I want Ray Kingsley to read what has been written and make the initial corrections. When I return I'll go through the concept as I see it."

"Raymond," Spink smiled and added, " you won. No one has ever bested Frank, but you did."

"Charles, how does it feel to be Frank's wet noodle?"

Just as I was leaving the office to head for San Francisco International Airport and my flight, Wakelin intercepted me. "Hoche-Mong, you were difficult with Charlie Spink." Indeed, I was not docile. Cain had changed the atmosphere of the department and I was not happy with the negative approach surfacing from his leadership. I felt sorry for Spink but that was not my problem; Spink had to deal with Frank Cain and not just roll over like a well-trained mongrel.

I caught the British Airways flight to London that afternoon. I was going to spend one day in London then catch a flight to Vienna, where I would spend three nights eating, sight-seeing, and playing. The three-hour train ride to Linz was something I was looking forward to. I had booked a lunch reservation and expected to be served royally in the restaurant car. Austrian's principal hobby is food, and I was ready to learn more about their favorite pastime.

I was on my way and ready for my clear and cold, with no ice, Tanqueray gin with three olives in business class. I wasn't disappointed. The appetizer was smoked Canadian salmon with a touch of fennel on a thin slice of black bread.

I sank into my seat and thought about the crazy week that I had just lived through. Was that a good way to earn a living? Dealing with the likes of Frank Cain spoiled much of the camaraderie of any department. I have had my quota of some good bosses and my share of some louses. On the whole the average gave me good superiors and I could get along with the toughest ones, if they made sense and were coherent in their demands. Cain was not. His ego was blinding him. He was unable to see how stupid his ego made him. What was it they called him in private? "The Undertaker." How he came about with that name I don't know but it fit. He was tall, gaunt, and always wore jackets that came down below his butt — much too long. He walked with a gait like a donkey on the run.

"Are you ready for a refill, sir?" the attendant jolted me out of my thoughts.

My seatmate was a young woman from London who worked in San Francisco. She was returning home for some family occasion and was looking forward to the traditional roast beef dinner that her mother had promised. She was working for the large accounting firm of Arthur Anderson, based in San Francisco, and although she was English, she had obtained her permanent residency in America soon after graduating from the University of California, Berkeley. Our conversation during the flight was light and offered no great insights into either of our personalities. I read a book and she watched a movie. I admit to having a bit of difficulty getting excited about accounting and the juggling of numbers. I knew the firm that employed her and today I wonder what has happened to my seatmate since her employer has been forced into bankruptcy because of a scandal about altering figures in Enron's accounting books to exaggerate profits in order to increase the value of their stocks; in other words, "cooking the books."

My arrival in London was uneventful and the weather was excellent. I headed for the Underground's Piccadilly Line for the long ride to the Gloucester hotel. After a shower and a very short rest, I called my friend Patrick Gavigan to see at what time he expected to meet me at the National Gallery. The Piccadilly Line took me to the vicinity of the gallery. I met Gavigan and we spent the afternoon and evening looking, walking, and discussing politics, especially the Northern Ireland conflict which affected him greatly because he was Irish and very much against the civil war. We stopped for dinner at a Lebanese restaurant near my hotel. After dinner, which was washed down with a couple of pints of ale, I had the hotel doorman hail a taxi for Gavigan. I prepaid the taxi fare, said goodbye to my friend, and headed to my room for a shower and bed. The next day I was to catch a mid-morning flight to Vienna.

Austria and Hitler's Birthplace

For me it is always a pleasure to go to Vienna. I was not going to stay at my favorite place, the Pension Christina, because it was full but they suggested I try the Pension Strauss. It was a bit inferior to the Christina but still in the 1010 sector of Vienna, the old center of the city.

Vienna is just one of the most charming cities in the world. The city always provides good music, delicious food, classic history, and cordial people. I cannot imagine the Viennese opting for right wing politics and Adolf Hitler, but they do have a right wing streak in their political composition. As much as they like to blame Hitler for being coerced into accepting the plebiscite for unification in 1936, I suspect that underneath their bon vivant aura, they maintain a deep feeling of inferiority that led them into extreme right wing behavior.

Could it be that when they lost their claim to the Austrian-Hungarian Empire, Austria retrenched into extreme political conservatism? Yet, Austrians need to be commended for standing firm against the Soviet occupation after WWII. It is their firmness that helped them remove the shackles of the Soviet boot, which allowed them to join the Western European National block in the early 1950s. Austria is not an easy nation to classify, but it is, nevertheless, a beautiful country to be in.

For my first afternoon in Vienna I had to visit the Hotel Sacher. This is the hotel that gave birth to the renowned chocolate and raspberry torte. The torte was created to satisfy the keen taste of Metternich who served as Austrian minister of foreign affairs and then chancellor from 1809 to 1848.

Sacher Torte

Much as he had good taste for food, his political leanings were harsh; he encouraged European powers to suppress liberal and nationalist activity by employing a network of spies to inform him of political threats. I suspect that

Klemens Wenzel Nepomuk Lothar von Metternich contributed greatly to Austrian antipathy for political liberalism. It mustn't be forgotten that under President Richard M. Nixon, Chancellor Metternich was really Secretary of State Henry Alfred Kissinger's hero and model.

At the Hotel Sacher I did not waste any time in ordering a piece of Sacher torte mit schlag and a cup of hot coffee. My mouth rejoiced and my soul was satisfied because it was well rewarded. The gods of chocolate knew how to please a lover of the cocoa bean and its product. In Austrian konditorei, and also at the Hotel Sacher, the lounges were well appointed and guests sat, talked, smoked, meditated, and read without being disturbed by much movement, loud conversations, or intrusive waiters. Most of the newspapers of Europe were posted on easy-to-handle wicker holders. I found a current copy of the *Herald Tribune* and *Le Monde Diplomatique* and sifted through the news. The waiter refilled coffee cups as soon as they were empty and stopped only upon instruction from the guest. After a couple of hours I decided to take a walk and explore, once again, the 1010 area around St. Stephen's Cathedral, the center of the old town.

The old "Inner City" forms the center of Vienna. This area includes many of the city's historical buildings and landmarks as well as its most fashionable shopping districts. The famous St. Stephen's Cathedral stands at the heart of the Inner City. Several blocks west is the Hofburg, a palace that consists of both modern buildings and medieval structures. The palace includes the royal apartments, now occupied by the president of Austria; the Imperial Library; several museums; and the Spanish Riding School.

Emily and I were privileged to attend a magnificent performance at the Spanish Riding School where they showed the famous Lipizzaner white horses performing extraordinary dances. Lipizzaner horses, or Lipizzaners, come from horses imported into Austria from Spain and Italy during the mid-1500s. These beautiful show horses have strong bones, short legs, and thick, arched necks. Their powerful hindquarters enable them to make difficult jumps. The best-known Lipizzaners are those trained at the Spanish Riding School of Vienna in Austria. These horses perform graceful jumping and dancing feats. Lipizzaners, although white in color as adult horses, are pitch black at birth. To see Lipizzaners perform is an unforgettable experience.

Near the 1010 district lie two of Vienna's most beautiful parks, the Burggarten and the Volksgarten, which is famed for its rose trees. A band of streets called the Ringstrassen encircles the Inner City. Some of Vienna's most impressive public buildings line these streets. They include the Museum of Art History, City Hall, the Opera House, the Parliament Building, and the Stock Exchange. Adjacent on Lothringerstrasse is the Konzerthaus famous for hosting Gustav Mahler and Hugo Wolf, and of course Mozart and Beethoven.

These buildings date from the second half of the 1800s. The noted Austrian architect Johann Bernhard Fischer von Erlach designed several Viennese buildings, including the Karlskirche and the Schonbrunn Palace. The palace stands at the southwestern edge of the city and its architecture follows the style made memorable in the Palace of Versailles with one major difference: Where Louis Le Vau and Jules Hardouin-Mansart designed fine, thin, delicate lines and columns for the splendid Baroque palace in Versailles, the Schonbrunn Palace has massive columns, thick lines, and none-too-delicate architecture. The Schonbrunn Zoo, which lies on the palace grounds, was built in 1752 and is the world's oldest zoo.

To the north on the bank of the Danube River and not far from the 1010 district is a long park called The Prater. The Prater has the largest Ferris wheel in the world and when a rider reaches the top of the wheel a magnificent view of Vienna and the famous Vienna Woods on the western edge of the city can be seen. Emily and I had correctly planned to ride the Ferris wheel at early evening so that the sparkling lights of Vienna could be appreciated.

Indeed, in Vienna I retraced some, but not all, of the steps I had taken several times before; each visit to the city marks a new level of affection for that extraordinary place. I cannot get enough of Vienna and I'm looking forward to the next visit and the next sausage sandwich, morning hot cross bun, fruit tarte, and, of course, a portion of Sacher torte with a cup of absolutely authentic Viennese coffee.

It was time for me to catch the train for Linz (to re-taste the famous Linzer torte), and see a good Austrian portion of the Danube River. My seat in the dining car was by the right window, the riverside. As soon as the train started to roll and leave the station, the waiter brought me a tall beer and some cheese. The Danube appeared in the window and Vienna slipped out of sight, replaced by rolling green hills and mountain peaks in the distance. The first stop would be the town of Krems, located across the river. Lunch was served and the main course was pork roast soaked in wine, with small pasta twists and several vegetables. The salad followed and then dessert arrived. Dessert was a substantial piece of Linzer torte with whipped cream on the side and fresh raspberries.

Coffee accompanied the dessert and it was followed by a small glass of powerful schnapps. My tummy was satisfied and my mouth was happy. Did I want a cigar, the waiter asked me? I was tempted but decided that I would behave and also avoid becoming ill to boot. Cigars look great on other people and they are impressive but I'm not a cigar smoker and never have been. In London I've been offered Cuban cigars on several occasions but, as I said, they are not tempting enough for me to light one and then feel nauseated.

The train stopped for a few minute at Kermes and then on it continued. There would be no other stops until Linz. I stayed in the dining car and sipped coffee; Viennese coffee is a dessert in itself. Soon the waiter stopped by my table to announce that Linz was only 10 minutes away and that my bag would be deposited on the station's platform. I tipped him handsomely and also thanked him for taking such good care of me.

Indeed, my green shoulder bag was delivered to me as I stepped off the train and the chauffeur from the conference had my name on a slate board. I was driven to the hotel, assigned an ample room with a large balcony overlooking the Danube River, and in an ice bucket a bottle of Riesling wine was waiting for me with a note from George Kozmetski welcoming me to Linz and inviting me to dinner at 1900 hours. Looking at my watch, dinner was five hours away so I had time to shower, change clothes, and walk through the hotel garden and on to the river. I needed the exercise and I needed to sort out my thoughts about the address for the next day.

After my walk to the river and to the garden, I proceeded to the hotel lounge for a Scotch but as I entered Dr. and Mrs. Kozmetski, who were sitting near a large window that overlooked the garden, waved me over. A bottle of Mosel white wine was chilling in a bucket of ice and I was poured a glass. Soon the mayor of Linz and Michael Dell, whom I already knew from a meeting and several dinners we had enjoyed in Austin (some under the auspices of Kozmetski and IC^2), joined us.

Michael, who had been a student of George's at the University of Texas, was interested in how I, a philosophy student, was able to fit in Bechtel's culture. We discussed this issue and the apologia that usually follows when asked this question. I said that good logical thinking could be applied and managed in any culture and environment.

When George, a Greek Orthodox Christian, let the cat out of the bag that I was also involved in the Episcopal Church, Michael wanted to know how this correlated with my work in IT and regional development. After a bit of explanation, Dell admitted that he too was courting the Episcopal Church, now that he found the Southern Baptists approach offensive to his thinking and Judaism too strange for his taste. Dell was currently attending a local Episcopal Church and taking Inquirers' classes to learn about Anglicanism, the Episcopal Church, and its thinking.

"Recently, I had the pleasure of meeting the bishop when he visited," Dell added.

"Which bishop was he?" I asked.

"Bishop Payne," he replied, and added "a most friendly person and a fine preacher of the liberal tradition."

I looked at him for a long moment, so Dell asked me "He is a good man isn't he?"

"Yes, he is a fine, substantial, wise, and loving person. He was my classmate in seminary. You can tell the bishop the next time you see him that I send my warm and affectionate regards."

We continued our conversation, not about the subject of IT, but about the Church and what all of us were about. The Kozmetskis were Eastern Orthodox Christians in their persuasion, but attended the Greek Orthodox Church

346 · RAYMOND HOCHE-MONG

because there were no Belarusian congregations in Austin, and they were not about to attend the local Roman Catholic parishes since his family had moved to Belarus so as to escape the Polish Roman Catholic church.

After a few sips of wine, the mayor of Linz began to participate in the conversation. We discussed the old city, its contribution to Austria, and of course I asked about Hitler and his family. He informed me that Hitler's house was not really in Linz but was located on the outskirts of the city in a small village called Braunau. The mayor was a charming Viennese who was delighted to host Americans and to be able to practice his very fluent English. He had visited Chicago, Los Angeles, Austin, and Miami — these cities had impressed him a great deal. He was hoping to return to America and George Kozmetski, I'm certain, would see to it that he did.

When we walked over to a restaurant, close by in the main part of the old town of Linz, our conversation continued on the same subject. Michael Dell was interested in how I was able to juggle my commitment to the Episcopal Church, my work at Bechtel, and, on top of that, being a partner in the operation of a bed and breakfast.

Dinner was exceptional, and the accompanying wines were well selected by George. Michael wanted to know my thoughts about the Eucharist but I wanted to get an image of what was going to happen in the morning at the conference. The conference was in essence a show-and-tell occasion for the West to introduce the East to IT with its developing process and its effect on the economy. The heart of the conference was to show how the free market operated vis-à-vis IT. Dell and others were going to connect entrepreneurship to IT; George Kozmetski was going to speak about IC^2's energizing approaches to IT and entrepreneurship development; my part was to compare Silicon Valley's free approach to IT emplacement with the French, Italian, Australian, and also other US formats and to elaborate on the manner by which the Silicon Valley pattern can be transplanted to other locations, and perhaps to other countries too. The three of us exchanged some ideas with the hope that we would avoid any duplication and certainly avoid boring the audience. George informed us that 556 registrations had been received of which 221 came from the Eastern bloc of nations. Indeed the curtain separating East from West was beginning to lift now that the Berlin wall had been reduced to rubble. In a few days I would fly to Berlin and would see the wall, or what was left of it, for myself.

The next morning after the greeting and usual introductions were made, Dr. Kozmetski gave a splendid address. George was followed by Michael Dell who used a slide projector to show the audience his computer design and assembly complex in Austin. Michael stressed that Dell Computer was more interested in outsourcing for assembly than in manufacturing. He conceived that his main contribution to IT was to offer inexpensive hardware, tailored to particular needs and tasks, and placed in the hands of customers in three days. Others could spend time in research and development, in creating new programs and new hardware; he would concentrate his research on providing low cost, quick delivery and fast applications.

When it was my turn, I spoke about IT facilities in the San Francisco-San Jose area, and the wealth of research and development that emerged from free incubators located in small shops, apartments, single dwelling houses, and coffee shops. I spoke about the European and Australian models and how they differed from those of Silicon Valley, and from other American models located in and around Boston, upstate New York, Austin, Seattle-Redmond, and elsewhere such as in some small towns of Nebraska, Montana, North Carolina, Virginia, and other places that I could neither remember nor recognize. Yet, none of these IT centers, complexes, or so-called parks were designed or managed by an "authority," and in most cases there was no land set aside for that purpose.

In Boston, IT established its roots initially in old abandoned factories around US Route 128. In Austin, properties around the decommissioned Air Force base of Bergstrom proved to be handy for IT because the land was inexpensive. Added to that was the incentive and hope that the city's airport would move to that decommissioned airbase. I mentioned many examples and compared them with non-American and even with some Canadian models.

At the Q&A session, the discussion progressed to details that we had anticipated. Representatives from Poland, Russia, and Ukraine were keen to learn the way funding was obtained. Dell indicated that he started with an old car, a trunk full of parts, and a substantial list of potential customers. George told them that he had been part of the very progressive firm Teledyne that was sold and whose sale gave him funds to use for the creation of IC^2, and he also had tenure as a professor at the University of Texas, Austin. I shared with the audience that I was the poorer of the threesome but that a major corporation employed me. Did any of us have governmental financial support? We assured them that we did not, except to borrow funds from lending organizations like banks. George allowed the audience to know that he was the least indebted of the three of us because he had his own personal wealth.

The conference continued for two more days and turned out to be successful, more so than we expected. Whether the contents that were shared helped anyone in the Eastern bloc is still hard to judge. I felt, and am still of that feeling, that it will take at least three generations to evolve before the Eastern bloc can shed totally the mentality of centralized authority and allow, with little restriction but some control, the free market and entrepreneurship to emerge.

Any free time that I had was used to visit and explore Linz. I wanted to see Adolf Hitler's birthplace. Adolf Hitler was born on April 20, 1889, in Braunau, Austria, a small town across the Inn River from Germany and a mere 52 kilometers west of Linz. In 1895 Hitler's family moved to Linz in a small cottage west of the city and that is where he went to public school. I wanted to see the several places that were connected to Adolf Hitler's (or Schicklgruber or Hiedler — his real names) beginnings.

The conference ended at noon of the third day and my flight to Berlin was scheduled for the next day at noon. Because I was free to do what I wanted after breakfast of the conference's last day, I asked the hotel if there was a taxi that could take me to Braunau. The hotel suggested a tour guide with a car instead of a taxi; the fixed price would be more reasonable and the guide could assist me with the historical facts. I accepted and made an appointment for 10:30 a.m.

At the appointed time, the guide arrived with a small Opel car. Anton, the middle-aged guide, spoke very good American English and was pleasant.

The price for the day was not exorbitant and it included lunch somewhere along the road. We left immediately for Braunau, the small village across the Inn River from Germany. It took about 50 minutes for the trip to Braunau's city limit and another 10 minutes to the house where Hitler was born. It was a small, miserable looking house with a double three-meter mesh wire fence around it. The house had become part of the Austrian National Historical Registry, but there was no attendant and the house was locked. Anton asked me to wait a moment to see if the neighbor across the road had a key. He soon returned to tell me that no key was available and visitors were not permitted inside; in fact he informed me that the inner fence around the house was electrified to discourage visitors poking around or vandals destroying the place. Anyway, I was glad to visit where one of the most criminal men of the 20th century had been born and where he had lived before moving to Linz.

My guide drove me to the center of Braunau. There was nothing special nor outstanding in the village. It looked like a typical Austrian small town, except that it was a border checkpoint to Germany. Anton mentioned that the language spoken in Braunau sounded more German than Austrian, but nevertheless it was not as high as the German of Berlin or Bonn.

The drive back to Linz was scenic and most pleasant. Anton stopped at a small restaurant close to the bank of the Danube River near Eferding (I believe) where we had lunch of several types of sausages, cheese, and bread, all washed down with a fine stein of Austrian beer. For dessert we had the traditional Linz torte. I noted that during my visit to Linz each piece of Linz torte I tasted was not quite like the previous one. I gathered that the recipe varied from baker to baker, but that was fine with me because they were all wonderful and delicious.

Anton was a history professor at the university in Linz. He acted as a guide for small groups when he needed some extra money; he had accepted this assignment because he was interested in the American point of view on Hitler. He was surprised that I was not a typical American but that made it all the more interesting for him. When we returned to the hotel, after paying and tipping him, I invited Anton to the lounge for a drink. We chatted for a couple of hours and I learned a great deal more of the history about the area, about the people in Linz and Braunau, and about the ongoing movement in Austria towards rightwing politics. Anton abhorred rightwing politics and assured me that he was a centrist and very devoted to opening up people's minds, especially his students', to a more liberal view of politics.

At the end of our drinks, I asked him if he would join me for dinner but he declined because he had to go home to his wife and daughter. His daughter was 19 and a student at the university reading history and international affairs; she hoped to work in some aspect of diplomacy, perhaps at the United Nations. As we said goodbye, Anton asked me if he could give me a ride to the airport in the morning. I thanked him and accepted gladly.

Later that evening over a sip of Cognac I said goodbye to Dr. and Mrs. Kozmetski and to Michael Dell and others who were associated with the East-West Conference. George told me that the conference numbers had increased to 670 people of whom 390 or so were from the Eastern bloc of nations, but most of them were from Russia and Ukraine. IC^2 would publish the papers and the commentaries as soon as everything was gathered in Austin.

The next morning Anton picked me up and drove me to the airport. He refused to take any money but accepted coffee and a Viennese breakfast goodie. I waited for the flight to Berlin. We said goodbye again and he reached into his satchel and gave me a large bar of Austrian chocolate and a well-wrapped piece of Linz torte that his wife had made. Unfortunately, I forgot to ask for his full name, his address or telephone number and the hotel could not recall (or were unwilling to tell me) whom they had recommended.

Also waiting for the flight were Dr. and Mrs. Kozmetski and their ten-year-old granddaughter, who were headed to Frankfurt on the same flight I had been booked on. My flight was scheduled to make a short stop in Frankfurt and then continue to Berlin. George and I talked about his and my work and how I'd become interested in knowledge cities and especially the people who lived in them. I recounted that I saw a city as an organism that nurtured the whole country because it contained the substance that could and did generate the imperative economic vitality that society required to survive. But with Bechtel I should consider building and construction, he reminded me.

Perhaps, but that was not my primary focus, because buildings without productive people were ultimately doomed to decay. I emphasized that it was industrious people that made a city possess life, dynamism, produce revenue, and become a wellspring of amenities for its residents to enjoy all the factors of good quality-of-life. George said that in a sense that was the reason that he had established IC^2: to demonstrate that knowledge and creative people are keys to a better world and that the city is the arena where both can bloom and produce.

Berlin and the New Germany

The Lufthansa flight departed on time for the 65-minute trip to Frankfurt am Main, Flughafen airport. Then I continued on a Pan American flight to Berlin's Flughafen Tegel airport. This was a strange flight arrangement because Germany's flag carrier was precluded from flying into Berlin by the Russian authorities; Pan American, Air France, and British Airways, as airlines of the occupier nations were permitted access to the city's main airport. Flughafen Templehof, the other airport closer to Berlin, was still in East Germany, but would soon become one of the principal airports for the city after the unification of the two Germanys took shape or which had already become a fact but still not a practice. Thus I was booked to fly from Linz, to Frankfurt, and then switch on Pan Am to Berlin. What should have taken 45 minutes if flown direct from Linz to Berlin, ended up by taking three hours and 30 minutes and two airlines.

At any rate, my arrival at Tegel was uneventful. My Japanese hosts whisked me off in a limousine to the hotel. After registering and unpacking, I was led to the conference hall at the hotel and given my assignment, which was pretty much the same as in Linz except for an adaptation to the current audience. The audience was made up of Germans, Japanese, Australians, Americans, Poles, and Hungarians and the conference was sponsored by the Japanese-German Institute of International Cooperation (which was funded by the Japanese) and by the Japanese Ministry of Industry, Technology, and Investment (MITI).

After an hour of listening to greetings, salutations, courtesy announcements, and official recognitions of important attendees (of which I was one because of my association with Bechtel), we were bussed to the Japanese Center, an impressive building styled after the Imperial Palace in Tokyo, but on a smaller scale. All participants were invited to sit around a long table, which must have been at least 45 feet in length, for the "intimate" conference. We were told that the hotel was too formal but this present building just completed a month earlier for the conference was less formal and much more intimate! The level of intimacy must be controlled by the culture gauging it. To me it felt as if I were asked to chat intimately with friends in the Salle Royale of the Grand Palais in Paris. The table was so long that we had microphones and speakers individually keyed for each person seated. Of course recorders, video cameras, and monitors were placed strategically so that we could see each other's grimacing when speaking. I should have expected this setting from Japanese hosts, but because I was substituting for Billo Puri, I had not been given all the gritty details.

Oh well, it was an acceptable experience and on the whole the conference was quite interesting, especially the trips exploring both sides of Berlin now that the Wall was in rubble (yes, I did pick up a fragment and had it mounted).

For the evening, after a buffet dinner, we were invited to attend a concert in the old Post Office Concert Hall in what was still East Berlin (the unification of Germany would not be official until October 1990). We were regaled with Johann Sebastian Bach's six Brandenburg Concertos.

After the concert I realized that I was exhausted and hence limp. A shower and bed consumed the last vestiges of energy from my body. Just as I was about to flip off the light switch by my bed the telephone rang. I thought of not answering it but then the red message light would flicker all night. "Hello," I said into the receiver.

"Raymond," it was the voice of Billo Puri, "I'm just checking that you've arrived and found the conference interesting. Have you seen my friend Dr. Soyamoto?"

I replied that I had seen him, had conveyed Billo's greeting to him, and that at this point the conference was expected to be interesting or so I hoped. "Billo, it is two o'clock in the morning and I must get my sleep so that I can be bright-eyed and bushy-tailed for the morning session. Adios and Ciao." I cradled the telephone.

Sleep came in seconds but morning arrived too soon. Was it the cracking sound of dawn that awakened me or was it room service knocking at the door? I got up to check the door. A pretty blond opened the door before I could reach it and entered with a silver tray carrying a coffee pot, several hard-boiled eggs, a variety of cheeses, a number of slices of various sausages, cream, sugar, several Kaiser rolls, a carafe of apple juice, and a red rose. It's a good thing that I sleep in pajamas because I had not thought of grabbing a robe. The waitress refused a tip by shaking her head, and left the room without saying a word.

Opening the curtains I overlooked Berlin's grand boulevard, called Unter den Linden, and on the left I could see a part of the Spree River and Museum Island. Emily had given me a good map of the city and that helped me orient myself in this extraordinary soon-to-be-again capital.

Because I was scheduled to speak before the noon recess I had some time to catch my breath and make some final adjustments to my speech (it was a few notes on one 3x5 card; this was before Power Point). I took the shuttle bus to the conference hall and found my place at the table. Because it was to be an informal conference each speaker would speak from his assigned place at the table. When my turn came I was pleased to see that everyone was in attendance. I spoke about economic globalization and the end of a partitioned globe suffering under fragmented financial systems, restricted political conditions, oppressed labor forces, and minimal educational opportunities. A practiced "technopolis" was a liberating and intellectually active organism. Dr. Soyamoto was particularly happy with my words, especially because MITI was intent on segregating IT firms into what it called Technopolis Complexes — just a different word for "park." The buffet lunch was served and each of us took a plate back to the giant table. A young Japanese woman, whose name I cannot recall, caught my attention and asked if I could have a word with her after the session was over. I agreed.

At the close of the afternoon session I climbed onto the shuttle bus for the ride back to the hotel. That evening we were to attend a play performed in the open arena near the Brandenburg Gate. On the bus the young Japanese woman sat next to me and told me that she was an urban planner with a master's degree from the University of California, Berkeley. Would Bechtel be interested in her? I said that I did not know but that I would look into it. "Are you Japanese or American?" I asked because her spoken English was quite American.

"I am Japanese but I cannot get a job in Japan." I inquired why that was so. "I am a woman and women are not readily offered professional positions in my country." That was a bit of news that I knew but assumed was being changed in the current society of Japan. "Not so. Japan is still a man's world. Women are not considered able to work in professional positions."

"Why did you come to California to obtain a degree knowing that you could not he employed in Japan?" She said nothing but acknowledged my question. "Don't you think that it would have been better to locate work while you were studying for your degree?" She agreed that she should have done that but procrastination and shyness held her back. Her courage surfaced when she heard my uplifting presentation about knowledge being a renewable commodity and not hampered by national or language boundaries. I said that I would see what Bechtel had to offer and she responded by telling me that she had a visa that permitted her to work in America for a few years.

The bus arrived at the hotel and we disembarked. It was time for a drink so I invited her to join me. Saronna Ikbato (I think that was her correct name) was a delightful young lady with a quick mind and a good sense of humor. After talking with her in the lounge I began to see that she could play a major role in the Infrastructure Department as a liaison to any Japanese project we might have. There were several projects that members of the department pursued and I would speak with them. I knew that my friend Bernard Catalinoto was involved in a possible project in Osaka, Chris Hartzell was looking at a project for a new-style office building in Tokyo, and Don Graff was involved with a potential project in Hokkaido. "I will look into the possibility of a slot for you," I said.

"Here is my vita," she reached into her bag.

"No, I will not need it at the moment. When we are in San Francisco I'll arrange for a meeting with a few of my colleagues," I said, then added, "You are still living in Berkeley?" Saronna confirmed that she would be in Berkeley in a couple of weeks. I gave her my card and ordered another drink. Dinner that evening would be served in a special dining room of the hotel. After our drinks I excused myself to go to my room to freshen up before dinner.

The Beckman Link

When I arrived in my room I had a message from Ligia. I called her to inquire what the message was about because the call had not come on my personal phone. She informed me that she had received a fax from the Beckman Laser Institute and Medical Research Center at the University of California, Irvine, asking that I contact them as soon as possible. It wasn't too late so I made the call.

Michael Berns, Ph.D., said that he was inviting me to attend a reception honoring Dr. Arnold Beckman, the founder and benefactor of the center and that the State Department had agreed to authorize two Russian physicians to attend the training and familiarization programs at the Center. "Raymond, would any of your contacts in Troitsk be interested and willing to come to the Center for a year's training?" Michael Berns asked.

I said that I would look into it as soon as I returned to San Francisco and that I would be delighted to come to the reception honoring Dr. Beckman. Berns and I chatted for a few minutes and then he told me that the training would cost $12,000 per candidate but the Beckman Institute would pay half of that as a matching fee. I had to not only identify two candidates but I had to find $12,000 for the program. The latter was a difficult task because to obtain funds from my department at Bechtel would require the signing approval of Frank Cain. That was going to be a no-win issue.

I had had good contact with the Beckman Laser Lab at the University of California, Irvine for several years because of my interest in the development of laser science. The Kurchatov researchers in Troitsk had been focused on powerful large laser technology and that had piqued my interest. Soon after in a conference I had met Dr. Berns and was introduced to Dr. Beckman and his work. I had inquired if Berns was interested in meeting Pismenny the next time he was in California. They did and found common ground for cooperation; the Kurchatov scientists worked on large laser and Berns worked on fine laser, best used for medical and industrial cutting purposes. In the course of my dealing with IT I had had several meetings with Dr. Berns and Dr. Beckman both in Irvine and in Palo Alto. Because Cain was not interested in this aspect of IT, I had contacted Dr. Harold Forsen, scientist and head of research and development at Bechtel (more about him soon).

I thought about how I could manage that little obstacle as I lay in bed awaiting sleep, which did not come quickly for me because my brain was moving at light-speed examining all the possibilities and options. I had to find a way to raise the funds because the laser training was too important not to have the Russians participate in it. It was good for Russia and it certainly was good for America; sharing science is a great bonding agent for long-term friendships. Anyway I thought that the exchange invitation would serve the Russian trainees well and would offer them a view of American culture. I fell asleep pleased with the Beckman opportunity and looked forward to making it a reality. I should have considered my naiveté.

Arnold and Mabel Beckman at the University of California, Irvine Campus, founded the Beckman Laser Institute (BLI) and Medical Clinic. The center was focused on micro-laser surgery procedures, cell biology, ophthalmology, and radiology research. The director was Michael W. Berns, and his assistant was Ann E. Siemens, vice president and manager of development & marketing.

BLI was doing extraordinary research in the application of laser technology in medicine, especially in surgery. Because the Russians were working on mega-laser applications at the Troitsk Kurchatov Nuclear Institute, there was research that could be tapped by BLI that would be beneficial to both the

USSR and America. The commonality in laser research was such that the USSR's research was quite advanced in the field of mega-laser while the American research was specifically geared to micro-laser applications. Creating the bridge between the USSR and America offered potential for great technological breakthroughs in laser research. In fact, the United States soon discovered that its "Star Wars" laser defense program promoted by Reagan was not as developed as that of the Russians. Fortunately for the United States, when the USSR imploded in 1991 all defense research on its laser programs ceased.

I would see what I could do. It was too important an opportunity to ignore.

Both the Republicans in America and Frank Cain had the same view of the USSR, and especially of Russia. Both looked at Russia as an "evil empire" that was out to do horrible things to the world. That Russians and members of the Soviet social fabric were caught in the grip of the Communist hierarchy never did register in either Reagan's brain or in Cain's cranial cavity. It was not all black and white between the USSR and America. The USSR was on the verge of an implosion and we in the west had to do something positive to bring about a good and substantive change. Working with Pismenny and the Beckman Institute was a small step in that direction, a very small step, but nevertheless a positive step as we discovered later. Pismenny had identified two physicians for the exchange, one of whom had a Ph.D. in physics in addition to his medical degree.

To get this program started, I shortened my trip and returned to San Francisco to search for the funding. Frank Cain did not want to allocate a single penny for the exchange. He thought that the entire scheme was stupid and would amount to naught. I did not waste a moment but went to Harold K. Forsen, Ph.D., senior vice president of Bechtel's research and development group.

Harold was a mentor, a friend, and a safe haven when conditions in my department were difficult and impossible to endure. Conversation with Forsen was always about concepts and not about the internal politics of Bechtel. Harold was a science-minded person who saw physics and philosophy as one discipline where one envisioned knowledge in mathematical language and the other, philosophy, articulated knowledge in concepts, events, and processes. We often discussed the works of A.N. Whitehead, especially his summa *Process and Reality*.

In the turbulent days under Cain's authority, Harold Forsen's company assured me that reason did prevail even when one is overwhelmed by incoherencies. Forsen was most kind to give me time to center myself when I was thrown off balance. All I needed was to telephone him and immediately he would tell me to come to his office, usually as soon as he was free. Dr. Forsen retired from Bechtel two years after I did in 1995. At Bechtel Harold was a mental giant condemned to function among inferiors (Forsen died in March 2012).

After briefing Harold, he was convinced that the exchange program had merit, great merit. He called in his finance people and his chief researcher and we all discussed what the gains and losses would be. No one could come up with any losses. The gains were extraordinary, especially since Bechtel would be further connected to the Soviet's excellent research in laser technology. After some further discussion, Harold approved the $12,000 for the program and he insisted that I telephone Dr. Berns to inform him that the funding would be transferred to the Beckman account the next day. I was to say nothing to Frank Cain, and if word leaked that Bechtel was supporting the exchange program, I was to refer all inquiries to Dr. Harold Forsen (who outranked Cain).

Harold Forsen was a prince of a person. In February of 2004, Dr. Forsen telephoned me during a layover in San Francisco International Airport on his return trip from Washington, DC. He had moved to Kirkland, WA to retire and to write a book.

Ignoring Frank Cain, Emily and I went to the reception at the Beckman Laser Center to honor Dr. Arnold Beckman and to wish him a happy 90th birthday. Dr. Forsen arrived at the center soon after I did and I introduced him to Dr. Beckman, Dr. Berns, Ann Siemens, and to the exchange physicians from Troitsk. We briefed the exchange physicians and asked them to keep Dr. Forsen and me informed about their programs, their research, and their progress. We asked them to send us quarterly reports.

As I look back at that program, one physician proved to be most valuable to the exchange venture, and one had to be sent back to Russia because he did not perform well at all. Dr. Natasha Sveltikava continued her work with Dr. Berns for an additional year on a fellowship advanced by the Beckman Institute and without Bechtel's participation. Natasha was the candidate with a Ph.D. in physics and an MD with specialization in cytology. When she returned to Russia a teaching chair was offered to her at one of Russia's prestigious medical universities in St. Petersburg. Unfortunately I have lost direct contact with her but every so often I hear about her from Dr. Pismenny.

My contact with the Beckman group was an experience that I shall cherish for many years if not forever. I learned a great deal, not only about laser technology, but also about how research is conducted and how intellectual property cannot be hidden in a safe place where no exchange of ideas can occur. While working with the Beckman group, especially with Dr. Beckman and Dr. Berns, I learned again that knowledge is unfathomably thrilling and rewarding. I also began to appreciate that knowledge is a renewable and lasting commodity and that once it becomes emergent it is practically eternal. Moreover, I saw firsthand that knowledge is cumulative; that is, each layer of information is placed on the previous layer to help build the mental library, the data base, that makes life exquisitely exciting, stimulating, and sacramental because of its precious gifts to a human being and to all beings. To learn, to know, and to experience are what life is all about; add love to these and human beings can ask for no more and no less.

When I returned to my office in San Francisco, I began putting Saronna's name and qualifications into the mill and telephoning people who needed a Japanese person for this or that project. Bernard Catalinoto was working on a planning project near Osaka and he would consider Saronna, if and when the funding for the project materialized. At the moment there was a study for a proposal to build an island airport location not too far from Osaka. This was an airport that I had discussed with the Japanese client when I informed them that we could place an airport anywhere in the world "if he had enough funds and patience!" The airport, which was to be built on a made-made island, was in the planning process and the civil engineering was scheduled to follow soon. I had suggested that they scrap the project because the island would invariably sink into the ocean. Years later I was proven to be correct; Kensai International Airport is sinking several centimeters into the ocean every year. Nevertheless, even if the island of Kensai is sinking and to keep it viable fill has to be brought to it regularly, it has offered the Japanese a splendid airport free of the restrictions that encumber inland aviation complexes. Hence I offer my apologies for having been negative.

The project that Catalinoto worked on never did materialize and Saronna was not hired. I approached Don Graff but in typical manner, he was interested, but never produced an offer for some work on his project in Hokkaido. I tried in other departments but projects for Bechtel were not surfacing and hiring was thin. I telephoned Saronna and told her that I had failed to help her, at least for the time being. I suggested that she try Parsons or Fluor and gave her some introductory names. Several weeks later I received a phone call from Saronna announcing that Fluor had offered her a planning position in their urban department. She would be working on a project in Okinawa but would remain in the United States and not travel to Japan. She was pleased and so was I. The last time I heard from Saronna was in 1992 and she was still employed by Fluor.

I completed my expense reports. This was to be a two-part report where one was sent to IC^2 for the conference in Linz and the other for the Berlin conference. IC^2 was prompt in reimbursing me for the exact amount I asked, which included the airfare in business class, but Frank Cain would not sign the report on the pretext that I should slip it in with the Linz conference and let IC^2 pay for it. That was not much of an ethical position and I just laughed at him. Spink was not sure how he should react to my response to Cain's preposterous call. I called Billo Puri to ask how he intended to pay for my expenses, and he suggested that the amount come from the department's overhead budget. Cain was not only incensed by Billo's recommendation but also suggested that Puri had sent me without obtaining proper authorization from him (Cain). I leafed through my expense report and showed Cain that he had signed my travel request twice, once for Linz and another for Berlin! Cain looked at me with a stare that suggested that if he could he would throw me out the 30th floor window. Ultimately he signed my expense report with some obvious embarrassment.

"What's next on your plate?" Cain asked me in an attempt to change the subject.

"I'll review the assignment you gave me."

"What assignment?"

I paused long enough to whet his curiosity. "Troitsk's report." He looked at me and said not a word.

I stopped in Kingsley's office and asked him if he was ready for a cup of coffee and had a few moments to discuss the state of the Troitsk report. He was ready. As I was waiting for the elevator we heard Wakelin's voice, "What's Hoche-Mong doing now?" The elevator took us down. After coffee and our discussion on the report, a report that Kingsley had polished rather well, I returned to my office and was intercepted by Wakelin.

"What have you said to Cain?" He asked me. I reiterated the details of my meeting with Cain and Spink. "Cain doesn't like you and will make your life impossible here," he warned me.

"Michael," I said, "he does bother me and he does add to the acid in my belly, but I cannot do much about his feelings towards me."

"He does control much in this department and you are here to do his bidding," Michael reminded me.

"Michael, that's too bad for Cain if his ego keeps him in conflict with me. He is just another of Bechtel's minions and his ego is of no interest to me. I'll avoid him as much as possible but at times we'll butt heads."

"You might give him wiggle room," Michael said.

"I will. I'll just ignore him."

My desk was a welcoming harbor, and the Troitsk report was a good task to pull me away from the silly politicking that floated around. My plate was full of work and I could not dwell much on what was going on vis-à-vis Cain. Both Troitsk and Bari demanded my attention and I needed to tend to Bari as soon as I completed the Russian task. Umberto Bozzo was anxious for me to come to Bari to discuss the next stage of the evolution of Tecnopolis, and I was ready to spend a few days or weeks in Puglia.

Just as I was becoming immersed in Troitsk, Riley Bechtel's assistant phoned me to ask if I would send Riley a copy of my trip report. I informed him that I had not planned to write one. Well, would I write an evaluation of what I learned in Berlin? Riley was also sending me the text of Prince Charles's speech on the new architecture of London, specifically his comments on the new Lloyd's of London Bank building.

"What am I to do with that speech?" I asked.

Well it seems that the prince was going to be at a conference in Miami and Riley had been asked to attend and to speak too. In sum, Riley wanted a few comments, a few ideas, and a few specific aesthetic bits from me on the subject of architecture.

"Why not ask the architectural people at Bechtel to tackle that for Riley?" I questioned.

"Raymond, Riley wants your comments and not those of the architects, and especially not any comment from Bob Reynolds." Robert Reynolds was the chief architect, a Harvard graduate, but not too terribly willing to offer his opinions, if and when he had any.

After I cradled the telephone, Michael Wakelin came to see me and inquired why Riley's assistant wanted to reach me. It seems that Wakelin had been called on the phone to learn if I was in San Francisco. I related my conversation to Michael but he reminded me that I was not an architect and that he was and he should do the task.

"Fine Michael," I said, "Wait a moment and I'll call Riley's office and inform him that Wakelin has pulled me off the architecture task because I'm not an architect and that he will do the task." I reached for the phone and called Riley's office. After some discussion with Riley's assistant and several moments of waiting until he checked with his boss, the assistant replied that I was to do the task and not have Michael take over, even if he was an architect. As diplomatically as I could make it I reported to Michael that Riley was interested in my point of view; he had already obtained other points of view. That piece of information did not endear me with Michael any more than poking him in the eye would have. My comments were taken by Riley and incorporated in his address at the City Outline Conference in Miami and I received name recognition.

Really I'm Not Trouble on the Hoof

In the past anecdotes it may appear that I am impossible to live with, constantly on the warpath, looking for fights and issues to support my quest for combat, and that I enjoy intimidating people by stepping over them. On the contrary, I would just as soon work on a project and would go to some length to avoid any altercation. But when push comes to shove, I'll stand my ground and will defend myself and those who are intimately associated with me. I do respect authority, especially when it is earned authority, but I will resist feeding authority the food of self-aggrandizement. Cain would have had no problem with me if he had not been so hungry to nourish his ego with credits that were not his. Once a foul condition surfaces I am constantly alert for any hints of threat or underhandedness.

Michael, however, on the whole was a pleasant sort, and at one time was considered a friend, and very much a visionary but an unabashed political games-player. As a department leader, Michael Wakelin had a genius for surrounding himself with excellent people. The people who reported to him, as I did, were first class thinkers, visionaries, and extraordinarily competent and adept in their craft. The problem arose when Michael competed with his team for some share of the rewards. He could never understand that by allowing his department to excel he would be reaping adulation, credit, and a great reputation. Michael was unable to see through his selfish need for glory.

In a way, Michael had the same ego issues that Cain possessed but he was not mean or nasty. All his people were involved in writing papers, making presentations, and producing reports — all of these works quite often penetrated through the membrane that separated the pedestrian, the ordinary, and the uninspired from that which is visionary, imaginative, and unrealized. Often that approach succeeded in giving Michael grief because it put him in difficult positions with some of his superiors, and he was one to kowtow to his higher-ups. When he gave in to the limiting attitudes of some of his superiors many of his best people chose to abandon him for other positions or projects that were totally removed from his purview.

Ultimately both Cain and Wakelin ended up in the backwaters of Bechtel; the first managing a non-essential department that eventually was terminated, and the latter given a false accolade with the title of "Bechtel Fellow," which led Michael to accept forced retirement as soon as he reached his 25th year at Bechtel. It was a sad situation because Michael was a visionary and tended to attract good people for his team, but then he would screw it all up by antagonizing those who supported him. Cain was finally removed and given a minor role without a department under his supervision and a couple of years later he was invited to retire.

Under those and other similar people at Bechtel, I was an unwilling practitioner in the art of self-defense, merely to keep my sanity and to protect my territory, my self-respect, and the needs of my clients. Being trampled over is not my goal in life. My person is too valuable to me to be crushed by people's heavy-handedness and authoritarianism. To be put down without responding to another person's egocentric quest is to admit that one is not important and it is an indication that one is either a coward or unwilling to defend his dignity. I am neither. To be overwhelmed by the whim of another is shameful, unethical, and stupid.

Attending to Odds and Ends

In May 1989 I had finished reviewing the Troitsk report and was called by Umberto Bozzo to come to Bari to discuss what I thought should be the next step for Tecnopolis. Umberto was being hounded by the new president of the University of Bari to come up with a plan that he could attach to his program, something that would clearly give a contrast to his university against Bari's Technological University — which had been created with the help of Tecnopolis, Bozzo, and Gianfranco Dioguardi, the current president of the board of Tecnopolis. In this situation Umberto was being squeezed to develop a plan or a program that would give the University of Bari greater presence than the Technological University. Bozzo didn't much like that idea because the University president usually acted as an impediment by vetoing anything that had anything to do with science, business, and the nurturing of intellectual capital unless it was based on classical literature.

I made arrangements to book a flight to London a few days later. My plan was to catch up on a few EU tasks in London, and then fly to Brussels for a meeting with a representative of the European Development Bank, Dr. Eileen York, and after that head for Rome and on to Bari.

Bari and the Department of Puglia were beautiful in May and this Friday the weather was balmy and not yet hot. After arriving in Bari, Umberto came to fetch me at the Palace Hotel located in the downtown area and whisked me to his office. We would go to his house for dinner that evening. We talked for a couple of hours about the future of Technopolis, Umberto's plans for his own future, and the options that were available to him. Dr. Gianfranco Dioguardi came to meet with us around six p.m. We still had not determined what it was that we would do. I had a hazy idea buzzing in my head but I wasn't sure how either Umberto or Gianfranco would receive it. Then I decided to let the idea fly out.

"Why not develop an ongoing art exhibit here at Technopolis?" I said. They both looked at me and their looks intimated some acquiescence. I continued, "An ongoing art exhibit here at Technopolis would not only fulfill some of the needs of the art department at the University of Bari, but could also bring the technical brains of the Technological University into the program, after all, 'techne' means art in Greek."

Dr. Dioguardi, who spoke French to me, proposed that such an exhibit could run for each semester, hence it would be a rotating and ongoing event that would call upon the talents residing in both universities.

"One university would contribute its fine art talents and the other its technical talents," Gianfranco Dioguardi added.

"After a while," Umberto suggested, "both universities would have blurred contribution of their talents and Technopolis would be the place where art would be displayed, encouraged, and nurtured."

Gianfranco Dioguardi declared that the idea was brilliant. I was charged with writing the program and making a brief presentation to both university rectors as soon as a time could be scheduled.

We went to Umberto's house for dinner and some wine. It was an interesting evening because Gianfranco Dioguardi, as I said, spoke French to me since he spoke no English; Umberto spoke English to me; and I struggled gladly in Italian in an attempt to resuscitate it as I spoke to Anna Bozzo, who spoke neither English nor French. It was not quite like the Tower of Babel, but pretty close to it in its level of cacophony — Italians are not a soft-speaking people but hearty eaters. It was a fine dinner and typical of one served in an Apulian home.

After a few days to gather information, to meet with art leagues and other groups, and to make the presentation to the university rectors — both liked the idea and the proposed program — I left Bari for London and on to San Francisco. My plan was to write a draft of the program and then return to Bari to discuss it with all the parties involved, which included the rectors, the contributors of funds, Dr. Dioguardi, and several of Umberto's supporting board members. I had identified mid-June as the time to head to Bari, a few weeks before the summer holidays that begin in August for the Europeans.

Because of other commitments at Bechtel, my plate was overflowing. There was a review of Moreno Valley to see if the new city council would accept a less complex program; a call to work on a proposed floating island airport in Japan; and a meeting in the Bahamas to discuss tourism and aviation with the government. The Moreno Valley revised program did not convince the city council one bit; the program died and that was that.

Bechtel, however, for the first time received FAA approval for an airport — the first in its long history of building airports. The floating island for the Japanese, in deference to all advice that it was a miserable idea, went ahead. Ultimately to be built and called Kansai International Airport, it was constructed totally on soil brought from the mainland and anchored by concrete perimeter walls supported by deeply sunk pylons. This was a concept that I had rejected but then it was built in spite of my negativity. Because the Kansai was created on landfill, it is sinking all the time and needs to be refilled constantly. As I mentioned earlier I apologized for being negative to this idea of a floating airport; now I believe that such airports have a future in places where land is limited and legal obstacles are too complex to overcome. Environmental concerns, however, should not be ignored when such airports are considered.

The Bahamas project was one of the successes I enjoyed immensely. The Bahamas are a chain of about 3,000 coral islands and reefs that make up an independent nation in the West Indies. They extend from about 50 miles (80 kilometers) off the eastern coast of Florida to the northeastern tip of Cuba, a distance of more than 500 miles (800 kilometers). Only about 20 of the islands are inhabited. About four-fifths of the Bahamian people live on two of the islands: New Providence and Grand Bahama. Nassau, the capital and largest city, lies on New Providence. The beauty and mild climate of the Bahamas have helped make tourism the basis of its economy in spite of hurricanes visiting it often.

I had worked on two projects in the Bahamas and now there was a request that I go to New Providence to discuss an expansion plan not only for the airport, but for Bahama Air, the quasi-national airline. My colleague Carol Austin was still working on a task that included a craft academy and a vocational school. I telephoned Carol and informed her that I would be in Nassau the next Friday for a rest over the weekend, and some intense meetings with government officials starting the following Monday. Carol offered to meet me at the airport and chauffeur me around in her leased car.

A flight to Nassau from San Francisco calls for a night's layover in Miami. The first Thursday of July 1989 I boarded a flight to Miami. In Miami I stayed at the Sheraton and had dinner in Coral Gables at a fresh fish restaurant that I knew. Swallowing a dozen Gulf oysters and a fine dish of three soft-shell crabs made for a good dinner. The next morning I boarded the early flight for the 50-minute jaunt to Nassau on the oldest continuously operating airline in America, Hawk Airways. Hawk operates two Martin amphibians from Miami to Nassau and I booked a seat on one of them. It was pure unadulterated pleasure for me. When we landed, Carol Austin was waiting for me in an old 10-passenger white limousine, the leased car for the duration of her stay in Nassau.

I enjoyed being back in Nassau and staying at the historic Queen Victoria Hotel on the waterfront. I was looking forward to the splendid fried conch fritters as an appetizer, followed by fish and good English Ale. Carol was full of good news about her project. She invited me to her suite before dinner and offered me a martini made with Tanqueray; she always was kind to remember my favorite libation. After exchanging news we boarded her long white car and headed for the western tip of Nassau where we both knew a good yet inexpensive restaurant that catered to locals and not to tourists. As expected the food was what I remembered: excellent. After dinner Carol drove me back to my hotel and I invited her to share a brandy.

The next day Carol offered to drive me around Nassau, which is the principal city of New Providence Island — the Bahamian center of government. I was thinking of catching a flight to Eleuthera Island to see my old friends, but the weather did not promise to be dry or clear. So I accepted the offer of a drive around Nassau and a visit to her two training centers. Carol's enthusiasm was catching and I became eager to see what she had accomplished. The weekend was pleasant, restful, and very entertaining. Carol was the perfect hostess.

On Monday morning Carol drove me to the International Airport for my meeting with the director of the Aviation Authority and his staff. After my meeting at the airport Carol drove me to the office of Bahama Air for a discussion on whether a fleet master plan was necessary. The airline operated six Fokker 28s for passenger service and three DC-6s as freighters, not a very large fleet by any means. Canadian, Venezuelan, and US carriers supply most of the services to the Bahamas, and on occasion a Cuban carrier brings goods and a few tourists.

After reviewing the routes, the freight loads, and the passenger services to the islands from Nassau, I made the suggestion that newer aircraft might produce more revenue, greater profit, and offer options for greater use of their proprietary routes. Replacing the Fokkers with used Boeing 737-100s might allow the airline to increase its cargo and passenger loads and decrease the fuel consumption (B-737s are more passenger-friendly than Fokkers) and give the line longer service distances. We discussed several possibilities that would surface from an upgraded fleet and I invited airline management to speak with Boeing and even with McDonnell to obtain direct data for their decisions. I was asked to help the management meet with the aircraft manufacturers and assist them in the selection process.

After several meetings with the airport authorities and the airline representatives that took me up to Thursday, I then made a reservation with American Airlines for the return flight to Miami and a connecting flight to San Francisco with a short stop in Dallas. Carol and I had a farewell dinner on Wednesday and she drove me to the airport for an early departure on Thursday. I was most pleased to have had Carol drive me around and be my company during the few days I dwelt in Nassau. Carol Austin was a charming and bright woman in possession of a sharp sense of humor and a ready smile. A professional trainer by choice, yet she was capable of tackling many tasks competently and with a creative zest that made her a valuable employee and colleague. Socially I can describe Carol as a single woman, but unmarried by choice and quite comfortable to be in that state. I think that Carol would make a fine partner for any man, but the man would have to be bright, caring, and self-assured to manage his relationship with this extraordinary woman. I have always enjoyed working with and socializing with Carol but I cannot remember ever receiving a hug from her, and that has puzzled me.

After I returned to San Francisco, I received a fax from Bahama Air asking if I would set up appointments with Boeing and McDonnell. Immediately after receiving this message I telephoned my contacts at the two aircraft manufacturers. Meetings were agreed for the next week and I conveyed the message to Bahama Air. Our first visit was at the Long Beach facility of McDonnell where we saw several MD-80s and received the necessary information on which the small airline could base its decision. From Los Angeles we flew directly to Seattle and on to Boeing's facility in Renton where we received an overwhelming amount of data on used B-737-100s and –200s.

The next day I spent in a conference room at the hotel with the team from Bahama Air. We sorted out the information and identified what was important and what were merely cosmetic add-ons. The conclusion was that Bahama Air would do better with the Boeing product, but we had to find a way to sell the Fokkers and the DC-6s. I telephoned Charlie Clark, who worked for Boeing and had been a friend for many years, and asked him if he had any suggestions for the old airplanes. Charlie thought that a Chinese customer in Hainan Island would be interested in the aircraft if they could be converted to combis (mixture of passenger and freighter). We worked on that issue before I left for San Francisco.

Several months later the Bahamian old aircraft were sold and transferred to China and Boeing delivered six practically new B-737-200s combis to the Bahamas. The DC-6s were sold to a Peruvian freight forwarder who served mainly central South America.

Desert Storm and Travel

With the Troitsk report completed and the Bari paper almost finished except for Umberto's review and comments, I was ready for my next trip. But under Saddam Hussein of Iraq and President George H.W. Bush, circumstances changed greatly. In August 1990, Iraq invaded the neighboring country of Kuwait. With that invasion the political balance of power around the Arabian-Persian Gulf changed dramatically. President Bush began to put together a coalition of nations willing to be partners in a military operation to evict the Iraqis from Kuwait. The US State Department called for reduced travel, and travel for Americans only when absolutely necessary.

The Department of Defense and the Joint Chiefs of Staff proposed, following General Colin Powell's rule, that an overwhelming force be used to remove the Iraqi military from the oil-rich nation of Kuwait. The military effort to force Iraq out of Kuwait became known as Operation Desert Storm. My problem with this proposed build up was that it took more than six months before any signs of a military operation appeared possible. I had to be in Italy and I had a profitable project that needed my attention now — not in a year or two. I made plans to travel to London on British Airways and then to transfer to a BA flight to Rome. I was warned that my travel was deemed dangerous but no one at Bechtel made any signs to stop me. Was I expendable? Or was I a revenue producer?

At 6:20 p.m. I boarded BA flight 267 to London's Heathrow International Airport. I was riding in a B-747-400 that normally carries more than 350 passengers but the purser announced that on this flight we had only 48 souls on board plus a crew that numbered 24. It was strange to be flying in such a huge machine with only a few people, but what was still stranger was Terminal 4 at Heathrow where I had a four-hour wait for a flight to Rome.

The terminal was empty except for the concessionaires, the cleaning people, the BA service staff, and passport and security personnel. I stopped at the center counter for a plate of fresh oysters and the server offered me a plate of smoked salmon to accompany it. When I had finished my meal, he announced that it was free, no charge, because he had to dispose of the food before it spoiled. It was either discard the fresh food or give it away to the few passengers. The terminal was not crowded and the low level of activity kept the noise level quite low. When I entered the BA Club to freshen up, there were only two people inside plus the hostesses.

I had never experienced the emptiness of a terminal as I did that mid-morning. The Kuwait occupation had chased passengers away from airlines in droves. Many flights to Saudi Arabia and other places were cancelled. Flights over the Middle East were rerouted over Africa to avoid the region and the possibility of being hit by an Iraqi Scud missile.

My flight to Rome was searched twice before we boarded the aircraft. It also had only a few passengers rattling around in a B-757. Rome's Leonardo Da Vinci Airport was also empty and very quiet. On the lower level where I usually boarded an Italia flight for the 50-minute flight to Bari, the waiting area had just 10 passengers!

Arriving in Bari I was met by Mario Marinazzo in his dilapidated Austin automobile, the car that he claimed no one would steal or vandalize. I was taken to my hotel and then to Tecnopolis for a meeting with Mario, Umberto, and Annamaria Annicchiarico. Each had reviewed my program and approval was directly given. In the morning I was to meet with university people and a few public officials for their evaluation, but I was assured that there was nothing to worry about because the program had been distributed and no negative comments had been returned to Umberto.

The next morning I attended a meeting where Italian was mainly spoken, but Mario acted as my interpreter when I was stuck or was not able to grasp the trend of the discussion because the speakers often spoke rapidly. Towards the end of the meeting, both university rectors asked for a detailed executive preface that could be circulated to the press, to the Ministry of Education, and to the local art guilds. The response was positive, supportive, and encouraging. I promised that I would have a draft sent to Umberto in a few weeks and would return to Bari to receive their comments before the final text was done. I would return in four weeks to obtain the comments from Umberto on the future plan for Technopolis, a report that I had worked on for several months.

Back in San Francisco I made my trip report to upper management, which included Spink, Gary Bechtel (now president of Bechtel Civil), and a couple of other people. Billo Puri, the titular business development point man, made the statement that Bari was a waste of time and that probably Bechtel was losing money dealing with them. I had expected this comment because Chip Tabor, my friend, had overheard Billo making that statement to Wakelin. Chip had immediately checked with the comptroller's office for the exact revenue total produced by the Tecnopolis for Bechtel. I pulled the accounting sheet out of my binder and read the total net revenue aloud that Tecnopolis had produced for Bechtel (Chip was present). The net total, not the gross but the net total, had put 1.8 million dollars in Bechtel's coffer since I had taken over the job. That piece of information sealed Billo Puri's mouth to an ever-noticeable silence.

Now it was time to put the finishing touches on Bari's art program and the evolution of *Bari's Tecnopolis*. The latter was a concept paper describing the next steps in Technopolis' continuing and effective development. Because Dr. Bozzo and his staff had reviewed both tasks, my immediate job was to flesh out the paper and bring it to quality for final approval and publication. My intention was to return to Bari in November 1990, just a month away. To get my tickets and reservations for the trip I asked Ligia to process my request then called Umberto to ask him if that was in agreement with his schedule and intentions. He would be happy to see me in November and wanted to know if I wished to attend one of the opera performances in the Bari Opera House that Dr. Gianfranco Dioguardi's firm had recently restored. Umberto also wanted to show me the restored Church of St. Nicholas, which was founded in 1087 and where the original Saint Nicholas is buried. Gianfranco's construction and engineering firm had done some amazing restorative work for the ancient city of Bari, that as early as the 400s B.C. was recognized as an important town. Both Gianfranco and Umberto reminded me often that Bari had been destroyed and rebuilt three times.

Just as I was about to leave for lunch and the noon lecture at the Commonwealth Club of San Francisco, Don Graff came to inform me that he was going with me to Bari because as overall manager of projects and at the invitation of Dr. Bozzo, it was his responsibility to visit every project. That piece of news surprised me for two reasons. Bari was not under Graff's purview and he was not my superior, at least I had not been informed that he was; moreover, he did not outrank me. The other reason was that Umberto had not informed me that he had asked Don Graff to accompany me. Had he done so, he would have told me. It was too late to call Umberto at the office, so I called him at home. Anna replied that Umberto was at a meeting but he would return my call in a couple of hours. I went to my luncheon.

Later that afternoon, Umberto Bozzo called me. We chatted about the task and I asked a few clarifying questions for which he had good answers and ideas. When the initial conversation was nearly spent, I asked if he had invited Don Graff to accompany me to Bari.

"I don't know anything about Mr. Graff's visit. I received a fax from Mr. Graff informing me that he was coming to Bari."

"Umberto, you did not invite him?" I questioned him.

"No, Raymond, I did not."

"In that case then you do not authorize his expenses to be taken from the Tecnopolis account."

"No, Raymond, I do not authorize his expenses from the Tecnopolis account," Umberto assured me.

After wishing him a good night over the phone, I went to Graff's office. When I arrived he showed me a memo that he was sending to Spink for authorization to go to Bari. In the memo he stated that Dr. Umberto Bozzo had requested his presence in Bari to review several issues about the project.

"Are you sending this memo to Spink?" I asked.

He was.

"Don, I'm not paying for your expenses out of the Bari Project account," I told him. As project manager for the Bari project I had to authorize all debits from that account.

Graff stared at me then said, "As overall manager of projects I must go to Bari to review certain issues."

"Good, you can go, but pay your expenses from your overhead account. No Bari funds will cover your expenses, especially since Dr. Bozzo has not invited you to visit Bari." That said I walked out of his office.

The upshot of this was that Don Graff did accompany me to Bari, he did pay his expenses from the department's overhead account, and Dr. Bozzo neither spent one minute alone with him nor did he discuss the project with him. While in Bari and out of courtesy, I acted as a guide to Graff. Even when he was present at a meeting, he was regarded as a non-entity.

One example of his non-entity presence occurred after Umberto and his staff discussed my two reports and if any changes needed to be made. I had informed Umberto that the report would be finalized and placed in his hand by 31 January 1991. Don Graff interjected by saying, "Oh, we can have the report in your hands by the end of the year, in December."

I looked at him but did not have to say anything, because Dr. Bozzo said explicitly, "When Raymond said 31 January that was good enough for me!"

It is always appropriate to set the rules and to maintain them whenever possible. In this situation, Bari was my project and I was accountable to the client and to the company that employed me and not to some employee who wanted to hedge in and claim some degree of importance for no reason at all. Perhaps it was overkill to be firm in this situation but when does one stay firm? In the final analysis, the Tecnopolis project was successfully completed and the client was pleased with the results — and it is still a productive complex. Dr. Bozzo is still my friend and I'm always a welcome guest in Bari, at his house, at Tecnopolis, at the universities, and in many of the firms.

Kuwait, USSR, and their Effect

Events in the world were changing rapidly between 1990 and 1992. As I mentioned earlier, Iraq had invaded Kuwait and the small oil-rich Sheikdom was being pillaged. In January 1991 the US-led coalition removed Iraqi forces from Kuwait.

In the USSR, Party Secretary and President Mikhail Sergeyevich Gorbachev was placed under arrest in his dacha on the Black Sea in Crimea. On Aug. 19, 1991, several conservative Soviet Communist officials tried to overthrow Gorbachev as president of the Soviet Union. Telephone conversations between Troitsk and Montara were numerous and Slava Pismenny was appalled at the turn of events although he was certain that Gorbachev would regain his position but not his power because he expected that the USSR was on its last gasp. The coup quickly collapsed in the face of widespread opposition, and Gorbachev retained his leadership, although his government was weakened by the attempt.

Soon afterward, most of the 15 republics that made up the Soviet Union declared independence but indicated their willingness to become part of a loose confederation of former Soviet republics. Four republics — Estonia, Latvia, Lithuania, and Georgia (part of it was retaken by Russia) — became independent nations. Gorbachev tried to prevent the complete breakup of the Soviet Union. However, on Dec. 8, 1991, the republics of Russia, Ukraine, and Belorussia broke away completely from the Soviet Union and formed the Commonwealth of Independent States (CIS) and were soon joined by all the remaining republics except the four just named that refused to be part of the CIS. On December 25, Gorbachev resigned as president, and the Soviet Union formally ceased to exist.

Gorbachev became Soviet Party Chair as the country's economy declined rapidly after years of mismanagement by both the Party and his predecessors. In 1985, he announced that the country was facing a major crisis and that drastic changes were needed. I was in Troitsk in 1987, when the physicist Andrei Dmitriyevich Sakharov was elected to the new DUMA and to the National Academy of Science after years of detention. Gorbachev announced that the most important task facing the nation was to modernize the economy and make it more productive. He proposed changes to move from the Communist centralized economic system to a more market-driven and democratic scheme. He called for a reduction in the power of the Communist Party — which controlled the country — and increased power for elected bodies. His program of economic and political reform was called *perestroika* (restructuring). His call for more openness was known as *glasnost*.

In 1989, the USSR held its first contested elections for the newly created Congress of People's Deputies (DUMA). The following year, the government voted to allow non-Communist political parties in the Soviet Union. Many Communist Party members and other Soviet officials opposed Gorbachev's reforms. But in March 1990, Gorbachev was elected by the Congress of People's Deputies to the newly created office of President of the Soviet Union. Hence Gorbachev became the first and the last president of the Union of Soviet Socialist Republics.

News from Troitsk was coming fast and furiously over my connection with the Moscow-San Francisco Teleport line, a line I had had installed to facilitate communication with the project. During this time a Technopolis Conference had been scheduled at the Mark Hopkins Hotel in San Francisco and Pismenny was one of the lead speakers. When Slava arrived and stayed at my house it was a sight to see him so jubilant and excited about what was developing in Russia and the former USSR. Democracy was emerging, free market economics were bubbling to the surface, entrepreneurship was becoming the choice for those who had interest in business, and travel abroad was no longer denied to Russians — the changes in Russia were breathtaking and also confusing. Needless to say, I was excited, enthralled, and fascinated by the changes and the fact that I was close to the action.

In 1988 after my visit to Troitsk and after the many discussions I had with Pismenny, Sobolenko, and others it had become obvious that the days for the continued existence of the USSR were numbered, perhaps to, at best, four to five more years, but definitely it would implode by 1994. I wrote a memo to Riley and copied Slavich about my information. The death knell for the USSR was finally heard on 31 December 1991. In the final analysis I was off by three years!

Return to Bari: Next Steps

Just before Christmas 1991, Umberto Bozzo telephoned me to ask if I would give some thought about the process of how he could begin to implement the next steps for Tecnopolis. My reply was direct and certain: I would put my thoughts down on paper and have something ready soon. Bozzo admitted that I need not rush into that task immediately but that I should keep in touch with him as my thinking progressed. On further conversation I learned from his hints that Umberto was having some major difficulties with the rector of the University of Bari. The university hierarchy, especially the rector, did not readily accept progress and change, but Tecnopolis was inevitably on the forefront of change. The art program had satisfied the University rector a little, but he wanted more stature than could be afforded to him as long as the technical university was flourishing. I thought that this represented the battleground between the static and dynamic and Bozzo the local boy was bringing good changes to an old region — perhaps too quickly. I then recognized that Umberto wanted my thoughts written in such a way as to convince the rector, and all who were like him, that Tecnopolis was about change, but not in a threatening way.

After reviewing my file on Bari and checking several times with Umberto by telephone, I began to list what I considered were important steps that needed to be considered for the future on Tecnopolis and the universities that served it. The rector of the Technical University was not a problem because he was Gianfranco Dioguardi, the major supporter of Tecnopolis. The rector of the University of Bari was difficult to deal with because he was under the false impression that all technical education was no more than tool shop training and not intellectually valid. My task was to convince him that technology, from the Greek word for art, "techne," was a necessary third leg for the stool upon which science, and liberal arts, stood. I often reminded him that my degree in physics was closely tied to my degree in philosophy — science and liberal arts worked hand in hand. Fortunately, when I expanded this concept it helped to convince the rector that both universities and Tecnopolis had vital roles in the promotion of the intellectual life of Bari, Apulia, Italy, Europe, and the world. Umberto and Gianfranco could not thank me enough.

The art program was a success because it included both the liberal side of education and the technical character of higher learning. We had artists from California, New York, Nice, Tempera, Bologna, and Kyoto and each artist or group of artists managed to merge both the plastic and performance forms of art with several levels of intellectually complex instances that employed many aspects of human thinking. The rector of the University of Bari admitted that he had never thought that science and technology could be entwined to the degree indicated with liberal education.

War and Ideas

The Persian Gulf War began on 17 January 1991 (January 16 US time) in Iraq by the bombing of Iraqi compounds in Iraq and Kuwait. The military effort to force Iraq out of Kuwait became known as Operation Desert Storm. Bush also ordered US participation in a massive ground attack that began on February 24 (February 23 US time). In this attack, coalition troops entered Iraq and Kuwait and defeated Iraq's military after about 100 hours of fighting. On 27 February (February 28 in the war area), President George H. W. Bush declared a halt to all allied military operations.

Iraq's occupation of Kuwait was troubling to the world and the effects of the Iraqi presence had repercussions that lasted well beyond the liberation of the land. After quickly gaining control of Kuwait, Iraq moved huge numbers of troops to Kuwait's border with Saudi Arabia, triggering fears that Iraq would invade Saudi Arabia next. Iraq's actions were viewed with alarm by the world's industrialized countries, which relied on Kuwait and Saudi Arabia as a primary source of petroleum. After the forces of Iraq's president were pushed out of Kuwait, retreating forces not only pillaged Kuwait but also set fire to many oil wells, and that became a complex ecological disaster.

I was working on the Bari task and listening to the news from Russia and C.I.S. The news reports were evenly divided between the old USSR and Kuwait. The aircraft of the US Air Force assigned to bombing and to patrolling Iraqi soil were based in Dammam, Saudi Arabia, at the new and yet unfinished King Fahd International Airport. King Fahd International Airport (KFIA) was designed as the biggest airport in the Kingdom and possibly in the world. Following the traditional historical pattern, this airport was to be a memorial for the dying current king.

King Fahd was in ill health, obese, and incapable of walking even for short distances. The country was awaiting his death. Crown Prince Abdullah, as the next in succession, had been de facto regent and hence ruler of Saudi Arabia since January 1, 1996, because King Fahd was incapacitated by a major stroke. My recollection of Abdullah is as a fine horseman racing his steed outside the boundary of King Khalid International Airport (KKIA) in Riyadh, the capital of the Kingdom. Standing in the new royal terminal of KKIA, Abdullah was an impressive man possessing the composure of strength with gentleness. When he addressed the members of the various firms that had built the terminal, a mix of multi-nationals from Korean to Swede, German, Philippine, Italian, American, and other ethnic representatives he was cautious to mention that the Kingdom was pleased to work with such a varied international group that represented many cultures, traditions, and religious orientations and that Saudi Arabia was struggling with the issue of granting religious freedom in the country. It was obvious that the Crown Prince could not quite grant religious freedom in Wahabi Saudi, but there was at least a spark of hope in his address. The Crown Prince spoke in Arabic but when the reception opened up for the higher echelons working under contract to Bechtel, he did not have any trouble switching to English in private conversations.

As the reader can notice, my time in the Kingdom of Saudi Arabia was delightful and the experience memorable. Apart from a few minor problems here and there, I was able to enjoy my work, my association with other employees, with the supporting firms, and with several Saudis. I've had the good fortune to be invited into Saudi homes, to discuss politics and religion with Saudi groups, to enjoy both Saudi art and Saudi elements of antiquity and literature, the latter in translation. I believe that in increments of no more than three months, my time in Saudi Arabia must have added at least to a year and a half with work performed in several locations but mostly anchored in Jeddah, Riyadh, Jubail, Dhahran, and Al Khobar — with 13 round trip flights.

ARAMCO'S Fleet Master Plan

In April of 1990 Gary Bechtel called me to come to his office immediately. That was curious because Gary usually asked me out for coffee.

He had been appointed president of Bechtel Civil Company (BCIV), a task that did not make him very happy because he was neither really interested in managing a large portion of Bechtel nor was he keen on working for the firm. Gary had worked with me on occasion, especially when he was being groomed to take over the firm when his father Steve would retire. Gary hated the idea of being "condemned," as he often said, to inherit the job of managing the engineering and construction company legacy of the Bechtel family. I sympathized with him but was never quite certain what I could do to assist him. In the long run his younger brother Riley was appointed to head the firm and Gary was "allowed" to leave the firm and seek his own way.

At any rate, we were good friends and often had face-to-face conversations but never in his office. There was a Viennese coffee shop not too far from Bechtel and that's where we met. To be summoned to Gary's office was very strange.

When I arrived, Michel Thomet, computer engineer, and Bill Small, an architect who was assigned to airport planning, met me. I was informed that ARAMCO was asking Bechtel to revise their 1982 Aircraft Fleet Master Plan. In essence my task, if I accepted it, was to handle the aviation part and Thomet would handle the rest, which included putting the document together and dealing with cost, scheduling, personnel force, and accounting requirements.

Was my part just the aviation portion, I kept asking? Neither Thomet nor Small were cognizant of aviation and specifically aircraft usage. Small was not going to be at all involved in the revision because he was being reassigned to the architectural group (an assignment that ultimately brought about his early retirement). Thomet, although he had a pilot's license and had flown a Cessna 150 and 172, had not flown in several years and knew very little, if anything, about large commercial aircraft. I was assured that aviation was my primary responsibility. If that was the case then I accepted the task.

In 1982 Dr. Stephen Gomes and Wang Ping had been the key people doing the fleet updating for ARAMCO's aviation department. Neither man was currently employed with Bechtel. When Gomes was doing the fleet plan, he had recruited me to review the aircraft choices that had been prepared by Wang Ping. Hence in 1992 when Mizel Snowbar, director of ARAMCO's aviation department had called Bechtel for a team to upgrade the fleet master plan, I was asked specifically if I would join the team. The other member of the team was Michel Thomet who was willing to manage the team and would be responsible for the final product.

I still had much work to do for Bari. I was also thinking of retiring now that the Goose and Turrets B&B was showing profitable potential. The economic health of the country was good and that of Silicon Valley was soaring. Yet I knew that the economy was prone to follow the standard sine curve: it could be up one quarter and begin a downward slide the next. With that in my head, I saw ARAMCO as a task that would give me time to make my retirement decision.

The Infrastructure Department under Cain was really in disarray and I could see the writing on the wall for either a restructuring or disbanding. Profits were down and many projects were stagnating because personnel assignments were made by stroking Cain's pets instead of encouraging competence. I was actively looking for another home at Bechtel. Dr. Harold Forsen, head of Bechtel Research and Development (BR&D), wanted me to join his team, but I suspected that he too was looking for an appropriate time to retire. His obvious replacement, John Patet, did not appear to me to be someone with whom I could work. Patet was a retread from a utilities firm and did not have the substance to lead Bechtel's Research and Development group. I was searching for a good place but there was no immediate pressure to transfer.

Once again, a few mornings later, Gary Bechtel phoned me to ask if I would have lunch with him. When I met with him he took me to the Banker's Club atop the Bank of America Building. He said that he had an offer to make. Because he was aware that I disliked Cain and the current condition of the Infrastructure Department and that I had mentioned my thoughts about retirement, Gary wanted to know if I would be interested in developing a program to convert Stapleton, the old international airport in Denver, into a multi-use technology center and cargo transshipment airport. The challenge appealed to me, especially since I knew that I'd be my own person in that project and could recruit like-minded people to help me. Gary allowed that I did not have to move to Denver but could commute as often as I wished. That was a good start from Gary because he was aware that I liked my place in Montara and my B&B. After lunch and informing Gary that I would give his offer serious thought we returned to our respective offices. He gave me 10 days for a final decision.

I called my architect friend Charles Sands and asked him if he was interested in such a project. His reply was positive and immediate. I also called Ray Kingsley, my colleague from the French and Russian projects, to ask him if he would be willing to handle the economic/financial side of the project. He too responded with a quick and positive answer. I phoned Gordon Linden and he too was very interested. I also called Steve Gomes for his help; he was very good at making contacts and networking. Steve accepted, especially since he would not be working for Bechtel. He'd had a bad experience with Cain and had been laid off without warning. With those four men in tow, I felt that the Stapleton project had some long-term merit, and I liked Gary Bechtel, the soon-to-retire president of BCIV.

I asked Gary what the schedule was and who would fund the conversion?

He replied that he had in tow a developer, also the support of the city of Denver, and the State of Colorado. Then Gary added that by keeping the airport operations for cargo and general aviation, the FAA would continue to give funds for upgrading the systems.

"Raymond," he added, "I'm meeting with several people this week and the next to secure the funds, and Denver is considering having us also operate the airport."

Then he added, "It will not be a Bechtel company!" It sounded good and promising. I had time to finish the current tasks.

I turned my attention to completing the work for Bari and beginning the ARAMCO project. Bari could be put in abeyance now that I was sure that Umberto was leaving the Tecnopolis and, anyway, I had finished the concept delineating its future options. After I retired, Umberto would call me to do one more task before he left Tecnopolis.

The ARAMCO master plan demanded that I return immediately to Saudi Arabia after a long hiatus. Returning to the Eastern Province, not particularly my favorite part of the Kingdom, was nevertheless a pleasant opportunity that would give me a chance to see what had been accomplished in the years that I had been away. Returning to Saudi Arabia was not tantamount to coming home, especially after eleven visits, but it was not quite an alien place because I knew what to expect and I could manage the complexity of the situations that would emerge. Saudi was not the friendliest place on earth but it was not the unfriendliest either. It was Saudi Arabia, a country with strict statutes supported by limiting laws and a culture that pushed (superficially at least) fundamental Islam down the throat of every person in the Kingdom. I chose to live with the strict situation by not arguing with it. My time in Saudi, especially in the mostly Shiite Eastern Province, which represented an extreme Islamic conservatism, was limited to a few weeks. I could manage that for a short time. Even the remnant of the Sunni population, all followers of the fundamentalism of the Wahabi theological movement, could be lived with for a few weeks or a few months, as I had done in the past. This visit to Dhahran and Dammam would last less than three weeks, and I would be able to visit old colleagues working at the new airport site, the future King Fahd International Airport.

I was looking forward to working with Michel Thomet, my French-Swiss colleague who was also a chocolate aficionado. I had never worked with him directly but thought that it would be fun. I had forgotten about his shenanigans in Gabon to bring back ivory illegally and his self-serving attitude.

After reviewing the work performed by the previous team in 1982 and reading the request agreed upon by Bechtel, I made my own work plan and schedule. My plan was to make three visits to Dhahran-Al Khobar, Saudi Arabia, to prepare a viable fleet plan and to visit both fixed-winged and rotary-winged aircraft manufacturers and suppliers for European and American brands; to ride in the jump seat on all ARAMCO's route flights in Saudi to review their routes and the quality of the runways; and to interview all key personnel working on flight management — pilots, cargo loaders, mechanics, schedulers, and training personnel. It was a daunting program but it would be interesting and satisfying.

After meeting with Thomet and sorting out the parts of the tasks and the schedule I had prepared, I announced that I would head to Dhahran in January 1992, right after the New Year's holiday and several months after the liberation of Kuwait with Operation Desert Storm. We were not to travel together because he wanted to overnight in Kuwait and I preferred to take the overnight layover in London or Paris. Because I would be the first to arrive in Saudi Arabia, I would meet him at the International Hotel in Dhahran when he arrived a few days later.

Arriving earlier in Dhahran would give me an opportunity to meet the client in Al Khobar (the city adjacent to Dhahran where ARAMCO's flight department was located — really at the end of the airport perimeter), to reconnoiter the surroundings, and to get an early start. I was also eager to meet Mizel Snowbar, director of ARAMCO's aviation department who was listed on Flight Safety's graduate records as an accomplished pilot with ratings for Gulfstream G-280, DC-6 and 10, Boeing 737-100 and 200, De Havilland Twin Otter, plus the Fokker F-27 and 50, and also qualified for transoceanic flights with passengers. There were few Saudi pilots with these varied ratings; in fact not many non-Saudi pilots had as many varied ratings.

Again taking my favorite BA flight to London, I chose to spend two days at the Bechtel office. I wanted to speak to a few of the representatives of European aircraft manufacturers, especially Fokkers and Airbus, and also to dispel some of the jet lag that was always the price I paid for crossing the Atlantic. That task done, I boarded another BA for the six-hour flight to Dhahran and a return to Saudi Arabia.

Much water had passed under the bridge at Bechtel in that decade. My attitude towards Bechtel had changed enormously and Bechtel's treatment of me had also changed. Yes, perhaps my arrogance had paid off from that day in Jeddah when I questioned Dr. Alexander's presentation on art for the airport and then Colonel Amin had given me permission to state my comments. My self-identity has never been dependent on Bechtel or on my job, any job, even within the hierarchy of the Episcopal Church. I was mulling over how I looked at my work, especially now that I was seriously considering retiring from Bechtel, and also retiring from the active priesthood. I did not depend on a job for my sense of self and I was not hostage to the job and to those who had power over me. Case in point was that I had been dismissed several times from jobs and each time that happened I was elevated to another and better position, and on a few occasions within the same organization. Someone whose identity is not job-dependent has the ability to walk away without engendering a personality crisis. In addition, without the tether of dependence on a job, I can be creative, ethical, and willing to push the limits to reach the possible. This made it easier for me both to be independent and candid in my views and to function in a high-pressure environment without hurting myself.

I have seen the devastation that can occur when someone is dependent on his job, his position, and on a certain level, authority. Then all of a sudden all that is taken away and he is left without any external psychological support. I have seen the results in the Church, in aviation (especially in the airlines when a senior pilot is furloughed or loses his seniority classification), and at Bechtel when a title is lost because of a layoff. In all these cases self-satisfaction and self-identity are dependent on external sources. Unplug the light from an external source of electricity and the lamp shines no more!

One person I knew wanted to become vice president; this was his goal and his identifier and, more than that, it defined him. Another I met had been furloughed by an airline and then the firm had filed for bankruptcy and soon went out of business. Because he was in his early fifties, other airlines could only hire him if he accepted a low seniority number which would place him on the same par as much younger pilots with much less experience. Recognizing all that, he was devastated and driven to depression and at times excessive drink. Here he was defined by his job as an airline pilot. The uniform, the stature, the special treatment, and most of all the respect he had obtained from passengers, now all that was gone. He was a hollow and dissatisfied person drained of his spirit and his vitality. I don't know if he ever regained his dignity or any satisfaction from inner strength, but it was certain that his inability to be satisfied was a chronic condition. A person should be his/her own container of self-definition!

The lighted flares of the exhaust stacks from the Ra's Tannurah oil field were beginning to be visible. The BA flight had entered Saudi territory, all alcohol was stowed, and passengers were organizing their papers for entry into the country. Magazines with illicit photographs were left on board for the crew to dispose of at the next stop, which was Dubai — a less restrictive country. Local time was now 1:15 a.m. I expected to be in bed by 3:00 — and that was too optimistic of me.

Anyway, I did finish passport control and customs at 2:45 and made it to bed by 3:45 after checking in at the International Hotel and taking a hot shower. With a sleeping pill, moments later I fell into a deep, though not restful, sleep. Awakened mid-morning by the hotel clerk announcing that the director of ARAMCO's aviation department was on the line, I quickly brushed away my sleep cobwebs and attempted to be coherent. Would I join Snowbar for lunch at one o'clock? He would come for me at the hotel.

I had spoken to Mr. Mizel Snowbar over the telephone from London to inform him of my arrival. Snowbar was very knowledgeable about aviation, but management of a department was not his forte. For that he had Mr. Ahmed Gibran, a Palestinian educated at Columbia and possessing also a Harvard MBA. At the beginning of my research for ARAMCO I thought that it had 50 to 60 aircraft. When I looked at the records I soon learned that ARAMCO operated 75 fixed-wing aircraft as a small airline ferrying passengers, supplies, and equipment to and from all its facilities including connections to Europe, Texas, and a few Arab countries. In addition ARAMCO operated 22 helicopters that it used to serve the oil and gas platforms in the Gulf, to fetch channel ship pilots off tankers coming into or leaving port, and patrolling oil and gas lines from wellheads to the refinery. Every decade, ARAMCO called a consultant to revise its fleet master plan and for the last two decades, Bechtel had been given the task, and for this revision Thomet and I were the key persons for the work.

At the appointed hour Mr. Snowbar arrived to whisk me off to a Lebanese restaurant in Dammam. The food was excellent, the service proper, and the prayer call interruptions were minimal and unobtrusive because we lunched in a private room.

It is customary that at the call of prayer all activities stop, as does the service. Muslims must say their prayers and non-Muslims must remain quiet throughout.

Snowbar ignored the call to prayer and we continued briefing. Were the Boeing aircraft still the preferred type for ARAMCO? Would ARAMCO continue to use the Bell helicopters or were the Eurocopters best suited for the tasks? Perhaps a mixture of both would be best, but that would increase the maintenance cost and the type rating training. I explained that before I could offer options and recommendations I would have to study the routes, the demands put upon the equipment, and the projections for the future of the aviation group.

"I will ride every route and every type of aircraft; I will speak to the chief pilot who is responsible for the training; I will speak with the maintenance chiefs of fixed and rotary aircraft; and I will interview, not once but several times, Mr. Ahmed Gibran and, of course, you."

"You have my authority to do what has to be done. Here is a letter with my signature and the signature of the chief of security giving you that authority in Arabic and in English."

Lunch was completed and I gathered that Snowbar was satisfied with my answers. He handed me another letter in order for me to obtain my temporary security badge from the security department. He would drive to Al Khobar, the ARAMCO complex, so that I could obtain my badge immediately. When done, a car would be waiting for me to return me to the hotel or to the aviation department, if I finished before five o'clock. I did not, and the car never did arrive to return me to the hotel! Good beginning for a project, I thought to myself. The security pass was valid for only one month. This meant that on my next visit to Saudi, I'd have to obtain another security pass. Not a good way to run an efficient program.

At the security office I asked if someone could telephone the aviation group for a car to be sent over for me. I was informed that the security person was not authorized to make personal calls. Could I make a business call to the aviation director, I asked. Well that was a possibility but his supervisor would have to give me permission. In the end, the supervisor decided to give me a ride to avoid more phone calls. I was taken in a squad car with lights flashing and sirens wailing to the International Hotel. At the hotel the doorman was most officious as he opened the car door and then the entry door. I was both embarrassed with my arrival in a squad car and annoyed that the aviation department had not sent me a car as Snowbar had promised.

At 6:30 a.m. the next day, I telephoned the aviation department to request transportation from the hotel to my office. Once at the aviation department, I walked directly into Snowbar's office. The moment he saw me I could tell from his face that yesterday he had forgotten to send transportation for me. After the apologies and the subsequent greetings he asked if I would like to fly with him to Jeddah to pick up an executive.

"We're taking the Gulfstream and we'll be back by dinner time," he tempted me. The temptation was too difficult to resist so I accepted. Sitting in the jump seat and wearing headsets, Snowbar and I discussed his vision for the aviation department. The copilot was an American retread from Pan American Airways. In Jeddah we had lunch at the new Marriott Hotel located on the shore of the Red Sea. The executive was a Saudi and an ARAMCO VIP. The return trip was filled with more conversation and specific wishes voiced by Snowbar for the aviation department. I also enjoyed chatting with the copilot who had been hired by Pan Am just a few months before it went bankrupt and closed all operations when Delta Airlines reneged on its letter of agreement. The copilot was fortunate to be hired by ARAMCO and because he had several ratings for aircraft that were operated out of Dhahran, he was in good stead with Snowbar and would be moving up the ranks to left seat in no time at all.

After all the excitement of the day, I returned to my hotel to prepare myself for a full day's work. The next day, once in my assigned office and after meeting key people, I settled myself at a desk to review the aviation program and begin to make some initial judgments about the direction I would take to revise the master plan. I expected Michel Thomet's arrival before the weekend (Thursday and Friday) and wanted to be ready to brief him. I was scheduled for a review flight to one of the oil wells in a De Havilland Twin Otter on Sunday, after Thomet's arrival.

When Thomet arrived, I was pretty much in control of the aviation program as it related to aircraft fleet and route needs. All I had to do was check each route to see if the correct aircraft was servicing it. I also had to visit Ra's Tannurah to review the rotary fleet, which serviced the northern offshore oil field up to Kuwait and east almost to the Jazireh-ya Khark Island, off the coast of Iran. The large rotary aircraft also supported the ship-pilots exchange program. This program called for ship-pilots who guided tankers through the channels of the Persian-Arabian Gulf to be picked up at the end of their trip from the vessels or be deposited onto an incoming vessel. These over water flights were dangerous missions that required extremely skilled pilots and helicopters in top operational conditions with good and stable hovering capabilities. These flights also demanded exact navigation because the Iranians were itching to shoot down a Saudi helicopter that entered their airspace.

Researching ARAMCO's Flight Fleet

In the course of my interviews, I became more interested in Mr. Ahmed Gibran, the Palestinian manager of the aviation department. I soon learned that every Monday there was a staff meeting held at Ra's Tannurah and Gibran was expected to be in attendance. Because I wanted to visit the Ra's Tannurah site, I asked him if I could drive up with him and return by air on the regular scheduled Boeing 737-100 passenger flight.

On the road north, Gibran and I had a good while to chat. He was born in Haifa of Muslim and Jewish parents. His father was Muslim, a university professor of political science at Hebrew University, and a strong advocate for Palestinian independence and statehood. Gibran's mother was Jewish and a physician, specializing in "favism," the genetic malady that affects many people in Arab countries, especially those who depend on a fava bean diet for their protein requirement. As a physician, Gibran's mother was on the staff of a prestigious Israeli hospital and research director at Hebrew University. Gibran, a Muslim, was married to an American Jew who had a degree from Princeton University in chemistry. Gibran was unable to find work in Israel or in the Palestinian sector; hence he applied at ARAMCO and was given a good position. On the Palestinian-Israeli issue he did not see any solution until both sides abjured their antagonism and Israel offered some progressive economic development for the Palestinian sector. None of the hardcore groups, in Israel or in Palestine, will achieve a peaceful status and the neighboring Arab states do not much care to help resolve the conflict. Even Saudi Arabia, in claiming to want a peaceful solution, was in the same breath, through Wahabi support, funding fundamentalist schools, "madrasahs," in Pakistan that produced manpower to supply Hamas and the other terrorist groups. Likewise Iran and Syria were supporting groups in Lebanon to destabilize Israel. Jordan seemed to be more inclined to help bring about peace, but it had only voice and no money and with a large aggressive population of Palestinians residing in the kingdom, it had no real leverage over the Arab hardcore groups.

Our conversation was most interesting and informative. Gibran's wife, as a Jew, was seen as a dangerous person in Palestine. In Israel, she was seen as a traitor to her people. As a Jew she had a difficult time obtaining a visa for Saudi Arabia. It was only after the intervention of several VIPs from ARAMCO that a limited visa was first issued, one that allowed her to arrive at Dhahran airport and travel to ARAMCO's compound and not leave it until she departed the country. Later on, with some leverage from Snowbar and others, that silly restriction was lifted and now she could move about freely, as long as her husband, like for all females, accompanied her. Currently Gibran's wife was on the college faculty at ARAMCO teaching chemistry.

Arriving at Ra's Tannurah, Gibran introduced me to the chief pilot of Rotorcraft and then he entered into a meeting room — and I did not see him again until the next day at the aviation complex. The chief pilot gave me a non-briefing, and by that I mean that it did not inform me one iota! After thanking him, I visited the maintenance facility and obtained some good solid data. When I returned to the main office, the chief pilot's secretary informed me that I was scheduled for a flight over the Gulf at 10:30. The helicopter I'd be riding in was scheduled to travel all the way to the farthest oil platform located near Jazireh-ya Khark Island to deliver a few workers and then return by way of Latitude 28 and Longitude 50 (they use whole numbers to eliminate confusion) or, in the pilots' jargon, "Waypoint 2850 to pick up a ship-pilot from a tanker." The pilot for that flight, I was informed, would be Herman (Butch) Peace, a senior pilot, and his copilot.

Before the flight was ready to be boarded, Michel Thomet arrived from Dhahran on an ARAMCO B-737. He had decided at the last minute to come see the helicopters and check out their operations. I entered his name on the manifest for the flight with Mr. Peace.

At 10:15 a.m. I heard a clear Texas voice bellowing from the anteroom and greeting everyone with "Hi y'all this mornin;" the voice unmistakably belonged to one who had a bounce in his demeanor and joy in his speech.

"I'm Butch Peace and you must be Dr. Raymond," Butch reached out and took my hand in a vise grip. His face was filled with a broad smile and sparkling eyes. I liked him immediately. "We're going flying over some big waters and you are going to have a hell of a ride here with my buddy who'll be flying most of the way," as he put his arm around a man we expected was his copilot. "Hank here will fly the stinking chopper and I'll just go for the ride to see the sights of the beautiful Gulf of Arabia." He chuckled and pointed at my badge. "You got some security badge," my badge had an awful picture of me, "but that's OK. In the Persian Gulf — that's the same gulf — no one will care how you look, not even them fishes." He was full of sound and laughter, but he seemed to be in definite control of what he was about. "Les go, for today we fly," it was more a command than just words. "Meet you all outside in 10 in that bird out there," he said as he pointed to a large Bell-412EP helicopter.

Ten minutes later I stood at the door of the whirly bird waiting for Butch or Hank to tell me where to sit. "Dr. Hoche-Mong you'll be sitting on the jump seat just behind the console and between us. This way you can talk with us and see through the large windshield," Hank helped me into the bird. Michel Thomet would be sitting in one of the passenger seats. Several other people joined us and seated themselves around me. The swing cable special-ist took the seat by the right door where he could manage the winch to hoist the fellow who would be picked up from the tanker.

Hank took the left seat (in helicopters that position is the copilot's seat) and Butch placed himself in the right seat. "OK folks get comfortable for the ride of your life."

At exactly 10:30 the rotors began to whirl around. Butch handed me a headset. Soon Hank lifted off, banked the bird across the fence and headed over the Arabian Gulf. Hank was flying and Butch was giving him pointers and handling the radio. Soon we flew over an oil platform, then another and another. We were flying at about 2,000 feet over the choppy waters. Butch indicated that there was a 30-knot wind and swell of 15 to 20 feet in the gulf. "It's going to be fun picking the dude up from the tanker," Butch said.

"Maybe, Butch, you'll fly that portion," Hank said to Butch.

"No way cowboy, it's your heifer and you'll lasso it. Piece of cherry pie it'll be."

The helicopter was bouncing a bit because of the gusting wind but I loved it. "They tell me you're a pilot. What do you fly?" Butch asked me.

"Not rotor aircraft. Just plain fixed wing birds," I replied.

"Big'uns or puddle jumpers?" he asked.

"Both kinds and my own 6-300," I added.

"Wow. Your very own bird!"

Up ahead I saw another oil platform. We were headed for it but the wind made us drift to the left of the landing spot. Hank maneuvered with some difficulty towards the landing spot, which was a rectangle of about 10x20 meters. Hank worked the aircraft to the spot and placed the wheels on the surface with a thud, but safely. Without shutting down the engines we disgorged all but two of our passengers and then took to flight again.

The next leg of the flight took us to another oil platform, one still closer to the coast of Kuwait. In the distance we could still see some of the smoldering smoke of the oil well fires ignited by Sadam Hussein's retreating army. The platform came into view and Hank had a little less difficulty landing the helicopter this time because the wind in this area was not gusting, at least not as much as for the previous platform. On this platform the two passengers we had on board deplaned and we enplaned six others. Off we went to the oil tanker lane to pick up a ship channel pilot. It was routine to deliver onto an in-coming vessel a ship's pilot or to off-load ship channel pilots when they had finished escorting ships out into the open waters; this was usually about 30 kilometers out from the Saudi port. So far we had been flying for 50 minutes and had made three landings.

Back in the open Gulf, the gusts picked up with a great deal of force and speed. The wind was blowing at 20 knots but gusting to 35 knots. The heavy Bell Helicopter was bouncing around in an unpredictable way. Hank was still flying because this was his day and he was completing the check out phase. Every pilot was required to have his flying reviewed every so many months by a qualified senior check pilot.

Hank had flown several small helicopters for the Army in Vietnam. He was a good pilot, attentive, determined, and careful, but this larger helicopter was heavy, fast, and a handful to maneuver, especially in gusty weather.

Butch was his appointed check pilot and as such he was patient, quiet, funny, and most helpful to Hank. Hank had to build up his confidence and resolve to handle this helicopter in any weather that was determined to be acceptable by the base dispatcher. All flights were flown in IFR conditions even if VFR weather was clear, especially at night or during sand storms. Because there were no landmarks over water, helicopter pilots always filed IFR plans even when the visibility was unlimited — locating platforms or tankers was not like shooting fish in a barrel. Moreover, every helicopter had to be tracked by ARAMCO's and Saudi ATC's radar because they flew over water, were in proximity of Iran and Iraq, and the Gulf waters were dangerous because the Saudi-exiled, religious reprobate Osama Bin Laden, founder of Al-Qaeda, had threatened to bomb a tanker or otherwise disrupt operations.

We soon saw the outgoing tanker in the distance. The wind was still gusting and we could see the flag on board flying straight out horizontally in the wind, then all of a sudden it would whip around 90 degrees from where it was, then whip back again or go the opposite direction. Hank tried to maneuver the helicopter so as to have the lifting cable reach the deck in the center to avoid the tall cranes, the masts, the communication cables that were strung from mast to mast, and the floodlight poles that were placed around the outer deck for night operations. We could see the ship pilot standing and waiting for the lifting harness to reach him. Hank tried several times but he could neither quite maneuver the helicopter into the proper position in the gusty winds nor hold it steady enough for the cable to be lowered. He kept being blown away from the spot where he needed to be. After trying five times he asked Butch to take over but Butch suggested he try one more time by starting his hover higher and long before he reached the pickup spot so that by the time the harness reached the pilot the helicopter would be in position to lift him up. The sixth time Hank did as Butch had suggested but still, he was blown past the critical point.

"Butch take over and you try," I heard Hank's plaintive voice over the intercom.

"Nah, you try once more and take it real early in your pass," Butch said.

"Butch I'm too tired to be careful. Take it now," Hank insisted. So Butch took control of the helicopter, made a pass, and ordered the cable and harness ready to be winched down when we were still crossing the bow of the tanker. High over the pickup spot, Butch just dropped the helicopter straight down as he ordered the cable cranked down with the harness. Butch canted the helicopter to resist the gusting wind, which was still blowing. He held it in place although it was being whipped every-which-way. He hovered over the deck in nearly a 45-degree angle facing the wind. He held the helicopter steady by playing with the power against the gusts. The harness reached the pilot who wasted no time putting it on. Butch firewalled the power and reversed course using the wind to help him gain altitude quickly. He shot up, pulling the pilot over the floodlights, the cranes, and the communication lines to safety. The cable lifted the ship pilot to the open helicopter door and the winch operator hauled him in.

Butch quietly turned the helicopter toward home base and asked Hank if he wanted to take us all back. Hank accepted the controls and added, "Butch, I wish I could fly the way you do."

"You will one day soon. These 'stinkin birds need to be tamed and they need to know who is boss — and you'll get the hang of it soon." I was impressed. We were all impressed.

"You're one hell of a pilot ole Tex," said the ship channel pilot.

The sling operator added, "They don't make them any better than ole Butch!"

Art After a Helicopter's Gusty Flight

When we returned to ARAMCO's helicopter base, it was time for lunch. Butch asked us if we had a place to eat or would we accompany him to the local "greasy chow hall"? Off we went in his four-wheel drive SUV to the chow hall for fried chicken, mashed potatoes, and a salad. It wasn't that bad. It wasn't that good either. But it passed for lunch and gave me the opportunity to have time with this fine helicopter pilot. I told him that I had admired his dexterity, his finesse, and his strategy for handling the helicopter for the pickup.

"Back in 'Nam it was not only gust that we had to deal with, but gun fire." He paused and stared at me for the longest time and I kept silent because it was obvious that he was recalling an incident or several incidents in Vietnam. "If I failed to haul a dogface, he soon was either captured or killed by the 'Cong." He paused again. "I failed several times because of my inexperience, but I soon learned that I'd get it right or get shot." Staring at me he continued, "Man, to get it right I had to make the fucking stinkin 'copter part of me or else auger it into the goddam 'Nam shit!" I understood his words and his attitude.

He asked me where I had gotten my name. I told him that it was of French origin. "Je parle Français," he exclaimed with a big smile on his face. "Je suis aussi un peintre," he told me. We continued in French and I learned that he was seriously studying the language because he wanted to improve his painting talent in France and do some copying of the masters at the Louvre. Michel, who was Swiss-French, spoke French too, and thus our conversation in Ra's Tannurah continued en Français, and Butch was delighted to be able to practice his beloved acquired language. That he spoke French with an obvious west Texas accent didn't matter much.

We soon discovered that Butch was a fine painter who particularly liked to work in oils. He invited us to his apartment. The apartment had been converted into a studio by using the full sunlight of his balcony to bathe the room in good natural light. He was copying many of the masters and doing a fine job of that. I saw that he was good but could use some professional guidance and he knew it. We discussed the options available to him and the most reasonable one was to study in France. He thought that in two years he would have enough savings for a year's worth of study in France. He planned to go to Paris for his R&R, which was due a couple of weeks hence. He wanted to obtain permission to do copying at the Louvre. Because I had met the assistant director of the Louvre, Mr. Jacques Corrisson, during one of my trips to Paris, I suggested he contact him by mail or telephone for the appropriate permission (I learned later that he had done as I suggested and had received permission).

After seeing many of his paintings, some finished and some still in process, we returned to the helicopter base to catch the returning B-737 to Dhahran. I wanted to stay over and discuss art with Butch but the ARAMCO task hampered that bit of luxury. Michel and I took the short flight back to Dhahran.

Ever since that serendipitous meeting, Butch and I have kept a running correspondence and I have maintained an interest in his artistic development. Butch will emerge as a fine artist but unfortunately painting is a profession that does not reward one too well financially. After eighteen months of instruction and coaching, Butch Peace did so well at the school that the administration asked him to remain and join the faculty as a teacher. He taught art for several years until his return to Texas because his teenage son no longer wanted to live with his mother.

Soon after returning to Texas he married a delightful woman from North Carolina with two children and then moved to Wilmington, NC and opened a small art school. The school operated quite well and brought him a good income until the downward trend in the economy that started after the presidential election of 2000. He had to shut the school, return to Texas, paint portraits for a pittance, and then accept a position as chief pilot for a helicopter firm.

In 2003 luck ran out on Butch Peace. He was discovered when he was examined to have a small heart tremor that immediately invalidated his first class medical certificate. Losing his first class medical certificate got him furloughed and forced him to join the ranks of the other 9.7% unemployed. Today, while awaiting the restoration of his medical certificate and an improving economy, Butch is driving his own long haul truck for a freight company and is negotiating with a bank to purchase a couple of trucks. He is still painting and we keep an active correspondence by email and telephone.

Hitting Uneven Project Surfaces

The ARAMCO aviation master plan progressed well in so far as my contribution was concerned. I reported all my comments and suggestions about both fixed and rotary winged aircraft on the plan, but many of my suggestions were counter to what Thomet wanted because they added another level of safety to the general operation of the fleet. Safety in Saudi Arabia was not a first-level concern and Thomet felt that the aviation department would balk at my insistence that it should be part of the master plan. Thomet and I ultimately parted ways on the master plan and I wrote a minority report that I insisted should be included in the final Aviation Master Plan.

Needless to say, Michel Thomet was unhappy and this opposition in approaches diminished any sense of friendship we might have had. I questioned his sense of ethics and he questioned my insistence in forcing ARAMCO to adopt recognized safety features even if the cost was greater. Ultimately, the minority report, which I had personally submitted to Mr. Snowbar, was accepted by ARAMCO because the aircraft used by the oil firm were registered in the United States and the FAA demanded that all the safety requirements I had demanded be included.

For example, one safety measure I insisted on was for the installation of intake screens for the turbines to prevent sand and small pebbles from striking the compressors. These screens had a short life of two or three flights and were expensive because they were designed not to impede the air necessary for the turbines. Cost in the larger sense was minimal, approximately $2,000 per aircraft but they would protect the life of the 1/3 million-dollar turbine engines. Most ARAMCO flights operated on runways that had sand and gravel blown onto them by the strong wind.

In the meantime I had come to the conclusion that I would never again work with Michel Thomet. That such a man as Thomet could ignore simple safety issues because he wanted the "bottom line" to be reduced in order to please the client while endangering the people using the equipment, was frustrating, surprising, and quite unethical.

Many weeks later, soon after my return from Saudi, I spoke to Gordon Linden and Michael Zachariah about Michel over lunch. Both had worked with Thomet in Gabon a few years back and had found him particularly unethical in his operations. They told me that after completing his assignment in Gabon he purchased two elephant tusks (I mentioned these ivory tusks earlier), items that were not only illegal to buy in Gabon, except on the black market, but also illegal to bring into the United States. To circumvent that issue he took a flight to Montreal, Canada by way of Paris, and then rented a car to cross the border into the United States to avoid the strict American Customs that forbids the importation of items from endangered species. Because he hand-carried the tusks into Canada and they were packed in document tubes, Canadian Customs at the airport assumed that they were business documents. Entering the United States in a rented car did not demand close scrutiny by Customs. Once in the United States he deposited the tusks in his border motel room and returned the rental car to Canada and went back by bus to his US hotel. He subsequently rented another car from a US rental agency and drove himself to California. This was quite an ingenious strategy but nevertheless illegal, unecological, and blatantly unethical.

Thomet, I was told, not only antagonized Linden and Zachariah with his unethical behavior, but bragged that he had out-maneuvered American law by bringing in the tusks — elephants were of no concern to him; the value of the ivory was.

To my knowledge, Thomet never corresponded with Butch or inquired about his artistic work or his wellbeing. On my last visit to Saudi Arabia and a few months before Butch was to terminate his contract with ARAMCO, he met me in Dhahran for dinner. Butch had enrolled in an art school located on the outskirts of Paris and had decided that painting was his calling and not flying helicopters, those "stinking machines," as he called them.

Not an Embryonic Airline

In November 1992, a few weeks before Thanksgiving while in my office in San Francisco, I received a phone call early in the morning from Mr. Mizel

Snowbar who had been director of ARAMCO's aviation department during my assignment for the preparation of their Fleet Master Plan. I was surprised to receive his call because as far as I was concerned the assignment was completed and I was no longer involved in it. Mr. Mizel Snowbar invited me to have lunch with him that day because he wanted to discuss a project that he was thinking of putting together. I accepted the gracious invitation and met him at the Sheraton Palace Hotel, in the Garden Court Restaurant, a wonderful place with a large glass dome, plants, and an atmosphere not unlike a garden but inside the building where it was quiet enough to conduct a conversation without being overwhelmed by the speaking voices of neighboring eaters.

Mr. Mizel Snowbar was interested in starting his own small airline in Saudi Arabia in competition with Saudia National Airline. He had gathered several investors and had contacted two or three aircraft-leasing firms. He wanted to have me prepare a fleet and route master plan and in return, as payment, I would be given stocks in the airline. It sounded good were it not that it would operate in Saudi Arabia. I doubted that such an airline would survive the pressures that the Royal Saudi family would exert on such a venture.

Who were his investors? They were mostly investors from neighboring Middle East countries who hoped to compete with Saudia by creating a low fare airline imitating the format of Southwest Airlines in America. He spoke to me about a management position with his potential airline and a good stock option package. It sounded intriguing but I was not convinced that such a venture would work. The package offered to me was good, rich — if it were successful — but I felt that it would never work. I told him that I would think about it and get back to him as soon as possible. Snowbar needed an answer before close of business that day. He had to discuss issues with several investors and I was key to his project.

"Give me a few hours to think about it," I requested.

"Give me your positive answer by this afternoon and we can sign an agreement tomorrow morning," he said. Then Snowbar added, "I don't want

Bechtel in this because they are in the same bed with the Royal Family." That was obvious.

After lunch I returned to my desk to think this through. What were my gains and losses? Did I see the venture as potentially successful or even possible? What passenger seat mile would make such an airline produce revenue and profit? Saudia obtained fuel support from the Kingdom; would this new airline get the same break? I doubted that it would, not as long as it competed with Saudia. I saw little possibility for success.

I placed a call to the chairman and CEO of American Airlines, Mr. Robert Crandall, whom I had met and with whom I could discuss such a venture. He was not available at the time but returned my call long before the deadline time. We discussed various options, the general political situation in Saudi Arabia in 1992, the possibility that Iraq would try again to overwhelm Kuwait and Saudi Arabia, the possible passenger mix and the seat mile revenue, and a score of other issues including the response from the Royal Family to a competitor to Saudia. The conclusion was that it would be a bad venture.

Before three I called Snowbar and informed him that if I were paid for the fleet master plan I might consider helping out but I just couldn't accept his stock options in lieu of payment because I thought that his project was not possible and could not possibly succeed in Saudi Arabia. He insisted that I rethink the offer again but he could not pay me just for doing the master plan; he wanted my collegial participation. I thanked him and hoped that his venture could be successful. We ended by saying a few friendly words and I wished him good fortune and, furthermore, offered to respond to any questions he might wish to ask me. Yet, I reminded him, that he had a not-too-plausible venture, especially in the Kingdom.

As it turned out it never did get off the ground. The King announced an edict in January 1993 that in the Kingdom of Saudi Arabia no competing airline could exist, other than Saudia Airline. Saudi Arabia is a closed society hence there is no reason why the government should allow competition to take away revenue from a national enterprise. Thus my short-lived opportunity to be part owner of an airline never did materialize and I was not in the least sad about it. In fact I was pleased that my good sense prevented me from making an unwise and stupid move, particularly because I planned to retire from Bechtel. I never spoke to Snowbar again but heard that he had left ARAMCO and had accepted a position as chief pilot with an airfreight firm in the Middle East.

Bergstrom, Lee, and a Response

Not long after Mr. Snowbar's call, I received a letter from the Honorable Lee Cooke, mayor of Austin, Texas, inviting me to come to his city to look at the Bergstrom Air Force Base (AFB), which was slated for decommissioning.

I had met Lee Cooke several times when I came to IC^2 to converse with George Kozmetski, and Lee had been invited to address the Technopolis Conference in San Francisco. I liked Mayor Cooke and found him a straight and honest person who had the best interest of his city in his plans. Lee was also a friend of Michael Dell and well regarded by Dr. Kozmetski. I accepted the invitation to come to Austin for a few days after discussing it with Spink, who authorized the trip.

When I arrived in Austin, a police officer was waiting for me at the arrival gate and a patrol car was illegally parked at the street level of the terminal. I was taken directly to the Marriott Hotel, shown my suite, given a few minutes to refresh myself, and then taken to the mayor's office. Lee Cooke greeted me warmly and introduced me to two gentlemen from Horizon Development Corporation, and to Mr. Palle F. Smidt, chairman and CEO of Mercantile Holdings, Inc. The issue before us was the conversion of BAFB from a military entity to a civilian commercial airport to replace the current municipal airport, which was slated to be closed or to be dedicated to general aviation.

After discussing the schedule for the transfer, the funding, the participation of the city and the state, the expected cleanup of the toxic waste by the Defense Department and the schedule for that task, and finally which airlines would be willing to contribute their support in funds and services to make Bergstrom a viable civilian airport, I asked, after a pause, if freight carriers were considered as tenants and if night operations would be permitted. The latter questions had not been broached by any of the gentlemen present. Mr. Smidt assured those present that he would look into the issue of freight carriers immediately. Mayor Cooke reached for the phone and called someone responsible for aviation traffic and consequential noise limits.

Because it was still early in the afternoon, I suggested that a visit to Bergstrom AFB was necessary before I could make any further contribution to the project. We all climbed into two waiting patrol cars and headed for BAFB at a good clip. At BAFB I scoped out what I could see and what was needed for the transfer, making it clear that this was only a cursory appraisal and that a more detailed one was imperative. Would Bechtel take on the task? The mayor asked me. Bechtel had experience with the conversion of Peace AFB, New Hampshire I informed Lee Cooke. I could not, however, say more at this stage because no official proposal had been made and no one knew exactly when the military would vacate the base.

At any rate, I gave them reasons to be assured that BAFB would make a good civilian airport with its 12,000-foot runways, its excellent NAVAIDs and weather farm, and sufficient space for several terminals and cargo facilities. The mayor and his team were pleased with my comments. After leaving BAFB, the mayor took me to IC^2 to meet George Kozmetski, who was waiting in his office.

After the hellos, Lee Cooke left for a meeting and George announced that I was invited to dinner at his house in the country. He had a beautiful house in a large garden surrounded by woods and a private lake. Mrs. Kozmetski, George announced, was away in California so she would not be joining us for dinner, but his cook and butler were quite able to do a fine dinner without the guiding direction of his wife, Rona.

George's driver brought the car from the garage and we proceeded to his house. Soon drinks were served and the mayor and his wife arrived. In the course of the dinner a question was directed to me about what went through my mind during the celebration of the Eucharist, especially when I was at the altar. George and his wife, I learned, were Eastern Orthodox and Lee Cooke and his wife were Lutheran. What did go through my head at the altar? My answer was quite general.

When dinner was over I was returned to my hotel. After a shower and some reading I adjourned to bed in the hope of treating myself to a good night's sleep. What was it that passed through my head at the altar? Sleep was being diverted until I answered that question.

I immediately realized that I don't always have the same thought. My thinking is mostly affected by what is going on in the world because I never accept that I'm out of the world, not for one moment. The Eucharist for me is the tool I use to get me to pay attention to the world, to look at life; it also reminds me again and again to love gracefully all living creatures — human, animal, etc.

I'm committed to life and not death, especially death when it means the final end. Death for me is inevitably the new beginning of a transitory stage (nothing to do with reincarnation, which is a stupid concept) that offers me another birthday, a "birthday into eternity" as Massey Shepherd would re-mind me. I think of my servanthood and how it can be best applied to benefit my fellow humanoids. Helping others, tough love helping, is what I like to do with my life.

The words of the Canon of the Eucharist act as prods to move me, or give me more momentum, towards my goal of helping others. They prod me also to recognize again and again that what I do at the altar is neither more nor less what I do and must do all the time in the world. Because the world and the Universe are sacred — holy places, special places, and signature items of our creator — I recognize the altar as being a sign of that sacredness. The bread, the wine, and the people are all active elements that reinforce for me the sacredness of the universe. "Holy, holy, holy," are words that sharpen for me the articulation of what I believe to be the primary characteristic of the universe.

To Jesus, the one who emphasized the doing of the simple meal, I say thank you. My thanks are in a small way what I feel in my inner being to be a response, a constant response, to God, however one defines that complex and symbolic word. Jesus for me is the way that I have chosen to follow to re-spond to God, to Abba my father, the source of my life, the primordial initiator of all.

Of course at times I think of flowers, seeds, ants, bees, tigers (especially Siberian), gorillas, fish, marine mammals, the ocean, rivers, volcanoes, atoms, quarks, and other interesting stuff, all of which are amazing emergences of the universe's creative power. Will I someday understand a little the process of creation? Will I someday no longer see, smell, touch, enjoy a rose, admire a gorilla, or appreciate the unseen effect of a meson? God, please tell me about black holes, tiny strings, water, love, and beauty! Explain to me, Jesus, why cruelty is a fact of life? Why do ants greet each other when they meet? Let me understand why one musical phrase is more touching than another. What makes art so important to humans and yet artists are not given their due support by society?

I ask lots of questions. I receive few immediate answers but I am not discouraged. I think, and for me that's prayer in the best sense of the word. Often I argue with God or Jesus, and that's acceptable to me, because they are both processive, hence open to interaction, change, and givers of the unmerited gift of grace. Then too often my mind wanders.

Much as I find many inconsistencies in Scripture, both in the Old Testament and in the New Testament, the dating of the canonical Gospels, and especially about Jesus, I'm fascinated that this one man so affected the world and still does.

The new non-canonical gospels recently found in Nag Hammadi are further indication that the man Jesus had enormous influence both when he was alive and now after his death. I must admit that I am greatly influenced by his life, the few authenticated words and actions we have of it, and his temperament. No it was not so much that he was a teacher but that he touched our lives, my life, and still does. I cannot let him out of me. I cannot dispense with him. I cannot ignore him. I am always wondering about him, his life, what I accept that he said, his influence, and the effect of what we now call the Eucharistic Paschal feast emanating from his life.

In bed my mind wandered and soon I fell asleep.

My trip to Austin was valuable in many ways. Bergstrom was acquired by the Municipal Aviation Department and did become the new commercial airport for the city and the region. Several IT firms located themselves

406 · RAYMOND HOCHE-MONG

around the airport and now Austin stands as another R&D center in technology. Mayor Lee Cooke finished his term and was immediately hired by Dell as vice president of marketing. The team that was engaged to convert Bergstrom produced a fine airport for the city of Austin. Bechtel, however, did not receive any of the work that was to be generated by the report because its aviation department, at the insistence of Frank Cain, never submitted a proposal, much as I urged them to. Cain's reluctance to offer a proposal was that he could not imagine that a reasonable profit could surface from the conversion; his interest was primarily directed to buildings, especially office building on the East Coast. Yet, the records show that the conversion of Peace AFB did bring good returns to Bechtel. Consequently, Bechtel missed out on Bergstrom AFB, then on George AFB, on Northrop AFB, and finally on Castle AFB.

What was sad and mainly caused by Frank Cain's limited vision is that Bergstrom has become a major high technology center with many aspects that are similar to Silicon Valley. The kernel of this development came from the report I had prepared for the conversion of Bergstrom from an Air Force Base to a joint-use airport serving not only Austin, the capital city, but the existing high-tech firms near the airport, firms such as Texas Instruments, Cisco, GM Data, DELL Computers, and others, which would soon be attracted to the area, its infrastructure, and its ready, skilled and professional work force. Moreover, the University of Texas was near and would contribute to the ongoing development of science and technology; intellectual properties that would further expand the hi-tech arena around Bergstrom. Bergstrom and Austin are currently functioning as an active Technopolis!

Politics or Shenanigans

When I returned from my short trip to Austin, Texas I learned that the Infrastructure Department was going to move to an adjacent building. Moves at Bechtel came with the style of how the firm operated. Moves were often called for because the building was being sold or leased (it would be repurchased three or four years later and by that maneuver some taxes were saved and some profit was accrued); location changes also followed either the expansion or the contraction of a department; then also location changes were the result of a department's acquisition by another entity within Bechtel.

As I indicated Cain was overseeing our department in San Francisco, and also was managing another department in Vienna, Virginia, one more in tune within his mode of operation. In fact, his principal office and residence were in Virginia. It was apparent that Cain was going to ask several people in my department to transfer to Vienna. Because I was floating in the department and was no longer managing the IT or technopolis program and was currently a consultant to the slowly deteriorating aviation department, my position was loose, flexible, and open to several options. I knew that Gary Bechtel was interested in having me become part of his team, especially for the Stapleton conversion in Denver, Colorado. I also knew that I was not about to go to Vienna under any circumstances but I also knew that Cain would never shackle himself with the likes of me. Were there other options?

Upon my return and a few days later, I noticed that people were practicing the art of political gamesmanship. A few wanted to relocate to Vienna, especially Cain's adopted minions. Others were looking at other departments within Bechtel. I had an offer from Harold Forsen to join his research and development group, but I was certain that Harold was not going to remain at Bechtel much longer than a couple of years. Charlie Spink, Cain's shadow, was going to be promoted to senior vice president so he could retire with that title in a couple of years; in the meantime Charlie was going to head the business development effort for BCIV.

I listened and kept my ears open to hear what was developing and if I wanted anything that surfaced. Apart from that internal pot stirring there was another pot being stirred, which was the political soup. A great effort was made in 1992-3 by Bechtel to promote the Republican point of view among its employees. That Bechtel claimed to be nonpartisan was a joke. Many of Ronald Reagan's and George Herbert Walker Bush's supporters and cabinet members were attached to or employed by Bechtel. It was very obvious to me that Bechtel was a haven for Republican aficionados, especially for some of the right-wing types. In my department I was known to be a progressive Democrat. But nonpartisan Bechtel did not miss a beat when it was time to influence and or attempt to change my position. That persuasive effort was not new, it had started with the MX Program, the ICBM silos, the nuclear power generation campaign, the corporate effort to keep George Herbert Walker Bush president for a second term, and mustered support for Newt Gingrich's "Contract with America."

One morning, when I opened my emails, I found a message from the PR office suggesting that Gingrich's proposal would reduce the debt and the deficit but that President Clinton was shirking his authority by not cooperating and signing the budget bill. I was tired of this campaign to persuade the employees to support not only the Republican plan but to reject Clinton's sound judgment (which was directed by the able Secretary of the Treasury, Robert Rubin). I called Flynn, head of PR and told him that he had already caused me a lot of problems by misunderstanding the Kerch issue, and now he was "annoying the hell out of me with his political rubbish."

Ten minutes later, Spink and Wakelin came to see me.

"Flynn called me to say that you spoke rudely to him over the phone," Spink said.

I looked at him, and called Flynn and switched on the speaker phone. Both Wakelin and Spink glared at me. "Mr. Flynn, I understand that you phoned Spink about our conversation?" He was silent. "Well did you?" I asked.

Spink and Wakelin waited.

"I just don't believe that you should call me and use that tone of voice," Flynn said.

"Then stop sending me those idiot political emails." I terminated the phone conversation then turned to Spink and Wakelin. "What can I do for you gentlemen?" I asked. They both looked at me and left without saying a word.

I was tired of Bechtel, of Spink, of Flynn, and particularly of Frank Cain. I was also very, very tired of Michael Wakelin. The firm had changed and not for the better. Lesser people had replaced many of the creative managers. It appeared that the replacements were timid and only interested in protecting their turf. Long-term vision, planning, innovating, strategizing, and preparing for the new and the unexpected had been cast aside, forgotten, and discounted. Frank Cain was a good example of this new perspective and I wanted no part of it.

I called Harold Forsen, manager of R&D and a director, and went to see him. I told him what happened and how I felt. He also had received the emails and the past implications about Bechtel's political opinions. He was tired of it too. The new directions that Bechtel was entertaining saddened Harold. After chatting for a bit, we both decided that it was time to don our hats and leave the firm.

Making the Decision

Retiring from Bechtel had been in my thoughts for several years. I had promised myself that at the age of three score I would shake the Bechtel dust off my sandals and seek some other way to occupy my remaining years. Because I was finishing my assignment with the Bari Tecnopolis and also Umberto Bozzo was thinking of resigning from the institution to seek his fortune as an independent consultant, my thoughts had been organized for the day when I could leave Bechtel. I telephoned Umberto to inform him of my pending decision. He assured me that we could continue to have an agreement to work together on projects as long as he was able to use me. He did remind me that his days were numbered at Tecnopolis; he was planning to exit at the end of 1993 and seek his fortune elsewhere. We agreed that we would try to work together.

On the second of January 1993 I rewrote my letter of retirement, a letter that had been on my computer for several months. After printing it out I took it home to discuss both its contents with Emily and the fact that we would be losing my salary. My next move was to make an appointment with Bob Hecht, our investment advisor, to review my portfolio.

The next day, after lunch, I went over to the Bank of America building to meet with Hecht. Bob had already reviewed my portfolio and advised that it was in good shape with some solid investments — I wouldn't become

410 · RAYMOND HOCHE-MONG

wealthy but I would have a good nest egg that would grow even if the economy took a dive (which it did in 2000). In fact today, with the economy of 2014 barely showing signs of life and growth, my investment portfolio is showing some small growth, not by a large amount, but still it is more positive than negative. We have so far survived President George W. Bush's miserable management of the economy, to say nothing of his leadership and vision. We have and are keeping our heads above the downturn caused by the greed of the banks, the insurance firms, and the many pyramid games that were conceived under the deregulations put forward by the Republican Administration.

Because Emily and I had started the Goose and Turrets Bed and Breakfast, I felt certain that our finances would be fairly stable even if the economy weakened. Our mortgages were not enormous and our rental house was rewarding us with a fair monthly income. It was in our plans to sell the rental house because we wanted to clear our debts and stop managing the mess the tenants were making. I also had to look at the possibility of not landing any project or not being caught so tightly in a financial web that I would have to accept any project offered to me. Remember: I work on what I like to work on and with people I like to work with — I always try to do it my way! Hence my finances had to be on solid footing.

It was customary for Bechtel to offer a consulting contract to retirees but I was certain that I did not want to continue working for the firm. With Frank Cain at the helm, Charles Spink as his deputy, Billo Puri as the business manager, Michael Wakelin as the line manager, and Donald Graff as the operations manager, I could not find anything that was sufficiently interesting for me to remain at Bechtel.

Riley Bechtel's leadership as president left a great deal to be desired and the new herd of directors now guiding the firm did not impress me enough to entice me to stay. Gary Bechtel, Riley's older brother and now president of Bechtel Civil Co. (BCiv) was a pleasant person but he knew little about the business and wanted to be as far away from it as was possible. Because of his great antipathy for the firm (and perhaps of his family) Gary did not obtain his father's blessing to become president — and nothing pleased him more.

As I mentioned earlier, I knew Gary from his training days; many persons were assigned to me for training and he was one of the first. Often Gary would come to me for conversation or to air a problem, and often I would go to him for advice or an informal chat. He wanted me, as I had indicated, to help him out now that he had leased the old Denver Stapleton airport for his racing car company and to develop an industrial park. His plan was to hire Bechtel for the work on the old airport and to have me become the program manager. A contract with Bechtel had been signed and it was just a matter of weeks before work would begin. Gary did not want me to move to Denver, Colorado, but to lease an apartment close to the airport and fly back and forth as the project and he required. The project had some interest but I would still have to remain under Frank Cain's umbrella if I stayed with Bechtel. Gary just did not have the infrastructure to support a team under the flag of his small company. I did review parts of the technical service agreement for Gary and estimated that my task would extend over three or four years, hence it was a safe bet that I'd be working for a while, with his promised support.

As I thought about Gary's offer, there was the possibility of my being able to create my own department and gather my own team and cut any ties with Cain's group. I would need an administrator because I was not willing to struggle with that side of the process. Yet it was not magnetic enough to attract me. After many discussions with Gary on the plan and the tasks that would surface from it, I decided that I wanted out of Bechtel completely. After 18 years the time was nearing for the exit. Bechtel had hired me on 24 January 1975 and I wanted to exit on 24 January 1993, exactly 18 years later. With that date in mind it was time to prepare my move for the door. It was customary to give Bechtel two weeks notice and this was January 3, 1993. In twenty days I wanted to be free from the clutches of this firm.

The next morning after my coffee I called Gary for an appointment. He could see me immediately. I took the retirement letter that I signed to his office. He read it and asked if this was for his file and action.

"No. This is just to inform you. Actions will be initiated by the department," I replied.

"Raymond you are laying off Bechtel. You know that you have work and a project waiting for you yet you are laying off Bechtel," he looked at me and smiled. "I'll be leaving the firm soon too but keep it under your hat please," he added.

We chatted for a few more moments and I pointed out that I suspected that he would cut the umbilical cord with Bechtel sooner rather than later. When he left, the project in Denver would fall under Cain's purview and that was unacceptable to me. Perhaps I could generate a new department but that was unlikely because Cain would fight me, with the help of Riley, at every turn. Moreover, Gary was just starting and could not carry a whole team without Bechtel or another firm to support him. My B&B was doing relatively well and I was not about to jeopardize it for a dream — and Denver was too uncertain and too far from Montara. Finally I explained to Gary that racing cars were not in my field of interest. I left his office and walked to Wakelin's.

Michael Wakelin was brooding because Cain had promoted Billo Puri to a level above him; it was Wakelin who had hired Billo 20 years earlier. Wakelin was in his office and plotting his next political strategy at Bechtel. He was doodling and drawing a rough organization chart; there were rectangles with names on pieces of paper in them. Wakelin was moving some here and there mumbling to himself. Before I said anything he asked, "Do you think that I am in competition with my people?" I looked at him, puzzled as to what that was all about. "Mort Dorris accused me of competing with my people and this morning Gary Bechtel accused me of the same thing."

I handed him the retirement letter without answering his question. "Why are you leaving?" he asked.

"It's in the letter," I replied.

"Yes, but why are you leaving?"

"Michael I'm tired of it all." I paused then added, "Yes, you do try to compete with your people but are not able to be successful at it." I paused for a moment then continued, "I want out." I wouldn't discuss the issue further.

Every day after this encounter he'd come to ask me if I had changed my mind.

"Two more years and you'd make twenty with Bechtel," he'd say.

My reply was succinct, "And what would that earn me?"

After Wakelin, I went to Charles Spink's office and handed him the letter. "You don't get along with Frank Cain?" he asked.

"I want out to do what I want to do," I answered.

He invited me to sit down at his conference table but nothing that he said could make me change my position. After a while he picked up the telephone and dialed a number. The recipient was Frank Cain. Spink spoke to him about my resignation; then Cain asked to speak with me.

"I suppose that's because we've had our differences that you want to opt out?" Cain said before saying "Hello."

"Frank you are not that important to me and you are not pleasant either," I replied.

"I like to run a tight ship," he said.

"Good, Frank. Run your tight ship but do it without me." I gave the receiver back to Spink who looked at me puzzled. He spoke for a moment more with Cain and cradled the receiver.

"Frank is sorry that you are leaving, and so am I."

"Thanks Charlie," I paused long enough for him to stop staring at me. "Please initiate the paper work because on 24 January I'm out the door and I'll be history to you and others in this department." I walked out.

Back at my office I called the personnel department to alert them that I was opting for retirement and that my letter was being sent to them that day. Monique Rivera came to speak to me about an office move we were scheduled to make at the end of January. I informed her that I knew about it and would act on it when I had time.

"About your vacation to Chile in February, I've noticed that you don't have enough for thirty days of paid time off," Monique said to me.

"Monique," I replied, "Don't worry your little head about that. I do have the PTO and more."

She looked puzzled and asked, "You do?"

With a broad smile I replied, "Yep, I do. Now how about an espresso?"

"I can't now. We have a BCiv meeting in five minutes. Are you coming?"

"Monique, I'm off to enjoy my espresso and read my new Economist."

"Raymond, are you skipping the meeting?"

"Of course!" And that was the beginning of my exit strategy from Bechtel Corporation.

After my espresso I returned to my office and called Monique. "Now would you come for lunch?" I asked her. She could and would.

At lunch at Caravansary, I explained to her that I was retiring and that my last day would be on 24 January 1993. She immediately had tears in her eyes but was too embarrassed to reach for a tissue so I handed her one. After she regained her composure she asked if I would permit her planning a lunch for me.

"Only if it is at Etrusca Restaurant," I said. Etrusca was my favorite restaurant in the downtown area and the food was first-rate. I'd often treat myself to dinner there after work. It was a lovely place, well appointed, the kitchen was extraordinary, and the food was superb.

"Have you colleagues that you'd like to have at the luncheon?" Monique asked. We discussed several names and excluded many from the list. Finally she decided that the day would be the one before my last. I agreed.

On the day we had the lunch, there were about 30 colleagues at the long table; many who were not on the list I'd given Monique but who had left Bechtel months or years earlier. I was surprised that so many wished to attend my departing luncheon. Denis Slavich, a director, and Forsen came to the lunch, as did Gary Bechtel. Denis stood and announced that he wanted to offer a toast to me. He spoke kind words but he finished by saying, "I would like to inform all of you that Raymond never, never worked for Bechtel." There was a long pause as Denis looked at the puzzled guests. "Bechtel worked for Raymond — now he is laying off Bechtel!"

Many voices exclaimed that it was a known fact: "He surely did." The occasion was joyous and peppered with many affectionate comments. I had tears in my eyes. Unbelievable as it was, the curmudgeon had a few friends!

Not more than several days after my luncheon Slavich and Jackson left Bechtel and Forsen left two years later.

After 18 years, a lot of maturing on my part, sufficient good times to overwhelm the difficult times, two dismissal events that never were finalized, thousand of miles and many countries visited, several life-long friends made, numerous occasions when personal limits were overcome by creativity, ingenuity, sheer determination, and patience, I was walking out the door of 50 Beale Street to experience a new horizon. I was retiring from one event to begin another. Now I had to reorder my occasions, select a few and discard a few, and fashion my new event or events. All options were on the table and once again it was choosing time.

Honi soit qui mal y pense (Shame be to him who thinks evil of it)

PART SIX

Which Facet is Shown?

A memoir is an exercise in fiction writing peppered with a modicum of selected facts. That is exactly what defines this autobiography, or better this memoir, because it is neither a chronicle of events that took place over several decades, nor is it a deposition listing what defines my life. This autobiography is the story of a person who has lived an interesting life. In this story there are instances reflecting elements of creativity and occasions when risks were taken. For me creative activity is a particularly good way to express myself after a process that demands solitude. Moreover, the ability to create and the result that is produced from it are often regarded as possessing value to society, to those around me. Thus in this autobiography, the message is not so much residing in the general chronology but in the essence of what I experienced, how I lived my life, what contributions I made, while not forgetting the mistakes that haunt me. That an event occurred one year or another, on a particular date or another, in a certain place or elsewhere is less important than that it occurred and also that from it emerged certain altering effects that changed the course of my small segment of history; a history that I have no need to relive because the future is still ahead and I can apply to it what lessons I have learned.

That I was born in Cairo, Egypt instead of Paris, France, or Memphis, Tennessee has value because it has affected the view of the world I live in. As a child born at the time when a global war was tearing apart the fabric of society, my understanding of society is a little different than that of a child born in peacetime Montreal, Canada. I was touched by the war. My family disappeared because it became a casualty of that war through death, exile, and by the forces that disenfranchised many of its members. War is a terrible event, especially as it affects the lives of children. Children never are able to overcome the marks that war makes on them even when they are not directly touched by it. Indirectly, the effects of war leave an indelible wound on children, a wound that they can scratch but which never heals. The world as a result is never a safe place for them because it reflects what man's inhumanity to man can engender. For children who have lived in the very bosom of war, the sound of marching men wearing boots, the high whistle of a siren, the bellowing cloud from a fire, the loud sound of an exploding firecracker will send shivers through a person's body. More than that is the caution, concern, even fear that bubbles up in the inner self when crossing a border, confronting a passport officer, or passing through customs. As a result the view of the world takes a different coloration, which affects one's perspective.

There are other aspects that surface from the conditions that come from having been touched by war. Time becomes precious and wasted time is something that must be avoided. Every moment counts because it may be the last, even if reasonably it is not. Life must be lived and cannot be squandered. People are important because some of them may die soon. Life, like the flickering flame of a candle, must be protected from the whiff of a breeze that might extinguish it. Maintaining some form of correspondence with friends and acquaintances is something that cannot be neglected because people are important, very important, and so, so temporal.

Another aspect in me that I can recognize and cherish is solitude. Solitude is the moment when I can live inside my head without being disturbed by the constant noises of the agitated world around me. A moment of silence, a few instants for thought, an introverted offer to reenter my own self without disturbances — these are precious to me. I love to read and I read regularly but I can also not read and just allow myself to think in my solitude. No constant entertainment is necessary for me; at the dentist I can merely think and need not read last year's National Geographic or last month's Times to entertain my poor brain. There is enough going on inside my mental library to keep me busy, entertained, and happily occupied. That is not solipsism but an attempt to gather myself for a few moments away from the cacophony of the world.

Not One but Several

Adults wage wars. Young people die in them. There are many ramifications surfacing from the wars apart from killing and physically maiming a good portion of the population involved. Wars alter the characters of the young, even the young who have not been directly fighting on the battlefields. The military call this collateral damages or effects. Children are psychologically wounded, always cheated of their youth, and affected by the violence of wars and the hostilities that surface from them. We currently have encountered the tragic changes on children that have occurred in Cambodia, Congo, Uganda, Rwanda, Liberia, Russia, China, North Vietnam, and other locations devastated by wars, instability, and oppression. Children forced to kill their parents to save their own miserable lives. Children who have been forced to take up arms against non-combatants merely because that was the only way they could survive. Most of these children received no education, only training to kill, and their only concern was to survive. They killed because adults forced them to, for causes that they neither understood nor cared about.

Beyond the blood and carnage of battle, there are other aspects of war that affect children. Being cheated of their youth, these children are never quite rid of the effect of the consequences of wars. Freedom and play are lost to the children of wars. Nourishing foods and desserts are suspended from their diet. Eating for children is reduced to belly-filling modes. Ice cream, chocolate, cookies, and other sweet things that add to the quality of a meal are not what they experience. I can remember what a rare delight a bar of Cadbury chocolate brought to me and to my classmates in boarding school. The food I was given was nourishing, good tasting, and quite adequate to prevent me from malnutrition but it wasn't fun food, happiness-imparting food, or frivolous food — the kind that a child eats because it is a reward to the palate. Living to eat is replaced by eating to live. Food becomes the source of energy to survive the next wretched hours. Perhaps that is why I've turned to cooking, to preparing interesting dishes, to experimenting with all sorts of ingredients, and to inviting dinner guests because watching people with good appetites is a joy for me, the cook. I love to have chefs of reputable restaurants as my dinner guests because it helps me recognize that food is important for good living. Food and the five senses are how life is moved beyond the dreary into the charming.

There are other items that children do not receive during wars. Orthodontia is a major item that bypasses children during wars because dentists are recruited to care for the battle wounded and reconstructive dentistry is essential. In my case, much as I needed the care of an orthodontist, such service was not available to me. By a good twist of genetic heritage my teeth were healthy but they remain unsightly. War denies other needs to children, some of which are much more serious than orthodontia.

Then there are the conditioning behaviors that mark a child for life. Children of wars become hoarders of supplies because in the back of their minds they fear penury. When in a grocery store a child of war in peacetime will often purchase twice what is needed because it is never known when the items selected will disappear from the shelves and be unavailable on another day. Such children unconsciously become hoarders of foodstuff. "Not just one but several" becomes the motto of a war child. To this day, I cannot buy one apple or even two; I have to purchase a dozen or a bag full of apples. The same applies to cucumbers, lettuce, tomatoes, and a score of other items; I cannot bring myself to limit the purchase to just one item. It all seems too silly when I see people purchasing one apple, one orange, one loaf of bread, etc. Children who have endured the time of wars are a strange bunch and it is high time for adults — the promoters of wars, the initiators of wars — to recognize the long-lasting effect of wars and hostilities on the young.

Here I say nothing about the casualties of wars, the combatants who return maimed for life. I say nothing about them because that aspect of war has not touched me, except vicariously. I have seen the wounded. I have transported the burned cases, the crippled casualties, the faceless gun-fodders, and the psychologically affected but for these I have been a mere empathetic observer. They are the casualties of wars, of wars unleashed by adults — be they just wars or unjust wars, the result is the same: carnage ensues in all its horrible forms.

For science wars are considered to be the driving force behind emerging new discoveries, or so some say. Perhaps. But it seems that in a civilized society, there might be other driving forces to spur science and technology. It is true that in aviation many new designs and capabilities are the stuff that comes from the military development of aircraft. Yet, there are many other innovations that have surfaced because the civilian and not the combatant side of aviation have demanded improvements that have had little immediate value for military aircraft. Necessity may be the mother of invention, but the father need not be a combatant! Economic requirements are just as good and valid driving forces for innovations in science and technology. Yet we tend to rely on the military, even though military funding for innovation is extraordinarily expensive and mostly unreliable because defense departments operate on the principle of pork barrel funding rather than that of rational planning.

Funding for research, especially when it originates from the coffers of governments, is limiting in scope, vision, and purpose. It seems to me that civilian sources of funding are more reliable, less prone to narrow vision, and more able to produce results that are economically viable. But it is true that commercial funding for research is not devoid of the need for quick profits. If profit does not come as quickly as anticipated, then funding for research and subsequent funding for development is minimized. At this point, firms turn to the government for a handout and the taxpayer is burdened with the expenses. But in time of national emergencies, such as when hostility and war are imminent or in effect, funding from public coffers is less likely to be questioned and firms involved in research and development take advantage of the easy source of cash — and in the process become great proponents of the military-industrial elements that support wars and hostilities because it is good for business. I have lived though threescore and ten years plus of military-industrial cash orgies and as a war child I am sick of it! Je suis désolé des circonstances (I am sorry for the circumstances).

The Age of Assessment

One goes along year after year without being confronted by the need to assess the social fabric that is an important part of a person's life. Then one day the challenge surfaces. You are in a new location, in a new region, one that straddles three states and encompasses several communities of which some are small cities, towns, hamlets, and still a few are merely collections of houses in hollows of hills. Your responsibility is to improve the economics, health, and general welfare of the people residing in the various communities. You have to learn more and then begin to make some coherent assessments to help you undertake the task.

Because I was a non-Appalachian, a person speaking with an obvious strange accent, and one whose heritage was not local but foreign and recently European, my task was to learn a great amount and yet not to offend anyone in the process. I approached the two universities located in proximity to my region. One was in Atlanta and the other one was in Knoxville. I read everything that I could find on what made a city, a region, become economically viable and what did not. I looked at Paris, New York City, Chicago, Brasilia, Rome, Nashville, and several others, especially Atlanta, the liberal city which is curiously located in one of the most conservative states of the South. My information had to be translated and applied to communities like Ducktown, McCaysville, Copperhill, Blue Ridge, and other still smaller communities like Epworth, Hell's Hollow, and Dog Town. At the time I thought that it was a daunting task, a task that was impossibly complex but I did not give up. I just plugged along like a blinded horse following a trail that was filled with ruts. Somehow I neither fell into a ditch nor dropped off a cliff. In the process the good folks of the region accepted the fact that I was trying to learn about them, understand their ways, and promote their wellbeing.

Assessing a community is not an easy task. Not only did I have to get to know the people of the region, to know the power groups so to speak, but to understand what it was that they considered to be their way for a good quality of life and how they managed to achieve it. I learned about bartering and how the people tried to be independent from the firm that excavated ore and historically controlled the finances of the community. As a company community, the region was to a large extent dependent on the sole major employer until its citizens realized that it could manage otherwise. Small businesses were encouraged to open in the small towns, food markets were invited to open in competition with the company's own market where employees could shop and deduct their purchases from their salaries, thus increasing their dependence on the major employer. Slowly the pieces that my due diligence assessment had identified came together and with the help of several local friends a plan was devised for the community to use as a guide. Active participants in the planning process were members of the Junior Chamber of Commerce (JCC) and a few leading and young entrepreneurs who had found their voices and spirits as the process of independence from the mining company took shape. In all this my education on economic development took shape and became less draft oriented and more fine-tuned for application. The region began to move ahead with gusto, a gusto that surprised and also worried the sole employer. People of the region recognized that as soon as mining was exhausted, the firm would liquidate its assets and the region would be abandoned. It was evident to the power groups in the community that something drastic had to be entertained to remove them from their economic doldrums. The plan that had been devised by the JCC members became a working document for real implementation.

Along the way the federal government got a whiff of what was bubbling in the tri-state region and offered its assistance under the aegis of President L.B. Johnson's Great Society and the indefatigable support of a bright Georgia legislator by the name of Jimmy Carter. The crystallization of the plan occurred early in 1966 with the legislation from the federal government that helped promote innovative approaches for economic development in the remote regions of Appalachia.

Much of what I learned during my residence in the tri-state region of Tennessee, Georgia, and North Carolina served me well in later years when I was involved with regional economic development in other corners of the world. When working in Italy, France, Finland, (USSR), Russia or in other locations, I often recalled how I had managed the situation, the problems, the people, and the general condition in the Tri-State region north of Atlanta. As I've often said, education is a cumulative process where one layer of learning is added on top of another layer to form a stronger basis for further learning and for its application to the puzzle that is a life's journey.

Learning at Any Speed

When my two children were young and I, as a parent, was occupied with some parts of the management of their education (Trudy participated quite assiduously in the process) it occurred to me that I had little in my own history to use as a gauge or a standard that would be applicable to their situation. Both children were bright, eager to learn, but retained information at very dissimilar rates. Moreover, depending on the subject, each had a different way and a different rate of understanding and of retaining the information they received. What intrigued me was the rate at which each learned a subject. Each was able to grasp a subject at a rate that suited their temperament. Never wanting to inflict upon them any prejudices towards a subject, or worse, to categorize a subject as more appropriate for girls and less so for boys, I constantly debunked such categorizing when it emerged.

In one of my parent-teacher conferences, one teacher of a very prestigious school suggested that one child was less capable of absorbing a subject because he or she was of the "wrong" gender. I had to convince the controllers of this prejudice that in most cases gender was irrelevant.

In addition when one child asked for some tutoring in computers, he was told that time was not available for tutoring because he did not show enough ability to absorb the intricacies required of the subject matter rapidly enough to fit the preset schedule of the school. After arguing with the teacher against the comment, I became more convinced (but never quite certain) that it was this implicit approach that contributed to the negative attitude that my child presented to his class teacher and to the school.

At the end of the school year the child was transferred to a different institution. In the very first month the child's attitude and comportment changed radically for the better, even to the point he was requesting private lessons in Latin and additional tutoring in computer programming. Much as I knew little about computers and considered them a bit frivolous at that time, I did not object to the tutoring, especially since the cost was negligible. But what is important to me is that the child neither needed to be subjected to any gender discrimination nor did the child need to be limited to a preset curriculum that allowed less flexibility or tailoring to a particular child's curiosity.

In my own education I encountered the same limiting obstacles, perhaps identified as the "teacher knows best" perspective. In preparatory school I wanted to learn more math and Italian but because my teacher felt that I did not have time I could not attend these special classes. When attending university I wanted to attend classes in the physics and the philosophy departments but since I was registered in engineering I was not allowed. After thinking and finding that I could take courses anywhere if the courses were in the same topic, I asked if I could take tensile mechanics in the physics department. That was acceptable. Hence with a little strategizing I shifted eventually to physics and philosophy but not before I was informed that the disciplines had nothing in common, and in fact were anathema to each other. I studied both anyway and encountered no psychological harm or academic conflict. One must strategize personally for one's education!

Adult Synthetic Constraints

This is a learning box constructed by adults to suit a preset schedule rather than one tailored for a child's curiosity, personal ability, and inherent speed of learning. Perhaps that takes too much of an institution's time and requires too much effort for a mass-produced society. But education is time consuming, and energy absorbing, and difficult because it is a process to mold the minds of students.

A teacher (or an institution of education) is entrusted with students and is responsible for developing their human capital. The result will yield direct benefits for them — they'll learn more, perhaps at their own pace, because they are better educated. In addition, this educated capital will benefit their future employers — banks, manufacturing businesses, government, universities (some might learn enough to become educators par excellence), scientific confraternities, art guilds, etc. Their skills and education will enhance the social, political, and economic infrastructure that makes life pleasant and possible for them as adults — safe streets, stable institutions, and an agile brain for fulfilling their fondest hopes.

Teaching institutions and their teachers mold the minds of their students to produce a better thinking organism. Teachers open windows to the world for their students. Teachers prove that the impossible simply takes a bit of learning to convert into the possible when each student is allowed to absorb knowledge at his or her individual pace, yet there are teachers who are neither competent nor sensitive to be helpful. A mind should not be wasted and a good teacher lures the students into not wasting it. As the Negro University Alliance's motto states: "The mind is such a terrible thing to waste." Teachers make certain that it is not.

In my own case and throughout my life I have been a slow learner and a learner who has a terrible time with testing when given multiple-choice questions. Why? Perhaps I cannot see life as a black-and-white tableau. I see variations, options, possibilities, and alternatives depending on the situation, the problem, and the condition — and the psychological baggage brought by both the examiner and the examined. And so if there are any apparent loopholes, I find them and argue with them — to the detriment of the expected answers resulting in my not passing the test. Thus for me it is not so much speed that is at issue but the format. Give me essay exams and I do very well. Give me multiple choices and I do poorly. The former is time consuming for the examiner; the latter is time economical for the examiner. The decision then before us is: Are we to make education fit the examiner's schedule or the student's learning and testing make-up? In most cases today we give in to examiners (read that also as "institutions"). Of course, essay answers can be filled with nonsense that attempts to cover for the ignorance of the writer. Nevertheless, an examiner can separate the wheat from the chaff.

In a very real sense this is why the academic profession has turned me off. In my experience the institutions have mostly taken precedence over the student. One example I encountered was when I challenged the need for residency at a university that did not quite offer a graduate program that suited a student's specific quest. With a program of inter-university support, thus using faculty from other recognized universities; I was able to proceed to my goal. When several years later I told a senior faculty member at another university about this program, the professor responded candidly by asking: "But how does it benefit the university?" My reply was direct and to the point: "It benefits the student and that's the purpose of a university!" The faculty member was not in agreement.

Granted, there are many institutions willing to spend the necessary time and to amend their policies for the benefit of the students in their charge, but on the whole they are few and far between.

What frightens me are two issues that surface from the pell-mell of the current educational system in America and also abroad. As I indicated above, we adults forget that educating the young is an investment in the future. Educate a child and the payoff is a life-long return for society. The second issue is that with such diverse cultural change in America and abroad because of the great migrations that are being experienced it is forgotten that the reality is that not all students come from Main Street. With Chinese, Indians, Vietnamese, Ugandans, and others moving into what was thought to be primarily a singular ethnic society, the character of teaching is changing. In one class a teacher may have several international students who speak several languages and who know little or none at all of the local language. How will the teacher from St. Joseph, Missouri or from Poitiers, France or from Singapore or Cairo, Egypt manage to communicate with the student? The problem is magnified further when teachers are not required to learn another language than their own. In America, the problem is truly problematic because Americans are limited in their learning of foreign languages, not that the opportunity is limited but the luring is non-existent. This condition is readily encountered in schools located in poor sections. How do we resolve this condition?

I was a child who, when he attended an English school, did not speak the language and was forced to learn the new language rather quickly. Yet, I remember that I could find one teacher who was able to help me understand something by using French, Italian, and even Arabic. Is that possible in the local school today in America, France, England or Portugal?

Upon returning from Finland in 1989 where even the bus and taxi drivers were able to communicate in English or French, I took a local bus in San Francisco, a very cosmopolitan city that prides itself for being ethnically mixed. I chose to speak only in French. Entering the bus I asked the driver how much the fare was. She did not understand what I was saying. I showed her my five-dollar banknote expecting her to make change even if she did not speak my language. She kept repeating in English: "Exact change only!" After several words were interchanged a passenger came over and explained in broken French that the driver did not speak French and that the policy of the bus company was that only the exact fare was acceptable. A non-English speaker was left out in the cold simply because he did not have the exact change for the fare. In a world where multiple languages are currently required human beings can no longer be limited to one language, and although English may be spoken in general, it is not universal. Lest it is forgotten, it is also an investment in the future!

Religion-osity

In a few months I will celebrate a half-century in the priesthood and have been an active participant in the Episcopal Church (ECUSA) throughout my ministry with service in both parochial and non-stipendiary arenas, but always attached to a parish. In writing my thoughts for this work, I speak of the many facets of Christianity, the reasonable aspects of it, and the unreasonable doctrines that have plagued it and continue to plague it. For the past several decades the United States of America has been beleaguered by the zeal of religious fundamentalism. This fundamentalism has overwhelmed every aspect of society and has especially affected the political arena on all levels. Issues that have been accented by this fundamentalism include:

- Abortion
- Ordination of women to holy orders
- Consecration of gays to the episcopacy
- Marriage between same sex partners
- Prayer in public meetings
- Acceptance of people who are not of a Christian persuasion
- Ascription of God in all affairs of society
- Consideration for the poor and the wretched
- Tending to the environment

These issues have so inflamed contemporary society that a large block of reasonable religious people avoid speaking or associating themselves with current thought lest they be lumped with the fundamentalists. The atmosphere is not only intolerably annoying but it is insulting to reasonably minded people. The established churches have not made too much of an effort to redress this inflammatory condition. The Roman Catholic Church (RC), and the Orthodox Churches (OC) to a lesser degree, has contributed to this chaotic situation by refusing to be reasonable and also by refusing to interpret its doctrines in light of contemporary science (if not contemporary thought). The RC, guided by their Pontiff's extreme conservatism (John Paul II or Benedict XVI), has sailed willy-nilly into sexism, pedophile activities, and unreasonable biblical exegesis, hence interpretation. The Episcopal Church has been battered by the objections of hard conservatives on the issues of ordination of women, consecration of gay bishops, and blatant misrepresentation of scriptural passages in support of their own narrow agenda. Other churches have not attempted to resolve the controversies with grace but have exacerbated the minds of their followers by pronouncements that denoted that God was passing judgment in many ways from weather patterns to earthquakes and tsunamis; America was being punished for its transgressions!

On the issue of same sex marriage the churches are shirking their responsibility by not making a genuine effort to define marriage and same sex union with all the legal attributes that should come with it. By and large the churches have simply said no to same sex marriages without offering alternatives. Moreover, in the 21st century how is the historic definition of marriage explained in the light of:

1. Extensive mobility to pursue employment (often both spouses have to go to different localities if they want to earn income)
2. Professional and personal growth that inherently moves spouses away from each other intellectually and socially?

After many decades I question if the traditional definition of marriage can be carried over without some amendment to the current century. I am not quarreling with the idea of long-term marriage but only with the adaptation of it to fit the times. Contemporary society is no longer confined to a village separated by great distances and where household chores require the physical energy of the entire family. The bonding phenomenon that held spouses tied together over the years is no longer strong enough to be effective. Indeed families need to be stable, offspring have a need for a loving and warm nest in which to mature, but spouses are no longer protected from dissolution by the strength of the social fabric — in fact interested neighbors are discouraged from interfering in the affairs of others. Everyone speaks of the sanctity of the family, the nuclear unit, but the forces of society are explicitly set in motion to corrupt the safety of the unit by the requirements of today's needs. When families require two incomes just to make ends meet, to pay the bills, to cater to the style of life offered through marketing, advertisement, and also to furnish education to offspring, it is impossible to demand that the unit of the family remain intact for more than a few years.

Let's not forget that a same sex gay couple is able to nurture children either through adoption, artificial insemination or because one person has been married to a member of the opposite sex and then decided that a gay relationship was more fulfilling. How are children to be regarded and raised in such an environment? What does the traditional family unit under these conditions mean? Indeed it is a conundrum that has not been addressed, and when it has, it has been coated with scriptural and other platitudes. The churches have avoided the issues because it is too explosive to make some clear pronouncement. In the meantime the civil society is assuming the responsibility of defining what marriage means, but in as much as marriage is a religious concept, the churches are resigned to total silence. Conservative bishops are more consumed by the election of a gay bishop instead of spending their energies on the state of marriage in their jurisdictions. Fundamentally oriented churches are more concerned about aspects of marriage that they interpret as contractual agreements, thus missing the very point of what marriage is supposed to be. Historically, the Church defined marriage as a "covenant" relationship wherein each spouse accepted the other unconditionally and without escape clauses that would permit any abrogation of the union. Contracts, however, by definition have escape clauses and these may be used to void the agreement. Hence, when fundamentally oriented churches promote the reaffirmation of "contractual" vows they are inherently treading on very dangerous and shaky ground, ground that will not sustain what they like to promote as the "sanctity of the family unit!" In many nations, a contractual marriage is required to affirm that a union is legal; a church marriage is not accepted as being legal.

In my weakening sight after all the years of service, I sense that the Christian church and the other religions such as the Jews, the Muslims, the Hindu, Buddhist, Shinto, Mormons, and others, including the offshoots of these and of the several newly created and fashionable branches have ignored the very issue that is tearing their social fabric apart. Nevertheless, for good or ill, the legislative bodies will concern themselves with the issue of marriage but the results may be distasteful to all. The results will be distasteful because they will be filled with compromises that will suit the wishes of no one but only those who write the corpus of laws without regard of how they will affect beliefs, sound theology (if such exists), common sense, and correct ethical processes. I exclude moral processes because they call for allegiance or commitment to a higher authority, often considered to be divine in character, whereas ethics is a secular concept that works as a social lubricant. In other words to be moral is to operate within the context of parameters set by a higher authority that may not be recognized by many people. To be ethical is to function with a set of established agreements within the fabric of society, which promotes a kind of social lubricant to oil the interchanges among people and make life together easier to accept, safer for all, and better to enjoy.

Approaching the end of my road in life I learned that a loving God does not in any way give me the right to coerce others to believe the same axioms that I do. I also learned that Christianity perhaps has never been practiced!

Unacceptable Poverty

I've witnessed poverty in every corner of the planet. I've seen debilitating poverty in Egypt, Chili, Argentina, Brazil, India, Russia, Ukraine, England, France, Germany, Italy, Switzerland, Spain, Saudi Arabia, Australia, Japan, Thailand, the Philippines, China, Canada, other places that are still filed in my memory, and also in the United States of America.

As a young boy I saw people sleeping in the streets of Cairo and Alexandria because there was no place for them to call home. I saw sick people, people with elephantiasis displaying huge legs and who were lying in the street unable to be mobile. I remember a young boy who had no nose, no ears, and less than part of one hand, which was the result of leprosy, hopping from tramway to tramway to beg for change.

In India I encountered the poor of a caste that literally lived in the streets because they were unable to be employed or were assumed to be less than human by fellow citizens; they were the poor of the poor who were discarded as being subhuman all because they belonged to a different caste, a lower class or an excluded group as historically recognized by the rest of the population.

It appears that in the first decade of the 21st century, the world, and especially the United States, will experience an increase in the homeless population — not too dissimilar from what I saw in historically underdeveloped countries.

In Chile, Brazil, and Argentina I walked through the "Bidonville" communities — large communities created by taking discarded tin containers and flattening them, then linking them to make walls for simple abodes, insulating the thin walls with cardboard, and where people slept on flea-infested straw beds and were visited by rats. As I walked through the shanties I ran over rats scurrying about without the least amount of concern for humans. Several children had fingers missing because rats had chewed them off. The bigger shock was seeing in contrast the wealth of Ipanema Beach, Rio de Janeiro — and just a few hundred meters away.

The People's Republic of China prides itself on being egalitarian and of providing good living conditions to its people. In 1999 in Guangdong Province, a labor-intensive manufacturing center, workers worked 16 to 18 hours a day and many of them were homeless, maimed, and had torn clothes because pay was minimal and social support was nil. They were treated as trash because they left their farms for a better life and in the hope of improving their existence by working in factories just to survive the harsher conditions of the hinterland. Farmers and country people need full access to urban services, such as education and health. Factory workers need to be given benefits to improve their lives such as housing, shorter hours of work, and to be recognized not so much as cheap laborers but as human beings who have the potential to contribute to China's future.

I can continue and mention dire poverty on the streets of Zurich and Geneva or in Rome, Milan, and even in San Francisco. Homelessness is a social disease that plagues all developing and developed countries and it is the product of the high cost of living and the lower value placed on human beings. It is also, consequently, the result of mismanaged financial conditions where the rich have hoarded wealth at the expense of the less wealthy and the poor. It is an economic fact that the very wealthy have tilted the playing field to their advantage. Wealth has been unevenly distributed, acquired, or inherited in such a way that the top few have a greater percentage of the wealth than the remainder of the population. We treat each other as if the other person is not quite a human being. The world's economic agenda is based on the wealthy with a consummate disregard for the poor, the disadvantaged, and those who fall through the cracks because of our refusal to accept them as partners in life's journey.

Moreover investment brokers have accumulated wealth by manipulating the funds of people who trusted them without regard to shared allocations. It doesn't matter who buys or who sells the likes of financial instruments, the investment broker receives a substantial fee either way. The fee has nothing to do with advice given, if any, and usually none is given, but merely for moving money from one person to another! No actual product is generated; payment is for the transaction performed electronically. Thus the top earners nickel and dime (read as millions or billions) the lower earners out of their earned benefits, to be relegated to a sub-status of society that does not even provide them with adequate health care or proper education because we mean to keep our profit margin ever higher at their expense. I am amazed to learn that California's Silicon Valley has an extraordinary large number of homeless living in a geographical area where wealth is noted in billions of dollars. Top earners, who are hard workers and producers, ignore the less fortunate or forget them. There is also the thought of "I've gotten mine, the hell with the others!" When chief executives earn 30 or 40 times (even 300 and 400 times) what people on lower rungs earn, there is an economic disjunction that occurs. I am seeing a split in the population in the United States and in other countries between the extremely wealthy and the less wealthy who make up the middle class. And this is not merely the fault of the high earners; it is the fault of the tax system that favors the extremely well off in society and the gargantuan corporations who benefit quite well by *legally* using tax loopholes.

That same degree of poverty is visible in Spain, Italy, France, Germany, and the United Kingdom as well as in many other European countries. It is also becoming readily visible in the United States. In the former Soviet Union countries such as Russia and Ukraine, the poor, homeless, and diseased

— in spite of the acclaimed free national health programs — languish in many parts of the cities, villages, and the hinterland where all of them suffer enormously, especially in the harsh winter months. Poverty and neglect are quite present in socialist and ex-socialist countries, and they are just as much an insult to humanity as they are in free-market societies. Indeed, the poor may be with us always, but in the 21st Century we should be able to minimize their misery, even do away with it.

It seems to me that the greatest shock to my senses was seeing extreme poverty in Japan, Canada, and the United States of America, nations that are known to have extraordinary wealth at their disposal. When I inquired how it was that many homeless persons were present in Tokyo, Nagoya, Osaka, Kobe, and especially the harbor city of Yokohama, I was told that the people were probably unwilling to work or to obtain appropriate training to satisfy work requirements. Perhaps that was possible. I'm certain that there are many people who have little incentive to work, less interest in caring for themselves or to exert much effort about self-improvement. Parasitic living is not limited to plant life but also finds a place among human beings. Nevertheless, in a culture that prides itself on its work ethics, its racial purity, and its devotion to profitability, seeing wasted human beings huddled in corners, in alleys, near transportation stations, and on busy sidewalks was disconcerting, especially when seen during the cold and icy months of winter. The second highest economy in the world was failing just as well as the highest in managing its poor. I am certain that no human being wants to be poor or strives to be impoverished. Certainly life is not always fair but human beings who are able to help could be fair!

In America Too...

The United States of America, the highest and most active economy was unable in 1999 to reduce the number of its poor population. Every major city in America had streets that were peppered with homeless people. Poverty and particularly malnourished people and children were to be found in every corner of American society. Indeed, in a society that is economically active, that flaunts the mightiest military in the world, and that invites the poor of the world to come to its shores to create a better life for themselves, America has failed and failed miserably in providing the means to help the economically disenfranchised — whether or not they want to be poor, to remain disenfranchised, or to vegetate as parasites but to lift themselves from the bottom of the social rung.

In America it seems that we have a distorted view of what a human being is worth. The country still values human beings as worth less, much less, than 10 dollars per hour when they work a full hour. The value of a human being is scaled down at every turn of the budget screw. Even in healthcare the country is unwilling to find a solution for providing every citizen rightful and adequate medical support. The preference is for insurance firms to be the monitoring provider of healthcare. Moreover, the country requires employers to provide healthcare insurance but of course that is limited only to when a worker is employed (that will change in later years with what will be called Obamacare). Americans claim that they distrust the government, at least this is what some congressional representatives claim; nevertheless the same congressional representatives trust the government to manage Medicare, healthcare for the military, and for themselves and to manage the Military and the Defense Department. How come they trust the government for these special cases but refuse to trust it for the general population? It is an issue that has to be resolved, not tomorrow or the day after, but now — immediately!

Cultural Changes: New Economies

I have been fortunate in my travels to meet several different types of ethnic people, not just groups, but individuals. I've watched them cook their food and have eaten their meals, shared their homes, and, often through signs and translators/interpreters, discussed with them their hopes, aspirations, political views, and ethical framework.

In the remote locations of many ethnic communities, my palate has tasted meat from whale, seal, moose, reindeer, bear, walrus, particular fish and crustaceans native to the Arctic, edible plants from the tundra, and many savories that were unidentifiable to me. My eyes have seen healthy primitive societies living well in the far northern regions and at the same time they have witnessed the destructive influence of modernization.

In western Alaska and eastern Siberia, where neither American nor Soviet Union authority could penetrate and modify the Eskimo culture, the natives could keep their ethnic identity, continue with their traditional ways, and manage their travels as they moved across the Bering Straits to reconnect with their families and friends.

Inland, where American or Soviet authority was more exacting, the native Indians of Alaska and the Asian peoples of northern Siberia were less able to maintain their traditional ways. Many if not most of them succumbed to dire poverty, alcoholism, and in many cases malnutrition. Was that a product of isolation from their social connection or was it just that they were not adequately prepared to manage their lives in the maelstrom of contemporary conditions?

In northern Scandinavia, Finland, and Russia, where national authority was minimal, the inhabitants of Lapland, the Sami people, were able to keep to their traditional ways of tending reindeer, fishing, and hunting. In addition, again because the nations were unable or disinterested in regulating the Laplanders whose territory they occupied, the culture, ethnic customs, and economic system flourished healthily. Herding reindeer, the Laplanders were able to cross borders from Norway to Russia without difficulty or documents, and although documents were required, they merely ignored them and proceeded to cross the dividing fences that modernity had installed. In the case of the Soviet Union, the bureaucrats at the border quickly learned not to interfere because it was impossible to control or prevent the influx of the Sami people and their herds. I was informed that during the occupation of Norway, Finland, and northern Russia by the Nazi military forces, the northern corridors remained open to Laplanders and the German forces reluctantly practiced a blind eye approach. Consequently, Laplanders were least affected by WWII or the Cold War, and their culture continued to function unimpeded by the effects of modernity, yet their trade outside of their group did suffer substantially.

Where primitive cultures are able to be unaffected by the driving forces of modernization, they continue to dwell well by maintaining their own sense of who they are and how they function. In places where primitive cultures have been forced into or altered by modernity, by and large they have not fared too well. Good examples of this societal breakdown from my experience are to be found in the Arctic regions and in the Americas, especially by the Aleut, Aluriiq, Northern Inuit, and Yupik people.

Other places where I have witnessed a similar societal breakdown because of a forced modernity foisted on primitive peoples is in the Arabian Peninsula, and on many islands of the South Pacific and also on the continent of Australia and the island of New Zealand. In Saudi Arabia the nomadic Bedouin are slowly disintegrating as a culture because of the strict authority of the current government and the rapid pace to drag them into modernity, which consequently impinges upon their societal fabric.

In Australia and in New Zealand the native inhabitants are diminishing at a frighteningly rapid pace. Aboriginal and Maori social groups have shrunk to such a level that they are minimally influential to settlers from Europe. Consequently, these token remnants of past primitive societies are in miserable conditions, suffer in extreme poverty, and large numbers have given themselves to alcoholism not unlike America's native Indians.

What is it that modernization offers primitive societies? What has contemporary American society offered to the Native Americans? In Brazil what has the government offered the Indians of the Amazon River basin to improve their traditional society? And is it a good thing that is being done by the occupying intruders to the natives of any region? I wonder.

Culture develops through a long and arduous process of testing, applying, and selecting the right format for this or that particular society. When foreigners arrive and proceed to change the local format of a society, is attention being given to what will happen down the line and how long it will take to stabilize the people involved? Centuries, many of them, are needed to reorient a people to a new mode of living. Not only is the economic system of a primitive people demanding adjustment but issues of health, welfare, and custom must be addressed and addressed slowly. Current experience shows explicitly that in most cases foreigners have botched the job of converting primitive people to modern times. In my travels I've not seen modernization offer too many successes to primitive societies. The urge to "bring these folks to the 20th or 21st century" cannot be curbed but must be paced and tempered with the understanding that it took us centuries to arrive at our current level of modernity. Anthropologists are the first to recognize that modernizing primitive societies is a long and tedious task requiring much forethought. But then the anthropologists and we must ask if modernizing the primitive natives of the Amazon River basin, the Inuit and Yupik, the American Natives, the Pygmies and other peoples of Africa is a good or even an ethical issue.

In the political arena, we must ask the same question about any form of government that is promoted. Is democracy or capitalism or communism better for all societies or are some societies more prone to live under one or another political system instead of being forced to change? Human rights are critical to all societies but the application of those rights is not universally equal. If the need to equalize the human rights surfaces, then the process for changing them must be approached with great respect for tradition, cultural format, and the makeup of the fabric of the society in question.

I admit that I've seen much disjunction when primitive societies come into contact with modern societies and the results have not been very encouraging. The intrusions by modern groups of primitive societies for whatever reason — for humane causes, for the sake of research, or for religious causes — have produced pathetic consequences.

My Island Home

In 1962, the late environmentalist Rachael Carson, in her extraordinary book *Silent Spring*, raised the issue of the care and nurture of our planet Earth to a level that had not been considered before the arrival of her work. At the time of the reading of Carson's book I was involved in the initial steps of part of my professional education and I was busy, therefore too occupied to give environmentalism too much attention. Yet even with the scant attention that I gave to the Earth's wellbeing, the very ideas that Carson put forward never left me; indeed they haunted me.

While living in north Georgia in the late 60s, after having gone through the Free Speech movement in Berkeley, California, and on occasion participating in it, I became more concerned with the care of the earth. Also in the early part of the 60s I began to read everything that the late Lauren Eiseley, also an anthropologist, wrote about the nurture of the earth. At that time I began to plant a vegetable garden and I also received pointers about composting, recycling paper and cardboard, reducing the use of plastic bags and Styrofoam, and not using poison for dispatching weeds and unfavorable insects. When I moved to California I began to recycle metal, plastic, and glass but often great distances had to be travelled to reach the facilities that accepted the items for recycling. The most difficult part of that effort was to convince the steel industry to accept cans for recycling in spite of the fact that in the making of steel some old steel is necessary as a catalyst for the smelter.

Today, my waste disposal is reduced to an amount that comes to less than two kilograms and often even less than that. Recycling is a fact of living on this earth and should begin before we buy items for our use. Do we need to purchase canned goods when fresh items are available? Do we need to use paper towels when we can use a washable cloth? Do we have to clutter the sewers with laundry water when that water may be applied to the garden and the residue soap in it is advantageous to our plants as a mild fertilizer and aphid remover? Can we not reuse plastic bags and aluminum foil several times before recycling them, and why do we need them at all? Bringing one's own bag to the store is not only a cost savings but also helps out with the recycling event. And so it goes if a little care is given to the items we use and can reuse.

In the 80s I began to be acquainted with the works of Lynn Margolis, the bacteriologist and fungicide scientist who proposed that (as she simply put it): "The Earth will outlast humankind's mistreatment but humankind will not!" By that time I was fully engaged in various aspects of environmentalism. But a more profound sense of concern overwhelmed me when I first met Julie Packard and Dr. Steven Webster, the initiators of the renowned Monterey Bay Aquarium (MBA).

I had been interested in the possibility of a new aquarium being considered in Monterey and at the suggestion of a friend (mentioned earlier) I attended in May 1978 a small and informal dinner at the coastal home of Lucille and David Packard. That evening after dinner the issue of an aquarium was discussed around a coffee table when dessert was served. Both Julie and Steve voiced their ideas and described the draft plans that had already been accepted and the funding that had been promised by David earlier. A sum of 50 million dollars was mentioned and both Julie and Steve made some comments that it would be sufficient for the first phase of the aquarium.

What mostly struck me and in a sense opened my eyes further were the comments by both Julie and Steve on the importance, condition, and effect of the oceans on the health of the planet Earth and on the education of the coming generations. That evening helped remove a portion of the cloud of ignorance from my brain and replaced it with a keen awareness that the ocean was one of the most critical aspects for the survival of the earth and for all living creatures upon it. As a flyer my focus had been on the sky and perhaps on Space but not much on the ocean, although I had crossed the Atlantic in a large passenger vessel and had flown over several oceans and seas. For me and in my ignorance, the ocean was vast, cold, and wet! In retrospect, I was not intimately aware of the value of the ocean.

After my encounter with the folks at the Packard house, I became convinced that I would be part of this new aquarium and its mission, as stated by Julie, especially that it would show the effect that the Elkhorn estuary had on the Monterey Bay and the condition of the bay itself as a living example of how the Pacific Ocean fared. On 20 October 1984 the Monterey Bay Aquarium opened to the public but on 18 October 1984 — two days before opening — I was given a personal tour of the facilities and an introduction to the scientific and technological staff. Ever since that momentous evening in 1978, I have been a great supporter of the aquarium and a small financial contributor for the promotion of its work.

As environmentalists, if that's what we're becoming under duress because of the garbage we produce, we must have a sense of humor as we tackle the problem to find solutions. I'm a fan of the writer on the environment T.C. Boyle, who alerts us that the environmental movement has become too preachy and mostly ineffective because it has not convinced the majority of voters that the problem of pollution and wanton consumption is deleterious to the planet. Boyle reminds us that the United States has been taken over by a "moral majority," a "religious right," and other similar groups with different names, that professes a faith that specifies that evolution doesn't exist and that creationism does, and that scientific facts are false. I ask the religious right that if faith tells them that creationism is the mode, why can't faith tell them that preserving the environment is more important than destroying it? Boyle has a solution to the environmental problem: if we all can agree — and no cheating — that if everyone on the planet would abstain from sexual relations for 100 years the problem would be definitely solved!

The environment and its care has become a major concern for me. On all airport, economic, and high technology projects on which I've had some influence, the issue of the environment has been foremost and has been made part of all developments. It is inescapable that we must be seriously concerned about our island home, the Earth. Few books made the point clearer for the public than Albert Gore's book, *Earth in the Balance*. The book is an indictment of the way humankind has treated the planet but I'm sorry to say that the good vice president did not emphasize his work enough when he ran for president in 2000 — in fact, in his numerous speeches he was mostly silent on the environment.

Today we have a critical issue that must be resolved, especially in the United States of America. The issue has to do with the reality of acid rain and carbon dioxide accelerating global warming. I shan't go into the details of the two problem issues but I want to remind my readers that if the United States does not take the lead in eradicating the earth's atmosphere of these two devastating conditions we might all end up living in an unhealthy and miserable place, made so by our own doing. Unless the United States acts boldly to reduce acid rain and global warming, the People's Republic of China, India,

Japan, Russia, and other polluters will not be moved to make the necessary effort to amend this devastating condition. In the United States where does the fault of inactivity rest? It rests on the shoulders of the voters who have elected uncaring and ignorant people as their representatives and president. Simply put, as New Yorkers would say, "Throw them bums out!"

Politics and Human Affairs

What New Yorkers say before voting leads me to the next commentary about my experience all these years. One of my New York colleagues and roommate assured me that voting was irrelevant, absurd, and silly. Is it? My first experience with voting began in 1954 with the mid-term elections in New Jersey where I was a resident. What was so important about voting (and this was the first time that I exercised my voting right, and by absentee ballot to boot)? Because I was with the military on a tour of duty in Alaska I had requested an absentee ballot. Many of my colleagues asked me why I was so interested in voting especially since they assured me my vote would not amount to any great change. I voted and was pleased to do so. Politics, many of my colleagues assured me, was a game for crooks, a silly exercise managed by dishonest people. I explained to those who were disparaging the process, that politics was in reality the management of human affairs; it was the process, the tool, with which we managed the business of a group of people. Yes, there existed possibilities for crooks to intervene in the process, politics could become the arena where dishonest politicians could corrupt the system of government, but removing ourselves from the arena merely gave the crooks more leverage to be corrupt. My vote, minuscule as it was, was what — added to all the other votes — would help make a difference.

In addition, I added, voting in ignorance was just as bad as not voting because it was the misuse of the privilege and it diluted one's right to influence the system of government. In a free society and for a representative government, each vote was paramount because it was part of the whole political fabric. My friends were surprised that a new member of the American community was seriously engaged in voting and in participating in the American electoral process. Moreover, my colleagues were intrigued that I had done my homework, in as much as I had read about the issues. Now I must admit that in the early mid-term election of the 50s my progressive democratic vote did not upset the cart of the entrenched conservative Republican pro-McCarthy supporters. But the very fact that I voted and those other, like-minded people voted did not give the opposition a mandate to rule.

It is unfortunate that many Americans have a low esteem of people who are in politics. Being called a "politician" is tantamount to insulting someone. Yet politics are the very backbone of a free democratic society and the re-quired duty of all informed citizens if good government is to be pursued. That a few politicians are unethical, that others are ineffective, is mainly the fault of the electorate. Indeed it is an unfortunate truism that people get the politi-cians they deserve and the leaders they merit. Understanding that politics is the management of human affairs, it then becomes every voter's responsibil-ity to exercise a voice for the selection of the politicians, nay, the representatives, who will speak for them in the arena of government. But this is only part of the responsibility; unless the voter educates himself/herself prior to voting what is cast becomes fundamentally useless. An ignorant vote is a vote for the opposition. Recalling John Adams:

"It becomes necessary to every subject then, to be in some degree a statesman: and to examine and judge for himself of the tendencies of political principles and measures." (The Papers of John Adams, Cambridge: Belknap Press, 1977, Vol. 1, p. 81, from "'U' to the Boston Gazette" written on August 29, 1763.)

I learned that important lesson when I was in Europe during WWII. I saw what happened in Nazi Germany, the Soviet Union, Italy, Egypt, and many other nations where the people abrogated their responsibilities to effective bands, groups, and parties of disreputable characters. That it could happen in the United States is not impossible if we look at the effect of the "moral ma-jority" at the time of President Nixon, the "religious right" now in the second half of the first decade of the 21st century, and of the wealthy contributors influencing the political parties to support their agendas in the 21st century. I suspect that if 90-plus percent of the voting population had exercised its right to cast a ballot, neither of these three despicable groups would have had any great effect. In addition, when the minority abandons its right to counter the majority through the channel of the election, then it remains unheard, silenced, and expunged from the mainstream of politics.

Politics is the stuff of political animals, be they bees, ants, chimpanzees, great apes, or human beings. Whenever two human beings are together, there in their midst is created a political system where each is chosen, appointed or selected by circumstances to fulfill a particular role. One selects the food and the other builds the fire. One constructs a lean-to and the other picks coconuts or cuts branches for the lean-to. Cooperation and management of chores is the stuff of politics. In a representative form of government, the chores are delegated to a few representatives who are held accountable by those who chose them. In a dictatorship that isn't the case, as even the dictator is not accountable directly to the people. Yet soon enough the process of world and internal development makes even dictators accountable, but it may take years, decades, and centuries to be implemented.

So politics is not ghastly, dreadful, rotten or appalling; it is merely that electors are irresponsibly managing the representatives selected.

Of course we can say that in 1999 the process suffered a major hiccup when the Supreme Court led by Chief Justice William H. Rehnquist trespassed over the electoral process and appointed George W. Bush as the 43rd President of the United States of America. For me that date will go down in history as a major day of judicial malpractice and a shameful treatment of the electoral process in America. At any rate, this is my judgment and the readers will have to accept it as it is.

Problems into Challenges

How do I look at the world, at life, and at the future? This question touches the core of every human being because it demands an answer to the correlative question: Who am I and where am I going? Several tougher questions follow. After many years of examining myself I am certain that I know pretty well who I am — and who I am not. My sense of integrity is clear. I

446 · RAYMOND HOCHE-MONG

am not perfect and I am not a rascal. I do have the tendency to push the limits and to walk, so to speak, the tightrope and without the advantage of a safety net below me. That I take calculated risks is no secret; any endeavor that depends on creativity is risky. Every step taken by me offers a chance of failure or success, and that in itself is risky. I just take more steps, cover more terrain, explore more situations, and tackle more ideas, concepts, and challenges. I take no risk that I judge to be beyond my capabilities. I take no pleasure in foolhardiness. That is not my style or the way I comport myself. Calculated risks are acceptable and often part of my mode of operation. The risks may give me a little tightness around the collar, a few additional heart beats, some uncomfortable pauses, sweaty palms, and uncomfortable moments or even hours but on the whole I accept the pressure that ensues because it is part of the process I call life, or life as I understand it.

Making mistakes is also part of the process of life. I've obtained a great amount of wisdom from the mistakes I've made. Few mistakes are not correctable and those that cannot be are the ones that taught me not to repeat them. As the carpenter would advise: measure twice but cut once! I measure twice and often more because some mistakes are terminal, devastating, and produce horrible consequences that affect human relationships for a very long time. Yes, I have made mistakes, some minor and several major ones. The consequences emerging from these mistakes have been difficult to live with, but none have crucially affected me or wrecked my life.

Any risk requires forethought, and forethought is a key element of planning, and planning is the tool that helps me cope reasonably with the future. But for planning I must consider evaluation or what biblical scholars call prophesy — the ability to analyze the current situation and draw from it options for new courses, new schemes, new tactics, and then implement revised plans. This is not too different from the political pundits and social critics who look at the current situations and anticipate what will evolve from them. No crystal ball approach here, just examining where the flow of the current will lead. The problem arises when I recognize that the future is always in front of me whereas the present is merely a fleeting moment that barely has any effect on me because it is gone before I'm aware of it. The future, however, is there, here, and everywhere and constantly makes demands on me. The future is affecting me in the long term and in the short term; it impinges on me constantly because it is forever emerging and is never stable, static, or arrested long enough for me to alter it. I can, however, influence it by the way I plan my own life. Yes, I can influence it in many ways by how I execute my plan or plans. I can be oblivious to the future by adopting an attitude that depends on fate, or what the Arabs call *maktoub*, written in the scroll of one's life, or I can tackle the future by affecting it with tactical and strategic planning. "If I do this, then this will happen...." If one does nothing then who knows what will surface.

It is worth sharing that I seldom, if ever, encounter problems, only challenges. No, I don't ignore the difficulties and vicissitudes that life showers on me; I just take them as challenges to be resolved. Often accused of placing myself in control, I consequently suggest that resolutions are not impossible to construct. It all depends how one looks at issues. If looked upon as problems then one can expect headaches and subsequent misery because of the difficulties that surface. Contrary to this approach, if I see the situation as a challenge calling upon me to muster all my talents, then I'm ready to search for all sorts of means to resolve it creatively. A challenge is fun because it requires the best efforts to be activated. Can a challenge be followed by failure? Of course. But as I said earlier, I learn from failure and then either start over again with a new approach after examining the circumstance and/or seek help from other people.

A good part of how challenging life is for me is my increased focus on being of help to my fellow citizens. Service is a major portion of what my responsibility entails. Indeed, it is a corporate world and all human beings, all living creatures, are linked somehow. It is inhuman to be uncaring of others, surely at times that care may tax us and wear out our energy, but there it is; we cannot live in isolation or assume that someone in Laos does not affect us here or that a person in Africa is totally unconnected to me here in California. We are all one on this, our island home. Moreover, none of us, in Africa, Asia, Europe, or elsewhere is the center of the Universe. There is no single center; we are all part of the center and responsible for our geometrical location and our geographical attitude. What did you do to deserve being born in a developed country? What did you do to be born an American, a Mexican, a North Korean, etc.? Nothing.

Onward with the B&B

The idea of a B&B was discussed as early as 1981. I've always been interested in owning and running a bed and breakfast. When I lived in the UK often I would stay in B&Bs and that was a good way to meet families, eat home cooking (which is much, much better than restaurant meals), and learn about the culture and the different folks who live in the various sectors of the British Isles. More than that, I was in the habit of entertaining guests in my home and I thought that a B&B was a good way to continue entertaining, but then I would get paid for it. Of course that is an inhospitable way of looking at entertaining. It was obvious that my house in Montara was not large enough for a B&B because it only had three rooms and a large basement, which was not sufficient nor was it adequate for privacy, namely mine. I needed a larger house and I wanted one with a particularly interesting history.

The concept was discussed with Emily, but at the time we were just friends and not married. I also checked with several realtors in the hope that a useful house could be found not too far from Montara. It appeared after much looking and with the help of several realtors that my request for a large house near Montara would not be fulfilled. Finally I was directed to a realtor in Montara. Janet Gray offered reassurance that a house could be located in or near Montara, but first she showed me several houses, including a beautiful house overlooking the Pacific Ocean. It was a fine and attractive house but not one that I could see as a B&B. I was not interested in the house because it was too close to the ocean, on a cliff, and within the Coastal Commission's sensitive zone — that would have given me difficulties with zoning restrictions, public access policies (in California coastal property is accessible to the public, which means that we would be often asked for the use of our toilets and other amenities), and with wind, ocean spray, and blowing sand it would have been difficult to keep the building in decent condition. Janet was understanding. She also had an idea. She said to me, "Are you interested in White Elephant house?"

"What's a white elephant?" I asked Emily.

"An unusual structure," she replied.

"Where is it?" I asked Janet.

Janet's response was that the house was located on George Street.

"Is that the house with two turrets on an acre of land with a high tree hedge bordering the property?"

She replied that it was. Without giving Emily any hint I told Janet that I would buy it but first needed to see the inside of the house. Emily was not only surprised that I committed so readily but she was concerned that, because I was leaving for an assignment in Europe that would last several weeks, I would not be around for the final details of the purchase.

Janet took us to see the house. It was a large house that was nearly one hundred years old. The inside was a mess. The upper level was fantastic and its floor was in excellent condition because it had been used as a dance studio. A musician and his significant other, who was a dance teacher, owned the house. The significant other was dying of cancer and he was no longer able to care for the house. The price was good and I knew that a great deal of money would be spent bringing the building to code.

We purchased the building in 1983 and received our first paying guests in the summer of 1986. My intention, and perhaps my plan for the long-term, was for the bed and breakfast to give me a financial platform that would allow me to be selective when I began working as a consultant after retiring from Bechtel.

Holiday to Europe

A recapping of certain events will refresh the readers:

I had planned to take my two offspring to Europe with Emily. This was to be part honeymoon and part one of the last trips with Daddy for my growing daughter and son. My goal was to show them especially Lascaux and a few other of my favorite places. Jacques Marsal had invited us to visit and join him and his wife for dinner at his home. When the time came during the Christmas holidays of 1983, the trip was initiated and we would be in England and France for a whole month. The calendar was divided with 10 days with Emily in Cornwall, Christmas in Cambridge and Ely, with Christmas Eve at Ely Cathedral, then a drive to Folkston for the crossing of the English Channel. Dominique and Michel, my children, would meet me at Heathrow airport after they completed their classes.

When in France a car would be hired for the rest of the trip. Paris was first on the agenda. We stayed near the Opera, which offered us access to many places just by walking. After Paris we headed south towards Montignac and the Dordogne. We stopped for an overnight visit in the town where Madame de Maintenon's Chateau could be visited. My mother had been on the faculty in Cairo of the Cours Maintenon, a French lyceum. Francoise d' Aubigne (Madame de Maintenon) was a modest woman and an educator who finally became Louis XIV's wife and advisor upon the death of his first wife.

We arrived in Montignac and were met by Jacques Marsal and given a regal tour of the famous grotto of Lascaux. That evening the dinner was more than a five-star event. We were regaled with local ham and lamb, local mushrooms and truffles, local veggies and greens, local wine, and finally a superb dessert that was heavenly. To complete the repast we were offered several local cheeses. We still remember that dinner and the graciousness extended to us by Marsal and Nounou, his wife.

I must admit that much as we had a wonderful time together I was ill at ease. I had trouble urinating and the thought that ahead for me was the re-reconstruction of the house and the search for a reputable contractor to do the job for a reasonable fee was daunting. This haunted me and I still was uncomfortably bloated because of my bladder problem or whatever caused the discomfort.

The return trip was uneventful. Everyone in the group was well satisfied that the holiday had been in reality a holiday. I was the only silent voice who was not terribly happy but like a good trouper I agreed that we all had had a fine time.

As I intimated earlier, the large house was purchased in 1983. The marriage to Emily had been an occasion in November 1983. What was now in front of us was getting the house in shape for what we intended. My good friend Don Koenig from St. Edward's Episcopal Parish in San Jose, a fellow pilot and a retired building inspector volunteered to be our project manager. There was a great deal of reconstruction to be done. Both the East and West walls were leaning out about four centimeters each. The West wall was pushing against the addition, which served as the garages and the two bedrooms and kitchen. On the East side the movement would ultimately crack the wall. It had to be repaired. There were two cables tied to the walls and these were taut enough to emit a sharp ping when touched. Don was concerned that this would cause other major problems if not repaired soon. We contacted two structural engineers but I accepted only one because he designed a supporting structure that was not a trellis type. In fact what he designed was simple, attractive, and reinforced the existing foundations without crowding our beautiful redwood high ceiling. It was time to call the San Mateo County building inspector to tell him what we were going to do to improve the building so we could operate it as a B&B. The restructuring plans, including the structural improvements, were drawn and given to the building department for approval.

Mostly what we planned to do was remove extraneous parts, repair what needed to be repaired, and make the house livable not only for guests but for us. We were determined to have very good living quarters for ourselves separated from the guest area.

The county inspector arrived and made his recommendations, none of which addressed the leaning walls. Structural deficiencies were apparently of little concern to the county. That was not right, we thought. Don raised the issue with the inspector and again showed him the structural drawings that our engineer, Mr. Schilling, had drawn for us. The county immediately put on its seal of approval and gave us the go ahead after we purchased the required building permit, which cost a pretty penny!

Goose & Turrets, a 100-year-old villa

I am regressing a bit about the purchase of what would become the
Goose and Turrets B&B because much of my progress to retirement hinged
on that small business. Anyway the Goose and Turrets Bed and Breakfast
was given birth soon after construction had been partially completed (for an
old house construction is never fully completed) in 1985. In fact we had our
first paying guests in 1986. Receiving the first payment was pure satisfaction
because it assured me the G&T could be a sustaining operation, which could
allow me to do some consulting without accepting the first job that came my
way.

Retirement from Bechtel

Anyway in January 1993 exactly 18 years after I was first hired, I retired
from Bechtel Corporation. My time with Bechtel covered many areas, several
projects, and numerous assignments. My travels were extensive and my
scope of operation reached beyond the horizon. My fingers touched oil shale,
conceived new cities, airports, air space, government interchanges, human
living conditions, ocean health, and the development of programs for eco-

nomic development with knowledge-based regional community creation. The last was my origination.

Intertwined in all those were interesting side issues that brought me face to face with presidents, princes, prime ministers, industry giants, physicists, and a score of other people of importance. My time at Bechtel was at times magnificent and at times saddened by internal stupidity and poor management appointments, decisions, and limited visions. The firm was characteristically a "job shop" where a person had to create and nurture projects that suited both his/her talents and the revenue requirements of a privately held and owned company. There is no doubt that I learned a great deal at Bechtel. My vision was enlarged enormously and my talents sharpened. I was able to test and use qualities that I had never expected to apply. My multidisciplinary background was well suited for a company such as Bechtel, especially if one had the agility to maneuver with dexterity through the vicissitudes and many of the ossified channels without cracking the supports that keep one sane. The key to working at Bechtel and to survive joyfully was to establish one's self as an indispensable part of the organization. In spite of being near termination twice because of conflicts with small-minded managers, I was able to survive and receive promotions. My interest in aviation was a path that allowed me to explore airports, cities, self-sustaining regions, and economic development in infrastructure. The engineering and construction firm learned to spell and support the idea of the "technopolis" program on a grand scale.

Bechtel grew from its core element of engineering and construction with a focus on turnkey contracts to project management, operation and maintenance, and then boldly to city development, regional economics, and knowledge revenue production, which was much more lucrative. Using the idea of infrastructure offered Bechtel more options for diversified work.

The Southern Cone

In February 1993 I scheduled a whole month for a holiday visit to the Southern Cone of South America. I had retired from Bechtel and therefore I was able to arrange my time without being concerned about projects, duties at the firm or calls for business travel. My intention was to return to Chile where I had been in 1989 for a week, visit Tierra del Fuego, and then board a de Havilland Twin Otter for the Falkland Islands before flying north to Buenos Aires, Mendoza, Cordova, and Iguazu Falls, Brazil.

The first stop was in the capital city of Santiago where we met our temporary guide Victor Hugo, who spoke not a word of French. Our intention was to spend a few days in the capital and take a one-day trip to Valparaiso, the old seaport on the Pacific Ocean. The time spent in this portion of central Chile was magnificent and I found Chile to be a country where things worked well, people were pleasant, and the wine and food were excellent.

My good friend, the attorney Zañartu Jose Luis Santa Maria, met us and whisked us to his home for a fantastic dinner with his wife and young adult children. We learned that Chilean society is not very fond of coffee; in fact they are not normally accustomed to drinking or serving coffee, especially fresh ground coffee. Dinner was served on fine china and silver and the main course was superb. When it was time for dessert a silver tray was brought by the butler and on it were the cups and accessories for what I assumed would be fresh coffee. But no! From a little silver container we witnessed the butler taking a spoon with flavored instant coffee, placing it in a china cup and then adding hot water. Oh, well; but for the lack of "real" coffee our dinner and company were exceptional.

A few days later we boarded a LAN Chile plane for the flight to the Cone of Tierra del Fuego and the city of Punta Arenas, our launching place for a trip to the Falklands and to Cordillera del Paine to see the Torres del Paine, and Grey Glacier.

We arrived in Punta Arenas and had an Avis Rental car awaiting us at the airport. The next day we headed north toward Torres del Paine on a road that had only the left side paved. Driving was an experience because traffic had to switch lanes when meeting on-coming vehicles. It was safe enough because all the drivers adopted a courteous approach.

Before entering Torres del Paine National Park, a UNESCO Heritage Preserve, we stopped in the small village of Puerto Natales because we needed to have a flat tire repaired and enjoyed lunch as we waited. Lunch cost less than $5.00 and the tire repair was $5.00, and we had to insist that we would not pay less because the mechanic asked for only one dollar. At any rate we filled the gas tank, explored the small village and headed for the park's entrance, which was approximately 10 miles away.

We had reservations at Lake Pehoé Hotel located in the middle of the lake. There was a small bridge and several wheelbarrows. The wheelbarrows were for the guests to load the luggage and wheel them to the hotel.

Torres de Paine

It was a wonderful lodging facility and the lake was beautiful. From our window we could see the three peaks of the Paine mountain chain.

The next day we drove the few miles then walked the remainder of the trek to Grey Glacier located at the base of the Torres de Paine. It was a crystal clear day. The glacier had a blue tint to it and the ice was almost translucent.

I broke off a piece and gave it to Emily to taste. I also took a piece. The ice was delicious, very cold, and had a slight taste of wild flowers. We spent the whole day at Grey Glacier to enjoy the blue ice and the view of the wonderful peaks. We were told that we were fortunate because the peaks had been blanketed in clouds for several weeks and several visitors had never seen them. In fact the American Consul General had come with his family from Santiago to see the Torres de Paine but the peaks had never been visible and his tour of duty was terminating with a reassignment to Gabon.

Our stay of a few days in Torres del Paine National Park was memorable and what I saw will be etched in my memory for as long as I live. The park is a natural event that is incomparably beautiful and when the Grey Glacier is added what can I say: I was overwhelmed and still am several years later.

We spent a couple of days in Punta Arenas to explore the small city and take a good and lasting look at the Strait of Magellan. We also met a family recommended by my friend Santa Maria. The family owned and operated an ovine business that specialized in top grade sheep, animals that were approved by both the United States and European Union for import. I was amazed that there were approximately 23 varieties of sheep and each was used for a particular purpose such as wool, meat, or breeding — most beyond my scope of knowledge. I found that I was not only a novice in knowledge but didn't even understand what the explanations really meant. On top of raising sheep, the family owned an abattoir and a processing plant that extracted every piece of the animal for commercial application, even the small pieces of bones, which one would have thought to be waste, but no, they produced buttons, hair combs, and even belt buckles and also other applications too numerous to list.

It was time to board a lovely old de Havilland Twin Otter at Punta Arenas International Airport for the five-hour flight to the Falkland Islands for a week's holiday.

Before boarding the de Havilland we were weighed and selected two seats in full view of the cockpit and between them and us was a ferry fuel tank to supply the aircraft for the long flight from Chile to the Falklands, first via the Straights of Magellan and then over the open waters of the South Atlantic. Once we reached cruising altitude we were served a lunch tray and a fruit juice drink. After three hours and 44 minutes we sighted the Western Island of the Falklands. We arrived in the vicinity of the capital, Stanley, at Mt. Pleasant International Airport after a four-hour and 52 minute flight, hence ahead of schedule. The aircraft was parked on the apron for about two hours to be loaded with freight for Chile and passengers and then to return to Punta Arenas. I enjoyed the flight and the conversation with the pilots who did the trip once a week every Friday. The only danger they were concerned about was venturing into Argentine airspace, which was forbidden for flights serving the British possession. On the flight over the Straights of Magellan the pilots had to stay on the Chilean side and not intrude by crossing on the Argentine side; radar operators in Argentina were always tracking outgoing and incoming flights.

I had been looking forward to visiting these remote islands, islands that were the reason for a war between Britain and Argentina. This war had been primarily between Iron Lady Thatcher, prime minister of Great Britain and the dictator generals of Argentina. The Kelpers, as the islanders call themselves, were in no way willing to be part of Argentina, neighbors they would willingly be, but not Argentines! This was a war for Argentina that was lost before it started. In addition what really defeated the Argentine Navy was the entanglement of their ships' screws in the giant kelp that grows all around the islands. It takes a very knowledgeable sailor to avoid the kelp and to know where access to ports are possible. Moreover, because the Falklands are geologically akin to Africa, South American sailors were unaware of how the island land mass differs from that of Argentina. The British Navy had inside information from the Kelpers, information that was not available to the Argentine Navy or on their nautical charts. It was similar to the lack of geological knowledge that was unavailable to the Nazi military during their invasion of Russia because Stalin had specific geographical information removed or falsified years before the war started as a precaution against any attempt by Europeans to repeat the Napoleonic venture. What the Argentine Navy did not have was information about the long strands of kelp that were in places 10 centimeters wide and four centimeters thick and many miles long. This kelp became entangled in the ships' screws, which consequently seized the engines.

I enjoyed my stay in the Falklands, my acquaintance with the Cathedral Canon, the residents of Stanley, and the managing family on Sea Lion Island situated off the coast of the Eastern Island and protected as a breeding place for the island's premier sheep stock. Having sheep on the islands did not preclude penguins, seals, and a rich variety of birds from residing there also. We stayed on Sea Lion Island for four days but wished it had been possible to stay longer. Visiting the Falklands, one is either able to come for two hours or in weekly increments. Besides the weekly flights from Chile's Punta Arenas, other access was possible from London via Ascension Islands with a layover; this flight was scheduled twice a month on a British Airlines Lockheed L-1011. We arrived on a Friday and departed on the following Friday — too short a visit admittedly but better than none.

My short visit to the Falklands was a memorable event on my list of travels. Many years ago, while serving in the US Air Force, I had the opportunity to visit the area by air and to execute a short mission. I had been transported on a British aircraft carrier to the island of South Georgia.

Many years later when I returned to the Falklands my South Georgia experience added to my enjoyment and I was able to appreciate the beauty of this, the Eastern Island. I have never set foot on the Western Island and viewed it only when I arrived and departed.

The Falklands are mostly dependent on sheep rearing, a few herds of cattle for local consumption and dairy products. There are several fishing ventures but the catch is mostly for export with some retained just for the local Kelpers. I stayed in Stanley, the capital and principal business and administrative city. Stanley is a community of approximately 2,000 Kelpers and a few transient sailors, visitors, and military personnel who reside mostly near the International airport at Mt. Pleasant Base, about 30 minutes by car from the capital.

I had the opportunity to meet the Anglican Cathedral Canon and was invited to address the congregation scattered around the islands on radio on my first Sunday evening.

We arrived in Stanley on a Friday afternoon and after obtaining our room at Emma's B&B we strolled around the city first to introduce myself to the Cathedral staff and its Resident Canon. That night we made reservations for dinner at the Upland Goose Hotel and we ordered a local South Atlantic fish.

It was excellent and the ale was flown in from the UK. After dinner we walked to the end of the harbor jetty where we enjoyed both the cool breeze and the extended light of the southern sky. Birds were having a great time swooping in and out and also landing on our heads, shoulders or buzzing us. It was a lovely evening. Back at Emma's we sat on her veranda and made ourselves tea.

The next morning, Saturday, we walked to the jetty again but the wind was blowing hard and I learned later that it had been steady at a speed of 55 miles per hour. When we walked into the wind we could easily lean forward almost to a 45 degree angle without falling. It was an experience that will be hard to forget.

It was interesting to see striated caracaras, also known as Johnny Rooks; those large birds brave the strong wind without fear or concern. The striated caracara is primarily a scavenger feeding on carrion, offal and small invertebrates, and it will also prey on weak or injured creatures, such as young seabirds and newborn lambs.

We also had the opportunity to visit Sea Lion Island, an island reserved for breeding sheep. We stayed at a lovely B&B and were given a Land Rover tour of the island. The next day we walked around the island on our own. A most interesting aspect of visiting the Falklands, and especially Sea Lion Island, was the discovery that birds are not shy and certainly not afraid of human beings. Birds will perch on one's head, shoulders or hand just when waving, reaching, or pointing. At first it was a little disconcerting to have a bird alight on your head when talking with another person. On one occasion I was sitting and reading on the balcony of the B&B when a bird perched on my book and just looked at me; our encounter lasted perhaps as much as 15 minutes.

I became fascinated with the Rock Hopper penguins. These small birds are dedicated to living on sheer cliffs in large groups congregating noisily. To feed they descend to the ocean at least twice a day. After feeding they return by climbing up the cliff, jumping from rock to rock until they reach their established place. The sight of them struggling up and down these sheer cliffs and managing the rocks with agility, dexterity, and energy is not only impressive but also fascinating.

Watching these little creatures struggle on a regular basis to sustain life is a reminder that most of us don't work that hard to survive. It is the sheer effort that the rock hoppers exert for surviving that humbled me. Overcoming danger is one aspect of their living condition, then searching and hunting for food and also avoiding predators makes for a most curious evolutionary circumstance for these Antarctic creatures. No exaggeration implied if I admit that I watched them for a long period and then returned at a later time to watch them again.

Sea Lion Island is a breeding reserve principally for prime sheep, producers of wool and not meat. Several thousand sheep populate the island and are cared for by the managers of the B&B, several dogs, and two men and their families. It is a magnificent enterprise that supplies prime sheep wool to the British Commonwealth, the European Union, the United States, Canada, and Finland. Across the separation to the Southern Cone, another reserve is active for sheep, but these are primarily for meat consumption and not much wool. It is interesting that the sheep of the Punta Arenas have a 99.5% usage not only for meat, but also for such items as leather, buttons, and other commercial products.

Other interesting animals on Sea Lion Island were Macaroni Penguins and Upland Geese. These geese are part of the shelduck subfamily and are quite common on the Falklands. Their plumage is a bit unkempt looking to the observer but the geese are lovely, friendly, and live in groups of six to a dozen and are mostly white with some grey feathers.

Of course Sea Lion Island is also the home of seals, sea lions, and a large variety of land birds. There was a colony of breeding Adelie penguins on the eastern side of the island and we could hear their voices, similar to baying donkeys, from far away. We approached them without threatening them, but we managed to disturb them a little. The main concern of the penguins was to discourage the marauding pomarine skuas, birds of prey that steal the eggs of Adelie for food.

Our center of operation in Stanley was Emma's B&B. This was a comfortable place, quite hospitably managed, but sparse in terms of amenities in our room, although we did have a shower and plenty of hot water when we turned on the water heater. The breakfast was a standard British menu of eggs, sausage or bacon, and potatoes accompanied by juice and canned fruit. Fresh fruit is not available all the time on the Falkland Islands but a shipment of fresh fruits and vegetables comes weekly from Chile, on the same flight that brings passengers from Punta Arenas.

Why did I want to go to the Falkland Islands? I had never been there and that was sufficient reason to motivate me to make arrangements for a visit. I regret, however, that I only had one week, was limited to Stanley and the Eastern Island, but I did have a few days on Sea Lion Island, the preserve for breeding pure strains of sheep. I also had the opportunity to do some thinking about the future, now that I had retired from Bechtel and was anticipating making new decisions for new plans. Apart from the operation of the B&B, which gave me a platform for some income (not much, but enough to take the edge off the thought of poverty), I was considering entering the field of consultancy. But what was I to offer clients as a consultant? I really did not want to be identified with airports, but aviation was still interesting to me. My interest was steering me to city development and particularly to regional economic development touching the technopolis program as it affected strategic communities or potentially strategic communities. Hence, time on the Falkland was exactly what I needed for some clear thinking.

While in the Falklands I also considered Punta Arenas as a possible venue for development. Punta Arenas was the principal city of Terra de Fuego; it had an international airport and a thriving commercial community that included a dynamic ovine industry. In addition, Punta Arenas had a small and struggling university that offered potential for reducing the region's brain drain. My attorney friend in Santiago had given me a connection in Punta Arenas, which I expected to explore. Chile also offered a stable environment for something like a technopolis program to emerge and possibly blossom.

There was something beyond my superficial comprehension that made me find Chile attractive in many ways. Chile is a nation that is attempting to emerge with a certain level of coherency. Historically it has survived through some extraordinarily stupid elements of its evolution and these have run the gamut of occupation by foreign troops, dictatorships of one type or another, legitimate and illegitimate administrations, and democratic rule — both weak and strong at times. Today, Chile is on the road to a better future. It has applied a few economic principles that appear to produce a more effective system of governance. It has stopped relying solely on the exportation of minerals and focused on production of agriculture, of wines, of high technology, and of education. The attempt, which seems to be working, is to reduce the poverty and to remove the traps that produce the poor class. Chile is fortunate that it has very little racial tension even though it has a large immigrant population. Expatriates who continue to come to Chile for work projects, for the prospects of a good future, for the way the country is a welcoming venue, often decide to remain as adopted citizens even when they continue to maintain dual citizenship.

For example, the American wealthy-businessman-turned-environmentalist Douglas Tompkins negotiated with the Chilean government to create a national wilderness public park on his property. The park has been named Pumalin Park, and is situated in south central Chile, near the city of Puerto Montt. This is one example of how foreigners often are attached to Chile. Other American, Yugoslavs, British, French, and Canadians have come to Chile and given of themselves in many ways — a few for greed but very many for altruistic reasons.

In a sense this approach also reflects on some aspects of my reasoning for going to Chile. I first visited Chile in March 1989 a few months after the plebiscite on October 5, 1988 when General Pinochet was denied a second eight-year term as president. There was a spirit of freedom and hope mixed with an urge to develop the country's economy, to reduce poverty, to create a new commercial middle class, and to clean up the image of Chile in the eyes of the world. Much talk was heard about the election of a new president and the majority of members of a two-chamber congress anticipated for December 14, 1989. General Pinochet's dictatorship was examined and much of his cruelty was being considered by the judicial system. Yet there was some understanding that the baby needed to be separated from the dirty bath water. Pinochet had moved Chile on a good path of commercially developed industrial growth and agricultural expansion. He had strengthened both the secular and parochial educational institutions and had instilled a great focus on science, business, and economics. When I arrived to do some work on the aviation and airport sectors, it was immediately obvious that work and the results thereof were serious to America: people went to work and worked for a full allotted day of the normal 8-5; lunches were of one hour, siesta was no longer the common practice, and the infrastructure and communication operated very well. Needless to say I was surprised.

Unlike my experience in other countries of South America I met with several top CEOs involved with agriculture, aviation, legal firms, and technology. I was especially impressed with the representatives from American Airlines and the CEO of LAN Chile when they negotiated code-sharing, funding, and proposed goals for the next decade. Today LAN Chile is the premier airline of South America and has a rating placing among the top three of the world. I mention this particular example because it reflects on the general approach that Chile has adopted in several areas and business endeavors.

After listing a few of the interesting facets of Chile that I've encountered I might add that I find the Chileans a people with a good sense of humor, a large margin of honesty, and several qualities that are delightful and are especially noticeable when they greet you and share their charm, warmth, and hospitality. One feels immediately that one is a stranger only for a moment!

At the first opportunity I will return to Chile to resume some of the projects that I believe need to be accomplished.

Cruising on the Mississippi *Delta Queen*

The reader will recall that I retired from Bechtel in 1993 and soon took time off with Emily to visit Chile. When we returned from Chile we plunged into making the Goose and Turrets productive. I also attempted to make GT

Ideas valuable as a consulting entity. Both tasks were managed and kept me busy.

Once retirement was in effect, in the spring of 1994 we decided to take a cruise on the Mississippi *Delta Queen*, which traveled from New Orleans to Memphis. It was to be a seven-day cruise and it was delightful, peaceful, and exciting because the river had received major floodwaters from Ohio, Missouri, Illinois, and from the Southern states bordering it. The normal banks were not visible because the river had widened so much that new edges had emerged.

Normally I avoid cruises and guided tours, but a week's cruise on the Mississippi in the springtime was something that I had wanted to do. The first opportunity to plan a trip was for Chile and the second opportunity presented to me when I could schedule a cruise, put down a deposit, and set aside dates without fearing that Bechtel would send me on some wild-goose chase. Because the cruise was for seven days, I added several days to visit New Orleans and several other days to visit friends in Memphis, Nashville, Knoxville, and Copperhill. I was determined to act and live like a retiree before I started searching for consultancies.

We made arrangements and invited Malcolm and Katie Usrey to join us in New Orleans for the first part of the holiday. We also placed reservations to have dinner at K-Paul's, the restaurant owned and operated by Paul Prudhomme, the great chef — great in talent and size. Breakfast was of course scheduled at Commander's Palace and morning coffee and beignés for other days was at the Grand Marché. One day we drove to Venice, situated at the mouth of the Mississippi River, to experience the open Gulf of Mexico as the river empties into it. Instead of driving on the highway, we found that we could drive on the levee and thus avoid the traffic and see more of the river. At the suggestion of one of the dredging crew members, about halfway to Venice we stopped at Tom's restaurant where I enjoyed several oysters au naturel. On the return trip I stopped again at Tom's and again enjoyed more oysters. I have no bottom when it comes to fresh, uncooked oysters!

The next day or the one after, we decided to visit the Tabasco producers because Malcolm was a great aficionado of the hot sauce, so much so that he carried a pouch with a small bottle in it to douse his food in the event that the restaurant did not provide it. We were off to Avery Island by way of the Bayou following a stream where turtles sunning themselves on logs kept flipping into the water as we drove by. Avery Island, the home of the McIlhenny Company, is a salt dome and on it stands the legendary Tabasco hot sauce producer.

We spent the day touring the factory, smelling the strong peppery scent of the tabasco peppers cooking in large vats. The peppers are grown mostly in Mexico where they originated. Outside the plant on the property were gardens with wild birds, alligators, and both tended and wild native flowers. The day was good and special and the weather was delightful.

When we left Avery Island we drove towards Baton Rouge to connect to the highway that would return us to New Orleans. It was time for dinner. We found an interesting restaurant that specialized in Bayou fare. The restaurant also had a dance floor and an orchestra that played Zydeco music.

Zydeco (French: "les haricots" or "le zaricot", English: "green beans" or "snap beans") is a form of American roots or folk music. It evolved in southwest Louisiana in the early 19th century from forms of Louisiana Creole music. The rural Creoles of southwest Louisiana and southeast Texas still sing in Creole French with the pronunciation corrupted. The Creoles residing in the Bayou were mostly small time farmers who cultivated food for cooking such as a wide variety of beans, onions, rice, tomatoes, cucumbers, peppers, and other vegetables that enriched their menus.

At any rate the food and the music were excellent. On the dance floor there were many couples dancing to the Zydeco music. There was one gentleman who was an extraordinary dancer and his movements were the focus of all eyes because he was a first rate performer but certainly not a professional one although he could have been. The dancing, the music, and the food enthralled me. It was a great evening and one to be remembered.

Malcolm and Katie left to return to Clemson the next day or the day after and Emily and I were invited to have lunch at the home of Ken and Ann Hamilton, who lived across Lake Pontchartrain near Covington, Louisiana. We had met the Hamiltons several times because Ann was a regular guest at the B&B before she married Ken. As expected lunch was had in a small restaurant located on the edge of the lake that specialized in local fare. I succumbed to oysters, ceviche and grilled vegetables doused in a mustard sauce. Time allotted for lunch was short because we had to return the rental automobile and then head to the dock to board the *Delta Queen* for the cruise up the river to Memphis.

Mississippi *Delta Queen*

After years of hoping to take the Mississippi cruise aboard the old Sacramento River cruiser the *Delta Queen*, Emily was able to secure reservations. The cruise would be a whole week on the Mississippi River. On board I learned that this old classic stern paddle wheeler was towed from Sacramento through the Panama Canal to New Orleans to work as a tour boat on the Mississippi River. It had been beautifully restored and its crew of 100 served 80 passengers. It was a first class experience, which will be hard to forget.

The first night of our boarding we met the master of the vessel who informed us that there were two captains manning the boat and one master supervising them and the whole ship's operation. Each captain worked a six-hour shift and must know almost every foot of the riverbank. This knowledge is imperative especially when the river is flowing after major rains. The master of the *Delta Queen* was Captain Clarke "Doc" Hawley who began his career as the musician who played the ship's calliope, the steam organ located on the stern of the *Queen*. Doc worked and studied his way from organ player to master of this historical stern paddle wheel riverboat.

At the introduction, the master showed us some pictures of historic boats and major occasions that made this stern paddle wheeler famous; it had been the winner of races between riverboats several times and the master was known for his talent for winning races.

We became friendly with the master and discussed many elements of the physics of tugboat operation, especially in the pushing mode.

Many great sessions with the master informed our trip and in the process we became his favorite passengers and soon we found ourselves regularly dining at his table. This experience was a treat because the conversation was exciting, informative, and the company excellent. Chatting with the master added to the enjoyment of the cruise.

The Mississippi River had crested above its normal bank because of great rains in the Ohio Valley. We could not see the bank and both captains were working from memory because practically all the markers were displaced or under the water. At night the boat's powerful sidelights were lit to ascertain that no floating objects were in its path and that it remained in the deep portion of the river channel.

It was a marvelous cruise and I loved every moment of it. Our cabin was compact but comfortable and our cabin attendant, Williams, was most attentive. The food on board was excellent and plentiful; in fact more was served than we could reasonably and wisely consume. The only issue that I encountered was the lack of 120/240-volt outlets in the public areas to operate the computer, but I could, and did, use the battery pack and recharged them in our cabin, where there was not a place for a desk. I worked mostly in the lounge, on deck, in the pilothouse, or in the library. The cruise was uneventful except for the rushing river, and we were moving against the current. One night we were met by another barge to transfer more drinking water for us. In the darkness of the night and with the fast moving flow of the river we were presented with a fantastic spectacle and a bit of good river maneuvering.

Upon our arrival to Memphis after seven days on the *Delta Queen* the boat could not tie at its regular dock, so the master opted to tie to a firm tree at the foot of the Cotton Exchange. Dr. Rebecca Moore Jernigan kindly met us as we landed. Becky has been a friend of some sixty years and I had been looking forward to seeing her again in Memphis, the city were I had started my clergy journey in 1964 at St. Mary's Cathedral.

The Memphis on the Mississippi River

Memphis has pleasant weather in the spring. My schedule was to spend a few days in the city, then drive to Nashville and on to Knoxville. The plan was to return to Memphis and catch a flight to San Francisco ten days hence.

I wanted to visit St. Mary's Cathedral, the place where I did my diaconate and had my first priestly celebration of the Eucharist. I also wanted to visit an old and dear friend, the Rev. Robert Watson who had served as an assistant at the cathedral and who had been a chaplain to the medical students at the University of Tennessee Medical School.

Bob had also been an active actor in my play reading and acting group. He had played the interesting part of the minister in *The Scarlet Letter,* and Becky had played the part of Tituba, the young black woman who accented the issue of forgiveness. As a native of Mississippi and a fine actress and playwright, Becky pulled off a great performance. Bob was excellent and managed to convey the austere role of the adulterer, who was both aware of the charges leveled against him and knew well that his affair with the woman he loved and who was branded with the letter "A" was not a lighthearted episode. I'm sorry to say that I cannot recall the names of the other actors and readers but I can still see them in my mind's eye. The play was both read and subsequently acted before a large audience.

On Sunday afternoon after the Eucharist at St. Mary's and lunch at the old Camel restaurant, which was under new management, we went to Robert Watson's house to pay a visit. Bob's wife was sitting quietly in a sofa chair in the adjoining room. We were informed that she had Alzheimer's and was unable to participate in any conversation. The degeneration of her mental capabilities had been sudden and she was not expected to last the year. Bob was still as fit as a well-tuned fiddle and served at Calvary Church, the largest parish in Memphis, and taught two courses in ethics at Memphis State University, now part of the University of Tennessee.

Bob Watson received us with warmth and said that I was an addition not only to the Church but also to civilization. That was very kind of him to say. I've often thought that Bob was a fine human being and a good friend and guide, especially for my early years in holy orders. Bob is the living symbol of kindness and wisdom. I remember his adult Sunday classes as being packed with people excited to listen to him explore a theological point, a philosophical axiom, or a social condition. I remembered that 1964 was the year when civil rights and integration were the topics discussed. We were in

Memphis, Tennessee. The population of the city was buzzing with issues that dealt with racism. Bob had been run out of town when he was rector of a major parish in Charleston, South Carolina because he allowed "negroes" as members of the congregation and had allowed a few to seek positions on the vestry. There was no place for him in Memphis except as an assistant priest. Dean Dimmick was delighted to have Bob on the staff of the Cathedral. I was honored to have him as a mentor and a friend.

We spent almost two hours chatting with Bob. His wife, sitting in the next room on a sofa with her back to us, never moved and apparently was neither watching television nor reading a book. She just sat in total silence. Bob explained his wife's condition but indicated that there was little that could be done. He expected that the end would be sooner rather than later. I was informed that she died in 1995.

Seeing Bob Watson brought me back to my first years in the Diocese of Tennessee as a neophyte deacon. I was academically wise but lost in the arena of pastoral care and priestly functions. I survived and a great deal of the credit for my survival goes to Bob. After happily reconnecting with this good man we left his home with my head full of resurrected memories. As a young deacon I was overwhelmed by the tasks given to me, by the sensitive relationships that were mine to nurture, and by my personal condition as husband, father, and churchman.

The next day after breakfast and bidding adieu to Becky, we drove to Nashville to visit several of Emily's friends, many of whom were her mother's longtime friends. We were invited to stay with Adele Smith, a longtime friend of Emily's parents. I enjoyed going to Nashville and renewing the conversations that had been suspended since the last time I visited that city. On this occasion the next day, I left Emily to tend to her "old ladies" and pushed on to Knoxville to see Bishop Bill Sanders and to meet with Sandy and Buddy Finch, friends from my Copper Basin days. I was to have lunch with Bill Sanders, whose wife was terminally ill with cancer. The Finches were driving from Blue Ridge, Georgia and were spending the night in Knoxville so that we could have dinner together. I would be in Knoxville just overnight and expected to return to Nashville the next day to visit more friends.

Because I attended the University of Tennessee in Knoxville and also worked in that state, and because Emily was from Nashville and had attended Vanderbilt University, a visit to Tennessee was never simple, quickly accomplished, and without making several visits to see friends. We had a visit with Uncle Craig and his family. Craig, also a pilot, was Emily's last living uncle and a charming person of whom I was quite fond. We had to pay a visit to Ann Hill and I needed to have a wee Scotch with her — that was a tradition. At any rate we had several people we were scheduled to visit and I enjoyed every one of them.

Ann was a great supporter of the children's theater, which she mainly funded and supported. The Nashville Children's Theater was an exceptional institution, which was the envy of other cities. Ann had consulted with some of the major theater directors and professors of drama in the country and had received the support of the theater unit from the University of Tennessee, a major university dramatic department. The head of the department, Paul Soper, and the lead director, Fred Fields, had both given much to help Ann and to make certain that the Children's Theater developed as a major dramatic institution for children and potential directors of such theater. There were classes for children and also classes to teach directing. The latter was recognized by the academic community as being of university quality; university credits were awarded towards degrees in theater arts.

Ann was also a painter of sorts. Her paintings were of mediocre quality but her passion was impressive. I have over the years received many of her watercolors and treated her kindly for sending them to me. In truth, however, I was never prone to hang them for my guests to see. Ann was a most talented person, but watercolors were not part of what she did well. She was a fine collector of art from sculptures to masks, to wooden fashioned toys, and etchings — all of which I thoroughly appreciated and enjoyed. When I visited Ann it was our custom to have a short Scotch in the afternoon. The conversation covered her travels, her work, her health, and the future of art. We never discussed politics because she was always on the opposite side of mine. We both knew that we did not agree politically so we avoided the subject. Nevertheless, we enjoyed each other's company. Currently, Ann is in an assisted living institution because she cannot care for herself beyond bathing, reading, and pouring her evening short Scotch. Arthritis has reduced the use of her hands but she still does minimal work with water coloring, especially for Christmas cards. Ann is one of my few Republican acquaintances that I like and admire very much.

After Nashville we drove to Memphis to return the rental car and catch the flight to San Francisco. We had been away for almost a month and it was time to return to the B&B, our nest, relieve our inn-sitters, and hope that the B&B had earned enough income to not only pay part of the expenses but to pay our sitters. If I remember correctly, the B&B had done quite well.

Canadian Holiday and Retracing My Arrival

For the next 12 months I concentrated on working to make the B&B earn income. The economy in Silicon Valley was churning well, California was financially solvent, and the Clinton Administration was reducing the nation's deficit and debt. All this meant that the Goose and Turrets was enjoying occupancy of more than 65 percent, way more than I wished to work for. I was looking for another adventure.

A thought occurred that Canada would be a good place for a long holiday and that I could introduce Emily to where I had started in the New World. I had entered the United States from Canada but had not returned to it since 1955, at least not for a holiday in Nova Scotia. I had visited with the US Air Force Labrador, the Northern-Western Territory, Yukon, Newfoundland, and, when I first arrived in 1950, Nova Scotia. I suggested to Emily that I wanted to return to Hubbards, Halifax, and tour the Maritime Province and New Brunswick, especially the Bay of Fundy to see firsthand the incoming giant tide.

My plan was to fly to Boston and drive north across the United States-Canadian international border to Halifax and then search for the old road to Hubbards and Butterfly Lake. Emily began to look into the details of the trip and often consulted with me. She finally came up with a good plan, which included a flight to Boston, a drive to Bar Harbor, Maine and then a six-hour ferry ride to Yarmouth, Nova Scotia, Canada. We would explore Nova Scotia, stay in Hubbard for several days then drive across the peninsula to St. John's, New Brunswick. After a few days of local exploration we would drive to Dorchester and into the small hamlet of Middleton to find the best place to view the tide's approach. Emily had gotten information on when high tide was known to be and from St. John we would obtain further details. Arrangements were made for the flight and for the ferry. We had added a week on Grand Manan Island to spend time at North Head, the main harbor and largest village, staying with an Elderhostel group in the main hotel. We planned after Grand Manan to cross into the United States on the International Bridge linking Calais, Maine and St. Stephen, New Brunswick over the St. Croix River separating Canada from the United States, and then to visit Campobello Island, Canada, President F.D. Roosevelt's home.

I was looking forward to the trip, the holiday, and revisiting old haunts in Canada. My brain was digging into some old thoughts and bringing them up to the surface. I was puzzling at how my fortune had altered my plans as a young man and placed me in the United States of America. Had that not happened, and it was not my plan as I indicated earlier, I would have become Canadian instead of American, possibly becoming entangled with Patsy Hagen. Indeed: L'homme propose et Dieu dispose!

The holiday was scheduled for the month of October 1995. We had hired inn-sitters to care for the B&B while we were away and because the economy was still in good order we expected to have enough income to pay for the trip, the inn-sitters, and to bank a small profit. These were good times.

An Unexpected Incident

Before our Canadian excursion, I was scheduled to take my aircraft to Auburn, less than 150 miles from Hayward, to have one of the gyroscopes checked or replaced and I wanted to do that before the trip. My neighbor Martin Sobelman, who had recently earned his pilot's ticket, was interested in going with me. Would I allow his daughter to join us? Emily's grandson, Russell, was also visiting with his parents in Oakland and his mother Ashley asked me if I would take him too. I was expecting good weather and a fine flight to the foothills of California. The instrument repair station was ready and awaiting my arrival. We took off from Hayward mid-morning and planned to have lunch in Auburn at the airport.

After lunch we took a little walk on the airport to show the kids the parked airplanes and a couple that took off. There were several old and interesting aircraft on the ramp that fascinated the children and the adults. The kids were happy and my new instrument was installed and operating very well. It was time to depart. With preflight completed we took off from Auburn Airport. Auburn is approximately 1600 feet above sea level and just a few miles east of Sacramento. Soon after takeoff I noticed that I could not adjust my constant speed propeller. I reduced the engine's rotation per minute (rpm) and reduced the fuel flow to reduce the speed. I could not adjust the propeller. Recognizing that I could incur a run-away propeller I called Sacramento traffic control to advise them of my problem.

Sac Approach (ATR): "04R are you declaring an emergency?"

N4004R: "Negative at this time. I'll check the prop again."

ATR: "Advise option."

N4004R: "Sac Approach please clear me for Executive Airport direct."

Sac Approach: "04R cleared for Runway 2-Zero. Negative contact Tower."

Runway 20 is 150 feet wide and 5503 feet long. It was located dead ahead from the nose of the aircraft. I asked Martin to locate a maintenance shop from my California Pilot Guide. The landing was one of the best I'd ever made. I didn't want to shake the engine in the event that something was broken loose. I taxied to Patterson Aviation and shut down. We were all safe on the ground. I walked to Patterson and told the chief maintenance person my problem. He suggested we do a restart but I was reluctant to shake the engine any more. "Well, what are my alternatives?" I asked.

He turned me over to Erick, the chief aircraft inspector (AI). I had approximately 1870 hours on the engine and it was due for rebuilding (if the aircraft is leased or used commercially, which it is not) at 2000 hours (TBO/time before overhaul). Although 04R was not on lease I followed the rule. With some reluctance I agreed to a restart, carefully avoiding high revolution. The propeller was still inoperative.

After checking my logs and doing some figuring Erick gave me two options. Tearing down the current engine and searching for the problem; that would cost approximately $9,000 plus repairing what was broken. The other option was for a rebuilt engine with zero-time; that would cost approximately $18,000 plus whatever else I wanted done while the engine was removed.

"May I call my wife?" I asked. He handed me the telephone. I called Emily and explained the problem and my choice. Emily, also a pilot, immediately said to replace the engine with a zero-time rebuilt one.

"Erick," I said, "Let's go with a zero-time rebuilt engine."

He looked at me and said, "Your wife said OK to the rebuilt engine?" He was puzzled because his experience told him that wives were never willing to pay that much for a repair.

I added quickly, "She is also a pilot."

I instructed Erick to replace the engine mounts, repair the exhaust system, add a quick-drain oil valve, and let me know if the crankshaft was in good condition. If the latter was in good condition the engine rebuilder gave a $4,000 rebate!

I called for a rental car and loaded everybody for the return trip home via Oakland to deposit Russell with his parents. The children had been very good and the excitement entertained them sufficiently that I heard no complaints. Martin informed me that he had learned something about handling potential emergencies. Russell was returned to his parents in time to attend a game at the Oakland Coliseum. I drove Martin and his daughter back to Montara. Home was good after an exciting day and an assurance that when an emergency surfaced I had the good sense to manage it properly and without an iota of panic. Of course this had not been a major emergency but it was a good trial that demanded much of the pilot-in-command, especially when carrying a precious cargo of children. I did well and inside I was a bit proud of how I'd reacted. The mechanic Erik commended me for being a calm, clear, and safe pilot in what could have been a major emergency with a runaway propeller, or worse, a seized engine.

A few days later Erick called to inform me that the teardown firm in Boca Raton, Florida had found that a small shaft from the propeller governor had broken and the three-inch piece had lodged itself merely a few inches from the crankshaft. Had it fallen into the crankshaft while the engine was running it would have demolished it. A seized engine is no fun in a flying aircraft! Erick also informed me that the crankshaft was in good shape and my rebate would be sent to him. I asked if the rebate covered the cost of what I'd asked Patterson to do in addition to the engine and I was assured that it would. At any rate when the aircraft was returned the total bill was approximately $20,000. In a sense, that small three-inch steel rod cost me a whole bunch of money.

Resuming the Canadian Excursion

In my scheme of what retirement was all about, I was happy to be able to include another vacation on my calendar. The B&B was doing well, I had some small consulting tasks, and we managed our finances safely.

Early in October 1995 we left for Boston on American Airlines. Arriving when it was dark and after obtaining our rental car we drove away from the Boston Big Dig (the road construction that had been going on for years) to Lynn, an old shoe manufacturing town on the Atlantic and not too far from the New Hampshire state line. The bed and breakfast was splendid and the hostess directed us to a small but good fish restaurant not too far from where we were lodging. It was a pleasant walk in the dark and the weather was balmy and fresh, filled with sea scent: the smell of iodine mixed with salt mist and kelp. The restaurant did not have any lobsters so my meal was grilled scrod, the fish of the day, which can be anything from cod, haddock, to whatever is fished that day. It was excellent.

After a restful night and a good breakfast we headed for Maine and for Bar Harbor. Crossing New Hampshire took just a few minutes, then we entered the state of Maine and soon we were in Kennebunkport. We drove to the door of Tom's of Maine, the Harvard Divinity Graduate who is an environmental toothpaste manufacturer, for a visit. The tour was light and not extensive but we enjoyed conversations with several people who had worked for the firm since its beginning. We were then directed to a local bookstore where we found copies of Tom's book, which tells about the history and the time Tom spent at Harvard Divinity School. Tom's purpose was to discover and learn how to be humane, considerate, environmentally respectful, and God-centered but without being overly "religious" in the pejorative sense. Tom wanted to be a good person and have a business that reflected the best of human beings. He had achieved much of what he was aiming for and is still working at it.

After the bookstore, and of course we purchased Tom's book, we headed to the local fish restaurant to have our first Maine lobsters. Maine lobster is a treat especially when the restaurant cooks it in ocean water. I like my one-pound lobster without butter or any seasoning, merely accompanied by fried Julienne potatoes and local ale at room temperature. Much to Emily's surprise I ordered two lobsters and left only empty shells and had a happy tummy.

Kennebunkport has been bustling with commerce since the 1800s when many ships were built there and sent to sea from its harbor. Historically, Kennebunkport has been very important in the shipping industry of Maine. Folks settling this area were bound to the sea, and even today the seafaring culture is still much in evidence. It is still a busy fishing port and a major resort community. People from New England come to Kennebunkport to spend the summer and many purchase houses on the waterfront; in fact President George H. Bush has a house with a dock on the bay. We walked through town and visited many of the shops, the vacation houses, and the harbor. It was time, however, for us to head north to Bar Harbor and to our bed and breakfast. We expected the drive to be about 45 minutes following the coast.

It was an easy drive and traffic was light. We found the B&B where we were booked and settled in our room after unloading and parking the Thunderbird, our Avis Rental. A short distance from the B&B we found a teashop with a good table overlooking Acadia National Park, which we planned to visit the next day. It was just past three o'clock in the afternoon so we decided to look over the town. Not too far from the teashop we saw the Jackson Laboratory and a welcoming sign. We entered the lobby and noticed several glass cages with white mice engaged in various activities. An attendant approached and asked if we were interested in a short lecture and a video; both would give us an overview of the Jackson Lab.

In the auditorium the lecturer was one of the scientists who was engaged in oncology research and had recently been awarded the Nobel Prize in medicine. After questions and answers we were invited to view the video, which described the history of the Lab, its goal in research, and the importance of the mice collection and what was involved in maintaining their mice-breeding program. The Jackson Lab was an extraordinary and complex research institution that contributed an enormous wealth of information to science, especially to the discipline of medicine. I left the Lab convinced that because of its value to science it needed funding and although I was not wealthy I could contribute a small amount regularly.

We returned to the B&B and considered our options for dinner. My thoughts were focused on the Jackson Lab and the research that was being accomplished within its walls. I decided that the next day, after our visit to Acadia National Park, I would return to the Jackson Lab to obtain more information about what it was pursuing and its goals.

The day at Acadia National Park was marvelous and the weather was just as good for an out-of-door event. We enjoyed many walks, many paths, many encounters with history, and a fine lunch at the Park restaurant. I climbed the only hill in the Park, which is no higher than 550 feet and acts as a promontory overlooking the Atlantic Ocean.

At three o' clock in the afternoon we walked over to the Jackson Laboratory and were soon met by one of the knowledgeable guides. I asked about the lab's pursuits and goals. At the moment many researchers were involved with cancer and coronary research as they were affected by genetic combination. The Lab was focusing on mouse genome information and this was grounded on the mouse Phenome database. The researchers at the Lab have made enormous advances in Isogenic strains (inbred strains and F1 hybrids) that have substantially contributed to biomedical research. Needless to say, I

was fascinated even if I did not understand much nor absorb the specific details that were presented to me.

My head was filled with information and hope. It was obvious that the
Lab, through its research with mice, its curricula for post-doctorate programs,
and its influence on science, was offering a great service to mankind. Stated
briefly, the Lab discovers the genetic basis for preventing, treating and curing
human disease, and enables research and education for the global biomedical
community. The Lab directs its attention to six major areas employing 38
principal researchers:

- Cancers: brain, leukemia, lung, lymphoma, mammary, cancer initia-
  tion and progression; cancer detection and therapies
- Computational biology and Bioinformatics: mouse genome informatics, comparative genomics
- Developmental and reproductive biology: birth defects, Down syn-
  drome, sex determination, aging, osteoporosis
- Immunology: HIV-AIDS, anemia, autoimmunity, immune system
  disorders, lupus, tissue transplant rejection
- Metabolic diseases: atherosclerosis, diabetes, gallstones, hyperten-
  sion, obesity
- Neurobiology: blindness, cerebellar disorders, deafness, epilepsy,
  glaucoma, macular degeneration, neurodegenerative diseases

Based on the following resources that include this information:

- JAX® Mice have been shipped to approximately 19,000 investigators
  in more than 900 institutions, in at least 50 countries.
- Approximately 27 million mice have been distributed
- More than 5,000 varieties are available as breeding mice, frozen em-
  bryos, or DNA samples.

- The Jackson Laboratory Mouse Repository: This resource, maintained by Genetic Resource Science group, currently offers a portfolio of over 1,800 targeted and 900 transgenic mutant mouse lines, many of which are models for cancer, heart disease, Alzheimer's disease, ALS, diabetes, Parkinson's disease, spinal muscular atrophy, Huntington's disease and various autoimmune diseases. More than 400 new lines are imported annually.

The Laboratory Animal Health Services program oversees the health, welfare, and husbandry of Jackson Laboratory mice and provides expertise in the evaluation of clinical diseases.

Following the information given by the technician who greeted us we were introduced to a scientist who was gracious enough to take us behind the scenes to where research was being accomplished. It was a most impressive tour and we met several scientists of whom two have received Nobel Prizes for work that had been performed at the Bar Harbor lab.

I was so moved by what the Jackson Laboratory was doing that I immediately committed to being a contributor and have been one since. I was invited for the opening of the Lab's new facility at UC Davis, California.

The next day would be our last in Bar Harbor before embarking on a ferry to Canada's Nova Scotia. The ferry crossing would take approximately six hours and we would dock at Yarmouth in the southeast end of Nova Scotia. We took a few moments to book our crossing and arrange for our rental car to be taken on board in time. For dinner we drove a few miles to Southwest Harbor to explore the coast and to enjoy a small restaurant located on a jetty that served fresh lobsters boiled in seawater. It was marvelous.

The next morning after a light breakfast we boarded the ferry and were fortunate to find a vacant cabin with sufficient electrical outlets that we could connect our computers. It was on this sea voyage in 1995 that I first began to write this autobiography as a testament to my children, to my friends, and to anyone who wondered how a life can be exciting, rewarding, graceful, and focused on helping people. The crossing was uneventful and the fact that I was able to work made me unaware of the rolling ocean, something that has, on occasion, given me some nausea.

During the crossing my thoughts were about 1950-51 when I first landed in Halifax after crossing the Atlantic from Italy. As a young man I would be looking at a new phase of my young life. My intention at the time was to settle in Canada and make a new home for myself. I had been accepted to be an aircraft pilot in the Royal Canadian Air Force. My landing in Halifax began with a 16-day incarceration in the Immigration jail! The readers may recall this from reading earlier sections.

Nova Scotia, Canada

The crossing to Yarmouth was uneventful, quiet in our cabin, and productive because I was able to write and think. This was 1995 and I had crossed from Canada's New Brunswick Province to Main in 1950, 45 years earlier. In 1955 I had the opportunity to visit Nova Scotia when I drove from New Jersey but that was such a long time ago and I wanted to revisit some of my favorite places and head west to the Bay of Fundy to see and hear the roaring tide, the highest in the world, and which supposedly begins in the Indian Ocean.

At Yarmouth, the port authorities were cordial and welcoming. Soon I drove the two-lane road towards the small village of Hubbards in Nova Scotia, which was approximately 30 to 45 minutes from the metropolis of Halifax.

When I lived in Halifax in 1950 often my hosts, the Longleys, would invite me to their vacation house on Butterfly Lake in Hubbards.

Reaching Hubbards in mid-afternoon I was immediately surprised at how developed the village had become. It was a vacation town and no longer a mere village. I couldn't find the gravel path to the lake without asking someone. The post office had been enlarged and the grocery store had become a large modern market. The drugstore where often I had ice cream sodas was now a restaurant with a bar on one side and an ice cream parlor on the other.

It was all a bit disappointing but no village can be protected from development and progress.

We found the resort hotel where we had reservations and were soon shown our room. The view was splendid and it overlooked the farms and fields surrounding Hubbards. I could also see the old Anglican Church where I had on occasion visited. That was long before I had committed to Episcopal Holy Orders.

After we settled into the room, it was on to the Tea Lounge for a refreshing cup of tea and a few goodies to restore the energy lost in travel. After the refreshment I was eager to walk around the village to renew my acquaintance with the old haunts. First was to the post office where I inquired about the various changes that I first noticed. The clerk was willing to chat and inform me that developers had arrived but on the whole the villagers had been able to limit what was planned. The lake remained as it had been with no power boats allowed but because more people had moved into the area, the old grocery had to be expanded. As for the gravel road that used to lead to the lake, well that road had been relocated, paved, and widened. At the end of the road where it met the lake a boat dock had been built to accommodate the greater number of boats and to provide space for rental boats. After thanking the clerk I meandered towards the lake and managed to dip my toe in the water for old times' sake. It was very cold.

After more investigating I crossed the road and headed for the church, which was closed, but a notice advised that it was open on certain days and Eucharist was celebrated at noon on Wednesdays and at eleven o'clock on Sundays. After visiting the church property I went toward what appeared to be a restaurant, but it was closed for the season. In fact I soon learned that the bar lounge and a fast-food facility were the only eating places available for non-residents. Thus the resort hotel where we were lodged was the only restaurant available for us. We ate there that night and fortunately it was satisfactory, acceptable, and reasonably priced, although not a place to brag about. Tomorrow we would go to Halifax to see if my favorite sea fare restaurant was still in existence. Because I had forgotten its name I could not look it up in the directory, but I hoped that fortune would be on our side. Before leaving the dining table I asked the waiter of the resort hotel if he knew the restaurant I was looking for. At the description of the place and the abundance of self-serve mussels, he immediately said: "Oh, the Five Fishermen on Argyle Street." He went to the counter and returned with the address and phone number: 1740 Argyle St. 902-422-4421.

After dinner, because the weather was clear and it wasn't cold, I took a walk and ended up at the local drugstore that still functioned as a hangout for the younger generation. A woman in her mid-fifties managed the ice cream and soda fountain. I ordered a cup of chocolate ice cream and struck up a conversation with her. The counter person had been living in Halifax all her life, except when she went to university in Montreal, where she majored in business. She returned to Halifax and found that a job was available at the drugstore. After five years working at the store she offered to buy it if the owner-pharmacist would carry her loan. A deal was reached wherein the pharmacist would continue to work but would be relieved of any business obligations since he had become an employee. A few years later a younger pharmacist was hired and trained by the older one who eventually retired. Helen, the owner and counter person, remembered the drugstore as a teenager meeting place and reminded me that on weekends activity levels increased with the presence of teens and young adults. We chatted about her youth in Halifax and the people she remembered, but she knew no one that I could recall. After bidding her farewell I continued my walk and proceeded to Lake Butterfly. The moon was shining over the water but I could not see the far shore where the cottage I had stayed in was located. My thoughts were in high-speed mode as I revisited the highlights of my past in Hubbards with Dorcas and John Longley and their daughter Barbara. There was the first time I took the canoe alone and explored the lake, skipped over the shallow rapids, very shallow and not dangerous but exciting nevertheless. Of course I remembered the first fish I caught and the inadvertent swim I took when I reached too far to bag the fish. I could remember the bacon frying in the morning and the coffee perking as I returned from my morning dip in the lake. I remembered conversations with John about my future and walks into the wood with Barbara to pick blackberries for the evening pie. These were some of the marvelous memories that occupied me as I returned to the hotel.

Before bed and while sipping a cognac, I recalled some of the less marvelous memories. Especially the ones that reminded me that both Dorcas and John had died and that I had lost Barbara's address and her married name. I think that she had moved to Toronto or Ottawa, but I wasn't certain. I recalled that both parents had tried to have Barbara and me find some common bond between us but that never materialized. I had a goal to reach but did not quite know how to manage the path to it. Barbara was a cigarette smoker and I just could not tolerate the smell or the habit. That later I took up pipe smoking and on occasion a few cigarettes never changed my dislike for smokers. My excuse for my smoking was that it kept me awake during long shifts working on security tasks for the US Air Force.

The next morning it was to Halifax that we drove. I had a meeting with a technopolis group that was interested in converting the military base located in Dartmouth, across the harbor. I also wanted to see if any of the Hagens still lived in Halifax. Mrs. Hagen had been the senior matron at the immigration detention center. When I first arrived I was detained for 16 days and upon my release Mrs. Hagen had offered to give me lodging in her home. Mrs. Hagen had three daughters and one of them, Patricia, had become my somewhat girlfriend. During the passing years, I had lost track of the daughters and had learned also that Mrs. Hagen had died in the mid-sixties. In 1961, I had had a few communications with Patricia, whose marriage was falling apart. Patricia wanted me to come to Nova Scotia but time had passed and I was engaged to Trudy and was ready to start seminary in California.

During my return visit, this time in 1995, I never did locate any of the Hagens but did have a long visit with the technopolis team and was driven after lunch to Dartmouth for a meeting with the commanding officer and his legal counsel. All in all no project surfaced from these various business meetings. I suspect that nothing surfaced because no decision had been made by the government for converting the military base either to all civilian use or to joint civilian-military operation. There had been some talk but nothing concrete had been passed down to the lower level. Also perhaps they were just testing the water by talking with me. I would have enjoyed a project in Halifax but there it was, no project was ever realized.

After looking at a few sites in Halifax, such as Citadel Hill and its tower, we walked over to the Five Fishermen for a scrumptious dinner. I was not disappointed, not one bit. The menu was still as good as I had known and the taste was still fresh and satisfying to my palate.

There was a couple sitting across from us who ordered two small salads and nothing more. The rule of the house was that with any main order the customer could have as many mussels as he wished to eat; there was no limit. That was a fair rule and few customers abused it, except for the couple across from us who had ordered only two small salads and then had filled soup plate after soup plate with mountains of mussels. We were wondering if a waiter would notice that abuse. When it came time for the couple to pay the check, they were incensed that a surcharge had been added to their bill. The waiter explained for all of us to hear that a small salad was not considered a main order but merely a side order. Without any fuss the couple paid the tab and left muttering words that no one could understand.

When dinner was over I walked to the wharf to look at a few of the shops and enjoy the pleasant night air and the perfume of the ocean. I bought a Greek fisherman's cap and some small souvenirs, but nothing extravagant. It was time to return to Hubbards.

The Tidal Bore: Bay of Fundy

I was ready to travel to New Brunswick to see and hear the famous tide arrive. The actual bore of the tide coming to the closed end of the Bay of Fundy was renowned for being spectacular. The bore has been recorded to be approximately 50 to 55 feet in height when it arrives and when it retreats that same height becomes negative — the water recedes by that much. Tides are the rise and fall of sea levels caused by the combined effects of the rotation of the Earth and the gravitational forces exerted by the moon and the sun. The tides occur with a period of approximately twelve and a half hours and are influenced by the shape of the sea bottom and the drift of the ocean water, and, for Fundy, possibly beginning in the Indian Ocean. I was eager to learn more about the tides and how they were caused having studied some of the causes in hydrology classes when I was learning physics.

Most coastal areas experience two daily high (and two low) tides. This is because at the point right "under" the moon (the sub-lunar point), the water is at its closest to the moon, so it experiences stronger gravity and rises. On the opposite side of the Earth, (the antipodal point) for Fundy, a location in the Indian Ocean, the water is at its farthest from the moon, so it is pulled less; at this point the Earth moves more toward the moon than the water does — causing that water to "rise" (relative to the Earth) as well. In between the sub-lunar and antipodal points, the force on the water is diagonal or transverse to the sub-lunar/antipodal axis (and always towards that axis), resulting in low tide.

My destination to see the activity of the tide in the Bay of Fundy was Moncton in New Brunswick. I was directed by the tourist office to drive out of the small city towards Moncton Riverview and follow the signs to a farm where we would be welcomed to view the activity of the tide. I was also informed that the bore was expected to arrive at 1:18 p.m. I had plenty of time to arrive at the farm for the occasion. When I reached the farm, the gentleman farmer invited us in and showed us the location where we would best see the incoming bore. The good farmer and host had benches for us to sit on while we waited for the bore and in the meantime he gave us a fine explanation of how it all worked. I learned that the "farmer" was a retired professor of oceanography at the University of Fredericton, New Brunswick. Yes, indeed, the tide had its beginning in the Indian Ocean but it was not the waters of the Indian Ocean that traveled to the Bay of Fundy but rather the force of the water that moved through the liquid mass that made the local seawater move as the bore. Yes, water did increase in volume and it does inundate the coast, but that was regional or local water and not molecules that had traveled from the Indian Ocean.

With the arrival of the bore at 1:18 p.m. birds, fish, and seals often preceded its arrival or arrived with it. It seemed that a new life came with the bore and I suspect that life waned a little when it receded. I have not witnessed the receding bore in the Bay of Fundy but I suspect that with the waters returning away from the shore, birds, fish, and seals would have less reason to be that close to the coast. Feeding creatures are found where food is abundant and the tide brings food. Ahead of the bore we could hear its rumbling sound, like the roar of a Boeing 747 taking off. It wasn't insignificant. It was memorable and a little frightening. My body vibrated because of the sound and the ground I was standing on trembled a little as when an earthquake occurs. The bore approached and I was at least 10 meters above on the bluff but I was concerned that, perhaps, it would not stop at the foot of the rise. It did, but for a moment I was a little edgy. When the noise of the bore diminished, the noise of the birds intensified and the disturbance of the water's surface increased as seals, fish, and birds did what they did when the bore arrived: sought food from the upwelling. It was an extraordinary act of nature. Mother Nature does what she does best: impress mankind with her power.

We stayed about two hours to watch how wildlife took advantage of the incoming tide. The farmer, our host, was very willing to answer my questions and to discuss the theory of tides around the world. Much as the Fundy bore was extraordinary and currently the highest on the globe, there were other tides that were impressive, even if not as high as the one in New Brunswick. It was the shape of the bottom of the ocean and the tight entrance to the Bay of Fundy that made it so spectacularly high. There was also a major tide at the western end of the Strait of Magellan, in Chile, which had a height of 30 feet, more or less. The tide in that strait was the reason that great salmon breeding was supported without enclosures — hence just monitoring and not isolating aqua farming. The water of the Magellan was cleansed twice a day and the fish could breed in a clean, cold, and food-abundant environment.

Saint John's River Bore

Another of the interesting natural occurrences that I wanted to see was the reverse bore of the St. John's River. The Saint John's River sees its flow reversed at high tide, causing a series of rapids at the famous Reversing Falls where the river empties into the bay in a gorge in the middle of the city of Saint John. After locating the Five Chimneys Bed and Breakfast operated by Linda Gates I walked over to the St. John's River to await the coming of the tide. I was not alone. There were many other interested people on the bridge and on the bank.

Soon enough the bore approached. I could hear it. Several seals and sea lions approached attracted by the fish that seem to be carried by the tide. A few minutes after the bore was heard, the water from the bay came and the river reversed its course as was expected. It was fascinating. The force of the tide was extraordinary and the sound was frightening. It sounded like an approaching train mixed with thunder but it was continuous and not explosive. The bore was approaching rapidly but slow enough to witness its effect. I could see fish jumping out of the water and seals and sea lions having a great feast catching their abundant meal. About a half hour later the effect of the high water settled and everything appeared normal again — at least until the return of the low water level and the reversal of the tide, which would occur 12.4 hours later. I wanted to be at the same spot, but it would be in darkness.

To share a few more details, the first thing that I noticed was the approaching seals moving up the river and then the great flutter in the water as the fresh water fish swam feverishly to avoid the brackish seawater that was moving inland. Following the movement of the seals and the fish I could see a lot of driftwood being carried inland also. This was not a calm and quiet movement of the water going inland; it was violent and noisy. I certainly would not want to be in those waters during the coming — or for that matter the receding — of the bore. I could appreciate the power of the water as it swept up everything in its path with force.

After I finished dinner in St. John and took a short walk through the nearby park I returned to the B&B and enjoyed a chat with Linda Gates. Linda was a charming person and a fine hostess. I was amused that she announced that for breakfast in the morning we would be served "cheesy eggs." It did not sound too appetizing, at least after dinner that night. The room was comfortable and the appointments were pleasant, especially after we removed all of Linda's family pictures and hid them in a drawer.

After setting the alarm clock for 2:00 a.m. I went to bed and quickly fell into a deep sleep. The drive from Truro through Moncton to Saint John had taken its toll and I was tired. When the alarm awakened me, Emily continued to sleep undisturbed but I went to the bridge. It was a short walk and it wasn't that dark. The city had been helpful enough to have several floodlights illuminating the river. The noise of the tide receding was not as impressive as when the bore arrived; nevertheless there was a high level of rumble and the water moved out at a good pace and the river's fresh water regained its usurped place. I stood on the bridge for approximately 45 minutes and that was sufficient time to give me the experience of how the tide operates in this high tidal geographical location.

When I was walking back to the B&B my thoughts dwelt on the origin of the bore. I recalled that the tide started somewhere in the Indian Ocean — almost at the opposite side from the geographical location of the Bay of Fundy. The idea was fascinating to me, especially because it reminded me that I had watched an act of nature that made a lot of human power insignificant; add tsunami, volcanic eruptions, earthquakes, hurricanes, cyclones, and typhoons, and the effects of our weapons of mass destruction and military operations were minimal, even with the advent of the nuclear bomb. After walking several blocks away from the bridge I could still hear the loud noise of the bore.

The next morning at breakfast I was introduced to Linda's "cheesy eggs." At first I thought that it would be repulsive but when she served it I found it quite appetizing. Linda's cooking was good and her approach to the preparation of breakfast made it all the more interesting, charming, and tasteful. A peek into her kitchen convinced me that it was a mess — not as in "mess hall" but as in messy. All in all, although the kitchen was quite disorganized, the food that emerged from it was very good, healthy, and rich in taste. Linda is an exceptional person and I've kept in email contact with her since 1995.

We correspond sporadically but still have maintained a solid friendship. Linda is a fine person and a delight to know. Years later when we visited Maine for a vacation, she and her husband drove all the way from St. John's, Canada to Southwest Harbor, Maine for a day visit and lunch with us. Linda has several serious allergies and food needs to be carefully selected. The restaurant we chose in Bar Harbor was accommodating to Linda and we all had a marvelous time and an enjoyable meeting. Linda announced that she was closing the B&B to join her husband, Peter, in his public accounting business. Apparently Linda had been an accountant but stopped working as such when she had children. Now that her children were out of university she was resuming her profession by helping her husband, but I'm assured that I'll always have a room at the old Five Chimneys Bed and Breakfast.

Linda is a special individual who not only has several allergies but has a phobia against flying. She refused to take a flight anywhere. This means of course that Peter has to drive her for many miles and for many hours when they want to see family. Canada is no small country and cities are quite distant from each other. Linda has been invited to visit us at the G&T but that trip is well beyond her because Peter is not about to drive from New Brunswick to California. I expect that the next time we go to Canada we'll make a definite trip to visit with the Gates.

After breakfast I returned to the bridge to await the receding tide and to witness what was going to occur. The tide was not quite ready to do its thing. On the bridge I had company. People from Asia, Europe, and South America had traveled to see the tide's activity at Saint John's. Because I had been to the end of the Bay of Fundy at Moncton Riverview, had seen the bore's activity, and had developed a solid friendship with Linda Gates, I suggested that the journey there was well worth it.

Grand Manan Island

Part of the reason for going to Canada, apart from seeing the Bay of Fundy, was to re-cross the frontier from Canada to the United States, or more clearly from New Brunswick to Maine, as I had done it in 1950 when I first entered the United States. En route we were to visit Grand Manan Island for a week, which in reality is part of New Brunswick. Emily had made reservations with a senior group that was going to make all the arrangements for the week's stay on the island. I was a little apprehensive about the pre-arrangements, especially when prepared by a senior group, but I went along.

The drive from St. John's was a breeze and we arrived at the dock to board the next ferry to Grand Manan. Once on board, the crossing was less than an hour and we arrived on terra firma quite close to the hotel where we had rooms. It was a fine old hotel and the rooms were pleasant and comfortable, except for sharing bathrooms with several other people in the senior group. That did not over-joy me but I could live with it for the week.

After an introductory lecture and tea and coffee we were informed when dinner was scheduled and that prior to that we would have a lecture on the history of Grand Manan. I enjoyed the lecture and especially learning about this island that was located off the coast of Canada but technically was in US waters.

At dinner I was confronted with the first issue that led me to wish I were not with the group. I must admit that I don't do very well with a large group and one that complains about illnesses that each member experiences. We were sitting for dinner at a table for four, hence there was another couple with us. The couple listed the various ills and pains that they experienced from lumbago, to rheumatism, to gastric surges when certain foods were served. Substantial topics were not in the conversation; we did not discuss the lectures or any other topic that would encourage some use of our grey matter. After dinner, because it was still light I went for a walk, a long walk. When I returned the television was on and the program was the criminal trial of O.J. Simpson and soon to follow would be the verdict, not really of great interest to me. I went to my room, fetched my book and sat on the porch by a good reading light.

The next morning after breakfast the group was going on a bus tour to explore the island. I announced that I was going to walk and handle my own exploration of the island.

There were not too many streets or roads on the island and distances were not great. I could walk and enjoy the sunshine and the people. My first stop was at the gift shop where I was engaged in an interesting conversation with the owner who was born and had lived on the island most of her life, except for the few years in college in Saint John's. Emma was a history buff and gave me lots of information that I had not received the previous night. Emma suggested that I walk to the Constable Station and meet the official in charge. After a cup of tea and cookies made by Emma we discussed the political situation of Canada and its relation with the Big Gorilla, the United States of America. Our conversation went along uninterrupted until a customer arrived. I excused myself and Emma asked me to return before I left.

At the Constable Station the chief constable, Henry Gibbs, met me. Mr. Gibbs was also a native islander and a ready speaker who loved the island. We spoke for a while and then he invited me to come with him on his regular daily tour of the island. We climbed into his Jeep and off we went to the village of Sealcove, one of the oldest on the island.

In a large building, workers were smoking herring that were hanging from overhead supports inside the structure. There was a small smoker that emitted just a little smoke from an alder wood fire that was not offensive to those who worked or visited, but certainly smelled good. It took several days for the herring to dry and absorb the scent of smoke before being shipped to Europe and the United States. I was shown the village and was introduced to many of the workers in what I learned was a cooperative.

After Sealcove, Mr. Gibbs drove across the island to the other coast and Dark Harbour where they were harvesting and drying seaweed, or kelp, known as dulsing or dulse. I tasted dulse and loved it. It has the taste of the sea and the smell of the fresh sea breeze. I often sprinkle the dulse over food such as pasta or lamb, even fish. It does add to the taste and enhances the flavor.

After visiting Dark Harbour, Mr. Gibbs drove back and stopped by the airport. There was a small airport with a 2,000-meter runway (approximately 6,500 feet), sufficient for a cargo aircraft and a small airline, which was well maintained and welcoming. The airport was beckoning for me to come with my Red Bird some day.

Past the airport we stopped by an apple orchard and I was introduced to the farmer who offered me a delicious apple followed by a cup of tea. Mr. Robson had moved to Grand Manan from Manitoba to escape the wind and cold weather, not that Grand Manan does not have cold weather but it's not like western Canada.

It was time for lunch, Mr. Gibbs announced as we left the orchard. We returned to the Constable Station and left the Jeep. Walking a few meters south, we stopped in a small restaurant that served fresh seafood. I had a lobster and potatoes washed down with a draft ale. Mr. Gibbs ordered the same. For dessert I ordered a piece of apple pie and was informed that the apples were grown in Mr. Robson's orchard. After a cup of coffee I said goodbye to Mr. Gibbs and walked back to the hotel for some reading and a nap. The tour had returned for lunch and vegetable soup was served. When asked if I would join the lunch I declined and told Emily what my lunch comprised. She wanted to tour with me later in the afternoon and would skip the next tour by bus.

We took a leisurely walk to the harbor and to the fishing holding section where wild herring were kept alive in an enclosure until they were ready for smoking, drying, freezing, or live shipping off the island. We proceeded to several parts of the east side of the island and reached Woodward Cove, where we found a pleasant teashop. The afternoon was pleasant and the weather was perfect. There a local couple, John and Judy Formet, gave us additional information on the island and told us about the building of the radio shack, Swallow-Tail Light on North Head, and the end of fishing for Bluefin tuna, which had been shipped to Japan. Bluefin tuna were no longer legal for fishing because they contained large quantities of mercury, most of which had been dumped into the Pacific Ocean in the 1970s when a chemical plant near Tokyo had released large amounts of mercury into the Bay.

The "minamata disease," as it became known, is the result of the Chisson Corporation dumping several tons of methyl mercury into the adjacent bay in the 1950s. The mercury had followed ocean currents and was soon found in the North Atlantic, especially in the pelagic fish. Of all the tunas, the Bluefin possessed the largest parts per million of methyl mercury. Because of the Bluefin's high position in the food chain, methyl mercury levels were higher than in other fish.

Mrs., or rather Dr. Formet, was an oceanographer doing research on the island and was writing a book. John was a retired biologist but had continued to do research on the island. He was studying the various cellular variations in single cell creatures in the coastal waters. The information that was shared with us was precious and I continued to correspond with both of them when I returned home.

We spent just four days on Grand Manan because we agreed that we had seen all that we wanted to see. It was an interesting sojourn and the island offered an environment for a tranquil stay, especially if I or someone else wanted a place to write, read, or do less than little. I did not appreciate the superficial lectures given by the hosts and I did not enjoy the group conversations that could be heard. The day before we had decided to leave, the O.J. Simpson jury had declared that he was not guilty of the double murder of which he'd been accused. Because the news was given on television, the cacophony produced by the numerous commentators exceeded my patience. Adding to the commentators were the several evaluations given by the hotel guests. There wasn't a quiet spot in the hotel were I could read or use my computer. My room had no desk or comfortable sitting chair; I was trapped inside a noisy building or I could leave and sit in the harbor, which I did.

That night we decided to abandon Grand Manan and cross into the United States by way of St. Stephen border town into Calais, Maine. The St. Croix River separates Maine from Charlotte County, New Brunswick, Canada. I was eager to return to the crossing location because it reminded me of my first experience into America as an invited immigrant.

We took the ferry the next morning and then drove to St. Stephen. It was a short drive to the town that years ago had a huge chocolate factory, the Ganong Chocolate Co., which had been converted into a museum because chocolate was no longer being produced in St. Stephen. The old bus and railway station (I had ridden the bus when I first entered the United States) had since been converted into an information center. I parked the car and walked to the edge of the bridge that spanned the St. Croix River. I asked the border guard if I could walk to the center of the bridge and place one foot in each country. I was allowed but he watched me. The US border guard came over to ask me what I was doing. After explaining my reason, he offered to take a photo of me with one foot in each country and he then reminded me that I was standing on the longest and most peaceful frontier between two nations.

Campobello Island, Canada

We drove over the bridge then stopped for a moment to show our identification and headed to Campobello Island, which is in Canada but must be entered via the FDR Bridge from the United States.

After reaching the small village of Lubec we presented our identification again and drove over the FDR Bridge to Roosevelt Estate and International Park, situated on Friar's Bay.

It was a warming experience to see the house of the New Deal President. We were allowed to wander through several rooms, including the children's rooms with their toys, Eleanor's (Mrs. Roosevelt) quarters, and also look at FDR's personal room with his special wheelchair, ashtrays, books, and cognac glasses. I perused the library and found that both Roosevelts were avid readers of literature, politics, philosophy, and history. He had a few books given to him by Winston Churchill and one book in Russian given to him by Joseph Stalin: a leather bound Russian edition of *War and Peace* and an English translation of the work given to him by Stalin's foreign minister, Vyacheslav Molotov.

It was pouring rain when we started our visit but the rain ended soon after. The Roosevelts' retreat was soon in the sun and we could enjoy the garden and chat with the docents, who were kind enough to accompany us around the building and then point us to the local grocery store nearby where we purchased a bit of lunch before heading back across the bridge to Maine. Our next stop was Bangor for an overnight stop.

The brain was revisiting much history. First I thought about my arrival to Canada and the developments in my life that followed from the early 1950s. I was a young, inexperienced fellow open to options, opportunities, and willing to enter doors, when they opened, to see what was available behind them.

Now I was in my second year of retirement, if that is what it was called, from a major firm. Much ground had been covered since my arrival in Canada. I could not have planned my trajectory; much of the travel had been the product of emergence. Had I set up certain potential occasions or recognized that they offered opportunities? I don't know. Nevertheless, I appreciated the road traveled, chosen with some deliberation, care, and anticipation that the goal would be reached. My goal was always more experience, more education, and more service to my fellow human beings — as long as I resided on this planet. This may appear to be a bit of a platitude, but I have lived it! I have lived a life that brought me excitement, satisfaction, and much love. There were a few rough spots, some disappointments, but many rewards with a network of friends all over the world. I believe that my legacy will be that I was helpful to people, used my brain as much as possible, and considered food to be a sacramental bridge between friends. Probably my complexity will produce timely entropy. Who knows and who cares?

Return to Moscow

I had worked in Russia in Troitsk and become friends with Dr. Viacheslav (Slava) Pismenny, the director of the Kurchatov Institute of Nuclear Research. After retiring from Bechtel, Slava had asked me several times when I would return to Moscow. I wanted to return to Troitsk but scheduling a visit was difficult because I could not justify the cost and the time, especially away from both the bed and breakfast and my consultancy. Nevertheless, I wanted to return to Russia to visit my friends, to see what changes had surfaced since the dissolution in 1991, and to learn more about the future of this enormous country. I informed Slava that I would return to Moscow if and when the conditions were convenient and justifiable.

The justification came when the invitation was extended during Dr. Pismenny's visit to our home in 1998 just when the Russian ruble underwent a devaluation crisis. This was also the time when Russia decided to stop protecting the ruble and permit it to reach a real value vis-à-vis other currencies.

For Russians that period was most difficult because the economy was weakened by a reduced and almost non-existent productivity, the inflated price of the protected ruble, and the beginning of total dependency on oil and gas extraction, which continues to this day in the first decade of the 21st century.

In addition, Russia was going through many internal social, political, health, and industrial problems, especially with the productivity doldrums. Russia's financial platform was totally resting on the extraction of minerals and fossil fuels. In terms of oil and natural gas, Russia was sitting on several lakes, some even greater than those of Saudi Arabia and Kuwait. Revenues from oil and gas were great and excellent, especially after the oil wells had been cleared from the mistakes made by previous Soviet technological mismanagement programs. Some of these mismanaged programs were based on greed, ignorance, expediency, and the results of the final gasps of an extinguished government.

In 1998, the ruble faltered and was no longer serviceable as a viable currency. Moreover, the ruble was not exchangeable with other currencies. Investment revenues made in Russia by foreign and Russian investors were placed in entities outside the country. In addition, Russia was suffering also from a critical brain drain. Also, because the economy was lackluster, unemployment was in the 35th to 40th percentile, local production of goods was practically nil, services non-existent, and alcoholism rampant. The conversion to a democratic government, an open economic system, and a productive industrial base was not possible at that time. A few entrepreneurs built up their wealth by appropriating the State property and wealth of the USSR to become the "New Russian Millionaires" (or billionaires to be more correct), and as a result the ruble collapsed and the financial house of cards tumbled.

On 17 August 1998, Russia and the ruble lost its value. The collapsed and value-less currency made Russia a financial non-entity. My friend Slava was my guest in Montara. He had come to discuss aspects of nuclear development with several scientists at the Lawrence Livermore Laboratories. If the Russian financial system was rock bottom its science was still elegant. Slava found himself unable to use his Russian-issued credit cards because the firm backing them was bankrupt. The large Inkombank whose billboards proudly stated its motto "We are for real, we are here to stay," collapsed and was closed. Inkombank was the first of several banks to go to zero assets overnight because the Russian financial fabric was woven with weak and deteriorated threads. Slava had no money and no credit card to use for making phone calls. He needed to report to the Minister of Nuclear Energy but no Russian credit card allowed him access to the telephone. He was at my house and was invited to use my phone. I remember that date quite well because the phone bill was around $200, but I was pleased to help him.

Russia has yet to move into an economy that is not dependent on natural resources, and particularly fossil (oil and gas) resources. The Russian economy produces nothing more than fossil material, mining extracts, and some nuclear by-products. Any attempt to move into high technology has been dragged out into several planning stages with results that generated little more than talk. Whatever pockets of high technologies that have been active have been relegated to minimal importance because of the enormous financial controls that have demanded complete subjugation to the will of the Moscow hierarchy, namely Mr. Putin.

For example, the science city of Troitsk, 25 kilometers southwest of Moscow but still in the Moscow Oblast (region), has 11 science institutes. Each institute is closely tied to some aspect of the defense industry and ranges from nuclear to laser and whatever is in between. The historical branch of Kurchatov Nuclear Institute is still functioning productively but since 1992 it has adopted the name of Triniti Institute of Advanced Science (www.nti.org/db/nisprofs/russia/reactor/research/without/triniti.htm).

The director, Dr. Viacheslav Pismenny, is my friend, as I indicated earlier, and an active entrepreneur who is quite open to new project developments. He does find, however, that the governmental system restrains his creativity, even after his retirement.

Soon After the Bolshoi

Often I said to my friends that before I abandon this planet I wanted to experience the Russian Bolshoi, eat beluga caviar, and have a glass or two of Russian champagne in Moscow. In 1998, Slava Pismenny asked me to come to Moscow and also visit Troitsk, located approximately 25 kilometers southwest of the capital city. Gathering my collection of frequent miles on British Airways, Emily and I went to Moscow by way of London. Slava had been insistent about my visit and wanted me in April, just when the snow season ended and when spring started and the flowers bloomed. We arrived at Moscow's Sheremetyevo International airport at 7:00 p.m. a few days before Russian Orthodox Easter. It was dark and cold but we were dressed for it and the flight had been easy and smooth. Slava met us with his driver and our good friends Dima Sobolenko and Tanya Kuzkina. Slava presented Emily with a dozen red roses. My greeting was the traditional bear hug, and is it a wrap-around mighty hug!

After the greetings and the ride to our apartment on the 16th floor of the building where Triniti has a permanent two-room flat, and where a feast was laid out on the dining table, we proceeded to discuss why I was invited to Moscow. I was given a schedule of events and places I would visit, such as the hill monument where Napoleon saw the burning of Moscow and his imminent defeat by both the weather and lack of food for his exhausted army.

We also noticed that Slava had listened to my request, a request made several years earlier that I wanted to visit Zagorsk, now renamed Sergey Prasad. Slava had given me a short tour of Zagorsk in 1988 when I first arrived in Troitsk. He had seen my resume and discovered that I was a priest and active in the Church. Sergei Prasad is the major Russian Orthodox Lavra, the ecclesiastical hub of the Russian Church and where the Patriarchy has its seat.

There were a few more places he had scheduled for us to visit and these included museums, interesting streets (such as Arbat street, the Rodeo Drive of Moscow), underground shopping complexes, and of course the Kremlin. It looked like my stay in Moscow-Troitsk would be busy. I was also slated to address the Rotary Club of Troitsk, which Slava had incubated following the format of American Rotary clubs.

The next morning we looked in the refrigerator for something to prepare for breakfast and found lots of goodies that included eggs, smoked salmon, fruits, Bulgarian yoghurts, cold cuts, beer, milk, thick cream and butter, and chocolates. Bread was in the breadbox on top of the fridge. Breaking the fast was easy and nourishing. Soon Irena called that she was waiting for us downstairs. Irena was a cultural guide, art critic, and general super historian.

We embarked for the day for our education of Russian history, Moscow's geography, review of icons, and a general exploration of the beauty of the Russian capital. Irena was a good teacher and very patient, especially with me. Professionally Irena was an art historian and because of Slava's appreciation of art he had set aside a section in one of Troitsk's buildings for a gallery, which she managed. Irena was also determined to revitalize the Russian art community, a community that had been intimidated by the old Soviet regime because artists had been forced to subjugate their creativity for the propaganda of the Communist Party. Now that Russia was tentatively a more free society, artists were emerging as the natural critics of the social and political system. Irena knew many of the current artists and sought to have them exhibit their works in her gallery. She was also experimenting with programs that encouraged artists to perform plays or read manuscripts in her gallery or in other venues in Troitsk. I was excited by Irena's work and she recognized my interest and hence support. To this day, I have kept up with Irena and every time I return to Russia we meet and explore some of her art in the gallery.

We were exploring Moscow from one end to the other and Irena was lecturing and pointing and expected us to remember all the details.

In mid-afternoon at a tea stop, Irena announced that she had obtained tickets for the following evening for the Bolshoi and that the Mariinsky (Kirov Ballet) of St.Petersburg would be performing. I was excited and was uncertain that I had understood what Irena had announced, so I made her repeat every word again and again. I would go to the Bolshoi, and more, I would see the Kirov. This was an unbelievable piece of news, especially for something that I had wanted to see for many years.

The next day was more of the same, touring the city. We saw the giant titanium statue of Yuri Gagarin, the first man in space. We passed several times by the Lenin Library and Irena always asked us what it was — a testing exercise. After the tour of the major historical sectors of Moscow we decided to stop at a McDonald's for a "cocktail of milk and chocolate" (a milkshake) and to use their clean washroom. Washrooms and toilets are not always clean in most places in Russia but one can be certain that at McDonald's they will be clean, even immaculate. We returned to our apartment to rest and change clothes for the Bolshoi. Irena's driver would fetch us in a couple of hours so we had time for a nap, shower, and change of clothes.

At the appointed time, we arrived at the Bolshoi and were asked to wait at the entrance for our tickets to arrive. Soon Slava arrived looking quite dapper and with a big smile on his face — one implying that he'd eaten the canary! We entered the theatre.

Slava insistently steered me toward the fancy restaurant with large crystal chandeliers, velvet drapes, and all the accouterments of La Belle Époque and Tsarist magnificence. A waiter stopped by and Slava said something in Russian. Soon champagne arrived and caviar followed. "Now you cannot die unhappy," Slava reminded me.

Decadence befits me! While enjoying the champagne and the caviar Slava spoke of Kerch, Crimea. He was born in Kerch and wanted to restore the ancient city now that the USSR was non-existent and Russia was not using the region for the repair of its ships. He wanted me to see Kerch at some point to see what could be done, something similar to what I helped create in Troitsk. He described Kerch, mentioned the archeological treasures still in need of excavation and exhibition, and the two friends he had who were working to restore the history and splendor. I had never been to Ukraine and considered that some day I might venture to the Black Sea and perhaps take a look at the peninsula, which was famous for Sebastopol, Yalta, and the Charge of the Light Brigade. Yes, I'd consider a future visit to Kerch, I told Slava.

The performance by the Kirov was superb. With three intermissions, lots of caviar, and champagne, the evening was glorious. It was almost midnight and we had another portion before the evening was over. In our seats awaiting the lights to dim for the last part, Slava handed me an envelope. "Airplane tickets for Kerch tomorrow morning," Slava said. The lights dimmed. I could not read what was contained in the envelope but the inserts did appear to be tickets.

At the end of the performance and after the applause when the lights came on, I looked at what was inside the envelope. Indeed, there were two round-trip tickets to Kerch and our passports had the necessary visas. He had asked for our passports earlier in the day to register us with the police, so I was informed. But as it turned out, it was for the visas to enter Ukraine.

I looked at Slava. The flight left at 8:00 a.m. and now it was past 1:30 a.m. Slava indicated that the car would fetch us at 6:30 and Dima Sobolenko would be "your baby sitter." Dima was the deputy director, the first person I met in San Francisco from Troitsk in 1988, and a very dear friend. We enjoy each other's company. By the time we arrived at the apartment it was almost 2:15 a.m. I was tired but packing was a priority, shower followed, and slipping into bed was next. At 6:00 a.m. I was up and ready for this new adventure. The car arrived on time and off we went to Sheremetyevo Airport, the domestic terminal, at flying speed. We went through security, which was minimal, and then to Aeroflot Airlines. We boarded a Tupolev TU-154M, which is a very polluting three-engine jet aircraft, but comfortable for passengers and the service and food were quite good. We were served breakfast when the flight reached the appointed altitude. The meal was good and the coffee was excellent. The breakfast included hardboiled eggs, black bread, canned fruits, yoghurt, and a piece of chocolate. Both tea and coffee were available. It was a pleasant flight and Dima was most entertaining; he always was.

Kerch, Crimea

The flight to Simferopol, Crimea was not long, about two-and-a-half hours. Tatyana Umrikina, a past member of the Demetra organization, and her driver met us at the airport and they drove us to Kerch. The time to Kerch would be approximately three hours with a short lunch stop midway at a Tartar restaurant. After some research I discovered that the Greeks called the peninsula of Crimea "Tauris," later Taurica, after the inhabitants, the Tauri. The Greek historian Herodotus mentions that Heracles plowed the land with huge oxen (Taurus) to grow grain. Crimea was the breadbasket of Greece for many centuries.

At any rate after the greeting and halfway to Kerch, we stopped at the Tartar restaurant for a bite, some tea, and a washroom relief, which was really a hole in the ground. We had tea and some excellent desserts often found in the Middle East. It was a welcome rest.

After purchasing some mixed nuts we continued our journey to Kerch, but before the ancient city we stopped to see the gallery in Feodosya where the famous marine painter Aivazovsky's works are displayed.

Tatyana informed me that we would make a short stop in Feodosya to look at Aivazovsky's paintings in the gallery that had the entire collection of his huge and magnificent works. Feodosya also has several structures reflecting the Islamic tradition from the remnants of the Tartars.

Aivazovsky was able to paint the glistening aspects of seawater, reproduce the color of the turbulent liquid, and add the reflection of the white foam in such detail that a viewer almost sensed the wind blowing off the sea. He was so talented that he could paint large canvasses of several meters in size and still offer to the viewer the exquisite details that made the seawater sparkle before one's eyes. Indeed, his canvasses were huge! Aivazovsky was a wonderful marine painter. The son of an Armenian merchant family, he was discovered by the town mayor when he painted his first picture on the walls of houses with coal. In 1845 Aivazovsky was sent to St. Petersburg to study at the Academy of Arts. In Feodosya there are 417 paintings by Aivazovsky.

After visiting Feodosya, we pushed on to Kerch where we were lodged in Slava's condominium, a modern unit with all the amenities expected in a first class apartment. We had a fine bedroom with two large beds, a dining room with a table where at least 20 people could be served, a major kitchen with all the needed appliances, a bathroom that included a shower over the spacious tub, toilet, washer and dryer, and two sinks. There was also a library room with computer and internet connection, telephone, veranda, and good reading couches and chairs, and adjacent to the library there was a reception hall that also was the entry with double doors to the outside for security. The apartment was most comfortable, well decorated, and a pleasure for our stay.

That afternoon, Tatyana Umrikina came to Dr. Pismenny's condo accompanied by Dr. Viktor Zinko and Elena, his wife. Dr. Zinko was the chief archeologist for Crimea and his particular interest was the great treasures existing in the Kerch region. Elena was the principal historian for the same region. Both had received their education at St. Petersburg University and had worked at the Hermitage and other important museums in the Soviet Union. When the USSR imploded, Viktor regained his Ukrainian citizenship but Elena maintained her Russian nationality. Thus the combination of the two allegiances offered them many advantages, connections, and access to research facilities that otherwise would not have been readily available for their use. Because the Hermitage had in the past acquired most of the treasures discovered in the Kerch region, currently with the separation of Ukraine from Russia and as an independent nation, Crimea could retain possession of anything unearthed after 1991 — to the unhappiness of Russian antiquarians and museum authorities.

Viktor, who understood English but refused to speak it because he was shy, was able to explain to me through Natasha, the hired interpreter, what had been occurring in and around Kerch in archeology. Elena, who had some minimal English, was able to fill in the gaps and also offered us a thumbnail sketch of the history of the area. For example, we learned that Kerch and the eastern portion of Crimea had been a secure military region during the USSR's rule. The area between Kerch and almost to Feodosya had been dedicated to naval repairs. Navy vessels of the USSR were repaired, refitted, and used for training. Because of the naval presence and the high security, wherein only certified residents were allowed access to Kerch, the city was maintained in its pristine condition and all excavations were securely protected, but of course, not from the antiquarians of the Hermitage. This condition offered many advantages because after the fragmentation of the Soviet Union, Crimea, which was a republic and yet part of Ukraine, was able to establish its own bureaus for the care and excavation of its archeological treasures. I learned that in 1993 the President of Crimea had officially appointed Dr. Viktor Zinko as chief archeologist for the peninsula. This appointment placed all excavations, findings, and identification plus other important facets under Viktor's jurisdiction, hence also supervision. In the Crimean budget some funding was allotted to Kerch but that was not sufficient for all that was required. It was at this point that my friend Dr. Slava Pismenny took the funding helm and began to raise money for the necessary work.

The Demetra Project

On the afternoon of our arrival and after a light lunch Tatyana opened the conversation in halting English with an introduction of Viktor and Elena. It did not take long for us to discover that we needed an interpreter before any further inroads could be made on the Kerch project. Elena went to the phone and summoned Natasha who arrived at the condo in less than 10 minutes. Natasha's English was pretty much dictionary English but understandable and she was very patient with the Zinkos and us. After giving us a thumbnail sketch of the history, the Zinkos decided, correctly, that a tour of the main sites would be more useful. So off we went walking to see several sites starting with the Mithridates' hill, also known as the Liberation Monument. We were all dressed and booted with walking shoes but Tatyana Umrikina wore high heels! That was a sight to behold.

From the top of the hill we saw not only the ancient city of Kerch but also the abandoned naval complex west of the city where military affairs were of such a level that security prevailed from 1937 to 1991, hence making the eastern portion of the Crimean peninsula out of bounds to most people, with access permissible to documented residents or directly assigned military personnel. Down the hill we proceeded to the foundation wall of Mithridates' structure where many festivals and plays were produced.

Once a year, to commemorate the historical significance of Mithridates' era, many plays are performed and on one evening large groups of locals and visitors climb the hill as a sign of solidarity. It is an amazing event and on one occasion I was part of that ascent. I was amazed.

I could not continue the trek up the hill because of another engagement scheduled for me in St. John's, the oldest existing Orthodox Church in Kerch. It was my birthday and Elena had scheduled the premier local choir to serenade me. This was to be a surprise. I had not been informed at all. After the first course of our dinner, I asked if I could go outside to photograph the horde climbing Mithridates' hill. I went out assuming that it would be for a moment but Elena followed me and Viktor took my arm with a firm grip. I tried to go up the hill but Viktor pulled me towards the old church. "Why are we going this way?" I asked. Viktor does not speak English but understands it. He just pulled me. I pulled to go the opposite way. He pulled me more firmly and in the process made it impossible for me to take pictures, although I was able to snap a few. I gave up and followed him. He then released my arm. I followed Viktor and became docile.

The Church of St. John's, Kerch

I was taken into an old church, a structure that appeared to be very ancient and oozed history. When I entered the dark nave and waited for my eyes to become accustomed, I noticed the presence of a large choir of men and boys and the conductor. I had met the conductor but was never aware that she was the principal director of an extraordinary choir. I soon realized that the music was specially prepared for my birthday but fortunately the choir never broke into "Happy Birthday," except at the very end of the concert. The selections were primarily from classical Russian, German, and

French, but the last section was my favorite from Vaughn Williams' "Fantasia."

I was in awe, a little embarrassed, and very much emotionally unbalanced. In as much as I had made a fool of myself by insisting on watching and photographing the crowd heading up Mithridates' hill, here a lovely choir performing in Crimea's oldest church was greeting me for my birthday. A splendid occasion enveloped in extraordinary music coming from lovely voices. Here I stood, camera in hand, listening and absorbing the good music.

When the event ended I was re-introduced to the choir director, a fine lady who had recruited, trained, nurtured, and conducted this fine group of men and boys. This was not a choir performing because the Communist Party had ordered it. It was not a choir that a factory, school, or university had gathered for some institutional cause. This was a choir composed of volunteers who merely wanted to sing and perform good music under an excellent director. The director was a graduate of a premier Ukrainian music academy and had offered her service now that Crimea was free of the shackles of party affiliation, control, and direction. To provide for funding — funding is always a requirement — she had established a small music school where students paid tuition, patrons were subject to membership fees, and performance tickets were open to the public for a small fee. The choral venture was almost self-supporting but a few donors gave substantial amounts to see the endeavor through its trying emerging years. The process of developing a choral group was not at all strange; every embryonic choral group was going or had gone through the same growth exercise. What added to its possible permanence was the excellent music that it produced.

After the performance, we resumed our dinner in the restaurant and I had the good fortune to sit next to Tanya, the choir director. She gave me a memento in the shape of a music clef, which is still decorating my wall. We talked about her career and how she managed to obtain her music education during the period of great upheaval in the USSR from 1981 to 1991 at which time the implosion terminated the great Soviet State.

"All of a sudden, while in Moscow, I found that I was without a country, so I took the first train to Crimea, the place of my birth." She continued by adding, "A few weeks after my arrival, I was given papers that stated that because I was in Crimea I was now considered a Ukraine citizen." She continued, "Had I stayed in Moscow I probably would have become Russian."

Tanya was very happy to be a Ukrainian and was determined to do what was necessary for her country. We continued our conversation and touched on issues that addressed the financial conditions of the citizens. Ukraine was in a financial mess although it had natural wealth, factories, nuclear power plants, and, of course, the burden of the disaster of Chernobyl. Ukraine was also in possession of great archeological treasures, good schools and universities, and a multi-ethnic population that was ready and willing to work. Many Russians had left Russia and chosen to reside in Ukraine because conditions offered better advantages for eventual upward mobility.

But the situation was not going to be as simple as it appeared in the coming years because Russia was not about to let Ukraine go its own way and become more a part of Europe and eventually of the European Union. There were many Ukrainians who looked longingly at Russia and wanted to continue to remain in its circle of influence. My own estimation was that it would require a generation before the dust settled and Ukraine emerged as a truly independent nation and without the shackles of Russian domination. It wasn't going to be easy.

Elena Zinko was one of them; she was still attached emotionally to Russia. She was Russian and married to a Ukrainian but she selected to be a resident of Kerch, Crimea and live with her husband Viktor, who was selected to become the senior archeologist for the State of Crimea, a segment of Ukraine that was considered to be an independent state with Ukraine. In 2010, Ukraine was still struggling to get its economy and government in order but the financial downturn in the world did not help it much. (Moreover, in 2014 Crimea was stolen from Ukraine and transferred to Russia's jurisdiction.)

Elena keeps her Russian citizenship, owns an apartment in St. Petersburg, and maintains her residency in Ukraine. Under the current conditions of the Confederation of Independent States (CIS), Crimea is in a good position to enjoy the advantages obtained both from Russia and Ukraine, and to a certain degree from Poland, the adjoining and common border state with Ukraine. Elena's primary concern is what will happen when Ukraine stabilizes its economy, accepts full and real independence from Russia, and then moves to join the European Union (EU). Western Ukraine is quite politically different from the Eastern portion. The West wants engagement with the EU. The East, under pressure from Russia, wants to remain under its umbrella. The knotty issue is a natural gas pipeline that supplies both Ukraine and Europe with Russian gas. Russia often threatens to cut off the gas to Ukraine when it needs leverage to make it toe the line. At the moment Ukraine is neither politically stable nor in control of an economy that could make it acceptable for membership in the EU. Nevertheless and in spite of its many problems, Ukraine hopes to have its affairs in order in the next decade (my forecast is a generation) or so to join the EU.

As I work in Crimea (that was absorbed into Russia in 2013) I realize that the project is not what one can call a piece of cake. The issues of Ukraine are complex to resolve, funding guarantees are tenuous, association with the Getty Museum (more on that will be given), and current financial conditions in Europe and America do not offer much promise for attracting foreign investment. Indeed, the project is placed in the proverbial "rock and a hard place!" I have not given up.

Economic Development: Success or Failure

Life never offers guarantees. Success comes after a long struggle. Risk of failure is always around the corner. Developing a project to promote economic expansion, even where employment is readily available or potentially possible, and where government is functioning properly is often a complex endeavor and at times impossible to accomplish. Kerch was no different. The supporting entities that were selected or had volunteered their services were also subject to the vagaries of failure or the offerings of success. Again Kerch and Eastern Crimea were not immune to these elements. Moreover, in Ukraine and especially in Crimea, neither the government nor the employment pool was in an acceptable condition. The dissolution of the Soviet

Union left a vacuum that was problematic. The USSR dissolved itself because it was unable to sustain an economic organism any longer. The Soviet economic organism was dying of cancer. In brief, the Soviet Union adopted an aspect of Marxism dialectics that made it focus mainly on relations and changes and avoided seeing the nation as made up of separate persons. Individuals were often irrelevant because it was society that was important. The individual citizen was as useful as a grain of sand because it was the beach, not the grains of sand that mattered.

Also, there was nothing to generate any financial growth, except natural resources such as petroleum, but the oil-producing infrastructure was in poor condition, there were no funds to reconstruct it, and foreign investment was not available as long as the USSR was in the process of imploding, disbanding, and self-destructing.

In 1999, much as the Confederation of Independent States (CIS), the successor of the USSR, had shown signs that it could manage its survival; it was still not functioning adequately. There were some new foreign investments arriving to redevelop the extraction industry, there was also some investment in agriculture, and there was some investment in banking but loans were generated at exorbitant interest rates. So much for the redevelopment of the new CIS; the going was tough but progress appeared to be possible.

When I first realized that the USSR was on its last legs and had notified Bechtel that it needed to enter the arena soon before the opportunity disappeared, I also suggested that in my appraisal I did not see a long life for the Soviet Union. In a memorandum to Denis Slavich with a copy to Riley Bechtel, the potential heir of the company, I stuck my neck out by saying that no later than 1994 we would witness the termination of the USSR. My reasons were: 1) I saw no production of anything that could be used for export or domestic consumption, even as food; 2) I saw little incentive for workers to work — many that I saw were idle, sleeping, or drunk, and many appeared to have lost their dignity; 3) I saw little concern to safeguard the wheat harvest or the potato gathering — much of the produce was wasted before going to market; 4) I saw that what was controlled by the central government was totally irrelevant or not necessary to the needs of society; and 5) I saw a nation that had isolated itself by its paranoia from the global community. My projection was off by a few years! On 31 December 1991, instead of 1994, the USSR ceased to exist as a nation.

Denis was very much aware that the USSR was on its last legs because we had discussed the subject several times and he had visited Troitsk and had met Dr. Pismenny on two occasions. Denis also was quite knowledgeable about how the financial situation in the USSR was developing, if at all. But Denis was about to be furloughed from Bechtel by Riley. The competition with the young Bechtel heir and the seasoned director and potential successor to Steve Bechtel Jr., was very obvious. Fortunately the competition did not become an obstacle to my persistence to have Bechtel establish a pied-à-terre in the Moscow region. Riley moved ahead with the creation of an office in Russia, but erred by placing the office in Moscow rather than in Troitsk, the city of high technology and science. Bechtel in Moscow was just another foreign firm searching for recognition. In Troitsk Bechtel would have been immediately connected to the ministries performing research and managing energy, nuclear, and software development. Nevertheless, an office in the Moscow region, the Moscow Oblast, was better than nothing.

But another obstacle was placed before me. Riley was appointed President and soon began to place his own team into position. One of his friends was Frank Cain who was running the Maryland office. Frank took over the directorship of the section that managed the department where I was located and his initial act was to consider the entry into the USSR as a useless effort because he saw no "immediate" profit return from a nation that had neither a convertible currency nor an apparent future in the developing world. The result, as I mentioned in another section, was that I was instructed to pull myself off any USSR or Troitsk endeavor. That did not stop me from continuing my friendship with Dr. Pismenny and others.

With all this geopolitical change I was still interested in the development of Troitsk, Russia. From Troitsk, Director Slava Pismenny pointed me towards his birthplace, Kerch, in Eastern Crimea. Hence after the performance at the Bolshoi and upon my arrival in Kerch, I had been introduced to the splendor of the archeological treasures and accepted the challenge to take it as a project. After preparing a concept development plan (CDP), which was implemented as soon as it was received (and continues to be implemented), I directed my attention to the archeological treasures and to the education of the young folks.

To Help Kerch

In 2010, ten years after I took upon myself the task of helping Kerch develop its economic base; I'm still agonizing that I encountered more failures than otherwise anticipated. Several political storms overwhelmed us including the global economic downturn, the several changes of leadership at the Getty Museum, the Italian conflict over "provenance" of archeological treasures that affected the director of antiquity, and the attack on New York City on 11 September 2001 that made it more difficult to move items internationally.

The key supporters at the Getty were Dr. Marion True, the senior antiquarian and director of the Villa, and her colleague, Janet Grossman; both have left the Museum. In addition, Karol Wight, who had stepped into the position of temporary senior manager, has also departed the institution. The temporary staff in place until a new senior antiquarian can be nominated was unable to commit to an exhibition of Kerch's treasures (in 2011 a new permanent replacement for Dr. True had yet to be appointed). All these obstacles and more precluded the efforts to develop financial support or initiate an exhibition at the Getty for Kerch.

There were many facets to the strategy to elicit economic expansion in Kerch. I had worked with the United Nations representatives to make Kerch a Heritage Region to protect it from destruction when economic growth would begin to change the eastern portion of Crimea. For the Heritage program it was necessary to build a fence or establish a security system for the critical sections but the necessary funding was unavailable and the will of the Russian-leaning authorities in Simferopol could not be mustered. There was also a project to initiate a student exchange program with American secondary schools. Several schools were approached and many were interested, but when push came to shove none of them moved to the final step to bring reality to the project. There were many hurdles to overcome, some of which were related to acquiring visas at the time when the United States was reeling from the attack on the World Trade Center buildings in New York City. Then there was the global financial melt down that dried up many sources of funding for foreign projects.

I can count Kerch as a failure for me. Yes, I know that one is supposed to learn from failures but that's a terrible way to have to be instructed. There were many issues involved in the program to save the treasures of Kerch, and most of them were negative. The Getty, as I already indicated, had serious internal management problems. Then there was the "provenance" accusation by the Italian and also Greek government that dynamited the illustrious senior antiquarian and director Dr. Marion True — a person who was not guilty but was caught in the grinding financial mechanism of the issue — and finally there was the exodus of the remaining senior antiquarian staff who either found new positions in other institutions or retired leaving vacuums in the department of antiquity. The Kerch potential exhibit program was left without any supporters. The personnel replacement were either ignorant of what Kerch could provide or were simply uninterested because of lack of knowledge. Any effort for an exhibit was trashed by the replacement staff under temporary leadership of Dr. Clair L. Lyons or worse postponed to 2020, if ever. I was crushed, as were the good folks in Kerch. It was a failure and I take full responsibility if that is of any assistance.

There is, at any rate, some good that surfaced from this failure.

Marion True and Patrick de Maisonneuve

Out of a soiled stall from which the proverbial pony came, I found a dear and wonderful friend. In addition, with this friend came her magnificent husband. Marion True and her extraordinary husband, Patrick de Maisonneuve have become two of my dear friends, friends of unimaginable value and affection. Marion was the senior antiquarian and director of the Getty Villa, which she had a principal hand in restoring and redesigning. She was caught in the accusations that the Italian government, and to some extent the Greek government, vented on her on the issue of provenance of articles that the Getty exhibited. The fact was that Marion had authored an important treatise on the ethics directing the source (*provenance*) of antiques; nevertheless, the Italian government, knowing that the Getty had deep pockets and that it would let Marion take the fall, turned the law on her. The Getty has done very little to defend Marion, except fund her legal team. She was never proven guilty because the Italian statute of limitations came into play and the trials ended (a decade later the Greek government pronounced a not-guilty verdict). It has become obvious that the Italian government's prosecution team counted on the statute of limitation because they consistently dragged out the trial process, mostly without apparent cause. Finally, the case against Marion was closed but she was never rewarded by the Italian government with a not-guilty pronouncement.

Without apologizing I will jump ahead a decade because I want you to meet the friends I acquired from the Getty fiasco. Patrick, Marion's husband, is a wonderful and adorable person. As a retired professor from the Sorbonne, he is also a fine watercolor artist and an architect focused on historical buildings. Patrick is a genuine delight and I'm grateful to have him include me as his friend.

Marion and Patrick reside in France in their own house located in the de Maisonneuve family complex in St Gilles-Croix de Vie. The complex is on the Atlantic coast and I visited them a couple of times. On one occasion both Marion and Patrick came for an overnight visit to our little cottage in Boismé, France; they brought with them a feast of oysters and lobsters, which they promptly cleaned and shelled for us.

It was certainly a feast for all occasions and one to have with wonderful friends.

On another occasion we had lunch with Marion and Patrick at the Château de la Tremblaye near Cholet. It was another extraordinary occasion because the lunch was superb, the company warm and graceful, and we collected the watercolors that Patrick had made.

Indeed, out of failure emerged a magnificent and graceful friendship. I must, however, add that I have not given up on Kerch and I still maintain the network to support the project and I'm still in contact with the key people involved, although not with the Getty staff.

The Social Lubricant: Ethics

Kerch, and the problems that it elicited as I attempted to assist it in 1999 to develop into a coherent and viable economic region, has given me pause in my understanding of how people relate to each other. Specifically how ethics functions in today's society or societies, for it is ethics that lubricates the inherent relationship between human beings.

Human beings do not live in a vacuum. Christians or members of other persuasions have to be reminded that no one lives on this planet in a sanitized and pure environment. Hence, relationships cannot develop in a vacuum that isolates people from the concrete issues that affect life. Human beings are of the world and live in the world. It is an inevitable condition that human beings are constantly required to rub elbows with fellow human beings. It is good that we are not alone but this also requires a mode of operation that helps us avoid conflict, distress, and all the difficulties that surface from close contacts. When two human beings are in a setting where close interchange is inevitable some sort of arrangement must be initiated to keep the relationship from turning sour. That social lubricant is called "ethics."

Ethics is not a condition that surfaces naturally from the wilderness. Ethics is the product of deliberations between humanoids. It is the result of agreements, concordats, conventions, love, respect, and other conditions of human endeavors that develop specifically so that human beings can get along and get on with life.

Here I am speaking of "ethics" but there is another constant that permits the interchange between humanoids that function under certain conditions and that is "morals." Morals are quite different from ethics, hence something needs to be said about morals and a distinction between the two is required. In delineating a distinction between ethics and morality there are many obvious obstacles that get in the way of a clear separation. In brief I need to point out that in ethics religion does not in reality play a leading role, and it should not because the construct of ethics is based on philosophically developed agreements; whereas for morality, religious axioms (or other codified axioms) are inherently part of its definition(s) because a supreme "cause" is overbearingly introduced in the outcome.

The construct of ethics is based on a mutual understanding. In other words, ethics emerges from agreements between two or more parties. For morality, implicit in the construct is the assumed direction of a higher authority such as God or his messenger, prophet, ambassador, representative, the religious organization, the faith persuasion, the doctrinal axioms that have been developed by others and not your own, and the idealized persuasion that frames the definition.

The difference between ethics and morals is multidimensional. The word ethics come from the Greek "tà ēthiká" and by definition indicates the established common rules of conduct, legal stature if you will, recognized in respect to a particular class of human actions or a particular group, culture, society or class. As for morals, which come from the Latin "morālis," they are founded on the fundamental principles of right conduct as delineated by an authority — a caesar or a king — rather than on legalities, enactment, custom or stature; hence society accepts certain moral obligations.

Of course at this juncture the question is posed as to who establishes either ethics or morals? The former, ethics, is put into place by human agreements, legal or otherwise, proclaimed. It is the product of decisions that emerge from conditions that are recognized as making human interchanges less cumbersome. Ethics is a social lubricant that allows people to function knowing that the conditions are respected, fair, and conducive to good behavior.

Morals are established by conditions that are assumed to emerge from either natural law (whatever that purports to be), divine codes, or accepted from higher sources that specify good modes of operation. In many cases religions have a hand in dictating the source of moral behavior. Often the codes of morality are not debatable, whereas ethics is generally debatable until an agreement emerges. For example, one must not commit murder because morality based on something such as the Ten Commandments precludes the killing of a human being. Based on ethics, one does not kill because a human being has value; killing destroys the social fabric; and killing is inevitably a contributing factor to other killings. Moreover, the laws that society has enacted after great deliberations forbid murder. Simply put, moral behavior is based on requirements that are received from outside society and ethical behavior surfaces from internal social agreements.

In past years I have been put in the position to teach ethics on the college level, including medical students. On a few occasions I have been involved with discussing ethics with clients or when contracts had to be written and signed. My interest with ethics stems from my own study of philosophy and my understanding of human intercourse such as in politics or religion. I have often pointed out that when two or three people are gathered, quite promptly a political system of agreement is established. Each individual is given the means for expression such that it does not inhibit any other individual. In effect this agreement may not be formal and merely unspoken but nevertheless it is present and quite recognizable by each individual and by outsiders. Thus ethics helps the process of the management of human affairs. It is a social lubricant.

I've struggled often in my life to explain the distinction between ethics and morals. Often my philosophical education and my religious training have been in apparent conflict. I admit that my tendency has always been to side with my philosophical education and to ignore my religious training. For example, during my seminary years I refused to sit in on a course in moral theology but instead attended seminars in ethics in a secular university or with a mentor. If morality cannot be debated then I want nothing to do with it and will not apply it to social conditions. I must be able to ask "why" and "why not."

Therefore it should be argued that ethics is the individual's ability to determine between right and wrong while morals are the societal values collectively received from a higher authority. Morals define personal character received from sources beyond the person, while ethics stress a social system determined by human beings.

In truth, I tend to place my ethics in the situation rather than in a legal, statutory or doctrinal framework. I reject the doctrinarian position, the casuistic approach, and the Shari'ah admonition or any other that proposes a response without considering the particular details of a specific case.

I prefer to examine the situation and then I apply what I consider to be the ethical frame for the event. Hence in one situation I may decide one way and in another I may either reverse my position or approach it from a different angle or perspective. This approach may cause some problems for people who have preconceived guidelines for a particular situation, especially religious people who confuse the moral decisions with the frame supplied by ethics. Is murdering another human being bad? Well, it depends on the situation that frames both the killer and the victim. Examining the situation, the conditions, the causes, and the relationship between the killer and the victim will inevitably offer reasons that are not obvious or clear. Do humans have the ability to see all facets of a situation beyond the facts? Often facts are merely the tip of the iceberg, the details of the issue are hidden or ignored because of the law, the statute, the constraints of the environment, the time required to reach a viable decision, and the faulty human assumptions coloring the situation. By saying this I may be accused of inviting anarchy. Murder is murder and requires no apology or philosophical coating: many people would rush to add. Nevertheless, life is neither simple nor neatly sized for a prepared frame. Situations are complex because life is complex. Hence the event of murder may have ramifications that are also complex and certainly beyond the specifics of the laws. Is this not why juries have such an important role to play in murder situations? Neither judges nor attorneys have the whole picture in a murder case, therefore juries are asked to look beyond and often (or seldom) they do think, as best they can, outside the legal box. Even juries see only the tip of the action; there is much below the surface that cannot be discerned.

If the judicial system were based solely on morality what would be the consequences that human beings would have to bear? For example how is murder treated in the United States — in the capital punishment states and the non-capital punishment states — in Saudi Arabia, in Iran, in China, in Singapore, in Russia, and in other nations that have laws concerning the act of killing? Do they all have a clear understanding of the causes behind each murder? Is their judicial understanding based on morality or ethics? Under which one would the reader prefer to be affected?

We also have the problem of "right or wrong" and added to it is the issue of "true or false" and they color ethics. I'm reminded of Alfred North White-head writing in *Modes of Thoughts* (p.15): "The simple-minded use of the notions 'right or wrong' is one of the chief obstacles to the progress of under-standing." Indeed, when we stoop to use what is considered "fool proof" methodologies in making a judgment, we are abandoning the methods of searching for the applicable cause that affected a situation and resorting to a simple-minded treatment for resolving an issue. In fact, ethics is supplanted by a sort of voodoo approach, and often that is the tool that the legal profes-sion, those protectors of laws, employ. Can we always rely on the safe haven of precedents? Just because some issue was settled a few decades ago is it still viable for today? Look at slavery and its justification a century or more ago. Is it justifiable today because of its precedent resolution?

In William James' treatise, *Pragmaticism* (p. 222) we read, "The true, to put it briefly, is only the excellent in the way of our thinking, just as the right is only the expedient in the way of our behaving." Do any of us really know what is true, absolute true or truth, in any situation? This does not mean that we must live in a sort of denial of what is possibly correct. But we must con-sider what can affect what is considered to be the truth in any situation we examine. What are the factors affecting that situation: friendship, love, grace-fulness, human frailty, prejudice — recognized or not, etc.? As I suggested earlier, an ethical understanding considers these and more as they can affect a situation. Morality abiding by dogma and higher causes skips over this un-derstanding and looks at the judgment based on non-humanly agreed delimiting factors. In other words, in morality one is subjected to the ration-ale or dogmas that others, not the person or even his peers, have developed.

It is obvious that my thinking endorses situationalism but not relativism as a way of life, rather relativism as a philosophical axiom. As a way of life relativism is not dependable because by this approach ethics is just subject to the whims of an individual, or society, or of a few with no general or reasonable agreement put into place, except perhaps some degree of subjectivism. Before I confuse the reader and cloud the issue more than I have already, let me say that relativism is a philosophical approach stating that there is no absolute truth, merely truth relative to the individual, a particular culture, or both. In fact, relativism may be said to deny objectivism (poor Ayn Rand), which states that all reality exists independent of the person or of consciousness.

For our purpose it can be assumed that there are two major relativistic tributaries that are identified as 1) epistemological (pertaining to knowledge) and 2) ethical (pertaining to morality and values). Epistemological relativism is probably best exemplified by those who deny the possibility of providing a justification for our knowledge and values. Otherwise, ethical relativism is said to be based on "morality," which is dependent, as I've already indicated, on a higher authority. With ethical relativism we are brought back to our old definition of morality, which is not dependent on reason or analytical exploration. It is given!

A close cousin to relativism is "subjectivism;" essentially the acceptance that all conclusions are purely matters of personal opinion. That aspect to me is the denial of reasonable exploration and tells me that nothing is for certain in anything that human beings do or accomplish.

But as a philosophical tool relativism is useful because it questions anything that tends towards absolutism and dogmatism. This may be difficult for some readers to accept or digest, because dogmatism and absolutism are short cuts — and humanoids have gotten accustomed to short cuts in thinking otherwise why are they so enamored with fundamentalism — to clear thinking and relegates the work required to achieve a solution for life to someone else or to an institution.

I am always on guard when I read or am confronted by dogmas or absolutes. In my life in the Church, refusing to accept or abide by dogmatic or absolute pronouncements has often put me in positions that were not those of my colleagues or of my superiors. I have had to stand firm to defend my position or positions. In the understanding of Christianity, dogmatism and absolutes have no place — and here I'm following the Christic position. It is a disservice to Christianity when it is coated with dogmatic and absolute veneers. My Christianity is anchored on being graceful, upholding the dignity of others, respecting my fellow human beings as I hope to be respected by them, and expressing love in its many ramifications whenever possible and when it is least expected. Christianity is what gives me the freedom to live an ethical life. Christianity reminds me that I am a sacred human being; that I have dignity; and that I can improve the World during my tenure upon it; and that even with my imperfections I can be a contributor of record for good, for peace, and for a better life for my fellow human beings. Christianity is extraordinarily difficult because it calls on me to be a thinking human being every instant of my existence. Christianity makes the "I" and the "We" fellow cooperative and decisive travelers on this Planet.

Fortunately we have gone beyond the age when one was burnt at the stake for exploring ideas that were not often part of the general understanding or in accord with common ideas. The position I've shared with you is one that has guided me throughout my life and there it is and I share it with the readers without apologies.

Integrity: Who am I?

This discussion began in 1999 when I was talking about Kerch and what the project was contributing to the community, if anything. There were several facets that were reflecting aspects of behavior by way of the Kerch project. I was unable to link schools from Kerch with American schools. I was unable to secure visas for the youth because of the heightened security in America after the attack on the World Trade Center on 11 September 2001. I was unable to convince the Getty museum to have an exhibit of the archeological treasures of Kerch and to this day, still have not done so. In many ways all these failures were the product of mismanaged practiced ethics by several people who were active in the process. The long chain of missteps was apparent: from the attackers of the World Trade Center to the Kerch teacher who misinformed us and hence annulled the application for her own visa to the several postponements of the exhibits by the antiquarians of the Getty, to the Italian government's accusation of the Getty's director of antiquities on false charges and subsequent resignation, to the mismanaged search for funding, each event reflected a certain degree of unethical behavior by the parties involved.

Now the question for the reader is not about ethics and the ethics involved but whether the people involved recognized their own less-than-sterling behavior. Does each person in the process see that his or her action was detrimental to the task? I doubt it and I'm just as certain that not one person has recognized his or her questionable level of integrity. Even my participation is questioned because I may not have been as forceful or demanding as I should have to move this project ahead. Thus it comes that it is not so much an issue of ethics or morality but of integrity — recognizing one's negative behavior. Of course I am part of this fiasco because I too assumed that I had performed my task clearly but I had not. I made little mistakes along the planning course, mistakes that magnified my own personal errors, errors that misidentified the final goal and hence accentuated my own pride. Indeed, the Kerch project was mine but it was not for my benefit or for my aggrandizement. Hence I had to admit finally that I had failed and my integrity was in the balance. I'll explain.

Integrity has much to do with one's ethical behavior. What is integrity? Explained in simple language it is knowing clearly who one is.

I'm reminded of the famous bank robber Willy Sutton. Willy robbed banks because he enjoyed solving the security puzzle of the locking system on the various safes. "Why did I rob banks? Because I enjoyed it; I loved it." It may be an apocryphal story but it is said that he knew that he was a thief but he also knew that he didn't care about the little money he stole, he just wanted to open safes and took enough cash to live comfortably but certainly not extravagantly. Sutton mismanaged the truth of his safe robbing activities but he never compromised his integrity (or we assume that he didn't).

In other words, do I know when I have mismanaged something? Do I recognize when I say something erroneous about someone? Do I know when I've mismanaged the truth? Do I know when I've intentionally falsified a fact? These and others are what affect my sense of integrity — and most of the time I know about it. I know that, as the lyrics say "I've done wrong!" I also know that I have a need to correct what I've done and often I do. I don't, however, display my correcting actions as a badge of honor. It is expressed quietly and surreptitiously whenever possible but at times it is postponed to a more propitious moment and perhaps to seek a modicum of forgiveness.

In the Anglican Community, and equally in the Episcopal Church in the United States, there is a tradition of promoting general confession in the liturgies. Unlike the requirements to participate in personal confession with a priest as found in the Roman community, the focus of the Episcopal approach is to take a moment to admit to one's self that he or she has participated in wrong behavior. This is one indication that one's level of integrity perhaps needs to be reviewed, needs adjustment, and requires a correction. The important quality of surveying one's integrity is not to tell other people about the personal attributes of self-behavior but to inform one's self about one's comportment. Who am I, how am I behaving, and what can I do to recognize and improve my attitude? This is the gist of how integrity is maintained; fundamentally it is the recognition, for me at least, that I have reviewed my actions and that I have taken the necessary steps to reform them — or not. Of course, this does not lead me to believe that I have lived a perfect life. It does not assure me to understand that my behavior is without reproach, but it does allow me to fine tune it in the hope that it may be improved to a more ethical state. Knowing who I am is the key for me. I am reminded that in Greek, to sin is to miss the mark — as in shooting arrows on a target. The Greek word is *hamartia* and suggests that with the next shot the bull's eye can be hit, if only I adjust my sight to improve my aim — my ethical comportment. There is always the option for another attempt. To be Scriptural it is, "Go and sin no more!" Quite different from the doctrinarian approach, isn't it?

Knowing who we are is a valuable asset. It allows us to adjust our behavior, and even to improve it. It gives us a direction and a road map for living.

Otherwise we are unable to manage our life coherently. We may go from pillar to post and never attain a level of satisfaction or even of repose. We may become muddled and even hurtful to ourselves. Our personhood is diminished and we are less than we could be. Having integrity is a tool that permits us to function on a course that we can manage; even when we insist on being less than we are, we can recognize the conditions that cause us to be less than we can be.

The effort spent in checking my integrity has given me an appreciation for who and what I am. I may not be in top form but I have a healthy approach to who I am — warts and all.

The Bishop of Ely

Before I reach the finishing portion of this period I would like to return to my first introduction of the Right Reverend Lord Bishop, Peter Walker, and ecclesiastical authority of the Anglican Diocese of Ely. The readers will recall that as a boy I frequented Ely Cathedral, and at times participated in what was loosely called a choir. Of course the real boys' choir was made up of the students of the King's School but our choir functioned as a training and supplemental unit.

Well, in 1987 I was invited to attend a reception at the Cathedral, which was to be held in mid-September.

Because I was in the UK and would be present at the reception, I contacted the office of the bishop and informed the secretary that I wanted to meet the bishop a few days before. The following day I received a phone call from the secretary informing me that the bishop would be happy to meet with me at his palace (home) at eleven o'clock the next day. Somehow I managed to arrive late. In fact I arrived at the front door at almost one o'clock. Embarrassed and apologetic, I knocked at the door. The bishop opened it and bid me come in and then invited me to lunch. At the table I was introduced to Jean, Mrs. Walker. Bishop Walker had obtained a great deal of information from the archives and thus knew that I had not only been an active member in decades past but had continued to be a contributor of record since 1973, when

I had returned to Cambridge after a hiatus of nearly twenty years. Bishop Walker had also telephoned my good friend Nan Youngman who lived at the Hawks, Water Beach because I had given her name to his secretary as a reference, and who had several of her works displayed at the Cathedral. Bishop Walker was a renowned art lover and connoisseur.

Thus began a wonderful friendship that spanned more than 20 years. Peter Walker died on 28 December 2010.

Mrs. Walker was a graduate of the University of Chicago, with a master of arts degree in history from that university. English though she was, her parents had sent her to America for an education that was to be different from what they had experienced; both parents had been educated at Cambridge University. Peter Walker had been the product of Oxford University and after his doctorate in philosophy, spent several years on the faculty and dean of Corpus Christi College, Cambridge, and then ordination to Anglican Holy Orders, plus a number of cures, he had been nominated to be bishop by then-Archbishop Donald Coggan. He was translated from the Diocese of Dorchester to Ely in 1977 and retired in 1990.

Peter Walker was a lovely man who possessed a great intellectual brain. We had many exciting conversations on art, philosophy, and history — at times we also discussed the condition of the Church, its theological perspective, and its influence on the world. Peter was fond of Bishop George Bell, who was the authority of the Diocese of Chichester and a supporter of the free Christian Community during Hitler's dictatorship. Peter often was called upon to speak on Bell and on several occasions wrote extensive articles on him.

One of my finest memories was being invited to have dinner with Peter Walker in the dining room of the House of Lords. It was a grand evening and I was introduced to several major members of the House of Lords. I was also taken to the debating hall of the House of Commons to hear the members speak out, especially when they spoke out against Prime Minister Margaret Thatcher. After the spectacle in the House of Commons I was taken to the Lords Pub and given a whisky especially distilled for the members. I still possess a sample bottle of the elixir, which probably will never be opened.

I've shared many meals with the Walkers and many conversations. The last time I ate with the Walkers was in a pub and we had pizza and ale. After the meal Jean asked me if I would plant several pots for her in the small lot she used as a garden. Jean was losing her eyesight because of macular degeneration; she could barely read, watch television, or manage in the kitchen. I was informed that when Peter died Jean was taken to a nursing home and that she had died in the winter of 2011.

Much of the problem with aging is that one loses one's friends sooner than one likes. I share this vignette about dear friends because Peter and Jean had a prominent place in me in the last decades of the 20th century.

A major subject of our discussion with Bishop Walker was the church's role in Nazi Germany during the war, and the response that surfaced from the Church of England to the conditions of the Germans. Bishop George Bell was a major speaker for the Christians in Germany who did not accept Hitler's form of the national church. We often exchanged ideas and accepted Bell's position that the Church of England (C of E) had dropped the ball when it came to supporting the non-Nazi affiliated congregations in Germany and also of not standing with Pastor Dietrich Bonheoffer when he voiced that the Nazi congregations were an abomination and should be so identified by the C of E. Those discussions led us to how racism and slavery were also supported by many congregations and pastors in Europe, in the USSR, and in America. The integrity of many proponents of Christianity and of other faiths came into question. And so our discussions covered many aspects, many issues, and many complex topics, which kept us talking for hours. I miss Peter Walker and his gentleness, quick mind, and astute perception of the human condition. Peter Walker was the last of my senior friends.

The Closing Century

When I was younger, I looked with great interest at the dawn of the 21st century, a time that I never expected to witness because it was bizarre to me to live in two spans of one hundred years and that type of required longevity was unexpected, at least for me. Anyway, I was thinking of the future, a task that I often indulged in my work. On several occasions I was classified as a futurist, a commentary that I often rejected yet recognized as somewhat valid because I saw the next stage as being more important than the current stage — but the importance of the past stage loomed high because it gave me lessons on what had come before the present or the future. My work had been directed towards the primacy of knowledge and the value of education for managing one's future, and also for managing a community's future. My conclusion as I spent my energy on several projects was that the future required human beings to be educated, not in one discipline but to be educated well enough to remain at ease in the ongoing learning process demanded by the economic pressures that were encountered on a daily basis.

If one were not adept at learning constantly, adept at learning to learn at every turn of one's existence, then the result would be misery. Misery because earning an income would no longer be the norm for any individual; the lack of knowledge would preclude finding ready employment in the new age of high technology, information technology, physical technology, and in any form of intellectual technos — art of life. In no way was I focusing on a university education with a terminal degree in a particular discipline, which would be good and certainly useful in the coming knowledge age. A self-education, but an education nonetheless, was necessary to be able to navigate the rough waters of the upcoming economic years. One has to be disciplined to continuously learn from experience, from curiosity, from others, and from books, classes, conferences, discussions, and from the pell-mell of information that comes along every moment of our existence.

As I looked at the development of California's high technology in what is referred to as Silicon Valley, I could see that employment was geared to allow for the knowledgeably adept to earn wages, whereas the lesser educated or uneducated adept are to be condemned to the unemployment realm. I could discern that there were many opportunities for employment and firms were hurting for people to work, but the pool of the unemployed was filled with good folks who were not skilled for the jobs available. Moreover, those unemployed who were in possession of technical degrees were unable to accept positions or were unable to be hired because their technological skills were attuned to a past era and they could not readily be reeducated.

The key for obtaining knowledge was education — both formal and informal. An academic degree was and is important but what is yet more important is the ability to learn and learn and learn, and employ what one has learned on a moment-by-moment basis.

For example, the shining knights of high technology were brilliant because they were focused on acquiring knowledge all the time, even outside the university umbrella, and through that knowledge they innovated, invented, transformed, modified, refashioned, and on and on. Many of these Czars of the high-tech industry did not have university degrees but they possessed the ability to learn what was necessary for them to accomplish their goals or realize their visions, even to hire the required people who had the fundamental information to complement them and help them attain the envisioned goals. Whatever the condition, the tool was undeniably knowledge, skill, and willingness to tackle the unknown because the implement pertaining to reason and the acquisition of information was at their disposal — because they knew how to learn.

Unlike the craft person who does the same thing over and over and probably very well, the knowledgeable person opened new outlooks and took calculated risks as a matter of course. What the past taught was that the present was volatile and impermanent because it moved directly into the future, then needed to be altered, improved, modified, and confronted with a new idea. Knowledge-driven developments became the source of economic augmentation.

The new century brought with it a great deal of financial upheaval. Apart from national conflicts, terrorism, religious frictions, and societal problems, there surfaced the issue of reduction in the number of those employed. There were more people for fewer jobs. Unemployment had moved from the traditional level of three percent to nine or ten in the United States, and more elsewhere. Yes there were jobs available but fewer people were qualified to fill them. Why? Because there were, so to speak, many blacksmiths but fewer horses or wagon wheels in need of them. Moreover, industry needed people who could not be replaced by robots. Industry needed workers who could think for themselves, who could be creative, and who could manage an idea and go off with it without too much supervision but yet be accountable, and be prepared to defend their product, accept critical suggestions, and proceed to the next level of accomplishment.

In my work with knowledge-driven revenue-producing entities it became obvious that the economic future depended on education and subsequently on knowledge. Gone were the days when one could find employment with merely a high school degree, even with a preliminary college degree obtaining a job was becoming difficult when there were so many owners of terminal degrees available. The new environment is dynamically and intellectually attuned to the fabric of change and hence requires education as a supporting platform for its survival, and also for the engagement of the citizens.

Why was a terminal degree or its equivalent in experience so important? Of course this is a rhetorical question and I'll answer it by saying that the doctoral degree suggests immediately that the person travelled new avenues of thought, did research, defended his subject, and was willing to risk in order to be an innovator by approaching a subject in a way that others have not. I was informed that 63% of candidates for a doctoral degree never achieve it or even finish their dissertations. This is a commendable reason for lauding the ones who have obtained terminal degrees, especially those who continue to earn post-doctoral levels and other means of learning for acquiring knowledge.

Again, from my experience and from my work, I've noticed that the majority of jobs are specifically designed for people who have a higher education or the equivalent level of experience or innovation. Low-level employment options are extremely limited even for such crafts as plumbers, electricians, masons, mechanics, etc. It is quite apparent that employment is limited to people who can maneuver through the difficult paths of intellectual accomplishments. Gone are the days when the unskilled and even the semi-skilled could obtain work by doing menial or repetitive work. Thus as the years pass the number of unemployed will rise precipitously and the texture of the economic fabric will become tighter and tighter restricting the less capable from earning a living.

Another point to be made is that in today's environment one does not look at want ads, employment requests in the news, or jobs offered by human resources organizations, private or government, because these are usually filled before they are publicized (by law they must be posted but most know that they are filled internally by workers who are known within the network). The key to a job is to investigate the potential firms to see what they are missing; to develop the necessary skills to fill the empty position; and to create a plan, an approach, and a vision that the firms in question cannot refuse or that will give the person the necessary tools to become a working and profitable employee or consultant. Again, knowledge is the key: know what is necessary and have the know-how to do the task(s).

What is being offered is a peek at the future. I project — although I am far from being a prophet I can appreciate the human and economic conditions looming ahead — that towards the end of the first decade of the 21st century the world will experience a major economic downturn, perhaps more severe than the one experienced during the 1930s (it happened in 2008-9). In most cases to ease the plight of the unemployed any action will be too late because training for the necessary tasks and obtaining an education for mastering the required professional disciplines takes time and long-term investment, but currently society is unwilling to make the required effort to tend to the issue. Society is ignoring investment in the necessary infrastructure for preparing the wage earners for the future. By infrastructure I mean more than just roads, bridges, housing, and physical improvements, although these are more than necessary. By infrastructure I mean training and education at all levels. Simply explained, infrastructure is the structure that holds the whole enchilada together and education at all levels is the principal supporting item. Society might begin by supporting both politically and financially all the levels of education, the guilds of excellent teachers, the facilities wherein education is offered, and the sources that permit students to obtain this education.

Now nearing the end of 1999 and the shift from the Clinton administration to the younger Bush system, a system that had been imposed by the Rehnquist Court because the popular and electoral college votes did not agree, it became clear to me that a major problem was looming for the nation. The new and still unsworn-in administration had assembled a team that was by and large subservient to the giants of Wall Street. It was on Friday 17 December 1999 that I realized that the financial playing field had been tilted overtly in favor of the wealthy. The very wealthy one or two percent of Americans were in for a great deal of support from the new administration. The rest of the people in the medium and lower financial realms were in for some hardship, because they were not considered to be supporters of the Bush team. I suspected that by the end of George W. Bush's first term he would be put to pasture because Americans would recognize that he was the wrong person to be president for the new century. If Bush were not to be removed then the nation was going to be in a deep recession and an even deeper financial crisis because of high unemployment. I could foresee that the first four years of the 21st century would be pivotal in how the country managed its economic fabric. It was a wait-and-see period for me as the 20th century eased into the 21st century. The issue was not about the computer calendar chips not being programmed to switch to the new century but about how the nation would manage under the new tilt towards the very wealthy. (The disappointment is that George W. Bush was reelected in 2004, which indicates once again we deserve the leadership we get!)

I've reached the closing moment for this autobiography. I've relived much of my life as I recorded some of its details. Very few, if any, regrets have been encountered as I've traveled the road of my life again. It was not a perfect and uneventful life but it was not one that I would trade or change; it was my life, my intimate life and I made the most of it.

EPILOGUE

The new millennium will soon be upon me. I've never expected to see the 21st century. But there it is shown on new calendars! I've lived as best I could. All my tasks have not been completed and I've not been in the habit of leaving before the last word is written. Yet, I sense that the end is soon around the corner but not quite at hand. Thus I consider death to be a graduating exercise when my fellow human beings may grade me, and if there is something beyond it, well and good. I understand death, as my mentor and professor Massey H. Shepherd Jr., would remind me: "Death is the birthday into eternity!"

So be it.

It has been a good life and it is not over yet. I've stepped onto the threshold of the 21st century and the ride continues until it stops, but that's not for a while yet, I believe. When the final chapter will be written is beyond my immediate thought. I suspect that I'll continue writing as long as I am able and I've already put a few words down as "thoughts" for consideration.

As I look back I am aware that I've forged my own path through very different types of institutions, not as a rebellious or even as a docile member but as one who attempted to humanize the institutions. I have been accused of being antiauthority but that was not a correct label for me. I have no problem with reasonable orders, commands, or policies but when they are injudiciously administered then, as I understand them, I point it out in order to correct them. Working within three mainly authoritarian institutions (US Air

Force, Church, and Bechtel) I was able to move about and get ahead, even promoted, eventually after a few bumps and loops were tended to.

Perhaps the occasions given by my own course through these institutions may offer some guidance to others who are in situations where authority is overwhelmingly difficult. My approach was always that institutions are made of human beings, human beings who don their pants the same way I do. Often policies are written for the convenience of some bureaucrat, some executive board, rather than for the effective accomplishment of a project, a task or when human beings are considered to be mere pawns. Moreover, institutions find it difficult to admit that a policy or a judgment is, and was, in error because that would suggest that it is managed loosely and previous edicts were wrong. But will the current change prove to be correct? Change may be initiated, but like a gargantuan aircraft carrier it does not turn on a dime! Nevertheless, change must be pointed out and noted.

Each one of us is called upon to right wrongs, to help change idiotic rules, to move for better and more equitable institutions. No one has the luxury to let a poor situation pass by unattended. And, of course, how right are we, if ever? Yet we must try and try as best we can. Taking the long view has corrective value because it reduces self-righteousness and limits self-aggrandizement.

In my involvement on many projects it has been my good fortune to meet several august human beings, from singers, executives, presidents, scientists, ecclesiastical authorities, and low ranking folks who each participated in making an effort to better or strengthen the social fabric, or so I discovered. No person is unimportant in my sight. No person is irrelevant in the scheme of creation, yet a few are notoriously troublesome, a handful is ignored to our own detriment, but many are helpful, creative, good contributors, and the very salt of the earth. It was my good fortune to recognize some and to make the best of our encounters. I would hope that the readers might see these examples and accept them as beneficial tokens for their life.

I have mentioned my involvement in the Church and I've allowed that I'm not in any sense "religious" in the pedestrian understanding. When asked if I am religious I always deny it and avoid giving an explanation. In brief let me now state that organized religion is of little concern to me. Yet I am a functioning element in an organized religious community. Nevertheless, it is not the organization that I respect as much as the incident of its reflection of what it is as a microcosm of society. The Church as understood theologically, as the living body of Christ, is not per se the organized institution: not at all. No priest, no bishop, no archbishop, no pope, no patriarch, is of any importance in the larger scheme of commitment to the presence of God (however one wishes to define that name). For religion to have a viable function for human beings it will have to change in the same spirit as science. Its principles may be valid and eternal, but the expression of those principles requires continual development and if given by so-called revelation, they need to be factually and reasonably substantiated. Yet there may be some modicum of mystery in its substantiation but let's not push the limit, no more than science pushes the limit in its understanding of the physical universe. Much of what we ascribe to "mystery" is merely enigmatic and subjected to our inherent laziness! Not for a moment am I ascribing that there are no mysteries in this universe; there are, but in limited quantity. There are mysteries, unexplainable issues, in science and as well in religion but philosophical thinking can come as a helpful tool to help us deal with them. In all candor, perhaps we prefer the offerings and proclamations of organized religions because they shortcut our own reasoning and relieve us from doing fundamental exploration and hard thinking. I suspect it is better for many to be told than to figure it out. Nevertheless it may be an insult to our thinking function.

A few more words about supporting organizations that do what we as individuals cannot do alone. The current condition of the world and of society is in need of much support, much corrective actions, much protection, especially for issues of the environment, and much monitoring. As individuals we cannot manage the task by ourselves. We need the assistance of organizations and they in turn require our support, our financial contributions, and our candor when sharing ideas, plans, and expectations. No one is able to support financially all that these organizations require: none of us is that wealthy. Yet, we earn some income and a small percentage of that income can be shared without affecting our own well-being, our tight budget, and the few dollars that we allocate for our leisure. A small financial contribution is always better than none. Moreover, when one contributes a few dollars one becomes immediately an "owner" of what the organization, the institution, or the group tasks itself to do. Finally, offering oneself as a volunteer is to be rewarded in many ways. Giving some effort and/or some time is soon recognized as the lubricant that makes a free society operate effectively; merely a few hours is all that is needed. Become an owner of society and a contributor of record and enrichment of the self will be yours. Life is a liturgy so volunteer yourself and be an active participant.

It's been a good ride on the toboggan of life. Many up slopes and many down slopes. Many hairpin curves and many frightful occasions. At times I felt like a trapeze artist or a tight-ropewalker with no safety net below but somehow and providentially I never fell off. Speaking of providence, I have been amazed that quite often when it was evident that unknowingly I would be making a catastrophic error in judgment some direction was given to me to redress and change my course. Providence? Perhaps? Nevertheless there it was, but I'm quite ready to call it divine participation in my life. My reluctance is not because of humility but because I am uncertain and yet I'm immensely grateful. This is as close as I want to come to call this guidance the emergence of grace. Providential grace.

I'll say no more!

There are no whole truths;

All truths are half-truths.

It is trying to treat them as whole truths that play the devil.

(Alfred North Whitehead, Prologue, 1954)

INDEX

ABOUT THE AUTHOR

Author in July 2016

Comments and questions for the author are welcomed at
nimon.adventures@gmail.com

Please visit www.adventuresofnimon.info for more photos and information.

Made in the USA
San Bernardino, CA
29 July 2016